CITATION-AT-A-GLANCE
REVISED EDITION
Citations For Use In Legal Memoranda and Documents.
West Publishing. Your Paralegal Publisher.

Each of the following discussions and examples is based upon *The Bluebook: A Uniform System of Citation* (16th ed. 1996). Citation forms are those discussed in the general rules of *The Bluebook,* and modified according to the "Practitioners' Notes" section of the book at pages 10-19.

CITATION FORMS FOR SPECIFIC AUTHORITIES

STATUTES AND PROCEDURAL LAW:

■ **Statutory citations** should include:

a) statutory code title number (federal statutes only);

b) abbreviated name of the statutory code;

c) section (or subdivision) number;

d) year of the code, in parentheses.

❏ **Examples:**

Federal:	*State:*
42 U.S.C. § 1983 (1994).	Colo. Rev. Stat. § 12-22-125 (1993).
42 U.S.C.A. § 1983 (West 1990).	Ill. Rev. Stat. ch. 410, para. 80/4 (1994).

Items to Remember:

1. The format for state statutory codes varies from state to state. Consult *The Bluebook,* Table T.1, United States Jurisdictions, for proper code names and abbreviations in each state.

2. Cite to the official state code, if there is one. When citing to an unofficial code, include the publisher's name in parentheses, ahead of the publication year.

❏ **Examples:**

Wash. Rev. Code Ann. § 4.24.040 (West 1993).

Cal. Civ. Proc. Code § 473 (West 1992).

■ **Procedural law citations** should include:

a) properly abbreviated name identifying the rule (rather than the statutory publication);

b) number that identifies the particular rule.

❏ **Examples:**

Fed. R. Civ. P. 4(c).

Minn. R. Civ. P. 52.01.

Item to remember:

The organization and format of information varies by jurisdiction, but can be found in *The Bluebook,* Table T.1, United States Jurisdictions.

ADMINISTRATIVE DECISIONS/REGULATIONS:

■ **Administrative decisions citations** should include:

a) complete name of the first party listed (underscored or italicized);

b) volume number;

c) page number;

d) properly abbreviated name of the publication in which the decision appears;

e) year of the decision, in parentheses.

❏ **Example:**

Charles M. Smith, 86 I. & N. Dec. 461 (1983).

■ **Federal administrative**

a) title number in the cc

b) abbreviation for *Code of Federal Regulations* (C.F.R.);

c) section number of the regulation;

d) year of publication, in parentheses. Use latest year unless earlier version is being cited.

❏ **Example:**

16 C.F.R. § 444 (1996).

Items to Remember:

1. If the regulation is commonly known by a particular name, the name can be included preceding the other information.

❏ **Example:**

FTC Credit Practices Rule, 16 C.F.R. § 444 (1996).

2. State administrative materials should be cited by analogy to federal materials. For guidance for specific states' materials, consult *The Bluebook,* Table T.1, United States Jurisdictions.

JUDICIAL LAW (CASES):

■ **Case citations** should include:

a) case name (underscored or italicized);

b) volume number, proper abbreviation of official publication, page number where case begins;

c) volume number, proper abbreviation of parallel (unofficial) publication, if any, and page number where case begins;

d) in parentheses, the proper abbreviation for court (if not obvious from name of reporter) and year of decision.

❏ **Examples:**

U.S. Supreme Court — United States Reports:
Press-Enterprise Co. v. Superior Court, 478 U.S. 1 (1986).
Unofficial/parallel citation — Supreme Court Reporter:
Press-Enterprise Co. v. Superior Court, 106 S. Ct. 2735 (1986).

U.S. Court of Appeals — Federal Reporter, Second Series:
United States v. Sterley, 764 F.2d 530 (8th Cir. 1985).

U.S. District Court — Federal Supplement:
Campbell v. Sirak, 476 F. Supp. 21 (S.D. Ohio 1980).

State decisions:
State v. Walker, 35 N.C. App. 182, 241 S.E.2d 89 (1978).

Items to Remember:

1. Case names include last name of plaintiff, v. (abbreviation for versus), last name of defendant.

2. If there are multiple plaintiffs, multiple defendants, or other parties to the lawsuit, provide only the names of the first listed plaintiff and defendant.

3. When citing a direct quotation, the citation should include the page number where the quoted material begins. Insert this after the page number for the first page of the decision. This is called a "pinpoint" citation.

❏ **Example:**

Including quotation with citation:
"Each essential element of an adverse possession claim must be proven by clear and convincing evidence." Downing v. Bird, 100 So. 2d 57, 64 (Fla. 1958).

4. The last element of the citation is the year of the decision, in parentheses. If the official publication includes decisions from more than one court, then the proper abbreviation for the court should also be included in the parentheses before the year. In the next example, *Southern Reporter, Second Series* is the official publication for cases from Alabama after 1976. (See *The Bluebook,* Table T.1, United States Jurisdictions). Because So. 2d publishes opinions from several courts, it is ⌐urt for this particular opinion.

1982).

Prepared by Edward H. Hein and Be

ISBN # 0-314-22430-0

5. When citing a decision that was subsequently considered on appeal to a higher court, this information should be duly noted and underscored following the parenthetical information of year and court of origin.

❑ **Example:**
Subsequent decision on appeal:
Campbell v. Sirak, 476 F. Supp. 21 (S.D. Ohio 1980), aff'd, 705 F.2d. 451 (6th Cir. 1982).

6. In documents to be submitted to a state court, cite **in-state cases** with the official public domain citation, if available; otherwise, use the official state reporter citation, if available. Also include the regional reporter citation. For **out-of-state** cases, and for **all state cases cited in legal memoranda** and other non-court documents, use the official public domain citation, if available; otherwise, use the regional reporter citation. An **official public domain citation** (medium neutral citation) includes case name, year of decision, name of issuing court, and sequential number of the decision; pinpoint cites are to paragraph numbers. For guidance in citing a particular state's reporters, consult *The Bluebook*, Table T.1, and local court rules. Generally, see Practitioners' Note P.3 and Rule 10.3.1.

RESTATEMENTS:

■ **Restatement citations** should include:
a) full name of the Restatement, with edition in parentheses (underscored or italicized);
b) Restatement section number;
c) year of publication.

❑ **Example:**
Restatement (Second) of Torts § 847A (1979).

TREATISES AND BOOKS:

■ **Treatise citations** should include:
a) volume number (if more than one);
b) full name of author or editor (if given);
c) title of the publication (underscored or italicized);
d) edition or series number;
e) year of publication.

❑ **Example:**
4 James W. Moore et al., Moore's Federal Practice Par. 42.01 (2d ed. 1985).
William P. Statsky, Torts: Personal Injury Litigation (2d ed. 1990).

LEGAL ENCYCLOPEDIAS:

■ **Encyclopedia citations** should include:
a) volume number;
b) properly abbreviated publication name;
c) topic name (underscored or italicized);
d) section number;
e) year of publication.

❑ **Example:**
89 C.J.S. Trial, § 761 (Supp. 1988).

ANNOTATED LAW REPORTS:

■ **Annotated law report citations** should include:
a) full name of the author;
b) the word "Annotation";
c) title of annotation (underscored or italicized);
d) volume number;
e) properly abbreviated name of publication;
f) page number where annotation begins;
g) year of publication.

❑ **Example:**
Damian Edward Okasinski, Annotation, Attorney Malpractice in Connection with Services Related to Adoption of Child, 18 A.L.R.5th 892 (1994).

LAW REVIEW/JOURNALS:

■ **Law Review/Journal citations** should include:
a) full name of the author;
b) title of the article (underscored or italicized);
c) volume number;
d) properly abbreviated title of the periodical;
e) page number where article begins;
f) year of publication.

❑ **Example:**
Catherine M. Valerio Barrad, Genetic Information and Property Theory, 87 Nw. U. L. Rev. 1037 (1993).

GENERAL NOTES

SENTENCE STRUCTURE: If citations are prepared as sentences or clauses, a single citation or one concluding a sentence is ended with a period.

❑ **Example:**
Scot Typewriter Co. v. Underwood Corp., 170 F. Supp. 862 (S.D.N.Y. 1959).
Multiple citations appearing consecutively are separated by semicolons.

❑ **Example:**
Busik v. Levine, 63 N.J. 351, 307 A.2d 571 (1973); Crudup v. Marrero, 57 N.J. 353, 273 A.2d 16 (1971).
Citations appearing within other text should be set off by a comma at the beginning and end of the citation, unless the citation begins or ends the sentence.

❑ **Example:**
In the landmark case, Roland v. Kravaco, Inc., 355 Pa. Super. 493, 513 A.2d 1029 (1986), the plaintiff fell in defendant's parking lot and commenced an action in trespass to recover for her injuries.

CAPITALIZATION: Proper nouns appearing in citations should appear with the first letter of each word in capital letters. Connecting terms, such as *the, or, and, of,* should not be capitalized.

ABBREVIATIONS: Generally, avoid abbreviations not listed in *The Bluebook* unless substantial space will be saved and the resulting abbreviation is unambiguous. Consult tables at the end of *The Bluebook* for specific abbreviations, and Rule 6.1 for guidance on spacing and use of periods in abbreviations. *The Bluebook* index begins with one-and-one-half pages of entries under the heading "Abbreviations."

SHORT FORMS OF REFERENCE: Generally, once an authority has been fully cited in a document, a short form of the citation may be used for subsequent references in the same discussion of that authority. For specific guidance, consult *The Bluebook*, Rule 4, Practitioners' Notes P.4 and P.7, and the final section in each of Rules 10 - 20.

SUPPLEMENTS: If a supplement is used, this should be indicated in the citation in parentheses before the year.

❑ **Examples:**
28 U.S.C. § 1441 (b) (Supp. 1993).
Fla. Stat. ch. 95.16 (Supp. 1994).

7-3519-2/© 1997 West

ISBN # 0-314-22430-0

PRACTICAL LEGAL WRITING FOR LEGAL ASSISTANTS

Celia C. Elwell

Adjunct Professor
Department of Legal Assistant Education
University of Oklahoma Law Center

Robert Barr Smith

Professor
University of Oklahoma College of Law

WEST PUBLISHING COMPANY

Mpls/St. Paul   New York   Los Angeles   San Francisco

w Dictionary®, Corpus Juris Secundum®, Federal Reporter®, Federal
plement®, New York Supplement®, North Western Reporter®, Pacific
Reporter , Southern Reporter®, South Eastern Reporter®
U.S.C.A.®, WESTMATE and WESTLAW® are registered trademarks and WIN™ is a trademark of
West Publishing.
Shepardize®, Shepardized®, and Shepard's® are registered trademarks and Sheparding™ is a trade-
mark of Shepard's/McGraw-Hill, Inc.
LEXIS® is a registered trademark of Reed Elsevier

Copyediting: Christianne Thillen
Cover and Text Design: Lois Stanfield, LightSource Images
Cover Image: Telegraph Colour Library/International Stock
Composition: Carlisle Communications
Index: Bernice Eisen

WEST'S COMMITMENT TO THE ENVIRONMENT

In 1906, West Publishing Company began recycling materials left over from the production of books. This began a tradition of efficient and responsible use of resources. Today, 100% of our legal bound volumes are printed on acid-free, recycled paper consisting of 50% new paper pulp and 50% paper that has undergone a de-inking process. We also use vegetable-based inks to print all of our books. West recycles nearly 22,650,000 pounds of scrap paper annually—the equivalent of 187,500 trees. Since the 1960s, West has devised ways to capture and recycle waste inks, solvents, oils, and vapors created in the printing process. We also recycle plastics of all kinds, wood, glass, corrugated cardboard, and batteries, and have eliminated the use of polystyrene book packaging. We at West are proud of the longevity and the scope of our commitment to our environment.

West pocket parts and advance sheets are printed on recyclable paper and can be collected and recycled with newspapers. Staples do not have to be removed. Bound volumes can be recycled after removing the cover.

Production, Prepress, Printing and Binding by West Publishing Company.

TEXT IS PRINTED ON 10% POST
CONSUMER RECYCLED PAPER

COPYRIGHT ©1996   By WEST PUBLISHING COMPANY
                      610 Opperman Drive
                      P.O. Box 64526
                      St. Paul, MN 55164-0526

LIBRARY OF CONGRESS CATALOGING-IN-PUBLICATION DATA
Elwell, Celia C.
    Practical legal writing for legal assistants / Celia C. Elwell,
Robert Barr Smith.
        p. cm.
    Includes index.
    ISBN 0-314-06115-0 (pbk. : alk. paper)
    1. Legal composition. 2. Legal assistants—United States-
-Handbooks, manuals, etc. I. Smith, Robert B. (Robert Barr), 1933-
.
KF250.E45 1996
808'.06634—dc20
                                                    95-32136
                                                       CIP

Dedicated to
The Hon. Marian P. Opala,
Justice of the Supreme Court of Oklahoma,
teacher, mentor, and friend.

CONTENTS IN BRIEF

CONTENTS

v

PREFACE

Most books on legal writing concentrate on writing legal memorandums and briefs. We both teach legal writing and analysis, and we both have experience teaching legal assistants, and we know that legal assistants must know how to write both. But legal memorandums and briefs are only a part of the legal writing that legal assistants are regularly called upon to write in most workplaces. In this book we teach you how to write legal memorandums and briefs, and we also teach you how to write the many other kinds of documents commonly written by most legal assistants today.

Ethics

In this book we touch on the basic ethical principals for legal assistants. Even though our main purpose in this book is to teach you about legal writing, we stress legal ethics throughout the text. We cannot overemphasize the importance of high ethical standards for legal assistant students and practicing paralegals, as well as for the rest of the legal community.

Organization of the Text

The book is divided into thirteen chapters, a glossary, and several appendixes. The first chapter introduces our **fact scenario,** which serves as the basis for the lawsuit that we follow throughout the remainder of the book. Although each chapter stands on its own, the book is designed so that each chapter builds upon the last. We did this to help you build confidence in your legal writing skills as you progress through the book.

The **exercises** at the end of each chapter are designed to reinforce the key points for that chapter and to give you the opportunity to practice what you have learned. **Practice Tips** and **Margin Definitions** are sprinkled throughout the text, and the **Key Words** and **Phrases** are emphasized in boldface and found at the end of each chapter. All are designed as aids to understanding the text and reinforcing the key elements of each chapter.

There are **numerous examples** of various types of legal writing throughout the text and the appendixes. We have used "real life" examples of good, and bad, legal writing as much as possible. The text also includes on-the-job tips, such as shortcuts, time-savers, and common pitfalls to avoid in legal writing.

Supplements

These supplements are available with this textbook:

- The **instructor's manual,** which includes teaching suggestions, additional exercises, test questions, and suggested solutions to the exercises found at the end of each chapter.
- **West's Paralegal Video Library,** including these videotapes: "Introduction to Legal Research," which is designed to teach the basics and rationale for legal research.

  "I Never Said I Was a Lawyer," created by the Colorado Bar Association Committee on Legal Assistants. This video is non-state-specific, and employs hypothetical scenarios to give students experience dealing with ethical dilemmas, such as unauthorized practice of law, confidentiality, and lack of attorney supervision.

  "The Making of a Case," in which a case is followed from the court system to the law library shelf. This video provides an introduction to significant aspects of our legal system, and aids students to better understand of what case law is and how cases are published. The tape is narrated by Richard Dysart, star of "L.A. Law."
- **WESTLAW.** West's online computerized legal research system, offers students a "hands-on" experience with a system commonly used in law offices. It can be accessed with Macintosh and IBM PCs and compatibles, and requires a modem. Ten hours are free to qualified adopters.
- **WESTMATE** Tutorial. Interactive software introducing students to WESTLAW capabilities including the WIN   (Natural Language Enhancement). It is available in DOS and Windows versions. WESTMATE runs on IBM PC/PS/2s and compatibles.
- *Strategies and Tips for Paralegal Educators,* written by Anita Tebbe of Johnson County Community College and designed for the special needs of paralegal educators. Professor Tebbe offers specific teaching ideas that will help instructors aid students in meeting their educational goals.
- *Citation-At-A Glance.* A quick, handy, portable reference card to the basic rules of citation for the most commonly cited research sources using the rules found in *A Uniform System of Citation,* 15th Edition, 1991.
- *How to Shepardize: Your Guide to Complete Legal Research Through Shepard's Citations,* **1993 WESTLAW Edition.** This 64-page pamphlet clearly explains the basic research technique of shepardizing.
- *Sample Pages,* **Third Edition.** A 225-page softcover text that introduces West legal research materials.
- *West's Law Finder.* This 77-page pamphlet describes various legal research sources and how they can be used.

For further information on any of these supplements, please contact your West Sales representative or write to West Publishing Co., College Division; 620 Opperman Drive, P.O. Box 64779, St. Paul, MN 55164-0779.

We hope that you will find this book to be a useful tool, not only now but as a future reference book to keep handy in your office. We know only one way to improve anyone's writing skills, and that is simply practice, practice, practice. If this book helps you anywhere along that journey, then it was worth all of the work we put into it.

Please do not hesitate to contact either one of us if you have any questions, ideas, or examples that you would like to share, especially if it teaches us a thing or two. If we have learned anything throughout our respective legal careers, it's that the more we know, the more we realize we don't know. You can find us both in the phone book in Norman, Oklahoma.

Robert Barr Smith
Celia C. Elwell
University of Oklahoma Law Center
Department of Legal Assistant Education
300 Timberdell Road
Norman, Oklahoma 73019

ACKNOWLEDGMENTS

No book is ever written by the authors alone, and this one is no exception. The writing process takes help, and we have had a lot of it. Our sincere and grateful thanks are sent to everyone who has helped and supported us throughout the writing of this book, but especially to those listed below.

Reviewers

To each of the reviewers of this textbook, thank you for your suggestions and criticisms, and for the time you spent on this project. Your assistance was invaluable.

Stacey Barone
Adelphi University

H. John Barnett
St. Mary-of-the Woods College

Cherie Calvin
Watterson College Pacific

Teresa L. Conaway
Pellissippi State Technical Community College

Katherine A. Currier
Elms College

T. Eric Evans
Ball State University

Vera Peaslee Haus
McIntosh College

John J. Keller
The Paralegal Institute

Jennifer Allen Labosky
Davidson County Community College

Cynthia Lauber
Community College of Aurora

Eric L. Lundt
Miami-Dade Community College
Wolfson Campus

Mary McLaughlin
Inver Hills Community College

Virginia C. Noonan
Northern Essex Community College

Elizabeth Raulerson
Indian River Community College

Brenda L. Rice
Johnson County Community College

Mary S. Urisko
Madonna University

West Publishing

We owe special thanks to the consideration, tact, and boundless patience of our editor, Elizabeth Hannan, our developmental editor Patty Bryant, our production editor, Amy C. Hanson, and promotion managers, Stacie Falvey and Kristen McCarthy, whose suggestions and guidance helped us enormously.

Others

In his or her own way, each of the following people had some involvement in the writing of this book. Each of you have our most profound thanks and appreciation.

- Research assistants Sandy Nowak, Sue Teschner, Marguerite Buechner, Tara Little, and Jandra Cox, each of whom made a significant contribution. All are bright, innovative, hard-working law students who will be outstanding attorneys. We were indeed fortunate to have persons of their caliber involved in this project.
- Cynthia Hines Majors, Esq. and Deborah Hobbs for sharing their insightful suggestions and copious resources and for their encouragement and support throughout this project.
- Professor Bill McNichols of the University of Oklahoma College of Law, for his invaluable assistance with the chapter on legal analysis.
- Professor Maria Protti, formerly of the University of Oklahoma College of Law, who was kind enough to read and comment on our chapter on research.
- Professor John Delaney of New York University Law School, who kindly permitted us to use, in our chapter on analysis, portions of his trenchant comments on briefing cases.
- Bobbie Moore, Tom Majors, Richard C. Smith, Richard Mann, Lt. (Ret.) W. B. Smith, Teresa Baker, William O. West, Diane Lewis, Patricia Sellers Dennis, James G. Hamill, David L. Kearney, Dino E. Viera, Tom Enis, Joseph Snider, Jr., Susan French Koran, Charlessa Allen, Kerry Fisbeck, and countless others, for sharing writing samples and forms and their copious legal expertise, and for their encouragement and support throughout this project.
- Our office co-workers, and particularly Linda Ivy, for their assistance, support, and patience throughout the writing of this book.
- Ms. Eugenia Sams and the other wizards in the College of Law's secretarial pool, who know everything there is to know about computers and the care and coddling of authors. Without them, we would still be back at Chapter 5.

- Elizabeth J. Campbell, CSR, CP, RPR, and Nancy Ripple, CSR, CP, RPR, who graciously gave their permission to use their name and the name of Ad Infinitum Reporting, Inc., and for Elizabeth's valuable time and invaluable assistance in preparing the deposition found in Appendix I.
- All of the students in the University of Oklahoma's paralegal legal writing class in Spring 1994—JoAnne Clark, Steve DiStephano, Barbara Jones, LeAnne Moffitt, Georjana Sites, Rhonda Stinnett, Carolyn Weeks, and Lisa Wilson—for their patience and graciousness as willing guinea pigs when the book was in its final stages.
- Rowena Scott, Program Coordinator at the University of Oklahoma Department of Legal Assistant Education, for her patience, support, encouragement, and assistance throughout every aspect of this project.

The authors gratefully acknowledge the use of definitions from *Black's Law Dictionary* and *Legal Thesaurus/Dictionary* by William Statsky as a basis for the definitions of key terms in this text. Most of the definitions were edited extensively from the original publications for length control.

And, finally, our grateful thanks and appreciation to our friends, but most of all to our families—Patty Smith and Phillip and Chris Elwell—whose patience and understanding supported and nurtured us during the writing of this book, and without which this book would not have been possible.

Celia C. Elwell   Robert Barr Smith

1

INTRODUCTION

This book is designed to teach you good legal writing. We intend that it be useful to you not only during your training, but long after you have completed your education and are at work in the legal profession.

As you will quickly discover, good legal writing is much like other good writing: simple, direct, and concise. Contrary to what many people think, good legal writing does not use long sentences, obscure words, or lots of Latin phrases. There once was a time when much legal writing was written in "lawyer speak," or what we call "legalese," a collection of six-syllable words often studded with antiquities and imbedded in monstrous paragraphs that sometimes went on for pages. This lumbering, redundant style is responsible for the reputation lawyers have for obscurity.

No more. Your employer, the modern lawyer, will expect your writing to be streamlined, accurate, and as concise as possible consistent with being thorough. He or she will demand proper English and spelling, and as few fifty-cent words as possible. In this book, we show you how to write that kind of English:

- Most important, we want to train you to write clear, concise, professional prose.
- We want to introduce you to the most common documents you will be called upon to draft in practice.
- We want you to understand basic legal research.

The skills of research and legal writing go hand-in-hand. This book is not a research text, of course. But our chapter on research—and the essential skill of citation—introduces you to the most common sources of legal authority. It also shows you how research is begun and developed, and how its results are used in legal writing.

Throughout this book, we give you exercises to do and documents to draft. Do them faithfully. They will cement in your mind the lessons taught by each chapter. Your instructor may give you other exercises to do and other documents to draft; do them faithfully as well. There is absolutely no substitute for practice.

Do not be discouraged; your first efforts will probably disappoint you. Nobody drafts legal documents well at the beginning. But everyone can improve his or her writing with practice, patience, and perseverance. Stick with it.

Listen to your instructor's critiques, and then rewrite with those comments in mind. Welcome critiques from your attorney when you begin working a law office. Carefully read the work of veteran legal professionals whose work is acknowledged to be first-class. Write and rewrite, and be hard on yourself. Excellence does not come easy, but it comes.

Do not copy someone else's legal document uncritically. By all means learn from the writing of other top-flight legal professionals. But remember that many people in the profession write poorly and carelessly; obviously, they are not good examples. Also beware of documents written "because we've always done it this way." Bad writing is often mindlessly repeated through custom or habit.

It is not up to you to change the way your office does things. If your attorney prescribes a particular format for a document, that is the format you will use. But also remember that each document is just a little different from others of the same kind. Slavish copying of anything, even a fine example, is not enough. Each document must be tailored to achieve its particular purpose.

When we give you a drafting assignment in this text, it will often be grounded in a hypothetical case, *Healy v. Allegretti*. We have set out the scenario below. Read it over, but do not form any hard-and-fast ideas of what the pertinent law is, or how a legal professional should proceed in preparing either side's case. All of these things you will discover as we go along.

FACT SCENARIO

This morning, your attorney called you into her office. "Sit down," she said, and handed you a slim manila folder containing a few sheets of paper. "We have just been retained by Ms. Jane Healy to represent her in this matter," she continued. "All we have thus far is a set of facts, probably incomplete. I want you to work this case from the beginning. Read over the factual background in this folder, and then come back and talk the case over with me. Remember that as always, everything we discuss is confidential—especially anything that comes from our client."

After leaving your attorney's office, you returned to your desk and opened the folder. You read this summary of the facts:

The client's name is Ms. Jane Healy, 483 Moore Drive, River City. She is thirty-two, single, and a successful public relations specialist. She works for Ajax, Inc., a large firm, and is number two in the public relations department. She earns $55,000 per year.

The firm likes her and her work. Jane has already been told that she will become head of her department when her boss retires in about four months. She can expect to be delegated a great deal of

responsibility, and given a raise of at least $15,000 per year.

At 6:30 p.m., eleven months and twenty-two days ago, Jane Healy was on her way home from work. Traffic was heavy, and Ms. Healy was late. She had a date at 7:00 p.m., and wanted to change clothes, feed her cat, and freshen up before her date arrived.

She was driving west on 14th Street, about four blocks from her home. As Jane approached the intersection of 14th Street and Childs Street, the signal light there turned yellow. Even though the speed limit in that area is twenty-five miles per hour, Jane admitted later to the investigating police officer that she had accelerated to about thirty-five m.p.h. as she tried to beat the yellow light through the intersection. As she entered the intersection, traffic in front of her unexpectedly stopped, and she had to step suddenly on her brakes to avoid hitting the car in front of her. When the light changed, Jane remained stranded in the intersection because the traffic in front of her remained at a standstill.

While Jane Healy was stranded in the middle of the intersection, Charles Raymond was driving south on Childs Street in his 1985 Trans-Am, and had stopped at the same intersection for the red light. Totally disregarding the fact that the intersection was not cleared of east/west traffic, Mr. Raymond pushed his car's gas pedal all the way to the floor the instant the light turned green. He roared into the intersection, striking Ms. Healy's BMW broadside, knocking Jane against the left door of her car, and smashing Jane's car into a steel power pole on the southwest corner of the intersection. At the moment of impact with the pole, Ms. Healy's seat belt broke. The accident report and a diagram of the accident scene prepared by the investigating officer are provided in Exhibit 1.1.

As a result of this accident, Jane's skull was fractured, three ribs were broken, one rib punctured her left lung, and her face was very badly slashed by broken glass. Although it has been four weeks since the accident, Jane is still a patient in the hospital. Her doctors have told her that she must expect at least two more plastic surgeries to repair the damage to her face. Since the accident, Jane has also suffered from severe migraine-type headaches. Because of her disfiguring injuries, she cannot face the public—a requirement of her job—for at least a year, and will probably carry some facial scars the rest of her life.

Jane Healy's firm, Ajax, Inc., is sympathetic, but has told Jane that it cannot leave open the assistant vice president's position to which she was to be promoted in approximately three months. Worse, if Jane cannot meet the public for an unknown period of time, they must hire somebody who can. Ajax, Inc. has offered Jane a year's pay as severance, but this accident has probably cost her her prospects and her present job.

Charles Raymond, the driver of the car who struck Jane Healy's automobile, is a mechanic at Allegretti & Sons, a large company that rebuilds automobile transmissions and engines.

Raymond was convicted of drunken driving in November 1986 and June 1990. On both occasions, he was sentenced to sixty days in the county jail and a $500 fine. In 1986, his sixty-day sentence was suspended; in 1990, Raymond served thirty-five days. Last year, he was arrested again for drunk driving, but plea-bargained to reckless driving, for which he served ten days and paid a $500 fine. On all three occasions, the court suspended Raymond's driving license, and Raymond's license was still suspended at the time of this accident.

On the day of the accident, Raymond's boss, Vincent Allegretti, asked Raymond, as he had many times in the past, to deliver a transmission to a body shop in River City on his way home from work. Raymond agreed. Mr. Allegretti knows of Raymond's fondness for strong spirits and also of his driving record, although Mr. Allegretti did not know whether Raymond's last suspension was still in effect when he asked him to do this errand. Mr. Allegretti was also aware that Raymond often stopped at Red's Tavern throughout the day whenever he was transporting parts for Mr. Allegretti's business or was on his lunch break. In fact, Mr. Allegretti had counseled Raymond in the past about staying sober during work hours.

Allegretti & Sons has a blanket liability policy on all its employees and vehicles, with a maximum limit of $1 million per person per accident, plus coverage for property damage.

After Raymond left work that day, he decided to stop at Red's Tavern before he delivered the transmission to the shop at River City. Charles Raymond is a regular customer at Red's, where he frequently gets obnoxiously and aggressively drunk. That day, Raymond had at least four straight shots of bourbon, plus four beers, all in approximately forty-five minutes. As Raymond staggered from the bar and left through the front door, one of Red's customers commented, "Man, is that guy loaded." The regular bartender, Tony Simpson, who often serves Raymond, responded, "So what else is new?"

FACT SCENARIO

EXHIBIT 1-1 *Collision Report and Fact Diagram*

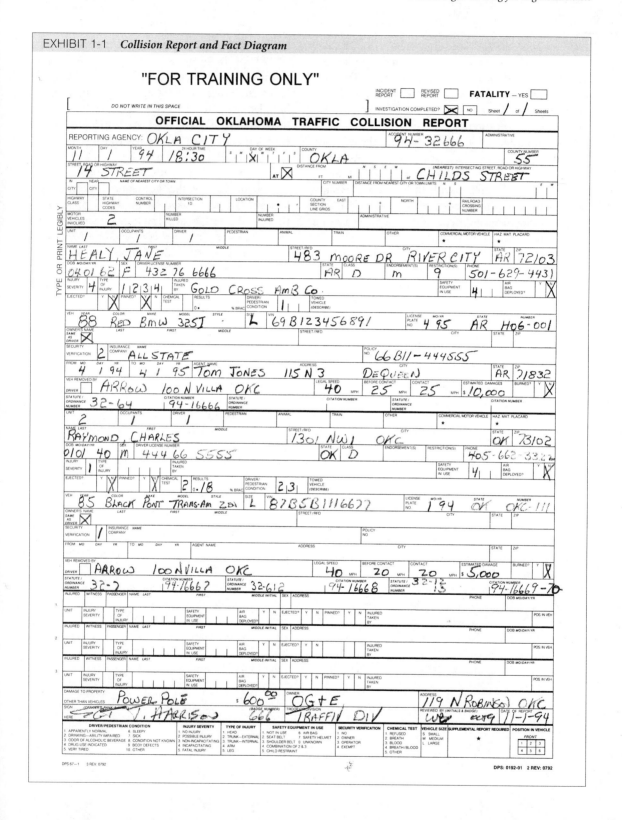

EXHIBIT 1-1 —*Continued*

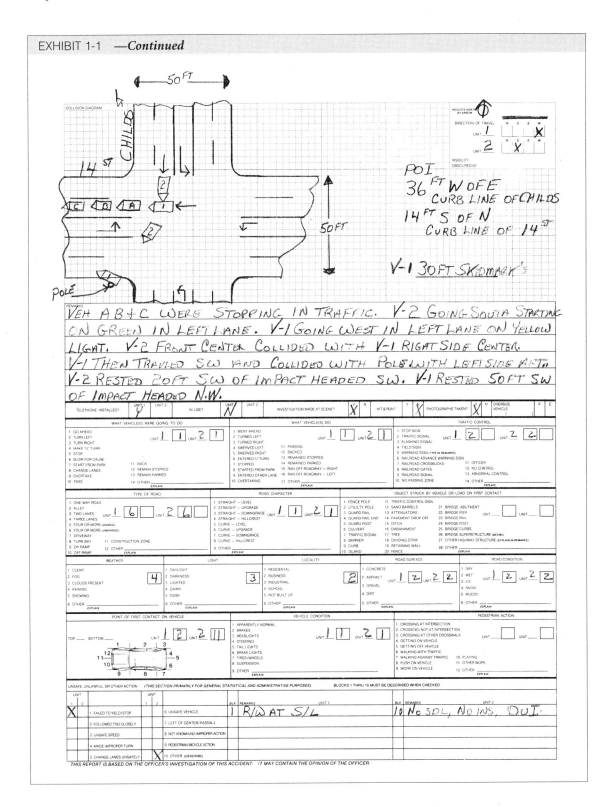

EXHIBIT 1-1 —*Continued*

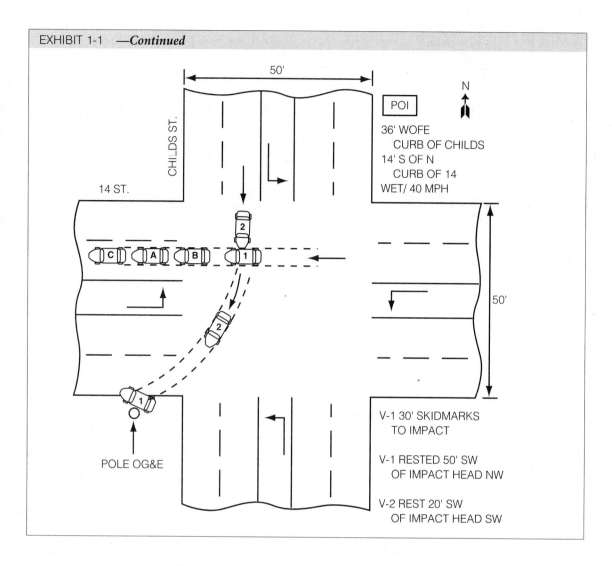

This is what you know about the case. It is, by the way, much more than you will ordinarily know at the beginning of such a case. You will need to find out other things as the case progresses; these things will be the subject of some of the exercises we will give you.

Before we get into the nuts and bolts of writing, research, and drafting, we will examine some other skills. Chapter Two deals with communication in the legal world—with clients, with co-workers, and with people outside the office.

2

COMMUNICATION SKILLS

Basic communication skills are invaluable to any legal assistant. Ideas, instructions, and questions—whether oral or written—must be understood, or they are not effective. We follow a philosophy somewhat akin to Murphy's Law: What can be misunderstood will be. Because much of what a legal assistant does is to obtain or request information, it is critical to be easily understood with no room for misinterpretation. If you feel you are often misunderstood or constantly have to explain, "that is not what I meant," perhaps your communication skills could use improvement.

◼ LISTENING SKILLS

Listening is one of the most important communication skills. How often do we find ourselves in a conversation thinking of what we will say in response before the other person has finished? It is no wonder that we understand only a portion of what the other person has said. Regardless of whether you are listening to a client or to your supervising attorney as he or she gives you an assignment, it is critical that you be able to *understand and translate* what is said. To *listen with understanding*, you must envision the speaker's expressed idea from his or her viewpoint, sense how it feels to that person, and use his or her frame of reference about the discussed topic.

Here are some suggestions for improving your listening techniques:

- *Pay attention to the answer given after you ask a question.* This sounds so simple, yet instead of listening to a response to our own question, we often concentrate on what we intend to say in response to the expected answer, or think instead about our next question. We may even think about unrelated things, such as plans for after work or for the weekend.
- *Maintain eye contact with the speaker.* This is one good way to avoid allowing yourself to be distracted or your thoughts to wander.
- *Avoid the tendency to anticipate, or jump to conclusions about, what is said before the speaker has finished.* Instead, listen closely even if you think you know what the other person is going to say.
- *Be sure that you fully understand what you have been told before offering any advice or suggestions.* Sometimes people are so eager to show their enthusi-

7

■ PRACTICE TIP

Remember that if we do not clearly understand what is being said, we often do one of two things. If we are interested in what the person has to say, we listen more closely to catch the meaning of what is said. Or, if we become bored or distracted, our attention on the speaker wanders until we have no idea what the other person has actually said.

asm or interest that they offer unsolicited solutions and suggestions without realizing that the speaker would prefer that they listen rather than give advice. That is not to say that solutions or suggestions are never appropriate. Of course they are if they are offered at the appropriate time.

■ *Stop what you are doing, and give the speaker your full attention.* It is nearly impossible to concentrate fully on someone else's words while you are doing something else. You may take in the gist of what is said, but will probably miss the details.

■ ORAL COMMUNICATION SKILLS

Almost three hundred years ago, British author and politician Joseph Addison said:

> If the minds of men were laid open, we should see but little difference between that of the wise man and that of the fool. The difference is that the first knows how to pick and cull his thoughts for conversation . . . whereas the other lets them all indifferently fly out in words.

You are judged, however fairly or unfairly, by what you say and how you say it.

Research has shown that, in face-to-face communications, the voice carries 38 percent of that communication, the body carries 55 percent, and the words carry 7 percent. Your voice, body, and words should convey confidence in what you are saying and how you say it to make your communication with others effective. Although your words may sound as if you are calm and self-confident, your foot beating a rhythm on the floor indicates something altogether different. When speaking, consider your inflection, tone, facial expression, gestures, and words; take into account the total impression you make.

PRACTICE TIP

Avoid slang, profanity, fad words, or other sloppy language.

Avoid slang, profanity, fad words, or other sloppy language. Consciously force yourself to find substitutes for these words, and eliminate them from your speech. This type of language makes the speaker appear coarse and unprofessional.

Sooner or later, everyone says the wrong thing. If you have blundered badly, simply say "I'm sorry," and move on to another topic. But if you have only flirted with danger, veer away as fast as you can. Do not cause a scene by making profuse apologies or by becoming flustered. Staying poised will help others do the same. If it is the other person who has blundered, help them out. Change the topic to a safer subject, and move on as if nothing had happened.

■ NOTE-TAKING SKILLS

Legal assistants are often asked to take notes during witness interviews, depositions, conferences, hearings, or trials. Train yourself to take notes quickly and accurately without losing the gist of what is said. Good note-taking is an acquired skill. It is difficult to listen and write at the same time—this is why your attorney needs you to take notes. Here are some guidelines for taking notes:

- *Note the key words and phrases.*   Some legal assistants find that some form of shorthand or speed-writing is invaluable when taking notes. Effective note-writing is more a matter of writing key words and phrases than attempting to capture every word. Noting key words and phrases will help you reconstruct the most important information in a memorandum. We can rarely read another person's handwritten notes. Usually you will transcribe your notes into memorandum form or some other format that can be reviewed by your attorney.
- *Transcribe your notes promptly.*   Few of us take precise, neatly written notes. More often than not, your notes will be hastily scrawled across a legal pad. It is extremely difficult to reconstruct events and dialogue from scribbled notes that are more than a few days old. It is best to transcribe your notes as soon as possible while everything is fresh in your memory.
- *Get the important details.*   When taking notes, listen closely for dates, names, and exhibit numbers and descriptions (as well as any key words and phrases) that will help to reconstruct the event later in your memorandum. Your notes do not have to be a verbatim transcript of what was said. Your role here is not as a court reporter, whose job it is to record and memorialize every single utterance made. Rather, your goal is to note the key points or other important information for your attorney. However, if you find that you are able to write down someone's words verbatim, be sure to indicate the same in your notes and your transcribed memorandum by quotation marks. Never use quotation marks when you are only paraphrasing what was said, or if you are unsure that your notes are accurate.

Here is one example of a situation in which you, as a legal assistant, can be an asset to your attorney by taking notes. Your attorney asks you to attend a **discovery conference** with her which has been scheduled in accordance with a local court rule that requires opposing counsel to meet and discuss disputes over discovery. The most common reason for this type of conference is one side's failure, or refusal, to produce requested discovery. Its purpose is to encourage the attorneys to work out whatever differences they may have during discovery before bringing the matter to the court to resolve.

In this situation, your attorney explains, she cannot give her full attention to hashing out differences with opposing counsel and take notes at the same time. She wants you there taking notes so that she will have an accurate account of the conference without relying on her memory alone.

If you are not currently working on the case or are unfamiliar with the discovery requests and responses of each party, review them before the conference. If you have studied the discovery requests and responses and do not understand what the discovery dispute

◼ PRACTICE TIP

Know the case. You will increase tenfold the quality of support you give to your attorney. If you know nothing about the case, then review the file's correspondence, pleadings, and other documents filed in the case. Do not be afraid to ask the attorney to fill you in on the latest developments.

is about, ask your supervising attorney to explain the problem to you. The better you understand the underlying reasons for the conference, the better you will note the nuances or inferences spoken by each side. Also, because you are taking notes, your attention will be more focused than your attorney's. You may even catch something that she misses.

During the discovery conference, be sure to note any agreements that are made, any promises or refusals to produce requested information or deponents by either side, and any arrangements agreed to by the attorneys to produce information, such as when or where the information, or person, will be produced. You can also assist by advising the attorney if any details are overlooked during the conference. During the heat of discussion, your attorney may forget to address a detail or two with opposing counsel. If this happens, you can discreetly advise your attorney so that the subject can be raised and, hopefully, resolved.

Exhibit 2.1 is a sample memorandum that might be written from notes taken during the discovery conference just discussed.

EXHIBIT 2.1 *Internal Memorandum on Discovery Conference*

TO: Amelia Pepper
FROM: Chris Roberts
DATE: July 25, 1993
RE: July 24, 1993 Rule 14(E) Discovery Conference
FILE: *Jane Healy v. Allegretti et al.*

This memorandum is a summary of notes taken on July 24, 1993, during the discovery conference held in our offices beginning at 1 p.m. and ending 3:05 p.m. Persons attending: Amelia Pepper and Chris Roberts, for Plaintiff Jane Healy, and Sean Oxford and Betsy Bates, for Defendant BMW.

After some discussion, Mr. Oxford agreed to produce John Cooper, BMW Senior Vice President of Production, for a deposition on August 11, 1993, at 9 a.m. The deposition is to be held in Mr. Oxford's office. We are to arrange for the court reporter. Each attorney agreed to use the same court reporter for all depositions to be taken in this case.

Further, Mr. Oxford agreed that the documents responsive to our Requests for Production Nos. 5–15 will be made available for our inspection and copying at Mr. Cooper's deposition. Part of those documents will most likely contain information, such as trade secrets or financial data. The parties agreed to sign a joint protective order, to be drafted by Mr. Oxford for our review and approval, for those documents. Any documents deemed by BMW or its counsel as relating to the protective order will be stamped in red ink with "CONFIDENTIAL—SUBJECT TO PROTECTIVE ORDER." Mr. Oxford will try to forward a draft of the protective order to you before July 30, 1993.

▓ DICTATION SKILLS

If you were to ask most legal assistants and lawyers, they would say that they never received any training on how to give dictation. It is just one of the skills developed on the job. Every legal secretary has her own stories about novice lawyers and paralegals whose dictation made them the comic relief at coffee breaks. Legal secretaries avoid transcribing the dictation of those attorneys and legal assistants whose dictation skills are bad to nonexistent. No one wants to touch it, and for good reason! If you find you are constantly frustrated because your secretary returns poor rough drafts of your dictation, it may be that your dictation habits are to blame rather than your secretary.

Dictation Equipment

Fundamental to good dictation is an understanding of, and familiarity with, the dictation equipment. Know how to stop, start, and rewind for prompts without overlapping. Remember that interruptions may cause you to lose your train of thought and create inconsistencies in your dictation. Rewind to the beginning of your last complete thought, reorganize your thoughts, and pick up where you left off.

Dictation Etiquette

When you are giving dictation, speak in a normal voice. Enunciate clearly. Do not try to dictate when you are eating or chewing gum or ice. Remember that the tape picks up any background noise, such as music or shuffling papers. If background noise cannot be avoided, compensate by using the speed and tone/volume controls to lessen the problem.

Editing

Good editing habits are a critical part of dictation skills. Indicate revisions in colored ink (but *not* blue or black) rather than pencil, and mark changes clearly. Be sure your handwriting is legible. Edit for clarity and conciseness. Avoid double or ambiguous meanings. Correct errors in grammar, spelling, and punctuation. Carefully proofread any names, addresses, numerical figures, definitions, and quotations. Use standard proofreading marks (see Exhibit 2.2 p. 12).

Dictation Dos and Don't

Here is a basic checklist of dictation dos and don't:

✔ *Organize your thoughts before you start to dictate.*   "You know where I said something about plaintiff's delinquent discovery responses? I think it was somewhere after that sentence about the hearing. Or maybe after the reference to the Scheduling Order—I'm not sure. Well, anyway, insert this stuff about the deposition I'm dictating now there." Need we say more?

✔ *When you are dictating, do not eat, chew ice, shuffle papers, or walk around the room.* All of these activities create noises that obliterate or obscure your words.

✔ *Always start any new dictation at the beginning of side A of the cassette tape.*   This helps your secretary avoid wasting time to search for the beginning of your dictation.

✔ *Give adequate instructions to the secretary for preparing the assignment.*   Give your secretary all the information he or she needs, whether it is an address, the correct spelling of a name, or the style of the case. If you cannot provide all the

---

EXHIBIT 2.2 *Proofreading Marks and Symbols*

Proofreaders' Marks

OPERATIONAL SIGNS

Mark	Meaning
ℛ	Delete
⌒	Close up; delete space
⌒℞	Delete and close up (use only when deleting letters *within* a word)
stet	Let it stand
#	Insert space
eq #	Make space between words equal; make space between lines equal
hr #	Insert hair space
ls	Letterspace
¶	Begin new paragraph
☐	Indent type one em from left or right
⊐	Move right
⊏	Move left
⊐⊏	Center
⊓	Move up
⊔	Move down
fl	Flush left
fr	Flush right
═	Straighten type; align horizontally
‖	Align vertically
tr	Transpose
(*sp*)	Spell out

TYPOGRAPHICAL SIGNS

Mark	Meaning
ital	Set in italic type
rom	Set in roman type
bf	Set in boldface type
lc	Set in lowercase
caps	Set in capital letters
sc	Set in small capitals
wf	Wrong font; set in correct type
X	Check type image; remove blemish
V	Insert here *or* make superscript
Λ	Insert here *or* make subscript

PUNCTUATION MARKS

Mark	Meaning
⌃	Insert comma
⌄ ⌄	Insert apostrophe *or* single quotation mark
⌄ ⌄	Insert quotation marks
⊙	Insert period
(*set*) ?	Insert question mark
;/	Insert semicolon
:/ *or* :/	Insert colon
=	Insert hyphen
M̲	Insert em dash
N̲	Insert en dash
⸦/⸧ *or* (/)	Insert parentheses

information needed to do the assignment, tell the secretary where it can be found, and *tell him or her clearly.* ("It's somewhere in the file" won't do). Most secretaries prefer to be given the file along with the dictation so that they can verify the spelling of names or details.

✓ *Always dictate the proper punctuation.* Secretaries cannot always determine punctuation by listening to voice inflection, even if it seems obvious to you where the punctuation belongs.

✓ *Do not assume the secretary knows how to spell everything you dictate.* Names, legal citations, and certain terminology (such as medical or legal terms) should be dictated in specific detail.

✓ *Spell out words that sound alike, such as* principle/principal *or* insure/ensure. A list of words such as these, and their correct spellings and definitions, can be found at Appendix A.

✓ *Indicate whether Co. should be typed as* Co. *or* Company, *or whether* Corp. *means just that or* Corporation. This is especially important when dictating the style or caption of the case, where accuracy of the proper name is critical.

✓ *Dictate when to double or single space, underline, italicize, bold, indent paragraphs, or capitalize certain words or phrases.* When dictating a parenthesis or quotation mark, be sure to dictate the closing parenthesis or quotation mark.

✓ *When dictating a quotation, provide a copy from the original for the secretary rather than dictating the quotation verbatim.* Quotations must be reproduced *exactly* as they are found in the original source. Commas or italics must be copied accurately. The secretary can accomplish this more efficiently with a copy of the original rather than from dictation.

✓ *Dictate columns, whether numerical or alphabetical, across the page from left to right.* Do not forget to indicate the position of decimal points. If possible, provide a written example of how you want the columns to look.

✓ *Label your dictation tapes.* If you are like most legal assistants, you share a secretary with other attorneys or legal assistants. To help your secretary manage her workload, put a sticky note on your dictation tape telling the secretary what is on the tape, such as "two letters" or "Answer to Interrogatories."

✓ *Always indicate the end of your dictation on the tape.* You will sometimes dictate more than one document on a tape to be transcribed by your secretary. How can you be sure your secretary will continue listening to the tape after the first document has been transcribed? If the gap on the tape between documents is significant, the secretary may mistakenly think you had finished dictating, and erase the tape. To avoid this problem, always say "end of tape" at the end of your dictation.

✓ *Do not rewind the tape after you have finished your dictation.* Your secretary can better determine the amount of time needed to transcribe a tape if he or she can see how much of the tape was used.

Good dictation habits are a skill usually acquired through experience rather than in a classroom. If you are unsure whether your dictation skills need improvement, ask your secretary. Your secretary, more than anyone, is an excellent judge of whether your dictation skills need polishing.

■ TELEPHONE SKILLS

Lawyers and legal assistants both use the telephone to accomplish many tasks. Good manners and courtesy should always be uppermost in your mind when talking on the telephone. Sometimes the telephone is the only means of contact you may have with someone. Therefore, that person has no other impression of you and your firm except your telephone communication.

Telephone Etiquette

As soon as your call is answered, identify yourself, then give the name of your firm or organization and the name of the person to whom you wish to speak.

> Hello. This is Elizabeth Simpson, Richard Barnes' legal assistant. May I speak to Diana Parker or her legal assistant?

If the person you are calling is not there or unable to take your call, leave a sufficiently detailed message to give the person an idea why you were calling or what information you are requesting.

Here is an example of what we mean. You are trying to reach a court reporter to request the transcription of a hearing, and she is unavailable when you call. Keep your message courteous, brief, and to the point:

> This is Elizabeth Simpson, Richard Barnes' legal assistant at Barnes & Barnes. Please tell Ms. Jones that I would like a transcript as soon as possible of the hearing held on March 1, 1991, in *Roberts v. Adelman.* That is spelled A-D-E-L-M-A-N. The case number is CJ–90–1661. Please ask her to call me at 325–1221 at her earliest convenience. Thank you.

Leaving this type of message should ultimately save time and extra telephone calls. After receiving the message given above, the court reporter should be able to gather the following information before returning your call: (1) the page count of the transcript (and therefore its cost) and (2) an estimate of when the transcript will be ready.

Organizing Your Thoughts

PRACTICE TIP

Organize your thoughts before making a phone call. If necessary, make a list of questions you need answered (or information you must obtain) and refer to your list during the call.

No one appreciates a telephone call from a person who takes forever to get to the point, and is unclear in what he is saying or asking. Garbled requests for information can only have one result—failure. This is why you need to organize your thoughts before making your telephone call. If necessary, write an outline of what questions need to be asked or what information must be obtained so you can refer to it during the call.

Putting the Caller On Hold

Never respond to a question with an abrupt "hold on a minute," and keep the caller waiting several minutes or longer while you try to get an answer. If you are asked a question you cannot answer quickly, say so, and ask the caller if you can call back once you have the requested information. Ask the caller for a number where he or she can be reached, and give an approximate time when you will return the call.

Taking Notes during the Call

Whether you are making a telephone call or receiving one, train yourself to make notes automatically during the call. Jot down the date, the person to whom you are speaking, and the information given or requested. These notes should always be placed in the appropriate file for future reference.

This may seem like a waste of time and valuable file space; it isn't. If there is ever any question as to whether the telephone call was made or what was said, you will have a record of the call to back you up. If you write out an outline or notes before you call, put them in the file as well. Further, just as it is a good practice to make notes during each telephone call, it is wise to follow up important telephone calls with a confirmation letter setting out your understanding of what was said.

Ending the Telephone Call

Usually the person who makes the call also ends it. This is not important unless the call seems to be dragging on and getting nowhere. When you have made tentative attempts to end the conversation by saying something appropriate such as, "Thank you for the information. I appreciate your help and cooperation," and have been totally ignored, take a more aggressive stance. Wait for the first pause, or interrupt if you must, and say, "I'm sorry, but my secretary just gave me a note saying I am needed by one of the attorneys," or "I'm sorry to interrupt, but I must leave for a meeting. Thank you again for your help."

Returning Calls Promptly

An important function of any legal assistant is to facilitate communication between the attorney and client. But communication can quickly break down when a client's telephone calls are not returned within a reasonable amount of time. Clients, as well as others, become quickly irritated when someone repeatedly fails to return their telephone calls.

A hectic and demanding schedule is no excuse for failing to return someone's telephone call. Have you ever tried to reach someone by telephone repeatedly, only to have them answer several days later and say, "I've been so busy I just couldn't return your call." Did you feel any irritation when you heard that response? If so, you can then easily imagine how a client might react. If you cannot return someone's call on the same day it was received, apologize for the delay. The person on the other end will appreciate your consideration and professionalism.

◼ COMMUNICATION BETWEEN LAWYERS AND LEGAL ASSISTANTS

Basic management skills are an important form of communication in any office. Many lawyers and legal assistants alike find it difficult either to give instructions, receive criticism, or both. These are skills that can, and must, be acquired to achieve your greatest level of effectiveness and professionalism.

Sometimes a legal assistant may feel that he or she has not received thorough instructions for an assignment or been adequately told what is expected by the supervising attorney. At times, instructions or guidelines are haphazardly given or overlooked because of the busy work environment. Also, attorneys may sometimes neglect details that they assume a legal assistant either knows or can figure out. Regardless of the reasons, this type of environment often leads to poor-quality work and frustration for the lawyer and legal assistant. These are good indicators that the quality of communication between the attorney and legal assistant needs improvement.

PRACTICE TIP

Develop a habit of returning telephone calls promptly. Make it a goal to return all calls the same day they are received. If necessary, return calls before or after normal business hours or during the noon hour.

PRACTICE TIP

All communication between two or more persons is subject to each person's individual interpretation. Since it is impossible to control how others present information to us, we should work on our own listening and speaking skills to improve communication.

Paraphrasing

Listen carefully when you are given instructions or assignments. Whenever possible, take notes, but only if you can do so without missing what is said. Do not interrupt with questions until after the speaker has finished. Then paraphrase your understanding of the assignment by repeating the instructions in your own words while referring to your notes, if you have any. The supervising attorney can then quickly determine whether the instructions were clear, and make whatever corrections or explanations are necessary.

Clarification

Once the attorney has given complete instructions for the assignment, think before you speak or ask questions. Take a minute, and think about the assignment. Did you fully understand everything the assignment entails? Do you know where to find the files you will need? Are there unanswered questions left hanging as to whom to contact or how to obtain certain information? Do not try to second-guess the attorney's meaning or intentions. If you are not sure, it is better to ask for clarification than to guess.

Don't Be Afraid of Saying "I Don't Know"

Even the most qualified, experienced, and highly paid lawyers and legal assistants do not know how to do everything. It is easy to say that no one knows everything, but it is sometimes hard to admit when we are given an assignment out of our experience.

Each of us wants to be thought of as a competent professional who can be trusted to complete any task efficiently and without mistakes. Perhaps we are afraid that if we admit we don't know how to do something, our superiors or peers will think less of us. A person who has trouble saying "I don't know" is often more afraid of putting his or her knowledge and qualifications into doubt than of being embarrassed by failure.

The Hon. Marian P. Opala, Justice of the Supreme Court, State of Oklahoma, believes that the ability to say "I don't know" is the mark of a true professional. Justice Opala stresses that one who admits not knowing how to do something often saves time and avoids making serious mistakes:

> Embarrassed to say *"I don't know,"* too many insecure professionals *pretend* to understand instructions they are really unable to follow. Whenever lawyers or legal assistants on my staff are stuck with an assignment they do not comprehend, I should welcome their call for explanation. People with oversized egos, who don't speak up to seek guidance, waste precious time and often court disasters.

PRACTICE TIP

There is no such thing as a stupid question. It is always better to admit that you don't know how to do something rather than wasting time trying to pretend that you do.

We agree. There is no such thing as a stupid question. If you don't know, you simply don't, and that is all there is to it. It is always better to admit you do not know how to do something than to flounder around trying to figure it out. At best, you will produce a substandard work product; at worst, something so totally wrong it is completely unusable and embarrassing to both you and your supervising attorney.

If you do not know how to do any part of an assignment, ask the attorney for more complete instructions when you are paraphrasing the directions given to you. Although you will still be expected to perform the work, the supervising attorney will probably give you more thorough instructions or direct you to resources that will help you complete the assignment accurately. If your supervising attorney is unable or unavailable to give you the instruction you need, request help from another legal assistant or attorney who specializes in that area or is familiar with the case. In either event, you will have made your best effort to complete the assignment as accurately as possible, and will have gained new experience in the process.

Prioritizing Assignments

Many people find it extremely difficult to say no to any assignment, even when their workload is already overwhelming them. No matter that you are already covered in work up to your eyeballs; it would be difficult to turn down a senior partner's assignment. Yet, it may be impossible to accept that assignment and still keep the commitments you have already made to other attorneys in the office. So what do you do? Either way you approach this problem, you lose. By taking on the new assignment and neglecting the ones you already had, you will disappoint the attorneys who were depending on you. But, if you refuse the new assignment, you may irritate the senior partner, someone whose opinion could easily affect your job stability.

Here is an example of what can happen when work assignment priorities become an issue. Suppose that on Monday, you accepted an assignment from one of the firm's young, associate lawyers to summarize ten depositions before the end of next week. On Wednesday, the senior partner asks you to monitor and take notes during a criminal trial in a lawsuit that is related to a case in your office. The trial should last until the end of the following week.

You cannot summarize all of the depositions and monitor the criminal trial. Once again, this is a no-win proposition. If you decide to bump the associate's assignment for that of the senior partner, what are the possible ramifications? Even if the associate assures you that he or she understands and will find someone else to do the work, the associate may resent you for giving preference to another attorney and not keeping your original commitment.

So, what if you choose instead to turn down the senior partner because of your prior obligation to the associate? Senior partners, for the most part, are accustomed to getting what they want, when they want it. Will the senior partner respect you for honoring a previous commitment to the junior lawyer, or simply be irritated, or worse?

We suggest that you take yourself out of the middle of this dilemma. No support person should be placed in the position of deciding whose work takes precedence over another's. If for no other reason, professional courtesy alone dictates that the attorneys should work out between themselves how each of their deadlines can be met.

Whenever you are working on one assignment and are approached to do yet another, ask the attorney what kind of deadline he or she needs. It may be that there is no conflict in getting both assignments done on time. But if it appears that meeting the deadline for one assignment will interfere with another, let the second attorney know about your prior assignment. Tell the second attorney that you would like to take on the assignment, but make it clear that you have already committed yourself to others, and say what those deadlines are. Discuss the new assignment's deadline, and how that will affect the other assignments you already have. If there is a conflict, the attorneys, not you, should decide whose assignment has priority and set the deadlines for the new, and the old, assignments.

PRACTICE TIP

If you are unable to take on the new assignment, tell the second attorney that, because of other commitments, you are unable to take on his or her assignment but hope that the attorney will keep you in mind for any future assignments.

Receiving Criticism Constructively

Even constructive criticism can be difficult to accept. Good management problem-solving requires that, when problems occur, they be fixed in two separate ways. First, deal with the current situation or problem, overcome it, and go forward. Second, go back and find the cause of the problem, and eliminate it. Constructive criticism should never be given or taken as a personal issue. Constructive criticism is not a personal insult; it is a problem-solving tool to keep that particular problem from surfacing in the future. Develop strategies on how to give and receive criticism constructively.

◼ COMMUNICATION BETWEEN LEGAL ASSISTANTS AND OTHER SUPPORT STAFF

In most law firms, a lawyer or legal administrator is responsible for managing the firm's secretaries and other support staff. At times, however, legal assistants perform this role together with other law-related duties. Of course, these responsibilities vary from office to office.

Office Etiquette and Procedures

Usually a legal assistant "shares" a secretary with one or more attorneys or other legal assistants. Here are some suggestions on supervising or sharing a secretary:

- *Learn when to give credit and when to allocate blame.* If an envelope is returned because you gave the secretary the wrong address, admit the error was your fault and apologize for causing the secretary the added work of revising the letter and retyping the envelope. This attitude encourages a better work atmosphere, because support staff do not feel that they will be held accountable, regardless of who or what is at fault, when something goes wrong. The point is to solve the problem, and learn from the experience to upgrade the quality of performance, rather than to place blame.
- *Promote the idea that there is no competition between you and your support staff.* You are each part of a team trying to accomplish a given goal together.
- *Make people feel good about themselves and their contribution—that they are worthwhile and important.*   This is the single most effective technique of good management. Productivity and the quality of work performed are directly tied to any employee's self-image. Therefore, take into account not only your support staff's abilities and skills, but also their personalities and how this combination of factors affects desired performance.
- *Be considerate when you give assignments.*   Try to give adequate instructions, and *be clear*. Although it may be convenient for you to leave details such as addresses and titles for the secretary to figure out, the result may be a reputation for not knowing what you are doing. Sloppy or incomplete instructions only increase the opportunity for mistakes, and program you and your support staff for failure.
- *Never ask a secretary to stop working on someone else's work and start on yours.* Your secretary does not appreciate being placed in that position any more than you do. Your secretary should never be placed in the untenable position of deciding whose work comes first. Some offices use a system such as "first in, first out." Other offices dictate that the decision be made by the persons shar-

ing the secretary or by the office manager. If you have a rush project for the secretary and there is work ahead of yours, request permission to "bump" your
work to the top of the stack from the people with whom you share the secretary or from the office manager.

In law offices, emergencies and deadlines are a fact of life. It is better to
reach an agreement on how these situations will be handled before the crisis
than to force the secretary to make these "no win" decisions.

- *Demand quality work.*   Minor errors in spelling, grammar, punctuation, or
  syntax reflect on you and your secretary. These errors give the impression that
  the writer is ignorant, sloppy, and unprofessional. Remember that most people
  will rise to whatever standard has been set. By keeping your standards high, you
  can ensure a better product for your firm and your client.

Handling Personnel Issues

But what do you do if the secretary continually bumps your work to the bottom of
the stack or just basically balks at doing your work? We doubt that there is any legal
assistant who has not encountered a situation such as this sometime during his or
her career. Unfortunately, some secretaries or other support staff resist receiving
instruction or assignments from a legal assistant regardless of the tact or consideration used.

In these situations, at times it is helpful simply to talk privately with that person
about the problem. Perhaps you are unaware that some misunderstanding or some
other small slight has occurred. If so, apologize and try get the relationship back on
track. It may be that your secretary feels that your instructions or your work-style are
creating unnecessary and time-consuming work. If that is the case, suggest a compromise. Ask for his or her opinion of what would work best for both of you, and *be
receptive* to suggestions.

If simply trying to talk it out with your secretary does not seem to have any effect,
it may be that you are both in a struggle for control. If you and your secretary cannot amicably meet at some common ground, then the problem can be approached
in another way. Although almost every legal assistant encounters this situation sometime during his or her career, it can be overcome with patience and professionalism.

Ideally, the firm for which you work has a strong, positive policy regarding its
legal assistants. In such an atmosphere, the majority of support staff choose to "go
with the flow." Few control situations occur because such problems are simply not
tolerated.

In other law offices, this obstacle is one best solved by the supervising attorney or
office manager, who could explain to the secretary or support person that he or she
does not work for a specific person, but *for the firm.* By not cooperating or doing a
legal assistant's work, that person is refusing to do the firm's work. This problem usually disappears when management makes it clear that such an attitude is not acceptable.

Should the problem persist despite management intervention, avoid doing anything to escalate the tension. Be courteous and professional. The office administrator
or supervising attorney should decide what steps should be taken to rectify the problem, just as if any other office rule had been breached.

Unfortunately, some supervising attorneys or law office administrators, who are
uncomfortable handling personnel issues, may fail to acknowledge or deal with this
problem. If that happens, there may be little else you can do to change the secretary's

> **PRACTICE TIP**
>
> Establish a reputa-
> tion among the sup-
> port staff as some-
> one who *demands*
> and *recognizes*
> quality work.

attitude. Should you find yourself in this situation, avoid confrontations; these only give the other person an excuse to find fault with you. Be pleasant, courteous, and professional. Try to compromise as much as you can without forfeiting quality. Then, if all else fails, ask to be assigned to another secretary who is easier to work with.

Do not be disheartened if you have this problem. Remember that many legal assistants have experienced it at some time during their careers. Talk about your problem with more experienced legal assistants, and find out how they dealt with it. Even if you do not find the solution to your problem, it will help to talk it over with someone.

■ COMMUNICATION BETWEEN THE LEGAL ASSISTANT AND CLIENT

Although this is not a book about ethics, you must have a clear understanding of these ethical issues to communicate professionally with any client.

Ethical Considerations

Before discussing communications between the legal assistant and client, we must recognize some key ethical issues:

- Conflict of interest
- Disclosure of legal assistant status
- Unauthorized practice of law
- Confidentiality

Lawyers are regulated by their state bar associations. These regulations include **ethical canons,** one of which governs the lawyer's use of legal assistants. As a legal assistant, you should be familiar with your state's ethical principles, and consider yourself bound by the same ethical considerations as lawyers.

The American Bar Association (ABA) Model Code of Professional Responsibility and the ABA Model Rules of Professional Conduct, although not binding on state and local bar associations, have nevertheless been adopted in total or in part by most of the state and local bar associations. The Model Rules, adopted by the ABA in 1983 as a revision of the Model Code, state the ABA's current position. Even so, the "old" Model Code still has tremendous influence.

Your state legislature or bar association may have already adopted model guidelines for the utilization of legal assistants. If so, those guidelines should address ethical issues for non-lawyers. We suggest that you review and become familiar with the **ABA Model Guidelines for the Utilization of Legal Assistant Services** drafted by the ABA Standing Committee on Legal Assistants and adopted by the ABA House of Delegates in August 1991, and the **National Association of Legal Assistants** (NALA) and **National Federation of Paralegal Associations'** (NFPA) Code of Ethics and Professional Responsibility and their respective Model Standards and Guidelines for the Utilization of Legal Assistants.

Conflicts of Interest.   Clients have the right to a lawyer's and legal assistant's undivided loyalty. A **conflict of interest** occurs when an attorney or legal assistant has an interest that is adverse to the client's. For example, a divorce action in which one attorney represents both the husband and wife would be a conflict of interest. Conflicts of interest can easily surface when one attorney represents co-parties in litigation who then become adversaries when one cross-claims against the other.

PRACTICE TIP

You should be familiar with your state's ethical principles, and consider yourself bound by the same ethical considerations as lawyers.

ethical canons
State bar association regulations governing attorney conduct, including the lawyer's use of legal assistants.

ABA Model Guidelines for the Utilization of Legal Assistant Services
Guidelines outlining recommended standards for using legal assistants.

National Federation of Paralegal Associations and National Association of Legal Assistants
The two major national legal assistant organizations.

conflict of interest
A situation in which an attorney's or legal assistant's regard for one duty leads to disregard of another duty.

The general rule is that, should one of a law firm's attorneys become disqualified because of a conflict of interest, the entire firm is disqualified. Most law firms conduct a conflict-of-interest check whenever a new client is brought into the firm by one of its attorneys. Some firms circulate the name of the client and a brief description of the legal matter, including opposing parties, throughout the law firm to each attorney. It is then the responsibility of each of that firm's attorneys to note whether a conflict of interest exists relating to the new client. More frequently, computers are used to conduct conflict-of-interest checks. Regardless of the system used, each law firm should have a thorough procedure for determining whether a conflict of interest exists for each new client.

It is not unusual for legal assistants or lawyers to leave one law firm for employment in another. When you move from one job to another, provide your new employer with basic, non-confidential information about clients for whom you did work at your previous employment. You should also advise your employer if you or your immediate family have any business or financial interests that could create possible future conflicts of interest. If a conflict of interest arises because of your involvement in matters at a previous job, advise your supervising attorney immediately. It may be possible for you to continue working on the matter, but only after consent has been obtained from the client.

Independent, or freelance, legal assistants have the most potential for conflicts of interest because they work on a contract basis for numerous attorneys from different law firms. For this reason, independent legal assistants should take particular care to prevent conflicts of interest or the disclosure of confidential information.

Disclosure of Legal Asssistant Status.   As a legal assistant, you will communicate with clients, opposing counsel and their legal assistants, the courts, and others. When your job necessitates contacts with others, you should always disclose your legal assistant status and act only within your delegated authority. If the contact is through conversation, then you or your attorney should make this disclosure at the beginning of the conversation. When writing correspondence on firm letterhead, always put your title under your name to prevent anyone from wrongfully assuming that you are an attorney for the firm. Regardless of the type of communication, it is imperative that the person you are communicating with be aware that you are a legal assistant, not an attorney.

PRACTICE TIP

Briefly, legal assistants cannot:
- Give legal advice
- Appear in court, except when permitted to do so by statute or regulation
- Accept cases or set fees on an attorney's behalf
- Perform any legal service without attorney supervision

◼ PRACTICE TIP

When your job necessitates contact with others, you should always disclose your legal assistant status and act only within your delegated authority. If you fail to disclose your legal assistant status, or if the disclosure is not made clearly enough, that person or the public may mistakenly assume either that you are an attorney, or that you are engaging in the unauthorized practice of law.

Many legal assistants carry business cards with name, title, address, and telephone and fax numbers printed on them. Business cards for legal assistants are generally allowed if the legal assistant's non-lawyer status is clear and it has no misleading or false information. However, your business card cannot be used to solicit business for your employer.

Business cards can be useful in situations where your status may be unclear to others. For example, you and your attorney attend the opposing party's deposition,

legal advice
Counsel given by attorneys to their clients consisting of an opinion or recommendation of a course of action.

unauthorized practice of law
When a non-lawyer performs those acts that only a lawyer in good standing may perform.

professional judgment test
The court considers whether the activity requires legal skills, knowledge, and training beyond that of the average layperson.

traditional areas of practice test
The court considers whether the activity would have been traditionally performed by an attorney or is commonly understood to be the practice of law.

incidental legal services test
The court considers whether the activity is frequently performed by laypersons depending on and secondary to some other business or transaction.

confidentiality
The ethical and legal obligation not to disclose oral or written communications between a lawyer and his or her client.

confidential
That which is meant to be held in confidence or kept secret.

privilege
The client's right to confidentiality of oral or written communications exchanged within the attorney-client relationship. The privilege can be broken only by the client.

where you meet with opposing counsel and her client for the first time. It appears to you that opposing counsel missed the fact that you were introduced as John Brown, legal assistant. By giving your business card to opposing counsel, you have made it clear that you are there in your capacity as your attorney's legal assistant.

If you fail to make the disclosure of your legal assistant status, or if that disclosure is not made clearly enough, that person or the public may mistakenly think you are an attorney. When this happens, you may appear to be engaging in the unauthorized practice of law. Intentional failure to disclose your legal assistant status could result in a criminal charge of the unauthorized practice of law. But what if the failure to disclose your legal assistant status was unintentional? If someone believes that you are an attorney, that person may ask you for **legal advice**—something that no legal assistant is allowed to give without the supervision of a lawyer or for which a lawyer is accountable.

Unauthorized Practice of Law.   There is no concrete definition for the **unauthorized practice of law,** and each state has its own interpretation. In June of 1995, the ABA Commission on Nonlawyer Practice issued a Report encouraging all states to reexamine and expand nonlawyer activity. The purpose of restricting the practice of law to members of the bar is to safeguard the public against legal services by unqualified persons. Throughout the years, the courts have created several general tests in an attempt to define this concept:

- Whether the activity requires legal skills, knowledge, and training beyond that of the average layperson, also referred to as the **professional judgment test.**
- Whether the activity is one that would have been traditionally performed by an attorney or is commonly understood to be the practice of law, also known as the **traditional areas of practice test.**
- Whether the activity is frequently performed by laypersons depending on and secondary to some other business or transaction, also known as the **incidental legal services test.**
- Whether the activity is characterized by a *direct relationship* between the attorney and the client.

Ethical codes and rules prohibit attorneys from aiding the unauthorized practice of law, and these same requirements hold attorneys responsible for the delegation and supervision of legal work to non-lawyers. The ABA Model Rules allow a layperson who is under the direct supervision of a lawyer to perform various legal tasks that would otherwise be considered as the unauthorized practice of law.

◼ PRACTICE TIP

Remember this definition of legal advice: When the result of an activity complex enough to require a lawyer's special training and skills is communicated to a client, it is considered legal advice. An attorney's legal advice or opinion to his or her client is an interpretation of the law and may also recommend a plan or course of action for the client to follow which the client may rely upon.

Confidentiality.   Oral or written communications between a lawyer and his or her client that contain legal advice are considered to be **confidential** and **privileged.** Lawyers are required to exercise reasonable care to prevent their employees from disclosing or using any confidential information. This prohibition applies to any information relating to the attorney's representation of the client, regardless of the source or form of the information.

Legal professionals, just like other working people, have a tendency to "talk shop" when they are together, regardless of whether the occasion is business or social. In the middle of a discussion, you may sometimes forget that there are others around you who may overhear your conversation about a client's case. Just because you have tuned out the conversations around you, that does not mean that others are ignoring your words. Elevators, restaurants, and coffee shops—or any other public place—are inappropriate places to discuss a client's legal matter.

Each of the ethical considerations summarized here deserves far more discussion. We offer these principles only as a refresher.

Client Communications

One of the most frequent complaints to bar associations is a lawyer's failure to communicate with his or her client. Clients complain that lawyers fail to return their telephone calls, send them copies of correspondence and pleadings, or keep them informed of developments in the case. These and other client communications could easily be delegated to a legal assistant.

Lawyers may properly delegate tasks to support laypersons if the lawyer (1) maintains a direct relationship with the client and (2) supervises, or is accountable for, the work performed by the layperson. The lawyer has complete professional responsibility for the work product, including all communications made by the layperson.

People hire attorneys because they have a problem. The worry and stress associated with this problem are commonly manifested by frequent telephone calls or correspondence to the lawyer from the client with suggestions or questions. Most clients have no intention of making unreasonable demands on their attorneys' time. They may only need to ask a question, give some information, or be reassured that their case is receiving adequate attention. Few attorneys have the time, or the patience, to respond to every inquiry from a nervous client. The simplest solution is for the lawyer to give the legal assistant the task of relaying communications directly to the client.

All contact with the client should be memorialized for the file. If you send something to the client by mail, use a **cover letter** (see Exhibit 2.3 p. 24).

If the contact with the client is verbal, such as a telephone call, make a written record for the client's file. This is a safeguard, not only for the client but also for you, should a dispute ever arise about what was said or done. This can be a quick note jotted on a piece of paper and put in the file, or a more formal memo to the file. Regardless, the important point is to make a written record of the contact noting the date, time, and the gist of the conversation. When verbal communication results in action to be taken, a confirmation letter is needed setting out your understanding of who will do what and when.

Whenever you, the legal assistant, have any communication with a client, you must remember that you are never allowed to give legal advice. You may convey whatever your supervising attorney tells you to say or write, even when it is legal advice, if you do not elaborate on, or explain, the message. Legal assistants who have frequent client contact are at the highest risk of crossing the thin line from giving information to giving legal advice. Clients often ask legal assistants questions that, if answered, would mean crossing this line. Should a client ever ask you a question that calls for legal advice, tell the client that as a legal assistant, you cannot advise them.

cover letter
A letter mailed with another document to introduce the other document.

EXHIBIT 2.3 *Cover Letter to Client*

[Date]

Ms. Priscilla Barker
517 Oakhurst
Ardmore, Oklahoma 73401

Re: *Barker v. State Insurance Company;* Case No. CJ–93–7234; District Court of
      Oklahoma County, Oklahoma
      Our File No.: BA0001

Dear Ms. Barker:

Enclosed is a copy of Defendant State Insurance Company's Answer to the Petition.

Please do not hesitate to contact me if you have any questions or would like additional information.

Sincerely,

Michael Masters
Legal Assistant

MM/lw
Enclosure

Offer instead to pass the question on to the attorney, and to communicate the attorney's response to the client as soon as possible.

CHAPTER SUMMARY

Communication skills, such as how to get along with your co-workers or your supervising attorney, may appear to be unrelated to legal writing. But we believe that the same basic principles for good communication skills apply to good writing skills as well. Each relies on clarity, good organization, and interpretation of ideas, instructions, or questions. Regardless of the type of communication, just remember—what can be misunderstood will be—and proceed accordingly.

KEY WORDS AND PHRASES

ABA Model Guidelines for the Utilization of Legal Assistant Services

attorney work product

confidential

confidentiality

conflict of interest

cover letter

disclosure of legal assistant status

discovery conference

ethical canons

incidental legal services test

legal advice

National Association of Legal Assistants (NALA)

National Federation of Paralegal Associations (NFPA)

privilege

professional judgment test

traditional areas of practice test

unauthorized practice of law

EXERCISES

The following statements contain *bad* advice for legal assistants. Armed with the principles you learned in Chapter Two, rewrite each statement and correct the inaccuracies.

1. To listen with understanding, you must incorporate your own viewpoint into what has been said, project what the speaker's next statement will be, and assess whether the speaker really means what he says.

2. The best way to demonstrate enthusiasm for what your client is saying is to offer advice immediately.

3. Research has shown that in face-to-face communications, the speaker's tone of voice has the greatest impact on her listener's interpretation of what has been said.

4. When a legal assistant is asked to take notes during a witness interview, her goal should be to record most of the interview verbatim.

5. Legal assistants are asked to take notes on client conferences, attorney meetings, and depositions. Because you are a legal assistant and not an attorney, there is no need to make yourself familiar with cases in advance. Having too much advance knowledge about a case may actually cause you to make dangerous assumptions and may interfere with your ability to be accurate.

6. The popular use of the dictation machine has improved the quality of legal writing. People tend to be more logical when they dictate, and dictation reduces the tendency toward verbosity.

7. Do not clutter your dictation with instructions to the secretary. Clerical support staff are professionals. They may be offended if you tell them when to punctuate, how to spell legal terminology, and how to set up columns.

8. When the attorney gives you an assignment, write down what is said and begin work as soon as possible. Do not ask too many questions because it is important to appear confident in your work environment.

9. When a client asks a legal question that you are fairly certain you can answer, by all means do so. If the client believes that you are an attorney, you have no obligation to correct that assumption. When you field questions for the attorney, you minimize some of the pressure that lawyers experience. Additionally, your demonstrated expertise increases your credibility with the client.

Practicing Communication Skills

The real test of what you have learned about communication skills arises when you apply what you have learned in the professional world. The following exercises may give you a preview of what lies ahead. Read each problem, and answer the question(s) that follow.

1. You have promised Ms. Pepper that you will interview all of the witnesses to Ms. Healy's car accident by the end of the day tomorrow. Much to your dismay, however, S. Lee Nowack, one of the senior partners, tells you that she needs you to take notes at a deposition she will be conducting this afternoon. She expects the deposition to continue through most of the day tomorrow as well. To make matters worse, you find a note on your desk from M. Ann Buechner, another senior partner, asking you to research a legal issue and to have the answer by noon. Obviously, you cannot meet all of these deadlines. What should you do?

2. You are now an experienced legal assistant, and a mentor to the newest legal assistant, Barney Jones. Barney comes to you for advice. It seems that the secretarial staff have grown increasingly antagonistic toward him, and he cannot understand why. Using the effective listening technique of clarifying what the speaker has said, you ask Barney what kind of problems he has been having with the secretaries.

   First, Barney mentions that many of his letters get returned in the mail due to wrong addresses. He explains that the secretaries type the letters and simply are not as careful as they should be.

   Second, whenever Barney has a project that he needs done quickly, the secretaries refuse to help him out. They just keep working on the project they were doing, and tell him that his work will have to wait. This particular problem has occurred three times in the past two days.

   Third, Barney has noticed a lot of typographical errors in his work. He has told the secretaries over and over again to "clean up their act." Still, the errors just keep coming.

How would you advise Barney on correcting these problems?

Practicing Your Memo Writing

Here is one more problem based on a real-life scenario. On Friday, November 17, the attorney working on Jane Healy's case asks you to sit in on a brief interview with a potential witness in the Healy lawsuit. The following is a transcription of that interview. Draft a memorandum to Ms. Pepper summarizing your notes taken during the interview.

Scenario

Ms. Pepper: (To Mr. Vierling) Thank you for coming in today. Will you tell me your name again?

Vierling: I'm Joe Vierling.

Ms. Pepper: And what is your address and telephone number?

Vierling: Well, right now I'm living with my brother, Steve, at the Lyrewood Apartments—number 17. He don't have no phone.

Ms. Pepper: Do you know the street address of the Lyrewood Apartments?

Vierling: Well, actually no, I don't.

Ms. Pepper: That's all right. I'm sure we can find that address. Tell me, why did you come today?

Vierling: Well, I heard you might be interested in anyone who, you know, saw the accident that happened at Childs and 14th Street the other day.

Ms. Pepper: How do you know about the accident? Did you see it?

Vierling: Well, sure. See, I hang out at the Dave's Bar and Grill there on the corner where the accident happened. I hang out there quite a bit—well, really every day ever since I lost my last job about three years ago. So, I was thinking, that if I did see the accident, you know, it could help your client's case quite a bit. It might even make all of the difference about who wins or who loses this thing. And, you know, if I am able to help your client win, well maybe she could help me out, too.

Ms. Pepper: What do you mean by "help you out, too"?

Vierling: Well, like maybe giving me a fee or percentage of whatever she gets from that crazy guy that hit her—because I would, like, be helping her win this thing.

Ms. Pepper: I see. Well, the way this works, we can't pay you anything for testifying except a statutory witness fee.

Vierling: Well, how much is that? It's quite a bit of money, isn't it? I mean, I heard that it's a lot of money.

Ms. Pepper: I'm afraid that it isn't very much—only about $40 a day for testifying at a deposition or at a trial. The legal system is set up that way because it is very important that a fact witness—and that's what you would be—not be biased because of what one side or the other has paid him but just to tell the truth. In fact, it would be against the law for me or my client to pay you or any other witness anything other than that statutory witness fee I just told you about, and we just couldn't do that. However, if you did see the accident, I am very interested in finding out what you saw and what you think about the accident itself.

Vierling: So, what you're saying is, you're saying that no one will pay to find out what I saw? 'Cause I really think that I could help your client win this lawsuit.

Ms. Pepper: No, I'm afraid that neither I nor the other parties' counsel are allowed to pay for someone's testimony like that. But I am still very interested in finding out what you know about the accident. Why don't you tell me about it from the beginning?

Vierling: Well then, I guess there's not much reason for me to be here. This ain't going to do me as much good like I thought it would. To tell the truth, I really don't remember much about that day except that I won $50 on a lottery ticket and, you know how it is, me and my buddies got stinking drunk to celebrate me winning. The part about being at Dave's, well that's true enough. I guess we started drinking sometime around noon that day, and didn't leave until Dave threw us out at closing time around 2 a.m. I think we drank old Dave's dry that day. Dang! I sure thought this would really work out good for both me and you, you know. Are you sure we can't work something out?

Ms. Pepper: Yes, Mr. Vierling, I'm very sure. I don't want to take up any more of your time, but I do want to thank you for coming in. My legal assistant will walk you out.

Vierling: Well, if you change your mind—like if things aren't going too well for your client—you can find me at Dave's.

3

LEGAL WRITING— THE BASICS

■ KEEP IT SIMPLE

Legal professionals are routinely guilty of several cardinal writing sins. Aside from a lack of clarity, which we deal with later in this chapter, the most persistent and irritating failing is unnecessary complication. Whatever you say must be said as ordinarily as possible.

Our minds comprehend words as though they are sifted through a coarse veil. When you use an unfamiliar word, or when your writing is unnecessarily complex, the reader either gets the meaning slowly—or not at all. The subject of law is intensely complex and easy to misunderstand. Precisely *because* you write about complicated things, you must keep your writing plain and simple.

The clearest writing we have ever seen is the stories we read in the first grade. Remember the two little kids and the dog? Dick said to Jane- or contrariwise- "Jane, there is Spot. Spot is a dog. He is running. See Spot run." You cannot beat that lean, plain writing for economy of words, or for clarity. What is it about "see Spot run" writing that makes it so clear?

Well, for one thing, there are no adjectives or adverbs, or only a very few. Most sentences contain little more than a subject, a verb, and an object. The subject and the verb come together right up front, with no unnecessary words inserted between them. The more words you put between subject and verb, the less likely you are to make sense.

Compare these two little paragraphs:

The subject of this paragraph, Spot, our old, trusted family friend, an eleven-year-old male of variegated neutral colors, is a member of the canine species.

This paragraph is about Spot, our faithful pet. He is a black-and-white male dog.

In the second paragraph, in addition to cutting out the fancy words, we have moved the verbs next to the subjects. You find out up front what or who does the acting, and immediately afterward you find out what he, she, or it did. The second example is clearer because we get right to the point. By contrast, the first paragraph is harder to read and understand in one quick reading. You have to wait even to find out that Spot is a dog; up until the seventeenth word, he could be the kid next door.

Simplicity has three other major enemies: pomposity, jargon, and verbosity. We will discuss them in that order.

27

■ PRACTICE TIP

Apply these secrets to good writing:
- ■ Delete every word that serves no function.
- ■ Edit each verbose phrase that could be a short word.
- ■ Delete every adverb meaning the same thing as the verb.
- ■ Avoid the passive voice, which leaves the reader uncertain about who did what.

Eliminating Pomposity

Legal professionals are human, after all, and as humans we tend to cultivate a good opinion of ourselves. We are bright people; we handle the English language well; we all know lots of words. When we write, therefore, many of us are sorely tempted to demonstrate the richness of our vocabulary for all the world to see. If we do, we are being just a bit pompous by unconsciously sacrificing clarity of expression for a boastful little demonstration of just how smart we are.

Now, when legal professionals talk informally together, we use ordinary words. After hearing a political debate, we say we thought one candidate "confused" the issue. That ordinary word, *confuse,* is the common word for a concept everybody understands. Why, then, on the job, do so many legal professionals write *obfuscate* instead of old commonplace *confuse?* Why do people write *facilitate* instead of *help* or *lead,* as the case may be? Why does *hairy* come out *hirsute,* and *go* become *proceed?*

We often carry our instinct for complication to even greater extremes, producing monstrosities that are almost parodies of the lawyer's art. Consider this real-world example:

> The critical component of the impairment theory devolves to a judgment analysis of whether section 1031(IV) review sub judice actually metastasizes federal law issue preclusion. . . . The metastasis would occur not only as to pure state law . . . but also as to heretofore pristine federal law issues. Academic scrutiny finds impairment to be more than conjecture.

This amazing statement, embedded in a document full of the same sort of talk, confuses and irritates the reader. Among other things, *metastasis* is not a legal doctrine, and words like *devolve* and *pristine* are hardly common language. The key word in this example is *academic.* Language such as this may well have a place in academe, where professors write mostly for other professors. It does not belong out where the rubber meets the road, where making sense is all that matters.

H. W. Fowler, perhaps the greatest writer on the English language, put his finger neatly on the great power of simple writing:

> There are very few of our notions that cannot be called by different names; but among these names there is usually one that may be regarded as the thing's proper name . . . the proper name . . . should not be rejected for another unless the rejector can give some better account . . . of his preference than that he thinks the other will look better in print.[1]

So that "proper name"—that ordinary term—is what you should always try to use. Dick and Jane do not say "see Spot proceed." The fire brigade commander does

---

1. H. W. Fowler, *Modern English Usage* (New York and Oxford: Oxford University Press). Reprinted by permission.

not shout, "Extinguish that conflagration!" We do not call one another on the telephone to say, "Susan, let's ingest lunch today."

Handling Jargon

Be careful, too, of incorporating jargon from other businesses or professions into your writing. Sometimes you will need to use some unusual word that is common in a particular business; if you do, then translate it for your reader, unless you know the reader is familiar with the particular business. Here is an example from a lawyer's letter to his client:

> Allegedly Mrs. Doe had a sensory deficit in the affected hip secondary to a prior surgery and could not detect that the hydrocollator was hot, and as a result sustained the aforedescribed burns.

> Well, we can guess at "sensory deficit"—that means she could not feel things. But how about "secondary to?" Doesn't that mean "caused by," a clear, common English construction? And what is a hydrocollator? If the reader does not know what one of those is, all meaning is lost. (And before you leave this sentence, strike out the nonsense word *aforedescribed;* it is purest **legalese**).

> You owe it to your attorneys, your clients, and yourselves to speak simply, to say things as you say them ordinarily. Your obligation is to write using the "proper names" of things, the language of everyday. Here is a fine rule that will help you keep your writing simple, a rule as simple as its meaning: If you don't say it, don't write it.

legalese
Outdated words, phrases, or other legal jargon that obscure meaning.

Trimming Verbosity

Wordiness, or verbosity, is another major threat to simple writing. It is terminal lawyer's disease, endemic to the profession. Much of the public is convinced that we legal professionals talk far too much; sadly, that opinion is at least partly right. The fact that we have much to say and make clear does not excuse a single unnecessary word.

It is particularly easy to let pomposity slip in if you dictate or fail to proofread. We have discussed proofreading and the pitfalls of dictation in Chapter 2. Suffice it to say now that "dictationitis" and failure to proofread carefully tend to produce windy letters like the example in Exhibit 3.1.

EXHIBIT 3.1   *Writing to Impress: A Letter from One Lawyer to Another*

Re: Pending Dispute

Dear Mr. Jones:

Due to my specialization in commercial law and related matters, I have been recently engaged by Mr. Brown to advise and additionally represent him regarding the above-referenced dispute. After reviewing the files on this matter, it appears to me that there are various ways in which the respective interests of our clients can be accommodated and settled as an alternative to the continuation of the pending litigation. Accordingly, I would appreciate your telephoning me at your earliest convenience so that we can discuss the matter and pursue possible settlement of this case.

I will be out of town on some unrelated litigation matters through Monday of next week, but will be available to discuss the matter with you after that time. I look forward to hearing from you.

Sincerely,

James Q. Dibell

Examine this letter for a moment, and then decide what the lawyer is really trying to say. Now quickly write out the message the way *you* would put it. It ought to look something like the letter in Exhibit 3.2.

EXHIBIT 3.2   ***Writing to Communicate: Revised Letter***

Re: Pending Dispute

Dear Mr. Jones:

   I represent Mr. Brown in this case. I think we can settle this matter. I shall be out of town through next Monday. Please call.

Sincerely,

James Q. Dibell

The rest of the original letter added nothing to the message, except to make it longer.

Consider some of the ways this writer inflated a simple message. First, nobody cares why the writer represents the client; it is enough that he does. Second, of course he represents him in the "above-referenced dispute"; what other dispute would it be but the one he writes about? Third, the reader does not care whether the writer has reviewed the files. Fourth, the reader is indifferent to why the writer will be out of town; all the reader cares about is when he can be reached by telephone.

You can help keep your writing simple by saying only the things you must say, and saying them only once. It is unnecessary to repeat yourself. It wastes words and reading time, and sounds as if you are patronizing your reader. Here is an example from Dan Rather on the "CBS Evening News":

> The hurricane is diminishing; it's not as strong as it was.

No doubt. Things that have diminished *are* less than they were before they diminished. Rather did not need to add this redundant second phrase. He wasted words, and sounded as if he was not sure whether we poor, dense TV-watchers understood what *diminish* meant.

Achieving Simplicity

Simplicity is not always as easy to achieve as it was in improving the clumsy letter we just rewrote, but you cannot go far wrong if you follow a few simple rules. These guidelines work in every situation, whether you are writing a letter, a memo, or a brief. They work regardless of who your audience is.

Write the Way You Speak. We have already mentioned this cardinal rule. Remember, no attorney or judge wants to waste time wading through sticky prose two or three times to ferret out its meaning. The judge will pick up the other side's brief to find out what the problem is; the lawyer will buck your memo back, with terse directions to write something he or she can understand.

We do not advocate that you always write with the stark simplicity of the first-grade primer. It is surely possible to be clear and do it with a little more style. But "see Spot run" does get down to basics: The message is clear, and there are no extra words to obscure it.

PRACTICE TIP

Write no more than you must to be clear, and do not repeat yourself.

PRACTICE TIP

If you do not use a word in everyday conversation, do not use it in a brief or memorandum unless it is a legal term of art with a specific legal meaning.

Write in Bite-Sized Pieces.   Justice Cardozo, one of the great legal writers of all time, used telegraphic sentences to present facts clearly:

> The defendant is a manufacturer of automobiles. It sold an automobile to a retail dealer. The retail dealer resold to the plaintiff. While the plaintiff was in the car, it suddenly collapsed. He was thrown out and injured.
>
> *MacPherson v. Buick Motor Co., 217 N.Y. 382, 384–85, 111 N.E. 1050 (1916)*

Like the person who wrote about Dick and Jane and Spot, Cardozo used short, plain sentences to state his facts. He gave his thoughts to the reader in short, bite-sized chunks that are easy to read and understand. There is no mistaking his meaning.

But there are other ways to break your writing into small, digestible pieces. For example, you can separate short, complete thoughts with a semicolon:

> American forces won the Gulf War with astonishing ease; speed, training, and firepower again proved superior to numbers.

Or, you can achieve the same effect by using a dash:

> The motion for summary judgment should have been granted—there were obviously no questions of fact remaining to be decided.

You can also state a proposition, close it with a colon, and then list subparts of the proposition, like this:

> Three elements are required to prove first-degree murder: the killing of a human, by the accused, with premeditation.

Within a complete thought ended by a period, semicolon, or dash, careful use of commas will keep the parts of each thought set off from one another.

Take as an example these classic lines from the Bible, and read them out loud:

> Thou shalt not fear for any evil by night, nor for the arrow that flieth by day, for the pestilence that walketh in darkness, nor for the sickness that destroyeth in the noon day.

Note how this passage breaks naturally after each comma, precisely where you would hesitate when speaking the lines aloud.

Using a combination of these techniques, you can create clear sentences of varying lengths, easy to read and understand the first time through. Whatever you do, try to keep big, fat dependent clauses and qualifying words from hanging about in the middle of sentences. For example:

> The following clause dealing with the $5.00 payment which the parties correctly call "rental" instead of making it clear, as our opinion stated, that the $25,000 was paid not as a bonus but rental, makes the opposite clear. For, in addition to flatly stating that this $5.00 per acre stipulated for was "rental" while not calling the $12.50 rental because it was not, it shows that the $5.00 payment was not, as the $12.50 was, required absolutely and in all events but only as an alternative to drilling.

What? This horror was written by a United States appellate judge in a tax case. Granted, tax cases commonly have a general air of obscurity, but there was no reason to use only two sentences, and cram both full of qualifiers.

PRACTICE TIP

As a general rule, you cannot go far wrong if you insert a comma where you would pause if you read the sentence out loud.

Just as bad is the next passage, in which a lawyer tried to state the "general rule" to be followed in cases such as the one he was arguing. In an earnest attempt to clearly lay down a rule, he produced the following mystery:

> Where there is a general plan or scheme adopted by an owner of a tract, for the development and improvement of the property by which it is divided into streets and lots, and which contemplated restriction as to the uses to which lots may be put, or the character and location of improvement thereon, to be secured by a covenant embodying the restrictions to be inserted in the deeds to purchasers, and it appears from the language of the deed itself, construed in the light of the surrounding circumstances, that such covenants are intended for the benefit of all the lands, and that each benefit thereof, and such covenants are inserted in all the deeds for lots sold in pursuance of the plan, a purchaser or his assigns may enforce the covenant against any other purchaser and his assigns if he has bought with actual or constructive knowledge of the scheme and the covenant was part of the subject matter of the purchase.

The whole statement is a single sentence that, if you read it repeatedly, turns out to have been carefully crafted. The trouble is, there are so many qualifications crammed into it that it is impossible to understand. And this meandering sentence was taken from an appellate brief filed before the highest court of Texas. The court deserved better.

What could the writer have done? Without reading further in the text, take your pencil and try to edit this humongous sentence so that it is easier to read and understand. After you have tried to solve this puzzle, read on, and see the solution we suggest.

It is always best to state the general rule or the result you are going to reach first, and then separately state qualifications or requisites. The sentence you have just read might be unravelled something like this:

> Where a tract owner adopts a plan to develop and improve property and restrict its uses, a buyer of part of the property may enforce the restrictions against the buyer of another part of the property. However, the following preconditions must be met:
>
> > First . . .
> > Second . . .
> > Third . . . .

A related way to confuse the issue is to refer to modifying facts that are not stated anywhere in the writing, facts that the reader must stop and read someplace else. Consider this puzzle taken from Section 509(a) of the Internal Revenue Code:

> For purposes of paragraph (3) an organization described in paragraph (2) shall be deemed to include an organization described in section 510(c)(4), (5) or (6) which would be described in paragraph (2) if it were an organization described in section 501(c)(3).

signposting
Structural writing tool in which elements of a statement are categorized and numbered. The sentence is then structured by each enumerated point (i.e., "first," "second," and "third").

Well, sure, we guess anybody can see that.

No doubt the reader can go to the code and read all these modifying sections, but while the reader is doing this, all understanding of Section 509(a) is totally lost. Such confusion is bad enough in a statute; it is unforgivable in ordinary writing.

The solution is to give the reader a rule or other statement, and separately list any qualifications there may be, much as we did earlier for the tract-owner and his restrictions. Here are some other ways to do it, setting each point off by numbering it. The process is called **signposting.**

Use *first, second,* and *third* when the point you want to make is enumerated in complete sentences, like this:

> The court focused on three things. First, it examined whether the defendant had breached his duty to the plaintiff hotel clerk. Second, the court considered whether the defendant had breached the standard of care for store security. Finally, the court analyzed whether inadequate store security was the **proximate cause** of the plaintiff's injuries.

Look at the last example again and consider another way to write it. Signpost your points using numbers to set them off, but describe them in fragments by using *whether.*

> The court focused on three things: (1) whether the defendant had breached his duty to the plaintiff hotel clerk; (2) whether the defendant had breached the **standard of care** for store security; and (3) whether inadequate store security was the **proximate cause** of the plaintiff's injuries.

standard of care
The degree of care that a reasonably prudent person should exercise under the same or similar circumstances.

If you can state your points briefly, you can simply spell them out in sentence form, signposting with numbers as before:

> The court focused on three things: (1) the defendant's duty to the plaintiff hotel clerk; (2) the standard of care for store security; and (3) the causal link between store security and the plaintiff's injuries.

proximate cause
A cause that, in natural and continuous sequence, unbroken by any efficient intervening cause, produces an injury (and without which the injury would not have occurred).

A common mistake is to signpost when the points are so brief that signposting is unnecessary. Look at this example of incorrect signposting:

> The court considered the child's (1) age; (2) mental competence; and (3) maturity level.

In this example it would have been more appropriate to separate these one- or two-word points by commas rather than semicolons, like this:

> The court considered the child's age, mental competence, and maturity level.

It is also possible to state points as a series of rhetorical questions, as in this example:

> The court asked three questions: (1) Did the defendant owe a duty to the plaintiff? (2) Did the defendant breach the standard of care? (3) Was the defendant's act the proximate cause of the plaintiff's injuries?

This technique tends to become awkward and cumbersome when making brief points. It is generally best to avoid it.

A second common mistake is to try to state too many points at once. Even though the next example is properly signposted and its points are stated in **parallel construction,** it ends up too long and cumbersome to be easily understood.

parallel construction
Consistent word form and verb tense among particular words and/or sentences.

> The defendant made the following mistakes: (1) leaving blood on his hands; (2) taking a blood-stained shirt to the dry cleaner; (3) leaving blood-stained carpet remnants on his front lawn to be picked up with the garbage; (4) running a classified advertisement for the sale of his knife collection; (5) asking his next-door neighbor if he could borrow a shovel, a pick, and a plastic bag; (6) donating his wife's blood-stained clothing to the Salvation Army; and (7) stopping by the police station to ask if he could be convicted of murder if the body could never be found.

When you list this many points, it is better to write them in paragraph form.

◼ KEEP IT SHORT

Keep it simple is cousin to the second vital rule of good writing: Keep it short. We have already talked about writing simply. Simple, common words are normally short words, one or two syllables long. Now we can take those short, simple words and put them into short, simple phrases, sentences, and paragraphs.

Writing Short Phrases

Ordinary legal writers have an astonishing genius for using four words where one would do. *At this point in time,* is a familiar example. What does it mean in fact? *Now.* So say so. Get in the habit of looking at little clusters of words and asking yourself whether there is a way to say the same thing with fewer words.

Cross out *on a regular basis,* and substitute *regularly.* Instead of *interpose an objection,* write *object.* Say *consider* instead of *take into consideration.* Use *soon* rather than *in the near future.* Erase *file an action against;* write *sue* instead. In Appendix B we provide a list of common verbose or stuffy words and phrases, and some suitable substitutes.

Our common speech is full of these obese phrases. Look for them, and delete them mercilessly wherever you find them. Once you get in the habit, you will save yourself perhaps ten or fifteen percent of the verbiage you otherwise would use. It will be second nature to cut out *for the purpose of* and insert plain old *to.*

Look for phrases containing redundancies (also called **tautologies**) and cut them down to their bare essentials. For example, take *prior experience.* Isn't *all* experience prior? Just say *experience.* Or, take the expression *remand back,* a redundancy often seen in lawyers' writing. Remand means "send back," so drop *back* and use *remand* alone. Cut *consensus of opinion* down to *consensus,* for that is what *consensus* means.

It takes practice to pick up some of these everyday redundancies, simply because they are so common. Take *join together;* have you ever tried to join something apart? And what about *handwritten manuscript?* A manuscript *is* handwritten; that is what the word means. Reduce these to one word, *join,* and *manuscript.*

Do the same for *end result, sum total,* and *complete stop.* Write *plan* instead of *pre-plan.* (How can you plan after you do whatever-it-is?) And say *audience* instead of *live audience;* can you imagine what it must be like to perform before a dead audience? More examples of alternatives to unnecessary verbiage and stuffy words can be found in Appendix C.

This simple editing process is particularly useful when drafting deposition summaries. The most common complaint by lawyers about deposition summaries is that the summary itself is too long. A deposition summary should be one-tenth the size of the deposition; if the deposition is 100 pages, the summary should be only 10 pages. The text of the summary should be clear and concise. After writing the first draft of the summary, go back and delete every unnecessary or redundant word or phrase. Not only will your writing be easier to read and understand, but your summary will also be shorter.

Writing Short Sentences

The incomprehensible sentence about tracts and restrictions is a fine example of what happens when sentences get out of hand; it is 174 words long. The two sentences in the tax case opinion are almost as bad, especially the second one. A good writer varies sentences in length and structure to avoid boring the reader. However, a sentence longer than about twenty words is almost surely harder to understand than it needs to be.

Of course it is possible to write beautiful legal prose and be understood, but if you have to choose between grace and clarity, choose clarity every time. And for clarity, short is always better—see Spot run. The best legal writers have always known and practiced the **rule of short.** Remember the gem from Justice Cardozo we set out earlier? Cardozo was one of the most scholarly justices ever to grace the United States Supreme Court; he had an enormous vocabulary. But for clarity, Cardozo chose to write as simply as he possibly could:

> The defendant is a manufacturer of automobiles. It sold an automobile to a retail dealer.
>
> *MacPherson v. Buick Motor Co.,* 217 N.Y. 382, 384, 111 N.E. 1050 (1916).

rule of short
The shorter the sentence, the easier it is to understand.

(By the way, that last line is what is called a **citation.** It tells you where to find the full opinion, if you want to read it. We discuss citations fully in Chapter 7. Most legal professionals follow the rules for citation form found in *The Bluebook, A Uniform System of Citation,* more commonly referred to as just The *Bluebook.* Whenever you are citing a case, statute, or any other legal citation, use The *Bluebook* as your guide unless your boss' preference dictates otherwise.)

citation
The reading, or production of, or reference to legal authorities and precedents in arguments to courts in law review articles, briefs, motions, treatises, and the like to substantiate or fortify the propositions advanced by the author of the document.

Cardozo's writing in *MacPherson* is almost telegraphic. To start, he uses short, plain sentences, each with the subject and the verb close together. There are no modifiers crammed in to lengthen and complicate these sentences. Toward the end of the passage, he varies his style. In one sentence, two short statements are coupled in a single sentence: Since each could stand alone, they are joined by a semicolon. All of his thoughts come in bite-sized pieces. His prose may not be the stuff of the Great American Novel, but it is absolutely clear on one reading.

Cardozo uses one sentence of nineteen words, about as long as a sentence ought ever to be. But even it is crystal clear. Its words—like the rest of Cardozo's words—are the simplest possible. They are also the shortest possible; they are the *common names* of the ideas for which they stand.

Writing Short Paragraphs

Law books are full of bulgy paragraphs that run on and on, sometimes for pages. They are tough to make sense of, however well-written, so break your paragraphs often, even if you have to make an artificial division. A pox on the rules of classic writing. All you should care about is being clear.

Many people will tell you that an idea must be expressed in a single paragraph. Do not believe them. The real rule is this: Do not express *more* than a single major idea in a single paragraph. If you need two or twenty short paragraphs to fully discuss an idea, by all means use them.

PRACTICE TIP

As a general rule, no paragraph longer than 15 or 16 lines should be allowed to live.

Eliminating Pleonasms

You can also streamline your writing by eliminating **pleonasms,** using more words than you need to give the sense intended. Several words are commonly found together, but mean the same thing. Here are some common pleonasms:

pleonasm
The use of more words than are necessary.

- bits and pieces
- whys and wherefores
- over and above
- pick and choose

- ways and means
- fair and just
- free and clear
- betwixt and between
- various and sundry
- bound and determined

tautology
Several words meaning the same thing used together.

The law has its share of pleonasms and **tautologies.** Our favorite is a triple-header: *null, void, and of no effect.* Our preference is to use *void* alone, but take your pick.

KEEP IT PROFESSIONAL

"Eschewing" Legalese

In the public mind, a hallmark of the legal profession is a fondness for using obscure lawyers' words when ordinary plain ones would do as well—or better. *Eschew* is a pretty fair example, a silly antique substitute for good old *avoid.* We have discussed the unnecessary use of eighty-five-cent English words when simpler ones will serve. Even worse is the use of antique Latin or Norman French expressions when there is a good English equivalent. Consider this unenlightening statement by an Illinois court:

> *Parens patriae* cannot be *ad fundandam jurisdictionem.* The zoning question is *res inter alios acta.*

PRACTICE TIP

Do not use Latin or Norman French expressions, unless they have become words of art with a specific meaning in the modern law.

legal terms of art
A word or phrase that has a fixed and known legal meaning.

We showed this passage to an erudite colleague, who told us that this gibberish means "we don't have jurisdiction" in plain English. Why did the court not say so in the first place? Everybody admires people who are comfortable with classical languages and other arcane lore, but precise legal writing is not the place to show off such esoteric knowledge.

Sometimes you will run into a Latin or Norman French expression that is still in regular use. Such expressions have become **legal terms of art;** they embody a bundle of legal ideas that are understood by all legal professionals. For example, there is *res ipsa loquitur,* which means generally "the thing speaks for itself." In tort law, this expression is used to describe a situation that could not have occurred without negligence. Since this Latin phrase is now a useful shorthand expression for a concept everybody understands, it is the most efficient way to express the concept.

Most important, avoid the boring affectation of using antique legal words that add nothing. Here is an example from an attorney's letter:

> Please answer said Fifth Set of Interrogatories and, if you have any objections thereto, which you obviously have by the import of your aforesaid letter . . . .

Words like *aforesaid* add nothing except an unpleasant odor of musty age; even worse are peculiar compound constructions such as *hereinbeforementioned* and *hereinbelow set out.* You can say the same thing, if you need to say it all, by simply writing *in paragraph two.*

Some of these silly legalisms are quite common. *Said,* for example, is often found in legal documents and in letters by lawyers who do not think about what they write. The word is useless and wholly unnecessary in every case; it *never* serves to clarify anything. To say *the said contract* about a contract you have referred to earlier adds nothing: of course it is the same contract you mentioned. What other contract would it be?

When a batch of these uninformative legalisms is crammed into the same writing, the result is even more ludicrous. Consider this hideous example, a pleading filed by a firm trying to withdraw from representing a criminal client.

> COMES NOW . . . X Law Firm . . . and hereby respectfully applies to this Court for it's [sic] Order withdrawing said law firm . . . from further representation of Defendant Y herein the premises for the reasons and upon the grounds that said Defendant . . . .

COMES NOW? This is an archaic usage that says nothing. Of course the law firm has come to court; it is filing this document. Phrases such as *comes now* and *in the premises* are holdovers from another age of legal writing. Many lawyers, young and old alike, cling to such legalese, misguidedly assuming that they are carrying on the lofty traditions of their craft.

On the contrary, such useless phrases can make legal documents cumbersome to read and understand. These expressions, unlike legal terms of art, add nothing to the "tradition" of legal writing. Here, from the same pleading, are some other illustrations of legalese that should be banished from good legal writing:

- *Said law firm.*   Surely this firm would not try to withdraw some other law firm. *Said* then, as always, adds nothing but length.
- *Defendant Y herein.*   Naturally the defendant is the defendant in this case. Why else would the pleading be filed in this case? Delete *herein*.
- *The premises for the reasons and upon the grounds.*   This is not only vintage legalese, but wonderfully redundant. *Premises* is an antique word for "the facts of this case." The writer then left out one or more words before *for,* so the sentence is gibberish. And finally, *premises, for the reasons,* and *upon the grounds* all mean the same thing. Why not say *because* and have done with it?

Legalese also includes the irritating custom, to which many lawyers are given, of spelling out a number and then giving the same number in numerals, thus: "thirty-seven (37) bushels." Nobody knows why so many lawyers do this. Such repetition may be marginally supportable when you write long and complicated numbers in the millions or hundreds of thousands. When you state ordinary numbers, however, it is just plain silly. Unless your attorney insists on it, do not do it.

When you do write dollar amounts, do not list zero cents when the number is rounded to an even dollar amount. For example, damages in the amount of $1,000,000 should *not* be written as "$1,000,000.00." Unless the figure contains some odd number of cents, drop the ".00."

Avoiding Babble

Many of the worst faults of legal writing can be traced to babble, the uncontrolled working of the vocal cords into a dictation machine. The dictating machine was surely the worst thing ever to happen to the legal profession. While it saves time, it also encourages verbosity, a sort of stream-of-consciousness writing that is long on sound and short on meaning. (Terminal babble is usually coupled with acute failure to proofread.)

Consider this example of babble, drawn from a real lawyer's letter:

> I have done as you have requested, and have reviewed the matter in my mind and have taken the time to review my file and the previous sets of interrogatories and defendant's answers, objections and responses thereto and I honestly am of the opinion, in good faith, that said interrogatories are not repetitive and that they are relevant and they were propounded before the effective date.

This rambling prose was obviously dictated in haste, probably while shuffling through papers in the case file. It was certainly never proofread, and incorporates most of the worst features of bad writing. To start with, it is far too complicated. This passage is only part of a single sentence, 185 words long. It is studded with unnecessary words:

- *Reviewed the matter in my mind.*   Of course it was in his mind. Where else?
- *Honestly of the opinion, in good faith.*   Can anybody be honestly in bad faith?
- *Taken the time to review my file.*   Doubtless it took time to review the file; why state the obvious?

And the whole letter—well over a page, single-spaced—is crammed full of useless legalisms: *said, thereto, thereof, therewith,* and *aforesaid,* none of which add anything to the letter, especially clarity.

Using the Right Word

malapropism
The mistaken use of a word that sounds similar to the correct word but has a different meaning.

Since legal professionals must be clearly understood, you must choose your words carefully. Even if the reader can puzzle out what you really meant, a glaring **malapropism** makes the reader wonder whether you are really very bright, and how much attention he or she should pay to the rest of your writing. This glitch, from a brief filed with a trial court, is the sort of thing we mean:

> The Plaintiffs asserted due to the disillusion of the Defendant partnership . . . . Where a partnership is in the process of disillusion . . . .

PRACTICE TIP

Using the wrong word always risks misunderstanding. *When in doubt, look it up.*

Now what the lawyer thought he was writing about was the *dissolution*—that is, the dissolving of the partnership. What he said was that the partners had lost their illusions. No doubt that was true, but it was not at all what he intended to say.

The reader probably was not misled. But what he or she did learn was that the lawyer or legal assistant who wrote this was careless. Either the writer did not know the difference between *disillusion* and *dissolution,* or did not care enough to proofread, or both. And who wants to hire a careless lawyer or legal assistant—or keep one?

A personal injury lawyer, writing to a corporate insurance client, produced this astonishing sentence:

> The mother testified that immediately after the March 1, 1978 vaccination, the child began a high-pitched scream which continued intermittently for years.

Good grief! Think about the picture this lawyer has painted. He has not only written something consummately silly, but he has left his reader confused. If the reader is trying to guess what reasonable damages in the case might be, surely he or she ought to know how often *intermittently* is.

If the child screamed once a month or so, damages might be reasonably low. If, however, *intermittent* means every few minutes, the insurance company is facing a major expenditure. The reader will certainly be on the telephone to the writer in short order; maybe he will start thinking about hiring another law firm, too.

Aim for Accuracy.   Make certain that the word you choose is as accurate as possible. Your reader is most likely to be misled by words that are ordinary enough on their face, and correctly assembled, but leave no clear picture of what they describe. For example, here is what one lawyer wrote to describe the demeanor of the key witness for the other side.

> During the plaintiff's deposition it became apparent that she creates a rather favorable impression. . . . She apparently is a nice-looking woman, 28 years of age with three chil-

dren and previously widowed. . . . Having had conversation with [witness X] I would conclude that he is an "everyday-type of person" whose testimony might not carry the same conviction.

Think, for a moment, about what a "rather favorable" impression might be. Is it less than favorable? Is it a little more favorable than the average, but not really engaging and persuasive? Or what? The lawyer has left the reader with no notion of how this witness really comes across. The whole point of his letter was to advise his client of the relative strength of his case. Because he did not write a clear assessment of the witnesses, he failed entirely in what he set out to do.

Equally mysterious is the statement "apparently a nice-looking woman." You are left with the feeling that she is nice-looking, whatever that means, but that there is something that might detract from that impression. If there really is something about her that detracts from her impact as a witness, it certainly is not specifically mentioned. And she has been "previously widowed," a rather intriguing expression. Can that mean that she is no longer widowed? Can somebody once widowed ever be unwidowed? Or does it mean, as it probably does, that she was a widow but has remarried?

The lawyer's correspondent must also have wondered what an "everyday-type of witness" might be. Why should an everyday person somehow lack credibility? Perhaps there was something about Witness X that indeed made him less credible than some other witness; if there was, the lawyer sure did not write about it. All you know is that there is something wrong about Witness X; you have no inkling what that might be.

If you have the slightest doubt about the precise meaning of a word, pick up that most valuable office aid, your dictionary. It ought to be on your desk, not down in the library. Always make certain your meaning is right by the book. Even when common words are widely and popularly misused, people who are careful with their English will know the difference.

One night Johnny Carson was relating a bout with some bad sushi or other spoiled food. "I was nauseous," he said, meaning that he was sick to his stomach. Wrong, Johnny. What he actually said was, "I inspired nausea," or something like it. He should have said *nauseated*. No doubt a lot of viewers did not know the difference. After all, *nauseous* is regularly misused by people generally. But a lot of viewers did know Carson was wrong, and those educated readers are the people for whom you write.

Commonly Misused Words.   Be especially careful of commonly misused words, such as *nauseous*. Even more egregious is the common misuse of *lie* and *lay*. *Lie* is what you do when you go to bed at night. *Lay* is its past tense, as in "yesterday I lay down for a nap." Otherwise, *lay* is what a chicken does with an egg, or what you do with something: for example, "lay the groceries on the counter." Writing "the doctor required her to lay down for an hour each day" marks you as darned near illiterate, and spoils the effect and power of your writing.

The reader gets the same negative impression of your writing when you use the wrong preposition. Proper usage requires that certain words be followed by certain prepositions. We have listed some of the most frequent combinations for you in Appendix B. If you are ever in doubt about which preposition should be used, take the time to look it up.

Here are some similar traps to watch for. Read them over, and see whether the differences in meaning between the first and second words are absolutely clear to you. Then check your dictionary. You will find there are very broad differences in meaning between these words, even though many of the pairs sound, and even look, very similar.

- apprise   - appraise
- discreet   - discrete
- disinterested   - uninterested
- emigrate   - immigrate
- eminent   - imminent
- illusion   - allusion
- imply   - infer
- masterful   - masterly
- prescribe   - proscribe

We have provided a list of commonly misspelled words in Appendix A. Knowing the difference, knowing the precise meaning, is not something nice to do. It is your *job*, and nothing less.

There are dozens more treacherous words, many of which will sneak up on you because intelligent people all around you are also misusing them. For example, *criteria* is a commonly used word, but many people forget—or do not know—that it is plural. The singular noun is *criterion*, so saying "the first criteria" is plainly wrong. Many people do not know that it is, but some educated, careful readers do, and they are your most important audience.

Avoid Using Slang and Fad Words.   Stay away from fad words, new expressions coined by the media, adopted from specialized professions, or made up by partisans of some political theory.

Consider the word *demonstrator*, which you read in the newspaper every day. In column one, it may refer to a group of senior citizens peacefully picketing to object to the closing of a public service. Two columns over, the same word may be used to describe a crowd of rioters attacking policemen and trying to burn down the state capitol in the name of some radical cause.

Or, take the word *ageist*, which has recently been invented to describe somebody who discriminates on account of age. The assigned meaning is illogical, of course: a flautist is one who plays the flute; a motorist is one who drives; a therapist is one who gives therapy. It follows that an ageist is one who ages, not one who discriminates.

And how about *viable?* This word once had a nice, reliable biological meaning. Now it can also mean "existing," "useful," "successful," and "possible," among other things.

Words like *viable, demonstrator,* and *ageist* have no consistent, reliable meaning, and no legal professional can afford to use a word that is not crystal clear. Nobody can be sure what these words mean from one sentence to the next. You can avoid the danger of using fad words by sticking to good old ordinary English words, the ones that immediately leap to mind when you think about a thing or a concept.

For example, take the word *kudos,* a sort of Hollywood word from the Greek for "praise." Remember the rule: If you have a solid Anglo-Saxon equivalent, use it. Do not borrow unusual or foreign words: *kudos* is both. That way, you avoid irritating and confusing somebody who does not know what *kudos* means. You also avoid the

PRACTICE TIP

Avoid unusual or exotic words, unless there are no common synonyms.

stupidity committed by writers who refer to "a kudo," never realizing that *kudos* is singular, not plural.

Then there are the jargon words you might consider borrowing from other professions. Legal professionals are often tempted to use medical terminology when discussing medical matters, particularly the injuries involved in a lawsuit to recover for personal injuries or medical malpractice. The worst vice of this habit is using technical language that means nothing to the average layperson. If you write about a "Colles fracture," you must tell the reader in ordinary terms what kind of break that is. Instead of *posterior to,* write *behind.* You will not sound like a doctor, but people will understand you better.

A few pages back, we included a rather murky paragraph dealing with burns from a hydrocollator. The lawyer who wrote it used the medical jargon *secondary to.* It was unnecessary, and could have been confusing. Doctors may say that "the patient Jones died secondary to a fifteen-story fall," but ordinary folk do not talk like that. You do not have to follow doctors' practice; it makes more sense simply to write that the fall killed Jones.

Using Correct Word Order

When you know your subject well, it is especially easy to get words out of order in a sentence. Sometimes the reader instantly recognizes your meaning, as when you write "we only include doctors' bills already paid," instead of "we include only doctors' bills already paid." But sometimes inaccurate word order produces a silly result:

> In the presence of the judge, the district attorney announced that he knew of attempts to bribe the jury.

How can the reader possibly know what the writer meant? The little pronoun *he* is so placed that nobody can know what was intended. If the DA is telling the court that he has learned of attempted jury tampering, why, good for him. He is doing his duty. But if he is telling the world that the *judge* knew somebody was fiddling with the jurors, then the DA had better be right; if he is not, he is in serious trouble with the judge.

How about this classic example of faulty word order:

> Being too stupid to understand directions, counsel argued that the defendant should not be held accountable.

In this case the reader suspects that the writer meant the defendant was unusually dense, not the lawyer. Although not all meaning is lost, the reader's train of thought is interrupted when he or she hesitates to decide what the sentence means. Worse, the reader wonders how this law office let a clunker like this out into the world; what else are they careless about?

◾ A TOUCH OF CLASS

As a legal professional, your first duty is to be clear, simple, and precise. That does not mean your writing must be dull. Your writing can be interesting, particularly when you are trying to persuade (as when you write a brief urging a judge to do a particular thing).

There are several useful ways to add interest and emphasis. Several others should be used sparingly or avoided altogether. Here are a couple to shun.

Avoiding Overemphasis

As a general rule, do not underline, italicize, or otherwise emphasize a word. Likewise, do not put words or sentences in capital letters for emphasis. It looks contrived, and gives your writing an unbalanced, amateurish appearance. If your writing is well crafted, the emphasis ought to be obvious. Artificial attention-getters tend to distract.

For the same reason, avoid emphasis by using a great army of quotations. As we discuss more fully later in this chapter, quotations should be used only rarely. A plague of quotations gives your writing a cluttered, disconnected character.

Now let us examine the ways in which you can achieve emphasis and power, ways that add to the persuasive force of your writing. These techniques must not be overused, but in moderation they will improve the power of your writing.

Using Repetition

When you repeat an important word or phrase, you add to its importance simply by driving it home in the memory of the reader. Repetition is used in two ways.

First, a single word can be used repeatedly in quick succession. The classic example is Sir Winston Churchill's great speech in the perilous summer of 1940:

> We shall fight in France; we shall fight on the seas and oceans; we shall fight with growing confidence and growing strength in the air; we shall defend our island, whatever the cost may be; we shall fight on the beaches; we shall fight on the landing-grounds; we shall fight in the fields and in the streets; we shall fight in the hills; we shall never surrender.

All very well for a speech, you say, but can a legal writer really use repetition this way? Consider this example:

> Never did Plaintiff make any effort to advise Defendant that the property was flooded; never did he write a warning letter; never did he call on Defendant; never did he so much as place a telephone call.

You can see the effect. The reader is left with the impression that the plaintiff was at best grossly negligent. He did absolutely nothing to help himself, and he failed to use any number of ways to tell the defendant that there was trouble so the defendant could take some action. There is a great deal more power to this paragraph than there is in the flat, rather puny statement that "the plaintiff failed to notify the defendant."

The second way in which repetition may be used to strengthen your writing is simply by writing a key word twice in quick succession. For example:

> By either definition Defendant's actions were plainly reckless, reckless of the lives and safety of everyone in the room.

alliteration
The deliberate repetition of similar sounds in close succession to emphasize particular words.

Using Alliteration

Alliteration is the deliberate repetition of similar sounds close together. It emphasizes what you are saying in two ways: It makes your words smooth and appealing, and its very sound can add a mood to what you write. Here is a famous example, written by the English poet Swinburne:

> Even the weariest river winds somewhere safe to sea.[2]

Consider this example of how alliteration might be used in legal writing:

> However facile such a shallow analysis appears, it cannot survive the withering wind of close, careful, consistent scrutiny.

"Withering wind" is one use of alliteration: Its *w* sounds add to the context of merciless examination. "Close, careful, consistent" is another: It serves to emphasize the need for intense scrutiny.

Be careful not to overdo the use of alliteration. You are not writing "Ode on a Grecian Urn." But sparingly applied, this technique adds both interest and emphasis to otherwise ordinary subjects.

Using Vivid Language

Legal writing is not the place for purple prose. Ours is, or ought to be, a dignified profession dealing in facts and principles of law, not emotion and invective. That does not mean, however, that word choice and context are unimportant.

Especially when you are writing for the court, you must do what you can in a dignified way to catch and hold the reader's attention. Even the most dedicated of judges have trouble concentrating on banal, boring material. Consider this report from a real-world court in England:

> Proceedings were interrupted during a debt case at Bristol County Court yesterday when a solicitor discovered that his gown had been set alight by an electric fire. When he apologized for creating a disturbance, the [judge] said he was only too glad to have some interest introduced into the case.

You must never depart from serious, professional speech to attract the court's attention, but you certainly should consider the words you use to make your point, and the context in which you use them.

Choose Your Words Carefully.   First, a little about word choice. Consider these four common words; they are very close to synonymous, but each has a different impact on the reader. All of them are ordinary words; all of them are simple. You can use any one of them. Which will you choose?

- *Dirty.*   The dust on the windowsill, the ring around the collar. Being dirty is probably no big thing. That is why we have washing machines
- *Soiled.*   A little more serious, a little less appealing, perhaps a stain instead of just general dust. Nevertheless, something soiled is not generally repulsive.
- *Grimy.*   This needs to be cleaned up immediately; nobody even wants to be around things that are grimy; the word implies ground-in, neglected dirt in quantity.
- *Filthy.*   Yech! This is the apartment you will not even consider renting, the T-shirt you have to pick up with a stick, the litter box that no self-respecting cat would use.

---

2. A. C. Swinburne, *The Garden of Proserpine* (New York: Harper & Row).

So word choice does matter. Do not overdramatize, but carefully consider the picture you are trying to paint for your reader. Choose the right word as you would choose the right color for a painting. Strictly within the bounds of honesty, your job is to persuade, and to persuade you must catch and hold the reader's attention. Vivid, precise language will help.

Consider the Context.   Also consider the context in which you will use your words. What sort of impression are you trying to create? Suppose you are dealing with the question whether a criminal defendant could have run six blocks fast enough to commit a crime at a particular time. If you wrote for the district attorney, you would probably characterize the distance as "only six ordinary blocks." On the other hand, a legal assistant writing for the defense might call the same distance "six full-sized city blocks." Is there any real difference in the distance? Of course not. Is there, however, a subtle difference in the impression left on the reader by these two contrasting statements?

Using Quotations Sparingly

Quotations are the bane of the legal professional. Even the best of us are often sorely tempted to borrow from legal opinions whole squadrons of quotes and enlist them in our own writing. After all, if the court said it, it must be both accurate and persuasive, right? Wrong.

To begin with, there is never an excuse for quoting banal, commonplace language. There is nothing to be gained by quoting a court's statement that "the judgment is affirmed." You can say that just as well. In fact, you can almost always paraphrase what the court said, and say the same thing more simply and in fewer words. Another reason to quote only occasionally is that using many quotations tends to produce dull prose. Moreover, a whole string of quotations gives a jerky, disconnected tone to any document.

Much judicial writing is dull and ponderous; filled with long, obscure words; and interminably verbose. It can take forever to make a simple point, a whole page to say what might be said in a line or two. Read over this example from an Oklahoma case, and try to say more briefly and plainly what the court took so many words to say:

> The party who purchases property from utter strangers and receives it under unusual circumstances, and especially where all the facts of the case are passed upon by a jury, and the jury has come to the conclusion after hearing the facts and circumstances, that the defendant had knowledge that it was stolen property, and by so rendering their verdict, it cannot be successfully maintained in an appellate court that defendant did not believe the property was stolen.
>
> *Camp v. State*, 89 P.2d 378, 380 (Okla.Crim.App. 1939).

Take a piece of paper and a few minutes, and try to translate this enormous sentence from a mass of verbiage into something clearer and simpler. Take your time. There are several ways to slim down this mess, but your translation ought to look something like this:

> The defendant purchased property from strangers under unusual circumstances; on this evidence the jury decided that he bought it knowing it was stolen. On appeal, this court cannot retry the factual issue of the defendant's knowledge.

Quotations also present a more subtle danger. Very seldom is the case you are writing about absolutely identical to the case you are quoting from; so, without some explanation, the statement of the law you quote is probably not precisely applicable to your own facts.

When *should* you quote, then? Quote when you cannot say whatever-it-is as well yourself, when the judicial language you quote expresses an important thought perfectly and memorably. How about this memorable opening to a Supreme Court argument:

> The question is whether a good Nazi can be a good American.

As an attention-getter, as a crisp, forceful statement of the problem, you cannot beat that line. So quote it, quote it because it is well said. What it says is not nearly as important as the way it is expressed.

◼ PROOFREAD

Failure to proofread is the most serious and unforgivable fault any legal writer can commit. It can produce simple nonsense, like this line from a lawyer's letter:

> He remembers leaks in the garden planters, but Mr. Jones had dirt pulled out of the planters and then repaired . . . .

A proofreading lapse can also miss a truly memorable silliness such as this:

> In the index to this brief, the Court will find an extensive copulation of authorities on this subject.

This ugly mistake was made in a written argument filed with a federal appeals court. You can imagine the court's reaction to that line. No doubt the judges knew the writer meant *compilation* instead of what he wrote, but the mistake almost surely produced both a break in the readers' concentration and a serious question in the readers' mind about the competence and reliability of the writer.

Failure to proofread also lets out into the world horrors like this next example. It is particularly dangerous because it has two meanings, and there is no way for the reader to decide which meaning was intended.

> She had to replace her 1984 Buick Skylark, four door, with a 1985 Buick Skylark, four door, with the additional cost thereof which was not reimbursed by insurance . . . in the sum of $3,056.33.

Thereof—an unnecessary piece of legalese in any case—adds nothing to the sentence except confusion. Maybe it refers to the '84 Skylark; maybe it means the '85 replacement. Is $3,056.33 the entire cost of the new car, or is it only the part not covered by insurance, or is it the difference between the value of the old car and the price she paid for the new one?

This sentence is a fine example of terminal babble, a piece of careless dictation never proofread. With just a little care, it might have come out something like this:

> She had to replace her 1984 Buick Skylark with a 1985 Skylark. The difference between the value of the old car and the cost of the new one is $3,056.33. This sum was not reimbursed by her insurance.

The writer could and should have caught and cleared up this confusion by careful proofreading. It was his duty to make sure his writing was clear. He cannot delegate that task to his secretary or anybody else. When any of us writes something, the obligation remains ours to make certain the finished product is right. Here are some time-tested suggestions for really effective proofreading.

Using a Proofreader

First, it is usually best not only to proofread your own copy, but to have somebody else do it, too. After spending a lot of time and sweat on a memo or brief or pleading, the writer herself often proofreads for what *ought* to be on the page, not for what is already there. It is easy to miss typographical errors and ludicrous or misleading constructions.

To avoid this, have somebody else read your writing. Best of all, have that person read it aloud in your presence. Language is only the spoken word reduced to symbols. You may be sure that if your writing sounds odd when read aloud, it needs some more work before it reads correctly, too. Never, never be content with something that is "almost" right. We are judged by what we write, and our reputation rides on every line.

Reading Slowly

PRACTICE TIP

When proofreading, force yourself to read slowly enough to check every letter and punctuation mark.

Most proofreading mistakes are made by failing to read slowly enough to catch the errors. Force yourself to read slowly and look at each letter and punctuation mark. If necessary, try this old typesetting trick: Using a pencil eraser, touch each character as you read to force yourself to read more slowly. You will eventually reach the point where you automatically proofread at a pace that allows you to spot each error. Proofreading is an acquired art that is mastered with patient practice.

When you can, have an intelligent layperson read what you write. That person may not understand a few legal expressions in your writing, but the sense of what you are driving at ought to come through. If it does, your writing has achieved its goal. If your reader turns to you and says, "I don't understand this," you may need to polish some more.

CHAPTER SUMMARY

Whatever you write, keep before you the basic rules of good writing:

- Keep it simple.
- Keep it concise.
- Say exactly what you mean; "close" is not good enough.
- Never use a long word when a short, familiar word will do. Remember, Spot runs; he does not perambulate or proceed.
- Unless you are using a legal term of art, never use a Latin or Norman-French expression when you have a clear English equivalent.
- Avoid fad words and words without clearly defined meanings.
- Edit and proofread. Cut unmercifully, and get somebody else to read your text before you put it in final form.

And remember the golden rule: If you don't say it, don't write it.

KEY WORDS AND PHRASES

alliteration	legal terms of art	pleonasm	standard of care
citation	malapropism	proximate cause	tautologies
deposition summary	parallel construction	rule of short	
legalese	pleading	signposting	

EXERCISES

Do the first three exercises. Then, compare your answers to the solutions given immediately after those exercises. Review Chapter 3 as necessary. Then proceed to exercises 4 through 8, which follow the solutions to exercises 1 through 3.

1. Consider the words and phrases printed below. Decide whether there is a simpler, easier way to say whatever-it-is and write your solution. By all means use a dictionary if you have the slightest doubt about any meaning. You will use one daily all your life as a legal professional.
   a. apprise
   b. evince
   c. afford an opportunity
   d. not later than
   e. terminate
   f. it is requested that
   g. adjacent to
   h. arising from the fact that
   i. take into consideration
   j. for the purpose of
   k. during the period when
   l. in view of the fact
   m. was in receipt of
   n. in the event of
   o. first of all
   p. make a decision about
   q. make an argument
   r. preliminary to
   s. posterior
   t. remunerate

2. Now let us try a few slightly longer phrases:
   a. There has been a cessation of hostilities.
   b. The decision should be held in abeyance pending resolution of the question as to whether a further extension of time is warranted.

   c. Theirs is a life marked by the allocation of a very limited portion of a person's resources, abilities, and energies to the ownership, maintenance, and adornment of residential structures.

3. Last, try your hand at unravelling this apparently ordinary letter. It is the most complicated problem so far, but do not let it stop you; you can turn it into much better prose than this author could. "Letters of Administration," by the way, means formal authority for somebody to administer the estate of a person who has died.

   [Date;]

   FEDERAL EXPRESS

   [Name;]
   [Address;]
   [City, State, and ZIP Code;]

   RE: Estate of _____
       File No.:_____

   Dear Mr. _____:

   Enclosed herein please find one (1) original and one (1) copy of the Petition for Letters of Administration in the above-referenced matter. I have sent same to your address via Federal Express, as you had earlier requested. Please review the same, and should same meet with your approval, attach your signature thereto and return same to my office. Upon my receipt of said Petition, I will obtain the signature of Mr. Brown, file same with the Court, and have a hearing date set for the issuance of the Letters of Administration. As we discussed, it will not be necessary for you to attend said hearing although I will require the presence of Mr. Brown.

   As we have discussed, please forward all documents reflecting expenses due and owing in the Estate to this office so that, following the issuance of the Letters of Administration, I may establish an

Estate bank account and begin the process of payment of same. Pursuant to your request, this account will require two signatures, your signature and that of your mother, for the issuance of all checks.

Sincerely,

Solutions to Exercises 1–3

(Reminder: Exercises 4 through 8 follow these solutions.)

1. a. tell   k. when
   b. show   l. because
   c. allow, let   m. received
   d. by   n. if
   e. end   o. first
   f. please   p. decide
   g. next to   q. argue
   h. because   r. before
   i. consider   s. behind
   j. to   t. pay

2. a. The fighting has stopped.
   b. We should not decide until we determine whether we need more time.
   c. They live in slums.

3. [Date;]

   FEDERAL EXPRESS

   [Name;]
   [Address;]
   [City, State, and ZIP Code;]

   RE: Estate of _____
       File No.: _____

   Dear Mr. _____:

   I enclose an original and a copy of the Petition for Letters of Administration. Please review, sign, and return both. I will have Mr. Brown sign, file the Petition, and set a date for a hearing to issue the Letters. You need not attend, but Mr. Brown must.

   Please send me all documents showing debts incurred by the estate. After the letters are issued, I will open an estate bank account and pay the bills. The checks will require both your signature and your mother's.

   Sincerely,

Now examine the original letter, and see why some of its verbiage can be cut out.

- *Enclosed herein please find.* No one talks like that.

- *One (1).* Redundant. Everybody knows what "one" means.
- *In the above-referenced matter.* Of course it is in the "above-referenced matter." What other matter would it be?
- *To your address via Federal Express.* Self-evident, since the addressee normally knows how something reached him, and how the letter was sent is stated plainly before the addressee's name.
- *As you had earlier requested.* Also redundant, unless there's some good reason for reminding the writer that he asked for whatever-it-is. Usually there is no such reason, and this language is repeated several times in this letter.
- *Should same meet with your approval.* Unless the addressee is a lawyer, he has no idea whether the petition is correct or not, so why ask him to "approve" it? And *same* is pure legalese: Never use it. Instead substitute the appropriate noun or pronoun. In this case, a simple *it* would do just fine.
- *Attach your signature thereto.* This ponderous phrase is pure legalese for good old *please sign.*

You get the idea. This letter is from the real world of law practice, by the way. It is a most extreme example of terminal lawyer's disease. Most of these extra or antique words are in the letter because the writer was long-winded; at least the reader can cut through this jungle and puzzle out what all this hot air is about.

But how about *forward all documents reflecting expenses due and owing in the Estate?* It is clumsy, certainly: *show* is a better word than *reflect; send* beats *forward; due and owing* is a pleonasm. But there is a more serious problem with the phrase, and it is this: What does it mean?

In particular, what does *in the estate* mean? Does the lawyer want documents showing debts owed *to* the estate, or debts owed *by* the estate? The context tells you he probably means *by* the estate, because he goes on to talk about paying "same." Now *same* properly refers to either *account* or *Letters of Administration,* and so makes no literal sense; even so, you can make a shrewd guess that *same* was intended to mean "debts."

Remember, though, your reader should never have to guess. What you say ought to be absolutely clear on one reading, without a chance of misunderstanding.

Look back again at the rewrite you did on the original letter. Before you move on to the next chapter, see whether you cannot perform even further useful surgery. We think you can.

More Chapter 3 Exercises

4. The flaws in these sentences should be obvious. Rewrite each using clearer, more concise language.

   a. Our client, Jane Healy, who worked in a public relations firm and had a promising career, was drastically delayed in her attempt to return to her abode, when the collision occurred.

   b. At the time that Jane Healy left the place of her employment, she had come to the recognition of the fact that she was running late.

   c. Ms. Healy planned to don evening apparel, provide her feline with nourishment, and reapply cosmetics to her facial surface upon reaching her abode.

   d. Prior to effectuating an attempt to navigate her way across the intersection, Ms. Healy beheld the traffic light as it changed color from green to burnt sienna.

   e. When the motor vehicles immediately anterior to Ms. Healy's automobile came to a halt, Ms. Healy found it necessary to apply her brakes, after which time she realized she was trapped in the middle of the intersection.

   f. Charles Raymond proceeded through the intersection subsequent to the traffic signal changing from red to green, and collided with Ms. Healy's vehicle.

   g. It is our hope that Mr. Raymond will henceforth cease and desist his practice of consuming malted beverages prior to his ventures into the intersections of public roadways.

   h. After he downed mega-brewskies, the dude t-boned that gal's car in a major way.

   i. This jurisdiction's prior case law in this area of jurisprudence suggests that the aforementioned male defendant may be totally and completely liable to Ms. Healy for her injuries.

   j. Mr. Raymond violated the statutorily articulated legal obligations required by all who attempt to travel by automobile on the public highways of this state, the fulfillment of which are required of all drivers, in that he ignored the dangers of alcohol consumption prior to such driving activity, he was inattentive to traffic conditions in existence in the vicinity into which he travels, and certainly, he failed to be consistent in the use of passenger restraining devices.

5. Ms. Pepper, your supervising attorney, has asked you and Fred to research a contributory negligence issue for Ms. Healy's case. Ms. Pepper takes a week's vacation, but asks you and Fred to send her a memorandum on your research. When you have prepared the memorandum, Fred writes the following cover letter. How would you rewrite it?

   June 1, 1994

   Amelia S. Pepper
   5300 Park Avenue, Suite 701
   New York, New York 10017

   Re: *Healy v. Raymond*
      File No.: A–6228

   Dear Ms. Pepper:

   Greetings and salutations! I hope you are enjoying your brief hiatus from the hurly-burly of the legal world!

   Enclosed herein please find the contributory negligence memorandum for the above-referenced matter. I have sent same to your address via Federal Express as you had earlier requested.

   Please review the same, and inform me if it meets with your approval. Said memorandum encompasses material from seventeen (17) cases in ten (10) jurisdictions.

   Your humble and faithful servant,

   Fred Wickam
   Legal Assistant

6. In Chapter 3, you learned about words that closely resemble one another but have entirely different meanings. The following sentences contain such words. Read each sentence. Decide whether each word has been used correctly. Change any words that have not been used properly.

   a. Although no express promise was ever made, Jane Healy implied from her employer that she would take over her supervisor's job when he retired.

   b. Before the accident, Jane Healy said that her car had been apprised at $27,000.00.

   c. Pulling into the intersection, Ms. Healy had no idea that she was in eminent danger of having an accident.

   d. Because of her extensive injuries, Ms. Healy's doctor had to proscribe a strong painkiller.

   e. Ms. Healy also has to lay awake at night because she is in so much pain.

7. Concise sentences are a hallmark of good legal writing. The following sentences are long-winded and convoluted. Rewrite them by breaking them down into shorter, more digestible sentences.

   a. Ms. Healy said that she bought her car new from a dealership in town and that the car had never been in an accident, so she had no opportunity to see whether the seatbelt would act as an effective restraint in an accident.

   b. What Ms. Healy did not know was that manufacturer of the car had issued a recall on that particular model because of seat belt problems and had advised local dealerships to warn them customers of the problem, but the dealership Ms. Healy bought her car from failed to notify her.

   c. When Charles Raymond broadsided Ms. Healy's car, the impact catapulted Ms. Healy's car out of the intersection and into a steel power pole, which is when the seatbelt broke, as a result of which Ms. Healy was flung up against her windshield and suffered a fractured skull, broken ribs, a punctured lung, and severe cuts.

   d. Doctors have told Ms. Healy that her face has been permanently scarred and that she will have to undergo two more plastic surgeries so she will probably be in the hospital a while; however, Ms. Healy's boss, Arthur Forbes, told her not to worry about rushing back to work, since she will not have a job to come back to because the firm does not want a public relations specialist with severe facial scars.

   e. Ms. Healy retorted that Mr. Forbes would not have a job to come back to, either, since she was going to tell the CEO about the large sums of money that Mr. Forbes had been withdrawing from company bank accounts and wiring to banks in the Caribbean, and about the fake expense reports Mr. Forbes

had been sending to the accounting department for trips he had not gone on.

8. Signposting is an important tool for breaking your writing down into bite-sized pieces. The sentences below suffer from these major flaws: (1) lacking signposting where it is needed; (2) including signposting, but following an incorrect format; and (3) using signposting where it is unnecessary. Rewrite the sentences to read as they should.

   a. Tom Collins, a bar customer, said Mr. Raymond downed at least five drinks in the hour before he left the bar. Mr. Raymond drank a shot of Jim Beam. Then he had a couple of beers. Then Mr. Raymond consumed a marguerita on the rocks. After that, Mr. Raymond had some peppermint schnapps.

   b. The witnesses to Mr. Raymond's intoxicated condition were (1) Roy Collins; (2) Tony Simpson; and (3) Sergeant Adams.

   c. Tony Simpson, the bartender, said he continued to serve Mr. Raymond drinks because he thought that he would get into trouble for refusing to serve a customer, that Mr. Raymond was just being his usual obnoxious self and wasn't really all that drunk, and that Mr. Raymond would have the sense to call a taxi if he really were intoxicated.

   d. When Sergeant Adams arrived at the scene of the accident, Mr. Raymond stumbled over to the police car. Although his speech was slightly slurred, Mr. Raymond made Sergeant Adams understand four things. First, that Mr. Raymond had been going the speed limit. Second, that he had flushed his driver's license down the toilet that morning by accident. Third, that he had stopped drinking after his last DUI. Fourth, that women drivers should be banned from the streets.

   e. Sergeant Adams, sizing up the situation quickly, (1) arrested Mr. Raymond; (2) handcuffed him; (3) read him his rights; and (4) took him down to the police station.

4

GRAMMAR AND PUNCTUATION

All of your learning and painstaking research will be ineffective if your writing does not follow the rules of English grammar and punctuation. In this chapter, we cannot tell you all there is to know about grammar and punctuation, but we shall try to give you at least the major rules. At the end, we also include a few of the rules of capitalization.

While this book cannot be a treatise on grammar, there are plenty of excellent handbooks on grammar and usage. The most famous one (and still very good indeed) is Strunk and White, *The Elements of Style*. Another, far more complete, is the Prentice-Hall *Handbook for Writers*. Finally, an authoritative source on the complexities of usage is the *United States Government Printing Office Style Manual*.

Get a good grammar book, put it beside your dictionary, and use it often. Some rules of grammar may seem picky to you, but to ignore them is just plain unprofessional.

◼ GRAMMAR

Using proper grammar is the mark of an educated, and careful, writer. Nothing destroys the reader's confidence in you more quickly than an obvious grammatical error; it tells the reader you are either ignorant or careless, or both. In either case, you are not the sort of legal professional anybody wants to hire.

You can feel that effect in this line from an article in a learned journal by, of all people, a law professor writing about law students:

Are we so much smarter than them?

Whoever wrote *them* instead of *they* sure did not sound smarter than anybody. The author used the wrong pronoun, and his carelessness spoiled the effect of a carefully crafted piece of writing. The writer forgot the rules of **pronoun references.**

pronoun reference
The noun to which the pronoun refers.

Pronoun References

Remember that a pronoun is only a substitute for a **noun.** So, with a pronoun in it, the sentence should read just as it would with the noun itself included in it. The writer of the example above did not stop to reflect that his short sentence, written out fully, would have read:

Are we so much smarter than they are?

That is, the verb *are* was implied, not expressed. If you write a sentence like this one, you cannot go wrong if you say the sentence as it would be with the implied word written out. Here is another example, using an **implied preposition:**

They gave the dirty jobs to her and him.

Written out fully, the sentence would read:

They gave the dirty jobs to her and to him.

As we said above, a pronoun is a substitute for a noun. It "refers" to that noun, which is called its **antecedent**, like this:

Johnson was a particularly ugly customer. When he appeared in court, he was always shackled.

Johnson is, of course, the noun. *He* is the pronoun that refers to Johnson. Because only one person is mentioned in the example, *he* can refer only to Johnson. Therefore, there is no confusion in this example. Sometimes, however, there can be, even in a comparatively simple sentence. Consider this example:

The congressman attacked the President, alleging that he knew of several secret scandals in the cabinet.

The sentence is ambiguous as written. *Who* knew of scandals in the cabinet? If it was the President, the inference is that he knew but did not act and, therefore, failed in his duty. But if *he* means the congressman, the inference is not quite so shameful: something is wrong in the cabinet, and the President must repair it. Here is a possible solution:

The congressman attacked the President, alleging that the Chief Executive knew of several secret scandals in the cabinet.

Try another example of the same pronoun confusion, this time in two related sentences:

The judge made a decision about the admissibility of evidence of a conspiracy between Jones and Smith. It will require a change of tactics by the state.

What will require a change of tactics by the state? Is it the decision by the court, or is it the evidence of a conspiracy? Sometimes what the writer intends is quite clear from the context in which the sentence appears, but often it is not. In any case, what a sentence means should be clear from the sentence itself, without depending on context. Here is one way to repair the last example:

The judge made a decision about the admissibility of evidence of a conspiracy between Jones and Smith. The ruling will require a change of tactics by the state.

As a general rule, errors like this do not obscure meaning entirely. They are, however, ludicrous. Like other silly mistakes, they make the reader wonder whether the writer is as careless about his or her research and reasoning as he or she was about failing to catch a stupid mistake. The writer's professional image is badly damaged as a result.

---

implied preposition
A preposition that is not stated in the sentence, but is implied from the sentence.

antecedent
The word or idea to which the pronoun refers.

Case Forms of Pronouns

Case refers to the status of a noun or pronoun, that is, whether it is the subject or object of a sentence. Remember, the subject acts, as in "the *lawyer* argued." The object is acted upon, as in "we set up the *tent*." Pronouns, such as who, he, she, and them, follow the same rules:

Jane and I arrived early yesterday.	I = subject.
The boss gave Jane and me a raise.	Me = object.
She and he failed the test.	She and he = subject.
I did not see either him or her.	Him or her = object.

The same rule controls the irritating problem of whether to use *who* or *whom*. To decide which to use, decide whether you want a subject (who) or an object (whom). Thus:

He is the attorney whom we want to retain.
(We want to retain whom?)

But:

He is the attorney who tried the *Jacobs* case.
(Who tried the case?)

Number

Nouns and verbs in the same sentence, referring to one another, must agree in **number**. That is, if the subject of the sentence is singular, the verb must also be singular. Be especially careful of words like *everybody, nobody,* and *somebody.* These may sometimes sound as if they refer to more than one person, but each word takes a singular verb: Everybody has the same assignment, *not* Everybody have . . . .

This sentence is grammatically correct:

Only one of thousands of lawyers reaches the Supreme Court.

This sentence is wrong:

Only one of thousands of lawyers reach the Supreme Court.

The number of the verb must be singular—*reaches,* as in *he reaches*—to match the subject of the sentence, which is *one. One* is the noun—the "thing" that *does* something, and is therefore the subject of the sentence. *Thousands* and *lawyers* are both plural, but neither is the subject.

Sometimes two or more nouns together will make up the subject of the sentence: Apples and oranges eaten together provides a complimentary taste. Wrong. While the two fruits are spoken of almost as a single thing, they are separate, so the verb must be *provide.* Also, each fruit has a taste of its own, so the sentence should say, "provide complimentary tastes."

Be especially careful where subject and verb are separated by several intervening words, as in this example:

The great number of instructions, memorandums, and other documents make it almost impossible for the secretarial pool to keep up.

The sentence looks all right; it even flows well when you say it aloud. Nevertheless, it is wrong. The subject of the sentence is *number*, which is singular. Therefore, the verb should be *makes,* which is also singular (not *make).*

---

case
The status of a noun or pronoun, referring to whether the noun or pronoun is the subject or the object of the sentence.

number
The form of a word indicating the word's singular or plural status.

Linking verbs are verbs that connect nouns. What should the verb's number be—singular or plural—if the noun on one side of it is plural, and the noun on the other side is singular? For example, consider this sentence:

Jury instructions are (is?) the heart of the disagreement.

Instructions is plural, of course, but *heart* is singular. Follow the old rule—which is not always easy—that the number of the *subject* decides the number of the verb. In this case the sentence should read, "instructions *are.*"

A similar problem arises with a verb that follows two nouns connected by *either-or* or *neither-nor.* See if you can solve this one:

Neither the defendants nor the government were (was) ready to compromise.

The rule here is to make the number of the verb match the number of the nearest noun. *Government,* the nearest noun, is singular, so the verb must be *was,* also singular.

A related rule is that a pronoun must be of the same number as the noun that is its antecedent. For example:

Each student must bring their books to class.

Now, what is wrong with that statement? Yes, people say things like that in common speech all the time. But when you must be precise, you recognize that the noun *student* is singular, and the pronoun *their* is plural. This common error is easy to fix. Simply say either:

Each student must bring his or her books to class.

Or:

All students must bring their books to class.

For clarity, *keep your pronoun close to its antecedent,* the word to which it refers. Be especially careful to do this when the sentence contains several nouns to which your pronoun can refer.

Because there is too much distance between pronoun and antecedent, this sentence is vague:

Storms on the north face of the Eiger produce rockfalls, ice-sheets, and torrents of water. They are very dangerous to the climbers.

What does *they* refer to? Is it storms? Or is it one, two, or all of the hazards produced by storms?

Be careful of using *it, which, that,* or *this* in reference to a preceding clause or sentence. For example:

The north face of the Eiger produces rockfalls, ice-sheets, and torrents of water, causing a high death-toll among climbers. It is often written about in the German newspapers.

Or:

Storms on the north face of the Eiger produce rockfalls, ice-sheets, and torrents of water, which have taken a deadly toll of climbers.

In the first sentence, *it* could refer to the death-toll, to the Eiger, or to the north face. In the second sentence, *which* could mean the storms, or one or more of the hazards produced by storms.

The uncertainty raised by the last three examples is easy to repair. Just be specific, like this:

> Storms on the north face of the Eiger produce rockfalls, ice-sheets, and torrents of water. These storms have taken a deadly toll of climbers.

Singular and Plural

This subject is closely related to number. The rule is simple: *a verb must be singular or plural according to whether its subject is singular or plural.*

If the subject of the sentence is clearly singular or clearly plural, it is easy enough to write the proper verb form:

> John and Mary *are* both students.

There are, however, some idiomatic expressions that do not follow the rules: Politics is a dirty business, or Bread and water is all the prisoners got to eat. These are also easy enough; they are common expressions, and you will know most of them automatically.

A more serious problem occurs when a singular noun is connected to other nouns by *with, plus, as well as, together with,* or *in addition to.* In such cases, the verb remains singular: The judge, as well as the lawyers, seems perplexed by Brown's testimony.

As a rule, use a singular verb after *each, somebody, everyone, nobody, neither,* and *either,* like this:

> Everybody in court was asleep by noon.

Or:

> Neither of them is prepared for the deposition today.

Making plurals of proper names is generally simple. Usually, you just add an *s.* If a proper name ends in *y,* add a singular *s,* as in "the two Marys," except for the few words that change form in the plural:

> We loved traveling in the Rockies.

Some two-word titles you make plural by pluralizing the noun and leaving the adjective alone, as in *brigadier generals* or *attorneys general.* Never use an apostrophe in making the plural of a proper name. "We went over to see the Markhams'" is wrong. Just say, "to see the Markhams."

Names that end in *s* form their plural by adding *es* after the final *s.* Examples are "the Joneses," or "the Collinses." A few plurals are mavericks. You just have to learn them. For example, the plural of *beau* is *beaux,* as it is in French.

There is no consistent rule. Here are some other odd plurals:

- Stadiums (not stadia)
- Strata (not stratums)
- Geese (not gooses)
- Mongooses (not mongeese)
- Curriculums (not curricula)
- Alumni (not alumnuses)

The plural of *datum* is *data,* which is often used—incorrectly—as both singular and plural. *Criteria* is always plural; the singular is *criterion.* If you have a choice between

PRACTICE TIP

A verb is singular or plural according to whether its subject is singular or plural.

PRACTICE TIP

Never use an apostrophe in making the plural of a proper name.

collective nouns
Nouns that refer to more
than one person or
thing, and may take
either a singular or plural verb (e.g., "group").

active voice
The sentence form in
which the subject is
doing something.

passive voice
The sentence form in
which the subject has
something done to him,
her, or it.

plurals, prefer the Americanized plural. Choose, for instance, *indexes,* instead of *indices,* and *appendixes* instead of *appendices.*

Some nouns, called **collective nouns,** may take either a singular or a plural verb. *Group* is a good example. Either "the group were busily harvesting," or "the group was busily harvesting" is considered correct.

British usage in these cases is to choose the plural, as in "the Army have finished training at Aldershot." American usage prefers the singular, as in "the government has again run out of money." Use whichever form you think makes the sentence smoother. *Court,* by the way, is not a collective noun, even though there may be several judges on the court. *Court* is always singular, as in "the court has adjourned for the day; it will reconvene tomorrow."

Active and Passive Voice

In the **active voice,** the subject of the sentence is doing something—he, she, or it is *acting.* For example:

Charley flew to Acapulco on the first of May.

In the **passive voice,** by contrast, the subject of the sentence has something done to him, her, or it. The subject is therefore *passive:*

Charley was flown to Acapulco on the first of May.

Here is a more extreme example of the passive voice:

He was fallen upon by the tree.

instead of, "the tree fell on him."

Write in the active voice as much as you can. When you do not, much of the life goes out of what you write, and your writing becomes less interesting and therefore much less persuasive. The passive voice may also introduce some unnecessary uncertainty to your writing, like this:

The bomb was left at the hotel at about two o'clock.

Who left the bomb at the hotel? The identity of the bomber, if you know it, is plainly important, but it is lost when you use the passive voice.

You may occasionally use the passive voice simply for convenience, to make your prose flow more smoothly. An example of such a harmless use of the passive voice appears at the end of the preceding paragraph: The identity of the bomber . . . is lost. . . . Ordinarily, however, try to state everything in the active voice. You will make your prose leaner and more forceful by doing so.

Occasionally, you may write a sentence in the passive voice because the actor (the doer) is unknown, or because the identity of the actor is immaterial:

The Complaint was filed Thursday afternoon.

There are situations in which you may deliberately choose to use passive rather than active voice. You may wish to emphasize the object of the sentence, rather than its subject. Suppose, for example, that you are writing for the district attorney, and you want to emphasize the plight of the victim of a crime, rather than the perpetrators. You might do it like this, using the passive voice:

The frail old man was viciously attacked by the defendants.

The passive voice is also used to be purposefully vague or evasive. This may be why legal professionals commonly use the passive voice when drafting answers to discovery requests. Notice the difference in these two sentences:

Active voice: The Governor made calls to the District Attorney.
Passive voice: Calls to the District Attorney were made.

Did you notice how the identity of the actor is omitted in the sentence using passive voice? Both statements are accurate, but the passive voice is more subtle and vague. Listen for the passive voice the next time you watch the evening news on the television. If someone is attempting to avoid giving a direct answer to a controversial question, we bet that they use the passive voice.

As we have discussed, there are situations in which using the passive voice is proper. But unless you are using the passive voice for a specific purpose, use it as little as possible. Even though your usage of the passive may be quite correct, it robs your prose of a little of its force and urgency, and makes it that much less persuasive.

Mood

The **indicative mood** is the verb form used for ordinary statements, as in "the judge instructed the jury," or, "the sun will rise at 6:30 tomorrow." The **imperative mood** refers to commands: "Be quiet," said the senior partner, "and listen." The mood with which writers often have trouble is the **subjunctive mood,** which you use when you are writing about a condition uncertain, or contrary to fact: I wish I were on the Supreme Court [but of course I am not].

You form the subjunctive mood by using *were* where you would ordinarily use *was,* or by substituting *have* for *has,* or by using *be* instead of *is, are, was,* or *am.*

Here are some examples of subjunctive mood, all of them talking about things that are not (or are uncertain):

If I were king, I'd exterminate Saddam Hussein. [I am not king.]
If he have a fault, it is talking too much, too often. [He may not have this fault.]
Though great care be exercised, the operation still could fail. [The operation may not succeed.]

As you can guess, the usage in the second example is almost extinct, even in the ivory tower of academe. We suggest that you forget about it, except to recognize it as a proper subjunctive if you see it in a letter.

Some subjunctive *be* expressions are still used occasionally. Everybody knows Patrick Henry's ringing words: "If this be treason, make the most of it." Even so, we think you can dispense with this form too, unless your boss insists.

On the other hand, subjunctive expressions using *were* are still common:

indicative mood
The verb form used for ordinary statements. "The legal assistant drafted the discovery request."

imperative mood
The verb form used for commands. "Order in the court," said the judge.

subjunctive mood
The verb form used when writing about an uncertain condition or one that is contrary to fact or reality. "If I were the judge, I would overrule the objection."

■ PRACTICE TIP

Verbs may be in one of three moods:
- The *indicative mood* is used for ordinary statements.
- The *imperative mood* is used for commands.
- The *subjunctive mood* is used when writing about an uncertain condition or one that is contrary to fact.

If it were only summer . . . .

If mosquito bites were money, I'd be rich.

Yesterday, George looked as though he were going to die.

If we were to offer even a small settlement, I think the defendant would accept.

Master the "were" form of the subjunctive mood. It is not only correct; it shows class and education. Educated readers of your prose will know the difference, and appreciate your care.

Double Negatives

Two negatives make a positive. For example, nobody has a doormat that says "Not Unwelcome." It is simpler and shorter simply to say "Welcome." We had trouble thinking of any instance in which we could acceptably use **double negatives.** We could not, particularly because legal writing must be clear and specific, and the double negative, by its nature, is less clear than a single positive.

The double negative is bad enough. Understanding becomes even harder when the writer introduces *three or more* negatives. Here is a horrible example, a single sentence that has no less than *four* negatives. We could not translate it, and yet it is part of a statute dealing with pension plans, a law meant to control peoples' lives:

> A plan shall not be treated as not satisfying the requirements of this section solely because the spouse of the participant is not entitled to receive a survivor annuity (whether or not an election has been made) . . . unless the participant and his spouse have been married.

As you see, there are four *nots* in the paragraph. Some would consider *unless* to be a fifth negative, because it changes the meaning of the sentence—if any—by attaching another condition.

Even less complex multiple negatives take time to understand:

> The book is not untranslatable unless one is not Hungarian by birth.

The careful reader will decipher this sentence by reading it carefully—again—but the delay will derail his or her train of thought and detract from the persuasive power of your work.

Avoid using double negatives in anything you write. The only "exception" to the rule is not really an exception at all. It occurs rarely, when you must write something like this:

> The brief for the government was not unclear.

This sentence would be proper in commenting on a litigant's assertion that "the government's brief was unclear." In short, the sentence does not mean that the government's brief was "clear," but rather quite simply that it was not unclear. If you otherwise avoid the double negative in your writing, your meaning will be quite plain on the rare occasion when you must write something like this example.

Nominalization

A **nominalization** is a noun made out of a verb. Avoid using them when you can. For example, instead of writing "the office made inquiries," simply say, "the office inquired." Strike out "we have reached a resolution of the dispute," and substitute "we have resolved the dispute." As you see, nominalizations require more words than does simply using the verb alone.

---

double negative
Two negative words used in the same sentence. Two negatives make a positive.

PRACTICE TIP

Remember that, when your writing is unnecessarily complex or cumbersome, the reader either gets the meaning slowly—or worse, not at all.

nominalization
A noun made out of a verb.

PRACTICE TIP

Avoid using nominalizations. "The office made inquiries," versus "the office inquired."

Parallel Construction

Parallel construction simply means expressing two or more ideas *using the same grammatical form.* For example:

> We have scheduled the depositions, the doctor's consultation, and Mr. Young's trip to the accident scene.

This sentence flows evenly, because the ideas in it were all formed as nouns. Compare it with this one:

> We have scheduled the depositions, the doctor's consultation, and to send Mr. Young to the accident scene.

As you see, the second sentence has a ragged, uneven cadence to it because, instead of three nouns, we used two nouns and an **infinitive** (*to send*).

Consider a second example:

> The next step is preparation and travel to the site of the conference.

Notice how this sentence smooths out when you add a preposition and a couple of commas:

> The next step is preparation for, and travel to, the site of the conference.

Parallel construction also requires that the writer express a series of things in identical form. To do this, either use an article before each item in the series, or just one article before the first item in the series. Here are a couple of examples:

> The package consists of a lease, a cleaning contract, and a quitclaim deed.
> The package consists of a lease, cleaning contract, and quitclaim deed.

Either sentence is correct. Here is a sentence that is not:

> The package consists of a lease, a cleaning contract, and quitclaim deed.

As a matter of style, observe another rule whenever you can: if you list a series of nouns, either modify all of them, or modify none of them. For example, write:

> The manager used vegetables as a centerpiece. Each table was decorated with deep green lettuce, bright red apples, and pale yellow grapefruit.

Not:

> The manager used vegetables as a centerpiece. Each table was decorated with deep green lettuce, bright red apples, and grapefruit.

The first sentence is a little longer, but much smoother and better balanced than the second.

Split Infinitives

The two parts of an **infinitive**—*to go, to travel, to relax, to argue*—normally should not be separated by another word or words. For example, "to be or to not be" grates on the reader, as well it should. But the rule against **splitting infinitives** is not absolute. Sometimes splitting an infinitive makes the sentence flow much more smoothly:

> Throughout the trial, counsel for the defendant managed to coolly and professionally frustrate repeated attempts to impeach his client.

---

parallel construction
Consistent word form and verb tense among particular words and/or sentences; expressing two or more ideas using the same grammatical form.

infinitive
A predictive or future verb form (e.g., "to send"):

PRACTICE TIP

State related ideas or a series of things in the same, parallel grammatical form.

split infinitive
A predictive or future verb form. Infinitives are split when the article *to* is separated from the verb by another word or words. "He decided to quickly send the memo."

We think this sentence is made clearer and smoother by splitting the infinitive rather than by keeping it intact, as it is in this example:

> Throughout the trial, counsel for the defendant managed coolly and professionally to frustrate repeated attempts to impeach his client.

Possessives

Possession is shown in two ways. First, you do it by word form (*his* briefcase, *their* vacation, *its* dimensions). Remember that pronouns like these do *not* take an apostrophe. Thus *it's* is not a possessive. Instead, it is a contraction of *it is*, and the apostrophe is used to show that a letter was left out.

Second, you show possession by adding an apostrophe (') and an *s* (the attorney's briefcase, the lot's dimensions). When you make a possessive out of a singular noun, just add an *'s*, no matter what the final letter of the word may be, as we did in the examples above.

But when the word ends in *ss*, as in *witness*, you may either add *'s*, or simply place an apostrophe outside the final *s* without adding a third *s* (the witness' testimony). You may also form the possessive in the same way if adding another *s* would make the word hard to say, usually when the word ends in a sibilant (an *s* sound). For example, write *Jones'* rather than *Jones's*; write *Texas' state flag*, instead of *Texas's state flag;* and prefer *indifference' penalty* to *indifference's penalty.*

Form the possessive for plural nouns simply by adding an apostrophe after the final *s*, (the marathoners' best times), unless the noun itself is plural in form (the women's golf association, or the children's toys).

That *or* Which

Consider this sentence:

> The judge will sustain the defense objections that she considers well founded.

Does it matter whether you use *that* or *which*? Indeed it does; it can affect the meaning. Which one you use depends on whether the four-word clause at the end of the sentence is restrictive, or nonrestrictive.

A **restrictive clause** follows a noun and defines it. Restrictive clauses generally begin with *that*. The example we gave above is restrictive, because the clause told us the judge would sustain *only* the objections she considers well founded. Put another way, the restrictive clause *limited* the noun.

On the other hand, a **non-restrictive clause** does *not* define or limit the noun:

> The judge will sustain the defense objections, which she considers well founded.

This means the judge is going to sustain *all* of the defense objections, because she thinks they are *all* well founded. A nonrestrictive clause always begins with *which*, and is separated from the noun by a comma, as it is in our last example.

Where, When, *and* In Which

The words *where, when,* and *in which* are not interchangeable in any sense. *Where* refers to physical location:

> We sat in the square where Washington's statue is.

PRACTICE TIP

One way to tell the difference between a restrictive and nonrestrictive clause is to look at the clause. If it is set off by commas and the sentence can manage without it, then it is nonrestrictive.

restrictive clause
A clause that follows and defines or limits a noun. Restrictive clauses generally begin with the word *that*.

non-restrictive clause
A clause that follows but does not define or limit a noun. Nonrestrictive clauses always begin with the word *which*.

When pertains to time:

> Dawn is when the fish bite best.

In which refers to a thing being contained in something else:

> *Brown v. Board* was the case in which . . . .

Or:

> This is the can in which we found the leftover beans and the nail.

Or:

> The court in which jai-alai is played was being renovated.

(*Where* would also be proper in this last example).
The following usages are *always* incorrect:

> *Brown v. Board* was the case where . . . .
> A mistrial is always granted in a trial where insurance is mentioned to the jury.

In both of these examples, use *in which* instead of *where.*

Dangling Modifiers

Misplacing a modifying word or phrase can cause all sorts of trouble. Here are some common errors made with **modifiers.**
Adverbs that limit—such as *only, nearly, hardly,* and *almost*—must go before the words they modify:

> The professor assigned almost the entire text.

Not:

> The professor almost assigned the entire text.

And:

> In a whole day, we managed to seat only two jurors.

Not:

> In a whole day, we only managed to seat two jurors.

When a **participial phrase** appears at the start of the sentence, it always refers to the *subject* of the sentence, as in these horrible examples:

> Seeing his rubber ducky floating in the pool, the lifeguard dove to the child's rescue.
> Lying under some papers at the back of the drawer, John saw yesterday's tuna sandwich.

Consider poor old John, all scrunched up inside his desk drawer, groping about for his now-odorous lunch. *John* is the subject of the sentence, so this dangling phrase refers to him, rather than *sandwich,* which was what the writer intended. We can fix the problem of John and his snack very simply:

> John found yesterday's tuna sandwich lying under some papers at the back of the drawer.

As for the lifeguard, he looks a lot more adult if we write:

> Seeing the child's rubber ducky floating in the pool, the lifeguard dove to the rescue.

modifiers
Any word or group of words which limits or qualifies the meaning of other parts of the sentence.

PRACTICE TIP

Limiting modifiers must go before the word or phrase that they modify.

participial phrase
A group of words that functions as a participle and refers to the subject of the sentence. "Hearing the woman's cry for help, the policeman ran to the scene of the crime."

Try not to separate modifying clauses or phrases from what they modify. If you do separate them, you may produce some mighty odd expressions. Here is a memorable example, printed in Strunk and White's classic *The Elements of Style:*

> New York's first commercial human-sperm bank opened Friday with semen samples from 18 men frozen in a stainless steel tank.

What an awful way to go! And we cannot resist adding an example used by Fowler, the word-master, in his *Modern English Usage:*

> For sale, a piano by a lady going abroad in an oak case with carved legs.

No matter where you put them in a sentence, *because* phrases can cause unusual trouble, like this:

> Corporate executives decided to reject the union's demands because they were unreasonable.

Fix this one by writing:

> The corporate executives decided to reject the union's demands, which they considered unreasonable.

Misplaced modifiers need not even include a verb:

> An advocate of real ability, the firm entrusted young Barebones with the defense of the Jones divorce litigation.

modifying phrase
A group of words that alters the quality, degree, or meaning of another word in a sentence.

Barebones is the advocate with real ability, of course, but the **modifying phrase** at the start of the sentence modifies the subject of the sentence, *the firm,* instead of *Barebones.* Problems like this one are easily repaired. Just move the modifying phrase—now "dangling"—over next to what it modifies, like this:

> The firm entrusted defense of the Jones divorce litigation to Barebones, an advocate with real ability.

Or:

> Barebones, an advocate of real ability, assumed the defense of the Jones divorce litigation.

Here is another possibility:

> Barebones, an advocate of real ability, was entrusted with the defense of the Jones divorce litigation.

Again we managed to move the modifying phrase where it belongs, but we also put the sentence in the passive voice. We have already explained why you should avoid the passive voice whenever possible. Therefore, either of the first two changes in the sentence is preferable to the last one.

dangling modifiers
Modifiers that modify a noun placed either before the modifier or after the modifier.

Beware also of **dangling modifiers,** which may modify either something before them or something after. Here is a good example:

> Mother told John frequently to exercise the dog.

Did Mother tell John often, or did she tell him to walk the dog often? To clarify this sentence, just change the word order:

> Mother frequently told John to exercise the dog.

Or:

> Mother told John to exercise the dog frequently.

Compound Words

Compound words are words made up of two or more words used together as one expression. For example, when we say that a boy is "fifteen years old," each word is used in its usual, individual sense. But when we say, "he is a fifteen-year-old boy," we use three words as one, as a single adjective. When we do that, it is proper to separate the parts of the compound words with hyphens. The same rule applies to a compound noun:

> He is a fifteen-year-old.

Usually, omitting the hyphens from a compound word does not obscure meaning. But in particular cases it can. Take, for example, this road sign on an Oklahoma turnpike:

> No East Bound On Ramp

On what ramp? It seems clear, on first glance, that there must be some ramp on which you cannot drive east. Not so. What the Highway Department really meant to say was this:

> No East-Bound On-Ramp

Upon reading this sign, you instantly understand that if you turn off at this point, going east, you cannot get back on the turnpike again. When deciding whether to hyphenate two or more words, you will find that a good style manual helps. Even more helpful is just a moment's thought about what you really want to say. For example, which of these two expressions says what you mean?

> An adult bookstore owner
> An adult-bookstore owner

Compound words are certainly useful, but use them as little as possible. Do not try to make up new ones. If you do, you run the risk of sounding silly, or even of confusing your reader. Take this made-up compound word, for example:

> Beware of the savage arrow-hunting tribesmen.

You have to guess at what *arrow-hunting* means. It probably refers to tribesmen who hunt with bows and arrows. But it just might mean tribesmen who go about hunting arrows, or material from which to make arrows.

Both . . . And

The rule for using the conjunctions *both* and *and* together is very like the rule of parallel construction. After each of them, use the same grammatical construction:

> I both cursed the heat and enjoyed the sun.

But not:

> I cursed both the heat and enjoyed the sun.

Here is another example:

compound words
Words made up of two or more words used together as one expression.

I addressed both the judges and the lawyers.

But not:

I both addressed the judges and the lawyers.

Run-On Sentences

If you leave out punctuation between main clauses in a sentence, you produce a **run-on sentence** in which two thoughts are jumbled together. Here is an example:

The dictionary is an indispensable tool it keeps me and my secretary from making silly mistakes.

Repairs are simple. Separate the thoughts with either a period or a semicolon, or perhaps a dash. If you use a comma, you should add *and* before *it*. Without *and*, you produce a "comma splice" (discussed under "Punctuation," later in this chapter).

Dangling Prepositions

Try not to leave a lonely preposition dangling at the end of a sentence, like this:

It was forty miles to the little town he lived in.

Instead, say:

It was forty miles to the little town in which he lived.

This rule, however, is far from absolute. Winston Churchill, the all-time master of the English language, heaped scorn on the idea of completely abolishing **dangling prepositions** at the ends of sentences. "This is the sort of arrant pedantry," he wrote, "up with which I will not put."

So let your ear be your guide. If a sentence sounds awkward *unless* you put the preposition at the end, break the rule. Here are two examples of such a case:

He could not understand what the fuss was about.
The lawyers did not know what they were getting into.

Surely those are both smoother, clearer sentences than the "arrant pedantry" of the following two:

He could not understand about what the fuss was.
The lawyers did not know into what they were getting.

Contractions

A contraction is a word made of two other words put together, with one or more letters omitted. *Aren't* is a good example, a word made up of *are* and *not*. The apostrophe indicates that something was left out, in this case the *o* in *not*. Other familiar examples are *can't* (cannot), *won't* (will not), and *haven't* (have not).

Whether (Or Not)

Write *whether*, rather than *whether or not*, in sentences like this one: "We could not tell whether the jury was impressed." Or this: "The judge will decide whether the temporary injunction will be made permanent." Use *whether or not* only to describe a situation in which it does not matter which alternative happens. Here are two examples:

Whether or not we win the marathon, we will lose the meet.
We are driving to Pittsburgh tonight, whether or not it rains.

▦ PUNCTUATION

Accurate punctuation helps understanding. Lack of it confuses, and advertises that the writer is either careless or ignorant. Here are some simple rules that will help you use the correct punctuation mark in the right place.

Commas

The comma marks natural pauses. If you use one where you would naturally hesitate when speaking, you cannot go far wrong. You can use the comma in several ways.

Commas in Series.   The comma separates the elements of a series of things:

> The expert witness will require an easel, an overhead projector, and a laser pointer.

Or:

> Four subjects were taught during the summer: torts, contracts, property and ethics.

There is no universal rule on whether the last item before *and* is followed by a comma. You will notice that we have done it both ways in our two examples. You may prefer to omit the comma before *and,* as we did in our second example.

Commas with Independent Clauses.   The comma separates two complete sentences (independent clauses), set apart by *and* or *but*:

> The judge ruled for the prosecution, but the defense will appeal.

Commas with Non-Restrictive Clauses.   The comma sets off *non-restrictive clauses*—clauses that are not essential to the point of the sentence (see *That* or *Which* above). In the following example, "Who was a Greek Cypriot" is a non-restrictive clause:

> The defendant, who was a Greek Cypriot, could not speak English.

Here, "a Greek Cypriot" is technically called an **appositive phrase:**

> The defendant, a Greek Cypriot, could not speak English.

Here, "claiming he was a Greek Cypriot," is a participial phrase (a verbal phrase that includes a participle and that may function as a noun):

> The defendant, claiming he was a Greek Cypriot, could not speak English.

Commas after Introductory Phrases.   The comma separates a long introductory phrase (also known as a **dependent clause**) from the rest of the sentence:

> Even though the jury had heard ten days of testimony, the jurors remained alert and interested.

Commas with Conjunctive Adverbs.   Two commas set off a modifier that interrupts the usual order of words:

appositive phrase
Nouns and their modifiers, which rename or describe other nouns that cannot stand alone as sentences.

dependent clause
A clause that begins with a subordinating word, such as *because, if, who,* or *that,* to express particular relationships between the clauses they introduce and the main clauses to which they are attached. A dependent clause never stands alone as a sentence.

We lost the case, unfortunately, in spite of brilliant advocacy by Ms. Mason.

By the way, be careful of constructions like this. They tend to cause an awkward break in the flow of the sentence, although they are not technically incorrect. The example would flow better if you did it this way:

Unfortunately we lost the case, in spite of brilliant advocacy by Ms. Mason.

Commas in Direct Address.   The comma is used to show direct address:

Ms. Anderson, please tell us what happened on July 24th.

Commas for Clarity.   Commas help avoid any chance of ambiguity in your sentence:

Twenty miles beyond, the mountains rose into the sky.

If you omit the comma here, the reader may first read:

Twenty miles beyond the mountains . . .

and then have to stop and re-read the sentence.

comma splice
A punctuation error in which two independent clauses are joined by only a comma.

independent clause
A clause that can stand alone as a sentence.

One major, and common, error is called the **comma splice.** It looks like this:

We drove farther into Idaho, the scenery was wonderful.

Here two **independent clauses**—clauses that can each stand alone as a sentence—are joined by only a comma. Independent clauses can be joined by punctuation more emphatic than a comma, such as a period, a semicolon, or a dash. More of those farther on.

Semicolons

The semicolon (;) indicates a pause in your sentence. It is not as strong as a period; it is stronger than a comma. It has two principal uses.

Semicolons with Independent Clauses.   The semicolon connects two independent clauses:

We drove farther into Idaho; the scenery was wonderful.

Semicolons as Separators.   The semicolon separates parts of a sentence that are lengthy, or that have their own internal punctuation:

There are three parts to the pack: a waterproof pocket for personal possessions; a large pocket, lined with plastic, for food; and a series of smaller pockets, each with a snap, for odds and ends.

Colons

The colon is used in several ways:

- *It introduces a list or series of things:* as in the example above about the parts of the pack.
- *It is routinely used in addressing someone:*

Dear Mrs. Hammerstein:

- *It signals that something important follows it:*

  The witness committed the ultimate sin: he lied.

- *It introduces an example, like this:*

  It is easy to infuriate Judge Grinch: chewing gum in court drives him into a rage.

Quotation Marks

Quotation marks (") are used to set off a direct quotation:

  "I find you in contempt of court," cried the judge.

Single quotation marks (') show a quotation inside another quotation:

  Mathers said, "The judge was furious. I heard him shout, 'I find you in contempt,' over all the courtroom noise."

Quotation marks go *outside* periods and commas, as in the last example, but *inside* all other punctuation. Thus:

  "The judge was furious."

Or:

  "The judge," he said, "was furious."

But:

  Mathers said, "The judge was furious"; I thought she looked benign.

Dashes and Hyphens

Dashes in Pairs.   Used in pairs, dashes are useful to set off parenthetical material with minimum disturbance to the flow of the sentence, like this:

  The M-1 tanks climbed the sand berm—a 30% grade—and easily crossed the ditch beyond.

Single Dashes.   A single dash lends emphasis to what follows it:

  The tidal wave was monstrous—so high it dwarfed the four-story waterfront motel.

Hyphens as Connectors.   The **hyphen**—some people call it a "little dash"—is used to connect the parts of compound words, where there is any chance of confusing meaning. Hemingway gave us a wonderful example in this line from *Death in the Afternoon:*

hyphen
Mark used either to divide a word or to form a compound word.

  All stories, if continued far enough, end in death, and he is no true-story teller who would keep that from you.

Without the hyphen, Hemingway's meaning becomes unclear. He could mean a true (in the sense of "real") storyteller, or one who tells true stories, the meaning Hemingway intended.

There is no iron rule governing when to hyphenate words, except that you ordinarily do not use a hyphen after a word ending in *ly*. The best rule of thumb we know is, if in doubt, hyphenate. Normally the meaning of most compound words is clearer if you use the hyphen.

PRACTICE TIP

Do not hyphenate after a word ending in "ly." Such words are adverbs and require no hyphen.

Locked-In Hyphens.   Sometimes you will use two successive hyphenated adjectives that have the same first word, such as *well-trained* and *well-supervised*. You could write your sentence this way:

We have well-trained and -supervised guards.

But we think it is better in this case to spell out both compound words to be absolutely clear:

We have well-trained and well-supervised guards.

PRACTICE TIP

Use the hyphen to show a close relationship between, or combination of, two words.

Hyphens Indicating Relationships.   You can also use the hyphen to show a close relationship between, or combination of, two words. For example, if you are writing about race relationships, you can properly use the phrase "black-white dialogue." If the subject is fashion, "yellow-orange" accurately portrays a combination of the two colors.

Apostrophes

The apostrophe has several uses.

- *It shows possession, as we discussed earlier under "Grammar":*

  We appealed the judge's ruling.

- *It shows contraction, as we also saw under "Grammar":*

  The sheriff's deputy said, "The defendant didn't appear in court."

- *It forms the plurals of numbers and letters used alone:*

  There are four s's in Mississippi.
  The diver scored all 9's on that last dive.

Parentheses

Parentheses (the singular is *parenthesis*) are used in the following ways:

- *They set off material inserted in a sentence to avoid ambiguity:*

  The procession wound down Piazza Street (the main artery that used to be called 8th Avenue) before it finally halted before the cathedral.

- *They set off material that interrupts the primary thought of the sentence, appropriately called* **parenthetical comments:**

parenthetical comments

Explanatory, supplementary, or transitional words or phrases usually set off by parentheses, commas, or dashes.

  The highway is a succession of potholes all the way to Sofia (a common condition everywhere in Bulgaria) and takes three dreary days to travel.

- *They are useful for enclosing numbers and letters that divide the text:*

  There are three elements to first-degree murder: (1) the intentional killing of a human being, (2) with premeditation, and (3) without excuse.

Many writers also use brackets for this purpose. We think it is better to reserve brackets for the uses we specify in the next section.

Brackets

Although brackets and parentheses look similar, their uses are very different.

Brackets inside Quotations.   Use **brackets** to set off a comment inside a quotation when the comment is not part of the quotation:

> "Dr. Marchibanks asserts that fully 20% of high school graduates are functionally illiterate [other educators think the percentage is too low] and unable to write understandable English."

Brackets at Beginning of Quotation.   Brackets are also used in a quotation whenever words from the beginning of the original sentence have been deleted. The brackets tell the reader that there is an omission from the original. For example, suppose you decide to quote only part of the following sentence:

> Sighting a snow leopard was only the start of his adventures high in the Hindu Kush.

You might do it this way:

> "[H]is adventures high in the Hindu Kush" were related to us on every occasion, *ad nauseam.*

The brackets here also indicate that you have changed the first letter of a quotation from lowercase to uppercase, or vice-versa. You have shown your reader that you have capitalized *H,* and that it was not capitalized in the original, but appeared in lowercase.

Brackets indicating Substitutions and Omissions.   Brackets are also used within a quotation to show a substituted word or letter that did not appear in the original text:

> "Each [enemy] soldier was shackled hand and foot."

Empty brackets are used to indicate the omission of a letter or letters, like this:

> legal assistant[]

Brackets Inside Parentheses.   You may, on rare occasions, use brackets to set off a statement within material that is already inside parentheses. Here is an example:

> The voters approved the new resolution (although a large number [45%] voted against), but no one at all voted for the motion of censure.

We have said you will use this construction rarely for this reason: So many modifiers, tumbling over one another, usually produce an inherently clumsy and confusing sentence.

Brackets Enclosing *Sic.*   Finally, you use brackets to enclose the Latin word *sic.* [Sic] shows the reader that some apparent error in the quotation was not your mistake, but appears in the original quotation. Suppose you quote a passage erroneously stating that David killed Sampson with a rock from his sling. You show the error was made by the author of the quotation in this way:

> "David, still a young boy, seized a stone from the ground, hurled it from his sling, and brought Sampson [sic] crumpling to the earth."

Ellipses

An **ellipsis** is three periods separated by spaces and set off by a space before *and* after the last period (" . . . "). Here are some uses for the ellipsis.

brackets
Symbols used when indicating an omission of letters or words or when changing a letter from uppercase to lowercase, or vice versa.

ellipsis
Punctuation generally used to indicate the omission of a word or words to take the place of the omission.

Ellipses within Quotations.   Within a quotation, an ellipsis is used to show the omission of a word or words to take the place of whatever was omitted, like this:

> "David, . . . , seized a stone from the ground, hurled it from his sling, and brought Goliath crumpling to the earth."

Ellipses at Beginning of Quotation.   An ellipsis should *never* be used at the beginning of a quotation. For example, the following is incorrect:

> ". . . The voters approved the new resolution, although a large number [45%] voted against, but no one at all voted for the motion of censure."

So is this:

> ". . . Although a large number [45%] voted against, no one at all voted for the motion of censure."

The proper way to show that the beginning of this sentence is omitted from the quotation is to use a bracket, as we discussed above:

> "[A]lthough a large number [45%] voted against, no one at all voted for the motion of censure."

Ellipses at End of Quotation.   When indicating an omission from the end of a quoted sentence, use an ellipsis *and* a period, like this:

> "The voters approved the new resolution, although a large number [45%] voted against [it] . . . ."

(The brackets around the word *it* merely indicate to the reader that the word was not in the original text.) In this example, the ellipsis comes *between* the last word quoted and the final punctuation of the quoted sentence. The exception to this rule comes into play whenever the quoted language is used as a phrase or clause, like this:

> In their brief, Plaintiffs now ask the court to designate Oklahoma City as the "permanent deposition site of corporate witnesses," evidently meaning any employee of defendant who is a potential witness, and to "require defendant to bring such witnesses to Oklahoma City at defendant's expense."

Using ellipses can be tricky, and it is easy to use them incorrectly. As always, whenever you are in doubt about the proper use of any punctuation or grammar, double-check yourself. A thorough, although somewhat confusing, guide to using ellipses can be found at Rules 5.2 through 5.4 of **The Bluebook.**

The Bluebook

The Bluebook, A Uniform System of Citation, is a reference book for citation format and rules published jointly by the Columbia Law Review, the Harvard Law Review, the University of Pennsylvania Law Review, and The Yale Law Journal.

Slashes

A slash is a useful punctuation tool, but it is often misused. Although some people, including many journalists, think a slash means "and," it does not; it means "*or.*" Therefore, *red/green* stands for red *or* green, not red *and* green, or some combination of the two. If you want to indicate a combination of the two colors, use a hyphen, like this: red-green.

■ CAPITALIZATION

As with our discussion of grammar and punctuation, we cannot take the space to cover every rule of capitalization. But we do include a few of those rules you will use the most.

Proper Names

Always capitalize the name of a particular person, thing, or place, such as

- London
- Wednesday
- George Washington
- November
- the Bible
- the Indian Ocean
- a working knowledge of Arabic

Do not capitalize proper names that are used to refer to things other than their original meaning, such as

- diesel engine
- venetian blinds
- arabic numerals
- a place-setting of china

A related rule requires capitalization of the names of the Deity and personal pronouns referring to Him: *God, He,* and *Him.*

Titles

Always capitalize a title that precedes a name: *Judge TeSelle, Professor Roberts, General Powell,* or *President Bush.* If the title is used alone, it normally is not capitalized. However, capitalize *President* used alone when you refer to the President of the United States (the President), and *Justice,* when it refers to a particular justice or the Justices collectively of the United States Supreme Court or a state appellate court.

The word *court* technically is never capitalized unless you refer to the United States Supreme Court or write the word as part of the full title of a court: "the Supreme Court of Alabama." But legal professionals frequently capitalize *court* as a gesture of respect when addressing a particular court or referring to a court in a document which that court will read. Thus, it is proper in a brief before the Colorado Supreme Court or the Federal District Court for the Northern District of California to say, "this Court should . . ." or "in the *Reilly* case, decided last year, this Court held that . . . ."

Capitalize *Constitution* when you write the full title of a state constitution. Capitalize it when you use it alone in referring to the United States Constitution. Also capitalize parts of the Constitution, such as *Article, Section,* or *Amendment,* unless you are using abbreviations of those parts in a citation. For these abbreviations, use lowercase as *The Bluebook* directs.

State is normally capitalized only when it is part of the full name of a state: "the State of New York." Many practitioners also capitalize *State* in legal documents when referring to the prosecution in a criminal matter, as in "the State has decided not to prosecute."

PRACTICE TIP
Capitalization rules may vary from law office to law office. Find out what your employer wants capitalized.

PRACTICE TIP
Your professional reputation depends upon your use of proper punctuation and good grammar.

Titles of books and articles are capitalized according to this rule: Capitalize all nouns, verbs, and pronouns; all other words of four letters or more; and prepositions and other short words that are more than mere connectors, such as *out* and *not.*

CHAPTER SUMMARY

We end this chapter as we began it, with a word of caution. Your use of proper grammar, punctuation, and capitalization, like your use of proper spelling, is a sign of professionalism. Do not mistakenly think that readers miss small errors in any of these areas. If what you write is correct in every small detail, the reader knows he or she is reading something written by a careful craftsperson. Your writing will be much more persuasive as a result.

Be especially careful to follow these basic rules:

- Pronouns must clearly refer to the correct noun.
- The number of related nouns and verbs must be the same.
- A verb must be singular or plural in form, according to whether its subject is singular or plural.
- Whenever possible, write in the active voice.
- Remember to use the subjunctive mood when you write about a condition that is uncertain or contrary to fact.
- Always avoid double negatives.
- Do not make nouns out of verbs (nominalization). Instead, use the verb itself.
- Keep your sentence construction parallel.
- Do not split infinitives unless the sentence sounds silly if you do not.
- Be careful of the case of pronouns. It changes depending on whether the pronoun is the object or subject of the sentence.
- Check the position of apostrophes used to show possession.
- Use *that* or *which* depending on whether you are writing a restrictive or nonrestrictive clause.
- Remember that *where, when,* and *in which* are not interchangeable.
- Keep modifiers close to the words they modify.
- Hyphenate compound words.
- When you use *both . . . and,* follow each of them with the same grammatical construction.
- Punctuate between independent clauses in a sentence.
- Avoid using prepositions at the end of a sentence.
- Do not use contractions in legal writing, unless they are part of a quotation.
- Check your use of punctuation. Poor punctuation can change the meaning of a sentence or make it meaningless.

KEY WORDS AND PHRASES

active voice	brackets	comma splice	dependent clause
antecedent	case (noun or pronoun)	compound words	double negatives
appositive phrase		dangling modifiers	ellipsis
The Bluebook	collective nouns	dangling prepositions	hyphen

imperative mood	linking verbs	number	pronoun references
implied preposition	modifiers	parallel construction	restrictive clause
independent clause	modifying phrase	parenthetical comments	run-on sentence
indicative mood	nominalization	participial phrase	split infinitive
infinitives	non-restrictive clause	passive voice	subjunctive mood

EXERCISES

Pronouns

The following sentences are tainted with pronoun errors. Indicate any pronoun errors that you find in each problem; there may be more than one. Then, rewrite the sentence correctly.

Potential Pronoun Errors

a. Pronoun reference is ambiguous.
b. Pronoun and verb do not agree in number.
c. Pronoun and antecedent do not agree in number.
d. Pronoun is in improper case.

____1. The phone rang. Amelia Pepper picked it up. "Is this Amelia Pepper?" a voice asked. "This is her," Ms. Pepper replied.

____2. "My name is Jane Healy," the caller said. "I've just been in an auto accident. Me and my boss have just had an argument. I think my firm is going to fire me because of my injuries and my medical bills. Can you help me?"

____3. "I'll be at your hospital in ten minutes," Ms. Pepper said, and hung up. Since neither of the receptionists were at the front desk, no one saw Ms. Pepper hurry out the office door.

____4. When Ms. Pepper arrived in Ms. Healy's room, Ms. Healy described the extent of her injuries. "Three of my ribs are broken, my skull is fractured, and my face is seriously cut. The doctors tell me it will take a long time to heal."

____5. "My firm sent me flowers and a card to show their support," said Ms. Healy. "Next thing I know, Mr. Forbes, my boss, told me that he and the company vice president had been talking, and that he thought I should look for another job."

____6. Ms. Healy told Ms. Pepper that each of her superiors have a reason for wanting to fire her. "I caught Mr. Forbes embezzling funds from our pension account," she said. "Then when I told the vice president, I realized that he was probably doing it with his knowledge, if not cooperation."

____7. "Just between you and I," Ms. Pepper said, "I think a court will be sympathetic when they hear your facts. The problem is that they are sometimes hard to persuade in whistleblower cases."

____8. At that point, a doctor walked in. "Everyone needs their rest," she said, looking pointedly at Ms. Pepper. "Visiting hours are over." Ms. Healy rolled her eyes. "One of the things I hate most in the world are pushy doctors," she said. "Besides, just who do you think you are ordering around?"

____9. The doctor smiled grimly and said, "You may not think much of doctors, but I am the one who will decide whom is well enough to eat dinner tonight, and whom will get only lime jello. Also, I think you should know that the hospital is concerned about their patients overexerting themselves on the way to the bathroom. If you aren't careful, I may have to order a catheter for you."

Ms. Healy winced and looked at Ms. Pepper. "A doctor's words of wisdom is worth listening to. Perhaps you had better leave now after all."

Passive Voice

Read the following sentences. Decide whether they are in active or passive voice. If a sentence is in passive voice, rewrite it so that it is in active voice.

1. Charles Raymond had been drinking at Red's Tavern for about an hour before he left the bar.

2. Two shots were consumed by Mr. Raymond, by whom two beers and a marguerita were also ingested.

3. Mr. Raymond had been arrested before for drunk driving.

4. One could not have known that Ms. Healy would become another traffic statistic.

5. Ms. Healy had braked for the cars in front of her just as the light turned orange.

6. Jane's car was hit broadside as Mr. Raymond raced through the intersection.

7. It should have been expected that a man with two DUIs would eventually have a bad accident.

8. At the time of the accident, Mr. Raymond was employed by Vincent Allegretti.

The Subjunctive Mood

The sentences below are written in the subjunctive mood. But some of them contain errors. Determine whether each sentence is correctly written. If it contains a mistake, rewrite the sentence to correct the error.

1. If Charles Raymond were wiser, he would have called a taxi instead of trying to drive.

2. As the first police car arrived, Mr. Raymond wished that he was more sober and less in trouble.

3. "If I was to take a blood-alcohol test right now, the result would probably have three digits," Mr. Raymond thought grimly to himself.

4. Mr. Raymond thought he should act as though he was sober, and thereby try to deflect suspicion from himself.

5. Though a veteran drinker be shrewd, there are some things that one cannot hide.

Double Negatives

You will find the following paragraph replete with double negatives. Rewrite it to eliminate them.

A not inexperienced attorney, Amelia Pepper grew more shocked as the facts of the case unfolded. First, she discovered that Mr. Raymond was not without prior convictions for drunk driving. Second, Ms. Pepper was not unable to uncover the fact that the car dealership not unknowingly did not warn Jane Healy of her

car's defective seat belt. Finally, Ms. Pepper found out that Ms. Healy's not uncalculating boss had not engaged in the most unquestionable of business practices. Furthermore, when he realized that Ms. Healy was not unaware of his embezzlement, he did not stop short of using Ms. Healy's misfortune as a pretext for firing her.

Nominalization

The following sentences use nouns where verbs would be more concise. Rewrite the sentences to eliminate the nominalizations.

1. Ms. Pepper made inquiries into Mr. Raymond's driving record and drinking habits.

2. Mr. Raymond made the argument that Ms. Healy ran a red light, and that was why he hit her.

3. Ms. Pepper made a request for an accident report to see whether Mr. Raymond's allegation could be true.

4. The police department has a requirement that people tender a $10 payment before they receive copies of accident reports.

5. Apparently, Mr. Raymond did not take his suspended driver's license into consideration when he made the decision to drive.

Parallel Construction

All of the following sentences contain parallel construction problems. Rewrite them to correct these errors.

1. To pay for his attorney's fees, Mr. Raymond sold his new motorcycle, elaborate stereo system, and television.

2. When Mr. Raymond crashed into Ms. Healy, Ms. Healy fractured her skull, a few facial bones, and she broke three ribs.

3. Ms. Healy had a hospital bill, a surgeon's bill, and attorney's fee.

4. Ms. Healy wanted a consultation and assistance from an attorney as soon as possible.

5. Mr. Forbes brought Ms. Healy beautiful yellow roses, an expensive get-well card, and books.

Possessives

Read the following sentences. Decide whether the possessive forms in each sentence are correct. Fix any errors that you find.

1. Jane Healy planned to give her cat it's dinner when she got home.

2. According to all the witness' affidavits, the light was yellow when Ms. Healy started across the intersection.

3. Two witnesses, Mr. and Mrs. Nicks, were standing near the intersection waiting for a friend of their's.

4. The Nicks' statements were particularly helpful.

5. A local womens' group donated money to pay for some of Ms. Healys' medical bills.

Where, When, and In Which

Where, when, and *in which* are words that are frequently confused. Check the following sentences to see whether these words are used properly. Correct any mistakes that you find.

1. The intersection where the accident occurred had a reputation for being unsafe.

2. Amelia Pepper's legal assistants found six cases where courts said running a red light constituted negligence.

3. The part of the court's opinion when it said running a red light constituted negligence was Part III.

4. The case in which the court made this statement was a personal injury case.

5. Where the plaintiff has suffered gruesome injuries, the attorney will often seek a jury trial.

Misplaced Modifiers

All of the following sentences contain misplaced modifiers. Rewrite the sentences so that the modifiers are placed correctly.

1. Now twisted around the steel utility pole, the onlookers gazed dumbstruck at Jane Healy's wrecked BMW.

2. The force of the collision almost destroyed the entire car.

3. Charles Raymond denied that he had driven drunk repeatedly.

4. Being visibly drunk, Sergeant Adams decided to administer a breathalyzer test to Mr. Raymond.

5. An officer of impeccable judgment, Charles Raymond agreed to go down to the police station with Sergeant Adams.

Punctuation

1. The following sentences lack proper punctuation. Rewrite them using commas, colons, semicolons, question marks, and quotation marks as needed.
   a. Charles Raymond admitted having the following drinks before leaving Red's Tavern a shot of Jim Beam two beers a marguerita and a shot of peppermint schnapps.
   b. Although the light had turned yellow Jane Healy figured she had time to clear the intersection.
   c. Tony Simpson the bartender at Red's Tavern knew that Mr. Raymond had had a lot to drink however he thought that Mr. Raymond would call a cab if he were too drunk to drive.
   d. Sergeant Adams said Mr. Raymond have you been drinking this afternoon.
   e. Would you mind coming down to the station with me to take a breathalyzer test Sergeant Adams asked Mr. Raymond.

2. Some of the following sentences are run-on sentences. Identify which are run-ons. Rewrite them properly, breaking them down into separate sentences where necessary.
   a. Hans Weber had learned two months ago that the seatbelts on 1988 BMW 325is were defective, he decided not to notify his customers because it would take too much effort.
   b. Mr. Weber did not realize that his failure to warn could create a devastating amount of legal liability, so he never worried about the effect of his decision.
   c. Mr. Weber finally consulted a lawyer after Jane Healy's accident it was too late to do anything to protect himself.
   d. When Mr. Weber explained his situation to his lawyer, his normally jovial lawyer suddenly became quite grave.

e. "I don't care what you have to do, I just don't want to lose everything I've worked so hard to get," Mr. Weber said.

3. The following sentences are excerpts from court opinions. Check them for correct usage of ellipses, quotation marks, and brackets, and correct as needed. Write "correct" if no changes are necessary.

   a. "[T]his Court must not depart from the standard of established law in this jurisdiction."

   b. "Without exception, courts in this state have viewed driving while under the influence . . . . as per se negligence."

   c. "the plaintiff in this case contends that the defendant owed her a duty of care.

   d. Beginning in 1987, the plaintiff worked for the defendant without taking a single absence . . . . after the car accident, the defendant fired her without explanation."

   e. "The plaintiff claims that she was dismissed from her job because she told the regulatory authorities...about illegal activities undertaken by her employer....[T]he defendant company has moved for summary judgment."

5

CORRESPONDENCE AND INTERNAL MEMORANDUMS

Later in this book, we discuss in detail some specialized kinds of legal writing: memorandums of law, legal briefs, and various other technical legal papers you will encounter. In this chapter, we deal with the "everyday" things you will write—correspondence and internal memorandums.

You will write thousands of letters and internal memos. Because you write so many of them, you may be tempted to think of letters and internal memos as routine and unimportant. Think again. Everything you write on the job is important, whether you write one or a thousand letters or memos in the course of a year. As you read on in this chapter, you will see that attention to detail is the hallmark of a real legal professional.

■ INTERNAL MEMORANDUMS

Leaving a paper trail through every matter on which you work is critical. Leave every file so complete that someone who knows nothing of the matter could pick up your file and work competently on it. That means you cannot keep the contents of conversations and telephone calls stowed away in your head. If you get sick or are unavailable for any reason, other people working on that file must have access to all the information relating to it. They cannot read your mind.

Realize that you cannot recall every detail of every matter on which you work. Six months after you have talked to the other side on some pending litigation, you may need to recall in detail what was said. You cannot be positive about who said what if you depend entirely on your memory. Moreover, if it comes to a dispute with another law firm about what was said, you will be far more convincing if you state what happened from notes made at the time of the conversation.

These notes are called **internal memorandums.** A simple memorandum might look like the one in Exhibit 5.1.

> **PRACTICE TIP**
> Always leave a paper trail.

> **internal memorandum**
> Memorialized information of some aspect of the case, to be used only in-house.

EXHIBIT 5.1. *Internal Memorandum of Telephone Call*

TO: File
FROM: JRJ
DATE: January 11, 1993
RE: Telephone conference with Fran Martin, Legal Assistant, of Emerson &
              Emerson
FILE: *Emery v. Bowen*
File No.: 92–677–11

Plaintiffs will stipulate to the expected testimony of Officer Thompson. I will draft the stipulation and send it to them for their review and approval prior to January 21, 1993.

Uses for Memos

Exhibit 5.1 is obviously a memo of a telephone call. It serves several purposes. First, it memorializes an oral agreement by the other side to what may be an important detail in some pending litigation. Anyone who may work on this file now knows, without asking you, that the other side has agreed to stipulate to Officer Thompson's testimony.

Second, this memo also serves as a written reminder to you—or anybody else who works on the file—that before January 21, you must get the **stipulation** to the other side for signature. Your attorney may draft the stipulation herself. Or she may want you to draft it, have her approve it, and make sure it is signed by opposing counsel. Either way, this little memo helps to nudge your memory.

Third, depending on your office procedures, a copy of this memo may further serve to inform your attorney of what the other side has agreed to. If it is not your firm's custom to pass information in this way, your memo reminds you to tell your attorney that the other side has agreed to stipulate. In any event, any agreement or understanding that you convey to other parties, or that is conveyed to you, must *always* be passed on to your supervising attorney. By writing a memo instead of relying on verbal communication, you lessen the chance for misunderstanding both with outsiders and in your own office.

Deadline Ticklers

Last, a copy of this memo may go to your **tickler file** or be used by you or your firm's docketing system. A lawyer's malpractice insurance requires that he or she use some type of docket or **tickler** system to note court dates and deadlines for filing documents or taking some other type of action. A tickler is simply a list of things that have to be done by certain dates.

Most law firms now use a computerized docketing system, but you may also want to devise your own method as a back-up or reminder for you and your attorney. You may wish to keep a large calendar or a datebook with reminders in it or memo copies clipped to appropriate pages. Or, you could use a folding file with a separate pocket for each date—you tuck a copy of your memo into the appropriate pocket. Whatever kind of tickler you set up, make sure that you can calendar at least 90 days ahead, and check the tickler system *every* day.

---

stipulation

A *stipulation* of expected testimony is an agreement by both sides that, if a witness were in court, he or she would testify substantially in the words of the stipulation. It saves calling the witness physically to testify at trial or at a deposition.

tickler file

A system used to store and retrieve ticklers.

tickler

A reminder of things that must be done by certain dates.

PRACTICE TIP

Whatever kind of tickler you set up, make sure that you can calendar at least 90 days ahead, and check the tickler system every day.

Do not say to yourself as you write a memo, "Oh, I'll remember that." You will be working on dozens of matters at once, and you cannot remember everything you have to do at the time you have to do it. When you make notes of something you have to do, make an entry not only on the day something is due, but several days before that. Give yourself some lead time to do whatever it is correctly.

When to Write a Memo

We suggest that you write a memo whenever you are called by somebody outside the firm on any matter. It usually takes only a few seconds to dictate a short note to the file or type the information you have received into the word processor. The rule here is *do it now.* If you put off recording the conversation, you increase the chance that you will forget exactly what was said.

How about writing a memo by hand? That will work, of course, but it is harder to read than a typed memo, and takes at least as long to do. If your memos are handwritten, make sure you write them on a full-sized piece of paper, however short the memo. Little notes—even stick-ons—have a way of losing themselves in the file, or falling out and disappearing forever. Also, make sure that your writing is legible and the meaning of the note can be understood. Many of us use our own shorthand or speed writing that is easily read by us, but indecipherable to anyone else. Keep in mind that any handwritten note to the file will also be referred to by others.

We discussed memorandums of telephone calls, but you may also want to record something on an internal memo at other times. *Make a written record of any conversation (whether by phone or face-to-face) with an opponent, court reporter, judge's clerk, client, witness, etc., unless it is absolutely without significance.* Even when you are not sure a conversation is important, make a memo of it. Any time that you expend on a client's case or other matter, especially if that time is billed to the client or someone else, must be accounted for in the file.

Here is a situation in which an internal memo to your attorney is appropriate. Your supervising attorney asks you to schedule a witness' **deposition,** and he gives you a list of the dates and times at which he will be available. You next call opposing counsel and, after explaining the reason for your call, agree on a specific date and time to hold the deposition. You then call to arrange for the **court reporter.**

Why not simply tell your attorney when the deposition has been scheduled and go on to your next project, instead of writing an internal memo? Something as important as a deposition—or anything requiring the attorney's attendance—should be written down for the file and noted on the firm's tickler system. If you simply say to your attorney, "The deposition has been set for "January 17 at 2 o'clock," one or both of you may forget when the deposition was scheduled.

Also, for most legal assistants, setting the date and time of the deposition and contacting the court reporter is only the first step. You must also arrange for a place to hold the deposition, usually a conference room in your firm's office, the court reporter's, or opposing counsel's. The legal assistant may also be expected to prepare deposition questions and to review and pull relevant documents to be discussed at the deposition.

Exhibit 5.2 (p. 80) is a sample internal memorandum from a legal assistant to his supervising attorney regarding a deposition. This memo would reassure the supervising attorney that all of the details surrounding the deposition either had been, or would be, taken care of by the paralegal.

PRACTICE TIP

When scheduling work deadlines, make two entries in your tickler file: one on the due date and one several days earlier, to give yourself lead time.

PRACTICE TIP

Make a written record of any conversation, whether by phone or face-to-face, with opposing counsel or staff, or with a court reporter, judge's clerk, your client, witnesses, etc.

deposition
A pretrial discovery device by which one party questions the other party, or a witness for the other party. Answers are given under oath in the presence of a stenographer or court reporter.

court reporter
A person who transcribes testimony by shorthand or stenography during court proceedings or other related proceedings, such as a deposition.

EXHIBIT 5.2.   *Internal Memorandum—Scheduling a Deposition*

MEMORANDUM

TO: Amelia Pepper

FROM: Chris Roberts
         Legal Assistant

DATE: October 12, 1994

RE: Deposition of Charles Raymond

FILE: *Healy v. Raymond et al.*
         File No. A–500.1

Charles Raymond's deposition has been scheduled for Friday, October 28, 1994, at 1:30 p.m. I have put this on the tickler for your docket and have noted it on your desk calendar. I have arranged with Elizabeth Campbell at Ad Infinitum Reporters to hold the deposition in one of their conference rooms; Elizabeth will be our court reporter. I have sent a confirmation letter to all counsel of record and to Elizabeth Campbell.

As we discussed, I will begin drafting questions for Mr. Raymond's deposition. I will deliver those to you by Friday with a suggested list of documents that relate to Mr. Raymond or about which you may wish to ask him.

Since this will be the first deposition taken in this case, I suggest that you and the other counsel involved agree to use the same court reporter for all of the depositions. In addition, since this will be a document-intensive case, I also suggest that all deposition exhibits be numbered sequentially. For example, ten exhibits may be used for Mr. Raymond's deposition (marked Exhibits 1 through 10). For the next deposition taken, the first exhibit should be marked as Exhibit 11, and so on. All deposition exhibits could be kept together in a bound volume to be used as reference or as exhibits for future depositions in this case.

Please let me know whether this plan meets with your approval and whether you need anything else done before Mr. Raymond's deposition.

PRACTICE TIP

Each file should be complete enough that a stranger to the matter could work on it without asking you or your attorney for information.

Remember, as we said before, each file should be complete enough that a stranger to the matter could work on it without asking you or your boss for information. If what you have just heard or otherwise learned is something you and your attorney need to process the case, you must get it in the file. When in doubt, write it down.

◼ PRACTICE TIP

Legal assistants are often the "keeper" of the documents produced by both sides in a lawsuit or any other important documents. We suggest that you have one "master" set of documents. It is up to you to maintain the integrity of these documents; therefore, you must make it clear that no one but you may touch the master set.

If your attorney needs the documents for whatever reason, pull and copy a "working" set of the documents he or she wants. Never allow attorneys or anyone else to cannibalize your master set of documents by removing even one page, regardless of promises to return it to the exact spot where they found it. By the same token, never use an original or the master copy of any documents for deposition preparation or as a deposition exhibit.

▦ CORRESPONDENCE

You will write thousands of letters every year. Especially at first, your attorney will review some or all of them. Later on, your attorney may ask you to draft most or all of the correspondence in a given case, or even to sign her name to some correspondence. But until your attorney pays you the compliment of giving you some latitude with correspondence, everything goes through her or him in draft.

Writing Letters

As with any legal writing, you should always carefully proofread and edit any letter. Delete any unnecessary words or legalese. Write as you speak. Use plain English rather than legalese, and omit outdated phrases such as "the above-referenced case" or "enclosed herein." Your goal is to write letters that are easy to read and understand.

Avoiding Common Errors.   There are three common errors in letter writing. Keep them in mind as we talk about the elements of correspondence. Whatever sort of letter you are writing, make every effort to avoid these three mistakes.

First, and worst, is writing so that your reader has trouble understanding you. Remember that your correspondent often knows little or nothing about the precise matter you are discussing. In any case, your knowledge is superior to that of your reader.

Second is talking down to your reader, insulting his or intelligence, or giving that appearance. You must be sure your correspondent understands you, but it is unnecessary to explain the obvious or define a common term. Save your definitions and explanations for legal expressions and other unusual terminology.

Third is failing to be clear about what you want your correspondent to do, and when. Anticipate the reader's questions or possible misunderstandings. Deadlines or requests for action must be stated in such a way that the reader knows exactly what is expected and when. If there is a question in your mind as to whether the reader will know what you are talking about, do not leave anything to chance. Ambiguous letters are costly. You lose valuable time in writing second letters or making follow-up telephone calls, and the additional time you spend solving the problem is passed on to the client in your fees.

> **PRACTICE TIP**
>
> Avoid making these three common errors:
> - Writing so the reader cannot understand you.
> - Writing so the reader feels patronized or insulted.
> - Writing so the reader cannot tell what you want done.

Being Professional.   Everything you write, whatever the subject matter and whoever the addressee, must be entirely professional in tone. Even when you are writing to a client you know well, do not say things such as:

The insurance company just can't seem to get it together.

What is wrong with that line? Well, to start with, the expression is slang, and using slang is always a bad idea in formal correspondence. Worse, the line is vague; it does not tell the addressee what the problem is. Taken altogether, this language has an unprofessional ring, and every lawyer wants his or her legal assistant to be always and entirely professional.

Sloppy English and careless writing also contribute to the impression of lack of professionalism. Consider these lines, taken from an important letter demanding a large sum of money for an injured client:

> **PRACTICE TIP**
>
> Everything you write, whatever the subject matter and whoever the addressee, must be entirely professional in tone.

In addition, the facts of this case, as you very well know, are quite aggravated in view of the fact that your insured was driving his vehicle under the influence of alcohol and in concert thereof, fled the scene.

When we take this paragraph apart, you will find that it can be said more professionally in much fewer words:

- *As you very well know* is pure surplusage, and a little insulting. Of course the other lawyer knows the facts, and probably does not appreciate the condescending tone of the phrase.
- *In view of the fact* is a sure sign of careless writing. *Because* would have been better and saved four words.
- *In concert* applies to people acting together. What this writer meant was simply *and* or *and also. Thereof* is advanced legalese and, in any case, it is wrongly used; *therewith* is the only word that fits with *in concert* and it too is pure legalese.

Altogether, the writer gave the other side the impression they were dealing with a confused mind, a legal assistant who could not be bothered with the details of an important letter. The attorney on the other side will not be impressed with his opponent's potential to beat him. Moreover, if this firm's client is intelligent and she sees this letter, it could shake her confidence in her lawyer and his support staff.

Sometimes you will write letters to people you know, perhaps a legal assistant or lawyer whom you see socially. Or, you will draft a letter for your attorney to somebody he knows well, perhaps a law school classmate. Stay away from first names. Should your client also receive this letter, he or she simply may not understand how a lawyer can represent him or her zealously and still call the other side's lawyer "Janet." Except in a purely social setting, always address other legal professionals as Mr. or Ms., no matter how well you (or your attorney) know them.

That also goes for anyone else you write to. Address everybody as Mr. or Ms., unless they have a title such as Judge, Reverend, Doctor, Major, etc., in which case you use their title. Never be tempted to address anybody you deal with for the firm, even a personal friend, by his or her first name unless the person asks you to do so.

PRACTICE TIP

Keep your letter professional in tone by referring to the addressee as Mr. or Ms., or by using the addressees' title if they have one.

Being Temperate. Being temperate is really part of being professional. It means, simply put, do not let yourself sound boastful and quarrelsome. Bombast and threats are not only highly unprofessional, but entirely unproductive. Here is a real-life example:

I have been a trial lawyer in the city of X for . . . 18 years and hold the record for the highest jury verdict . . . awarded . . . in the sum of $2.1 million dollars.

The implication is, of course, that the opponent ought to immediately give in and settle the suit, but lawyers and other legal professionals are not intimidated that easily. Legal professionals' reactions to boasting like this are usually quite different. They simply redouble their efforts to frustrate the writer's efforts to obtain whatever it is the writer wants. Any cooperation the writer might have otherwise received, he will get no more, and he will acquire the reputation of a braggart into the bargain.

Even if you receive letters that are downright nasty, do not be tempted to descend to the writer's level. Tell your attorney immediately, of course; she may wish to deal with the matter personally. But in any case, *you* should remain entirely civil and professional. When an opponent becomes uncivil, sarcastic, or abusive—and sooner or later somebody will—your first instinct may be to strike back with the same weapons. Do not. *Ever.* Your own cool professionalism will be even more appreciated by your attorney, the court, and the client; it will stand out in sharp contrast to the actions of the other side.

Being Understood.   No matter who the addressee may be, plain language is always best. The cardinal rule of legal writing applies here, as it does everywhere else—*if you don't say it, don't write it.* Keeping it simple helps ensure that everybody you write to understands what you are talking about, no matter what their education.

Even if you keep it simple, however, you must consider your audience. For a client with an eighth-grade education, you will have to take special pains to be clear. Short, simple writing may be the only thing that your addressee can easily follow. At the same time, you must be careful not to appear to talk down to people. Nothing is more insulting. Unless you are quite positive you are writing to somebody with sharply limited education or intelligence, ordinary language will do just fine for both layperson and learned lawyer.

Even when you know you are writing to an educated person, remember he or she probably will not understand legal words of art and the jargon of other professional disciplines. Do not write glibly about **res ipsa loquitur** or *magnetic resonation* without telling your addressee what these terms mean.

Avoid legalese—everywhere, of course—but especially in letters. It adds nothing but length, and has a particularly discouraging effect on clients and other laypeople. It does not impress them. "Whenever I read something and I don't understand it," said Will Rogers, "I know it was written by a lawyer." Most of the public share Rogers' opinion of lawyer's language, so make very sure you keep out all *saids* and *hereinbefores* and similar ancient terms.

Stay away from other antique language, too. Oddly, many lawyers who normally speak good, modern English regress a couple of centuries when they write letters. "Yours of the 18th instant to hand," they write, instead of "I have received your May 18, 1994 letter." Legal assistants, in a misguided attempt to sound more professional, also sometimes adopt this writing style. Keep it simple.

All the usual rules of good, readable legal writing apply to letters with double force. Short paragraphs are even more important in letters than they are in memorandums or briefs. Where the normal paragraph length in a memorandum should be fifteen lines or less, your paragraphs in a letter should not exceed eight or ten. The same goes for sentence length. Keep sentences short, preferably not more than ten or twelve words.

Above all, make every effort to be clear. Say carefully what you want, and proofread everything before you send it. Consider this example, written by a lawyer representing the plaintiff in a personal injury case. In this "demand letter," the lawyer for one side is telling the opposition what his client's damages were and demanding a sum in settlement of the lawsuit.

> Moreover, she lost eight months of vacation if she would have stayed on the job as to an accrual in the sum of $981.60, including therein analogously sick leave for one day per month for a total of eight days in the sum of $785.28.

Imagine the dilemma of the addressee in trying to figure out what the writer wants.

- *Eight months of vacation*—does that mean she could have taken off eight months from work? Probably not, because her vacation was worth only $981.60. Or was it?

PRACTICE TIP

There is no such thing as a routine letter. Both you and your firm are judged by the quality and accuracy of what you write.

res ipsa loquitur
A Latin phrase meaning "the thing speaks for itself" used in tort law. The event would not have happened without negligence.

PRACTICE TIP

Keep it simple. If you don't say it, don't write it.

PRACTICE TIP

Use these length guidelines in correspondence: No more than 10 to 12 words for each sentence and 8 to 10 lines for each paragraph.

- What did the writer mean by *as to an accrual in the sum of $981.60?* Does that mean all her vacation was worth that sum? Or each month? Or what?
- *Including therein analogously* is a real mystery. Is sick leave included within vacation? It sounds like it, but if that is so, why is a separate value ($785.28) placed on sick leave?

Generally, a letter is something more than a means for passing on information. Often you will want a decision from the addressee, or an opinion, or an action. Here, especially, you must be very clear about precisely what you want, from whom, and when.

Remember, if something you write can be misunderstood, it surely will be. Here is a simple example:

> Please tell us if you can attend the deposition on Thursday, May 18, at 10:00 a.m. in the offices of Addams & Greene, located at 700 North Broadway.

At first glance this paragraph seems clear enough, but it really is not. Suppose your reader cannot attend the deposition at the time set, but takes your letter literally. She will not call, and you will spend additional time trying to contact her to confirm her attendance. This confusion and extra work could have been avoided had you thought about what your letter was really asking of the reader. Had you thought about it, you would have written, instead:

> Please tell us whether you can attend the deposition on Thursday, May 18, at 10:00 a.m. in the offices of Adams & Greene, located at 700 North Broadway.

As first written, your letter plainly told the addressee to call *if* she could make the deposition at the time scheduled. She could not attend, so she did not call. As rewritten, your letter told her to let you know *whether* she could attend the deposition—to call or write you—in either case.

Sometimes mere words are not enough. Consider this paragraph from a lawyer's letter, in this case written to the firm's client, an insurance company:

> Jones, operating the westernmost of the three vehicles in the collision, contends that the plaintiff's vehicle (the middle one) impacted the easternmost vehicle, operated by Brown, before her vehicle collided with the plaintiff. Mr. Smith testified that he felt, but obviously did not observe, two separate impacts, the initial impact being the greater of the two.

What happened here? After reading the paragraph, the reader has more questions than answers. Which way was everybody going? The plaintiff was sandwiched in the middle, but who was on each end? And what was everyone driving? A "vehicle" can be anything from a bicycle to a truck and semi-trailer. If everybody here is driving a mid-sized passenger car, we have one case. On the other hand, if the crash involved a car, a tractor, and an 18-wheeler, the case is a different one altogether.

Careful drafting would have answered these questions. But even with clear, concise writing, some fact situations are better understood if a simple diagram is also included. It need not be draftsman's work; a simple diagram in ink will serve to make your words much easier to follow. It can be your own work or a xerox of the diagram on a police report, just as long as it accurately illustrates the situation you are describing in words.

Jogging the Addressee's Memory.   Sometimes you must remind your addressees of something you asked them about earlier, but to which they have not yet responded. Be diplomatic. People are usually embarrassed when reminded that they forgot to do something important. Try words like this:

You will recall that on March 25, 1994, I asked for a copy of the inventory sheets for the first six months of operation in 1992. I need the sheets soon so that I can complete our report. Please have the inventory sheets sent to me before June 1, 1994. If you have any questions or need additional information, please do not hesitate to contact me.

Following Up.   If you have asked for something by telephone or in person, and the matter is important, it is best to follow up your request with a letter. You can often gracefully couch your follow-up as a thank-you note, something like this:

Thank you for agreeing to send me the maps of United Aggregate's gravel claims. Please let me know if there are copying or other costs involved.

When you have arranged for somebody—say, your client or a witness—to be in court or someplace else at a particular time, *always* write a follow-up letter, no matter how alert and vigorous your addressee may be. Everybody forgets things, and your reminder letter will be a handy memo for your correspondent. If a number of weeks or months will go by before the addressee has to do whatever-it-is, it is both courteous and careful to send another reminder shortly before the event.

Follow-up or confirmation letters serve another important purpose. If a dispute later arises about who promised what to whom, it helps immensely to have a clear, specific written record in the form of a copy of a letter sent to the other side. When you produce your copy, the opposition has the choice of either caving in, or arguing lamely that the letter never arrived.

Earlier in this chapter, we discussed a scenario in which the legal assistant was asked by her attorney to schedule a deposition. Exhibit 5.3 (p. 86) is a sample of a confirmation letter to opposing counsel.

Look at the bottom left of the letter, below the legal assistant's signature. The abbreviation *pc* means "photocopy to." You may be more accustomed to seeing *cc* meaning "carbon copy to." By noting on the letter that copies have been sent to counsel for the other party in the lawsuit and to the court reporter, you have accomplished two things. First, you have done the same thing with one letter that otherwise would have taken three separate letters containing identical information. Second, you have a written memorial of an oral agreement between you and opposing counsel.

Getting Things Done.   You will frequently need to ask your correspondent to do something, sometimes several things. It is up to you to make certain that what you want done does not get lost in the rest of your letter. To be sure your addressee sees and identifies what is wanted, spell out what he must do and when he must do it, and put everything you want done in the same paragraph.

Take the following paragraphs from a lawyer's letter. Identify what the writer wants the addressee to do and when he must do it, and spell those tasks out in a single, clear paragraph. You will find our sample solution below the paragraph.

If the Plaintiff continues to suffer from neck and back pain, we recommend you authorize the added precaution of an independent medical evaluation by an experienced neurologist.

Assuming the Plaintiff's injuries are as alleged, and long-term therapy is prescribed, the judgment could run well into six figures. We therefore request you confirm that the policy limit is one million dollars.

We intend to draft interrogatories to obtain more information about the Plaintiff's job history and previous injuries. We will also obtain her medical records from the company clinic. Finally, since she testified in her deposition that she was hurt in a 1979 accident in Detroit, we will obtain the records of her treatment there. We need your approval for this procedure; it will be expensive, requiring that we send someone to Michigan.

PRACTICE TIP

Follow-up letters serve as reminders and as written records of information given or received.

EXHIBIT 5.3.   *Confirmation Letter to Opposing Counsel*

October 12, 1994

James B. Baxter
Baxter & Associates
200 North Robinson, Suite 1700
Oklahoma City, Oklahoma 73102

RE: *Healy v. Raymond et al.*; Case No. CIV–94–1742–H;
     United States District Court for the Western District of Oklahoma
     File No. A–500.1

Dear Mr. Baxter:

   This letter is confirm your agreement by telephone today to schedule the deposition of your client, Charles Raymond, on Friday, October 28, 1994, at 1:30 p.m. The deposition will be held at Ad Infinitum Reporters, located at 228 Robert S. Kerr Avenue in Oklahoma City. This office will arrange for the court reporter.

Thank you for your cooperation.

Sincerely,

Christopher B. Roberts
Legal Assistant

pc: Troy Garner, Esq.
Garner & Pinckert

Elizabeth Campbell, CSR
Ad Infinitum Reporters

Here is our suggested solution:

> We ask that you (1) authorize retention of an experienced neurologist to examine Plaintiff; (2) confirm that the policy limit is one million dollars; and (3) approve sending an attorney to Michigan to obtain Plaintiff's Detroit medical records.

This little paragraph goes at the end of the letter. It collects in one obvious place all the things you want your correspondent to do, even though those same requests may be stated elsewhere in your letter. In the letter from which we took our paragraphs, the requests were scattered here and there throughout two pages of thick verbiage. It would have been easy to miss one of the tasks, especially by a busy person for whom this letter was only one of dozens of matters to be dealt with during a single day.

Numbering phrases or sentences does not lend itself to literary perfection, but it helps your reader pick up on those things he or she must take action on. A short paragraph like our example can then become a memo for action.

This last example is a letter to a sophisticated client, an insurance company that deals regularly with claims and litigation. When the client has little or no experience in legal matters, it pays to be even more careful with directions as we were in Exhibit 5.4.

Always remember that what seems simple and routine to you may be complex and strange to a layperson. Take special care with correspondents who are elderly or

---

EXHIBIT 5.4.   *Sample Letter to Client*

Ms. Eva Wolleson
416 Elm Northwest
Ardmore, Oklahoma 73401

RE: Contract for Sale of Southwest Half of Section 31, Carter County, Oklahoma

Dear Ms. Wolleson:

Enclosed are the original and five copies of your contract. One copy is for your files. For the original and the other four copies, please do the following things, in this order:

1. In the presence of the notary public, sign and date the original and each of the four copies on the lines just above your name, as indicated by the red arrows.

2. Then have the notary sign and notarize the original and each of the four copies. If it would be more convenient for you, bring these documents to our office, and one of our notaries will perform this service for you.

3. Mail the original and three copies to me in the enclosed self-addressed, stamped envelope no later than October 1, 1994. Keep the fourth copy for your files.

I will deliver an executed copy to Jeezlix, Inc.

If you have any questions or need additional information, please do not hesitate to contact me.

Sincerely,

Christopher B. Roberts
Legal Assistant
For the Firm

CBR/cce
Enclosure

---

unaccustomed to business or legal matters. Your efforts will help get things done smoothly and on time, and your clients will appreciate your courtesy and attention to detail.

When you want something from an opponent, it is sometimes desirable to put the burden of getting the task done on time on opposing counsel. Lawyers are notorious foot-draggers. At times, neither they nor their clients will place a high priority on doing things you want them to do. Therefore, try to craft your letter so that they cannot simply choose to do nothing as a response.

Contrast these two sentences:

We have scheduled examination of the property for 1:00 p.m. on April 28, 1994. Please let us know whether that date and time will be satisfactory.

We have scheduled examination of the property for 1:00 p.m. on April 28, 1994. If we do not hear from you to the contrary by 5 p.m. on April 25, 1994, we shall assume that this date and time are satisfactory.

The first sentence is clear, but it leaves the decision in the hands of the other side. They are quite likely to delay up to the last minute, and then decide they cannot make it. Or they may not respond at all, leaving you to play telephone tag to get a decision from them. The second sentence puts the burden on them. They may decide that April 28 is inconvenient, but at least they have to take the initiative and call you.

We have said this elsewhere in this book, but it is worth saying again here: When someone (other than your client) is represented by a lawyer, you must thereafter make any contact with that person through his or her lawyer, *not* directly with the person. For example, when you are advised that Brown, the tenant your client is trying to evict, has retained Jones & Jones to represent him in the eviction dispute, you will thereafter deal with Jones & Jones in the matter. Your letters will be addressed to Jones & Jones, not Brown.

Watching Your Language.   By watching your language, we do not mean avoid using vulgar language. We mean, rather, to always remember that what you write to someone today may come back to haunt you six months or a year from now.

To begin with, only your attorney can speak for the client on matters addressing the client's legal position, so you must avoid every appearance of doing so in any letter you personally sign. In this circumstance as in all others, remember you are a legal assistant, not the attorney.

Next, be very careful of seeming to commit the firm to any course of action unless you have plain authority to do so. Even an estimate or "maybe" must be carefully considered before putting it in a letter. What can be misconstrued will be, especially by opposing counsel in a legal dispute. So, unless your attorney has authorized you to do so, make no promise or statement of fact to your client, a witness, or opposing counsel without clearing it with your supervising attorney. If in doubt whether you have authority to make a statement, it is always better to ask.

Following the Golden Rule.   The golden rule in letter writing is easy enough to remember:

> If you don't need to say it, don't say it at all.

Remember that your letters are being read by busy professionals who do not have the time to wade through long, rambling letters. Make your point as succinctly as possible. Your brevity and clarity will be appreciated, and will reflect well on you and your supervising attorney.

Do not put anything in a letter that does not have to be said to get your business done. Do not add gratuitous opinions; do not give information you do not have to; do not make estimates unless the nature of your letter requires you to. If you do, you can be sure that somebody may later try to hold you to any guess you make, any estimate you give, or any opinion you offer.

Being Human.   Having said all these things about being careful, being professional, and not using first names, we must remind you that there is still room for humanity. For example, if you know that some correspondent's spouse has been seriously ill, there is nothing wrong with adding—even to the opposition—"Best wishes from us all for your wife's speedy recovery." If a correspondent has been recently promoted, by all means congratulate him or her. There is nothing unprofessional about courtesy, or concern for others.

PRACTICE TIP

When someone (other than your client) is represented by a lawyer, you may not contact that person directly. Any contact made with that person must be through his or her lawyer.

Formatting Letters

First impressions are lasting ones. If the appearance of your correspondence is not professional, it reflects on you and your attorney. Well-trained legal secretaries are experts in this area and know how to make your letters look their best. If you are not sure of what format to use or where something should be positioned on the page, do not be afraid to ask your secretary for help. After all, that is his or her domain, not yours. Having said all that, here are some tips on formatting your letters to flow smoothly, to look their best, and to avoid embarrassing errors.

Starting the Letter.   At the top of the page, under the address, include a subject line that instantly tells your reader what the subject matter is. The reader is then immediately focused on what the letter is about. Use *RE:*, *SUBJECT:*, or *SUBJ:*, followed by a short description of the matter. In litigation matters, the subject line is generally the name of the plaintiff *v.* or *vs.* the name of the defendant, with the case number of the lawsuit, and the name of the court where the lawsuit was filed. Your subject line can be, and normally is, a general one:

> RE: *Strawberry v. Panoply Enterprises;* Case No. 91–8769; United States Court of Appeals for the Tenth Circuit
> File No. STRAW–004

Notice that the law office's file number is included after the description of the subject matter. This is your own office's system or code, which should be included on all correspondence. Other offices prefer to jot the file ID number in ink on the retained copy of the correspondence. Wherever the number is placed, it helps ensure that a copy of this letter will come to rest in the right file.

The **re** or **subject line** can be much more specific, like this:

> RE: *Strawberry v. Panoply Enterprises*
> Demand Letter

> or

> RE: *Strawberry v. Panoply Enterprises*
> Status Report
> File No. STRAW–004

RE or subject line
A standard part of a legal letter or memorandum heading that states the subject matter of the correspondence.

Our preference is to limit the subject line to identifying the general subject matter of the letter and the file number. In this, as in all other matters of procedure and format, you will be guided by your attorney's preference.

When you write the court about any case already filed with that court, always include the **docket number** of the case in your *subject* or *re* line, as shown in the first example above. The docket number is the number assigned by the court administration to identify each new piece of litigation.

Many law offices require that the addressee's name appear at the top of the first page of a letter—usually at the top left. If the letter is not sent by regular mail, show how the letter was transmitted, as in these examples:

docket number
The case number assigned by the court administration to identify each new piece of litigation.

July 10, 1993

VIA FAX (or FACSIMILE)

Mr. Ernest T. Esterbrook
200 North Walker, Suite 1700
Cincinnati, Ohio 45207

July 10, 1993

VIA HAND DELIVERY

Mr. Ernest T. Esterbrook
200 North Walker, Suite 1700
Cincinnati, Ohio 45207

July 10, 1993

CERTIFIED MAIL,
RETURN RECEIPT REQUESTED

Mr. Ernest T. Esterbrook
200 North Walker, Suite 1700
Cincinnati, Ohio 45207

header
Information placed at the top lefthand corner of the second and subsequent pages of correspondence to identify them in case the pages are separated.

If a letter has more than one page, make a **header** on the second and all subsequent pages. Type the name of the addressee at the top left and then, after it, add the letter date and the page number, like this:

Mr. Thomas Mahrer
July 10, 1992
Page Two

Besides lending a professional polish to your correspondence, a header helps to keep the pages organized for the reader. It can also help you keep multipage letters organized when several are being assembled and sent at once. If a letter has exhibits attached, put a header at the top of the exhibit as well, like this:

Page 1 of 3
Exhibit "A"

footer
A specific line of text, page numbers, or both, at the bottom of a page.

If you prefer, this information can be placed at the bottom of the page. In that case, it would be called a **footer.** Some law firms have rubber stamps made that can be used to mark exhibits. Take care when marking or numbering any exhibit or other document. For example, if the words *Exhibit A* were stamped or typed over a number, making it impossible to read or decipher, the exhibit's integrity would be irreparably damaged. Regardless of what method you choose to mark or number exhibits or other documents, be aware that the number or mark must not cover any part of the actual document or exhibit.

Organizing Your Thoughts.   Many lawyers write by opening a file and dictating the first thing that comes into their heads. The result is often a confused mess in which topics and subtopics are all mixed together, leaving an irritated reader to waste time sorting everything out. As we discussed in Chapter 2, it takes only a moment to make a note or two, or an outline, about what you want to say before you start to say it. Then you can write smoothly in short paragraphs, dealing with one topic at a time.

Start by telling your correspondent why you are writing. The subject line across the top of the letter will give her a general idea, but the first paragraph ought to set out specifically why you wrote, for example:

Our client has authorized us to make an offer of settlement. . . .

PRACTICE TIP

Regardless of what method you use to mark or number exhibits or other documents, do not place the number or mark where it covers any part of the actual exhibit.

Lawyers are fond of saying "in the above-entitled matter" or "in the above-referenced matter" at least once in any correspondence. Of course whatever they are writing about is "in the above-entitled matter." That is the reason for the subject line. Using "in the above-entitled matter" or "in the above-referenced matter" is always unnecessary; leave it out.

If you have not corresponded with the addressee before, introduce the firm before you state the purpose of the letter, like this:

> This firm represents the Estate of Mr. Charles Emory Martin, who on May 14, 1992, was killed in a collision with a truck driven by your employee, Mr. Thomas A. Rodgers.

In the body of your letter, group similar things together. For example, suppose you are reporting on witness interviews, discussing what you found in medical reports, estimating the chances that your client will win or lose, and asking the client to do something, all in the same letter. Deal with one topic only, such as the witness interviews, in as many paragraphs as you need. Finish that topic completely, then move on the medical reports. Your letter will be easier for the reader to digest.

For example, consider the letter in Exhibit 5.5, reporting on the progress of a personal injury action.

As we did in the sample letter above, group similar things (each topic) in one paragraph.

Bear in mind, by the way, that only the lawyer makes tactical judgments or predictions in a letter ("a 70% chance of winning"). You must never make such judgment calls yourself. If they are included in a letter, your supervising attorney must be the one to sign it.

As a matter of style, some law offices use headings for each topic, or require that such headings be numbered. Others require that each request be spelled out in a complete sentence, or they place other requirements on the format of letters. You must follow the office guidelines. In every case, however, you must try to organize each letter logically, making it as easy as possible for the addressee to understand and comply.

For simple letters covering one or two uncomplicated matters, you need not worry about careful organization and headings and such. If you are clear, your reader will understand without them. Even with short, simple letters, however, it is best to emphasize in the last paragraph anything the reader must do or supply or remember.

When you are answering a question posed to you in a letter from the correspondent, always restate that question, preferably in the exact words the reader used to you. For example:

> In your letter of April 28, 1993, you asked whether you could reoccupy the land leased to Mr. Thomas without notice to him and without getting **leave of the court** to do so before you enter.
>
>   The answer is this:. . . .

leave of court
The court's permission to take a particular action that would otherwise be prohibited.

Sending Copies.   You will sometimes want to send copies of correspondence to somebody besides the addressee. For example, you may wish to keep the client advised by sending copies of letters you have sent to opposing counsel, or to the other party to a dispute in which you represent the client.

Normally, you indicate that a copy has been sent by putting a line below and to the left of the signature block, like this:

pc: Mr. Grover T. Williams

or

cc: Mr. Grover T. Williams

EXHIBIT 5.5. *Letter to Client in Personal Injury Lawsuit*

Mr. George Lewis
ACME Liability Insurance Companies
500 West Main
La Jolla, California 92037

RE: *Jane Doe v. Hansen's Delivery Service, Inc. and Joseph L. Brown;* Case No. CIV–94–5523; United
      States District Court for the Western District of Oklahoma

Dear Mr. Hansen:

We took Plaintiff Jane Doe's deposition on January 21, 1993. She is 28, an attractive widow, and mother of three young children. She is articulate and made an excellent impression. Ms. Doe is clearly convinced that the insured's driver—Brown—caused the accident.

Ms. Doe claims that, as a result of this accident, (1) she received a concussion that has caused head, neck, and back pain; (2) this pain has continued since the accident to the extent that she cannot work; (3) her injuries are permanent; and (4) she needs a laminectomy and spinal fusion. Ms. Doe has a previous foot injury, unrelated to this accident, that she received in 1979 when she lived in Ohio.

The police report and witnesses' statements support Ms. Doe's testimony. Mr. Brown, the driver, will not be as convincing on the witness stand at trial as Jane Doe or the witnesses to this accident. I estimate that Plaintiff has a 70% chance of winning a jury verdict at trial of probably $100,000 or more.

We have sent discovery requests to Plaintiff Jane Doe to determine (1) Plaintiff's and her husband's earning capacity and work history; (2) Plaintiff's destination on the day of the accident; (3) the frequency with which she traveled the road on which the accident occurred; (4) whether she was taking any type of medication at the time of the accident; and (5) whether she may have been running late or was distracted in some other way at the time of the accident. We have forwarded Plaintiff's x-rays to our expert witness, radiologist Dr. Olson, and have asked him to examine them and prepare his opinion in a written report.

At this point, I recommend that we employ an accident reconstructionist to analyze how the accident happened and to testify, if necessary, at trial. I also recommend that we obtain Ms. Doe's Ohio medical records to discover whether she previously complained of head, neck, and back pain. Lastly, I recommend that Ms. Doe be examined by a neurologist.

Please authorize the actions recommended in the preceding paragraph. Please note that, to get the Ohio records, we must send someone there. Also, please consider whether you wish to make a settlement offer and whether the amount of my settlement authority includes the $1,000,000 policy limit.

Please let me know your decision by June 15, 1994.

Sincerely,

George Hidalgo
For the Firm

The pc means "photocopy to." The cc stands for "courtesy copy" or "carbon copy," even though carbon paper is no longer used.

Sometimes you want to send someone else a copy without advising the addressee that you have done so. In that case, do not note on the original that a copy has been sent. Instead, show it only on the copy you send and on the one you retain for your own file, like this:

bcc: Mr. Grover T. Williams

The bcc stands for "blind carbon copy," that is, one not revealed to the letter's original addressee. Sending blind copies is a delicate matter. A correspondent may be offended by discovering that, without his knowledge, someone received a copy of a letter written to him. It is your responsibility to make sure that your secretary knows who gets what, and to check the original and all copies yourself before anything is sent.

Always remember that there is no such thing as a "routine" letter. Every piece of correspondence has at least some importance. That means you should not treat correspondence casually, and you should not let a letter out of the office without reading it carefully in final form.

Using Form Books.   You will find that law libraries are full of **form books,** volume after volume of sample writings for every occasion. Many law offices also keep samples of their own forms for future reference. These forms certainly have their place. They can be useful in framing **pleadings,** contracts, and other documents, including some types of letters. Much of their standard language, called **boilerplate,** you will retain and use in every similar document.

But be careful—remember that no two lawsuits are precisely the same. You may certainly use forms, but you must always be sure to tailor them to fit your precise purpose. Treat forms, especially letter forms, as models to be followed for general format and not necessarily for content. Your attorney will tell you what standard language he or she wants retained in particular kinds of letters, and what should be modified.

Writing Different Kinds of Letters

You will learn more on the job about constructing particular types of letters to your attorney's satisfaction. But that process will come easier if we discuss these general types here. First, however, an important piece of advice: When you are asked to draft such a letter—or any other kind of document—you must find out what office policy requires or forbids for this particular kind of document.

Some offices keep a file of sample documents to help new lawyers and legal assistants with format; they can be very helpful. Better still, ask your supervising attorney about ground rules when you get the assignment; she is the one you must please. It also helps to get a sample of a similar letter or document that she has done. Use it as a model, but do not copy it. Remember, seldom are two documents exactly the same. Perhaps the best source of information on office forms and policy is an experienced legal secretary or legal assistant.

Information Letter.   The **information letter** is the standard letter used to tell somebody about something. We have already given some examples of information letters. In general, they are written when you or your supervising attorney have information to pass on. Sometimes, however, they are written when there is nothing new to say. Never forget that the client has hired your supervising attorney because the client has some type of problem. Like any problem, legal difficulties can be worrisome for your client. A protracted silence from the attorney hired to solve that problem is irritating to a client and bad business for the lawyer. It is good, professional policy to contact each client from time to time, even when there is nothing new to report in the case. A few lines from the lawyer or legal assistant reassures clients that you and your attorney are on the job and have not forgotten them.

form books
Collections of sample legal documents to be used as models for creating other documents.

pleadings
A legal term of art describing documents that contain *claims* and *defenses* filed by the parties to a lawsuit with the court. Pleadings set out the issues to be tried.

boilerplate forms
Standard language that, if used in a particular type of form or pleading, retains the same specific meaning from form to form.

PRACTICE TIP

Always revise any form you use to fit your precise purpose, and carefully proofread the final draft to avoid embarrassing errors.

information letter
A standard type of letter used to give information.

◼ PRACTICE TIP

State bar associations have noticed that the most frequent complaint about lawyers by their clients is the lawyer's failure to communicate with the client. Avoid this problem by:

- ■ Returning a client's calls promptly
- ■ Keeping the client advised of the status of the case by letter or telephone
- ■ Forwarding to the client copies of important documents filed in the case

advice or opinion letter
A letter addressing a client's question of law and containing legal authority to support its conclusion; it may also recommend a particular course of action.

Advice or Opinion Letter.   As the title implies, **advice** or **opinion letters** are more complex letters advising clients what or what not to do in a particular situation. You must use special care in drafting these letters. In most offices, they follow a rigidly prescribed format. Even if your supervising attorney allows you to sign some other types of letters, you may never sign a letter that gives advice or a legal opinion. To do so is actually practicing law, which only a lawyer may do.

Opinion letters usually begin with a clear statement of the question to be answered. For example, "In your letter of July 15, 1993, you asked whether. . . ." This statement is generally followed by a summary of the conclusion. Next comes a paragraph setting out the facts and assumptions on which the opinion is based. Following that is a discussion of the question, showing how the writer reasoned to arrive at the conclusion he or she reached.

case law
Law created by decisions of the court.

statutory law
Law created by acts of the legislature.

administrative regulations
Law created by administrative agencies.

Often the discussion portion of an opinion letter refers to **case law, statutory law,** and **administrative regulations.** You may be called upon to apply these authorities to your factual situation, much as you do when writing a memorandum of law or a brief to be filed with the court. When you rely on a case, do as you would do in a legal memorandum or brief: Give a brief synopsis of the facts of the case, the result reached by the court, and the reasoning the court followed in reaching that result.

If you are writing to an attorney, citations of authority are appropriate and often required. Your **citations** should be in proper standard format, just as you would write them in a brief for the court.

citation
The reference to or quotation of legal authority.

If your opinion letter is written to a layperson, as it often is, you need not formally cite the authority you are relying on unless, of course, it is office policy to do so. For clarity, however, you will sometimes want to identify the authority on which you rely, perhaps like this:

> The answer to your question depends on the interpretation of a state statute, Title 10, Section 344 of the Oklahoma Code. That section has been construed by the Oklahoma Supreme Court in two cases, *Creswell v. Temple Mill. Co.,* 499 P.2d 421 (Okla. 1972) and *Paris Bank of Texas v. Custer,* 681 P.2d 71 (Okla. 1984).
>
> Section 344 provides that. . . .
>
> In *Creswell,* a corporate board of directors decided that. . . .

Like most rules, this one has a major exception. When your correspondent must comply with certain rules to achieve, or avoid, the result reached in the letter, give the full citation to the rules so he or she can find them. You may even attach a copy of the pertinent case, statute, or regulation as an enclosure to the letter itself. If, for example, the opinion letter says your client may operate his plant only by abiding by certain federal safety regulations, tell him exactly what they are and where to find them.

Often, office policy will be to state carefully the information upon which the opinion is based, not only in the opinion, but in a separate paragraph at the end of

◼ PRACTICE TIP

Guideline 3 of the ABA Model Guidelines for Utilization of Legal Assistant Services lists three functions that a lawyer *may not* delegate to a legal assistant:

- Responsibility for establishing an attorney-client relationship
- Responsibility for establishing the amount of fees to be charged for a legal service
- Responsibility for publishing a legal opinion to a client

the letter. Because opinion letters are extremely delicate matters, we also recommend this practice. If the client encounters difficulties later and defends himself by saying that he followed his attorney's advice, the opinion letter should plainly reflect what the lawyer considered when rendering the opinion. A typical **limiting paragraph** might look like this:

> This opinion is based only on those facts that you furnished and that are set out in the first three paragraphs of this letter. Should these facts change, or should you learn of additional facts, please call us at once. Any change in the facts, or new facts, may change the result of the opinion.

Opinion letters tend to be more formal than other sorts of letters, but you must draft them in the same clean, clear prose you use for any other type of legal writing. Use the same sharp tools: short sentences, short paragraphs, simple language.

limiting paragraph
In an opinion letter, a statement of the information upon which the opinion is based.

Demand Letter.   **Demand letters** are sent to the opposing party in a controversy, demanding whatever action or compensation will satisfy your client. These are not letters "asking" for something; such letters are merely requests. Demand letters have an altogether different tone, a tone of command. They must be courteous and professional, of course, but they are also quite formal and firm. A demand letter speaks with an air of assurance and certainty, requiring the addressee to do something that the writer demands as a matter of right. They are of two basic types.

First, the **general demand letter.** This one is used for many things, such as a letter to a client's tenant who has not paid the rent, a letter to a father who is behind in child support for the client's child, or a letter to the owner of a junk car who has not removed it from the client's property.

These letters demand that the addressees do something or cease doing something, and tell them why they must (see Exhibit 5.6).

In every demand letter, be quite specific. It is not enough to demand that the addressee "fix" whatever is wrong. State in detail what your client wants done, and how it is to be accomplished. You must also state *why* the addressee must comply with your demand. For example:

> Compliance is required by paragraph seven of the lease, which states in part. . . .

If some statute or other provision of law requires the addressee to comply with the demand, then identify that provision. You may also wish to attach a copy of the pertinent statute or regulation as an enclosure to the letter.

When the addressee is represented by an attorney, the letter will be addressed to that attorney. In this case, it is often a good idea to include with your letter copies of any document upon which your demand relies. Not only is this good, professional practice, but it saves time. No competent attorney will advise a client to comply with any demand without being satisfied of the basis for it. Supply opposing lawyers with

demand letter
A form of legal correspondence sent to the opposing party in a controversy demanding whatever action or compensation will satisfy the client; it speaks with an air of assurance and certainty, requiring the addressee to do something that the writer demands as a matter of right.

general demand letter
A letter commanding that the addressee do something or cease doing something and telling him why he must do so.

PRACTICE TIP

A demand letter speaks with an air of assurance and certainty requiring the addressee to do something that the writer demands as a matter of right.

EXHIBIT 5.6   *Sample Demand Letter*

Mr. Samuel D. Bates
President
Worldwide Foods Distributors, Inc.
600 West 4th Street
Ferryville, New Jersey 07632

RE: Ferryville Plant

Dear Mr. Bates:

This firm represents Johnson Products, Inc., headquartered in Midville, with plants there and at 680 Front Street in Ferryville. Trucks delivering and picking up merchandise at the Main Street gate to your Ferryville plant persist in blocking access to the loading dock of Johnson Products. This practice violates City Ordinance 702(c) of the Municipal Code of Ferryville, and does substantial financial harm to my client's business.

Your plant manager was notified orally (April 3, 1995 and May 1, 1995) and by letter (June 10, 1995) that allowing trucks to obstruct the Johnson Products' dock is unlawful and damaging to Johnson Products' business. These notices have been ignored.

If this practice is not stopped by July 1, 1995, we will have no choice but to seek **damages** and **injunctive relief** in the courts. Please advise us of your intentions or have your attorneys contact us immediately.

Sincerely,

Tara Little
Associate for the Firm

TL/cce

---

damages
Monetary compensation that may be recovered in court by someone who has suffered injury or loss to person, property, or rights through an unlawful act or omission of another.

injunctive relief
A court-ordered equitable remedy prohibiting someone from doing some specified act or commanding someone to undo some wrong or injury.

■ PRACTICE TIP

A demand letter should state in detail:
- What your client wants done
- Why
- How that action is to be accomplished
- A date by which the action must be done

information necessary to decide what action they should advise the client to take in response to the demand letter. It can only speed up the process, and it also demonstrates that your client means business.

Simply demanding payment—or whatever it is—is not enough. Be certain that the letter sets a "not-later-than" date by which payment must be made.

The second type of letter, a demand for settlement, is more specialized. It is most often found in personal injury litigation as the tool a plaintiff uses to present his or her claim to the defendant as persuasively as possible, and it sets the stage for actual trial of a case. *This type of letter is typically broken into six topics, presented in this order:*

■■ PRACTICE TIP

Preparing a **settlement demand letter** has several advantages for you and your attorney:

- It forces you to analyze the strengths and weaknesses of your case
- It forces you to gather and analyze all of the evidence
- It gives you and your attorney a rehearsal for trial should settlement not occur

settlement demand letter
Legal correspondence often found in personal injury litigation, in which the plaintiff's attorney demands a sum settlement from the defendant or defendants.

1. *Description of the plaintiff.*   In one to two brief paragraphs, tell about the plaintiff—who she is, her achievements and goals, her work, her pertinent medical history, and what her life was like before the accident.

2. *The facts of the case.*   Briefly, tell how the accident happened. While it is acceptable to state your client's version of how the accident occurred, you must never distort or misstate the facts. Doing so only makes the possibility of settlement less likely, because your client's demands will appear unreasonable and unrealistic. Refer to any documents, diagrams, exhibits, or deposition testimony that supports the facts and attach that evidence as an exhibit to the letter.

3. *The theories of liability and recovery.*   State whatever legal theories are relied upon to recover from the defendant and how those theories apply to the facts of this case. Use citations of authority where applicable.

4. *Description of plaintiff's injuries.*   Briefly explain the injuries that the plaintiff received and the medical procedures used to effect her recovery. Describe any temporary or permanent disabilities suffered by the plaintiff as a result of the accident. Refer to photographs or other documentation of your client's injuries, and attach them as exhibits.

5. *Statement of the amount of damages.*   This part can be simply a list of medical or other expenses incurred by the plaintiff. While the list should leave no expense unaccounted for, it should not be an itemized list of each pill or bandage bought. Rather, list each medical provider and the total amount charged by that provider for medical services to your client. Group the expenses in subcategories, such as hospitals, pharmacies, physical therapy, etc. Include separate totals for actual expenses incurred to date and anticipated expenses.

6. *Analysis of damages and demand of settlement amount.*   This analysis should be no longer than one to two paragraphs. Briefly summarize the damages being demanded and include their costs. State what an anticipated jury verdict in your client's favor would be. Then, state the amount of settlement that would be acceptable to your client.

Settlement demand letters require considerable thought and crafting. The tone of such a letter must be professional and formal. Make use of any document, exhibit, or deposition testimony that supports your statements. Do not threaten or boast to the opposition about your firm's ability and winning record. Those tactics do not work. Rather, lay out the facts on which your demand rests and state what you are demanding; it is not always money, or only money.

For example, suppose the addressee's client has illegally dammed a creek, forcing water onto your client's property. Your client wants to demand that the dam be removed—maybe even demand that it be removed during low-water season—and seeks monetary compensation for damage already done.

Make certain you leave the door open for settlement negotiations, even if both sides seem pretty well fixed in position. Do not be specific about settling the dispute; speak only generally:

> We shall be happy to discuss this matter further.

Responding to letters like this is a real art. It is often useful to correct significant errors of fact made by the other side, or to cite case or statutory law that favors your side. Sometimes, however, tactics may demand that you keep your own counsel, no matter what the other side says. Your supervising attorney will decide how deeply your letter should go into the facts or law.

CHAPTER SUMMARY

Whenever you are drafting a letter or internal memorandum, keep the following points in mind:

- Always keep careful notes and memos of all you do in a case.
- Make your notes and memos quickly, while a call or conversation is still fresh in your mind.
- Keep letters courteous, clear, professional, and as brief as possible. Avoid legalese.
- Avoid using first names and other personal references in letters.
- Remember to follow up important oral requests or agreements by writing a letter.
- Remember to include a clear reference line at the head of your letters, to use headers on each page after the first, and to include a docket number, if there is one.
- Organize and proofread your letters.
- Outline a substantial letter on an important subject. Group similar matters together.
- Courteously but plainly tell your correspondents what you want them to do. Group the things you want done together.
- When a correspondent poses a question in a letter to your firm, repeat the question when you write back in answer.
- Be careful of forms. They are often good models, but remember that every case and situation is different.
- Be especially careful with opinion letters. They are always signed by a lawyer, and must follow a careful, narrow format, including a restatement of the facts upon which the opinion is based.
- A demand letter states in detail what your client wants done and why, how the requested action is to be accomplished, and a date by which the action must be done.
- A settlement demand letter consists of (1) a description of the plaintiff, (2) the facts, (3) the theory of liability or recovery, (4) the medical expenses, (5) a list of damages, and (6) an analysis of damages and the amount demanded as settlement.
- Carefully monitor who gets copies of letters, including "blind copies." Personally make certain that all enclosures are correct and are directed to the proper person.

KEY WORDS AND PHRASES

administrative regulations

advice letter

boilerplate forms

case law

citation

court reporter

damages

demand letter

deposition

docket number

footer

form books

general demand letter

header

information letter

injunctive relief

internal memorandum

letter

leave of court

limiting paragraph

opinion letter

pleadings

re or subject line

res ipsa loquitur

settlement demand

statutory law

stipulation

tickler

tickler file

EXERCISES

1. Ms. Pepper has filed Jane Healy's Complaint. Now Ms. Pepper asks you to set up a deposition for Charles Raymond. At the deposition, Mr. Raymond will appear with his attorney, Mr. Austin. Ms. Pepper will ask Mr. Raymond detailed, fact-specific questions about the accident and his driving record, which Mr. Raymond will have to answer under oath. A court reporter will record Mr. Raymond's responses.

   You call Mr. Austin to request the deposition and schedule a time for it. Mr. Austin agrees to have the deposition next Thursday at 10 a.m. at your office. You next call the court reporter and arrange for her to take the deposition. Because it is the end of the day and you are tired, you do not make a memorandum of either of these phone calls. Is this a good decision? Why or why not?

2. You ask your co-worker, Fred Wickham, to write a letter to Mr. Austin confirming the deposition that you have scheduled. Fred writes the following letter and gives it to you to proofread. What problems do you see? How should those problems be corrected?

   June 1, 1994

   Mr. Richard Austin
   Austin & Burkes
   Attorneys at Law
   122 S. Robinson St.
   Oklahoma City, OK 73212

   Re: *Healy v. Allegretti*
   CIV 94–1742–H

   Dear Rich:

   This letter is to confirm the depo we have scheduled for 10 a.m. on Thursday, June 16 for the above-referenced matter, per your telephonic contact with us yesterday.

   As you well know, your client Charles Raymond is theperson we want to question. It is our impression that Mr. Raymond is a real flake. Therefore, we ask that you take special measures to ensure his presence at the depo.

   If Mr. Raymond fails to appear, we will take action against you both. After twenty years of successful legal practice, a prestigious firm like Nowack & Buechner has little patence with pre-trial maneuvering.

   Cordially yours,

   Fred Wickham
   Legal Assistant

3. Yesterday, you dictated a letter to Jane Healy updating her on her case. But you forgot to dictate where the paragraphs were supposed to break. In addition, you were in a good mood and consequently rather long-winded.

   When your secretary shows you what she has transcribed, you shudder. Your letter appears below. Edit it, paying special attention to sentence length and paragraph breaks.

   June 5, 1994

   Ms. Jane Healy
   483 Moore Drive
   River City, OK 72211

Re: *Healy v. Allegretti*
    CIV 94–1742–H

Dear Ms. Healy:

This letter is for the purpose of updating you on what has happened on your case and what is going on so that you know what the situation is. First, Amelia Pepper and I have interviewed and talked to all the witnesses and people who saw Mr. Raymond at Red's Tavern, in addition to all the people who watched the accident occur. Second, Ms. Pepper filed a petition on your behalf on June 4 against Mr. Raymond, Mr. Allegretti, Red's Tavern, Ajax, Inc., your car dealership, and the manufacturer of your car, and we are currently waiting for all of these parties to respond, which they should do within the next twenty days. Finally, Ms. Pepper and I have scheduled a deposition next Thursday for Mr. Raymond, which will give us a chance to hear what his story is and what he might say at trial. Please let me know if you have any questions about your case.

Sincerely,

Your Name
Legal Assistant

4. Jane Healy's employer, Ajax, Inc., is served with a summons and a copy of the Complaint. Shortly afterwards, Lisa Skinner, an attorney from Ajax's legal department, writes you a letter. Ms. Skinner says that the company is willing to let Ms. Healy have her old job back if she will dismiss her claims against Ajax. However, Ms. Healy would have to accept a fifteen percent pay cut, since her injuries will restrict her contact with the public.

You think this is an excellent offer, but you want to respond quickly before Ajax changes its mind. Ms. Pepper is out of the office; and Ms. Healy, who is heavily sedated from her pain medication, is not answering her phone. Applying your initiative, you draft the letter below and send it to Ms. Skinner.

Assume the letter is perfectly grammatical. Are there any problems with the letter? If so, what are they?

June 10, 1994

Ms. Lisa Skinner
Ajax, Inc.
Department of Legal Counsel
112 South Burgess Parkway
River City, Oklahoma 72211

Re: *Healy v. Allegretti et al.;* Case No. CIV–94–1742–H; United States District Court for the Western District of Oklahoma File No. A–500.1(a)

Dear Ms. Skinner:

I have received your letter of June 9. In it you offered to give Jane Healy her old job back with a fifteen percent pay cut if she would dismiss her lawsuit against you.

Thank you for your generous offer. Ms. Healy will be happy to accept it.

I will put the agreement in writing and have Ms. Healy sign it by the end of this week. I will then send the agreement to you so that you can look it over and sign it if you approve of the language.

Once again, I appreciate your willingness to settle the case. I will be in touch with you soon.

Sincerely,

Your Name
Legal Assistant

Practicing Your Letter Writing

The most effective way to perfect your correspondence skills is to write letters. In the following exercises, you will practice drafting the kind of correspondence you will be asked to write in the real world. Read the scenarios, and then do the exercises.

Scenario: Attorney R. W. Buckley, 1212 Bleak Valley, Suite 523, Nashville, Tennessee, represents Judy Davis, the engineer who designed the seat belts in Ms. Healy's car. The attorney with whom you work, Harry Mason, needs to depose Ms. Davis as soon as possible. In a recent telephone conversation, you and Mr. Buckley finally agreed that the deposition will take place on November 17 at 2 p.m.

This agreement did not come easily. Mr. Mason and Mr. Buckley were once on a planning committee for the State Bar Association's annual awards dinner, and had a heated dispute over the type of punch to be served.

Although the two attorneys deal professionally with one another, they intensely dislike each other. Mr. Mason finds Mr. Buckley moody and unpredictable. Mr. Buckley thinks Mr. Mason is pushy and uncompromising. In fact, Mr. Buckley does tend to be irresponsible, and Mr. Mason is a bit controlling.

In your conversation with Mr. Buckley, he reluctantly agreed that the deposition will take place in your office at 110 Park Place, Suite 1117, New York City. You will arrange for the court reporter. Mr. Buckley will notify his client of the date, time, and place of the deposition and has told you that no subpoena will be necessary to ensure that his client will show up for the deposition.

Mr. Mason is concerned that Mr. Buckley will botch his responsibility and fail to notify his client of the deposition. If that happens and Ms. Davis fails to appear for her deposition, Mr. Buckley or his client may have to pay any costs associated with rescheduling the deposition. However, Mr. Mason is more concerned with the time factor. He simply needs to get this deposition done quickly.

1. Write a letter to Attorney R. W. Buckley, of the firm Buckley, Hines & Majors, P.C., confirming the deposition arrangements. Other persons who should be told about the deposition are Richard C. Smith of Smith & Associates, Mr. Allegretti's attorney, and the court reporter, Elizabeth Campbell at Ad Infinitum Reporting Inc. You will need to remind Mr. Buckley of his responsibility, but take care not to create more hostility.

Scenario: When Mr. Buckley receives your letter regarding Ms. Davis' deposition, he has a change of heart. He realizes that it is silly to continue his feud with Mr. Mason. He calls you and says he talked to Ms. Davis on the phone but did not send her a confirmation letter. Then he blithely mentions that he forgot to make the payment on his office equipment, and half of his office equipment has been repossessed.

You decide to take advantage of Mr. Buckley's amiable mood swing. You are aware that Mr. Buckley has a working model of the type of seat belt that was in Ms. Healy's car, and Mr. Mason has said that he would like examine the model before trial. "Sure thing. No problem," says Mr. Buckley, "I'll send a runner over with it tomorrow . . . Thursday at the latest."

2. Because you have been well trained, you understand the importance of immediately documenting telephone conversations. Before you do anything else, write a memo to the Healy file memorializing your conversation with Mr. Buckley.

3. As you might have guessed, Mr. Buckley forgot to send the seat belt model. At least you hope he forgot, and that his failure to send it isn't indicating another mood swing. Write a reminder letter, disguised as a thank you letter, to spur Mr. Buckley into action.

4. Draft a settlement demand letter on behalf of your client, Ms. Jane Healy, to Richard C. Smith of Smith & Associates, Mr. Allegretti's attorney.

5. Draft a response to Amelia Pepper, Jane Healy's lawyer, from Richard Smith, Mr. Allegretti's attorney, in response to the settlement demand letter you wrote for exercise 4 above.

6

LEGAL RESEARCH

This chapter is not a full discussion of the research process and all its sources. Full treatment of this subject requires a book-length text. This chapter is a quick reference source only, a place to go to check your memory of the steps in basic research. We deal only with the most-used sources of legal authority. We do not touch on some sources at all, such as those you use in researching administrative law and in finding legislative intent. This chapter also deals only with research in books, and does not address computer-assisted legal research.

◼ LEGAL AUTHORITY

Legal research is the tool by which legal professionals determine (1) a client's legal rights and/or liabilities, (2) the appropriate course of action for the client's case, and (3) what the client must do to follow the law. **Legal authority** is the written material you use to decide what the law is in a particular case, and from which you analyze what the result is liable to be in a pending case. Legal authorities take two forms.

Primary Authority

Primary authority is predominantly **case law**—judicial opinions from the same jurisdiction your case is in—and **statutes,** both federal and state. It also includes administrative law or the regulations and rulings of government agencies. If it is law in the jurisdiction with which you are concerned—your state, for example—and deals with the very same question you are researching, it is **mandatory authority;** that is, the court will have to follow it.

For example, when the Supreme Court of Nebraska decides a point of law, a Nebraska trial court faced with the same point cannot decide it some other way; it is *bound* by the higher court's decision. Conversely, an opinion from the Supreme Court of Oklahoma would be **persuasive authority** only for a Nebraska trial court, meaning that the Nebraska court may be persuaded by the arguments made in that opinion but would not be bound to follow it. If the Supreme Court

legal authority
A source relied upon for a legal argument or theory.

primary authority
Any law on which a court could rely in reaching its decision; predominantly case law.

case law
The body of reported cases interpreting statutes, regulations, and constitutional provisions; used to decide what the law is and what a court will do when facing a certain question in a particular fact scenario.

statutes
Laws passed by the legislature at all levels—national, state, and local.

mandatory authority
Any primary authority that a court must follow in reaching its decision.

persuasive authority
Non-mandatory, primary authority and any secondary authority that may influence or give guidance to the court or administrative tribunal by its arguments or reasons offered, but is not binding on the court.

secondary authority
Any non-law on which a court could rely in reaching its decision.

legal periodical
Journals or newspapers prepared by a private publisher containing recent decisions, notices of local court proceedings, and news of general interest to the legal profession.

legal encyclopedia
A type of secondary authority that is a general source of information.

treatise
A type of secondary authority that focuses on a particular area of the law.

of the United States decides a question about the United States Constitution, that interpretation is binding on all federal courts and state courts faced with the identical question.

By the same token, the statutory law of your jurisdiction is binding as well, if it deals with the precise question you are researching and has not been otherwise modified or held unconstitutional by the courts.

Secondary Authority

Secondary authority includes a variety of sources that serve to explain or collect the law, or to help you find case law or statutes. Secondary authorities are called persuasive authorities, meaning they may influence the court or administrative tribunal by the arguments or reasons offered, but are not binding on the court. Secondary authorities include legal encyclopedias, treatises, citators, annotations, and **legal periodicals** of several kinds. We shall talk about them all in this chapter.

◼ THE RESEARCH PROCESS

Imagine that you have been given a question to research on your first day in the new job. Where on earth do you start?

First, you must understand the nature of the problem, and a little about the general area of the law in which you will be researching. Never hesitate to ask questions of your supervising attorney. He or she will be happy to clarify terms and tell you a little about the area of the law to which your problem belongs. Remember that, especially when you are just starting out, *there is no such thing as a dumb question.*

Legal Encyclopedias and Treatises

Now, off to the library. Unless you are very comfortable with the area of the law in which you will be researching, it is always best to start with some general information. You can use either a **legal encyclopedia** or a **treatise** to bone up on the law generally. A treatise is simply a book about a particular area of the law, such as *Williston on Contracts*. Most have both a table of contents and an index, and you can soon begin to read generally about the law affecting your question. You will gain general information about the law, and you will find references to some important judicial opinions in the area.

The legal encyclopedia is an even better source of general information. Two legal encyclopedias are in general use: *Corpus Juris Secundum* (C.J.S.) and *American Jurisprudence Second Series* (Am.Jur.2d). Both are excellent research sources. We shall deal mostly with *Corpus Juris Secundum*—legal professionals call it C.J.S.—because it is part of the West system of nationwide research materials, and can therefore lead you into that system. Do not confuse C.J.S. with *Corpus Juris,* the old legal encyclopedia. It has been replaced by C.J.S.

C.J.S. and Am.Jur.2d work just like ordinary encyclopedias, and both have a large index you can use to search for words and phrases that describe your problem. The digest explains the law in an orderly way, and supports its statements by references to case law. So, in addition to gaining some understanding of the law, you may pick up a case or two that will provide a good starting point for the rest of your research.

◼ PRACTICE TIP

In tort law, contributory negligence is an unreasonable act or omission by the plaintiff which, together with the defendant's negligence, is the *proximate cause* of the injury. Proximate cause is that cause which, in a natural and continuous sequence, unbroken by an efficient intervening cause, produces the injury and without which the injury would not have occurred.

Corpus Juris Secundum

Let us take a walk through *Corpus Juris Secundum.* We shall start with a problem you have been given to research.

Your firm represents the Ajax Hotel. Here is what happened there last month, and became the subject of a lawsuit just filed against the hotel, alleging it was negligent. The hotel left an open elevator shaft unguarded. The plaintiff walked into the open shaft and fell two stories. The plaintiff is blind. She did not use a cane as she walked to the elevator.

The question your attorney wants answered is whether the blind woman was **contributorily negligent** in not using a cane to help compensate for her blindness. If she was contributorily negligent, her negligence may substantially reduce the hotel's liability.

contributory negligence
In tort law, a defense that the plaintiff contributed to his or her own injuries and should therefore be barred from recovery.

The General Index.   You are going to begin with the *C.J.S. General Index,* a multi-volume set at the end of the encyclopedia. Before you start, think about words and phrases that will describe your problem and lead you quickly to the right section of C.J.S. Consider descriptive words and phrases in these contexts:

- Parties to the litigation
- Places and things involved in the case
- The basis of the action, or the issue to be decided
- Any defenses involved in the case
- The relief sought by any party to the case

Considering our scenario, you think of these clues:

- Blind persons; handicapped persons; disabled persons
- Elevators
- Negligence
- Contributory negligence

Write down your descriptive words and phrases, and begin by searching the index for the most likely word or words (in this case, probably *blind* or *handicapped persons*). Exhibit 6.1 (p. 106) is a reproduction of the page dealing with blind persons.

Notice in the righthand column of Exhibit 6.1, where the arrow is, the entry "Contributory negligence." That is one of your descriptive phrases, so that entry sounds as if it bears on your problem. Make a note of the section number that follows it: Neglig § 142.

After the section number, it is a good idea to add a description of what it pertains to—in this case, "blind persons, contributory negligence"—because you may end up with several section numbers to follow up, each one pertaining to some different topic.

PRACTICE TIP

As a general rule, your legal research will be more useful and productive if you make clear and copious notes from the beginning.

EXHIBIT 6.1   *General Index to* Corpus Juris Secundum

BLIGHT ELIMINATION
Eminent domain, **Em Dom § 64(1)**
  Particular property, necessity for taking, **Em Dom
    § 90**
  Site location, **Em Dom § 91**

BLIGHTED AREAS
Housing, generally, this index

BLIMP
Defined, **Vol. 11**

BLIND
Defined, **Vol. 11**

BLIND ALLEY
Cul de Sac, generally, this index

BLIND AMENDMENTS
Statutes, constitutional prohibition, **Stat § 260**

BLIND BILLED
Carriers, defined, **Carr § 122**

BLIND CAR
Railroads, defined, **R R § 1**

BLIND CROSSING
Evidence, conclusion of witness, **Evid § 453**

BLIND FLUE
Railroads, defined, **R R § 1**

BLIND HORSES
Highways and roads, driving on contributory negli-
  gence, **High § 274**
Streets or other public ways, negligence in driving on,
  Mun Corp §§ 854, 855

BLIND INTERSECTIONS
Generally, see **Title Index to Motor Vehicles**

BLIND PERSONS
  Generally, see **Title Index to Social Security and
    Public Welfare**
Abatement and revival, blindness caused by wood alco-
  hol, **Abate & R § 144**

Civil rights, complaint charging discrimination against
  teacher, **Civil R § 153**
Contracts, capacity to contract, **Contracts § 133(1)**
Contributory negligence, **Neglig § 142**   ◄─────
  Question of law or fact, **Neglig § 260**
  Streets or other public ways, injuries from defects
    or obstructions, **Mun Corp § 849**
County liabilities, equal protection of law, **Const Law
  § 553**
Criminal law, new trial, blindness of accused, **Crim Law
  § 1462**
Damages, **Damag § 238**
  Jury questions, proximate cause, **Damag § 176(4)**
  Medical expenses, **Damag § 91(3)**
Deeds and conveyances, validity, **Deeds § 54**
Elections,
  Assistance to voters on ground of blindness, **Elec-
    tions § 208**
  Manner of voting, observance of statutory regula-
    tions, **Elections § 208**
  Secret ballots, exception, **Elections § 201(2)**
  Writing in names of candidates, **Elections § 208**
Equal protection of law, county liabilities, **Const Law
  § 553**
Fraud,
  Bills and notes, defense **Bills & N § 498**
  Signing instrument misread by defendant, recovery
    for fraud, **Fraud § 34**
Highways and roads, injuries from defects or obstruc-
  tions, contributory negligence, **High § 269**
Indigent persons, participation in general distribution of
  poor relief funds,
  Paupers § 1
  Pension, § 82
Inns, hotels, and eating places,
  Personal injuries, contributory negligence, **Inn § 28**
  Safety of premises, **Inn § 25**
Institutions, exemption from taxation, **Tax §§ 285, 296**
Landlord and tenant, contributory negligence descend-
  ing stairway with assistance, **Land & Ten
  § 417(19)**

SOURCE: Reprinted from *General Index to Corpus Juris Secundum.* Copyright by West
Publishing Company.

PRACTICE TIP

Your research is
never complete
until it is brought up
to date.

pocket part
A cumulative supple-
ment found at the back
of a book that updates
or consolidates all earlier
volumes.

topic
The general area of law
in which a particular set
of circumstances or
issues falls; also a type
of legal research that
uses West's key numbers
for researching digests.

Pocket Parts.   Now remember, as with every other research source, *you are never
through until you bring your research up to date.* That means you must consult the latest index to C.J.S. You will find it at the end of the bound volume, a pamphlet hooked
by a cardboard tab into a pocket in the back cover of the volume. It is called, for obvious reasons, a **pocket part.** You use it just like you use the bound volume, consulting
the same index entries you consulted in the hardcover book.

The Topic Index.   There is another way to get into the legal encyclopedia. If you
know the **topic** under which your problem falls, you can go directly to the encyclopedia volume in which that topic appears. At the end of the topic, you will find a separate index for that topic only. Exhibit 6.2a is a sample page from the topic index to
Negligence.

EXHIBIT 6.2(a)   *Topic Index to* Negligence

NEGLIGENCE

Beds,
    Dealer's liability for injury from faulty design, § 100(3), p. 1113, n. 50
    Failure of dealer representing himself as manufacturer to test, § 100(3), p. 1114, n. 58
    Products liability, weight of evidence, § 243(10), p. 699
    Purchaser's duty to inspect, § 100(3), p. 1110, n. 33
Beer containers, explosion,
    Evidence of defective regulator, § 222, n. 30
    Proximate cause, fermentation pressure, § 265, p. 933, n. 42
    Weight of evidence, § 243(10), p. 701
Beer distributor, duty to inspect cases, § 100(3), p. 1112, n. 48
Bees, poisonous insecticides, weight and sufficiency of evidence, § 243(1), p. 671, n. 28
Belief of person charged as to existence or nonexistence of danger, § 5(3), p. 512
Beneficiaries of estate, notice of injury and claim, § 180, p. 316
Beverages,
    Bottles and bottling, generally, post
    Products liability, § 100(2), p. 1092
Bicycles,
    Imputation of contributory negligence of operator to guest, § 168(10), p. 236
    Tripping over bicycle in hallway, weight of evidence, § 243(11), p. 704, n. 48
Bill collector, negligence toward, jury question, § 272, p. 960, n. 31
Billboards, construction, weight of evidence, § 243(10), p. 697
Bills, persons entering premises to pay, § 63(149)
    Service station invitee, § 63(128), n. 20
Bills of particulars,
    Complaint alleging acts in violation of statutes and ordinances, § 187(4), n. 42
    General averment of negligence as ground for bill by plaintiff, § 187(9)
    Res ipsa loquitur where plaintiff furnishes bill of defendant's negligence, § 220.23, p. 607, n. 62
Bingo,
    Injuries on premises, evidence, § 243(11), p. 705
    Liability for injury to invitee, § 63(45), p. 730, n. 95
    Persons entering halls, rules governing, § 63(133)
Blameworthy conduct, culpable negligence distinguished, § 1(13), p. 456
Blank form, status of person entering bank to obtain note form, licensee, § 63(133), n. 94
➤ **Blind persons,**
    Contributory negligence, § 142
        Question of law or fact, § 260, p. 894
    Sufficiency of care exercised as to, § 12, p. 587
Blocks, concrete blocks, attractive nuisance, § 63(96)
Blood donors, reasonable care in testing and examining by donee, § 66, p. 943, n. 30
Blood poisoning, Boncilla treatment, weight and sufficiency of evidence, § 243(8), n. 84
Blood tests, intoxication, evidence of contributory negligence, § 242, n. 91
Blowtorch,
    Evidence of negligence and fire caused by, § 243(9), n. 90
    Infant trespasser, burns, § 63(61), n. 50

Blowtorch—Continued
    Pleading willfulness or wantonness, injuries to child, § 190, n. 40
Blueberries, burning blueberry lands, weight of evidence, § 243(9), n. 92
Boarding and lodging houses, transmission of contagious diseases by placing of afflicted children, § 71
Boards and commissions, violation of rules and regulations, contributory negligence, § 127
Boats,
    Contributory negligence of operator, imputation to passenger or guest, § 168(10), p. 236
    Duty to invitees, § 63(46), p. 747
    Engines, purchaser's liability for injury from condition of boat after removal, § 95, p. 1061, n. 5
    Sinking, questions of law and fact, § 252, p. 813, n. 12.40
Boilers,
    Contributory negligence, failure to observe or take precaution against danger, § 257(2), p. 890
    Evidence of negligence in erection, maintenance, etc., § 243(10), p. 697
    Explosions, weight of evidence, § 243(10), p. 701
    Increase of water pressure in boiler as proximate cause, § 112, n. 9
    Lifting of section, physical possibility, § 251(1), p. 777, n. 70
    Partial defense of contributory negligence of employee injured by violation of boiler inspection act, § 172, p. 280
    Products liability, weight of evidence, § 243(10), p. 699
    Res ipsa loquitur doctrine, bursting or exploding, § 220.24, p. 615
    State inspection as affecting manufacturer's liability for negligent construction, § 100(3), p. 1098, n. 94
Boncilla treatment, evidence of negligence, § 243(8), n. 84
Bond, criminal proceeding, forfeiture, evidence, § 239, n. 69.5
Bonfires,
    Nuisance per se, § 72, p. 952, n. 1
    Safeguarding children from injury, § 72, p. 955
Booking agent, business invitee by invitation, § 63(137), n. 92
Bottles and bottling,
    Contributory negligence, breaking or explosion, § 257(2), p. 890
    Denatured alcohol, attractive nuisance, § 63(102)
    Evidence,
        Cause of injury, § 244(6)
        Contributory negligence of person injured by explosion, § 247(3), p. 760, n. 95
        Custom or usage in handling, § 232, p. 640, n. 2
        Defendant's precaution against injury from explosion, § 243(14), n. 13
        Expert testimony, injury by explosion, § 244(4), n. 72
        Medical testimony, dead mouse in bottle, § 244(4), n. 74
        Negligence,
            Injury by exploding bottle to one watching bottling machine, § 243(10), **p. 697,** n. 95

EXHIBIT 6.2(b) *Topic Index to* Negligence

NEGLIGENCE

SOURCE: Reprinted from C.J.S. *Topic Index to Negligence.*

■ PRACTICE TIP

West's key number system is the organizational principle used to classify the small paragraph summaries of the opinions in the digests. Every topic and subtopic in the law is assigned a key topic and number by West.

Look down the lefthand column, at the bottom where the arrow is. You see that this index also lists "blind persons" as a subtopic, and leads you directly to the same section—"Contributory negligence, § 142"—that you found in the general index. Now continue to scan this index for more descriptive phrases. Look at Exhibit 6.2(b), the second page from the topic index to negligence.

On this page you looked under "Contributory negligence" in the lefthand column, beginning eight lines from the top. Sure enough, farther down, at the arrow, you find the entry "Blind persons, § 142."

Two descriptive phrases, but the same result. You can also check this index in the pocket part.

C.J.S. Now you are ready to open the encyclopedia itself. You open the volume covering *Negligence* to Section 142, and begin to read.

As you can see in Exhibit 6.3(a), Section 142 ("Persons under Physical Disability") opens with a "black-letter" paragraph giving you the general rule of law. The next entry is "Library References," which is followed by this line: Negligence ☜ 86.

EXHIBIT 6.3(a) *Excerpt from 65A C.J.S. § 142*

§§ 141–142 NEGLIGENCE   65A C. J. S.

jury, but is merely of dull mind, is chargeable with the same degree of care for his personal safety as one of brighter intellect.[5]

§ 142. Persons under Physical Disability

A person under any physical disability is required to exercise ordinary care to avoid injury, and if he fails to do so, and such failure contributes proximately to the injury, he is guilty of contributory negligence.

Library References

Negligence ☜86.

A person laboring under any physical disability increasing his liability to injury must nevertheless exercise ordinary care to avoid injury;[6] and if he fails to exercise that degree of care, and such failure contributes proximately to cause his injury, he is guilty of contributory negligence.[7] Such a person is not required to exercise a higher degree of care to that end than is required of a person under no disability;[8] ordinary care is all that is required.[9]

However, in determining whether such a person exercised ordinary care for his own safety, his disa-

bility is a circumstance to be considered.[10] Thus, while it has been said that ordinary care is such care as an ordinarily prudent person with the same disability would exercise under the same or similar circumstances,[11] it has also been held that it may be incumbent on one with a physical disability to put forth a greater degree of effort than would otherwise be necessary in order to attain that standard of care which is required of everyone.[12]

Blind persons and persons with defective vision. The fact that a person is wholly or partially blind does not relieve him of the duty to exercise ordinary care for his own safety;[13] and if he fails to exercise such care, and his failure to do so contributes proximately to cause his injury, he is guilty of contributory negligence.[14] It is not negligence as a matter of law for a blind person to be present in a public place[15] or to walk unattended on a public street.[16] In the absence of knowledge to the contrary, actual or imputed, such a person may assume that he is not exposed to, or threatened by, injury which can come to him only from a breach of the duty which others owe to avoid injury to him.[17]

Continued

EXHIBIT 6.3(a) *—Continued*

5. Ala.—Worthington v. Mencer, 11 So. 72, 96 Ala. 310, 17 L.R.A. 407. 45 C.J. p 995 note 54.

6. Iowa.—**Corpus Juris Secundum cited in** Tisserat v. Peters, 99 N.W. 2d 924, 926, 251 Iowa 250.
Mass.—Keith v. Worcester, etc., R. Co., 82 N.E. 680, 196 Mass. 478, 14 L.R.A.,N.S., 648.
N.J.—Berger v. Shapiro, 152 A.2d 20, 30 N.J 89.
Karmazin v. Pennsylvania R. Co., 196 A.2d 803, 82 N.J.Super. 123, rehearing denied 198 A.2d 97, 82 N.J. Super. 435.
45 C.J. p 995 note 56.
Care required to avoid injury to person under physical disability see supra § 12.

Knowledge of danger
(1) Old woman of frail and slight physique suing for injuries resulting from fall sustained when salesman in provision, fruit, and vegetable market slightly brushed woman's elbow or arm must be charged with knowledge of her physical condition and of the risk she incurred in stationing herself so near to salesman that an ordinary movement on his part might jeopardize her safety.
Cal.—Ury v. Fredkin's Markets, 79 P.2d 749, 26 C.A.2d 501.

(2) Person whose faculties of observation are temporarily suspended as regards a dangerous condition is virtually in the same mental position as one who has never acquired knowledge of such condition.
Kan.—Cox v. City of Coffeyville, 110 P.2d 772, 153 Kan. 392.

7. Tenn.—Felton v. Horner, 37 S.W. 696, 97 Tenn. 579.
45 C.J. p 995 note 57.
Failure of passengers on trains to have an attendant as contributory negligence see **Carriers** § 776 a.

8. Cal.—Jones v. Bayley, 122 P.2d 293, 49 C.A.2d 647.
Me.—McCullough v. Lalumiere, 166 A.2d 702, 156 Me. 479.
S.C. **Corpus Juris Secundum cited in** Conner v. Farmers and Merchants Bank, 132 S.E.2d 385, 392, 243 S.C. 132.
45 C.J. p 996 note 58.

9. Cal.—Jones v. Bayley, 122 P.2d 293, 49 C.A.2d 647.
S.C.—Conner v. Farmers and Merchants Bank, 132 S.E.2d 385, 243 S.C. 132.
45 C.J. p 996 note 59.

10. Conn.—Goodman v. Norwalk Jewish Center, Inc., 139 A.2d 812, 145 Conn. 146.
Mass.—Keith v. Worcester, etc., R. Co., 82 N.E. 680, 196 Mass. 478, 14 L.R.A.,N.S., 648.
45 C.J. p 996 note 60.

11. Cal.—Conjorsky v. Murray, 287 P.2d 505, 135 C.A.2d 478—Jones v. Bayley, 122 P.2d 293, 49 C.A.2d 647.
Conn.—Goodman v. Norwalk Jewish Center, Inc., 139 A.2d 812, 145 Conn. 146.
Me.—Ham v. Lewiston, 47 A. 548, 94 Me. 265.
S.C.—**Corpus Juris Secundum cited in** Conner v. Farmers and Merchants Bank, 132 S.E.2d 385, 392, 243 S.C. 132.

12. U.S.—Darter v. Greenville Community Hotel Corp., C.A.S.C., 301 F.2d 70.
Cal.—Jones v. Bayley, 122 P.2d 293, 49 C.A.2d 647—Armstrong v. Day, 284 P. 1083, 103 C.A. 465.
Me.—McCullough v. Lalumiere, 166 A.2d 702, 156 Me. 479.
Neb.—Trumbley v. Moore, 39 N.W.2d 613, 151 Neb. 780.
45 C.J. p 996 note 62.

Requirement stated in terms of degree of care
In some cases the text requirement has been stated in terms of a commensurately greater degree of care.
U.S.—Darter v. Greenville Community Hotel Corporation, C.A.S.C., 301 F.2d 70.

13. Cal.—**Corpus Juris Secundum cited in** Krause v. Apodaca, 186 C. A.2d 413, 9 Cal.Rptr. 10, 12.
Iowa.—Balcom v. Independence, 160 N.W. 305, 178 Iowa 685, L.R.A.1917C 120.
Pa.—Davis v. Feinstein, 88 A.2d 695, 370 Pa. 449.
45 C.J. p 996 note 64.
Care required to avoid injury to blind person see supra § 12.

14. Pa.—Karl v. Juniata County, 56 A. 78, 206 Pa. 633.
45 C.J. p 996 note 65.

15. N.Y.—Harris v. Uebelhoer, 75 N. Y. 169.

16. Or.—Weinstein v. Wheeler, 271 P. 733, 127 Or. 406, 62 A.L.R. 574.

17. Tenn.—**Corpus Juris cited in** East Tennessee Light & Power Co.

SOURCE: Reprinted from *Corpus Juris Secundum*. Copyright by West Publishing Company.

---

key number
A number identifying where a particular topic falls in West's outline of the law; West's key number system is the organizational principle used to classify small paragraph summaries of the opinions in the digests.

This is a **key number** that identifies where this topic falls in West Publishing Company's outline of the law. *Write it down*, not only the number but also the word or words—called the *topic*. It is your "key" to finding cases in this precise topic, a technique we discuss below under "Digests." Note that the key number is *not* the same as the topic paragraph numbers in C.J.S.

Notice, as you read on through the discussion under § 142, that every statement about the law is supported by a footnote containing one or more citations to appellate opinions. Pay attention not only to the text of the section but also to citations to cases that may discuss the law bearing on your precise problem. For example, look at the first paragraph in the lefthand column of the page shown in Exhibit 6.3(b):

> Thus, the fact that he is blind, or has defective vision, may make it incumbent on him to make greater use of his other senses to prevent injury than if in full possession of his faculty of sight.[19]

Now look down at footnote 19 in Exhibit 6.3 (b). It contains several cases discussing the "due care" required of a person with impaired sight. Even more to the point of your problem, in the center column of footnotes on this page, you will see this entry:

EXHIBIT 6.3(b)   *Excerpt from 65A C.J.S. § 142*

65A C. J. S.   NEGLIGENCE §§ 142–143

In determining what constitutes ordinary care on his part, his blindness, and all other circumstances affecting the question as to what care was reasonably necessary to avoid injury, should be considered.[18] Thus, the fact that he is blind, or has defective vision, may make it incumbent on him to make greater use of his other senses to prevent injury than if in full possession of his faculty of sight.[19] Ordinary care to protect himself from injury, however, is all that is required of him.[20] Ordinary care in the case of such a person is such care as an ordinarily prudent person with a like infirmity would have exercised under the same or similar circumstances.[21]

Deaf persons. It is the duty of a person who is deaf, or whose hearing is defective, to use ordinary care for his own safety;[22] and if he fails to use such care, and such failure contributes proximately to cause his injury, he is guilty of contributory negligence.[23] The fact that he is deaf, or has defec-

tive hearing, may impose on him a duty to make greater use of his other senses to protect himself from injury than if in full possession of his faculty of hearing;[24] but ordinary care, such as an ordinarily prudent person laboring under a like infirmity would exercise under the same or similar circumstances, is all that is required of him.[25]

§ 143.   Intoxicated Persons

The voluntary intoxication of a person does not excuse him from exercising the due care required of a sober person, and where such intoxication prevents him from using the necessary care, and his negligent conduct contributes directly to the injury, he cannot recover.

Library References

Negligence ⟜88.

The care required of a person who has become intoxicated voluntarily is the same as that required of one who is sober.[26] Accordingly, the voluntary

v. Gose, 130 S.W.2d 984, 987, 23 Tenn.App. 280.
45 C.J. p 996 note 66.
Intrusting safety to others
Blind persons may, within reasonable limits, intrust their safety to those who are younger and stronger mentally and physically than themselves without being guilty of negligence.
Minn.—Anderson v. Winkle, 5 N.W. 2d 355, 213 Minn. 77.
18. Iowa.—Hill v. Glenwood, 100 N. W. 522, 124 Iowa 479.
45 C.J. p 996 note 67.
19. Cal.—**Corpus Juris Secundum cited in** Pennington v. Southern Pac. Co., 304 P.2d 22, 29, 146 C.A.2d 605, 65 A.L.R.2d 690—**Corpus Juris cited in** Jones v. Bayley, 122 P.2d 293, 297, 49 C.A.2d 647—**Corpus Juris cited in** Armstrong v. Day, 284 P. 1083, 1086, 103 C.A. 465.
N.J.—Berger v. Shapiro, 144 A.2d 900, 52 N.J.Super. 94, affirmed 152 A.2d 20, 30 N.J. 89.
Pa.—Taylor v. Rollins, Com.Pl., 9 Chest.Co. 65.
Tenn.—Riddell v. Great Atlantic & Pac. Tea Co., 241 S.W.2d 406, 192 Tenn. 304.
45 C.J. p 996 note 68.
Care required of sighted person compared
(1) As a rule in determination of liability in a tort action, a person with defective vision will be held to a greater degree of care than a person of normal vision when confronted with unfamiliar, dark surroundings.
La.—Mahfouz v. United Broth. of Carpenters and Joiners of America —Local Union No. 403, App., 117 So. 2d 295.

(2) Where persons have defective vision, they should use greater care in proportion to the dangers to which men are constantly exposed than is required of those in full possession of the faculty of sight.
Tenn.—Riddell v. Great Atlantic & Pac. Tea Co., 241 S.W.2d 406, 192 Tenn. 304.
Use of artificial aids required
Due care for a blind person includes a reasonable effort to compensate for his unfortunate affliction by the use of artificial aids for discerning obstacles in his path.
Pa.—Davis v. Feinstein, 88 A.2d 695, 370 Pa. 449.
20. Cal.—**Corpus Juris Secundum cited in** Pennington v. Southern Pac. Co., 304 P.2d 22, 29, 146 C.A.2d 605, 65 A.L.R.2d 690—**Corpus Juris cited in** Jones v. Bayley, 122 P.2d 293, 297, 49 C.A.2d 647.
45 C.J. p 996 note 69.
21. Cal.—**Corpus Juris cited in** Jones v. Bayley, 122 P.2d 293, 297, 49 C.A. 2d 647.
Conn.—**Corpus Juris cited in** Muse v. Page, 4 A.2d 329, 331, 125 Conn. 219.
Iowa.—**Corpus Juris Secundum quoted in** Tisserat v. Peters, 99 N.W.2d 924, 926, 251 Iowa 250.
Ky.—Gill v. Sable Hide & Fur Co., 4 S.W.2d 676, 223 Ky. 679.
N.C.—**Corpus Juris Secundum cited in** Cook v. City of Winston-Salem, 85 S.E.2d 696, 701, 241 N.C. 422.
45 C.J. p 996 note 70.
Care commensurate with risk
Where defendant's mother-in-law was over seventy years old, had suffered a stroke, walked with a shuffling gait and was afflicted with "barrel" or "tunnel" vision, mother-in-law had a duty to exercise a degree

of care for her own safety which would be commensurate with risk involved.
Wis.—Cordula v. Dietrich, 101 N.W. 2d 126, 9 Wis.2d 211.
22. Me.—McCullough v. Lalumiere, 166 A.2d 702, 156 Me. 479.
Md.—Fenneman v. Holden, 22 A. 1049, 75 Md. 1.
45 C.J. p 996 note 72.
Care required to avoid injury to deaf person see supra § 12.
23. Wash.—Hamlin v. Columbia, etc., R. Co., 79 P. 991, 37 Wash. 448.
45 C.J. p 996 note 73.
24. Cal.—**Corpus Juris cited in** Jones v. Bayley, 122 P.2d 293, 297, 49 C.A.2d 647—**Corpus Juris cited in** Armstrong v. Day, 284 P. 1083, 1086, 103 C.A. 465.
Me.—McCullough v. Lalumiere, 166 A. 2d 702, 156 Me. 479.
45 C.J. p 997 note 74.
25. Cal.—**Corpus Juris cited in** Jones v. Bayley, 122 P.2d 293, 297, 49 C. A.2d 647.
Conn.—Kerr v. Connecticut Co., 140 A. 751, 107 Conn. 304.
45 C.J. p 997 note 75.
26. Cal.—**Corpus Juris cited in** Cloud v. Market St. Ry. Co., 168 P.2d 191, 194, 74 C.A.2d 92—**Corpus Juris cited in** Emery v. Los Angeles R. Corporation, 143 P.2d 112, 115, 61 C. A.2d 455.
Ga.—Southland Butane Gas Co. v. Blackwell, 88 S.E.2d 6, 211 Ga. 665, conformed to 88 S.E.2d 424, 92 Ga. App. 288.
Idaho.—**Corpus Juris cited in** Geist v. Moore, 70 P.2d 403, 409, 58 Idaho 149.
Kan.—Townsend v. Jones, 331 P.2d 890, 183 Kan. 543.

PRACTICE TIP
Your research is never finished until you have checked the pocket parts.

citation
A reference to legal authorities and precedents used to fortify the propositions advanced by the writer of the document.

Use of artificial aids required

Due care for a blind person includes a reasonable effort to compensate for his unfortunate affliction by the use of artificial aids for discerning obstacles in his path.

Pa.—Davis v. Feinstein, 88 A.2d 695, 370 Pa. 449.

This sounds like exactly the sort of authority you have been looking for. You will want to read *Davis,* and the **citations** show you where to go to find it. In *Davis,* you will find research tools, in particular key numbers, that will help you discover other similar authority (perhaps in your own state). We discuss key numbers in more detail later, under "Case Law."

Are you finished with the encyclopedia? Emphatically, *no.* You are *never* finished with any research source until you have made sure you have gotten right up-to-date. If you turn to the back of this volume of C.J.S., you will find another pocket part. Like other supplements, it contains pertinent material that appeared after the bound volume was published.

You use it by turning to "Negligence § 142," the same place you found pertinent material in the bound volume (see Exhibit 6.4). Under an entry for page 173 and footnote 19, another case is shown, *Argo v. Good Co.,* that deals with the use of artificial aids by a blind person.

In our example, the index referred you repeatedly to the same section, "Negligence § 142," and we have followed it through the pocket part. Sometimes the index refers you to two or more sections in the encyclopedia. When it does, *read them all,* bound volume and pocket part both, before you leave the encyclopedia. That way, if the first encyclopedia section you chose does not lead you to anything useful, you need not return to the encyclopedia.

Now that you have finished with the encyclopedia, where do you go from here? Well, you have a couple of cases to read, cases that you know deal with the responsibility of a person with defective sight to compensate by using an artificial aid. You may want to read those cases first. Or, you may choose to follow up on that key number you found under "Library References" right up in the front of "Negligence § 142." We choose to follow up the key number first. To do that, we use a **digest.**

digest
Volumes organized by subject containing paragraph summaries (called headnotes) at the beginning of an opinion or point of law within that opinion which are primarily used as case finders.

Digests

A digest collects—by subject—a summary of each legal point arising in each reported case that is listed in the digest by its key number.

You first decide which digest to use. There is one general digest, covering the entire United States. But it is cumbersome to use, because it has so many entries. Therefore, it is better to begin with a more limited digest, usually the one covering your own state, or the federal courts, if your case is in the federal system. There is also a digest for the United States Supreme Court, and one for most of the geographical regions into which West divides its reporter system.

Key numbers. Sometimes you will already have a key number when you begin research in a digest. If you have one, simply turn to that topic and number in the appropriate digest and begin. You will find a series of paragraphs, each describing a point of law discussed in an appellate opinion. You will need to read each little paragraph under your key number to decide which of these cases is pertinent to your

EXHIBIT 6.4   *Excerpt from Pocket Part for 65A CJS § 142*

§ 141   NEGLIGENCE

65A CJS 20

Page 171

However, it has also been held that the standard of care to be used in determining whether a mentally deficient person is contributorily negligent is the same standard of care as is required of an ordinarily careful person under the same circumstances.[2.10]

2.10 Ariz.—Galindo v. TMT Transport, Inc., App., 733 P.2d 631, 152 Ariz. 434.

3. N.Y.—Young v. State Dept. of Social Services, Dept. of Mental Hygiene, 401 N.Y.S.2d 955, 92 Misc.2d 795.

Okl.—Warner v. Kiowa County Hospital Authority, App., 551 P.2d 1179.

A mentally deficient person can be incapable of negligent conduct only where he or she is so functionally incapacitated as to be incapable of negligence as a matter of law.[3.5]

3.5 Wis.—Burch v. American Family Mut. Ins. Co., App., 492 N.W.2d 338, 171 Wis.2d 607, review den. 494 N.W.2d 211.

§ 142.   Persons Under Physical Disability

page 172

6. Ind.—C.J.S. quoted at length in Memorial Hospital of South Bend, Inc. v. Scott, 300 N.E.2d 50, 58, 261 Ind. 27.

Iowa—Chevraux v. Nahas, 150 N.W.2d 78, 260 Iowa 817.

7. La.—King v. Investment Equities, Inc., App., 264 So.2d 297.

N.Y.—Schreiber v. Philip & Morris Restaurant Corp., 268 N.Y.S.2d 510, 25 A.D.2d 262, affd. 226 N.E.2d 537, 19 N.Y.2d 786, 279 N.Y.S.2d 730.

8. Ill.—Borus v. Yellow Cab Co., 367 N.E.2d 277, 9 Ill.Dec. 843, 52 Ill.App.3d 194.

10. N.H.—Perry v. Fredette, 261 A.2d 431, 110 N.H. 114.

Infirmities of old age

La.—Garner v. Crawford, App., 288 So.2d 886.

11. U.S.—Sterling v. New England Fish Co., D.C.Wash., 410 F.Supp. 164.

Ala.—Shepherd v. Gardner Wholesale, Inc., 256 So.2d 877, 288 Ala. 43.

N.H.—Mutterperl v. Lake Spofford Hotel, Inc., 216 A.2d 35, 106 N.H. 538.

Wis.—Merkley v. Schramm, 142 N.W.2d 173, 31 Wis.2d 134.

12. Ill.—C.J.S. quoted in Atchley v. Berlen, 461 N.E.2d 1177, 1179, 42 Ill.Dec. 468, 87 Ill.App.3d 61.

page 173

19. Pa.—Argo v. Good Co., 53 Del.Co. 275.

20. Ala.—Shepherd v. Gardner Wholesale, Inc., 256 So.2d 877, 288 Ala. 43.

§ 143.   Intoxicated Persons

26. Ga.—Shuman v. Mashburn, 223 S.E.2d 268, 137 Ga.App. 231, 85 A.L.R.3d 741.

Ill.—Dursch v. Fair, 209 N.E.2d 509, 61 Ill.App.2d 273.

Ky.—Harlow v. Connelly, App., 548 S.W.2d 143.

La.—Vaughn v. Cortez, App., 180 So.2d 796.

Neb.—Webber v. City of Omaha, 211 N.W.2d 911, 190 Neb. 678.

page 174

26.5. Alaska—Wilson v. City of Kotzebue, 627 P.2d 623.

Ga.—Shuman v. Mashburn, 223 S.E.2d 268, 137 Ga.App. 231, 85 A.L.R.3d 741.

Ill.—Dezort v. Village of Hinsdale, 342 N.E.2d 468, 35 Ill.App.3d 703, 79 A.L.R.3d 1199, app. after remand 396 N.E.2d 855, 33 Ill.Dec. 328, 77 Ill.App.3d 775 and 441 N.E.2d 367, 65 Ill.Dec. 454, 109 Ill.App.3d 976.

N.J.—Tiger v. American Legion Post No. 43, 311 A.2d 179, 125 N.J.Super. 361.

Rule not applicable where evidence insufficient

La.—Barlow v. City of New Orleans, App., 228 So.2d 47, affd. 241 So.2d 501, 257 La. 91—C.J.S. cited in Barlow v. City of New Orleans, 241 So.2d 501, 505, 257 La. 91.

27. U.S.—Guss v. Jack Tar Management Co., C.A.La., 407 F.2d 859.

La.—C.J.S. cited in Lee v. Peerless Ins. Co., 183 So.2d 328, 330, 248 La. 982.

N.Y.—Rodak v. Fury, 298 N.Y.S.2d 50, 31 A.D.2d 816.

N.C.—Brower v. Robert Chappell & Associates, Inc., 328 S.E.2d 45, 74 N.C.App. 317, review den. 335 S.E.2d 313, 314 N.C. 537.

28. U.S.—Lambert v. Ford Motor Co., D.C.Ga., 46 F.R.D. 46.

Ill.—Dezort v. Village of Hinsdale, 342 N.E.2d 468, 35 Ill.App.3d 703, 79 A.L.R.3d 1199, app. after remand 396 N.E.2d 855, 33 Ill.Dec. 328, 77 Ill.App.3d 775 and 441 N.E.2d 367, 65 Ill.Dec. 454, 109 Ill.App.3d 976.

Md.—Quinn Freight Lines, Inc. v. Woods, 292 A.2d 669, 266 Md. 381.

Neb.—Webber v. City of Omaha, 211 N.W.2d 911, 190 Neb. 678.

N.Y.—Coleman v. New York City Transit Authority, 332 N.E.2d 850, 37 N.Y.2d 137, 371 N.Y.S.2d 663.

Voluntary drunkenness ordinarily constitutes contributory negligence

N.J.—Anslinger v. Martinsville Inn, Inc., 298 A.2d 84, 121 N.J.Super. 525.

29. Ill.—French v. City of Springfield, 283 N.E.2d 18, 5 Ill.App.3d 209.

Tex.—Hemmenway v. Skibo, Civ.App., 498 S.W.2d 9, err. ref. no rev. err.

§ 144.   Children

page 175

33. U.S.—Howland v. Sears, Roebuck & Co., C.A.Ohio, 438 F.2d 725.

Fla.—Sparks v. Casselberry Gardens, Inc., App., 227 So.2d 686.

Ind.—Smith v. Diamond, App., 421 N.E.2d 1172, 32 A.L.R.4th 43.

Mo.—Bollman v. Kark Rendering Plant, 418 S.W.2d 39.

Or.—Grant v. Lake Oswego School Dist. No. 7, Clackamas County, 515 P.2d 947, 15 Or.App. 325.

34. La.—Freeman v. Wilcox, App., 303 So.2d 840, writ den. 307 So.2d 630.

36. Colo.—Kushnir v. Benson, App., 520 P.2d 134.

Ill.—Mack v. Davis, 221 N.E.2d 121, 76 Ill.App.2d 88.

Kan.—Gerchberg v. Loney, 576 P.2d 593, 223 Kan. 446.

La.—Bruno v. Fontan, App., 338 So.2d 713, writ ref. 341 So.2d 895.

Va.—Sullivan v. Sutherland, 143 S.E.2d 920, 206 Va. 377.

No distinction is made between charging a minor with negligence or with contributory negligence.[37.5]

37.5. N.H.—Hamel v. Crosietier, 256 A.2d 143, 109 N.H. 505.

§ 145.   ——— Age at Which Contributory Negligence is Chargeable

37.50. Kan.—Talley v. J & L Oil Co., Inc., 579 P.2d 706, 224 Kan. 214.

N.C.—Welch v. Jenkins, 155 S.W.2d 763.

38. Ark.—Sherman v. Mountaire Poultry Co., 419 S.W.2d 619, 243 Ark. 301.

Ga.—Mitchell v. Cox, 190 S.E.2d 154, 126 Ga.App. 151.

La.—Babin v. Zurich Ins. Co., App., 336 So.2d 900, cert. den., Sup., 339 So.2d 847.

Ohio—Parker v. Hansen, 217 N.E.2d 706, 6 Ohio App.2d 214.

Child over age

Kan.—Talley v. J & L Oil Co., Inc., 579 P.2d 706, 224 Kan. 214.

page 176

39. Ind.—Wozniczka v. McKean, 247 N.E.2d 215, 144 Ind.App. 471.

40. U.S.—Echevarria v. U.S. Steel Corp., C.A.Ind., 392 F.2d 885.

La.—Outlaw v. Bituminous Ins. Co., App., 357 So.2d 1350, writ den., Sup., 359 So.2d 1293.

Mo.—Bollman v. Kark Rendering Plant, 418 S.W.2d 39.

Okl.—Warner v. Kiowa County Hospital Authority, App., 551 P.2d 1179.

Tex.—Molina v. Payless Foods, Inc., Civ.App., 615 S.W.2d 944.

41. U.S.—Drayton v. Jiffee Chemical Corp., D.C.Ohio, 395 F.Supp. 1081.

Md.—Palms v. Shell Oil Co., 332 A.2d 300, 24 Md. App. 540.

N.M.—Sanchez v. J. Barron Rice, Inc., 427 P.2d 240, 77 N.M. 717.

42. Ga.—Jones v. Jones, 168 S.E.2d 883, 119 Ga. App. 788—Carter v. Brannon, 178 S.E.2d 755, 122 Ga.App. 812.

Ill.—Cusick v. Clark, 360 N.E.2d 160, 4 Ill.Dec. 413, 45 Ill.App.3d 763.

Md.—Mulligan v. Pruitt, 223 A.2d 574, 244 Md. 338.

Mich.—Snider v. Jennings, 161 N.W.2d 594, 11 Mich. App. 562.

Mo.—Woods v. Gould, App., 515 S.W.2d 592.

43. Cal.—Bauman v. Beaujean, 53 Cal.Rptr. 55, 244 C.A.2d 384.

Ga.—Harris v. Hardman, 212 S.E.2d 883, 133 Ga.App. 941.

Ill.—Rios v. Sifuentes, 347 N.E.2d 337, 38 Ill.App.3d 128.

La.—Schexnayder v. Zurich Ins., App., 257 So.2d 764.

Mich.—Robinson v. Russ, 226 N.W.2d 848, 58 Mich. App. 27.

N.Y.—Yun Jeong Koo v. St. Bernard, 392 N.Y.S.2d 815, 89 Misc.2d 775.

Tenn.—Cleghorn v. Thomas, 432 S.W.2d 507, 58 Tenn. App. 481.

Va.—Shelton v. Mullins, 147 S.E.2d 754, 207 Va. 17.

Under strict liability dog-bite statute

Ohio—Ramsey v. King, 470 N.E.2d 241, 14 Ohio App.3d 138, 14 O.B.R. 154.

page 177

44. Ariz.—Vigue v. Noyes, 550 P.2d 234, 113 Ariz. 237.

Ky.—Brown v. Wilson, 401 S.W.2d 77.

La.—Smith v. Trahan, App., 398 So.2d 572.

Wash.—Arnold v. Laird, 621 P.2d 138, 94 Wash.2d 867.

Under five years of age

Tex.—MacConnell v. Hill, Civ.App., 569 S.W.2d 524.

In the absence of evidence, etc.

The statement in Gottesman v. City of Cleveland which in effect makes freedom from contributory negligence of a child between the ages of four and five years dependent on the absence of evidence of his discretion and understanding to appreciate danger, has been disapproved, the court holding that a child under seven years of age is conclusively presumed incapable of contributory negligence.

Ohio—Holbrock v. Hamilton Distributing, Inc., 228 N.E.2d 628, 11 Ohio St.2d 185.

45. U.S.—Porter v. United Steel & Wire Co., D.C.Iowa, 436 F.Supp. 1376.

descriptive word index
A tool used in legal research when using a digest to lead you to other areas and case law.

graph under your key number to decide which of these cases is pertinent to your question.

If you find case summaries indicating some cases that might be on point for you, make a note of the citation to each case. Once you have finished with the digest, you will then read each of these cases. However accurate an editor may be, you must never, never rely on a digest summary of a case in doing your research. Read the case yourself. Only then can you assess the impact of the case, be sure you know all the facts, and fully understand the court's reasoning.

Sometimes you must consult a digest without already having a key number. In that case, you must find a key number before you can use the digest. You begin by turning to the **descriptive word index** to the digest. It works very much like any other index. Here is an example.

Suppose that your office has a client who has been charged by federal authorities with possession and manufacture of an illegal drug. Here is what happened:

> Government agents saw your client buying chemicals that could be used to make the illegal drug. Without a warrant, they stuck a magnetized tracking device—a "beeper"—under the fender of his car. Staying out of sight, they then followed him to the warehouse where the drug was made, by monitoring the transmissions from the beeper.

Your supervising attorney is considering a motion to exclude, or suppress, the evidence seized as a result of attaching the beeper to the client's car. You are to research the question. How do you get into the digest?

Our procedure is a little like the one we followed in finding information in C.J.S., the legal encyclopedia. Think a little about words and phrases that describe your problem. It may help to think about descriptive terms in the context of these general areas:

1. Parties to the case
2. Places and things involved in the case
3. The basis of the lawsuit, or the issue involved
4. Any defenses that might be raised
5. The relief one or both parties are seeking

What can we fit into each category?

1. *Drug-manufacturer,* maybe, or *drug-seller.* Neither is specific enough to give a high probability of help.
2. *Beeper,* or *electronic tracking device.* A very likely source of help.
3. *Motion to suppress evidence,* perhaps.
4. How about *illegal search and seizure?*
5. *Motion to suppress* might fit here, too.

Now that you have some descriptive words and phrases to work with, you have to select the proper digest.

Digests.   If you are working on a state problem, it is easy to find the proper digest. West produces a series of state digests, each of which collects and digests judicial opinions from a single state. If you find nothing helpful in the state digest, you may expand into a regional digest, corresponding to the regional reporters in which West prints judicial opinions.

If, for example, your case is in California, you will research in the *Pacific Digest,* because California falls within West's Pacific area. If your case is in Texas, you will use the *Southwestern Digest.* A regional digest will give you cases from nearby states. While this authority is not binding on courts of your state, it may be persuasive.

If your case deals with a federal question, you will probably use the *Federal Practice Digest.* There are several of these, and they are not cumulative, so you will start with the latest one. If you have a federal constitutional issue, you may decide to begin with the *Supreme Court Digest.*

Once you have chosen your digest, you simply run through its index the descriptive words and phrases you have chosen. In the example above, the question is a federal one, so you will use the *Federal Practice Digest.*

Now think back to the point when we had just finished using the legal encyclopedia. We chose at that point to go directly to the digest, using the key number we got from the encyclopedia. In the digest, we found more cases under the key number "Negligence 86." Because we found them under the key number that pertained to our subject, all the cases were relevant to our problem. Those cases cited other cases, and some of those we also read.

When we finished with the encyclopedia, we could have chosen to let the key number wait, and immediately read the two cases we found under footnote 19. Had we done so, we might have found other relevant case law cited in those two cases. We might also have found another relevant key number in a **headnote** to one of those cases: remember that these cases, too, have headnotes summarizing their important points, and each one of those headnotes has its own topic and key number.

After we had read the cases we found in the encyclopedia under footnote 19, we would have followed up what clues they gave us, run any new key number through the appropriate digest, and read any cited cases that looked good.

And so on. Research is an upside-down pyramid. A single case will lead you to a key number or another case. These will in turn give you more cases, which may lead you to more. Sometimes it is hard to find anything relevant to your problem—**on point,** as the lawyers say. At other times, you will be inundated in useful cases. Then you will have to carefully select the best cases, using the criteria set out under "Case Law."

Case Law

Case law—judicial opinions—is the heart of legal research and the most-used source of legal research. Generally speaking, case law consists of opinions written by appellate courts, like the United States or a state supreme court. Except in New York, written decisions by state trial courts virtually never appear in print. In the federal system, United States trial courts (the federal district courts) often write opinions that are published and form a valuable research source. In the legal profession, judicial opinions are generally called, simply, *cases.*

Something like 10,000 judicial opinions are approved for publication each year. Many others remain unpublished. Published opinions, the real meat of research, appear in sets of books called **reporters.** There are several types.

- *Official reporters.* Some jurisdictions, including the Supreme Court and about half the states, publish their own judicial opinions. Because they are produced or endorsed by the government, the reporters in which these opinions appear are called *official.* Some other states once had official reporters of their own, but have since ceased publication.
- *Unofficial reporters.* These reporters are published by private publishers, and are the main sources for your research. The text of the opinion is of course the same in both official and unofficial reporters. But the unofficial reporters also

headnote
A brief paragraph summary, located at the head or beginning of the opinion, of the points or issues decided in the case.

on point
Or "on all fours," means the facts and issues of the opinion are the same as or substantially similar to your client's.

reporters
The books that contain the opinions written by the courts.

PRACTICE TIP

Occasionally, you
will come across a
case in which the
court has written its
own syllabus at the
beginning of the
opinion. Since it
was written by the
court and not
West's editors, you
may quote from it.

◼ PRACTICE TIP

Case law is useful in deciding what the law is and what a court will do when faced with a certain question in a particular scenario. Simply put, you use case law to reason from what courts
have done, to what they would *now* do under similar circumstances.

contain a number of research tools in addition to the text of the opinion. The
official reporters do not have these, and that is why you will prefer the unofficial reporters in your research. We discuss these research tools next.

The major publisher of unofficial judicial opinions is West Publishing Company,
the only firm to cover all jurisdictions in the United States. West calls its reporting
apparatus the National Reporter System, and it works like this.

Headnotes.   A judicial opinion released by its court for publication is considered by
a West editor, who extracts from the case its salient legal points. The editor then
writes a one-sentence synopsis of each point of law, called a *headnote*. The editor
then decides where each headnote fits in West's outline of the law, and assigns it the
appropriate *topic* and *key number*. Remember that the key number is formed from
the name of the topic under which the subject fits, plus a number indicating the subheading to which it relates.

**case synopsis,
syllabus**
A brief statement sum-
marizing the rulings of a
court opinion which,
unless written by the
court itself, constitutes
no part of the court's
opinion but is prepared
by the publisher for the
convenience of the
reader.

The Case Synopsis.   The West editor also writes a short **case synopsis,** or **syllabus**—a brief summary of what happened in the action. This, together with the
headnote or headnotes, is inserted ahead of the text. The completed job looks like
the one shown in Exhibit 6.5.

The Headnote Numbering System.   Notice in Exhibit 6.5 that the headnotes are
numbered 1 through 5, just before the topic and key number. When you read
through the text of the opinion itself, you will come to [1] in brackets at the start of
a paragraph—it tells you that you are at the beginning of discussion of the material
summarized in headnote 1.

This numbering feature is very helpful, especially in a long case. You may be
interested only in the point of law discussed in a single headnote out of many. To read
what the court said about that point without wading through the rest of the opinion,
you can skim down the text until you come to the appropriate headnote number in
brackets. If, for example, only the material in headnote 11 is of use to you, read the
facts of the case to understand it, then skim down to [11] in the text to read about
the point important to your research.

Headnote numbers have one other important use, which we will talk about when
we come to *Shepard's Citator.* For now, just remember that when you find a case that
addresses the legal question you are trying to solve, *write down* the numbers of the
headnotes ([1], [2], [3] or whatever) that summarize the points important to you.

PRACTICE TIP

Choose those
cases closest to
your own on the
facts, and pick
cases decided as
recently as possi-
ble. Choose cases
decided by the
highest court in
your state, if there
are any.

The Criteria for Choosing Cases.   What kinds of cases, then, are most useful in pre-
dicting the answer to a legal question?

◼ *Cases from the jurisdiction in which the question arises.*   Obviously, in a ques-
    tion of Oklahoma law, you are much more interested in the position of the
    Oklahoma courts on that or similar questions than you are in what some New
    York court thinks about the same matter. Sometimes there is no local case law

EXHIBIT 6.5   *Asher v. Exxon Company, U.S.A.*

---

728 Mich.   **504 NORTH WESTERN REPORTER, 2d SERIES**

200 Mich.App. 635

**Farmer ASHER and Lucy Marie Asher,
his wife, Plaintiffs–Appellants,**

v.

**EXXON COMPANY, U.S.A., a Division
of Exxon Corporation, a Foreign
Corporation, Defendant–Appellee,**

and

**Product–Sol, Inc., a Michigan Corpora-
tion, U.S. Industrial Lubricants, Inc., a
Foreign Corporation, Chemical Solvents Inc., a Foreign Corporation, 3M
Company, a Foreign Corporation, Tech-
no Adhesives Company, a Foreign Corporation, and Dubois Chemicals, Inc.,
Jointly and Severally, Defendants.**

Docket No. 140366.

Court of Appeals of Michigan.

Submitted March 10, 1993, at Detroit.

Decided July 19, 1993, at 9:25 a.m.

Released for Publication Sept. 23, 1993.

Case Synopsis →

Employee who was allegedly injured as
result of his exposure to toxic chemical
manufactured by defendant sued to recover on products liability theory, and the Circuit Court, Wayne County, John H. Gillis,
Jr., J., granted manufacturer's motion for
summary disposition on statute of limitations grounds. Employee appealed. The
Court of Appeals, Holbrook, J., held that:
(1) continuing-wrongful-acts doctrine did
not toll period of limitations on employee's
products liability action until date of employee's most recent exposure to chemical
manufactured by defendant, and (2) employee failed to establish that he was suffering from any "mental derangement"
such as would prevent limitations from
running.

*Digest Topic &
Key Number*

Affirmed.

1. Limitation of Actions ⚿95(4)

Cause of action for damages arising
out of tortious injury to person accrues, for
limitations purposes, when all of the ele-

ments of cause of action have occurred and
can be alleged in proper complaint.

2. Limitation of Actions ⚿95(4.1)

Products liability cause of action accrues when plaintiff knows or should have
known of injury, and not at time of exposure to product or at time of diagnosable
injury.

3. Limitation of Actions ⚿55(6)

Continuing-wrongful-acts doctrine did
not toll statute of limitations on products
liability action arising out of employee's
exposure to toxic chemicals in workplace
until employee's most recent exposure to
product manufactured by defendant, given
employee's admission, at time he first developed symptoms of illness, that he believed his symptoms were caused by chemicals he used at work.

4. Limitation of Actions ⚿74(1)

Employee who allegedly experienced
some memory loss and difficulty in finding
his way around employer's plant as result
of his exposure to chemical manufactured
by defendant failed to establish that he
was suffering from "mental derangement"
such as would toll statute of limitations on
his products liability action. M.C.L.A.
§ 600.5851. ←   *— Statutes
                         Construed*

5. Limitation of Actions ⚿74(1)

Mere fact that employee was able to
work was not dispositive of whether he
was suffering from any "mental derangement" such as would toll statute of limitations on his products liability action against
chemical manufacturer. M.C.L.A. § 600.-
5851.

See publication Words and Phrases
for other judicial constructions and
definitions. ←   *— Words &
                          Phrases
                          Construed*

Mark Granzotto, Detroit and Jerome G.
Quinn, Bloomfield Hills, for plaintiffs-appellants.

Dykema Gossett by Joseph C. Basta,
Kathleen McCree Lewis, and Darleen Dar-
nall, Detroit, for defendant-appellee. ←   *— Attorneys*

Continued

EXHIBIT 6.5   *—Continued*

ASHER v. EXXON CO.   Mich.   **729**
Cite as 504 N.W.2d 728 (Mich.App. 1993)

Judges ———▶ Before GRIBBS, P.J., and HOLBROOK, and NEFF, JJ.

HOLBROOK, Judge.

In this products liability case, the circuit court granted defendant Exxon Company, U.S.A., summary disposition under MCR 2.116(C)(7). Plaintiffs appeal as of right. We affirm.

Farmer Asher (plaintiff) worked for General Motors Corporation from February 10, 1966, to May 15, 1987. Plaintiff's work involved cleaning glue residue from the walls and floors of spray booths. During the course of plaintiff's employment at
Complete Text ——▶ General Motors, he was exposed to various
of Opinion industrial adhesives and cleaning solvents manufactured and sold by Exxon Company, U.S.A. (defendant) and other defendants. Plaintiff used one of these products, "Fab cleaner," throughout his tenure at General Motors. Defendant's product, 587 Naphtha, was first sold to General Motors in July of 1985 for use as a component of Fab cleaner.

Plaintiff initially avoided going to a doctor because he did not want to be placed on sick leave and suffer reduced income. Dr. Jerry Walker first treated plaintiff in December of 1979 for chronic rhinitis, anxiety, boils, and breathing difficulty. Walker diagnosed that these conditions were caused by plaintiff's exposure to chemicals at his workplace.

During the 1980s, plaintiff began to experience memory loss, difficulty finding his way around the General Motors plant, and chronic lethargy. Plaintiff failed to heed Walker's advice to find a different job. In May of 1987, Walker declared plaintiff permanently disabled. Plaintiff and his wife filed their complaint on April 18, 1989.

Defendant moved for summary disposition under MCR 2.116(C)(7), arguing that plaintiffs' complaint was not filed within the period of limitation. The other defendants joined in defendant's motion. After plaintiffs had settled with all six other de-

fendants, the circuit court heard oral arguments regarding the motion. Defendant argued that plaintiff knew of his claim for several years by the time he began using Fab cleaner containing 587 Naphtha in July of 1985 because he knew from the onset of his first symptoms that the chemicals were a possible cause of his illness. Defendant argued that plaintiff had three years from the date of his first exposure to its product in July of 1985 to file timely his cause of action. Plaintiff responded that the complaint was filed timely because he was continuously subjected to defendant's tortious conduct through plaintiff's last day of employment with General Motors on May 15, 1987. Alternatively, plaintiff argued that the period of limitation had been tolled because he had been suffering from mental derangement. The circuit court found that plaintiff was not mentally deranged because he was able to work and function. The circuit court then granted defendant summary disposition.

When reviewing a motion for summary disposition under MCR 2.116(C)(7), this Court accepts all well-pleaded allegations as true and construes them most favorably to the plaintiff. *Bonner v. Chicago Title Ins. Co.,* 194 Mich.App. 462, 469, 487 N.W.2d 807 (1992). If the pleadings show that a party is entitled to judgment as a matter of law, or if affidavits or other documentary evidence show that there is no genuine issue of material fact, the trial court must render judgment without delay. MCR 2.116(I)(1); *Nationwide Mutual Ins. Co. v. Quality Builders, Inc.,* 192 Mich. App. 643, 648, 482 N.W.2d 474 (1992). If no facts are in dispute, the court must decide as a matter of law whether the claim is statutorily barred. *Harris v. Allen Park,* 193 Mich.App. 103, 106, 483 N.W.2d 434 (1992).

It is undisputed that the period of limitation for a products liability action is three years. M.C.L. § 600.5805(9); M.S.A. § 27A.5805(9). The issue [1] presented in

1. In *Scott v. Monroe Co. Bd. of Road Comm'rs,* unpublished opinion per curiam of the Court of Appeals, decided November 8, 1989 (Docket Nos. 108566, 108567), lv. vacated 438 Mich. 869,

474 N.W.2d 592 (1991), this Court rejected the argument that the products liability statute of limitations began to run on the date of the

504 N.W.2d—17

EXHIBIT 6.5   —*Continued*

730 Mich.   **504 NORTH WESTERN REPORTER, 2d SERIES**

this case is whether the continuing-wrongful-acts doctrine tolls the period of limitation in a products liability action until the time of the most recent exposure to the product.

M.C.L. § 600.5827; M.S.A. § 27A.5827 provides:

> Except as otherwise expressly provided, the period of limitations runs from the time the claim accrues....

> [T]he claim accrues at the time the wrong upon which the claim is based was done regardless of the time when damage results.

[1] A cause of action for damages arising out of tortious injury to a person accrues when all the elements of the cause of action have occurred and can be alleged in a proper complaint. *Connelly v. Paul Ruddy's Equipment Repair & Service Co.*, 388 Mich. 146, 150, 200 N.W.2d 70 (1972). Under the discovery rule, an action for products liability accrues when the plaintiff discovers or should have discovered a possible cause of action. *Bonney v. Upjohn Co.*, 129 Mich.App. 18, 35, 342 N.W.2d 551 (1983).

In *Defnet v. Detroit*, 327 Mich. 254, 258, 41 N.W.2d 539 (1950), our Supreme Court held that continuing wrongful acts occurring within the period of limitation prevent the accrual of an action in trespass. Since then, the continuing-wrongful-acts doctrine has been applied to other claims. See, e.g., *Moore v. Pontiac*, 143 Mich.App. 610, 614, 372 N.W.2d 627 (1985) (nuisance); *Sumner v. Goodyear Tire & Rubber Co.*, 427 Mich. 505, 510, 398 N.W.2d 368 (1986) (civil rights). Plaintiffs argue that the continuing-wrongful-acts doctrine should apply to products liability actions for personal injury damages.

[2, 3] In *Larson v. Johns–Manville Sales Corp.*, 427 Mich. 301, 304–305, 399 N.W.2d 1 (1986), our Supreme Court held in part that a cause of action for asbestosis accrues in accordance with the discovery rule rather than at the time of the exposure to asbestos or at the time of diagnosable injury. A products liability cause of

action accrues at the time a person knows or should have known of the injury and not at the time of exposure to the product or at the time of diagnosable injury. *Stinnett v. Tool Chemical Co., Inc.*, 161 Mich.App. 467, 472–473, 411 N.W.2d 740 (1987), citing *Larson.* The Court in *Stinnett, supra* at 473, 411 N.W.2d 740, further held that the plaintiff's claim was barred by the statute of limitations because he failed to file his complaint within three years after he knew or should have known of the injury. Consequently, a cause of action for products liability accrues when the plaintiff discovers, or through the exercise of reasonable diligence should discover, an injury and its likely cause. *Mascarenas v. Union Carbide Corp.*, 196 Mich.App. 240, 244, 492 N.W.2d 512 (1992), citing *Moll v. Abbott Laboratories*, 192 Mich.App. 724, 731, 482 N.W.2d 197 (1992). Accordingly, we conclude that the accrual of a products liability action is determined by reference to the discovery rule. Thus, the continuing-wrongful-acts-doctrine does not toll the period of limitation in a products liability action until the most recent exposure to the product. Rather, the period of limitation in a products liability case begins to run when the plaintiff discovers, or through the exercise of reasonable diligence should discover, an injury and its likely cause. At that time, all the elements of the cause of action have occurred and can be alleged in a proper complaint. *Connelly, supra.*

In this case, plaintiff admitted that at the time he first developed symptoms of illness in the late 1970s, he believed that his symptoms were caused by the chemicals he used at work. Plaintiff's first exposure to defendant's product occurred in July of 1985. Like in *Stinnett, supra*, and *Mascarenas, supra* at 246, 492 N.W.2d 512, the circuit court in this case could have relied on plaintiff's own statements to find his cause of action barred. We agree with defendant that plaintiff had three years from July of 1985 to file a claim. Because plaintiffs' complaint was filed after July of 1988, it was barred by the statute of limitations.

plaintiff's last exposure to toxic substances in   the workplace.

PRACTICE TIP

A writer "distinguishes" a case by showing the reader essential differences between that case and another.

directly addressing the question you must answer. Even so, there may be cases from whose facts you can reason to a conclusion. Choose those cases closest to your own on the facts, and pick cases decided as recently as possible. Choose cases decided by the highest court in your state, if there are any.

- *Cases from outside the jurisdiction.* If you must use opinions from outside your own jurisdiction, rely on cases decided on facts as near to your own as possible. They are not binding on your court, but they may be persuasive. If your scenario includes local statutory law, then try, when you can, to use cases that also deal with a reasonably similar statute. Choose those best reasoned and most recently decided. But remember that just because a case is "old" does not mean it is worthless as authority.

Be very careful to choose cases for their closeness to your own on the facts and their similarity to your own situation. Do not use them just because they come out the way your client would like his case to come out. If there is law both pro and con on your question, you need to show both sides.

Unfavorable law does not go away if you ignore it. When you write a memo, your duty to your attorney and your client is to be absolutely Olympian and unbiased. You have the duty to tell your client he or she does not have a case, if that is the way the law comes out, regardless of whether the client likes it.

If you are writing a brief for the court, you have the ethical duty to inform the court of the existence of contrary law, regardless of whether the other side has found that law. You can certainly argue that it should not influence the case—"**distinguish** it," as the lawyers say—but you have to tell the court it is there, and what it held.

So, when you research, choose the influential cases not for their partisan value but for their closeness on the facts, the power of their reasoning, and the other facts we have just talked about.

As one of the criteria for choosing cases, we mentioned a preference for more recent decisions. But that alone is not a good reason for relying on a case, if it is not very close to your own on the facts. It is much better to use an older case closely similar to your own. You may even *prefer* an older case because it is very close on the facts, and it is well reasoned. Especially is this so if the opinion is a so-called "**seminal case**," an opinion cited repeatedly and with approval in subsequent decisions.

The Advance Sheets. Now we have talked about reporters, those series of solemn-looking books that enshrine (some say embalm) judicial opinions forever. It takes a while to publish them, of course. But how do you find new law just handed down? Well, aside from computer-assisted legal research, you rely on what the professional calls **advance sheets.**

An advance sheet is not a sheet at all; it is a paper pamphlet that collects the most recent opinions in advance of the bound, hardcover reporters. When the bound volume arrives from the publisher, the advance sheets are thrown away.

Each reporter series has one or more of these sheets on the shelf, following the last bound volume. They have all the same research tools as the bound volumes, such as headnotes and key numbers. They remain on the shelf until the publisher decides there are enough of them to collect into yet another hardcover volume.

Some courts publish—officially—what are called **slip opinions,** flimsy paper prints of new opinions. A good example is the Supreme Court of the United States, whose opinions always appear first in this form. These are among the earliest forms in which you may read a new opinion. The others are printouts in the loose-leaf services and, of course, the WESTLAW and LEXIS computer legal research systems.

distinguish

To point out an essential difference; to prove a case cited as applicable or inapplicable.

seminal case

An opinion cited repeatedly and with approval in subsequent decisions.

advance sheet

A pamphlet containing the most recently reported opinions of specific courts or the courts of several jurisdictions.

slip opinion

An individual court opinion published separately shortly after it is "handed down," or rendered, by the court.

EXHIBIT 6.6   *United States Supreme Court Slip Opinion*

SUPREME COURT OF THE UNITED STATES

Syllabus

BOWERS, ATTORNEY GENERAL OF GEORGIA
v. HARDWICK ET AL.

CERTIORARI TO THE UNITED STATES COURT OF APPEALS FOR THE ELEVENTH CIRCUIT

No. 85–140.   Argued March 31, 1986—Decided June 30, 1986

After being charged with violating the Georgia statute criminalizing sodomy by committing that act with another adult male in the bedroom of his home, respondent Hardwick (respondent) brought suit in Federal District Court, challenging the constitutionality of the statute insofar as it criminalized consensual sodomy. The court granted the defendants' motion to dismiss for failure to state a claim. The Court of Appeals reversed and remanded, holding that the Georgia statute violated respondent's fundamental rights.

Held: The Georgia statute is constitutional.   Pp. 3–9.

Exhibit 6.6 shows the first page of a Supreme Court slip opinion.

Some new opinions can also be found in privately printed loose-leaf publications. An example is *U.S. Law Week,* a letter-size periodical that comes already punched for a three-hole binder. It appears weekly, and gives you the full text of new Supreme Court opinions and important new opinions from certain other courts. Many state opinions are printed first (or only) in a state bar periodical, like the *Oklahoma Bar Journal.* Depending on local practice, some of these opinions may never be printed anywhere else, but still have the full force of law.

The Statutes

Increasingly, our lives are controlled by statutory law passed at all levels: national, state, and local. The most important of these are United States and state statutes that are passed, amended, and repealed in vast numbers every year. Fortunately, they are labeled and printed in an orderly fashion, usually according to what is called the **code system.** We shall illustrate that system by exploring the federal statutory scheme.

The Federal Statutory Scheme.   Here is a short review of the legislative process. A bill may originate in either house of the Congress, except for money bills, which must come from the House of Representatives. If a bill survives the tortuous process of committee hearings and is signed by the President, it becomes law. When that happens it receives a **Public Law number,** which looks something like this: 92–179. The number means that it is the 179th public law to come out of the 92nd Congress. It is first separately printed on flimsy paper, and called a **slip law.**

New federal statutes are also printed in a set called *United States Code Congressional and Administrative News* (USCCAN). It is published monthly while

---

PRACTICE TIP

A *code* is a collection of laws or rules that have been classified by subject matter. Before statutes are "codified," they are organized chronologically. After codification, statutes are organized by subject matter.

code system
A system that labels and prints statutes by subject matter rather than in chronological order.

Public Law number
The number assigned to a law identifying the Congress from which the law came and the law's number.

slip law
A legislative enactment that is promptly published in a pamphlet or in single sheets after it has been passed into law.

Congress is in session, and prints all new laws in full. It also includes—and here is USCCAN's greatest value—reprints of the most important congressional committee reports on the legislation. These reports give you some insight into the *intent* of the Congress in passing this particular legislation. Some new laws that are thought to be particularly important also appear in *U.S. Law Week.*

The first hardbound collection of new federal legislation is called the *Statutes at Large,* and publishes new laws in order of passage. It has a rudimentary index—not very complete and not intended to be so. The *Statutes at Large* is not normally a fruitful research source, since a statute in one volume may well have been amended or repealed in a subsequent volume or volumes, and the index is next to useless. But it does contain useful tables showing amendments and repeals in the annotated code.

Even so, the *Statutes at Large* can be useful, especially when you are researching a statute just passed and not yet codified (see below) in permanent form. Even when enough time has passed that a new law has been encoded in permanent form, a *Statutes at Large* citation can lead you into the permanent statutory collection. Tables in West's *United States Code Annotated* (U.S.C.A.) cite the *Statutes at Large* by date of enactment, chapter, volume, and beginning page, like this:

Act of June 25, 1948, ch. 646, 62 Stat. 954.

codify
To collect and systematically arrange by subject matter the laws, rules, or regulations of a particular geographic location, or a certain area of the law.

Fortunately, federal law is **codified,** meaning that for permanent reference, federal law is arranged by subject matter, in a series of subdivisions called **titles.** Each title is devoted to a certain subject matter: Title 10, for instance, deals with the Armed Forces. That way, each section of each title can be kept up to date, reflecting changes made in it from time to time. This statutory collection is called the *United States Code* (U.S.C.), and is officially printed by the United States government.

titles
A unit or part of a statute, usually one of its major subdivisions devoted to a certain subject matter.

The U.S.C.A.   As with much case law, however, the most useful statutory collection is unofficial. It is published by West, and is called the *United States Code Annotated* (U.S.C.A.). It is updated regularly, both by pocket part and separate paperback supplement, and contains a number of useful research tools not found in the official code. Your research will be done in U.S.C.A. Let us look at a page from it (see Exhibit 6.7).

EXHIBIT 6.7   *Excerpt from West's Lawyer's Guide to U.S.C.A.*

§ 1915.   Proceedings in forma pauperis

(a) Any court of the United States may authorize the commencement, prosecution or defense of any suit, action or proceeding, civil or criminal, or appeal therein, without prepayment of fees and costs or security therefor, by a person who makes affidavit that he is unable to pay such costs or give security therefor. Such affidavit shall state the nature of the action, defense or appeal and affiant's belief that he is entitled to redress.

An appeal may not be taken in forma pauperis if the trial court certifies in writing that it is not taken in good faith.

Subsections (b) to (e) omitted in this example

June 25, 1948, c. 646, 62 Stat. 954; May 24, 1949, c. 139, § 98, 63 Stat. 104; Oct. 31, 1951, c. 655, § 51(b, c), 65 Stat. 727; Sept. 21, 1959, Pub.L. 86–320, 73 Stat. 590; Oct. 10, 1979, Pub.L. 96–82, § 6, 93 Stat. 645.

SOURCE: Reprinted from *West's Lawyer's Guide to U.S.C.A.* Copyright by West Publishing Company.

Examine this page. First you see the section's number and short title:

§ 1915. Proceedings in forma pauperis

Next you see the actual text of Section 1915. We have omitted subsections (b) through (e) for this example.

Below the actual statute, you are given some history, that is, the origins of § 1915. Here is part of that history:

June 25, 1948, c. 646, 62 Stat. 954;
May 24, 1949, c. 139, §98 63 Stat. 104;

And so on. Here is a translation: This section was originally enacted June 25, 1948, and appeared in chapter 646, volume 62 of the *Statutes at Large,* page 954. The first amendment to the section was made May 24, 1949, and is contained in chapter 139, section 98, volume 63 of the *Statutes at Large,* page 104.

Complicated? Not really. To find the original enactment, just pull down volume 62 of the *Statutes at Large.* Now, open that volume to page 954; eh, voila!

Now, since we have talked about the research tools you find in the unofficial version of the federal code (U.S.C.A.), let's take a look at them.

First, you will come to an **Historical Note** that will give you a brief summary of how the present section came to look the way it does, including notes about what each amendment added or changed. Exhibit 6.8, for example, contains an Historical Note from 21 U.S.C.A. § 881 that deals with forfeiting property connected with illicit drug transactions.

Second, you will normally find a bold subheading called **Cross References** that leads you to different but related sections of the Code.

Next, and very useful, is a subheading called **Library References.** Library References lead you to other reference materials within the West system. Here is a sample:

Drugs and Narcotics § 191. C.J.S. Drugs and Narcotics § 141.

The first reference is a *topic* and *key number.* With it, as you now know, you can pull down any digest and use the key number to find cases dealing with the subject matter treated in this statutory section.

The second reference is to the legal encyclopedia *Corpus Juris Secundum.* In section 141 of C.J.S., Drugs and Narcotics you can read about the area this code section deals with, and maybe pick up a useful case or two.

Finally, and the most important, you will find another black-letter subheading called **Notes of Decisions.** This section gives you little synopses (like headnotes) of cases that have interpreted this statute. Lawyers call this process of interpretation *construing* the statute. There are often several of these Notes of Decisions, sometimes so many that they are collected in groups according to their subject matter.

For example, the Notes of Decisions following § 1915—printed in full here—are broken down into three major subdivisions:

Notes of Decisions
  I. GENERALLY 1-30
 II. PRACTICE AND PROCEDURE 31-80
III. APPEAL 81-123

historical note
The first research tool found in the unofficial version of the federal code, U.S.C.A., that briefly summarizes how the present section got to look the way it does, including notes about what each amendment added or changed.

cross reference
The second research tool found in the unofficial version of the federal code, U.S.C.A., which will lead to different but related sections of the Code.

library reference
The third research tool found in the unofficial version of the federal code, U.S.C.A., which leads to other reference materials within the West system.

notes of decisions
The fourth and final research tool found in the unofficial version of the federal code, U.S.C.A., that provides short synopses—like headnotes—of cases that have interpreted this statute.

EXHIBIT 6.8 *Historical Note from U.S.C.A.*

10. Suppression of evidence

Where inspection of defendant's premises was conducted following issuance of inspection warrant under this section, inspection was limited to administrative inspection and was conducted in accordance with this section, any matters revealed by such inspection were not subject to suppression in criminal proceeding. U. S. v. Prendergast, D.C.Pa.1077, 436 F.Supp. 931, affirmed 585 F.2d 69.

Where subsequent statements made by defendant were directly related to information gathered by Drug Enforcement Agency compliance officers as result of illegal search of defendant's pharmacy, defendant was entitled to suppression of such statements. U. S. v. Enserro, D.C. N.Y.1975, 401 F.Supp. 460.

§ 881. Forfeitures

Property subject

(a) The following shall be subject to forfeiture to the United States and no property right shall exist in them:

(1) All controlled substances which have been manufactured, distributed, dispensed, or acquired in violation of this subchapter.

(2) All raw materials, products, and equipment of any kind which are used, or intended for use, in manufacturing, compounding, processing, delivering, importing, or exporting any controlled substance in violation of this subchapter.

(3) All property which is used, or intended for use, as a container for property described in paragraph (1) or (2).

(4) All conveyances, including aircraft, vehicles, or vessels, which are used, or are intended for use, to transport, or in any manner to facilitate the transportation, sale, receipt, possession, or concealment of property described in paragraph (1) or (2), except that—

(A) no conveyance used by any person as a common carrier in the transaction of business as a common carrier shall be forfeited under the provisions of this section unless it shall appear that the owner or other person in charge of such conveyance was a consenting party or privy to a violation of this subchapter or subchapter II of this chapter; and

(B) no conveyance shall be forfeited under the provisions of this section by reason of any act or omission established by the owner thereof to have been committed or omitted by any person other than such owner while such conveyance was unlawfully in the possession of a person other than the owner in violation of the criminal laws of the United States, or of any State.

(5) All books, records, and research, including formulas, microfilm, tapes, and data which are used, or intended for use, in violation of this subchapter.

(6) All moneys, negotiable instruments, securities, or other things of value furnished or intended to be furnished by any

EXHIBIT 6.8 — *Continued*

Ch. 13   DRUG ABUSE PREVENTION   **21 § 881**

tivators are unknown, or which are wild growths, may be seized and summarily forfeited to the United States.

(2) The failure, upon demand by the Attorney General or his duly authorized agent, of the person in occupancy or in control of land or premises upon which such species of plants are growing or being stored, to produce an appropriate registration, or proof that he is the holder thereof, shall constitute authority for the seizure and forfeiture.

(3) The Attorney General, or his duly authorized agent, shall have authority to enter upon any lands, or into any dwelling pursuant to a search warrant, to cut, harvest, carry off, or destroy such plants.

Pub.L. 91–513, Title II, § 511, Oct. 27, 1970, 84 Stat. 1276; Pub.L. 95–633, Title III, § 301(a), Nov. 10, 1978, 92 Stat. 3777; Pub.L. 96–132, § 14, Nov. 30, 1979, 93 Stat. 1048.

Historical Note

References in Text. "This subchapter", referred to in text, was in the original "this title" which was Title II of Pub.L. 91–513, Oct. 27, 1970, 84 Stat. 1242, and is popularly known as the "Controlled Substances Act". For complete classification of Title II to the Code, see Short Title note set out under section 801 of this title and Tables volume.

"Subchapter II of this chapter", referred to in subsec. (a)(4)(A), was in the original "title III", meaning Title III of Pub.L. 91–513, Oct. 27, 1970, 84 Stat. 1285. Part A of Title III comprises subchapter II of this chapter. For classification of Part B, consisting of sections 1101 to 1105 of Title III, see Tables volume.

The criminal laws of the United States, referred to in subsec. (a)(4)(B), are classified generally to Title 18, Crimes and Criminal Procedure.

The Supplemental Rules for Certain Admiralty and Maritime Claims, referred to in subsec. (b), are set out in Title 28, Judiciary and Judicial Procedure.

The customs laws, referred to in subsec. (d), are classified generally to Title 19, Customs Duties.

Schedules I and II, referred to in subsecs. (f) and (g)(1), are set out in section 812(c) of this title.

Codification. "Drug Enforcement Administration" was substituted for "Bureau of Narcotics and Dangerous Drugs"

in subsec. (e)(4) to conform to congressional intent manifest in amendment of section 802(4) of this title by Pub.L. 96–132, § 16(a), Nov. 30, 1979, 93 Stat. 1049, now defining term "Drug Enforcement Administration" as used in this subchapter.

1979 Amendment. Subsec. (d). Pub.L. 96–132 substituted "The provisions" for "All provisions", and struck out "and the award of compensation to informers in respect of such forfeitures" following "compromise of claims".

1978 Amendment. Subsec. (a)(6). Pub.L. 95–633, § 301(1), added par. (6).

Subsec. (e). Pub.L. 95–633, § 301(a)(2), (3), struck out of cl. (2) provisions relating to use of proceeds of sale and added provision relating to the forwarding by the Attorney General of money and proceeds remaining after payment of expenses.

Effective Date. Section effective Oct. 27, 1970, see section 704(b) of Pub.L. 91–513, set out as an Effective Date note under section 801 of this title.

Legislative History. For legislative history and purpose of Pub.L. 91–513, see 1970 U.S.Code Cong. and Adm. News, p. 4566. See, also, Pub.L. 95–633, 1978 U.S. Code Cong. and Adm.News, p. 9496; Pub. L. 96–132, 1979 U.S.Code Cong and Adm. News, p. 2003.

Cross References

Contraband articles, including narcotic drugs, seizure and forfeiture of carriers transporting, see section 781 et seq. of Title 49, Transportation.

Narcotic drug defined, see section 787 of Title 49.

Just below these subdivisions, you will see an alphabetically arranged list of the subheadings under which Notes of Decisions for this section are arranged. Exhibit 6.9 is a sample.

EXHIBIT 6.9   *U.S.C.A. Excerpt*

Absence of
    Good faith on appeal 106
    Meritorious claim on appeal 107
Affidavit
    Generally 32
    Allegation of citizenship 33
    Attorney 37
    Fraudulent 34
    Habeas corpus proceedings 109
    Interested parties 38
    Merits 35
    Necessity of 36
    Poverty 39
    Sufficiency 40
    Time for 41
    Poverty on appeal 99
Allegation of citizenship, affidavit 33
Allowance of appeal 102–104
    Generally 102
    Good faith 103
    Meritorious claim 104
Appeal 81–123
Appointment of counsel 48
    On appeal 118
Attorney, affidavit of 37
Burden of proof 46
    Appeal 115
Certificate of trial court 93–98
    Generally 93
    As denial of leave to appeal 94
    Conclusiveness of 97
    Lack of 95
    Necessity of 96
    Setting aside 98
Conclusiveness of certificate of trial court 97
Constitutionality 1
Construction 2, 3
    With other laws 3
Costs 55
Counsel 48–50
    Appointment of 48
    Appointment on appeal 118
    Fee or allowance 49
    Security by 50
Courts applicable 6
Decisions applicable 86–90
    Extension of time 90
    Necessity of notice of appeal 87
    Perfection of appeal or record 88
    Time to appeal 89
Discretion of court 8
Dismissal 54
Dismissal of appeal 105–107

Generally 105
    Absence of good faith 106
    Absence of meritorious claim 107
Dismissal of habeas corpus petition on appeal 112
Duty of court 9
Evidence 116
    Sufficiency of 47
Extension of time, decisions applicable 90
Fee or allowance of counsel 49
Fraudulent affidavit 34
    On appeal 101
Good faith of appeal 103
Grant of petition 43
Habeas corpus proceedings 108–113
    Generally 108
    Affidavit 109
    Court in which made 110
    Dismissal of 112
    Merit of action 111
Indigent, rights of 85
In propria persona 114
Interested parties, affidavit of 38
Judicial notice 45
Lack of certificate of trial court 95
Law governing 5
Mandamus as remedy 91
Merit of action, habeas corpus proceedings 111
Merits, affidavit of 35
Meritorious claim on appeal 104
Moot questions 113
Nature of right
    Privilege 10
    Statutory 11
Nature of right to appeal
    Privilege 83
    Statutory 82
Necessity of
    Affidavit 36
    Certificate of trial court 96
    Notice of appeal, decisions applicable 87
Parties 31
    On appeal 84
Perfection of appeal or record, decisions applicable 88
Petition
    Generally 42
    Grant of 43
Poverty, affidavit of 39
Power of court 7
Practice and procedure 31–80
Prepayment of costs 121

SOURCE: Reprinted from *United States Code Annotated*. Copyright by West Publishing Company.

Sometimes a code section has been construed so little that there is no need for major divisions in the Notes of Decisions. In that case, you will find only a series of alphabetically arranged headings.

In addition to the main index, there may also be a **subdivision index** for each of the Roman-numeraled major divisions. Exhibit 6.10 is an index from the notes on Section 1915.

subdivision index
An index, in addition to the main index, for each of the major divisions (with Roman numerals).

EXHIBIT 6.10   *Section 1915—Notes of Decisions*

III. APPEAL
Subdivision Index

Generally 81
Absence of
    Good faith on appeal 106
    Meritorious claim on appeal 107
Affidavit, habeas corpus proceedings 109
Affidavit of poverty 99
Allowance of appeal 102–104
    Generally 102
    Good faith 103
    Meritorious claim 104
Appointment of counsel on appeal 118
Burden of proof 115
Certificate of trial court 93–98
    Generally 93
    As denial of leave to appeal 94
    Conclusiveness of 97
    Lack of 95
    Necessity of 96
    Setting aside 98
Conclusiveness of certificate of trial court 97
Counsel, appointment of 118
Decisions applicable 86–90
    Extension of time 90
    Necessity of notice of appeal 87
    Perfection of appeal or record 88
    Time to appeal 89
Dismissal of appeal 105–107
    Generally 105
    Absence of good faith 106
    Absence of meritorious claim 107
Dismissal of habeas corpus proceedings 112
Evidence 116
Extension of time, decisions applicable 90
Fraudulent affidavit 101
Good faith of appeal 103

Habeas corpus proceedings 108–112
    Generally 108
    Affidavit 109
    Court in which made 110
    Dismissal of 112
    Merit of action 111
Indigent, rights of 85
In propria persona 114
Lack of certificate of trial court 95
Mandamus as remedy 91
Merit of action, habeas corpus proceedings 111
Meritorious claim on appeal 104
Moot questions 113
Nature of right
    Privilege 83
    Statutory 82
Necessity of
    Certificate of trial court 96
    Notice of appeal, decisions applicable 87
Parties 84
Perfection of appeal or record, decisions applicable 88
Prepayment of costs 121
Privilege, nature of right 83
Questions for court 117
Record, right to 119
Rehearing 123
Remand 122
Setting aside certificate of trial court 98
Statutory nature of right 82
Sufficiency of affidavit 100
Time to appeal, decisions applicable 89
Transcript, right to 120
Writ of certiorari as remedy 92

SOURCE: Reprinted from *Notes of Decisions*. Copyright by West Publishing Company.

What do the actual Notes of Decisions look like? Exhibit 6.11 shows some, drawn from the Section of Title 21 dealing with forfeiture of property used in drug transactions.

Take a look at this subheading:

6. Transportation, concealment, etc. as grounds for forfeiture

The first extract under this subheading tells you generally what the court decided in a case called *United States v. One 1974 Cadillac Eldorado Sedan*. If this decision looks pertinent to the problem you are researching, you will read the case. Indeed, you *must* read the case. *Never* take somebody else's word for a case's facts, holding, or

PRACTICE TIP

Never assume that any writer's or editor's summary of an important case is correct. It usually is, but *you must decide for yourself. Read the case.*

EXHIBIT 6.11   *Title 21—Notes of Decisions*

Ch. 13   DRUG ABUSE PREVENTION   **21 § 881**

4. Purpose

A primary purpose of this section providing for forfeiture of conveyances used, or intended for use, to transport, or in any manner to facilitate transportation, sale, receipt, possession or concealment of contraband is to cripple illegal drug trafficking and narcotic activity by depriving narcotics peddlers of the operating tools of their trade. U. S. v. One 1972 Datsun, Vehicle Identification No. LB1100355950, D.C.N.H.1974, 378 F.Supp. 1200.

5. Property subject to forfeiture

Evidence which was received to support charge of unlawful acquisition of marihuana in violation of narcotics laws was "contraband" and not repleviable. Rea v. U. S., N.M.1956, 76 S.Ct. 292, 350 U.S. 214, 100 L.Ed. 233.

"Traditional or per se contraband" are objects the possession of which, without more, constitutes a crime, and claimant has no right to have per se contraband returned to him. U. S. v. Farrell, 1979, 606 F.2d 1341, 196 U.S.App.D.C. 434.

In absence of statutory authority, there is no basis for confiscation of derivative contraband merely because it is derivative contraband. Id.

Money used by defendant in attempt to purchase narcotics from undercover agent was used in unlawful manner as an instrumentality of crime, and thus it fell within category of derivative contraband for purposes of deciding defendant's claim for return of money following conviction for attempt to distribute heroin. Id.

Derivative contraband must be substantially and instrumentally connected with illegal behavior before such contraband is subject of forfeiture. U. S. v. One 1972 Datsun, Vehicle Identification No. LB1100355950, D.C.N.H.1974, 378 F.Supp. 1200.

There must be a substantially significant connection with criminal activity before an ordinary automobile may be seized and forfeited to government. Id.

6. Transportation, concealment, etc. as grounds for forfeiture

Forfeiture of vehicle used by party to illegal drug transaction did not depend upon accident of whether dope was physically present in vehicle, but vehicle's use to transport peddler or his confederates to scene of sale or to meeting where sale was proposed was sufficient. U. S. v. One 1974 Cadillac Eldorado Sedan, Serial No. 6L47S4Q407966, C.A.N.Y.1977, 548 F.2d 421.

Plain meaning of "to transport" as used in this section is simply to carry or convey from one place to another, and, this section being silent as to purpose for which the transportation is undertaken, no limitations such as limitation to commercial trafficking will be read into words used. U. S. v. One Clipper Bow Ketch Nisku, C.A.Mass.1977, 548 F.2d 8.

Forfeiture provisions are not limited to commercial trafficking, and it is not role of the courts to mitigate harshness of the statutes. Id.

This section does not limit forfeiture of vehicles to transportation situations, and where automobile was used to help sale of contraband, in that government informant paid another person for heroin while both were in the automobile, automobile was subject to forfeiture. U. S. v. One 1970 Pontiac GTO, 2-Door Hardtop, C.A.Cal.1976, 529 F.2d 65.

Intentional transportation or concealment of marijuana in a vehicle, no matter how small the amount, will subject the conveyance to forfeiture. U. S. v. One 1975 Chevrolet K–5 Blazer Vehicle No. CKY185F135794, D.C.Mich.1980, 495 F. Supp. 737.

Even the presence within vehicle of small amount of marijuana, strictly for personal consumption, will justify forfeiture of the vehicle. Id.

Uncontradicted testimony of three government witnesses established that truck was used to transport methamphetamine, justifying its forfeiture. U. S. v. One 1975 Ford Ranger XLT Serial No. F26YCV47607, D.C.Pa.1979, 463 F.Supp. 1389.

Aircraft which was found to be intended to be used to transport controlled substances in the future was subject to forfeiture and application of this section to such aircraft was constitutionally permissible. U. S. v. One 1945 Douglas (C–54–DC–4) Aircraft, D.C.Mo.1978, 461 F. Supp. 324 remanded on other grounds 604 F.2d 27.

Automobile which claimant was driving while carrying cocaine on his person and in which a suitcase containing traces of marijuana was found was subject to forfeiture as it has been used to "transport" controlled substances, even though only small amounts were found. U. S. v. One 1975 Mercury Monarch Serial No. 5E35L539729, D.C.N.Y.1976, 423 F.Supp. 1026.

Mere fact that there was an empty green suitcase, with a residue of marijuana, in trunk of vehicle in question was insufficient to support forfeiture of the vehicle on theory that it was intended to be used to transport marijuana away from a particular address to which four

629

PRACTICE TIP

When you are using WESTLAW or LEXIS to cite-check cases, we suggest that you also use WESTLAW's InstaCite, Shepard's Preview, and QuickCite or LEXIS' AutoCite to get the most up-to-date and comprehensive information available for that citation.

PRACTICE TIP

Always shepardize. There is never an excuse for failing to bring your research up to date.

reasoning. However reliable you find summaries in law books to be, there is no excuse for depending on them. The duty to read and decide is yours, and your supervising attorney expects you to have carefully read any case on which you base your research.

The citation tells you that the *1974 Cadillac* case was decided by a federal court of appeals (C.A.) and arose in New York (N.Y.). The citation is not a proper one, of course, nor is it intended to be. In *Bluebook* form, it would look like this:

United States v. One 1974 Cadillac Eldorado Sedan, 549 F.2d 421 (7th Cir. 1977).

This case may prove to be exactly the law you want. Whether it does or not, do not stop with *1974 Cadillac.* Go on through every division and subdivision of the Notes of Decisions that might contain useful case law. You have to read *every* one of these summaries under likely subheadings to be certain you have found all the pertinent cases summarized for this code section.

Now, turn to the pocket part (and separate supplement, if any) for this volume of the code, and consult the same headings and subheadings you have just been over. Read every case listed in these headings and subheadings to be sure you are up-to-date. Also in the pocket part, check the table of contents under your code section for Notes of Decisions, to see whether a new subheading has been added for the first time in the pocket part.

Remember *always* that with statutory research, as with research in every other area, you are never finished until you have gotten up-to-date. Check the pocket part and any separate paperback supplement, if there is one. Either pocket part or separate supplement may lead you to new decisions interpreting your code section, decisions handed down since publication of the hardcover volume. You may even find that the code section has been *amended* since the hardcover volume of U.S.C.A. was printed. However unlikely you think it is that anything new has appeared since the hardcover volume was printed, *check all the same.*

Shepard's Citator

For many legal professionals, **Shepard's Citator**[1] is the toughest research source to handle. To a few, it is and remains a mystery. But it is really not that complicated, and it can be your best friend.

The Reasons to Shephardize.   *Shepard's* is used for two important research purposes. First, a **citator** can help you find useful case law once you have found one good case. Simply put, *Shepard's* leads you to every subsequent case that has even mentioned the case you are researching. Since many of these later cases will deal with the same legal point your case did, they may be helpful in solving your research problem.

Shepard's Citator
The most widely used set of citators, it provides, through letter-form abbreviations or words, the subsequent judicial history and interpretation of reported decisions; it also denotes the legislative and amendment history, and cases that have cited or construed, constitutions, statutes, rules, regulations, etc.

citator
A research book containing lists of references or cites to help you assess the current validity of a case, statute, or other law and to provide leads to additional laws.

---

[1] *Shepard's Citations* (4th ed.). Colorado Springs, CO: Shepard's/McGraw-Hill, Inc., 1987.

sheparizing
The process of determining the subsequent history of a particular case and how subsequent cases have cited or interpreted a particular case.

overrule
An opinion is overruled when a later decision, rendered by the same court or by a superior court, expresses a judgment on the same question of law directly opposite to that which was given before, thereby depriving the earlier opinion of all authority as a precedent.

The process of running your case or cases through the *Shepard's* system is called **sheparizing** in the trade.

The second major use of *Shepard's* is to help you keep your job. Running a case—or a statute—through *Shepard's* will tell what has happened to it since it was handed down. A case that once was good law may have been reversed on appeal. Or, a subsequent case may have **overruled** your case, perhaps many years after it was first decided. Relying on a case that has been overruled, especially in arguing to the court, is the quickest way to acquire massive amounts of egg on your face, and maybe get yourself fired or your attorney sued for malpractice.

Always sheparize, both your authority and the opposition's. Remember, the other side gets tired too, and may forget to sheparize something they file with the court. It is your duty to check any case or other authority on which the opposition relies, on the chance they are relying on something that is no longer good law. Make sheparizing automatic practice, done without fail.

How to Sheparize. Let us run a case through *Shepard's* by way of example. We shall use *Thompson v. State,* 451 P.2d 704 (Nev. 1969). *Thompson* is reported officially in Nevada's own reporter, in addition to the regional Pacific Reporter. Its *official* citation is 85 Nev. 134. Although, as you know, your research will be done almost exclusively in the regional, unofficial reporters, this official citation will prove useful to you when the time comes to sheparize.

When you look at the library shelf on which *Shepard's* sits, you may be overwhelmed by the number of thick red volumes confronting you. Nearly every jurisdiction requires more than one volume—the basic book plus one or more supplements published to update the basic book. On top of those are one or more paper supplements, giving the most recent *Shepard's* entries. Where on earth do you start?

You can begin with the first volume of *Shepard's* in which your case appears and work forward to the latest supplement. But as a practical matter, most researchers prefer to begin with the most recent *Shepard's*—the paperback supplement. On the front of the most recent one of those (they are all dated), smack in the middle of the cover, is a black box in which you are told which *Shepard's* books ought to be on the library shelves. Exhibit 6.12 is a sample from *Shepard's Pacific Reporter Citations,* the one you will use to sheparize the *Thompson* case.

EXHIBIT 6.12 *What Your Library Should Contain*

WHAT YOUR LIBRARY SHOULD CONTAIN

1987 Bound Volume, Cases (Parts 1-5)*
1987 Bound Volume, Statutes (Parts 1 and 2)*
1987-1990 Bound Supplement (Parts 1 and 2)*
1990-1991 Bound Supplement*
*Supplemented with:
  —*April, 1992 Annual Cumulative Supplement Vol. 86 No. 8*
  —*February, 1993 Cumulative Supplement Vol. 87 No. 6*
  —*March, 1993 Advance Sheet Vol. 87 No. 7*
Subscribers to Shepard's Illinois EXPRESS Citations should retain the latest blue-covered issue.

SOURCE: Reproduced by permission of Sheperd's McGraw-Hill, Inc. Further reproduction is strictly prohibited.

Now you can open up the supplement, and read the table that tells you which citations are included in the volume (see Exhibit 6.13).

EXHIBIT 6.13   *Table of Citations Included*

THE CITATIONS INCLUDED IN THIS VOLUME (PARTS 1–5)
APPEAR IN

Pacific Reporter, Second Series, Vols. 1–725
United States Supreme Court Reporter, Vols. 282–469
Lawyers' Edition, United States Supreme Court Reports, Vols. 75 LE–91 LE
Supreme Court Reporter, Vols. 51–106
Federal Reporter, Second Series, Vols. 50–799
Federal Supplement, Vols. 1–640
Federal Rules Decisions, Vols. 1–110
Bankruptcy Reporter, Vols. 1–63
Claims Court Reporter, Vols. 1–9
Military Justice Reporter, Vols. 1–22
Atlantic Reporter, Vols. 155 At–515 A2d
California Reporter, Vols. 1–229
New York Supplement, Vols. 251 NYS–505 NYS2d
Northeastern Reporter, Vols. 177 NE–497 NE
Northwestern Reporter, Vols. 237 NW–392 NW

SOURCE: Reproduced by permission of Sheperd's McGraw-Hill, Inc. Further reproduction is strictly prohibited.

Now open up the citator itself, and track down the *Thompson* case. To trace *Thompson's* history, you need to turn to the correct page. You find that page by turning until you see the *volume number* of *Thompson* at the top of the page. As Exhibit 6.14 shows, *Thompson* is in volume 451 of the *Pacific Reporter,* Second Series (P.2d).

Now, having found the number of the volume containing your case, you look (in Exhibit 6.14 p. 132) down the black-letter numbers below it until you find number 704, the *starting page* of *Thompson.*

What follows looks a little like it came from the wall of an Egyptian tomb, doesn't it? But it is easy to read.

First you see a set of symbols in parentheses. They stand for 85 Nev. 134, the official citation to *Thompson.* Any time you find a citation in parentheses in *Shepard's,* it is a **parallel citation,** the same opinion in the same case, but in a different reporter. Parallel citations are shown in *Shepard's,* but *only* in the first volume in which your case appears.

Next comes any subsequent appellate history of *Thompson.* Here an attempt was made to get the United States Supreme Court to review the case. The attempt was unsuccessful, as the citation indicates: "US cert den in 396 US 893." The High Court declined to review the case (denied **certiorari**) in a decision reported in 396 U.S. 893.

Next you find an abbreviated citation to any case that cited *Thompson.* First come cases reported elsewhere in the *Pacific Reporter,* followed by Supreme Court cases, then by other federal cases collected by the federal circuit from which they come.

After that you find citations to any state cases that cited *Thompson,* designated by their unofficial citations and arranged alphabetically by state. Finally, *Shepard's* gives you citations to other sources that are also mentioned in *Thompson.* Here, last in the

parallel citation
A citation reference to another set of books or reporters in which the same case—word for word—can be located.

certiorari
A Latin word meaning "to be informed of"; most commonly used to refer to supreme courts, which use the writ of certiorari as a discretionary devise to choose the cases they wish to hear.

EXHIBIT 6.14 *Volume 451 of P.2d*

Vol. 451　　　　　　　　　　PACIFIC REPORTER, 2d SERIES

492P2d¹458
496P2d¹879
f 507P2d⁴1008
542P2d¹418
546P2d¹45
586P2d⁴208

—648—

Arizona
v Taylor
1969

(9AzA290)
452P2d⁶536
452P2d⁷536
458P2d³965
468P2d¹¹394
475P2d³295
e 481P2d⁹517
489P2d¹²875
490P2d¹27
490P2d²27
490P2d³27
509P2d⁷1072
546P2d⁶48
589P2d¹²14
643P2d⁷12
645P2d1256
707P2d953
781P2d50
Alk
479P2d¹²335
552P2d¹⁴144
Ark
458SW139
94Æ352n
24Æ348n

—653—

Essex Wire
Corporation
of California
v Salt River
Project
Agricultural
Improvement
and Power
District
1969

(9AzA295)
453P2d¹³236
453P2d¹⁰369
479P2d¹³720
522P2d¹⁰779
622P2d⁷48
Tex
558SW861

—662—

Troxler v
Holohan
1969

(9AzA304)

Nev
528P2d⁸1022

—666—

Washington
v Holden
1969

(75Wsh2d413)
521P2d¹962
700P2d³767
851P2d682

—667—

Colella v
King County
1969

(75Wsh2d953)
s 433P2d154

—669—

Moore v
Mayfair
Tavern Inc.
1969

(75Wsh2d401)
468P2d⁷1013
478P2d²782
492P2d⁶1064
496P2d⁶531
500P2d¹⁴1280
503P2d⁷761
510P2d⁶1110
521P2d¹¹933
523P2d⁵198
523P2d⁶215
526P2d1232
538P2d⁵518
538P2d¹³1252
547P2d⁵1226
550P2d¹¹77
550P2d⁷1181
567P2d⁶641
567P2d⁷641
603P2d⁵843
780P2d²1315
780P2d¹1320
j 780P2d1325
814P2d229
827P2d⁶1032
Colo
780P2d⁴468
43Æ289n
43Æ315n
43Æ374n

—675—

Weld v Bjork
1969

(75Wsh2d410)
484P2d³488
521P2d³1219

613P2d³162
665P2d²412
665P2d³412
Pa
547A2d1216

—677—

Rivard v
Rivard
1969

(75Wsh2d415)
498P2d¹914
529P2d²487
529P2d¹488
617P2d707
792P2d¹1262
792P2d²1262
f 801P2d⁵261
Mont
623P2d¹1389
f 663P2d²331

—681—

McAlester
v Nave
1969

e 518P2d⁷⁻⁴313
560P2d⁶⁻²565
570P2d¹1167
572P2d¹989
591P2d³⁻304

—684—

Independent
School District
No. 4
Sequoyah
County v
Oklahoma
Board of
Education
1969

531P2d²⁻337
553P2d⁴⁻¹152
642P2d²⁻¹620
648P2d²⁻828
702P2d²⁻53
741P2d²⁻459
Ore
679P2d1353

—687—

Nisbet v
Midwest
Oil Corp.
1968

459P2d²591
459P2d³⁻591
463P2d²⁻³683
471P2d²905

471P2d³⁻905
500P2d⁴⁻³288
541P2d⁶⁻⁵198
633P2d²1275
Cir. DC
465F2d⁴⁻³565

—698—

Cassidy v
Harding
1969

488P2d³⁻1279
527P2d¹1368
527P2d²⁻1368
531P2d³⁻1366
535P2d³⁻692
549P2d²⁻77
590P2d⁵⁻¹200
590P2d¹1181
590P2d²⁻1181
620P2d⁵⁻¹922
638P2d⁵⁻¹474
771P2d240
793P2d³⁻311
f 829P2d26
829P2d³⁻29
Ariz
776P2d801

—700—

Jake's Casing
Crews Inc. v
Grant
1969

469P2d²245
470P2d²992
542P2d⁵⁻512
d 619P2d¹629
694P2d²939
755P2d⁵⁻660
782P2d¹911
804P2d²⁻²442

—704—

Thompson
v Nevada
1969

(85Nev134)
US cert den
in 396US893
455P2d⁵916
460P2d¹113
460P2d²113
460P2d⁵161
462P2d⁴762
464P2d¹501
f 467P2d¹109
471P2d⁴217
471P2d²217
471P2d⁷217
484P2d¹722
490P2d⁹1246
490P2d³1247
490P2d⁵1247

492P2d¹1308
492P2d²1308
492P2d³1309
492P2d⁵1309
498P2d⁴1311
498P2d⁷1312
498P2d⁵1313
538P2d⁹583
d 541P2d³527
d 541P2d⁴527
547P2d³671
d 554P2d¹272
h 600P2d³221
h 600P2d⁷221
604P2d⁵352
h 611P2d⁷207
643P2d⁸1226
801P2d²1375
j 406US704
413US¹302
413US⁶302
j 32LE427
37LE¹622
37LE⁶622
j 92SC1890
93SC¹2570
93SC⁶2570
Cir. DC
e 427F2d⁴612
461F2d¹99
j 461F2d¹112
j 461F2d⁷112
j 461F2d⁴150
Cir. 3
415F2d⁷162
329FS¹17
Cir. 6
338FS⁹895
Cir. 9
427F2d⁵1037
Ariz
498P2d⁸147
Calif
481P2d⁴216
93CaR⁴208
Colo
f 497P2d1251
Conn
288A2d85
Del
281A2d146
Ill
265NE637
265NE688
La
234So2d188
Md
283A2d428
Mass
282NE76
Mich
172NW548
194NW912
205NW475
N J
273A2d579
N Y
308NYS2d951

N C
175SE593
Ohio
265NE328
Va
191SE180
39Æ1005n

—708—

Brown v
Washoe County
1969

(85Nev149)
553P2d⁵421
f 555P2d¹492
f 555P2d⁵493
557P2d⁴1154
d 669P2d721
855P2d¹540
f 855P2d⁵541
N M
487P2d⁵914
Ore
604P2d³394
Fla
464So2d1286
N H
394A2d837
3Æ581n

—711—

Havas v Carter
1969

(85Nev132)
464P2d¹779
620P2d¹867
741P2d¹804
Ore
d 495P2d²1204
55Æ289n

—713—

Eagle Thrifty
Drugs &
Markets
Inc. v Hunter
Lake Parent
Teachers Assoc.
1969

(85Nev162)
s 443P2d608
530P2d¹1189
646P2d551
654P2d⁴1017
Cir. 9
385FS1134

---

column of citations for *Thompson,* you see a reference to 39 ALR3d 1005n. ALR3d stands for the third edition of the *American Law Reports,* which we discuss below. In this citation, 39 is the volume of the ALR3d, and 1005n means that *Thompson* is mentioned in a note at page 1005.

That is easy enough to understand. But what are all those other symbols in the *Thompson* entries? First are the letters that precede some citations. These all stand for the way a subsequent case has treated the case you are sheparding; they are all defined in a table at the front of every volume of *Shepard's.* The first one you see is an *f* before 467 P.2d 109. That means the later case "followed" *Thompson.* It therefore may be a case you will want to read. The next one down is a *d,* preceding 541 P.2d 527. That tells you the subsequent case (the one at 541 P.2d 527) "distinguished" *Thompson.* You will probably want to read that one too. You need not try to memorize all of *Shepard's* codes. They are conveniently summarized in the front of each *Shepard's* volume.

How about the tiny raised numbers just before the page numbers in the cites? Well, remember that we told you to write down the *headnote number* of the pertinent headnotes in any case that seemed useful to you? This is why. The first case in the column of cases that cited *Thompson* (455 P.2d 916) carries a tiny number 5 before the 916. The 5 tells you that the citing case dealt particularly with the material summarized in headnote 5 of *Thompson.* If that legal point is the one you are particularly interested in, then of course you will want to read the case cited as 455 P.2d 916 in *Shepard's.*

One more thing to remember about sheparding: The page given you by a citing reference is *not* the beginning page of the citing source. It is the page of the case or other source on which your case is *cited.*

Run each important case through every volume of *Shepard's* in which it appears, and you have achieved two things. First, you're sure that the case is still good law; if there has been some modification or qualification of it, at least you will know about it. Second, you will have found every subsequent case that cited yours, with some clue as to why.

Is that all? No. If you forget everything we tell you in this section on sheparding, remember this:

> When a case is reported both officially and unofficially, shepardize it through *Shepard's* for both official and unofficial reporters.

If you do not, you may miss some materials that have cited your case. By way of example, we shall shepardize *Thompson* through the *Shepard's* for the *Nevada Reports.* Exhibit 6.15 shows the appropriate excerpt from that *Shepard's.*

From the top, notice first the parallel citation, in parentheses: it is to 451 P.2d 704, the unofficial reporter we just shepardized. Next you see the same reference to subsequent appellate history. After that comes a line of cases that have cited *Thompson,* but this time listed by their *official* citations. After that you find the same citing federal cases you picked up when you shepardized the unofficial citation. Finally, you get the two references to A.L.R. and the one to C.L.C.P.

But notice there are no references to other state decisions; you had a lot of them in the *Shepard's* for P.2d. And there is another difference: See the reference to 72 McL 731. You check the table of abbreviations in the front of the *Shepard's* volume, and you find that means *Thompson* has been cited in volume 72 of the *Michigan Law Review,* on page 731.

EXHIBIT 6.15
Thompson v. Nevada, *from the Nevada Reports*

Nevada Reports

Vol. 85

– 134 –
(451 P2d 704)

US cert den in396US893 — 1

85Nev^{5}387
85Nev^{1}579
85Nev^{2}579
85Nev^{5}599
85Nev^{4}723
86Nev^{1}103
f86Nev^{1}206
86Nev^{7}502
86Nev^{4}503
87Nev^{1}215
87Nev^{3}556
87Nev^{5}556
87Nev^{9}556
88Nev^{1}22
88Nev^{2}22
88Nev^{3}22
88Nev^{5}23
88Nev^{4}372
88Nev^{7}373
88Nev^{5}375
91Nev^{9}502
d91Nev^{3}633
92Nev^{3}190
d92Nev^{1}519
h95Nev^{3}590
h95Nev^{7}590
96Nev^{5}16
f96Nev^{7}454
98Nev^{8}181 — 2

j406US704
413US^{1}302
j32L$\mathbb{E}$427
37L$\mathbb{E}$^{1}622
j92SC1890
93SC^{1}2570
Cir. CD
461F2d^{1}99
j461F2d^{1}112
j461F2d^{4}150
Cir. 3
415F2d^{7}162
e427F2d^{4}612
329FS^{1}17
Cir. 6
338FS^{9}895
Cir. 9
427F2d^{5}1037 — 3

72McL731 — 4

71A^{2}449s
39A^{3}1006n — 5

CLCP§6.03 — 6

annotation
Explanatory commentary designed to give the reader basic information on a statute, case, or regulation.

Now a brief word about annotations. An **annotation** is an article on some area of the law. They are found in a set of volumes called *American Law Reports.* A.L.R.s, as they are called, come in six sets, 1st through 5th and A.L.R. Federal. The publishers choose a current case because it addresses an important or new area of the law, and print the case verbatim, just like any other reporter. They add to it, however, a commentary, the annotation, written by someone learned in that area of the law.

The annotation addresses other cases in the same area, and generally analyzes the law across the nation. An annotation can be a good source of case law; you may not find anything in your own jurisdiction, but you may find a case on point from someplace else. That case will give you one or more key numbers, which you may then take to the digests for cases in your own jurisdiction.

There is a consolidated *descriptive word index* that will get you into A.L.R.s 2d, 3d, 4th, 5th, and Federal, as well as some annotations in *Supreme Court Reporter, Lawyer's Edition,* the only reporter of Supreme Court cases that also carries annotations.

You may also get into A.L.R. through *Shepards,* in one of two ways:

- If you find a good case and shepardize it, you may find a parallel citation (in parentheses) to A.L.R. That means your case was selected as the example, or lead case for the point of law to be explored in the accompanying annotation. You will obviously want to read that annotation, because it almost surely deals with the point of law for which you read the case in the first place.
- *Shepard's* may also lead you to A.L.R. by showing that your case was *cited* in an A.L.R. annotation. It is not the lead case, but it is mentioned. You may want to check that annotation, because it may very well be in the area you are exploring.

annotation history table
A table indicating whether an annotation has been superseded or supplemented.

Remember one critical thing about A.L.R. Before you ever read an annotation, no matter where you got a reference to it, *make sure it is the latest annotation.* You do this by going to the index and opening up the **Annotation History Table.** Look up the annotation you have found. The table will tell you if it has been superseded (many annotations have) or supplemented. If your annotation is not shown at all, you know it is the latest one.

■ RESEARCH HINTS

We said at the beginning of this chapter that this book is not a treatise on research. Since that is so, we shall go no further in discussing research, except to add a few hints in addition to the rules we have already given you.

First, remember that you have to understand a problem before you can adequately research it. That means talking to other legal professionals and using broad-range secondary sources. Of these, the legal encyclopedia is generally the best place to start. It gives you a clear discussion of the law in your area and furnishes you cases and key numbers as well. Treatises can also be useful in giving you a general understanding of the law pertaining to your problem, and even giving you a case or two.

Second, there are lots of "how-to" handbooks describing common research sources distributed by the publishers. They are uniformly excellent. Best of all, they are free. West, for example, publishes a small paperback called *Sample Pages,* which introduces you the workings of West's legal encyclopedia, digests, and United States Code Annotated. Like the other publisher's guides, *Sample Pages* is profusely illustrated, and takes you step-by-step through the process of using each research source.

Third, remember to *read the directions*. Most research sources have an introductory section that tells you what is in the source and how to dig it out. When you tackle a research source you have never used before, do not neglect to spend a few minutes in getting familiar with using it.

CHAPTER SUMMARY

Research is a painstaking process, and it can be frustrating. It will go more smoothly if you follow a few basic rules in every research job, whether simple or complex. Here are those helpful rules.

- Understand your problem before you begin research. Never hesitate to ask questions.
- Use the encyclopedias and treatises to learn generally about the law bearing on your problem, and to find a few judicial opinions to start with. Check the pocket parts for the latest law.
- Use the digest that most closely relates to the jurisdiction you are researching (e.g., for Oregon, the *Pacific Digest*). Go completely through the digest, including the pocket part, and cover all relevant key numbers.
- Read the cases thoroughly. *Never* be content with a headnote summary. Read the text of the case itself to see what the case really stands for.
- Use the headnotes from, and citations in, relevant cases to find more relevant cases.
- Remember that statutory law plays an ever-larger role in the law. Check the statutes early in your research.
- Your research is never complete until you have shepardized, bringing your research current to the last possible minute. Carefully check not only your research, but your opponent's, to see that it is valid and is the latest law on the subject.
- Never forget the value of legal periodicals. They can be a rich source of case and statute law, and will sometimes suggest a useful theory you can use in urging your client's case.
- Remember that loose-leaf services may be useful in researching a particular area, since they generally are kept quite current, and will often give you the latest judicial, administrative, and statutory law all in one place.
- Use the A.L.R.s to enhance your knowledge of a subject, as well as to find useful law. Remember to watch for A.L.R. parallel citations while shepardizing. If a case on point is the "lead opinion" in an annotation, you know that annotation will be especially useful.

KEY WORDS AND PHRASES

advance sheets	case law	citation	codify
annotation	case synopsis	citator	contributory negligence
Annotation History Table	certiorari	code system	Cross References

descriptive word index	legal periodical	pocket part	slip law
digest	Library References	primary authority	slip opinion
distinguish	mandatory authority	Public Law number	statutes
headnote	Notes of Decisions	reporters	subdivision index
Historical Note	on point	secondary authority	syllabus
key number	overrule	seminal case	title
legal authority	parallel citation	shepardizing	topic
legal encyclopedia	persuasive authority	*Shepard's Citator*	treatise

EXERCISES

A Walk-Through Problem

We will talk you through this problem. Take your book, and go to the library. At the library, follow along with us as we discuss the problem. Pull down the books as we tell you to. Look up what we tell you to find, and you will arrive at the solution. This problem will be done within the scenario of *Healy v. Allegretti & Sons.*

Your supervising attorney expects one defense for Allegretti to be that Raymond was not in the course and scope of his employment when he struck your client. Therefore, they will argue, he alone is responsible for your client's injuries. Since Raymond has neither assets nor insurance, a judgment against him will be worthless. You want to keep his employer in the case if possible; Allegretti is insured.

Your attorney has asked you to write a memorandum exploring these questions:

Was Raymond an employee of Allegretti at the time of the accident, and acting within the scope of his employment?

Think about how you will begin this research. The first thing you have to do is make certain you understand the meaning of the question you have been asked to solve. Assume that your attorney is in court, so you cannot slip up to her office and ask. You must find out for yourself.

Do you understand the legal meaning of the "master-servant" (employer-employee) relationship?

Do you understand what "scope of employment" means in the law? You are not sure. Good. *Never assume anything,* and be quick to admit that you are not sure about something. Remember always that other legal professionals do not expect you to know everything or be infallible—what they expect is full-time professionalism, and that includes asking when you are not sure.

Where, then, do you go to find out generally about the area in which you must research? How about an encyclopedia?

Down in the office library is C.J.S., *Corpus Juris Secundum.* Remember you can get into C.J.S. in a couple of ways. You can turn directly to the correct topic, if you are sure which one you want. Or, and usually, you can go to the big General Index at the end of the set, and look up alphabetically the descriptive words you think may fit your problem.

Now you have pulled down the General Index to C.J.S. What descriptive words would you use to get into C.J.S.? Always start with the simplest descriptive word or phrase. For example, if you are looking for information on a case in which your client slipped and fell on slippery mud at the entrance to the defendant's store, your descriptive words should include *mud* and *slip and fall.*

In your case, how about *employer-employee?*

When you look up *employer-employee* in the index, you find that **"EMPLOYER-EMPLOYEE RELATIONSHIP"** is a major topic in volume 30 of C.J.S. If you look down the list of index topics under **"EMPLOYER-EMPLOYEE RELATIONSHIP,"** you find a likely subtopic: "Liability for injuries to third persons, acts or omissions of employee." As you see, the index then refers you to § 181 and following in the topic **"EMPLOYER-EMPLOYEE RELATION-SHIP."**

As an alternative to running down a promising subtopic in the index, you could have pulled down volume 30 and turned to the "Analysis" on page 1, a sort of detailed table of contents. Running your finger through the analysis (you are now on page 2 of the analysis), you come to **"V. LIABILITY FOR INJURIES TO THIRD PERSONS."** Whichever route you took, you arrived at the same subpart, which seems likely to give you a start toward the answer to your question. Let us take a look at the pages of this topic.

V. LIABILITY FOR INJURIES TO THIRD PERSONS - A. ACTS OR OMISSIONS OF EMPLOYEE-

You find that under item A. there are two major subheadings:

2. Liability of Employer Based on his Contribution or Participation.
3. Liability of Employer Based on Doctrine of Respondeat Superior.

Your next step is to read through these sections and, when you have, you have an understanding of the two possible bases for the liability of Raymond's employer:

- Maybe he negligently selected Raymond for delivery of the transmission, knowing Raymond's fondness for the bottle and horrible driving record.
- Maybe he is liable under the old doctrine of *respondeat superior,* the responsibility of an employer for his employee's acts done in the "scope of employment."

Now you have a general understanding of the law you have to apply. But what is the precise law in your own state? After all, that is the law that matters, not what the general rules are. How do you go from the general to the particular?

To do that, you have to explore what the courts of your own state have said. That means you have to find and read the right appellate opinions. How do you find them? Let us assume that you are going to research Allegretti's possible negligence in choosing Raymond, and that your state is Texas. Begin reading now at section 186, starting on page 262. As you read on into the second column on the page, you come to this line:

The basis of responsibility under the negligent hiring doctrine is the master's own negligence in hiring an incompetent servant who the master or employer knew or should have known, *or by the exercise of reasonable or ordinary care should have known,* was incompetent or unfit. [Emphasis added.]

The emphasized line is followed by a footnote—50—and a glance at that footnote gives you a Texas case: *Arrington's Estate v. Fields.* That is a case you will want to read. Even if you read it and find it is not precisely on point, it may very well lead you to other Texas cases that will help you. In passing, note that the citation given in C.J.S. is **not** *Bluebook* style. While it gives enough information for you to find the case, it illustrates the rule that you *never* use a citation from any research book; the *Bluebook* is the only authority.

Sometimes, as we did here, you will find a useful case from your jurisdiction right in the encyclopedia. As we explained in our chapter on research, that case can lead you to more. You read it carefully first, of course, to make certain it is in the area you want. If it is, you can then take from its headnotes the *key numbers* that correspond with the points of law in which you are interested.

You can also pick up a useful key number from the encyclopedia itself. Look again at the beginning of **§ 186.** The first thing you see below the title of the section is the black-letter summary of the law laid out in the section. Just below that, you read this:

Library References
Master and Servant 303.

These key numbers will get you into the digests. Remember the function of a digest: It organizes cases by *subject matter,* whereas the reporters simply print opinions in rough chronological order. You get into the digest by using a key number, which you can find in any of three ways.

The first we have just discussed; you find a case on point, and take from it the key numbers beginning the headnotes that deal with the points you are researching. Second, you can use the index to the digest to run down key numbers by looking up descriptive words and phrases. Third, you can acquire the appropriate key number from another research source.

As you have just seen, one such place is in C.J.S. Remember it is part of the West system, so it will give you key numbers to lead you into other parts of the same system. Knowing this, you have jotted down key numbers as you read along. Remember always that the key "number" includes *both* words and numbers; the number alone will do you no good, because you will not know which topic it appears in.

Now turn to **§ 190** of C.J.S., and read about liability based on the doctrine of *respondeat superior* ("let the master answer"). One of the sections that will interest you is **§ 204.** Read through it. As you see, it deals with the stipulation of the doctrine that requires the employee's act be within the "scope of employment" before the employer can be responsible for it. As you read through this alternative theory of liability under *respondeat superior,* you acquire at least two more useful key numbers, **Master and Servant (1) and (2).**

Now you have your way to enter the digests. Your first step is to select the right digest. Let us assume the case occurred in Oklahoma: you will pull down the *Oklahoma Digest,* if you have it in the library. It deals entirely with Oklahoma cases (and federal court cases arising in Oklahoma) and thus is the quickest way to find Oklahoma law.

You find only a few entries under **303. Incompetency of Servant** in the Oklahoma digest. It does not take long to read the little summaries. Very quickly, you find this one:

> **Okl. 1980.** When recovery against employer for act of a servant is rested on prior knowledge of servant's propensity to commit very harm for which damages were sought, basis of liability invoked is not respondeat superior but rather employer's own negligence in not discharging unfit servant. 25 O.S. 1971, § 6.
>
> Dayton Hudson Corp. v. American Mut. Liability Ins. Co., 621 P.2d 1155
> 16 A.L.R.4th 1.

This case sounds useful, so you make a note of it. Notice three important things about the summary of *Dayton Hudson.* First, the citations are not correct according to the *Bluebook,* but the capsule contains all the information you need to put together a correct cite.

Second, notice the citation **16 A.L.R.4th 1.** Remember that when your case carries a citation not only to the regional reporter (P.2d) but also to A.L.R., it means that your case was the "lead case" to an annotation. You will recall that an annotation is

an article on a particular point of law, represented by a lead case. If your case is chosen to be that lead case, there is every chance that the annotation deals with the precise point of law for which you are using the case. That makes the annotation worth reading, or at least scanning, for whatever insight into the law it may give you.

Third, notice the reference to "25 O.S., 1971 § 6." This is a reference to Section 6, Title 25, of the Oklahoma Statutes. It tells you that Oklahoma has a statute that bears on this very question. If you have not already found it, you should read it immediately.

Now if you do not have access to the *Oklahoma Digest,* you would look in the *Pacific Digest,* because Oklahoma cases are included in West's Pacific area. Next, you choose the volume dealing with the topic "Master and Servant." Then simply open that volume to the key number you want, say, **Master and Servant 303,** and begin to read the little capsule descriptions of the cases. It might take a little longer to find *Dayton Hudson,* because the *Pacific Digest* covers a number of states, but you would surely find it, summarized exactly as it is in the *Oklahoma Digest.*

Whichever digest you use, you are never through until you consult the pocket part at the end of the volume, to be sure you are entirely up-to-date. Remember you use the pocket part just as you do the hardcover volume. In our example, once you have read through the case summaries in the main volume under **"Master and Servant 303,"** you will turn to the pocket part and read any case summary you find there under **"Master and Servant 303."**

Once you have culled the digests for useful cases, including the pocket part, you are ready to read the cases that seemed on point. Start with the cases that sound closest to your own. If there are lots of them, begin with the most recent ones.

A little at a time, you will sort out the cases that seem controlling or persuasive. At first, this process will seem a little frustrating, because you will not always choose the key number that precisely fits the subject you are researching. It gets easier with practice, and you can help yourself by reading over West's little paperback book called *Sample Pages.* It is free, and it gives you some useful examples of digest research.

When you find a case that is on point, make notes, including its citation. Also write down the numbers of the headnotes that deal with your subject (1, 2, 3, or whatever). Later on, you will run the cases you have found through *Shepard's.* There you may find references to later cases citing your case and paying special attention to points made in specific headnotes of your case. Obviously, those are the cases that will be most likely to help your research, since you know just by looking at *Shepard's* that they concentrate on the points most important to you.

Let us look at the first page from one of the cases you saw in the digest (see Exhibit 6.16).

A reading of the headnotes of *Dayton Hudson* tells you that the main thrust of the case deals with insurance coverage for punitive damages, that is, damages imposed on a defendant to *punish,* rather than to recompense the injured plaintiff. But it does make clear that the basis for liability of Allegretti is probably Allegretti's own negligence rather than the doctrine of *respondeat superior.* You learn this from **headnote 5.** Although the behavior of the employee in *Dayton Hudson* (false arrest of a customer) is different from Raymond's propensity for drunken driving, you may be able to draw a logical parallel between the two, establishing Allegretti's liability on the basis of its own negligence.

In any case, *Dayton Hudson* is worth making notes on. Jot down enough of its facts, so that you can clearly remember the case if you decide to include it in your memo. Make a note also of headnote 5—that way you can watch for it later when you shepardize *Dayton Hudson.*

Since Allegretti knew a good deal about Raymond's horrible driving record, and about his propensity to drink far beyond excess, your attorney might want to consider adding a request for punitive damages when you file the Complaint against Allegretti. Remember, however, that *Dayton Hudson* tells you the insurance company will not have to pay the punitive part of the judgment, only the actual damages suffered by your client.

Practicing Your Research Skills

We did the previous research problem with you. Now, on your own, go to the library, look up each of the research sources to which we direct you, and answer the question we pose for each source.

1. Find 10 U.S.C.A. § 1005. Then determine:
   a. The name of the cited title
   b. The general subject matter addressed by the section

2. Find 52 Okla.Stat.Ann. § 271. Then determine:
   a. The name of the cited title
   b. The general subject matter of the title
   c. The subject matter addressed by the section
   d. The *Bluebook* citation form for this statute.

3. Find the case reported in 566 P.2d 1104. Then:
   a. Abbreviate the title of the case as it would appear in a *Bluebook* citation.
   b. Find the name of the court that decided the case.
   c. Find the date on which the case was decided.
   d. Read the case and determine the principal *holdings* by the court.

4. Find the case reported in 793 F. Supp. 461. Then:
   a. Abbreviate the title of the case as it would appear in a *Bluebook* citation.
   b. Find the name of the court that decided the case.
   c. Find the date on which the case was decided.

5. Find the case reported in 593 F.2d 893. Then:
   a. Abbreviate the title of the case as it would appear in a *Bluebook* citation.
   b. Find the name of the lower court from which the appeal was taken.
   c. Find the name of the court deciding the case on appeal.
   d. State the disposition of the appeal by this court.

6. Find the case reported in 101 S.Ct. 970. Then:
   a. Abbreviate the title of the case as it would appear in a *Bluebook* citation.
   b. State the name of the lower court from which this appeal was taken.
   c. State the name of the justice who wrote the majority opinion.
   d. State the disposition of the appeal.
   e. Give the parallel citations to this opinion as it is reported in other Supreme Court reporters. [Hint: remember you can find parallel citations to any case in the *first* volume of *Shepard's* in which the case appears.]

7. Find 42 Okla. L. Rev. 459.
   a. State the full name of this publication. What kind of publication is it?
   b. Give the name of the author of the article.
   c. Give the title of the article.
   d. Give the date of publication for the volume.

EXHIBIT 6.16   *Dayton Hudson Corp. v. American Mut. Lia. Ins.*

DAYTON HUDSON CORP. v. AMERICAN MUT. LIA. INS.   Okl.   **1155**

Cite as, Okl., 621 P.2d 1155

LAVENDER, C. J., IRWIN, V. C. J., and HODGES, SIMMS, DOOLIN and HAR-GRAVE, JJ., concur.

OPALA, J., concurs in result.

BARNES, J., dissents.

DAYTON HUDSON CORPORATION, a corporation, Plaintiff,

v.

AMERICAN MUTUAL LIABILITY INSURANCE COMPANY, a corporation, Defendant.

No. 54683.

Supreme Court of Oklahoma.

Dec. 23, 1980.

The United States District Court for the Western District of Oklahoma, Fred Daugherty, J., certified questions to the Supreme Court. The Supreme Court, Opala, J., held that: (1) a policy obligating insurer to pay for all sums which insured might become legally obligated to pay was sufficiently broad to include liability for punitive damages; (2) purpose of exemplary damages is to punish and deter, and culpable insured would not be permitted to escape civil consequences of its wrong by imposing liability upon insurer; and (3) public policy against insurance protection for punitive damages does not preclude recovery from insurer by employer to whom willfulness or gross negligence of employee became imputable only under respondeat superior doctrine; and (4) if employer's knowledge of employees' propensities makes employer's negligence ordinary, employer's liability can be shifted to insurer, but if employer's negligence is gross, i. e., if there is equivalent of positive wrongdoing, then public policy prohibits employer from

shifting burden of punitive damages to insurer, and whether there was positive wrongdoing was fact issue.

Questions answered.

Williams, J., concurred in result.

Hodges, J., filed a statement concurring in part and dissenting in part, in which Simms and Doolin, JJ., concurred.

1. Insurance ⬤═146.6

Liability policies are to be liberally construed in favor of object to be accomplished. 36 O.S.1971, § 3621.

2. Insurance ⬤═512(1)

Policy providing protection "for all sums which the insured had become legally obligated to pay" was sufficiently broad to include liability for punitive damages. 23 O.S.1971, § 9; 36 O.S.1971, § 3621.

3. Insurance ⬤═512(1)

Purpose of exemplary damages is to punish and deter, and culpable insured would not be permitted to escape civil consequences of its wrong by imposing liability upon insurer. 23 O.S.1971, § 9.

4. Insurance ⬤═512(1)

Public policy against insurance protection for punitive damages does not preclude recovery from insurer by employer to whom willfulness or gross negligence of employee became imputable under respondeat superior doctrine. 23 O.S.1971, § 9; 25 O.S.1971, § 6.

5. Master and Servant ⬤═303

When recovery against employer for act of a servant is rested on prior knowledge of servant's propensity to commit very harm for which damages were sought, basis of liability invoked is not respondeat superior but rather employer's own negligence in not discharging unfit servant. 25 O.S.1971, § 6.

6. Insurance ⬤═512(1), 514.22

If employer's knowledge of employees' propensities makes employer's negligence ordinary, employer's liability can be shifted to insurer, but if employer's negligence is

7

CITATION FORM

Now we have surveyed the sources in which you will find the law. In Chapter 9, "Legal Memorandums," we show you how to answer a legal question by analyzing legal authority and applying it to your own fact situation. In this chapter, we describe in some detail how to identify your authorities for your reader. The reference terms we use to identify authorities are called citations. There are hundreds of them, and together they make up the common language of research.

All legal professionals use the same language—citations—in referring to legal authority. The terms we use to identify authority may sometimes seem overly fussy and complex, but they are carefully designed as a common language for all professionals to use, so that we all instantly understand one another.

■ THE BLUEBOOK

The "code book" for the language of citation is called **The Bluebook: A Uniform System of Citation,**[1] more commonly referred to as just **The Bluebook,** a paperback reference book published jointly by several law schools, including Harvard, Columbia, and Yale.

The *Bluebook* contains a set of rules designed to ensure that everybody uses exactly the same terminology in referring to a legal authority. It also has a section laying out specific rules for citations of the federal and state courts; it gives examples of how particular citations ought to look.

The *Bluebook* is fussy: for example, it refuses to use postal abbreviations to designate states, but invents its own abbreviations. It is sometimes a bit difficult to find things in, but you must learn to use it. It is the bible of the profession.

You can also find some excellent help in selecting citation format in a valuable book called *Current American Legal Citations,*[2] written by a legal librarian named

The *Bluebook*
Published jointly by several law schools as a reference for general and technical rules of legal citation and style.

---

[1] *The Bluebook: A Uniform System of Citation* (15th ed.). Cambridge, MA: Harvard Law Review Association, 1991.
[2] M.M. Price, Bieber's *Current American Legal Citations* (4th ed). Buffalo, NY: William S. Hein & Co., 1992.

cite
A reference to or quotation of an authority; to name in citation or to mention in support, illustration, or proof of.

Bieber. Her extremely useful book organizes sample citations alphabetically, and gives upward of 2,000 examples. You must be familiar with the rules of the *Bluebook*. But once you are, *Current American Legal Citations* is a fine quick reference to virtually any citation form. It is the best investment any legal professional can make.

A correct citation—**cite** for short—leads the reader to the right book without a chance of error. An incorrect one, however, is double trouble. First, it may mislead the reader so badly that he or she cannot find the authority on which you rely. Second, and almost as bad, an incorrect cite tells the reader that you and your firm are unprofessional, that you do not know your job. The reader who sees inaccurate or nonstandard citations wonders immediately what else may be wrong with what you have written.

Use the *Bluebook*. Memorize the rules for basic citation format. Consult it any time you have the slightest doubt about how a particular citation ought to look. A little later on, we suggest that you use a couple of citation forms that do not follow *Bluebook* rules. Be aware that some law firms do not follow the *Bluebook's* rules for citations exactly. Local court rules may also require a citation form different from that specified in the *Bluebook*. Aside from these few variations, however, particularly when you begin work, check *everything* against the *Bluebook* or Bieber.

In the following sections, we give you some broad general rules to help you cite correctly and understand the *Bluebook* faster. Here they are.

PRACTICE TIP

Before filing any document with the court clerk, find out if there are court rules that require a specific format for citations. Be sure to check the local court rules, too. Follow the court rules rather than the *Bluebook*.

■ SPACING IN CITATIONS

You may have noticed already that some symbols in citation abbreviation are separated by a space, and some are not. The *Bluebook* also establishes rules for spacing between abbreviations in citations. Briefly, these are the rules:

- *Do not leave a space between single letters,* as in this abbreviation for a legal periodical, the American Bar Association Journal: A.B.A.J. The exception is when a single letter stands for a "geographic or institutional entity," such as a university. In that case, the single letter gets a space on each side, as in this abbreviation for the Boston College Law Review: B.C. L. Rev.
- *Leave a space on both sides of any abbreviation that contains two or more letters,* as in the abbreviation for another periodical, the *University of Oklahoma Law Review:* Okla. L. Rev. There is an exception to this rule also: "2d" and "3d" count as only a single symbol, as in this abbreviation for *Federal Reporter, Second Series:* 54 F.2d 111.

■ CASE LAW

Every citation to the opinion of a court must give the reader this information:

1. The name of the case
2. The volume in which the case appears
3. The identity of the book (the "reporter") in which it is published
4. The page on which the case begins
5. The identity of the court
6. The year in which the opinion was decided

◼ PRACTICE TIP

Every case citation must include the following information, in this order:
1. The name of the case
2. The volume in which it appears
3. The reporter in which it is published
4. The page on which it begins
5. The abbreviation of the court
6. The year in which the opinion was written

Here is an example:

Broadnax v. Symposium Players Inc., 362 N.W.2d 212 (Neb. 1984).
            (1)   (2)   (3) (4) (5) (6)

At a single glance, you know:

1. The title of the case, made from the names of the first-mentioned litigants on each side
2. The reporter volume in which the case appears
3. The name of the reporter (*Northwest Reporter*, 2d Series)
4. The beginning page of the case
5. The identity of the court (Neb. stands for the Nebraska Supreme Court)
6. The year of decision

The *Bluebook* gives you a number of rules to help you decide what to put in the title of the case. Generally speaking, however, the rule is this: Use the last name of the first litigant mentioned on each side of the case. For example, take a case whose full title is *Charles Broadnax and Martin King v. Symposium Players Incorporated and Charles Jordan, Jr.* The *v.*, by the way, stands for the Latin **versus** which means "against." In your citation, you would show the title of the case as *Broadnax v. Symposium Players Inc.* The official case title often adds ***et al.*** (meaning "and others") to the name of the case, or other obscure jargon like et ux. ("and wife"). Omit these and all other additions to the names, except words that show one of the litigants is a business entity (e.g., "Inc."). Also, omit the party's litigation status, e.g., plaintiff or defendant.

Federal Cases

The United States federal court system has three levels. At the top is the **Supreme Court of the United States.**

    Below it, presiding over well-defined areas of responsibility, are the intermediate appellate courts. They are called the **United States Courts of Appeals,** and their areas

◼ PRACTICE TIP

The United States is divided into thirteen federal judicial circuits, each with a court of appeals known as the United States Court of Appeals for the circuit. The Court of Appeals for the District of Columbia and the Court of Appeals for the Federal Circuit are included in these thirteen judicial circuits.

PRACTICE TIP

When there are multiple parties on each side of the litigation, include only the first party mentioned on each side. Omit *et al.*, but not **ex rel.** :

NAACP v. Alabama ex rel. Patterson

ex rel.
A Latin abbreviation for *ex relatione*, meaning upon relation or information.

versus
A Latin word meaning "against"; the abbreviation for "versus" is "v."

et al.
A Latin abbreviation of *et alii*, meaning " and others" that is often added after the name of the first party to replace names of the remaining parties.

Supreme Court of the United States
The highest appellate court, or court of last resort, in the federal judicial system, comprised of the Chief Justice of the United States and eight Associate Justices.

United States Courts of Appeals
The Circuit Courts; the first level of federal appellate courts which preside over well-defined areas of responsibility.

Circuit Courts
In the federal judicial system, the first level of appellate review for cases from the federal district court whose jurisdiction extends over several federal districts.

District Courts
In federal courts, the trial courts with general jurisdiction over cases involving federal laws and actions between citizens of different states; in state courts, a trial court having full jurisdiction within its own jurisdictional area over both civil and criminal cases involving state laws or offenses.

districts
The territorial area into which an entire state or country, county, municipality, or other political subdivision is divided for judicial, political, electoral, or administrative purposes.

of responsibility are the **Circuit Courts.** Usually these areas of responsibility are defined geographically: for example, the Court of Appeals for the Tenth Circuit presides over appellate questions arising in Wyoming, Utah, Colorado, New Mexico, Kansas, and Oklahoma.

At the bottom of the federal judicial pyramid are the **District Courts,** where cases are actually tried, evidence taken, and juries empaneled. These courts are responsible for geographical areas, called **districts.** A state may have one or more districts. These federal trial courts also publish opinions on important questions, although most state trial courts do not.

In writing citations to federal courts, follow the general rule we gave you earlier: Tell the reader what specific court wrote the opinion and when, and give the volume and page of the reporter in which the opinion appears. For example, a citation to a case from the Court of Appeals for the Tenth Circuit should look like this:

Morris v. Seymour, 686 F.2d 117 (10th Cir. 1990).

When you cite to a District Court case, the same rules apply. In these citations, however, the identity of the court will be its *district.* For example, here is a citation of an opinion from the United States District Court for the Western District of Oklahoma:

Lollie v. Trotline, Inc., 488 F. Supp. 282 (W.D. Okla. 1982).

The rules for citation to opinions of the Supreme Court of the United States are a little different. There are three reporters that report those decisions. One is the official reporter, published by the United States. The other two are unofficial reporters, published by commercial publishers. The text of the opinion is exactly the same in all of them.

The official reporter takes the abbreviation U.S. The unofficial reporter by West Publishing Company is shown as S. Ct., and that by Lawyers Cooperative Publishing Company appears as L. Ed. or L. Ed. 2d (*Lawyers' Edition,* or *Lawyers Edition,* 2d Series).

Now the *Bluebook,* for no discernible reason, directs that we cite only to the official reporter. The rule makes little practical sense for the world of practice, since most law offices and judges' chambers do not maintain the official set of reporters. They are produced with glacial slowness, and contain no research aids. (Research aids are described in detail in Chapter 6, "Legal Research.") Many lawyers and judges do, however, maintain an unofficial set of reporters, such as *Lawyers' Edition* and *Lawyers' Edition,* 2d Series, and these do contain helpful research aids.

The better rule, unless your supervising attorney or local court rules direct otherwise, is this: Cite to all three reporters, so that your reader (the court) can easily pull down whichever set he or she has and read the case. This is called **parallel citation**—listing the locations of an opinion that appears in more than one reporter. When you are writing parallel citations for opinions from the United States Supreme Court, give them in this order:

New York Times Co. v. Jascalevich, 439 U.S. 1317, 99 S. Ct. 6, 58 L. Ed. 2d 25 (1978).

You will note that there is no abbreviation in the parentheses to identify the court. This is because the U.S., S. Ct., and L. Ed. citations can refer only to the Supreme Court.

PRACTICE TIP

Use parallel cites to all three reporters unless the local court rules instruct otherwise.

parallel citation
A citation reference to the same case printed in two or more different reports.

State Cases

Some states have official reporters of their own appellate decisions. Some used to have them, but have since discontinued publication. Legal writers were once required to cite to both official and unofficial reporters if a state decision appeared in both. No more. Here is the modern rule: Cite only to the unofficial (commercial) version of a state decision.

The Bluebook does not require citation to the official state report—if there is one—unless your citation is in a document that will be submitted to a court in that state. Generally, state cases are published by West Publishing Company in volumes called **regional reporters,** which collect the appellate opinions of several contiguous states in a single volume. For example, the Pacific Reporter (P.) and Pacific Reporter, 2d Series (P.2d) publish the opinions of appellate courts in California, Nevada, Hawaii, Oregon and Washington, and several other western states.

regional reporters
Volumes of state court opinions that collect the appellate opinions of several contiguous states in a single volume.

So, follow the case citation rule set out earlier: Cite the case name, volume, reporter, first page, court identity, and date. Your citation will look like this:

Burns v. Blackwell, 231 P.2d 311 (Okla. 1951).

Now when *Burns* was decided, Oklahoma had its own official reporter—the official reporter was not discontinued until 1953. Even so, you need not refer to the official reporter as a parallel citation under the *Bluebook* rule. When you do include the official citation, it always goes first, as it does in this example:

Burns v. Blackwell, 204 Okla. 400, 231 P. 2d 311 (1951).

As with any citation to an official reporter (such as U.S.), *you do not need to identify the court in parentheses with the date of decision.* The official citation Okla. does that for you: Okla. means the Supreme Court of Oklahoma, and none other.

How, you may ask, do I know whether a particular state has an official reporter, or ever had one in the past? That information is easy to come by. In Chapter 6 "Legal Research," we discuss *Shepard's Citators,*[3] and the process called shepardizing. *Shepard's* tells you whether any case you look up has an official citation, and gives you that citation.

---

[3]Shepard's Citations (4th ed.) Colorado Springs, CO: Shepard's/McGraw-Hill, Inc., 1987.

■ PRACTICE TIP

Follow these general rules for citing case law:
- Use only the last name of the first persons on each side of the litigation. If the party is a corporation, use its full name.
- Do not include the party's litigation status (e.g., plaintiff, defendant, appellant, or appellee).
- If there are multiple parties on either side of the litigation, include only the *first* party mentioned.
- Omit *et al.* but not *ex rel.*
- If two or more different cases are consolidated, use the parties from the first case for the case name.
- Do not abbreviate *United States.*

The *Bluebook,* in section T, gives you the correct abbreviations for all courts. No two are identical. For instance, if *Burns* were a criminal case, its citation to the official and unofficial reporters would then look like this, cited in a brief to an Oklahoma court:

> *Burns v. State,* 189 Okla. Crim. App. 761, 231 P.2d 311 (1951).

An Oklahoma criminal case on appeal is decided by a court called the Court of Criminal Appeals. The official reporter was abbreviated Okla. Crim. App. by the *Bluebook.*

Subsequent History of Cases

The *Bluebook* requires a citation to reflect appellate action subsequent to the opinion you are citing. For example, suppose you are citing a case decided by the Oklahoma Supreme Court. The losing litigant sought and received review of the case by the United States Supreme Court. When you cite the Oklahoma Supreme Court opinion, you also show what the United States Supreme Court did with the case, like this:

> *Madison v. Hollyhock Enterprises, Inc.,* 465 P.2d 214 (Okla. 1977), *aff'd,* 437 U.S. 700, 98 S. Ct. 22, 56 L. Ed.2d 416 (1978).

signals
Indicators provided to show the purposes for which the citations are made and the degree of support the citations give.

affirmed
The declaration by an appellate court that the judgment, decree, or order of a lower court is valid and must stand as rendered.

subsequent history
The appellate court's treatment of the cited case after the date of the cited case.

writ of certiorari
An order by the appellate court which is used by that court when it has discretion on whether to hear an appeal from a ‹lower court.

introductory signals
Signals before a citation provided to show the purposes for which the citation is made and the degree of support the citation gives.

The *Bluebook* provides several **signals** (such as *aff'd*— **affirmed**) to give the reader some idea of what the final reviewing authority did with the case. In the preceding example, the United States Supreme Court agreed with the decision of the Oklahoma Supreme Court.

Here is an example of another signal. We take the same case, but have the United States Supreme Court reverse it, on some ground that is not connected to the reason for which you cite the case:

> *Madison v. Hollyhock Enterprises, Inc.,* 465 P.2d 214 (Okla. 1977), *rev'd on other grounds,* 437 U.S. 700, 98 S. Ct. 22, 56 L. Ed.2d 416 (1978).

Let us run through a final example of **subsequent history.** Review by the Court is technically approved by granting a **writ of certiorari** ("to be informed"). The writ is directed to the court that last decided the case, and simply means, "we shall review the case." Suppose now that in the same case, the United States Supreme Court decided not to review the case. Your subsequent history would look like this:

> *Madison v. Hollyhock Enterprises, Inc.,* 465 P.2d 214 (Okla. 1977), *cert. denied,* 437 U.S. 700, 98 S. Ct. 22, 56 L. Ed.2d 416 (1978).

You can easily find out whether a case you cite has a subsequent appellate history. Simply consult *Shepard's Citator,* which we mentioned above.

Introductory Signals

Earlier in this chapter, we talked about using signals to indicate subsequent history. **Introductory signals** are placed before a citation to tell the reader something about the citation. Rules 1.2 through 1.4 of the *Bluebook* give a list of introductory signals, the order in which more than one signal is used, and the order of authorities within each signal. Basically, introductory signals indicate one of the following:

- The citations following the signal support your proposition (*See, See also, E.g., Accord, Cf.*).

- The citations following the signal suggest a favorable comparison to your proposition (*Compare [ ] with [ ]*).
- The citations following the signal indicate a contradiction to your proposition (*Contra, But see, But cf.*).
- The citations following the signal indicate background material related to your proposition (*See generally*).

Two signals may be used together, as in "*See, e.g.* "

Underline or italicize signals whenever you use them. No comma separates the signal from the rest of the citation:

> *See W.R. Grace & Co. v. Pullman Inc.,* 74 F.R.D. 80 (W.D. Okla. 1977).

But if you use two signals together, put a comma before and after the second signal, like this:

> *See, e.g., W.R. Grace & Co v. Pullman Inc.,* 74 F.R.D. 80 (W.D. Okla. 1977).

Short Citations

Whenever you refer to the **holding** in a case, or the court's **rationale (or reasoning)** in that case, you are required to give a "**short** " or "**spot**" **cite.** This is a citation which tells your reader the precise page in the opinion that contains the information to which you refer. We gave you some examples in Chapter 9 on legal memorandums. Here is a little more discussion on how it is done.

Take for example the case of *Palfrey v. Charger,* 776 P.2d 283 (Cal. 1990). Remember the parts of a case citation: Palfrey is the first-named plaintiff; Charger is the first-named defendant. The opinion is printed in volume 776 of the *Pacific Reporter,* Second Series, starting at page 283. Cal. is the *Bluebook* abbreviation for the California Supreme Court that wrote the opinion. The date, 1990, is the year in which the opinion was decided by the court.

The first time you mention *Palfrey,* or any other case, you give its full citation. But suppose that as your first mention of *Palfrey,* you give the holding of the case. That requires you give your reader a citation to the exact page on which that holding occurs, like this:

> *Palfrey v. Charger,* 776 P.2d 283, 286 (Cal. 1990).

After you have given the full citation to the case, you are still required to give a citation each time you refer to particular language, to the court's holding, or to the rationale of the court. But you can now give a short or spot cite. This is how you do it.

One common—and useful—short cite looks like this:

> *Palfrey* at 286.

If you are short citing to a case for which you gave parallel citations the first time you cited it, you must tell your reader which reporter your short cite is to. For example, say you have cited a Supreme Court case, like this:

> *New York Times Co. v. Jascalevich,* 439 U.S. 11, 99 S. Ct. 6, 58 L. Ed.2d 9 (1978).

Here is your short cite:

> *Jascalevich,* 439 U.S. at 13.

With the short cite in this form, there is no chance of your reader being confused about which reporter you are citing to.

holding
The Court's answer to or resolution of the legal issue before it; the legal principle to be drawn from the opinion (decision) of the court.

reasoning or rationale
The court's explanation of why it decided a legal issue as it did.

short or spot cite
A citation that tells your reader the precise page in the opinion on which the reference discussed by the author may be found.

PRACTICE TIP
Your citation must clearly direct your reader to the precise authority to which you refer.

id.
An abbreviation meaning "the same" used to indicate reference to the immediately preceding authority; indicates an exact repetition of the last citation given.

You can also use **id.** *Id.* means that you are repeating exactly the last citation you gave. Or, if you are citing to the same case you last cited, but to a different page, you can use *Id.* at 286.

Above all, remember this: Your citation must clearly direct your reader to the precise authority to which you refer. To achieve this end you must be exact, and you should use the framework specified in the *Bluebook.* Everybody else does; and you are no exception. You are expected to speak good *Bluebook,* just as other legal professionals do.

Never forget that in citation, as in every other area of legal research and writing, "pretty close" is simply not good enough. If what you do is not precise, do it again. You owe it to your supervising attorney, to your client, and to your own professional reputation.

◼ STATUTES

code system
A system by which statutes are organized in sections, often called "titles," according to subject matter.

statute
A formal written enactment (law) of a legislative body, whether federal or state, which declares, commands, or prohibits something.

titles
Under a code system, a unit or part of a statute, usually one of its major subdivisions.

The federal government and the states organize their statutes in what is called a **code system.** Under a code system, **statutes** are organized in sections (often called **titles**) according to subject matter.

After a legislative session has finished passing bills into law, each new statute is distributed to the code title in which its subject matter belongs. In this way, statutory law is collected in an orderly fashion. Codes are normally provided with a detailed index, and "unofficial" versions (commercially printed) contain a variety of research tools.

Code citation is generally quite simple. A citation to the United States Code, for example, looks like this:

10 U.S.C. § 1284(c) (1988).

You have told your reader (in order) the number of the title, the identity of the code, the section and subsection of the title, and the date of the edition you have used (normally the latest).

How do you establish the date of the code edition you are using? The date may occur in three places:

- If there is a date on the spine of the book or the pocket part, use that date.
- If there is no date on the spine, but there is a date on the title page, use the date on the title page.
- If the code has neither of these dates, use the copyright date.

The *Bluebook* requires you to cite to the official version of the code. But research is ordinarily done using an *unofficial* version, for two reasons. First, unlike the official version, the unofficial one contains numerous research tools. Second, the unof-

◼ PRACTICE TIP

A basic citation to a statute contains the following information, in this order:
1. The number of the title;
2. The abbreviated name of the code (U.S.C.)
3. A section sign (§) with the section number and subsection of the title
4. The year of the edition you have used

ficial version is usually the most current. In both versions, of course, the statutory language is precisely the same.

Your office may require you to cite to the unofficial version if you used it. The abbreviations for unofficial versions are also in the *Bluebook*. For example, our federal code citation, if made to West's unofficial version, would look like this:

> 10 U.S.C.A. § 1284(c) (West 1983).

Three things are different about this citation. First, the codal abbreviation is U.S.C.A., United States Code Annotated, which tells your reader this is a citation to the unofficial version. Second, the publisher is shown. The *Bluebook* requires this form for unofficial versions of codes. Third, the date is different.

If you were using the other unofficial federal code, United States Code Service, your citation to the same code section would look like this:

> 10 U.S.C.S. § 1284(c) (Law Co-op 1983).

As we said, unofficial codes are generally kept much more up-to-date than are official ones. They are kept current by regular supplements. Some supplements are separate booklets. Most are what lawyers call **pocket parts,** pamphlets mounted on cardboard tabs that fit into a pocket in the back of the hardcover volume of the code.

If your citation is to a pocket part, direct your reader to the supplement. The citation should look like this:

> 10 U.S.C. § 1284(c) (Supp. 1992).

There is another school of thought, however; some advocate using the year in which the statute was enacted or became effective rather than the date of the book or pocket part. The reasoning is this: Suppose that a statute about contracts was revised, and those revisions became effective in 1992. Then the statute was revised again, and those revisions became effective in 1994. Now suppose that you are citing to that statute in a brief to the court in a case involving a contract signed in 1993. According to the *Bluebook,* you would use the date of the pocket part, which could be 1994, 1995, and so on. But the law that applies to the contract in this case is *the law that was in effect at the time* —the 1992 version. Using the latest date of the pocket part may be correct format according to the *Bluebook,* but it may mislead readers who want to look up the statute in effect at the time the contract was signed.

If the statutory material to which you refer is found in both the hardcover volume and a supplement, tell your reader that also:

> 10 U.S.C. § 1284(c) (1988 and Supp. 1992).

The citation rules for state statutes are generally the same as those for federal law. Some states have both official code collections and unofficial ones. Some get along with only an unofficial version. All are based on a code system, although the names vary from state to state. Usually, the unofficial version is called an **annotated code.** Unofficial state code citations differ a little from citations to official codes, just as U.S.C.A. differs from U.S.C. As an example, consider Oklahoma, which has both official and unofficial codes:

> 57 Okla. Stat. § 212 (1991).   [the official version]
> 57 Okla. Stat. Ann. § 212 (West 1991).   [the annotated, or unofficial version]

Often, the publication dates of unofficial and official versions are different. In this example, the publication dates of both hardcover codes were 1991. The pocket

pocket part
A cumulative supplement in pamphlet form found in the back of a book that updates or consolidates all earlier volumes.

annotated code
The unofficial version of state statutes containing brief summaries of the law and facts of cases interpreting or applying statutes passed by Congress or state legislatures which are normally included following the text of the statute.

part in the annotated (unofficial) version shows that there have been no changes to § 212 after the unofficial code was published in 1991.

When you are citing to the United States Constitution, cite provisions without the date unless the cited provisions have been repealed or amended:

> U.S. Const. art. I, § 9, cl. 2.
> U.S. Const. amend. XIV, § 2 (year).

There are other citation rules pertaining to statutes, all of which you can find in the *Bluebook*. Check it often, and get to know it well.

◾ SECONDARY AUTHORITY

secondary authority
Any non-law (e.g., treatise, legal encyclopedia, or law review article) relied upon by a court in reaching its decision.

Secondary authority is legal research material other than cases and statutes. Generally speaking, you do not often use secondary authority to persuade a court. It is, however, extremely useful in finding cases and in otherwise aiding your research and understanding of your problem.

Citation of secondary authority also follows rules laid down in the *Bluebook*. You must know how to cite secondary authority as well as primary, because you will cite it often in office memoranda and occasionally in briefs for the court. Secondary authority is of several kinds, which we describe in the following sections.

Treatises

treatise
Books that are a type of secondary authority focusing on a particular area of law.

hornbook
Popular reference to a series of textbooks which review various fields of law in summary, narrative form, as opposed to casebooks which are designed as primary teaching tools and include many reprints of court opinions.

Treatises are textbooks on specific areas of the law, such as contracts or criminal law. Lawyers call some of them **hornbooks,** a term dating from the days in which precious paper pages in basic reading books were protected by a thin sheet of horn. Many times a treatise will tell you at the front of the book how its citation should be written. If that information is not provided, then a treatise is cited by volume (if there is more than one); author (first initial and last name); page, paragraph, or section—whichever is applicable; edition; and publication date, like this:

> 3 B. Bittker and L. Lokken, *Federal Taxation of Income, Estates and Gifts* § 74 (2d ed. 1991).

Or:

> Restatement (Second) of Torts § 37 (1980).

Or:

> 1 A. Corbin, *Contracts* § 36 (2d ed. 1950).

When the book is arranged by numbered paragraphs or sections, as Corbin is, you can add the page number, if you think it helpful:

> 1 A. Corbin, *Contracts* § 36, at 137 (2d ed. 1950).

If the book has a supplement, and you rely on material in it, say so like this:

> 1 A. Corbin, *Contracts* § 36 (2d ed., 1950, Supp. 1971).

◾ PRACTICE TIP

Remember that a court is never required to follow secondary authorities. Unlike primary authorities, secondary authorities are not mandatory.

Legal Encyclopedias

You use encyclopedias of the law just like you would ordinary encyclopedias. The fabric of the law is broken down into many subtopics, arranged alphabetically. **Legal encyclopedias** are great beginning places where you can start to understand the law controlling your question and find citations to some pertinent case law. Remember the two major encyclopedias are *Corpus Juris Secundum* and *American Jurisprudence, 2d Series.* They are cited similarly, giving their title abbreviation, the section cited, the title of the subtopic, and the date of the volume. For *Corpus Juris Secundum,* you add the volume, putting it first. The citations look like this:

> 88 C.J.S. *Trial* § 122 (1955).
> Am.Jur.2d *Zoning and Planning* § 117 (1976).

legal encyclopedia
An encyclopedia in which the fabric of the law is broken down into many subtopics, arranged alphabetically; a type of secondary authority which is a good general source of information.

Legal Periodicals

Legal periodicals appear as magazines, newspapers, or paperback books. They are produced by a variety of sources, including bar associations and commercial publishers, and include such publications as the *American Bar Association Journal.*

By far the most important type of periodical is the **law review.** These are published by law schools, and contain carefully researched and edited articles on a wide variety of legal subjects. They can be enormously valuable to you in understanding your question and in collecting both law and ideas that affect the answer. Law review pieces are of three kinds: articles, comments, and notes. Articles are generally written by lawyers, judges, or professors. Notes and comments are written by law students.

You cite law reviews by author's name, title of piece, law review title, volume, page, and year of publication. If you are referring to a note or comment rather than an article, say so. Here is an example:

> Barry G. Burkhart, Comment, *Leases: Farmland Lease Provisions in Oklahoma,* 44 Okla. L. Rev. 461 (1991).

If you are citing to an article, you need not identify it as such. Write your citation like this:

> Rodney J. Uphoff, *The New Criminal Discovery Code in Oklahoma: A Two-Way Street in the Wrong Direction,* 44 Okla. L. Rev. 387 (1991).

legal periodical
Secondary authorities, such as magazines, journals, newspapers, or paperback books, published from various sources, including bar associations and commercial publishers.

law review
A periodic publication of most law schools containing topical articles by law professors, judges, or attorneys, and case summaries by law review member-students.

Another important legal periodical is the state **bar journal.** Each state bar association publishes its own bar journal. The bar journal publishes the recently decided opinions by the appellate courts for that state. It can contain various announcements, such as address changes, obituaries, seminars, meetings, and conventions. Like a law review, a bar journal also contains carefully researched articles written by lawyers on a wide variety of legal subjects. A bar journal is also one method used by the courts to advise the bar of changes in court rules and to post the court's fees and filing requirements (such as the number of copies required).

You cite articles from bar journals by author's name, title of article, volume, abbreviated initials of the bar journal's name, page where article begins, and date of publication. Here is an example:

> Robert Richardson, *Should We Allow the Hinckley Backlash to Cause Bad Law? The Insanity Defense,* 53 Okla. B.J. 2180 (1982).

In most firms, at least one copy of the state's bar journal is kept in the law library for everyone's use, but it usually takes a week or two for a copy to reach the library.

bar journal
A regular publication by a state or the national bar association.

If there is a change in the court rules, fees, or requirements, you need to know about it as soon as it happens. Rather than waiting for a copy of the bar journal to be routed to you as it makes its rounds through the firm, we suggest that you invest in your own subscription. In most states, the cost is nominal for the valuable information the bar journal contains (about $20 to $30).

As with all other kinds of legal authority, you must not guess at the correct abbreviation for legal periodicals. You can find the proper abbreviation by consulting either the *Bluebook* or Bieber.

▨ LOCAL RULES AND CUSTOMS

local court rules
Court rules adopted by an individual court which supplement the Rules of Civil Procedure applicable to that court.

When you are constructing citations, remember also that **local court rules** sometimes require a citation form slightly different from the *Bluebook*. For example, the *Bluebook* abbreviates the Oklahoma Court of Criminal Appeals as Okla. Crim. App. But that very court requires lawyers filing briefs with it to use the abbreviation Okl. Cr.

Always follow local custom as well, if your firm subscribes to it. For example, you will not find the Oklahoma Statutes abbreviated in the Bluebook as O.S., but this citation form is commonly accepted in Oklahoma. If you are writing for a court outside Oklahoma, however, you would use the standard *Bluebook* abbreviation, Okla. Stat.

PRACTICE TIP

Know the local court rules, and follow them.

CHAPTER SUMMARY

Precise, correct citation is the hallmark of a legal professional. Sloppy cites tell the reader you do not care about the accuracy of your writing. Remember these basic rules:

- Always cite according to the *Bluebook*. Use other citation forms only if they are required by court rules or authorized by your employer.
- The first time you mention a case in a brief or memo, include the full citation to the case.
- Do not forget to use short or spot citations to identify the precise page of either the holding or reasoning of the court in any case you discuss.
- You need not place a short citation at the end of every sentence that discusses a holding or the reasoning of the court. Instead, you may use a single short cite at the end of the paragraph, but *only* if everything in the paragraph comes from the same page of the opinion.
- When you begin discussion of a case with a statement about its holding or rationale, your full citation should include a page cite to the source of your statement (*e.g.,* "In a later case, the same court held that. . . . *Jones v. State,* 501 P. 111, 114 (Okla. Crim. App. 1988)."
- If you quote from any source, give a spot citation to the precise page from which the quotation came. If you quote from a statute, cite to the precise section and subsection from which you quote.
- You can use *Id.* to show that your short cite is identical to the last citation you gave. If your citation is identical to the last citation except for the page, use *Id.* plus the page number (e.g., *Id.* at 147.)
- When your case citation contains both official and unofficial cites, your first short cite thereafter must tell the reader which reporter you refer to (e.g., *Jones,* 671 P.2d at 28).

- When your attorney permits it, give all three parallel citations to the United States Supreme Court opinions unless the court rules require otherwise. Although the *Bluebook* rule is to cite only to the official reporter, giving all three cites is a professional courtesy to anyone who may read what you write.
- Use correct spacing between numbers and abbreviations in citations. Correct spacing not only makes cites easier to read but also shows you are professional and painstaking.

KEY WORDS AND PHRASES

affirmed	*ex rel.*	pocket parts	Supreme Court of the United States
annotated code	holding	rationale (or reasoning)	titles
bar journal	hornbook	regional reporters	treatise
Bluebook	*id.*	secondary authority	United States Court of Appeals
Circuit Courts	introductory signals	short cite	
cite	law review	signals	versus
code system	legal encyclopedia	spot cite	writ of certiorari
districts	legal periodical	statutes	
District Courts	local court rules	subsequent history	
et al.	parallel citation		

EXERCISES

Imagine that you have found a number of legal authorities pertinent to the memo on which you are now working. Use the *Bluebook,* and give the correct citations for each one.

1. A 1989 case from the Supreme Court of the State of Washington. Its full title is *Charles Dunstan and Martin Frobisher v. Tubular Products, Inc.* You have found the case in volume 763 of the Pacific Reporter, Second Series, beginning on page 27.

2. A 1978 case from the Missouri Court of Appeals (*not* the Missouri Supreme Court). You have read it in volume 583 of the *Southwestern Reporter,* Second Series, beginning at page 211. The parties are *Continental Confections* suing *Anton Slivovitz et ux.* You are quoting from the opinion at page 217.

3. A case from the United States Court of Appeals for the 10th Circuit, decided in 1975. The parties are *Jason and the Argonauts, Inc. v. Perpetual Motion Exhibits Co.* The opinion is printed in the 525th volume of the *Federal Reporter,* Second

Series, starting on page 300. The holding in the case, which you discuss, occurs on page 317.

4. Section 845 of a federal statute. You found it in Title 10 of the United States Code Annotated. The hardcover volume of Title 10 was published in 1983. You check the pocket part (the supplement) but there has been no change ot the language of § 845.

5. Section 2A–104 of the Oklahoma Statutes Annotated, in Title 12A of that code. Section 2A–104 does not appear in the hardcover volume, but shows up for the first time in the supplement (the pocket part). The pocket part is dated 1992.

6. A discussion in Section 2513, on page 181 of a treatise on the rules of evidence in Oklahoma, by Leo H. Whinery. Professor Whinery's book is called *Oklahoma Evidence,* and was published in 1985. It has not been supplemented, and there has been only one edition. (A hint: Check Rule 15 in the *Bluebook.*)

7. A discussion in volume 22 of the encyclopedia, *Corpus Juris Secundum.* The topic is called "Criminal Law," and the material you cite is found in § 50, on pages 57–58. The hardcover volume was copyrighted in 1989, and carries no other dates. There is a 1991 pocket part, which shows no change to § 50. (A hint: Look further in Rule 15 of the *Bluebook.*)

8. An article in the *Harvard Law Review* by Frank H. Easterbrook, called "Foreward: The Court and the Economic System." It appeared in volume 98 in November 1984, beginning at page 4. You are citing it for reasoning appearing on page 10. (Yet another hint: Check *Bluebook* Rule 16. The *Harvard Law Review* is a consecutively paged journal, meaning that while it is published in a series of pamphlets, the page numbering of each pamphlet picks up where the numbering of the last one left off.)

8

LEGAL ANALYSIS

This chapter deals with "thinking like a lawyer." This term refers simply to a method of dissecting, understanding, and applying legal authority. The process applies to statutes and regulations as well as to case law, and some very general rules apply, whatever you are trying to interpret.

First, both courts and legislatures would rather decide less than decide more. That is, they will ordinarily make no rule broader than is necessary to accomplish whatever it is they want to do.

Second, language, either legislative or judicial, should be read in its ordinary sense unless, in a statute, that language is specifically defined as having some unusual meaning. In the sample brief of a case we give you in this chapter, the court follows this rule and chooses the ordinary meaning of a term as the meaning intended by Congress in a statute, rather than a strained and unusual meaning.

Third, as to statutes and regulations, courts prefer to read them in such a manner that they make sense, rather than require some bizarre result, or one contrary to common sense.

Fourth, if what a court says may have two meanings, you normally choose the meaning that makes the opinion consistent with other decisions by the court. Appellate courts are reluctant to change existing law if they can decide a new case somehow in harmony with cases they have decided in the past.

We spend most of our time in this chapter dealing with analysis of case law, the main path by which the law evolves. You will learn what to look for in a court's opinion, and how to "brief" the case. This brief is not the written legal argument that we deal with later in this book. It is a **case brief**: a summary of the salient facts of the case, together with a succinct account of the court's decision, and, especially, the *rationale* by which the court reached that decision.

As long as you work in the law, remember that you can *never* accept somebody else's idea of what particular legal authority means. Headnotes and other summaries are very helpful, and usually accurate. The same is true of discussions of an opinion in another case or in a law review article. Nevertheless, in the end, it is *your* analysis on which your supervising attorney must rely. That means you must *always* read authority on which you rely, and make your own analysis of its effect.

case brief
A summary of the salient facts of the case, together with a succinct account of the court's *decision* or *holding;* and especially, the *rationale* or *reasoning* by which the court reached that decision.

155

■ CASE BRIEFS

The easiest way to show you how to brief a case is to construct a sample case brief that includes all the essential elements of a good brief. You will develop your own method of briefing as you gain experience, but this example gives you a solid framework.

Facts

First, obviously, you must read the case. You will find it below: *McBoyle v. United States*, a 1931 decision of the United States Supreme Court.[1] Read it over without taking notes. Then we shall talk about what information you need to take from this case (and any other.) Then read the case again, the next time making notes.

---

[1] The authors gratefully acknowledge the inspiration for using this case, and permission to use the sample briefs that follow it. Both came from Professor John Delaney, a veteran law teacher and demystifier of legal learning. We recommend his commonsense paperback: *How to Brief a Case* (Bogota, New York: Delaney Publications), 1987.

CASE

McBoyle v. United States.

CERTIORARI TO THE CIRCUIT COURT OF APPEALS FOR THE TENTH CIRCUIT.
No. 552. Argued February 26, 27, 1931—Decided March 9, 1931.

CERTIORARI, 282 U.S. 835 515, ct. 181, 75 L. Ed. 742, to review a judgment affirming a conviction under the Motor Vehicle Theft Act.

Mr. Harry F. Brown for petitioner.

Mr. Claude R. Branch, Special Assistant to the Attorney General, with whom *Solicitor General Thacher, Assistant Attorney General Dodds* and *Messrs. Harry S. Ridgely* and *W. Marvin Smith* were on the brief, for the United States.

MR. JUSTICE HOLMES delivered the opinion of the Court.

The petitioner was convicted of transporting from Ottawa, Illinois, to Guymon, Oklahoma, an airplane that he knew to have been stolen, and was sentenced to serve three years' imprisonment and to pay a fine of $2,000. The judgment was affirmed by the Circuit Court of Appeals for the Tenth Circuit. 43 F.2d 273. A writ of certiorari was granted by this Court on the question whether the National Motor Vehicle Theft Act applies to air-craft. Act of October 29, 1919, c. 89, 41 Stat. 324; U.S. Code, Title 18, § 408. That Act provides: "Sec. 2. That when used in this Act: (a) The term 'motor vehicle' shall include an automobile, automobile truck, automobile wagon, motor cycle, or any other self-propelled vehicle not designed for running on rails; . . . Sec. 3. That whoever shall transport or cause to be transported in interstate or foreign commerce a motor vehicle, knowing the same to have been stolen, shall be punished by a fine of not more than $5,000, or by imprisonment of not more than five years, or both."

Section 2 defines the motor vehicles of which the transportation in interstate commerce is punished in § 3. The question is the meaning of the word 'vehicle' in the phrase "any other self-propelled vehicle not designed for running on rails." No doubt etymologically it is possible to use the word to signify a conveyance working on land, water or air, and sometimes legislation extends the

CASE—*Continued*

use in that direction, *e.g.*, land and air, water being separately provided for, in the Tariff Act, September 22, 1922, c. 356, § 401(b), 42 Stat. 858, 948. But in everyday speech 'vehicle' calls up the picture of a thing moving on land. Thus in Rev. Stats. § 4, intended, the Government suggests, rather to enlarge than to restrict the definition, vehicle includes every contrivance capable of being used "as a means of transportation on land." And this is repeated, expressly excluding aircraft, in the Tariff Act, June 17, 1930, c. 997, § 401(b); 46 Stat. 590, 708. So here, the phrase under discussion calls up the popular picture. For after including automobile truck, automobile wagon and motor cycle, the words "any other self-propelled vehicle not designed for running on rails" still indicate that a vehicle in the popular sense, that is a vehicle running on land, is the theme. It is a vehicle that runs, not something, not commonly called a vehicle, that flies. Airplanes were well known in 1919, when this statute was passed; but it is admitted that they were not mentioned in the reports or in the debates in Congress. It is impossible to read words that so carefully enumerate the different forms of motor vehicles and have no reference of any kind to aircraft, as including air-

planes under a term that usage more and more precisely confines to a different class. The counsel for the petitioner have shown that the phraseology of the statute as to motor vehicles follows that of earlier statutes of Connecticut, Delaware, Ohio, Michigan and Missouri, not to mention the late Regulations of Traffic for the District of Columbia, Title 6, c. 9, § 242, none of which can be supposed to leave the earth.

Although it is not likely that a criminal will carefully consider the text of the law before he murders or steals, it is reasonable that a fair warning should be given to the world in language that the common world will understand, of what the law intends to do if a certain line is passed. To make the warning fair, so far as possible the line should be clear. When a rule of conduct is laid down in words that evoke in the common mind only the picture of vehicles moving on land, the statute should not be extended to aircraft, simply because it may seem to us that a similar policy applies, or upon the speculation that, if the legislature had thought of it, very likely broader words would have been used. *United States v. Thind*, 261 U.S. 204, 209.

Judgment reversed.

Now we shall walk through the case together, pointing out its parts, and extracting the information you require from this or any other case.

Your notes can be in shorthand or your own code, just so you can always read them accurately. Most legal professionals develop their own abbreviations. In *McBoyle,* for example, you would ordinarily write "S.Ct." for Supreme Court, and "10th Cir." for Circuit Court of Appeals for the Tenth Circuit.

Title and Citation

First comes the title of the case: *McBoyle v. United States.*

Just below the case name, you find this information:

Certiorari to the Circuit Court of Appeals for the Tenth Circuit.

This line tells you where the case came from. ***Certiorari*** is the name of an ancient writ by which a higher court told a lower court to send up the case for review. *Certiorari* is still used for the same purpose. Legal professionals informally call it *cert.*

The date of decision is included in the **citation.** Note that, if the years of argument and decision are different, use the year of decision in your citation; the year of argument is not important.

certiorari
An appellate court uses the writ of certiorari as a discretionary devise to choose the cases it wishes to hear.

citation
Reference to legal authorities and precedents to fortify the propositions advanced by the document's author.

Note the title of the case, including the citation. You will need the citation for your brief or memo, or to return to the case to read it again or to check some detail.

Note the parties in the case and identify them by name (e.g., International Steel), by their relationship or by categorizing their identity (e.g., employer and employee), or by their litigation status (e.g., plaintiff and defendant or appellant and appellee).

Procedural History

Most litigation occurs in stages. For example, the first stage is from the time the law-suit is filed until it goes to trial. The second stage begins when the party who lost at trial appeals that decision. Then, should the appellate court remand the case to the trial court for further proceedings or a new trial, the third stage begins, and so on. The stages of litigation that occur *before* the opinion is written are called **prior proceedings** or **prior history.** Likewise, any stages of litigation that occur *after* the opinion is written are called **subsequent proceedings** or **subsequent history.**

Not all opinions discuss prior proceedings. Some, such as those from a trial court, may not have any. It is also possible that the prior proceedings were not significant enough to merit mention in the court's written opinion. If any prior proceedings are mentioned in the opinion, note in your brief who brought the proceeding, summarize what that party wanted, identify the court that was involved, and briefly state the outcome.

You do not need show who represented whom in the case. Omit that from your brief.

Note that the case came to the Supreme Court from the Tenth Circuit. Your brief should always include the **procedural history** of the case. That includes who sued whom and for what, and exactly what the trial court decided. Also include any intermediate appellate action, such as the 10th Circuit's decision in *McBoyle.*

Also include a brief mention of who is appealing (both sides do, sometimes) and what they are asking for. Usually the plaintiff is seeking to obtain something from the defendant, or is trying to stop the defendant from doing something. The defendant's objective may simply be to prevent the plaintiff from reaching that goal.

This information is usually in the first few paragraphs of the opinion. If there is no clear indication of the parties' objectives, you can infer them from the dispute or from any other clues you find in the opinion. If the opinion describes the plaintiff's objectives but not the defendant's, you can assume that the defendant's only goal is to prevent the plaintiff from obtaining his or her objective. Look for the *ultimate* objective—the *end result* that the party hopes to achieve.

The Opinion

Next you learn that Justice Holmes, one of the most famous of Supreme Court Justices, wrote the opinion for the entire Court. In this case none of the other justices disagreed with Holmes, although unanimous decisions are by no means usual. There may be one or more opinions in any case; briefly, these are the forms they may take:

- *Majority Opinion.* One justice writes for him- or herself and for others, making up a majority of the judges hearing the case. This is the opinion handed down in the usual case, as in *McBoyle.*

prior proceedings, prior history
The stages of litigation that occurred before the cited opinion was written.

subsequent proceedings, subsequent history
The stages of litigation that occurred after the cited opinion was written.

procedural history
The entire history of a given case, both the prior and subsequent history, which includes who sued whom and for what, and exactly what was decided by each court.

majority opinion
The opinion of an appellate court in which the majority of its members join.

- *Plurality Opinion.*   An opinion written for the greatest number of judges who can agree on a single opinion. It is less than a majority.
- *Dissenting Opinion.*   One or more justices opine that the case should be decided in a way other than the one chosen by the majority.
- *Concurring Opinion.*   One or more justices agree that the result reached by the majority or plurality opinion is correct, but wish to add their own thoughts on the reasons for the decision.
- *Per Curiam Opinion.*   *Per curiam* simply means "by the court." It is a decision, normally on a fairly routine matter, without a designated author. The term does not imply unanimity.

When you are analyzing a less-than-unanimous opinion from a court in your jurisdiction, it may be useful to note who wrote for the majority, who joined with that person, who concurred, who dissented, and so on. If the composition of the court has changed since the decision of the case you are analyzing, the change in personnel may indicate whether the court is likely to decide an identical case in the same way today.

Legal Theories of the Parties

Next, make a note of the reason for the litigation. What is the **legal theory** on which the plaintiff relies to recover against the defendant? This legal theory is not the injury for which the plaintiff seeks relief. Rather, it is a right recognized by the law which the plaintiff seeks to enforce: Is this a suit for breach of contract, or for personal injury caused by negligence, or for trespass to real property? The legal reason a plaintiff offers to support his claim is called a **cause of action** or, simply, a **claim**. Sometimes both sides will have claims against the other and defenses to their opponent's claim.

Now, note the **defense** or defenses raised by the defendant. A defense, simply put, is a legal theory offered by the defendant to show why he or she has committed no legal wrong; therefore, the plaintiff should not prevail and the claim should be dismissed. A defense may assert a contrary theory of the principle of law relied on by the plaintiff. It may be an *affirmative defense*, which is basically the assertion that the defendant had the legal right to do whatever the plaintiff complains of in the Petition or Complaint. For example, in an action for the shooting death of the plaintiff's spouse, the defendant might assert the defense of justifiable homicide—self-defense.

The most common defense is a **denial** of one or more facts necessary to support the claim. The denial is based upon a *different* view of the *same* rule of law raised by the opponent. The party asserting the denial is saying that the rule of law on which

■ PRACTICE TIP

The two types of theories of litigation are
- The *cause of action,* or *claim*
- The *defense*
A claim or defense is *always* based on one or more rules of law. A claim is the legally accepted reason for suing. The defense is the legal theory raised in response to the claim.

plurality opinion
Where there are not enough agreeing justices to form a majority of the court, a plurality opinion is one in which more justices join than in any concurring opinion.

dissenting opinion
The explicit disagreement of one or more judges of a court with the decision passed by the majority.

concurring opinion
An opinion in which one or more justices agree that the result reached by the majority or plurality opinion is correct, but wish to add their own thoughts on the reasons for the decision.

per curiam
A Latin phrase meaning "by the court."

per curiam opinion
A phrase used to distinguish an opinion of the whole court as opposed to one from an opinion written by any one judge.

legal theory
In litigation, either the cause of action, or claim, and the defense, all of which are always based upon one or more rules of law.

cause of action or claim
The fact or facts that give a person a right to judicial relief against another; the legally accepted reason for suing.

defense
Allegations of fact or legal theories offered to offset or defeat the other side's claims or demands.

affirmative defense
A defense that will
defeat the plaintiff's
claim even if the plaintiff
is able to prove all allegations in its Complaint.

denial
A type of defense in
which the defendant
denies one or more
facts necessary to sup-
port the claim.

**key fact, essential
fact, material fact,
operative fact**
A fact that is so crucial
that, if it were changed,
the holding of the opin-
ion would also have
changed; one which
tends to establish any of
the issues raised and
one upon which the out-
come of litigation
depends.

the claim is founded cannot be established because the other party has failed to prove an essential element of that rule.

The Facts

Next, read the facts of *McBoyle.* Your case brief begins with a summary of those facts, and most lawyers agree that the facts of any legal matter are its most important com-ponent. *Make sure you understand the facts of this or any case completely.* Judicial deci-sions are *fact-specific.* Courts normally do not set out to lay down ringing rules to solve cosmic questions of law. Rather, courts face a particular problem based on par-ticular facts, and it is *that* question they address, on *those* facts. The rule the court establishes in a given case may later control an identical or very similar question based on the same or very similar facts. But the rule is not intended to solve any ques-tion except the one presented in the case before the court.

The trick is determining which facts are the most important. These are called **key facts**. In other words, which facts are so crucial that, if they were changed, the hold-ing of the opinion would also have changed? Key facts are also sometimes referred to as **essential facts, material facts,** or **operative facts**. You must be able to recognize these key facts and determine during your research whether the cases you have found are relevant to your problem.

One way to find the key facts in an opinion is to note how the opinion discusses whatever prior proceedings occurred before the opinion was written. Sometimes an opinion discusses the prior proceedings but only to the extent that it tells who won at trial and who is appealing the trial court's decision. But, if you are lucky, the opin-ion will discuss *what happened* below (in the lower court). If so, then the higher court is telling you what facts it considered to be important or unimportant, and whether it agreed with the decision made by the lower court and why.

Generally speaking, judicial writers put the facts of the matter up front. But you must still watch for additional important facts that are buried elsewhere in the opin-ion. Be especially alert for extra facts that appear only in a dissent or concurring opinion. *Your brief must contain the essential facts of the case, the facts on which the court rested its opinion.* The facts must be stated in enough detail that you can easily remember what happened when you refer to your case brief again.

As you will see in the sample briefs at the end of this chapter, not all facts in a case are important enough to put in your brief. At the beginning, however, follow this rule: If you are not sure whether a fact is important enough to include in your case brief, include it. It is much better to have some extraneous facts in your brief than to omit something essential.

In *McBoyle,* your notes should reflect that McBoyle was the defendant in a crimi-nal action, accused of violating the National Motor Vehicle Theft Act. You also need to show exactly what McBoyle *did:* those acts for which he was prosecuted. Note also the citation of the Act: 18 U.S.C. § 408. The exact definition of "motor vehicle" under the act is crucial to the decision. Therefore, that language should be written *verbatim* in your brief.

Nobody can give you an infallible rule that tells you which facts to include and which to omit. But here are some rules of thumb that may help:

- Your notes should show who the parties to the litigation are, what they want, and what their relationship is. Maybe the plaintiff is a landlord, and he is suing the defendant, his tenant, for damage to the property. Here is how you might express these facts:

P landlord v. D tenant

You will develop your own abbreviations. Many people, for example, use the Greek delta (Δ) to mean "defendant," and pi (π) to mean "plaintiff." By all means use abbreviations; just be sure you can go back to your case brief later and understand what you wrote.

- Your facts must also include what the litigation is about, that is, the cause of action on which the plaintiff is suing:

π landlord v. Δ tenant for damage to aptmt & furn. caused by Δ's 12 cats.

- If the defendant has raised some sort of defense to the suit, and it bears on the question to be answered, include the facts that pertain to the defense:

π landlord v. Δ tenant for damage to aptmt & furn. caused by Δ's 12 cats. Δ relies on lease clause permitting keeping of pets & excusing damage from fair wear & tear.

Frequently you will need no more facts than this short paragraph. Sometimes you will need more. Suppose, for example, the tenant wants to defend on the ground that the landlord assured him orally, contrary to the written lease, that the tenant could keep any number of pets, and the landlord did not care what they did. The question would then be whether evidence of the oral assurance would be admissible. In that case, your facts might look like this:

π landlord v. Δ tenant for damage to aptmt & furn. caused by Δ's 12 cats. Lease says it's entire agreement betw. parties, bans pets, & holds Δ strictly liab. for all dam. Δ offers evid. of oral assurance by π that pets ok and π doesn't care what they do.

Sometimes the opinion itself draws your attention to those facts the court considers most important. Such language as "the pivotal language of the lease," or "it is critical that," or "the case turns on the fact that" points the way to facts that the court considered vital to its decision.

The Issues

Now make sure you understand, and write down, the precise question the court is deciding. Legal professionals call that question the **issue.**

> We recommend that you give the issue a separate small paragraph of its own, putting it between the facts and the reasoning of the court. Some writers put it up higher in the brief, just after the title and history of the case.

There are usually several issues, or questions of law, in an opinion. The issues roughly fall into two categories: **substantive** and **procedural**. A procedural question deals with the technicalities of bringing or defending the litigation (e.g., the format of the Complaint, the jurisdiction of the court, or the admissibility of evidence). Everything else is substantive, (e.g., the pollution of a river, the breach of a contract, or the commission of a crime).

issue
The precise question the court is deciding.

substantive issue
A question dealing with the actual law at hand.

procedural issue
A question dealing with the technicalities of bringing or defending the litigation.

Some opinions contain only procedural issues. Some contain both procedural and substantive. Pay attention to the headings or subheadings in the opinion. These will most likely tell you what the issues are (e.g., the appellant claims that Section 45 does not apply here, or the defendant asserts that this court lacks jurisdiction).

We think the issue is usually easier to understand if you put it after the facts in your case brief. An issue statement might look like this:

> **Issue:** Does the legal domicile of a married female Army officer follow the domicile of her husband, or is it determined by where she is stationed on military orders?

That, then, is the question the court must answer, the legal issue raised by the appeal. Remember that appellate courts normally do not decide broad, cosmic issues of law. What they solve are *particular,* limited questions in *particular* cases, usually grounded closely in the facts of those cases. The court usually limits its decision strictly to the facts of the case it addresses. To quote an eminent state supreme court justice:

> Why decide more when you can decide less?

As you read the sample briefs of *McBoyle* (Exhibits 8.1 and 8.2), you will see that the issue the Supreme Court addresses is the meaning of the phrase *motor vehicle* in a particular federal statute. The *McBoyle* Court does not deal with the meaning of that phrase generally, or even in every federal statute having to do with aviation law or with vehicles or with commerce. The Court limits its decision to the precise question raised on appeal:

> Does "motor vehicle" in the National Motor Vehicle Theft Act include airplanes?

Your issue must be the precise question decided by the court. You cannot loosely state a proposition "like" the question the court decided; you must be exact. In the "poor" *McBoyle* brief (Exhibit 8.2), you will see how the student framed the issue like this:

> [W]hether in federal aviation law the word "vehicle" applies to aircraft.

Wrong. First, the phrase the Court set out to interpret was *motor vehicle,* not *vehicle.* There is obviously a great difference between the two terms. Second, as we have seen, the question in *McBoyle* was limited to the meaning of *motor vehicle* under a particular act, not under the general law pertaining to aviation.

The Holding of the Court

holding
A court's answer to, or resolution of, the legal issue before it.

After you formulate the issue, your next step is to decide *how* the court answered that question. The answer to the question is called the **holding** of the court. The holding is the legal principle to be drawn from the opinion or decision of the court.

> Carefully formulate and write down the *holding* of the case. The holding is the court's answer to the *issue,* the question the court set out to solve. The court's *reasoning* is why the court answered the issues the way it did.

Some writers place the holding right after their statement of the issue in their case brief. Others put it at the end of the brief section dealing with the court's reasoning. Your statement of the court's holding should look something like this:

> **Held:** Where a female Army officer lives is decided by military orders. Therefore, her domicile is the place where she is stationed, and is not affected by the domicile of her husband.

The Court's Rationale

Next you must deal with *why* the court answered the question in the way it did, that part of the judicial opinion which applies law to fact to solve the question before the court. This is the **rationale** or **reasoning** of the court, and it must be reflected in your brief.

Condensing the court's reasoning into some manageable form is usually the toughest part of briefing a case. The court's rationale often goes on for pages. Always read the court's reasoning carefully, at least once, before trying to express it in your own words. Here is how you might state the court's reasoning in your brief of *McBoyle*:

Rationale: Congress did not intend to include aircraft under the Act. The Act applies to "motor vehicles," and:

1. "Vehicle," in ordinary use, means vehicles that run on land, but is not generally used to describe airplanes.

2. "Vehicle," where Congress and state legislatures used it elsewhere, means land-based vehicles, not aircraft.

3. Nowhere in debate or committee reports on the Act did Congress mention aircraft, although the airplane was a common means of transportation at the time of enactment.

Headnotes in the reporter will often help you in understanding the court's reasoning. They also can assist you in formulating both issue and holding. For example, consider this headnote, taken from a Nevada case, *McKinney v. Sheriff, Clark County*, 93 Nev. 70, 560 P.2d 151 (1977).

In *McKinney*, a criminal defendant challenged an indictment by the grand jury. He claimed that he could not be indicted for murder where he had conspired with other defendants to steal the victim's car, but did not know that the other conspirators murdered the victim and, in fact, ordered them not to use deadly force. The court disagreed, and one headnote summed up the court's decision this way:

Where purpose of conspiracy is to commit a dangerous felony, each member runs risk of having the venture end in homicide, even if he has forbidden others to make use of deadly force, and each is guilty of murder if one of them commits homicide in perpetration of an agreed-upon robbery.

Suppose you are reading *McKinney* to solve the question whether a criminal conspirator may escape liability for a crime he did not contemplate and even forbade. *McKinney* obviously will help you, since it deals with that very question. And the headnote above plainly spells out both the problem the court addressed and the court's answer to that question; in short, it gives you both your issue and your holding.

A reminder: As we have said several times, do *not* rely entirely on the headnote in *McKinney* to formulate your statement of the issue or the holding; the headnote is only an aid. Remember that your duty is to read the case. Pull out for yourself the issue and the holding as they are formulated in the case. Remember also, if you use *McKinney* later in a memo or brief, that you *never* cite to a headnote. Always cite the opinion in the case itself. Likewise, never quote a headnote.

Note: When you find a useful case such as *McKinney*, you will want to expand your research by running the case through *Shepard's Citator*,[2] to identify later cases

---

[2] *Shepard's Citations* (4th ed.) Colorado Springs, CO: Sheperd's/McGraw Hill, Inc., 1987.

dictum, dicta
A non-binding comment or observation made by a judge in an opinion that is *not* essential to the determination of the case.

judgment
The official decision of a court in a case brought before it.

disposition
The final decision by the court.

affirmed
A declaration by an appellate court that a judgment, decree, or order of a lower court is valid and must stand as rendered.

reversed
The setting aside by an appellate court of a decision of a lower court.

remand
To send a case back to an inferior court for some kind of further action or proceeding.

that cited *McKinney.* In preparation for this, include in your case brief the number of the *McKinney* headnote dealing with the point of law that interests you. So, after you note the holding in *McKinney,* add this: (HN 4).

Not all questions raised in a judicial opinion are issues, and not all comments by the court are holdings. Remember that an issue is the ultimate question the court must answer to decide the case. Only the *answer* to that issue can be called a holding. Often the court will deliver itself of an opinion on some point of law, a non-binding comment that is not essential to the decision in the case. Such comments are called *dicta* (singular *dictum*), a shortened version of *obiter dictum.*

You need not include *dicta* in your brief, with this exception: Where some *dictum* by a court supports or opposes whatever your firm is trying to accomplish, by all means make a note of it. It may be persuasive to another court, even though it is not binding on that court. It may also indicate what the court rendering the *dictum* will do with the matter to which the *dictum* pertains, if that court is ever called upon to address the question the *dictum* seems to answer.

The Judgment

Finally, after you have carefully stated the issue and written down the reasoning of the court and the court's holding, record what the court *did* with the case, the **judgment** it rendered, which is sometimes referred to as the court's **disposition** of the case. Often you can express that disposition in a single word: **affirmed** or **reversed**. Sometimes the court reverses the decision and **remands** it—sends it back—to an inferior court for some kind of further proceedings.

Sometimes you may want to include a dissenting or concurring opinion in your brief. A particularly well-written opinion, even if it ended up in the minority in the case for which it was written, may be persuasive to a court later considering the same or a similar problem.

In short, these are the elements of a case brief. As you get used to briefing cases, the process will become easier. You will almost automatically pick out the important facts and the reasoning of the court. The more you formulate issues and holdings, the better you will get at that exacting task.

It is very important that you brief each case *in your own words.* If you copy what the court said word for word, your brief simply parrots the language of the opinion, and you learn very little. Only if you grasp the meaning of the case and express it in your own way can you really understand what the opinion is all about. As you will see in the sample "poor brief" (Exhibit 8.2), extensive copying of the court's language produces only an overlong, uninformative attempt at a summary.

As we said at the beginning of this section, there occasionally is room for quotation in a case brief. We recommended that you quote the precise language of the National Motor Vehicle Theft Act, because the precise wording was what the Court was examining in *McBoyle.* Otherwise, however, use your own words.

■ SAMPLE CASE BRIEFS

Now take a look at two sample case briefs for McBoyle. The first one is an excellent job. The second one is so poor as to be worse than useless; it is inaccurate and incomplete, and therefore misleading. Along with both of the sample case briefs, you will find commentary assessing how effective and accurate they are, where they are satisfactory, and where they fail.

We recommend that you use this format:

- Case Name and Citation
- Facts
- Procedural History
- Issues
- Holdings
- Rationale
- Judgment

As you see in the sample case briefs, you can vary the order of the case brief's parts according to the system that works best for you. However you arrange these parts, they must all be included. We recommend that you begin with the facts; they are always the most important element in any case. As a general rule, you cannot understand either the problem or the solution without knowing what happened in the case.

There is no need to type case briefs that are for your use alone. They can be handwritten, as long as your writing is legible. We suggest that you do your case briefs on plain three-hole paper. That way, you can keep a three-ring binder for your research, and put in it all your case briefs, notes from your boss, photocopies of statutes and cases, and so on. Your research material stays neatly together, and none of it gets misplaced or lost. We also suggest that you leave a three-inch margin in your case briefs, so you can add notes later as you discover new material or come to new conclusions about the law.

Exhibit 8.1 gives an excellent example of a case brief. Reread *McBoyle v. United States,* and make a note of the necessary components of a case brief as you come to them. Then compare your notes to this sample.

EXHIBIT 8.1   *An Excellent Beginner's Case Brief*

McBoyle v. U.S.
283 U.S. 25, 51 S. Ct. 340, 75 L.Ed. 816 (1931)

Facts   The petit. on appeal, McBoyle, was prosecuted by the Fed. Govern. and convicted at trial of violating the Nat. Motor Veh. Theft Act for transporting an airplane from Ill. to Okla., knowing plane to have been stolen.

That Act (Sec. 3) specifies that

    A)   whoever
    B)   transports (or causes to be transported)
    C)   in interstate (or foreign) commerce
    D)   a motor vehicle
    E)   knowing it to have been stolen—is liable.

Section 2 of Act defines motor vehicle as "automobile, auto truck, auto wagon, motorcycle or any other self-propelled vehicle not designed for running on rails."

Procedural History
    Judg. of convic. of McBoyle by trial ct. of Sec. 3 of Act affirmed by U.S. Ct. of Appeals (10th Cir.) and U.S. Sup. Ct. granted *writ of certiorari.*

Issue   Whether the meaning of the word "vehicle" specified in part of Section 2 of the National Motor Vehicle Theft Act—"any other self-propelled vehicle not designed for running on rails"—applies to aircraft?

Continued

EXHIBIT 8.1 —*Continued*

Holding   The meaning of the word "vehicle" specified in part of Section 2 of the Nat. Motor Veh. Theft Act—"any other self-propelled vehicle not designed for running on rails"—does not apply to aircraft.

Judgment   The judgment of the United States Court of Appeals (10th Cir.), affirming the trial court judgment of conviction of *McBoyle,* is reversed. (The effect of this reversal is to over-turn the trial court judgment of conviction).

Reasoning

Determining Congressional Intent

     1)   In everyday, popular usage, the meaning of vehicle and airplane is different. A vehicle runs on land; an airplane flies.

     2)   State statutes (e.g., Conn., Ohio & Michigan), and weight of federal statutes (e.g., Traffic Act of 1930) agree with popular usage.

     3)   No evidence of congressional intent to include aircraft when this statute was passed in 1919—no mention in committee reports or in congressional debate (though airplanes were well known in 1919).

Policy

     4)   Holding serves objective that criminal statutes give fair warning of penalty if "a certain line is passed." Fairness requires a "clear" line.

     5)   Holding serves objective of judicial restraint. Court will not extend the statute because policy served is identical in punishing the transporting of either a stolen vehicle or a stolen aircraft in interstate commerce; or because Congress may simply have forgotten planes and would "very likely" have used "broader words" if it had thought of the matter.

Contrast this excellent brief of *McBoyle* with a poor brief, as shown in Exhibit 8.2. We have added the comments on the left to specify weaknesses.

EXHIBIT 8.2   *A Poor Case Brief*

McBoyle v. U.S.
283 U.S. 25 (1931)

Comments

McBoyle was the defendant in trial court. Here on appeal, he is described in the opinion as a petitioner. Use label of appellate court to avoid confusion.

Omission of statement of statutory rule violated (Sec. 3) and its elements and definition of "vehicle" (Sec. 2). This omission impedes pinpointing exactly what issue is in controversy on appeal.

Omits appeal to, and affirmance of judgment of conviction by, intermediate appellate court (U.S. Ct. of Appeals, 10th Cir.).

Facts

The defendant, McBoyle, was convicted of violating the Nat. Mot. Veh. Theft Act. He transported an airplane from Ill. to Okla., knowing plane to be stolen.

Procedural History

McBoyle was convicted by trial court and now appeals to U.S. Sup. Ct.

EXHIBIT 8.2 *—Continued*

Wrong. Far too broad—where does "aviation law" come from?

Wrong. Again, far too broad. Unsurprisingly, a wrong formulation of the issue leads to a wrong formulation of the holding.

Omits judgment.

This merely repeats what is in opinion, virtually word for word. The objective, however, is not repetition but succinct ordering, categorizing and, hence, understanding.

Issue
The issue is whether in federal aviation law the word "vehicle" applies to aircraft?

Holding
The holding is that in federal aviation law the word "vehicle" does *not* apply to aircraft.

Reasoning
No doubt etymologically it is possible to use the word to signify a conveyance working on land, water, or air, and sometimes legislation extends the use in that direction, e.g., land and air, water being separately provided for, in the Tariff Act, September 22, 1922. But in everyday speech "vehicle" calls up the picture of a thing moving on land. Thus in Rev. Stats. § 4, intended, the government suggests, rather to enlarge than to restrict the definition, vehicle includes every contrivance capable of being used "as a means of transportation on land." And this is repeated, expressly excluding aircraft, in the Tariff Act, June 17, 1930. So here, the phrase under discussion calls up the popular picture. For after including automobile truck, automobile wagon and motor cycle, the words "any other self-propelled vehicle not designed for running on rails" still indicate that a vehicle in the popular sense, that is a vehicle running on land, is the theme. It is a vehicle that runs, not something, not commonly called a vehicle, that flies. Airplanes were well known in 1919, when this statute was passed; but it is admitted that they were not mentioned in the reports or in the debates in Congress. It is impossible to read words that so carefully enumerate the different forms of motor vehicles and have no reference of any kind to aircraft, as including airplanes under a term that usage more and more precisely confines to a different class. The counsel for the petitioner have shown that the phraseology of the statute as to motor vehicles follows that of earlier statutes of Connecticut, Delaware, Ohio, Michigan and Missouri, not to mention the late Regulations of Traffic for the District of Columbia, Title 6, c. 9, § 242, none of which can be supposed to leave the earth.

Although it is not likely that a criminal will carefully consider the text of the law before he murders or steals, it is reasonable that a fair warning should be given to the world in language that the common world will understand, of what the law intends to do if a certain line is passed. To make the warning fair, so far as possible the line should be clear. When a rule of conduct is laid down in words that evoke in the common mind only the picture of vehicles moving on land, the statute should not be extended to aircraft, simply because it may seem to us that a similar policy applies, or upon the speculation that, if the legislature had thought of it, very likely broader words would have been used. *United States v. Thind*, 261 U.S. 204, 209.

CHAPTER SUMMARY

Case analysis is critical to good legal writing. Follow these rules to fully analyze any case.

- In deciding what a case means, never rely on the headnotes. Read the case and decide for yourself.
- Always assume the judge who wrote the opinion intended to be consistent with other law, and intended to make sense.
- When a case analyzes a statute, assume the court intended to interpret the statute so that it made sense.
- Carefully frame the precise issue the court was solving. Remember that appellate courts ordinarily decide the case on the narrowest possible basis.
- Your case brief must include the salient facts of the case, the holding, and the court's rationale.
- Make a note of the numbers of the headnotes that pertain to your problems. Those numbers will be useful when you shepardize the case.
- Record the complete title and citation of the case when you analyze it.
- If the case is in your own jurisdiction, it is worthwhile to note a strong, logical dissent, if there is one.

KEY WORDS AND PHRASES

affirmative defense	*dictum, dicta*	majority opinion	rationale (or reasoning)
affirmed	disposition	material fact	remand
case brief	dissenting opinion	operative fact	reversed
cause of action	essential fact	*per curiam*	*stare decisis*
certiorari	headnote	*per curiam* opinion	subsequent history
citation	holding	plurality opinion	subsequent proceedings
claim	issue	prior history	
concurring opinion	judgment	prior proceedings	substantive issue
defense	key fact	procedural history	
denial	legal theory	procedural issue	

EXERCISES

1. What is the recommended format for briefing cases? Explain each element in one or two sentences.

2. What does the term *certiorari* refer to, and how is it used in modern legal analysis?

3. If the date of the argument and the date of decision differ, which is most significant for citation purposes?

4. Explain the difference between a majority and a plurality decision.

5. What does a concurring opinion indicate?

6. What information pertaining to the litigants should be included in the "facts section" in a case brief?

7. Why is it important to state the issue or issues in a case in specific terms?

8. What is the term for the way the court ruled in a case?

9. Explain the proper use of West headnotes in case analysis.

10. How can use of headnote numbers help you to expand your research efficiently?

11. What is dicta? When is it relevant?

12. How does the court's judgment differ from the holding?

13. Why is it important to paraphrase opinions in case briefs?

Walk-Through Problem

You have been inundated with work on the Healy case, when the attorney you work with calls you into her office.

"There's an old law on the books in our state which suggests that we might be able to nail Red's Tavern for serving Charles Raymond that fourth bourbon" she says. "I have a meeting with Ms. Buechner tomorrow morning, and I haven't had a chance to research the issue yet. I did find one case, but I won't have a chance to read it before morning. I'd like you to brief the case for me, and get ready to explain it to me before my meeting. I just want the basics, but make sure you know enough about the case to make me look brilliant."

CASE

Cruse v. Aden.
SUPREME COURT OF ILLINOIS.
January 26, 1889.

APPEAL FROM APPELLATE COURT, FOURTH DISTRICT.

1. Intoxicating Liquors—Civil Damage Act—Gift by Friend.

The title of the Illinois dram-shop act, as given in the Revised Statutes of 1874, is 'Dram-Shops,' and the title of the act in full is 'An act to provide for the licensing of, and against the evils arising from, the sale of intoxicating liquors.' Section 6 provides for a penalty against 'whoever shall sell or give away liquors to minors' 'or to persons intoxicated, or who are in the habit of getting intoxicated.' Section 9 gives a right of action to persons injured in person or means of support in consequence of intoxication, against 'any person who shall by selling or giving intoxicating liquors have caused the intoxication.' All the other sections are directed exclusively against keepers of dram-shops. Const. Ill. 1870, art. 4, s 13, provides that no act shall embrace more than one subject, and that shall be expressed in the title. Held, that section 9 does not apply to persons who are not, either directly or indirectly, or in any way or to any extent, engaged in the liquor traffic, and does not give a right of action against one who gives, in his own home or elsewhere, a glass of liquor to a friend as a mere act of courtesy and politeness, without any purpose or expectancy of pecuniary gain or profit.

2. Intoxicating Liquors—Tort at Common Law.

It was not a tort at common law to either sell or give intoxicating liquors to a strong and able-bodied man.

*234 **74 W. S. Day, P. E. Hileman, and D. W. Karraker, for appellant. Monroe C. Crawford and H. F. Bussey, for appellee.

*232 **73 On the 4th day of November, 1884, George A. Cruse, husband of appellant, Julia Ann Cruse, was, while intoxicated, thrown from his

Continued

CASE—*Continued*

horse, and received injuries from which he shortly afterwards died. Thereupon said Julia Ann Cruse, his widow, prosecuted this suit in the circuit court of Union county against Adde Aden, since deceased, and obtained against him judgment for $800 damages. The suit was brought to recover damages for injury to her means of support, and the declaration concluded: 'And by force of the statute in such case made and provided an action has accrued to her against defendant for the recovery of her said damages in the premises, and therefore she brings her suit,' etc. Upon the appeal of the said Adde Aden to the appellate court of the Fourth district, the judgment of the circuit court was reversed, and the final order and judgment of said appellate court found and **74 recited the facts of the case to be as follows: 'Julia Ann Cruse, appellee and plaintiff below, at the time of the commencement of her suit was the widow of George A. Cruse, who died intestate; that during his life he furnished means of support to said appellee, and died intestate, leaving *233 a farm and other property of which he died seised and possessed; in his life-time he carried on his farm and was a strong and able-bodied man, capable of working as a farmer up to the time of his death; that by his death his widow was injured in her means of support; that the proximate cause of the accident which resulted in his death was intoxication, and that two drinks given him by appellant contributed to cause such intoxication; that said two drinks of intoxicating liquor were given to said husband of appellee by appellant as an act of mere courtesy and politeness, and not for any pay, profit, benefit, or advantage to appellant, or intended by appellant to gain for him any pay, profit, benefit, or advantage; and that appellant and said husband of appellee, at the time said two drinks were so given, were friends and acquaintances, and appellant was not then engaged, directly or indirectly, in the sale or traffic in intoxicating liquors.' Upon application of said Julia Ann Cruse, appellee in the appellate court and appellant here, the appellate court certified that 'the case involves questions of law of such importance on account of principal and collateral interests as that it should be passed upon by the supreme court,' and granted to said Julia Ann Cruse an appeal to this court, which was duly perfected.

Said appellate court further certified to this court the following grounds for granting said appeal, to-wit: 'First. That said supreme court may pass upon and decide whether or not, under section 9 of the dram-shop act of this state, a recovery can be had against a person other than a dram-shop keeper, or person who makes a business of dealing in intoxicating liquors; and whether, under said section 9, all person, though not engaged in the liquor traffic, can be held liable for selling or giving intoxicating drinks to another, thereby in whole or in part causing intoxication and injury, etc. Second. Whether or not, upon the facts found by this court in its judgment of reversal, a recovery can be had under said section 9 by appellee against appellant.' *234 Since the pendency of the appeal in the supreme court the death of said Adde Aden has been suggested, and Caroline Aden, his administratrix, has been substituted as appellee in his place and stead.

BAKER, J., (AFTER STATING THE FACTS AS ABOVE.)

If we rightly apprehend one of the claims made by counsel for appellant in his argument presented to this court, it is this: that it is not the character of the transaction or of the individual that controls the right of action involved in this suit; that such right of action existed before the statute was enacted; that every person is answerable under the law for an injury done to another; and that section 9 of the dram-shop act simply saves all remedies, and even enlarges them, so that it cannot be claimed that dram-shop keepers are exempt from damage suits of the character here in question simply because they are operating under a license from public authority for which they have paid large sums into the public treasury. This position is not tenable. It was not a tort at common law to either sell or give intoxicating liquor to 'a strong and able-bodied man,' and it can be said safely that it is not anywhere laid down in the books that such act was even held at common law to be culpable negligence that would impose legal liability for damages upon the vendor or donor of such liquor. The present suit can in no sense be regarded as an action of tort at common law. Meidel v. Anthis, 71 Ill. 241.

CASE—*Continued*

The cause of action here is necessarily purely statutory, and the question whether it is a valid cause of action must depend upon the proper construction ***75 of section 9 of the dram-shop act. *235 It is admitted by counsel for appellant that the various sections and provisions of the dram-shop law, except sections 6 and 9, are directed exclusively against dram-shop keepers and those engaged, lawfully or otherwise, in the liquor traffic; but it is insisted, in substance, that as the sixth section denounces a penalty against 'whoever shall sell or give intoxicating liquor to any minor,' 'or to any person intoxicated, or who is in the habit of getting intoxicated;' and that, as the ninth section provides in express terms that 'every husband, wife, child, parent, guardian, employer, or other person who shall be injured in person or property or means of support by any intoxicated person, or in consequence of the intoxication, habitual or otherwise, of any person, shall have a right of action in his or her own name, severally or jointly, against any person or persons who shall, by selling or giving intoxicating liquors, have caused the intoxication, in whole or in part, of such person or persons;' and that, as these sections, respectively, use the words 'sell or give,' and the phrase 'by selling or giving,' there is no occasion for construing such language, it needing no construction; and that the plain intention of section 6 is to protect minors, intoxicated persons, and habitual drunkards from either sales or gifts of intoxicating liquors, not on the ground that the giver is a dram-shop keeper, but for the protection of the minor, intoxicated person, and drunkard, and family; and that section 9 is intended to provide a remedy for those who are injured in person, property, or means of support by the conduct of others, be they dram-shop keepers or other persons. Section 13, art. 4, of the constitution of 1870, provides: 'No act hereafter passed shall embrace more than one subject, and that shall be expressed in the title. But if any subject shall be embraced in an act which shall not be expressed in the title, such act shall be void only as to so much thereof as shall not be so expressed.' In the Revised Statutes of 1874 the title of the act under consideration is 'Dram-*236 Shops,' and the title of the act in full is: 'An act to provide for the licensing of and against the evils arising from the sale of intoxicating liquors.' If the intent and scope of said sections 6 and 9 are as broad as the contention of appellant claims they are, and include the acts of a person who is not engaged, either directly or indirectly, in selling intoxicating liquor, but who merely gives at his private residence or elsewhere a drink or two of wine, beer, or other liquor, to a guest, friend, or neighbor, as a mere courtesy or act of politeness, and without any consideration whatever, pecuniary or otherwise, then it would seem such sections would, to the extent they include such acts of such person, be in violation of the constitutional provision we have cited, and void. The matters contained in said sections 6 and 9, and in section 13, even including the provisions in respect to gifts of intoxicating liquor, if limited to those who are in some way connected with the sale of intoxicating liquor, legitimately appertain and are germane to the subject expressed in the title of the act, but in respect to mere gifts of liquor by persons not connected directly or indirectly with the liquor traffic, or with any sale of liquor, it cannot fairly be said such gifts by them are embraced or expressed in such title. But we do not think said sections, or either of them, when properly interpreted, are in any respect whatever invalid. The title of an act, and especially where there is a constitutional provision, such as we have above mentioned, may very properly be regarded in seeking to ascertain the legislative intention and the real meaning of such act. Both the general title, 'Dram-Shops,' and the title of the act itself, indicates that the various provisions of the statute are aimed at dram-shops, and at those who are engaged, either lawfully or unlawfully, directly or indirectly, in the liquor traffic.

In determining the scope of the statute, and arriving at the true intent of its several provisions, not only should the title of the act be taken into consideration, but every other part of the same statute *237 should be considered, for the real object and intention of the legislature is to be gathered from an examination ***76 and comparison of the context of the whole act, thereby ascertaining its spirit, import, and meaning.

Continued

CASE—*Continued*

People v. Canal Com'rs, 3 Scam. 153; Perteet v. People, 65 Ill. 230; Biggs v. Clapp, 74 Ill. 335. It is admitted, as we have seen, that all the other sections of dram-shops, and those who make a sale or sales of intoxicating liquor. It seems useless, therefore, to analyze and examine said several sections for the purpose of demonstrating and showing the general scope of the statute. In three only of the sections of the act is any notice taken of 'gifts' of liquor. The thirteenth section provides that 'the giving away of intoxicating liquors, or other shift or device to evade the provisions of this act, shall be held to be an unlawful selling.' If in this section the words, 'the giving away of intoxicating liquors, * * * shall be held to be an unlawful selling,' are construed as meaning that the mere act of giving away intoxicating liquor by any person is an unlawful selling, then it would not only leave the remaining clause, 'or other shift or device to evade the provisions of this act,' without significance but it would render any person who, at his own table, at his private residence, gave a glass of wine to a guest as an act of hospitality, liable to the fines and penalties imposed by section 2 of the act, without such person had a license to keep a dram-shop. It is unreasonable to suppose such result was contemplated. Said section 13 does not in express terms say that it is applicable only to persons engaged in the liquor traffic; and yet it is plain from the context that only such persons are within its purview, and that in respect to them, and them only, a 'giving away of intoxicating liquors' is regarded as a 'shift or device to evade the provisions of this act.'

It is but reasonable to presume, since there is nothing in the context to rebut such presumption, and it is in conformity with the title and general scope of the act, that the legislature, *238 in using these words 'give' and 'giving' in these three sections of the same act, intended they should have one and the same meaning. Since the expression, 'the giving away of intoxicating liquors,' found in section 13 has reference only to those who are engaged or participate in the liquor traffic, or make a sale or sale of liquor as a matter of business, we may conclude the expression, 'against any person or persons who shall by selling or giving intoxicating liquors,' found in section 9, have a like restricted sense and signification. This court some years ago virtually decided the question here at issue in respect to the construction to be given the words, 'against any person or persons who shall by selling or giving intoxicating liquors,' contained in section 9 by the construction it gave to the words, 'whoever shall sell or give intoxicating liquor,' contained in section 6. The first-mentioned set of words are no broader or more inclusive than the latter, and it is evident that both expressions stand upon the same footing.

In Albrecht v. People, 78 Ill. 510, it was held that the provisions of section 6 do not apply to a person who, at his private house, and as an act of hospitality, gives a glass of beer to a visitor or friend alleged to be intoxicated, and that such a case was not one contemplated by said section. The decision in the later case of Johnson v. People, 83 Ill. 431, did not, as seems to be supposed, overrule the decision in the Albrecht Case. In the Johnson Case it was held that, whether a person is or is not the keeper of a dram-shop, he cannot sell intoxicating liquors to minors without incurring the penalties prescribed by said section 6 of the statute; and further held that a person employed in making change for parties engaged in unlawfully selling intoxicating liquors to minors may be convicted on indictment for selling the liquors, on the ground he aided, abetted, and assisted in such sales. In the opinion filed in that case it was said: 'It is not necessary to now determine whether a person would incur the penalty *239 of this section by giving liquors as an act of **77 hospitality at his house, as that question is not before the court.' The decisions in the two cases above mentioned were both undoubtedly right, and entirely consistent with each other; but expressions were used in the opinions in each of the cases which were unnecessary, and probably not entirely accurate.

In the construction of a statute, the courts are not confined to the literal meaning of the words in the statute, but the intention may be collected from the necessity or objects of the act, and its words may be enlarged or restricted, according to its true intent. Castner v. Walrod, 83 Ill. 171. The

CASE—*Continued*

dram-shop act now under consideration is a statute of a highly penal character, and provides rights of action unknown to the common law, and should, according to well understood canons, receive a strict construction. Taylor v. Sprinkle, Breese *1, 17; Pickering v. Misner, 11 Ill. 597; Freese v. Tripp, 70 Ill. 496; Meided v. Anthis, 71 Ill. 241; Albrecht v. People, 78 Ill. 510. A very full and elaborate discussion and comparison of the several sections and provisions of the dram-shop act, as bearing upon the question of the construction to be given section 9 of said act, will be found in the opinion of the appellate court, by GREEN, J., delivered in this cause, and reported in Aden v. Cruse, 21 Bradw. 401; and it

is deemed unnecessary to repeat the reasoning of that opinion.

We concur in the conclusion reached by the appellate court, that section 9 of the dram-shop act does not apply to persons who are not either directly or indirectly, or in any way, or to any extent, engaged in the liquor traffic, and that the right of action given by said section to one injured in her means of support is not intended to be given against a person who, in his own house or elsewhere, gives a glass of intoxicating liquor to a friend as a mere act of courtesy and politeness, and without any purpose or expectation of pecuniary gain or profit. The judgment of the appellate court was clearly right, and is affirmed.

source: Copr. (C) West 1994 No claim to orig. U.S. govt. works (Cite as: 127 Ill. 231. *238, 20 N.E. 73, *76)

The attorney gives you a copy of *Cruse v. Aden*, 127 Ill. 231, 20 N.E. 73 (1889). First, read the case carefully, without taking notes, and get ready to brief the case using the method described in this chapter. We will walk you through this case and help you pinpoint what you need for your case brief.

But before you do any writing, check to see how carefully you have read the case and whether you have grasped the important points. Try to answer these questions from memory:

- Which court heard this case?
- What is significant about the date of the case?

1. Now think about how the case got to the Illinois Supreme Court.
   a. Is this a civil or criminal matter? How do you know?
   b. Who brought the suit, and why?
   c. What were the parties' objectives?
   d. Who was the other party in the suit?
   e. What was the theory (or theories) of the litigation?
   f. What was the trial court's decision?
   g. How did Mr. Aden respond to the trial court's decision?
   h. How did the appeal turn out?
   i. Who brought the case to the Illinois Supreme Court?

   j. When the case came to the Illinois Supreme Court, who was the appellant?
   k. On what basis did the appellate court approve the appeal to the Illinois Supreme Court?
   l. Who wrote the majority opinion?
   m. Which of his peers wrote the dissent?

2. Now, state the facts of the case in three or four sentences.
   a. On what authority did the Widow Cruse base her claim?
   b. What was Mr. Aden's defense to the widow's claim?
   c. What were the issues in the case?
   d. Did the Illinois Supreme Court accept the appellant's or the appellee's argument?

3. We can hardly bear to think of poor Widow Cruse being left without a cause of action. So, we are going to turn back the hands of time, and ask you to change the facts of this case. *Think about which facts were central to the court's holding.* What fact(s) would you change if you wanted the court to find for Widow Cruse?

Do not be discouraged if you could not answer all of the questions above. This exercise was to emphasize how important it is to read carefully and comprehend your research.

Practicing Your Writing

1. You now have an opportunity to redeem yourself:
   Write a case brief of *Cruse v. Aden* following the
   format outlined in this chapter.

   To get the most out of this exercise, after,—and
   only after—you have drafted your own case brief
   of *Cruse v. Aden,* compare it to the sample in
   Appendix D. It is not important that your case
   brief match ours word for word, but it should
   contain the same basic information. If the content of your case brief differs significantly from
   the sample provided in Appendix D, reread *Cruse
   v. Aden* and, as you come across the information
   in our case brief, highlight or underline that language in *Cruse.* Go back and correct your case
   brief where necessary.

2. Jane Healy is calling you from her hospital bed.
   "My cousin Paul is an attorney in Wisconsin. He
   said that I might have a cause of action against
   the automobile manufacturer because of the
   faulty seat belt in my car. Paul even gave me the
   citation for a case that he says will support my
   claim."

   Jane's attorney is interested in the case, but
   really does not have the time to explore its relevance.

   She asks you to brief the case for a meeting
   tomorrow.

   Carefully read *Arbet v. Gussarson,* 66 Wis. 2d
   551, 225 N.W.2d 431 (1975), which begins on the
   following page. The following questions will help
   you to work through the process of case analysis.
   Try to answer the questions below from memory.
   If you paid attention to the proper elements of
   the case as you read it, you should be able to
   answer the questions without referring to the

   case. Do not worry. Regardless of how well you
   do with this exercise, your comprehension and
   analytic skills will improve with practice.
   a. Which court heard this case?
   b. Is this a civil or a criminal case? How do you
      know?
   c. What happened to this case at the trial level?
   d. Who brought the suit, and why?
   e. What damages did the injured parties seek?
   f. What single issue did the court consider?
   g. Which justice wrote the opinion?
   h. State the facts of the case in three or four sen-
      tences.
   i. Upon what legal theory did the plaintiffs base
      their cause of action?
   j. In Wisconsin, what must the plaintiff show to
      establish a manufacturer's strict liability?
   k. If the plaintiff meets its burden of establish-
      ing those elements of a claim, how may the
      defendant refute the claim?
   l. What did the Wisconsin Supreme Court say
      about the difference between negligent
      design and negligent manufacturing?
   m. Was it significant that the flaws in the design
      were not apparent to the casual observer?
   n. What was the defendant's argument for non-
      liability?
   o. Who won?

3. Now draft the case brief on *Arbet v. Gussarson.*
   After you have briefed the case, go to the next
   exercise to discuss the process of applying this
   case to Jane Healy's circumstances.

4. How are the facts in *Arbet v. Gussarson* similar to
   the facts in Jane Healy's situation?

5. What factors are different in our scenario and in
   Arbet?

CASE

ARBET v. GUSSARSON   Wis.   **431**
Cite as 225 N.W.2d 431

the building is constructed in accordance with accepted practices, even though some other practice might have rendered the building more safe. This is a recognition that construction involves the balancing of many considerations.[2] *Spote* is distinguishable, because there was no question that the nails, if they protruded, constituted a hazard.

[5–7] At common law, the highest duty owed by an owner of land toward someone on the premises was that of ordinary care, owed to an invitee.[3] This duty could be satisfied by alternative means. The landowner might either have his premises in a reasonably safe condition or give the invitee adequate and timely warning of latent and concealed perils which are known to the invitor but not to the invitee.[4] Another way of stating this same proposition is that there is no duty to inspect and warn unless it is shown that the premises were not in a reasonably safe condition. The statutory safe place duty to construct and maintain a public building as safe as its nature will reasonably permit is not a lesser standard than that imposed by the common law.[5] *A fortiori* no violation of a common law duty is shown if violation of the safe place statute cannot be established.

[8, 9] Plaintiff argues that defendant breached its common law duty of ordinary care by failing to warn her that the machine was topheavy. However, the evidence shows that the topheavy machine presented a danger only when it was wheeled into the delivery area to clean it with the air hose. Moreover, she had cleaned the machine in the delivery area at least 52 times prior to the accident. Her opportunity to observe and to discover any danger was greater than the opportunity of

any employee of the defendant. If the danger here was discoverable in the exercise of ordinary care, plaintiff was at least as negligent for her own safety as the defendant was in failing to warn her of the condition.[6]

Judgment affirmed.

66 Wis.2d 551

Jane ARBET et al., Appellants,

v.

**Mark GUSSARSON et al., Defendants,
American Motors Corp., Respondent.**

No. 462.

Supreme Court of Wisconsin.

Feb. 4, 1975.

Automobile driver and passenger brought action against second automobile driver and manufacturer to recover for injuries sustained when automobile was rear-ended by another automobile and the gas tank ruptured and fuel ignited. The Circuit Court, Kenosha County, Harold M. Bode, J., sustained manufacturer's demurrer and passenger and driver appealed. The Supreme Court, Wilkie, C. J., held that an automobile manufacturer could incur liability for injury to occupants of an automobile arising from manufacturer's negligence in designing the car so that it was unreasonably unsafe in an accident, even though the defect in design did not cause the acci-

2. An exception is where such general usage is inherently dangerous or obviously improper. Patterson v. Silverdale Resort, Inc. (1959), 8 Wis.2d 572, 99 N.W.2d 730.

3. Carr v. Amusement, Inc. (1970), 47 Wis.2d 368, 177 N.W.2d 388.

4. Schlicht v. Thesing (1964), 25 Wis.2d 436, 130 N.W.2d 763.

5. Rosholt v. Worden-Allen Co. (1913), 155 Wis. 168, 144 N.W. 650.

6. The comparative negligence law applicable to this case bars recovery unless the defendant's negligence was greater than that of the plaintiff. Holzem v. Mueller (1972), 54 Wis.2d 388, 195 N.W.2d 635.

Continued

CASE—*Continued*

dent; that complaint stated a cause of action for strict liability; that driver and passenger did not misuse the automobile by being rear-ended; that public policy did not preclude recovery; and that Congress had not preempted the field of automobile safety regulation.

Reversed and remanded.

Day, J., did not participate.

1. Automobiles ⊜ 16

Automobile manufacturer may incur liability for injuries to occupants of an automobile arising from the manufacturer's negligence in designing the car so that it is unreasonably unsafe in an accident.

2. Automobiles ⊜ 16

Complaint which alleged that when automobile in which plaintiffs were riding was struck in the rear, the front seat failed, causing passenger to be propelled into the rearmost portion of the automobile, that all four doors jammed, blocking all possiblity of normal exit, that gas tank ruptured spreading gasoline on the highway which was ignited by a unknown source, and that heat from the fire melted a gas line plastic vent container in the passenger compartment causing fire inside the car, severely burning passenger and burning driver as he tried to free the passenger, stated a cause of action for strict liability under Wisconsin products liability law.

3. Products Liability ⊜ 75

Where plaintiff shows that a manufacturer markets a product in a defective condition, which was unreasonably dangerous to the user, the manufacturer then has the burden to prove lack of negligence.

4. Products Liability ⊜ 11

Fact that defect in product relates to design rather than negligent manufacture does not excuse manufacturer from strict liability.

5. Products Liability ⊜ 11

In order for manufacturer to be held strictly liable for defect in design in product, the product must contain a dangerous defect whose presence an ordinary consumer would not reasonably expect.

6. Products Liability ⊜ 11

Fact that defect in design did not actually cause initial accident does not prevent recovery from manufacturer in strict liability as long as the defect was a substantial factor in causing the injury as alleged in the complaint.

7. Automobiles ⊜ 16

Passenger and driver in automobile which was rear-ended by another automobile did not misuse their automobile, and thus were not precluded from recovering from manufacturer for defect in design of the automobile which made the automobile uncrashworthy.

8. Automobiles ⊜ 16

Even if actions of automobile driver and passenger struck in the rear by another automobile did misuse the automobile, such a "misuse" was reasonably foreseeable by the manufacturer and that alleged misuse would not preclude driver and passenger from recovering from the manufacturer in strict liability for defect in the design of the automobile which made it uncrashworthy.

9. Automobiles ⊜ 16

Automobile manufacturer, in designing automobile, has a duty to anticipate risk that the automobile may be rear-ended.

10. Automobiles ⊜ 16

Neither possibility of deluge of litigation, nor possibility that unsophisticated juries would be unable to evaluate complex economic and engineering data presented at trial, nor fact that automobile manufacturers might be subjected to piecemeal regulation by different juries in different states precluded, on basis of public policy considerations, driver and passenger in automobile from recovering from manufacturer for injuries caused by defect in design of the

CASE—*Continued*

ARBET v. GUSSARSON   Wis.   **433**
Cite as 225 N.W.2d 431

automobile which made it uncrashworthy, even though the defect did not cause the accident.

11. States ⇐4.14

Federal safety regulations established by the National Highway Traffic Safety Administration, pursuant to the National Traffic and Motor Vehicle Safety Act do not preempt the field of automobile safety regulation and do not render state courts powerless to award damages to persons who are injured by defect in design of automobile which causes the automobile to be uncrashworthy. National Traffic and Motor Vehicle Safety Act of 1966, §§ 1 et seq., 108(c), 15 U.S.C.A. §§ 1381 et seq., 1397(c).

12. Automobiles ⇐16

Problem of automobile design is not exclusively legislative and courts may award damages under doctrine of products liability for negligent design which causes an automobile to be uncrashworthy. National Traffic and Motor Vehicle Safety Act of 1966, § 108(c), 15 U.S.C.A. § 1397(c).

Habush, Gillick, Habush, Davis & Murphy, Milwaukee, for appellants; Howard A. Davis, Milwaukee, of counsel.

Schoone, McManus, Hanson & Grady, S. C., Racine, for respondent; Kevin M. O'Donnell and Leah M. Lampone, of counsel.

WILKIE, Chief Justice.

This is a "crashworthiness" products liability case arising from an automobile accident in which plaintiffs-appellants, Jane and Raymond Arbet were burned following the rupture of their vehicle's gasoline tank and ignition of the fuel. The Arbets sued defendant Mark Gussarson, the driver of the car that rear-ended their car, and defendant-respondent American Motors Corporation, the manufacturer of the Arbets' car. Gussarson is not a party to this appeal. The Arbets allege American Motors negligently designed and manufactured

their car and that such negligence, while not causing the collision itself, did proximately cause the burn injuries. The trial court sustained American Motors' demurrer to plaintiffs' second amended complaint and judgment was entered accordingly. Plaintiffs appeal and we reverse.

[1]   The sole issue raised by this appeal is whether an automobile manufacturer may incur liability for injuries to occupants of a car arising from the manufacturer's negligence in designing the car such that it is unreasonably unsafe in an accident.

We conclude that the automobile manufacturer may, and we therefore uphold the complaint as against the demurrer of American Motors Corporation.

The second amended complaint alleges the following facts: On February 15, 1972, in Kenosha county, Raymond Arbet was driving and his wife Jane was a passenger in a 1967 Rambler Station Wagon that the couple had purchased new directly from American Motors. Raymond was waiting to make a left turn when the allegedly intoxicated defendant Gussarson allegedly negligently rammed his car into the rear of the Arbets' car. The sequence of events following the collision was as follows: The front seat failed, causing Jane Arbet to be propelled into the rearmost portion of the station wagon; all four doors jammed "blocking all possibility of normal exit," and preventing Raymond, who apparently escaped through a window, from quickly freeing his wife. The gas tank ruptured, spreading gasoline on the highway that was ignited by an unknown source; the heat from the fire melted a gas line "plastic vent container in the passenger compartment" causing fire inside the car, severely burning Jane Arbet and also burning Raymond as he tried to free his wife. The complaint then alleges that "neither plaintiff would have been injured by the fire if the station wagon had not been negligently designed."

The second amended complaint attempts to state causes of action against American

Continued

CASE—*Continued*

Motors based upon ordinary negligence and upon strict liability.[1] The complaint contains substantially similar allegations of negligent conduct to support both theories: (1) design of the gas tank so that it would completely rupture following impact, despite feasible means within the then-existing state of the art to build a gas tank that would retard leakage upon impact; (2) design of body and frame resulting in buckling and jamming of doors upon impact; (3) use of plastic breather mechanism retaining gasoline in passenger compartment where plastic could melt from heat from fire below vehicle, thus spreading gasoline inside car. The plastic mechanism was allegedly only used on 1967 Rambler three-seater station wagons and was subsequently replaced with a breather that would not retain gasoline in the passenger compartment; (4) failure to properly manufacture and inspect to insure that cars sold were not unreasonably dangerous; (5) failure to test and to establish quality controls to insure that the plastic breather mechanism would operate properly; (6) failure to warn potential users of the car of the above hidden dangers in the event of a collision. In addition, to support the strict liability theory the complaint alleges the car was defective and unreasonably dangerous, that American Motors was in the business of selling automobiles, and that the car was expected to and did reach the Arbets in substantially the same condition as when it was sold. The complaint seeks total damages of $2,550,000.

[2] This complaint states a cause of action for strict liability under Wisconsin products liability law.

[3] The doctrine of strict products liability under sec. 402A of the Restatement of Torts 2d [2] was first adopted by this court in Dippel v. Sciano [3] and was most recently restated in Powers v. Hunt-Wesson Foods, Inc.[4] Under this doctrine, where plaintiff shows that a manufacturer markets a product in a "defective condition" which is "unreasonably dangerous to the user," the manufacturer then has the burden to prove lack of negligence.

In the instant case, plaintiffs primarily allege that the car was defectively designed so that it was unreasonably dangerous in an accident. Plaintiffs do not ask that cars be built like Sherman tanks; rather, merely that they not contain design features rendering them unreasonably unsafe in an accident.

There is no question that the complaint alleges facts showing the car to be "unreasonably dangerous" in an accident—particularly the allegations concerning the plastic apparatus retaining gasoline in the passenger compartment indicate unreasonable danger.

---

1. The second amended complaint actually alleges six causes of action. The first three are based upon the negligence theory: the first in Jane Arbet's behalf for personal injuries, the second on Raymond Arbet's behalf for personal injuries, and the third also on Raymond's behalf for medical expenses arising from Jane's injuries and for loss of society and companionship. The latter three causes of action are based upon strict liability and are divided in a manner similar to the first three causes of action.

2. This section provides:
"Special Liability of Seller of Product for Physical Harm to User or Consumer
"(1) One who sells any product in a defective condition unreasonably dangerous to the user or consumer or to his property is subject to liability for physical harm thereby caused to the ultimate user or consumer, or to his property, if
"(a) the seller is engaged in the business of selling such a product, and
"(b) it is expected to and does reach the user or consumer without substantial change in the condition in which it is sold.
"(2) The rule stated in Subsection (1) applies although
"(a) the seller has exercised all possible care in the preparation and sale of his product, and
"(b) the user or consumer has not bought the product from or entered into any contractual relation with the seller."
Restatement, 2 Torts 2d, pp. 347, 348, sec. 402A.

3. (1967), 37 Wis.2d 443, 155 N.W.2d 55.

4. (1974), 64 Wis.2d 532, 219 N.W.2d 393.

CASE—*Continued*

ARBET v. GUSSARSON

Wis. **435**

Cite as 225 N.W.2d 431

[4, 5] The fact that the defect relates to *design* rather than *negligent manufacture* makes no difference. In Schuh v. Fox River Tractor Co.[5] this court held that a manufacturer could be liable under a strict products liability theory where it had designed a machine such that it was unreasonably dangerous. The plaintiff had tried the case under the theory that the defendant manufacturer had located the clutch lever on a crop blower machine in a place where the machine operator might be misled as to the lever's function. This court held that plaintiff had sustained his burden of proof that this design was unreasonably dangerous within the meaning of sec. 402A of the Restatement:

"We are of the opinion that there is credible evidence upon which the jury could find that the positioning of the lever was unusual and misleading. There is credible evidence that the location of the clutch lever contradicted the custom and practice of other manufacturers, who designed their machines in accordance with the accepted functional design engineering rule explained by Dr. Wardle. The jury could well have concluded that the placement of this lever could lead a potential user of the machine to believe he was stopping both the auger and the fan when he pulled the lever. In the absence of a warning to the contrary, the jury could well conclude that the machine was unreasonably dangerous and defective in its design by locating the control lever in such a misleading position without an appropriate warning." [6]

It must be noted also that the design characteristics complained of in the instant case were hidden dangers, not apparent to the buyer of the car, and not the subject of a manufacturer's warning. This is a different case, therefore, then a case where a plaintiff sues the manufacturer of a Volkswagen and complains that the car was designed too small to be safe. Such a defect could hardly be said to be hidden. To be an "unreasonably dangerous" defect for strict products liability purposes, comment *i* to sec. 402A, Restatement, 2 Torts 2d, says in part:

" . . . The article sold must be dangerous to an extent beyond that which would be contemplated by the ordinary consumer who purchases it, with the ordinary knowledge common to the community as to its characteristics."

Thus, under this definition, since the ordinary consumer would expect a Volkswagen to be less safe in an accident than, say, a Cadillac, the smallness of the car with the attendant danger would not *per se* render it inherently dangerous. Rather it must contain a dangerous defect whose presence an ordinary consumer would not reasonably expect.

[6] Additionally it is not important that the defect did not actually cause the initial accident, as long as it was a substantial factor in causing injury as alleged in plaintiffs' complaint. As this court held in Schnabl v. Ford Motor Co.: [7]

" . . . Appellant is not suing for total injuries, but for the death alleged to have been caused by the incremental injury which occurred because of the faulty seat belt.

"This court has held that 'The test of cause in Wisconsin is whether the defendant's negligence was a substantial factor in contributing to the result.' It need not be the sole factor, the primary factor, only 'a substantial factor.' Whether the delivery in Wisconsin of a faulty seat belt could have been a substantial factor in causing the death of deceased, even if it played no part in the accident, is a question of fact to be determined by the trier of fact."

Defendant argues that there can be no liability here because plaintiffs *misused* the

5. (1974), 63 Wis.2d 728, 218 N.W.2d 279.

6. *Id.* at page 737, 218 N.W.2d at page 284.

7. (1972), 54 Wis.2d 345, 353, 354, 195 N.W.2d 602, 198 N.W.2d 161.

Continued

CASE—*Continued*

car, *i. e.* cars were not intended to be "used" to have an accident. Defendant argues that even though accidents are foreseeable, that does not establish a duty on the part of the manufacturer to design a reasonably safe car.

[7–9] For two reasons, however, defendant is wrong. First, plaintiffs did not misuse the car. They did not intentionally have an accident or use the car to knock down trees in a forest. The accident occurred while plaintiffs were using the car for the purpose for which it was intended, normal driving on the highway. Second, even if the plaintiffs did misuse the car, that would not *ipso facto* defeat their claim if the misuse, or risk of an accident, was reasonably foreseeable. Clearly the risk that a car may be in a rear-end accident is reasonably foreseeable by defendant. Therefore, defendant has a duty to anticipate that risk. As the court said in *Schuh*: [8]

    " ' . . . "Intended use" is but a convenient adaptation of the basic test of "reasonable foreseeability" framed to more specifically fit the factual situations out of which arise questions of a manufacturer's liability for negligence. "Intended use" is not an inflexible formula to be apodictically applied to every case. Normally a seller or manufacturer is entitled to anticipate that the product he deals in will be used only for the purposes for which it is manufactured and sold; thus he is expected to reasonably foresee only injuries arising in the course of such use.

    " 'However, he must also be expected to anticipate the environment which is normal for the use of his product and where, as here, that environment is the home, *he must anticipate the reasonably foreseeable risks of the use of his product*

in such an environment. These are risks which are inherent in the proper use for which his product is manufactured. . . . " (Emphasis supplied.)

However, as the court also noted in *Schuh*, misuse of a product may be considered contributory negligence:

    " . . . Every manufacturer intends his machinery to be used *safely*. But it is not necessarily a complete defense to liability to show that the machine was being used otherwise. Under certain circumstances, misuse may constitute contributory negligence and thus be a factor in the comparison of negligence." [9]

Thus it is clear that plaintiffs' complaint states a cause of action for strict products liability under Wisconsin law. In view of our conclusion, it is unnecessary to extensively examine the numerous cases cited by the parties from other jurisdictions.[10] The leading case in this area is Larsen v. General Motors Corp.,[11] a decision of the Eighth Federal Circuit Court of Appeals applying Michigan law.

In *Larsen*, plaintiff sued General Motors for injuries caused by the allegedly negligent design of a Corvair's steering column which, in a head-on collision, allegedly acted as a spear propelled with great force directly at the driver's head. The court reversed the trial court's grant of summary judgment, and allowed plaintiff to proceed to trial. Concerning the problem of misuse the court said:

    "Accepting, therefore, the principle that a manufacturer's duty of design and construction extends to producing a product that is reasonably fit for its intended use and free of hidden defects that could render it unsafe for such use, the issue narrows on the proper interpretation of

---

8. 63 Wis.2d at 741, 218 N.W.2d at 607.

9. *Id.*

10. For a good review of recent cases on this subject, *see* Volkswagen of America, Inc. v. Young (1974), 272 Md. 201, 321 A.2d 737.

11. (8th Cir. 1968), 391 F.2d 495. *Contra,* Evans v. General Motors Corp. (7th Cir. 1966), 359 F.2d 822, certiorari denied, 385 U.S. 836, 87 S.Ct. 83, 17 L.Ed.2d 70; *but see* Nanda v. Ford Motor Co., 509 F.2d 213 (7th Cir. 1974).

CASE—*Continued*

'intended use'. Automobiles are made for use on the roads and highways in transporting persons and cargo to and from various points. This intended use cannot be carried out without encountering in varying degrees the statistically proved hazard of injury-producing impacts of various types. The manufacturer should not be heard to say that it does not intend its product to be involved in any accident when it can easily foresee and when it knows that the probability over the life of its product is high, that it will be involved in some type of injury-producing accident. O'Connell in his article 'Taming the Automobile,' 58 Nw.U.L.Rev. 299, 348 (1963) cites that between one-fourth to two-thirds of all automobiles during their use at some time are involved in an accident producing injury or death. . . . It should be recognized that the environment in which a product is used must be taken into consideration by the manufacturer." [12]

Concerning the problem of imposing liability based upon design as opposed to construction defects, the court said:

" . . . We perceive of no sound reason, either in logic or experience, nor any command in precedent, why the manufacturer should not be held to a reasonable duty of care in the design of its vehicle consonant with the state of the art to minimize the effect of accidents. The manufacturers are not insurers but should be held to a standard of reasonable care in design to provide a reasonably safe vehicle in which to travel. . . .

" . . . The duty of reasonable care in design should be viewed in light of the risk. While all risks cannot be eliminated nor can a crash-proof vehicle be designed under the present state of the art, there are many common-sense factors in design, which are or should be well known

to the manufacturer that will minimize or lessen the injurious effects of a collision.

The standard of reasonable care is applied in many other negligence situations and should be applied here.

"The courts since MacPherson v. Buick Motor Co., 217 N.Y. 382, 111 N.E. 1050, L.R.A.1916F., 696 (1916) have held that a manufacturer of automobiles is under a duty to construct a vehicle that is free of latent and hidden defects. We can perceive of no significant difference in imposing a common law duty of a reasonable standard of care in design the same as in construction. A defect in either can cause severe injury or death and a negligent design defect should be actionable. Any design defect not causing the accident would not subject the manufacturer to liability for the entire damage, but the manufacturer should be liable for that portion of the damage or injury caused by the defective design over and above the damage or injury that probably would have occurred as a result of the impact or collision absent the defective design." [13]

[10] Defendant finally argues that several public policy considerations dictate that no liability should flow from injuries caused by an automobile designed so that it is unreasonably dangerous. We disagree.

First, defendant raises the spectre of a deluge of litigation flooding both the courts and automobile manufacturers. It seems doubtful that a large number of additional actions would be commenced, although it does seem likely that automobile manufacturers will more frequently be joined as parties defendant. However, regardless of the amount of increased litigation that might arise it would be highly inequitable to create a special exception to the products liability doctrine for automobiles.

---

12. 391 F.2d 501, 502.

13. *Id.* at page 503.

Continued

CASE—*Continued*

Second, defendant asserts that unsophisticated juries would not be able to properly evaluate the complex economic and engineering data that would be presented at trial. However, juries are always called upon to make decisions based upon complex facts in many different kinds of litigation. Skillful trial lawyers should be able to reduce complicated concepts to ideas readily understandable to lay juries. The problems presented in products liability jury trials would appear no more insurmountable than similar problems in other areas of the law.

[11, 12] Finally, defendant argues that the national character of the automobile industry dictates that automobile design not be subject to piecemeal regulation by different juries in different states. Defendant argues that the problem of designing safe cars is for the Congress, not state courts, and that federal safety regulations established by the National Highway Traffic Safety Administration, pursuant to the National Traffic and Motor Vehicle Safety Act of 1966,[14] preempt the field of automobile safety regulation thus rendering state courts powerless to act in this area. Defendant completely overlooks, however, 15 U.S.Code, sec. 1397(c), which provides as follows:

> "Continuation of common law liability
>
> "(c) Compliance with any Federal motor vehicle safety standard issued under this subchapter does not exempt any person from any liability under common law."

Thus Congress felt that federal regulations should be supplementary to the common law of products liability. Defendant's argument that the problem of automobile design is exclusively legislative must therefore be rejected.

Order and judgment reversed; cause remanded for further proceedings not inconsistent with this opinion.

DAY, J., did not participate.

14. 15 U.S.Code, sec. 1381 et seq. (1970).

66 Wis.2d 602

STATE of Wisconsin, Plaintiff,

v.

Brenda SIDNEY, Defendant.

Joseph J. ATTWELL, Appellant,

v.

MILWAUKEE COUNTY, Respondent.

No. State 108.

Supreme Court of Wisconsin.

Feb. 4, 1975.

Court-appointed attorney, who had represented indigent client in connection with petition for habeas corpus to challenge probation revocation, filed petition for fees. The County Court, Milwaukee County, Fred P. Kessler, J., made an award in an amount less than that sought and attorney appealed. The Supreme Court, Wilkie, C. J., held that trial court did not sufficiently explore question of the amount of time which attorney spent in court and out of court; that compensation should be determined on a basis of $20 per hour for both in-court and out-of-court work; and that, henceforth, legal work performed on behalf of indigent criminal defendants should be compensated on the basis of $30 per hour.

Reversed and remanded.

1. Attorney and Client ⬅132

Things to be taken into consideration in determining compensation to be received by court-appointed attorney are the amount and character of the services rendered, the labor, the time, and the trouble involved, the character and importance of the litigation, the amount of money or value of the property affected, the professional skill and experience called for, and the standing of the attorney in his profession. W.S.A. 967.-06.

9
LEGAL
MEMORANDUMS

As we have emphasized throughout this book, *the primary purpose of legal writing is to be clearly understood.* Never is this purpose more important than when you are writing a **legal memorandum**. Your supervisors will judge your ability in large part by the quality of the memos you write, by the clarity of your writing, and by the research you have done before writing.

Distinguish between legal memorandums, internal to your law office, and those sometimes filed with the court in support of or in opposition to some motion or other matter. These are often called **briefs,** and are discussed later in our chapters dealing with trial briefs and discovery.

Legal memorandums—memoranda, if you prefer—are written within a law office to solve some problem that office faces. For example, it may be a question addressed to the firm by a client; it may be a problem raised by a case the office is about to try, or is actually trying; it may be a query by an attorney who is devising a new provision for a will or contract.

Your memorandum will attempt to answer the question by applying to it the pertinent judicial opinions (cases) and statutes that your research has discovered.

■ CASES

Our law constantly evolves. It does so as appellate courts address problems of legal interpretation and solve them in written opinions. With few exceptions, appellate courts do not take evidence; they deal with a case already tried, and so consider only questions of law. You will be most interested in appellate opinions from your own jurisdiction (your state) or, if your case is a federal one, the federal appellate area—the **circuit**—in which your case will be tried.

You will also want to rely on cases decided *as recently as possible.* Most important, you will *reason from cases as close as possible factually to your own.* You will seldom find a case exactly like yours, "on all fours" with your case, as the lawyers say. What cases you do use, you must analyze in some depth in your memo. We explain how below, when we discuss the main body of the memo.

legal memorandum
An internal memorandum written to solve a legal problem by applying pertinent cases and statutes.

brief
Legal memorandum containing arguments and authorities filed with the court in support of, or in opposition to, some motion or other matter.

circuit
In the federal judicial system, the first level of appellate review for cases from the federal district court.

◼ PRACTICE TIP

If a case is "on all fours," it is exactly on point with another case as to result, facts, or both. "On all fours" is most commonly used when a particular case is in all points similar to another because the facts are similar and the same questions of law are involved.

citation
Reference to legal authorities and precedents.

spot or short cite
A citation that tells your reader the precise page in the opinion on which the reference may be found within the cited opinion.

PRACTICE TIP

When choosing cases from your research for your memo, rely on cases decided as recently as possible and as close as possible factually to your own.

As you write your memo, always tell your reader where you got the ideas and propositions of law you are discussing. When you first mention a case or statute, give your reader the full **citation** of that case or statute. The citation is the combination of words and numbers that tells your reader *exactly* where to find the case or statute in the library.

Then, as you discuss a case, refer to the specific page on which you found the reasoning you are discussing. This is called **spot** or **short citing,** and helps your reader go directly to the critical part of a case you rely on, if he or she wants to read the case. (You will recall that this was discussed fully in Chapter 7.)

The whole idea of a memorandum is to predict, from the law as it is, what a court—or administrative panel—would do with the situation about which you are writing. Would a particular piece of evidence be admitted? Would a contract be interpreted by a court as your client thinks it should be? Would a special will provision achieve your client's goal if it were challenged in court?

◼ ELEMENTS OF THE LEGAL MEMORANDUM

Whatever the question is, you will write about it in the same general format. We have given you a useful format in Exhibit 9.1, which includes all the essential things a memo must address. Your law office may have its own. If it does, it will not be very different from ours, because any good memo must contain certain critical parts.

Heading or Caption

heading or caption
The section of a legal memorandum which identifies the person for whom the memorandum was prepared, the author, the date, what the memorandum is about, and the file to which it belongs.

brief bank
An index of the legal research done within a law office.

The **heading,** or **caption** of a legal memorandum is a purely administrative section that varies in format from office to office. It identifies the person for whom the memorandum was prepared, the writer of the memo, the date of final typing, and what the memo is about. We think it is also useful to include the specific file name and/or number and/or office code as part of the heading. This identifies where the memo fits into the office files and identifies the client for whom the memo has been written.

Give special attention to the "RE:" line. In instances involving complex litigation, or where one or more memorandums may be written on similar issues, a carefully written "RE" line helps you to distinguish one memorandum from another. Also, in many offices, the memo remains not only in the case file for which it was written, but also in the office research memory, usually referred to as a **brief bank**. More and more law offices carefully index and preserve research memorandums so that they may be easily retrieved: there is no point in reinventing the wheel, redoing the same research in the future for a similar question. Keep the "RE:" line brief and concise, but give enough detailed information so that the memorandum can be accurately indexed later for inclusion in the firm's form file or brief bank.

EXHIBIT 9.1 *Elements of a Legal Memorandum*

MEMORANDUM

TO: Senior Partner
FROM: Jane Paralegal
DATE: [Date of completion of the memorandum]
RE: [Brief description of issue or question]
FILE: [Identity of client and file number]

INTRODUCTION
[Optional]
Keep the Introduction brief, no more than one or two paragraphs. Do not include any legal citations.

STATEMENT OF FACTS
This section should set out all of the facts needed to understand and solve the problem by somebody *who knows nothing about it except what is contained in the memorandum.* Use only those relevant facts that are necessary to the reader's understanding of the issues.
The facts must be written objectively and accurately. Do not attempt to interpret them in their best light for your client. N*ever* omit a fact just because it supports the opposition. Do not include any legal citations.

QUESTION(S) PRESENTED
Keep this section brief, usually only *one sentence in question form.* Omit legal citations unless necessary to state the problem to be solved.

BRIEF ANSWER
This section is a summary of the answer to the question presented. It gives the reader a quick yes or no to the question raised, with a brief statement of the reason for the answer. Again, omit legal citations.

DISCUSSION
Start the Discussion by repeating the first Question Presented, then discuss the legal analysis of the issue the question raises. Begin with any statutory authorities, then follow with case law.

CONCLUSION
In the Conclusion, briefly restate the general points made in the Discussion section, and give the overall result.

Introduction

The **Introduction** is an optional paragraph at the beginning of your memo. It is used to explain briefly what has already happened in the case. It brings your reader up-to-date. It can also be used to explain why you were asked to write the memo, or how the issue arose. Its purpose is to give the reader a clearer understanding of the issues to be presented within the memo. Keep this section brief, no more than one to two paragraphs in length, and do not use legal citations.

Statement of Facts

In the **Statement of Facts,** write all of the relevant facts necessary to the reader's understanding of the issues. Do not include legal citations. Include all of the facts upon which the Discussion and Conclusion are based.

Introduction
An optional paragraph at the beginning of a legal memorandum or other document used to explain briefly what has already happened in the case, how the issue arose, or the event which caused the document to be written.

Statement of Facts
A section of a legal memorandum that provides all of the relevant facts necessary to the reader's understanding of the issues.

adversarial
An argument for one
side or the other.

This section should contain all the facts needed to understand and solve the problem by somebody who knows nothing about it except what is contained in the memo. Much of the time you are writing your memo for the person who gave you the problem; that person often knows the facts of the case as well as you do. Even so, carefully lay out all the pertinent facts. Your attorney may forget something about the case. So may you, if you come back to your memo weeks or months after you have written it. Moreover, other lawyers and legal assistants may rely on your memo. For example, if the case on which you are working goes to litigation, somebody else entirely may prepare the case for trial. That person must understand your memo without having to go to other sources for facts and background.

The facts must be written objectively, accurately, and concisely. A legal memo is not meant to be **adversarial**, that is, an argument for one side or the other. Rather, it should objectively point out the pros and cons in a clear, concise manner.

Do not attempt to interpret facts in the best light for your client. You must be careful to set out *all* the pertinent facts your reader needs to understand the problem, including those favoring the other side. Nothing is more useless than a one-sided memo. It is easy to become partisan when you are assembling your memo; be sure you do not omit a crucial fact just because it favors the other side.

At the same time, you must omit facts your reader does not need to understand and solve the problem. Do not include unnecessary dates, legal descriptions, or other details relating to the facts unless they are pertinent to the issues.

Time and practice will teach you which facts must be included in your Statement of Facts, and which may safely be omitted. Until you become expert in assessing facts, follow the safe rule: If in doubt whether to include a fact, always include it.

As an example here, let us take the case of an elderly couple who kill a burglar with a shotgun rigged to the locked door of their rural store. They have been accused of murder; may they plead self-defense?

Before you write your first word, make sure you fully understand the problem. Do not hesitate to ask questions of your supervising attorney. If there is already a file on the case, read it. The conclusion you draw in your memorandum will depend as much on the precise facts of your case as it does on the law. You must know those facts exactly.

Once you are entirely familiar with the facts, sit down and write a Statement of Facts for your memo. Incorporate all the facts the reader will require to understand the case and reach a conclusion about it. Your Statement of Facts should look something like this:

> George and Mary Block are a couple in their sixties. They own a small rural store west of Stillwater. The store is on the first floor, and their living quarters are on the second, separated by an interior door that they lock every night. Twice, attempts were made to break into the store, and the Blocks responded by setting a shotgun to shoot anyone entering through the locked front door. They also posted large, plain signs, visible to anyone approaching the front door: "Warning! Trespassers will be shot!"
>
> Last week, their shotgun killed an unarmed fifteen-year-old male, who broke in the front door with a crowbar. The Blocks were arrested, and their family has retained this firm to defend them.

Questions Presented and Brief Answers

Your reader will understand your memo more readily if you begin with a terse, clear statement of the *legal question* or questions the memo is intended to solve. Each question should be only one sentence in length. Remember, these are *legal* questions, not factual ones. If a question is particularly complex and hard to understand, your reader will not be interested in following your analysis and result. To avoid losing your reader, break the question down into several, separate issues.

The **Question Presented** should look something like this:

> **Question:** Is the residence of a female military officer determined by the residence of her husband?

Having asked the question as briefly and clearly as possible, answer it in the same way, in a **Brief Answer** (without citations), like this:

> **Brief Answer:** No. Because she moves on military orders directed to her, her residence is the place where she is stationed, or another place where she intentionally establishes and keeps residence.

When your memo includes many issues or questions presented, you may wish to state each question at the beginning of the analysis of that issue.

Let us go back to our problem with George and Mary Block, which we discussed earlier. After writing the statement of the facts, you now go on to carefully write your questions. Obviously, the short answers will have to wait until you have finished your research and have written the body of the memo. You may have to do some research first, if the area you are writing about is new to you. Usually, however, you will be able to frame your questions once you have mastered the facts.

You may need to do some preliminary reading before you even draft the questions, particularly when the problem is in an area you do not know well. For instance, in the Blocks' case, you will soon learn that, in the law, a firearm, set to fire automatically when tripped, is called a "spring gun."

Careful drafting of the questions will help you begin your research. In the Blocks' case, your question might look like this:

> May a commercial building be defended by deadly force in the form of a spring gun, if the defendants also live in the building?

Notice that the question is stated in the *present tense.* Use the present tense for your answer as well.

Pertinent Statutes

Many memos will involve interpretation of statutes or regulations. In your memo, you will paraphrase those statutes ("the statute requires that . . .") and may quote a short, vital section as the beginning of your discussion. But your reader may wish to read all of a pertinent provision, and so all important sections should be included somewhere **verbatim** in your memo.

If you quote a sizable section of statute in the middle of your Discussion, it will destroy your reader's train of thought and understanding. We suggest you include statutory material—if it is less than a page—in a separate section at the beginning of your Discussion, just after your questions and answers. Any essential statutory material longer than that may be put in an annex at the end of the memo or attached for the reader's reference as an exhibit.

Discussion

The **Discussion** is the heart of the memorandum, your discussion of the law as it applies to your question. The Discussion achieves three main goals: (1) it collects and preserves your legal research; (2) it educates the readers in what they must know to

---

Question Presented
A terse, clear statement of the legal question or questions the legal memorandum is intended to solve.

Brief Answer
A brief, clear answer to the Question Presented.

PRACTICE TIP
Use the present tense when drafting the Question Presented and the Brief Answer.

verbatim
To repeat something in exactly the same words; corresponding word for word to the original source or text.

Discussion
Within a legal memorandum, the section that gives an impartial analysis of the law as it applies to the question answered by the legal memorandum.

◼ PRACTICE TIP

The Discussion serves these goals:
- Collects and preserves your legal research
- Educates the readers in what they must know to understand the law that applies to each of the questions presented
- Methodically shows the readers the writer's rationale or reasoning used to reach the answer.

understand the law that applies to each of the questions presented; and (3) it methodically shows the readers the writer's rationale or reasoning used to reach the answer.

Above all, remember this about your Discussion: It is *impartial.* You owe your attorney and client an unbiased, judicious analysis of the problem you have been given. Do not take sides; do not identify with the client. Try to approach the problem as if it had nothing to do with people. That is very hard sometimes: try being impartial as you write a memo on the case of a battered-woman client. Nevertheless, you *must* analyze the law as a judge would, without passion or prejudice. Sometimes the best service you can provide a client is to render a clear, well-reasoned memo concluding that the client has no case and should save his money.

Restating the Legal Questions.   Begin your Discussion by restating each of the Questions Presented. We prefer to use headings and subheadings to do this. Restate the Question Presented as a heading or subheading within the Discussion of your memo.

For example, here is the Question Presented in the spring-gun case:

May a commercial building be defended by deadly force in the form of a spring gun, if the defendants also live in the building?

If the Brief Answer to this question was yes, then the question might be restated as a proposition, like this:

I. Defendants May Defend A Commercial Building With Deadly Force In The Form Of A Spring Gun If They Live In The Building.

Writing the Discussion.   Now you will go to the law library or the computer, and begin your research. Once you have gathered the case law and any pertinent statutes, you will sit down to write the Discussion of your memo. Do not save your best cases for last. Lead your Discussion with your most compelling authority, analyze it, and apply it to your own facts. Discuss cases *in the order of their importance.*

When discussing each case, follow this procedure:

1. State the facts and holding in the case.
2. Then give the court's rationale (its reasoning) for its holding.
3. Then compare the facts of that case to your own case situation.

Never forget that your memo should *educate the reader.* Lead the reader through a logical progression of thought. Remember that you should assume that the reader *knows nothing.* Do not make any jumps in logic from point A to point C and expect your reader to follow your train of thought.

■ PRACTICE TIP

Keep the reader with you at all times. Your points must be made *step by step* and backed up with solid authorities and reasoning.

First, *tell* the reader the facts of the case, the court's holding, and the court's reasoning. Then *show* the reader why the case is relevant to the question presented. Then *explain* the similarities or the differences between the cited case and your client's situation. At the end of your analysis, the reader should be subconsciously nodding his or her head in agreement if you have led the reader to the result in a logical progression of thought.

You must "keep the reader with you" *at all times.* Your points must be made step by step and backed up with solid authorities and reasoning if you and the reader are to reach the same conclusion. If you do not keep the reader with you, your reader will lose interest, or worse, be unpersuaded by your analysis and result.

Do not merely say that "*Kirkland* held . . . ." *Tell* the reader the facts of the case, the court's holding, and the court's reasoning. *Show* the reader *why* the case is relevant to the question presented. Then *explain* the similarities or the differences between the cited case and your client's situation. Be convincing, clear, and methodical. At the end of your analysis, the reader should be subconsciously nodding his or her head in agreement, *if* you have led the reader to the result in a logical progression of thought.

Remember that statutes are **mandatory authority.** If a statute applies to your problem, discuss it *first*, and then any case law that interprets it.

In our spring-gun case, assume your research discloses only some older cases. We shall analyze and apply one of them. Your Discussion might begin something like this:

> The general rule is that a spring gun cannot lawfully be used to defend property. *Pierce v. Commonwealth*, 115 S.E. 686 (Va. 1923).

Citing the Legal Authority.   You have stated a proposition of law in your first sentence, so you must immediately tell the reader the *authority* for that proposition. Here it is the decision on appeal in a case called *Pierce v. Commonwealth*. The rest of the citation tells your reader that the full text of the opinion can be read in volume 115 of the Southeastern Reporter, starting on page 686. Finally, the citation tells the reader that the Virginia Supreme Court decided the case in 1923. (See Chapter 7, "Citation Form," for the mechanics of citing cases and other legal authorities).

PRACTICE TIP
Write so that the reader cannot possibly miss your point. Remember, what can be misunderstood will be!

mandatory authority
Any primary authority that a court must follow in reaching its decision.

■ PRACTICE TIP

Primary authorities are mainly *case law* (judicial opinions from the same jurisdiction your case is in), *statutes* (both federal and state), and administrative law of government agency regulations and rulings.

If a primary authority is law in the jurisdiction with which you are concerned and deals with the very same question you are researching, it is then also *mandatory authority;* that is, the court has to follow it.

PRACTICE TIP

Never cite a case without giving its facts, rationale, and holding. Without those important elements, your reader is unable to determine why your cited case is important and how it affects your problem.

Discussing Case Law. *Never* submit a memorandum that merely makes statements about the law, and then follows those statements with citations alone. That is the equivalent of asking your reader to take the statements you make on faith alone. For each case you cite, you must tell your reader what the facts were, the court's reasoning, and the court's holding.

Review the Case. Explain to your reader what happened in *Pierce*, something like this:

> The defendant in *Pierce* owned a small store that had been plagued by burglaries. Pierce did not occupy any part of his store as a dwelling. To protect his store, he rigged a spring gun at the front door, but the lock was faulty and gave way when a policeman tested it during a night patrol. The officer was killed, and Pierce convicted of second-degree murder.

Report the Court's Holding. Next you will tell your reader what the appellate court decided in *Pierce*. As you explain the court's **holding**—the actual answer to the legal question it decided—and its reasoning, you will tell the reader the *exact* page on which the court did these things. Again, this is called a spot or short citation. It works like this:

holding
The court's answer to or resolution of the legal issue before it; the legal principle to be drawn from the opinion (decision) of the court.

> The court held that one may not kill, directly or indirectly, to prevent a mere trespass or theft of property. *Pierce*, 115 S.E. at 689.

Notice that this sentence is in the *past tense*. Use the past tense throughout your discussion of cases ("the plaintiff alleged that," or "the court reasoned that"). But if you back up a page, you will see that a statement of *what the law is* is written in the *present tense*: "the general rule is that one may not lawfully use a spring gun."

This is the rule you will use in your memorandums, and in briefs written for the court as well:

PRACTICE TIP

State the law of a case in the present tense; otherwise, stay in the past tense.

> Use the past tense throughout, except when you state what the law is; that goes in the present tense.

Read over the sample legal memorandum in Appendix E in the back of the book; you will see how tenses are handled there.

Give the Court's Rationale. Ordinarily, you will now go on to explain the court's **rationale**, the reasons it gave for deciding as it did. Any discussion of that reasoning, and any quotation from the opinion, must be followed by short cites, like this:

reasoning, rationale
The court's explanation of why it decided a legal issue as it did.

> The court reasoned that deadly force may be used in person only to avert the threat of death or great bodily injury. Since that is so, no one may use deadly force—a spring gun—to do what he could not do in person. *Pierce*, 115 S.E. at 688. The court concluded that Pierce was defending only property, not life, and affirmed his conviction. *Pierce*, 115 S.E. at 689.
>
> However, in *dictum*, the court speculated that burglaries of dwellings sometimes result in death or injury to occupants. Therefore, it said, deadly force might be lawful where the building to be defended was an occupied dwelling. *Id.*

dictum, dicta
Observations or comments by a judge in an opinion that is not essential to the holding in the case.

Dictum (plural **dicta**) is reasoning or other language by the court that is not *essential* to the holding in the case; such language is therefore not binding on other, inferior courts. It may be, however, quite persuasive as an indication of what the court may do when faced with a situation different from the one it solved in its opinion.

If you wish to quote from the opinion, remember to quote sparingly and only for *how* something is said. If you do quote from the opinion, you must also use a spot cite:

> "There is a recklessness—a wanton disregard of humanity and social duty, in taking . . . the life of a fellow being, in order to save oneself from a comparatively slight wrong . . . ." *Id.* at 688.

Id. is another form of short cite, explained in our chapter on citation. Remember that it means we are citing the same case we last cited—*Pierce*—at page 688.

Apply the Case to Your Facts.   Now that you have explained what happened in *Pierce,* and what the court decided there, your next step is to apply *Pierce* to your own set of facts.

> Under *Pierce,* the Blocks would clearly be guilty of unlawful homicide if they set a spring gun to defend only their store. However, because they live in the same building, we may argue that they acted in self-defense, doing only what they could have done personally had they been present. Once an intruder breaks through the outer door, the Blocks are threatened just as surely as their merchandise is.
>
> The existence of a locked interior door between the store and the Blocks' quarters should not defeat a claim that they set the gun to defend themselves, not the store. The interior door cannot be distinguished from an interior door within a dwelling, a bedroom door, for example.
>
> The most serious danger to the defense of self-defense is that the Blocks were not present to decide whether an intruder was reasonably a threat to their personal safety. Judicial objection to spring guns is based on the fact that the gun is mindless, and cannot exercise the discretion that human beings can. One court put it this way:
>
>> [I]f his trespass was merely technical—if it was a child, a madman, or an idiot, carelessly, thoughtlessly entering and wandering on the premises, the owner would withhold all violence . . . or . . . graduate his violence to the character of the trespass. [The gun] is without mercy or discretion . . . .
>>
>> *State v. Childers,* 14 N.E.2d 767, 769 (Ohio 1938).

This last quotation uses **block indentation,** that is, single-spaced and indented on both margins, so that it stands out. The *Bluebook* requires block indenting when the quotation is fifty words or more. We think the better rule is this: If something is worth quoting, it is worth block-indenting if it is more than a few words.

To return to your discussion and analysis of the cases:

> In *Childers,* the owner of a melon patch set a spring gun to protect his melons from vandalism. When a trespassing boy was hurt by the gun, the owner was convicted of assault. The court affirmed the conviction on reasoning identical to that in *Pierce.* However, the *Childers* court also speculated that a spring gun might lawfully be used to protect a dwelling.
>
> The District Attorney will argue that one must be physically present at the point of danger in order to act in self-defense. The D.A. will probably also argue that one who uses a spring gun is criminally responsible even where he would have been justified in shooting had he been personally present. This argument would rest on a powerful public policy against employing a mindless, discretionless deadly device.

Id.
A Latin abbreviation meaning "the same" used to indicate reference to the immediately preceding authority.

block indentation
Text that is normally single-spaced and indented on both margins, usually used for quoted material.

PRACTICE TIP

If you wish to quote from the opinion, quote sparingly, and only for *how* something is said. Be sure to use a spot cite for any quotation.

PRACTICE TIP

- Before you even think about string citing, you *must* carefully analyze and apply four or five of the best cases to your problem.
- Do not string cite more than four cases together.
- Never string cite without using parentheticals, even though the signal will tell the reader something about the cases that follow.

string citation, string cite
A series of case citations separated by semicolons and preceded by a signal. String cites are often used to emphasize a particular point in a legal memorandum or brief.

signal
Indicators provided to show the purposes for which the citations are made.

parenthetical
An abbreviated summary of the case in parentheses located immediately after the citation.

Conclusion
Within a legal memorandum, a brief summary of the analysis of the Discussion and the answer to the Questions Presented.

The length of the body of your memorandum (the Discussion) depends on the complexity of the problem and on the amount of useful authority available. Sometimes you will have an abundance of authority, and must choose which you will use. Generally speaking, however, four or five good cases ought to be enough to reach a conclusion on any question.

In Appendix E, we have included a sample legal memorandum. Use it as a model as you write your first memos. Whatever the problem you are writing about, the process of analyzing and applying case law should work about the same in every memo.

What is a "good case"? Remember, as we discussed above, it is a case that is as close as possible factually to your question, as recent as possible and, when possible, in your own jurisdiction. Sometimes you will want to show your reader there are other important cases in addition to those you fully discussed and applied. To do this, you may use **string citations.**

String Citations

Your research may have unearthed several opinions from other courts (jurisdictions) that followed the same rationale and have come to the same conclusion. When you cite each of those cases to emphasize your point, that successive chain of cases is called a **string cite.** A string cite is a series of case citations separated by semicolons and preceded by a **signal.** For example, take the signal *see*, which means the citations that follow are to cases generally reaching the same result as the cases just discussed. (For more on signals, see Chapter 7).

Suppose you have finished analyzing your best cases on spring guns and want to show the reader other cases that hold the same way. Your string cite might look something like this:

> *See Henderson v State*, 546 P.2d 11 (Okla. Crim. App. 1968)(defense of isolated barn with spring gun unlawful); *State v. Johnston*, 288 N.E. 2d 429 (Ohio 1962) (spring-gun killing in vacant house is homicide, but dictum that gun might be justified in occupied dwelling where inhabitant could have fired if personally present).

You will see that each citation in this string cite is followed by an abbreviated summary of the case in parentheses. These are called **parentheticals,** and help the reader understand why the cases are similar in import to the ones you analyzed at length. Never string cite without using parentheticals, even though the signal will tell the reader something about the cases that follow. Parentheticals normally should not be more than two lines long, and you may omit articles and other words not crucial to meaning.

Do not string cite more than four cases together. If you do, the result is likely to be a confusing, unwieldy mass of words and numbers in which the significance of the cases is lost. Instead, in that rare instance when you want to tell your reader that a whole regiment of similar cases is available, put them in an annex. List them there, *with parentheticals*, four or five to a paragraph; in the text of your memo, simply refer your reader to the annex.

Conclusion

The **Conclusion** is a summary of the analysis of the Discussion and the answer to the Questions Presented. It may also recommend action to be taken based on the result reached. The Conclusion should answer the Questions Presented and touch on the major legal issues that must be resolved to reach that conclusion. It may be that your research indicated that there was no general consensus among the various courts as to how an issue should be decided. If so, state the status of the law relating to the Question Presented by pointing out that some courts have held one way while others have come to a different, perhaps opposite, conclusion.

▨ OTHER CONSIDERATIONS

Up to this point, we have discussed the format for a legal memorandum and how to discuss and answer the questions raised by the memorandum. But there are still other more technical factors to consider when writing a legal memorandum.

Focus of the Memorandum

You are writing an analysis of, and an answer to, a specific question or questions. Your reader wants the answer and the reasons for it. He or she wants an analysis of the authorities that are important to *this question*, not a general treatise on the law. Stick with what is germane to your problem; forget tangential matters, however interesting.

Omit cases that are ancient history and no longer apply to the law as it stood at the time of the cause of action. History may be interesting, but not on the client's money and the firm's time. What the law is not, but used to be, is occasionally useful in understanding the law *as it now is*. Otherwise, it has no place in your memo.

Length of the Memorandum

Nobody can predict how long a memo will be. Many are only a page or two, but others may reach fifteen or twenty pages. Obviously, as with everything else you write, brevity is a virtue in writing a memo. But you cannot sacrifice clarity and completeness in the name of fewer words. Keep it simple and it will remain clear, no matter how many pages you have to use to cover your subject adequately.

Designation of Parties, Events, Documents, and Things

Designating a specific name for each of the parties or other actors, or for some other important event, document, or thing, helps to make the text of any document more readable and understandable. Lawsuits, and the documents generated from them, deal not only with the parties but also with contracts, legal descriptions, events, and dates. Commonly, they are described in lengthy and cumbersome legalese. We advocate using **designations** whenever a particular person (such as a party) or thing (such as the contract on which the lawsuit is based) appears repeatedly throughout a document.

designation
A specific name used whenever a particular person or thing appears repeatedly throughout a document.

There are three basic ways to refer to parties in a case:

- By the party's *name* or *abbreviation* of the name
- By a *functional* or *descriptive name*
- By their *relationship* in the lawsuit—plaintiff or defendant

Here is how it works. Suppose that the case involved one plaintiff and one defendant, and both are individual persons. You could refer to the plaintiff as "Plaintiff," "Plaintiff Rebecca Caufield," or "Plaintiff Caufield," and to the defendant as "Defendant," "Defendant James Baxter," or "Defendant Baxter." However, "Plaintiff

descriptive name
A designated name used to describe the parties when there are multiple plaintiffs or defendants.

functional designations
Descriptive names that indicate the relationship between the parties other than plaintiff and defendant.

Rebecca Caufield" or "Plaintiff Caufield" are redundant. The style of the case clearly shows who is the plaintiff and who is the defendant. Use one designation or the other, but not both.

Here is how you show the reader the designation assigned to each of the parties:

Plaintiff Rebecca Caufield ("Plaintiff") sued Defendant James Baxter ("Defendant") . . . .

It is obvious to the reader that the designation within the quotation marks and parentheses means "hereinafter referred to as." Therefore, that onerous bit of legalese is unnecessary, and should always be omitted. If you had preferred, you could have chosen to refer to the parties by their last names—Caufield and Baxter. After you have formally designated how you will refer to each of the parties, be sure that you consistently refer to the party in that way throughout the document.

When there are multiple plaintiffs or defendants, we suggest avoiding designations by plaintiff or defendant without adding something to help the reader distinguish between *which* plaintiff and *which* defendant. Instead, use a **descriptive name**, such as "plaintiff driver" and "plaintiff passenger." If the party is a corporation or some other type of business entity, use an abbreviation of the company's name, such as "GM" for General Motors.

Functional designations are descriptive names that indicate the relationship between the parties other than plaintiff and defendant, such as "landlord" and "tenant," or "manufacturer" and "distributor," or "buyer" and "seller." Functional names work especially well when you want to refer to a group of plaintiffs or defendants with a common characteristic ("limited partners") or when the party's technical name is too lengthy or difficult to abbreviate ("union" or "school district").

Consistent with your duty to write as simply and clearly as possible, we suggest that you do not refer to people and entities *in your client's case* by abstract names such as "defendant" or "accused" or "appellant." Call them "Ms. Brown," "Rev. Davis," "Bosco Corporation," "the school," or whatever term makes your writing clearest. This is especially useful in impressing on the reader that your client is a "real" person with whom the reader will be able to empathize.

However, *when analyzing cases*, it is usually best to name the characters in them according to their status in the case: "petitioner," "plaintiff," or whatever. Using these impersonal terms also helps keep them separate from the characters in your own case when your case is being compared with an authority case.

Up to this point, we have only talked about designations of the parties or other actors in the litigation. But litigation also involves events, contracts, property, and other things that may have lengthy or complicated names.

Say, for example, that your client, a municipality, is being sued by the Fraternal Order of Police, the police union, for an alleged breach of the Collective Bargaining Agreement and two amendments to that contract entered into by both parties. Obvious designations for the parties would be the "City" and the "Union."

How would you designate the Collective Bargaining Agreement, one of the key factors of the lawsuit? You could call it simply the "Contract" or refer to it by its initials, "CBA." Or, if the date of the contract was pivotal to understanding of the event that brought about the lawsuit, or if there is more than one floating about, you might want to refer to it as the "6/10/94 Contract" or "6/10/94 CBA."

The same thing works for finding designations for the two amendments. Each was signed at a different time, so you could use that to differentiate between them: "First Amendment" and "Second Amendment." But it is better to use the date the document was signed or became effective, like this: "7/10/94 Amendment" and

"10/10/94 Amendment." If one dealt with health benefits and the other with wages, you might refer to them as "Benefits Amendment" and "Wage Amendment," especially if benefits and wages are part of the issue being litigated.

Designations help your reader only *if you keep them short and make them descriptive enough* for the reader to understand immediately to what you refer. Designations are useless if you fail to use them consistently throughout the document. Once you designate an identity for something or someone, stick with it until you reach the **prayer**, or final closing paragraph of the document. Then, because you adopt a slightly more formal tone in that paragraph to ask the court to give you whatever it is you want, drop the designation and substitute the full names or titles of the litigants, like this:

> WHEREFORE, Plaintiff Rebecca Caufield requests that this court deny Defendant James Baxter's Motion for Summary Judgment.

PRACTICE TIP
Designations are useless if you fail to use them consistently throughout the document.

prayer
The final closing paragraph of a document which requests that the court do something.

Legal Authority

In Chapter 6, we discuss the different sources of legal authority. Remember that the usual source on which you will rely is called **primary authority**. It is of two basic kinds:

First, there are statutes—passed by the Congress or a state legislature or local government—and regulatory rules and regulations. Second, you will use case law. These cases are almost always the opinions written by appellate courts, with one important exception: the federal district courts. Although federal district courts are basically trial courts, their published opinions are also valuable as authority.

Although primary authority usually decides legal questions, do not ignore **secondary authority**. This authority includes treatises on the law and articles in legal journals. Secondary authorities are discussed in detail in Chapter 6. While these authorities will not compel a result in any case, they may be very persuasive to a court, as well as a fine starting place for your research.

primary authority
Any law on which a court could rely in reaching its decision.

secondary authority
Any non-law on which a court could rely in reaching its decision.

CHAPTER SUMMARY

When writing legal memorandums, keep these guidelines in mind:

- Give your reader the full citation of any case you discuss, when you first mention the case.
- Give page citations when you discuss the holding or rationale of any court.
- Begin the memo with a concise statement of the question you are addressing, and a brief answer to that question.
- Include in your Statement of Facts *all* the facts necessary to understand the problem even if the reader knows nothing at all about the case.
- Include pertinent statutes verbatim, in the memo if short, in an appendix if lengthy.
- Write generally in the past tense. If stating the law, use the present tense.
- Begin with your most important point. Lead with the most persuasive case or mandatory authority.
- Keep the reader with you at all times.
- Remain unbiased. Discuss both sides of the case.
- If you use string citations, include a parenthetical for each case.

- Refer to parties in a case (1) by the party's name or abbreviation of the name; (2) by a "functional" or descriptive name; or (3) by the party's relationship in the lawsuit—plaintiff or defendant.
- Designate parties in authority cases generically, e.g., as "plaintiff" or "defendant."

KEY WORDS AND PHRASES

adversarial	descriptive name	Introduction	secondary authority
block indentation	designation	legal memorandum	signal
brief	dictum, dicta	mandatory authority	spot, or short, cite
Brief Answer	Discussion	parenthetical	Statement of Facts
Conclusion	functional designation	prayer	string citation
brief bank	heading or caption	primary authority	verbatim
circuit	holding	Question Presented	
citation	*id.*	reasoning, rationale	

EXERCISES

The following exercises for this chapter are "fill in the blank." Complete each of the following statements.

1. The intended use of a legal memorandum is__
   _____.

2. In a legal memorandum, you are attempting to predict_____.

3. A memorandum attempts to answer a legal question by_____.

4. In selecting appropriate cases for your memorandum, you will be most concerned with opinions from _____ courts from _____ jurisdiction.

5. The _____ is the combination of words and numbers that tells your reader exactly where to find the case or statute.

6. *Spot citing* means_____.

7. The critical parts of a legal memorandum are
   a._____
   b._____
   c._____

   d._____
   e._____

8. The Statement of Facts should provide information needed to _____ by someone_____
   _____.

9. A memorandum should be nonpartisan because
   _____.

10. If your memo involves interpretation of statutes, you will generally _____ all but the most vital sections. If you wish to include the entire pertinent statute, it should be placed in one of two possible locations within the memorandum. If the statute is less than one page, _____. More lengthy excerpts should be printed_____.

11. Your guiding premise in discussing the law as it applies to your case is to analyze the problem__
   _____.

12. Statutes are mandatory authority. This means that_____. If a statute applies to your case, it should be discussed _____ case law.

13. The rule for use of present and past tense in legal memorandums is:_____.

14. Direct quotes from authority cases should be used_____.

15. Although the *Bluebook* requires block-indenting quotations of more than 50 words, we recommend_____.

16. A string cite is _____ preceded by a signal. Never string-cite without using_____.

17. The rule for designating parties is: Refer to parties and entities in your case _____, but refer to characters in the cases you analyze_____.

18. The proper use of secondary authorities in legal memorandum is_____.

Practicing Your Writing

The following assignment is a writing exercise. When drafting your legal memorandum, you may wish to refer to the Sample Memorandum found at Appendix E.

1. Impressed with your work on the *Cruse* brief, Ms. Pepper wants you to fully explore the dram-shop liability issue. Specifically, she wants to know whether Jane Healy has a valid cause of action against Tony Simpson, the bartender and owner of Red's Tavern.

   Ms. Pepper asks you to write a legal memorandum addressing only the issue of Simpson's liability. Use the Jane Healy scenario found in Chapter 1 and the following four cases. Assume you are writing for a state district court in the State of Anxiety, where no case precedent exists. The State of Anxiety does not have a statute authorizing a cause of action for negligent sale of liquor to an intoxicated driver. A civil damage law, enacted during Prohibition, was repealed in 1933.

   For purposes of this exercise, assume that your research has produced the following cases, which are the only relevant cases in existence:

   - *Brigance v. Velvet Dove Restaurant, Inc.,* 725 P.2d 300 (Okla. 1986)
   - *Connolly v. Conlan,* 371 N.W.2d 832 (Iowa 1985)
   - *Campbell v. Carpenter,* 276 Or. 237, 566 P.2d 893 (1977)
   - *Rappaport v. Nichols,* 31 N.J. 188, 156 A.2d 1 (1959)

CASE

300 Okl.   **725 PACIFIC REPORTER, 2d SERIES**

purchase gas from potential producers whom the statute prohibits from producing because they lack such a market for their possible product. Plaintiffs' operations are neither causing nor threatening any overground or underground waste. Every well owner in the field is free to produce the gas, provided he does not do so wastefully. He is legally and, so far as appears, physically free to provide himself with a market and with transportation and marketing facilities.

.   .   .   .   .

[T]he purpose of the Commission underlying these orders was, upon a theory of protecting correlative rights, to coerce complainant and other [others] similarly situated to buy gas from, and thus to share their private marketing contracts and commitments and the use of their pipe lines and other facilities for transmitting their gas to market with the owners of wells not now connected to pipe lines, who have not contributed in money, services, negotiations, skill, forethought or otherwise to the development of such markets and the construction of such pipe lines and other facilities. In short to compel complainants to afford markets to those having none."

The act examined in this case has substantially the same effect as that examined in *Thompson, supra.* The statutory scheme established by the act simply rearranges the contractual obligations of private individuals for the benefit of a subclass of well owners not having a contract to sell their product. As such it is not a proper exercise of the state's police power, for the law benefits one subclass of well owners at the expense of others and is thus not designed to benefit the general welfare of the people of the state. Nor can the act be said to prevent waste or protect correlative rights. The Corporation Commission has attempted to ameliorate the obvious constitutional flaws with the act by enacting rules which, in effect, emasculate the act. Statutes should be construed so as to uphold their constitutionality, but in this instance it is obvious that the construction given the act

is not supportable by a plain reading of it. The construction given the act by the Commission's rules is an attempt to rewrite the act, not interpret it.

Shawn **BRIGANCE, a minor, and Earle Brigance, his father, individually and as parent and natural guardian of Shawn Brigance, Appellants,**

v.

The **VELVET DOVE RESTAURANT, INC., Richard Stubbs, and Jerry Rimele, Appellees.**

No. 62005.

Supreme Court of Oklahoma.

July 8, 1986.

Rehearing Denied Sept. 23, 1986.

Third-party passenger injured in collision brought action with her father against restaurant and its owner for alleged negligence in serving alcoholic beverages to noticeably intoxicated driver. The District Court, Oklahoma County, William Saied, J., entered judgment sustaining defendants' demurrer and dismissing complaint, and plaintiffs appealed. The Supreme Court, Hodges, J., held that third-party passenger injured by intoxicated driver had a civil action against commercial vendor for on the premises consumption for negligent sale of an intoxicating beverage to a person the vendor knew or should have known was noticeably intoxicated and whose consumption of alcohol was the alleged cause of the injuries.

Reversed and remanded.

Hargrave, J., concurred in result.

Simms, C.J., concurred and filed opinion in which Doolin, V.C.J., and Opala, J., joined.

CASE—*Continued*

BRIGANCE v. VELVET DOVE RESTAURANT, INC.   Okl. **301**
Cite as 725 P.2d 300 (Okl. 1986)

1. Intoxicating Liquors ⚖=288

A commercial vendor for on the premises consumption is under a duty, imposed both by statute and common-law principles, to exercise reasonable care in selling or furnishing liquor to persons who by previous intoxication may lack full capacity or self-control to operate a motor vehicle and who may subsequently injure a third party. 37 O.S.Supp.1985, § 537; 37 O.S.1981, § 501 et seq.; 37 O.S.1951, §§ 1–7, 9–131.

2. Intoxicating Liquors ⚖=297

Third-party passenger injured by intoxicated driver had a civil action against commercial vendor for on the premises consumption for negligent sale of an intoxicating beverage to a person the vendor knew or should have known was noticeably intoxicated and whose consumption of alcohol was the alleged cause of the injuries. 37 O.S.Supp.1985, § 537; 37 O.S.1981, § 501 et seq.; 37 O.S.1951, §§ 1–7, 9–131.

3. Intoxicating Liquors ⚖=291

A commercial vendor for on the premises consumption, found to have breached its duty to exercise reasonable care not to sell liquor to a noticeably intoxicated driver whose actions thereafter cause injury to a third-party passenger, cannot be held liable unless it is shown that the illegal sale of liquor led to the impairment of the ability of the driver and that there was a causal connection between the sale and the foreseeable ensuing injury.

4. Intoxicating Liquors ⚖=291

An intervening cause which will break the causal nexus between a tavern owner's negligence in selling liquor to a noticeably intoxicated driver and the resulting injury to a third-party passenger is a supervening cause which is established by showing that the act is independent of the original act, is adequate of itself to bring about the result, and is one whose occurrence was not reasonably foreseeable. 37 O.S.Supp.1985, § 537; 37 O.S.1981, § 501 et seq.; 37 O.S. 1951, §§ 1–7, 9–131.

5. Courts ⚖=100(1)

Rule creating a civil cause of action against a commercial vendor for on the premises consumption for breach of duty to exercise reasonable care not to sell liquor to a noticeably intoxicated driver is prospective in application.

———

Appeal from the District Court of Oklahoma County; William Saied, Judge.

Parent and natural guardian of minor brought action individually and on behalf of minor against vendor of alcoholic beverages for on the premises consumption, the vendor owner and its employee for common law negligence in serving alcoholic beverages to an intoxicated driver of an automobile in which the minor plaintiff was a passenger that allegedly resulted in an automobile accident causing injuries to the minor. The District Court of Oklahoma County dismissed the complaint for failure to state a claim upon which relief could be granted, and parent appeals.

Reversed and Remanded

Istook & Associates, P.C. by Ernest J. Istook, Jr., and Mark A. Wright, Oklahoma City, for appellants.

Huckaby, Fleming, Frailey, Chaffin & Darrah by Michael R. Chaffin, Chickasha, for appellees.

HODGES, Judge.

Shawn Brigance and Earle Brigance, Shawn's father, (appellants) brought an action against The Velvet Dove Restaurant, Inc., Richard Stubbs and Jerry Rimele (appellees) for negligence in serving alcoholic beverages to a noticeably intoxicated person, allegedly resulting in an automobile accident causing injuries to Shawn, a minor at the time of the injuries. The District Court of Oklahoma County dismissed the complaint for failure to state a claim upon which relief could be granted, and appellants perfected this appeal.

For purposes of this appeal, appellees concur in the statement of facts set forth in appellants' brief in chief. The uncontroverted facts are as follows: the Velvet Dove Restaurant, Inc. (Velvet Dove), by

Continued

CASE—*Continued*

and through its president and principal stockholder, Richard Stubbs, and employee, Jerry Rimele, served intoxicating beverages to a group of minors, including one Jeff Johnson. Appellees knew Jeff Johnson drove the group to the restaurant as its employee assisted Johnson to his car upon the group's departure. Appellants allege beverages served by appellees caused Johnson to become intoxicated or increased his prior intoxication thereby causing a one-car accident in which Shawn was injured.

The issue before this Court is whether, absent statutory authority to the contrary, a third party passenger injured by an intoxicated driver has a civil action against a commercial vendor for on the premises consumption for the negligent sale of an intoxicating beverage to a person the vendor knew or should have known was noticeably intoxicated and whose consumption of alcohol was the alleged cause of injuries. The issue presented is one of considerable significance as the magnitude of intoxication-caused automobile accidents is well known.

The trial court, having no dram shop legislation or precedent in this jurisdiction on which to rely, dismissed appellants' complaint for failure to state a claim upon which relief could be granted. We find that, under the facts set out in appellants' pleadings, a cause of action for negligence against the vendor has been stated and reverse the judgment of the district court for the reasons to be stated below.

In 1959, the Oklahoma Legislature enacted the Oklahoma Alcoholic Beverage Control Act, 37 O.S. 1981 § 501 et seq., and repealed 37 O.S. 1951 §§ 1–7 and 9–131, as amended, and all laws or parts of laws in conflict with the Act.

Since the Legislature's repeal which included 37 O.S. 1951 § 121 (originally enacted in 1910), Oklahoma's dram shop act, there has been no occasion for this Court to consider the issue of whether a liquor vendor for on the premises consumption may be held civilly liable for injuries due to the acts of a noticeably intoxicated patron upon common law principles of negligence.

The elements of common law negligence have been summarized by this Court as "(1) the existence of a duty on part of defendant to protect plaintiff from injury; (2) a violation of that duty; and (3) injury proximately resulting therefrom." *Sloan v. Owen*, 579 P.2d 812, 814 (Okla.1977).

At common law a tavern owner who furnishes alcoholic beverages to another is not civilly liable for a third person's injuries that are caused by the acts of an intoxicated patron.[1] Such rule is principally based upon concepts of causation that, as a matter of law, it is not the *sale* of liquor by the tavern owner, but the voluntary *consumption* by the intoxicated person, which is the proximate cause of resulting injuries, so that the tavern owner is therefore not liable for negligence in selling the liquor.

In recent years, many states have retreated from the common law rule of nonliability for a liquor vendor regarding it as antiquated and illogical.[2] Several states with dram shop laws have also recognized a new common law right of action against a vendor of liquor.[3] Many of the jurisdictions which now recognize a civil right of action do so on the theory enunciated in

1. *See Cruse v. Aden*, 127 Ill. 231, 234, 20 N.E. 73, 74 (1889); *Waller's Adm'r v. Collingsworth*, 144 Ky. 3, 6, 137 S.W. 766, 767 (1911). *See also* cases cited in 45 Am.Jr.2d *Intoxicating Liquors* § 553 (1969).

2. *E.g., Ontiveros v. Borak*, 136 Ariz. 500, 667 P.2d 200 (1983); *Michnik-Zilberman v. Gordon's Liquor, Inc.*, 390 Mass. 6, 453 N.E.2d 430 (1983); *Campbell v. Carpenter*, 279 Or. 237, 566 P.2d 893 (1977); *Pfeifer v. Copperstone Restaurant and Lounge*, 71 Or.App. 599, 693 P.2d 644 (1985); *Sorensen v. Jarvis*, 119 Wis.2d 627, 350 N.W.2d

108 (1984); *see generally* W. Prosser, *Handbook of the Law of Torts* § 104, at 718–719 (5th ed. 1984).

3. *E.g., Connolly v. Conlan*, 371 N.W.2d 832 (Iowa 1985); *Thaut v. Finley*, 50 Mich.App. 611, 213 N.W.2d 820 (1973); *Trail v. Christian*, 298 Minn. 101, 213 N.W.2d 618 (1973); *Berkeley v. Park*, 47 Misc.2d 381, 262 N.Y.S.2d 290 (1965); *Hutchens v. Hankins*, 63 N.C.App. 1, 303 S.E.2d 584 (1983); *Mason v. Roberts*, 33 Ohio St.2d 29, 294 N.E.2d 884 (1973).

CASE—*Continued*

BRIGANCE v. VELVET DOVE RESTAURANT, INC.   Okl. **303**
Cite as 725 P.2d 300 (Okl. 1986)

Rappaport v. Nichols, 31 N.J. 188, 156 A.2d 1 (1959):

> "When alcoholic beverages are sold by a tavern keeper to a minor or to an intoxicated person, the unreasonable risk of harm ... to members of the traveling public may readily be recognized and foreseen; this is particularly evident in current times when traveling by car to and from the tavern is so commonplace and accidents resulting from drinking are so frequent."

As shown by the modern trend, the old common law rule of nonliability has been changed by judicial opinion:

> "Inherent in the common law is a dynamic principle which allows it to grow and to tailor itself to meet changing needs within the doctrine of stare decisis, which, if correctly understood, was not static and did not forever prevent the courts from reversing themselves or from applying principles of common law to new situations as the need arose. If this were not so, we must succumb to a rule that a judge should let others 'long dead and unaware of the problems of the age in which he lives do his thinking for him.'" [4]

This Court has similarly followed the concept that the common law "is a dynamic and growing thing and its rules arise from the application of reason to the changing condition of society." [5] The common law is not static.

The development of the law of torts is peculiarly a function of the judiciary. Because duty and liability are matters of public policy they are subject to the changing attitudes and needs of society.[6] The in-

stant case presents before us today the common law rule of nonliability for tavern owners and affords us the opportunity to reexamine the viability and efficacy of that rule in the State of Oklahoma.

Appellees assert that we are not free to change the common law because the Legislature has expressly spoken in this area by its 1959 repeal of Oklahoma's dram shop act and its failure to reenact such provision since that time. We are not persuaded by this argument. The dram shop act was not selectively repealed for it was repealed when intoxicants were legalized in 1959. Because the Legislature has failed to act to impose civil liability, for reasons unknown, does not unequivocally demonstrate legislative intent. To hold otherwise, would be indulging in a type of psychoanalysis of the Legislature. We simply cannot conclude that statutory silence is here indicative of legislative intent to bar the cause of action before us.

We also cannot accede to the view urged by appellees that this area of law is better dealt with by the Legislature. We find that on the basis of the clear trend in this area we are free to establish a civil cause of action by an injured third person against a commercial vendor of liquor for on the premises consumption. In rendering the opinion of *Vanderpool v. State*, 672 P.2d 1153, 1157 (Okla.1983), which modified the common law doctrine of governmental immunity, this Court stated in response to the oft-expressed view that if the doctrine is to be abrogated such should be done by the Legislature and not the courts of this State:

---

4. *Bielski v. Schulze*, 16 Wis.2d 1, 114 N.W.2d 105, 110 (1962) (quoting W. Douglas, *Stare Decisis*, 49 Colum.L.Rev. 735, 736 (1949)). This decision was quoted with approval by the Court of Appeals of Arizona, Div. 2, in *Lewis v. Wolf*, 122 Ariz. 567, 596 P.2d 705 (1979), wherein such court was constrained to affirm the trial court's summary judgment that in the absence of a dram shop law the bar owner is not liable in a negligence case because it was only an intermediate appellate court but stated "[w]ere we the Supreme Court of this state, we would abolish the anachronistic and illogical common law

rule and subject the bar owner to liability." In 1983, the Supreme Court of Arizona in *Ontiveros v. Borak*, 667 P.2d at 204, quoted with approval this language when abolishing the common law doctrine of tavern owner nonliability.

5. *McCormack v. Oklahoma Pub. Co.*, 613 P.2d 737, 740 (Okla.1980). *See also Vanderpool v. State*, 672 P.2d 1153, 1157 (Okla.1983).

6. *Vance v. United States*, 355 F.Supp. 756, 761 (D.Alaska 1973).

Continued

CASE—*Continued*

"But having come to the conclusions that the judicially recognized doctrine of governmental immunity in its present state under the case law is no longer supportable in reason, justice or in light of the overwhelming trend against its recognition, our duty is clear. Where the reason for the rule no longer exists, that alone should toll its death knell."

We believe the application of the old common law rule of a tavern owner's nonliability in today's automotive society is unrealistic, inconsistent with modern tort theories and is a complete anachronism within today's society.

The automobile is a constant reminder of a changed and changing America. It has made a tremendous impact on every segment of society, including the field of jurisprudence. In the "horse and buggy" days the common law may not have been significantly affected by the sale of liquor to an intoxicated person. The common law of nonliability was satisfactory. With today's car of steel and speed it becomes a lethal weapon in the hands of a drunken imbiber. The frequency of accidents involving drunk drivers are commonplace. Its affliction of bodily injury to an unsuspecting public is also of common knowledge. Under such circumstances we are compelled to widen the scope of the common law.

[1] We, thus, hold that one who sells intoxicating beverages for on the premises consumption has a duty to exercise reasonable care not to sell liquor to a noticeably intoxicated person. It is not unreasonable to expect a commercial vendor who sells alcoholic beverages for on the premises consumption to a person he knows or should know from the circumstances is already intoxicated, to foresee the unreasonable risk of harm to others who may be injured by such person's impaired ability to operate an automobile.

[2] In so concluding, we find the commercial vendor for on the premises consumption is under a duty, imposed both by statute and common law principles, to exercise reasonable care in selling or furnishing liquor to persons who by previous intoxication may lack full capacity of self-control to operate a motor vehicle and who may subsequently injure a third party. A person owes a duty to others not to subject them to an unreasonable risk of harm. We also note that a breach of duty for which we impose civil liability by this opinion constitutes a public offense under 37 O.S. Supp.1985 § 537.[7]

A commercial vendor for on the premises consumption is under a common law duty to exercise ordinary care under the circumstances.[8] We reach our conclusion in accordance with other courts finding a common law duty, relying on the general rule expressed in Restatement (Second) of Torts § 308 (1965):

"It is negligence to permit a third person to use a thing or to engage in an activity which is under the control of the actor, if the actor knows or should know that such person intends or is likely to use the thing or to conduct himself in the activity in such a manner as to create an unreasonable risk of harm to others."

And, Restatement (Second) of Torts § 390 (1965):

"One who supplies ... a chattel for the use of another whom the supplier knows or has reason to know to be likely because of his youth, inexperience or otherwise to use it in a manner involving unreasonable risk of physical harm to himself and others ... is subject to liability for physical harm resulting to them."

---

7.   37 O.S.Supp.1985 § 537 provides in pertinent part:

"(A) No person shall:
(1) Knowingly sell, deliver, or furnish alcoholic beverages to any person under twenty-one (21) years of age;
(2) Sell, deliver or knowingly furnish alcoholic beverages to an intoxicated person or to any person who has been adjudged insane or mentally deficient;"

8.   *Nazareno v. Urie,* 638 P.2d 671 (Alaska 1981); *Rappaport v. Nichols,* 31 N.J. 188, 156 A.2d 1 (1959).

CASE—*Continued*

BRIGANCE v. VELVET DOVE RESTAURANT, INC.   Okl.   **305**
Cite as 725 P.2d 300 (Okl. 1986)

[3, 4] Even if a commercial vendor for on the premises consumption is found to have breached its duty, a plaintiff must still show the illegal sale of alcohol led to the impairment of the ability of the driver which was the proximate cause of the injury and there was a causal connection between the sale and a foreseeable ensuing injury. *Ontiveros v. Borak, supra; Smith v. Clark*, 411 Pa. 142, 190 A.2d 441 (1963). As previously noted, the common law rule of a tavern owner's nonliability is based primarily on principles of causation, i.e., the chain of legal causation between the negligent selling of the alcoholic beverage and the injury is broken by the voluntary act of the patron in consuming the alcohol. *Ontiveros*, 667 P.2d at 206. An intervening cause which will break the causal nexus between the tavern owner's negligence and the resulting injury is called a supervening cause. In Oklahoma, the test to determine whether a cause is supervening is whether it is: "(1) independent of the original act, (2) adequate of itself to bring about the result and (3) one whose occurrence was not reasonably foreseeable."[9]

The Supreme Court of New Jersey in *Rappaport v. Nichols*, 31 N.J. 188, 204, 156 A.2d 1, 9 (1959), speaks to the issue of proximate cause:

"If, as we must assume at this stage of the proceeding, the defendant tavern keepers unlawfully and negligently sold alcoholic beverages to Nichols causing his intoxication, which in turn caused or contributed to his negligent operation of the motor vehicle at the time of the fatal accident, then a jury could reasonably find that the plaintiff's injuries resulted in the ordinary course of events from the defendants' negligence and that such negligence was in fact a substantial factor in bringing them about. And a jury could also reasonably find that Nichols' negligent operation of his motor vehicle after leaving the defendants' tav-

erns was a normal incident of the risk they created, or an event which they could reasonably have foreseen, and that consequently there was no effective breach in the chain of causation."

From the facts alleged in the present case, we cannot conclude as a matter of law that appellees' sale of the alcoholic beverage to the noticeably intoxicated patron could not have been the proximate cause of Shawn's alleged injuries. Concerning proximate causation, we find no distinction as does the old common law view, between the voluntary *consumption* of alcoholic beverages and the *sale* of the beverages in the chain of causation because the consumption, resulting intoxication and subsequent impaired driving ability of an intoxicated patron who is then involved in an accident are foreseeable intervening causes. A jury could find that appellees could have reasonably foreseen and anticipated the possible consequences in selling alcoholic beverages to a noticeably intoxicated patron who intended to drive an automobile and that the sale may have been a proximate cause of the alleged injuries. Ordinarily the question of causation in a negligent tort case is one of fact for the jury and becomes one of law only when there is no evidence from which the jury could reasonably find a causal nexus between the negligent act and the resulting injuries.[10]

We hold today that public policy is better served by holding that the common law principles of negligence are applicable where a commercial vendor for on the premises consumption is shown to have sold or furnished intoxicating beverages to a person who was noticeably intoxicated from which a jury could determine that such conduct creates an unreasonable risk of harm to others who may be injured by the person's impaired ability to operate a motor vehicle.[11] Based upon compelling reasons we, thus, reject the common law

---

9. *Thompson v. Presbyterian Hosp., Inc.*, 652 P.2d 260, 264 (Okla.1982).

10. *Id.* at 263.

11. By this decision we do not reach the question of whether a consumer-intoxicated driver has a new cause of action against the commercial vendor for on the premises consumption.

Continued

CASE—*Continued*

306 Okl.   **725 PACIFIC REPORTER, 2d SERIES**

doctrine of tavern owner nonliability in Oklahoma.[12]

[5] In adopting a new rule of liability which creates a civil cause of action, we specifically hold that the law hereby established will be applied prospectively to all causes of action occurring from and after the date the mandate issues herein.

We apply the rule of liability adopted herein to the parties in the case before us. We address appellants' theory of action on the assumption the facts pleaded are true and are sufficient to prove all the essential elements of a negligence action: duty, breach, cause and damages. If they are unable to prove negligence they will obviously fail to recover.

The judgment sustaining appellees' demurrer and dismissing appellants' complaint is REVERSED and the cause REMANDED for further proceedings not inconsistent with this opinion.

DOOLIN, V.C.J., and LAVENDER, OPALA, WILSON, KAUGER and SUMMERS, JJ., concur.

HARGRAVE, J., concurs in result.

SIMMS, C.J., concurs specially.

SIMMS, Chief Justice, concurring:

I fully concur in the opinion of the Court changing the common-law rule of nonliability for injuries to third parties. I add this comment only to point out that the opinion does not alter the traditional common-law causation concept to benefit a consumer driver's claim against the vendor. While the vendor of liquor for on premises consumption owes a duty not to provide alcohol to a driver who is noticably intoxicated, the driver also owes a duty to exercise ordinary care for his own safety and the safety of others by desisting from voluntary overconsumption. In a dispute brought by the consumer seeking recovery against the vendor, the common-law notion that it is the consumer whose consumption constitutes the proximate cause of harm remains viable.

12. We do not by this opinion address the issue

I am authorized to state that Vice Chief Justice DOOLIN and Justice OPALA join with the views expressed herein.

STATE of Oklahoma, ex rel., OKLAHOMA BAR ASSOCIATION, Complainant,

v.

Carroll SAMARA, Respondent.

SCBD No. 2830.
OBAD No. 563.

Supreme Court of Oklahoma.

July 25, 1986.

Rehearing Denied Sept. 15, 1986.

In an attorney reinstatement proceeding, the Supreme Court, Doolin, V.C.J., held that continuing to practice law after original suspension justifies denial of petition for reinstatement to practice law.

Reinstatement denied.

Hodges, Lavender, and Summers, JJ., dissented.

1. Attorney and Client ⬥57

Review of report of trial panel of professional responsibility tribunal is not limited to weighing of evidence or sustaining of decision on basis of substantial evidence from record. Disciplinary Proceedings Rules 6.15, 11.6, 5 O.S.A. Ch. 1, App. 1–A.

2. Attorney and Client ⬥61

Continuing to practice law after original suspension justifies denial of petition for reinstatement to practice law.

of a social host's civil liability.

CASE

832 Iowa 371 NORTH WESTERN REPORTER, 2d SERIES

Maurice J. CONNOLLY, as Administrator of the Estate of Jeffery J. Connolly, Maurice J. Connolly and Joan Connolly, Appellants,

v.

Joseph William CONLAN, d/b/a Twelve Mile House, Appellee.

No. 84–853.

Supreme Court of Iowa.

July 31, 1985.

A wrongful death action was instituted on several theories including a common-law theory for acts falling outside parameters of dramshop statute. The District Court, Dubuque County, William G. Klotzbach, J., entered order dismissing claim premised on a common-law theory, and interlocutory appeal was granted. The Supreme Court, Harris, J., held that claim in wrongful death action, arising from fatal injury sustained by plaintiffs' minor decedent in a single motor vehicle accident after decedent and another youth were served intoxicating liquor or beer by defendant, could not be premised on a common-law theory for acts falling outside parameters of dramshop statute.

Affirmed.

Schultz, J., dissented and filed opinion in which Reynoldson, C.J., McCormick and Larson, JJ., joined.

1. Intoxicating Liquors ⚿282

Dramshop statute, pertaining to sales or gifts of intoxicants to intoxicated persons or serving of such persons to point of intoxication, makes licensees and permittees strictly liable and, as such, preempts tort field as to them and precludes a common-law action for illegal sale of intoxicants to minors. I.C.A. § 123.92.

2. Intoxicating Liquors ⚿282

Claim in wrongful death action, arising from fatal injury sustained by plaintiffs' minor decedent in a single motor vehicle accident after decedent and another youth were served intoxicating liquor or beer by defendant, could not be premised on a common-law theory for acts falling outside parameters of dramshop statute. I.C.A. § 123.92.

Paula M. Stenlund, Dennis J. Naughton and Francis W. Henkels, Dubuque, appellants.

Gerry M. Rinden and Michael E. Sheehy of Klockau, McCarthy, Ellison & Rinden, Rock Island, Illinois, and Lawrence H. Fautsch, Dubuque, for appellee.

Considered en banc.

HARRIS, Justice.

This wrongful death action against a tavern owner-operator was brought in several divisions. Two divisions were based on the claim that a tavern operator is liable on a common-law theory for acts falling outside the parameters of Iowa Code section 123.92. This was the question on which this court was equally divided in *Haafke v. Mitchell,* 347 N.W.2d 381 (Iowa 1984). The trial court sustained defendant's motion to dismiss these two divisions. We granted plaintiffs' application to bring this interlocutory appeal from that ruling which we now affirm.

Plaintiffs' decedent was killed in a single motor vehicle accident after he and another youth were served intoxicating liquor or beer by defendant. According to the petition, which of course we assume here to be true, defendant knew the youths were minors and the sale was wanton, reckless, and malicious.

In dismissing, the trial court determined the dram shop act "is the exclusive method of recovery in civil damages against liquor licensees." Plaintiffs challenge this ruling, arguing that the dram-shop statute, section 123.92, provides but does not limit recoveries. They contend the section does not preempt all dram-shop theories of recovery so that there should remain a common-law right of action against licensees for their

Continued

CASE—*Continued*

CONNOLLY v. CONLAN   Iowa   **833**
Cite as 371 N.W.2d 832 (Iowa 1985)

acts which fall outside the parameters of section 123.92. More specifically, they urge that the statute addresses only sales or gifts of intoxicants to intoxicated persons or the serving of such persons to the point of intoxication, leaving unaffected a common-law action for the illegal sale of intoxicants to minors.

We agree with the trial court in rejecting these contentions. It would be repetitious to again trace the history of our views on statutory and common-law recoveries in dram-shop claims. *See Golden v. O'Neill*, 366 N.W.2d 178, 179–80 (Iowa 1985); *Clark v. Mincks*, 364 N.W.2d 226, 228–31 (Iowa 1985); *Haafke v. Mitchell*, 347 N.W.2d at 388; *Nelson v. Restaurants of Iowa, Inc.*, 338 N.W.2d 881, 883–85 (Iowa 1983); *Snyder v. Davenport*, 323 N.W.2d 225, 226–27 (Iowa 1982); *Lewis v. State*, 256 N.W.2d 181, 191–92 (Iowa 1977); *Cowman v. Hansen*, 250 Iowa 358, 373, 92 N.W.2d 682, 690 (1958).

[1, 2] The narrow question here has only to do with licensees and permittees. Section 123.92 makes them strictly liable and, for the reasons stated in the dissenting opinions in *Haafke*, 347 N.W.2d at 390–92, we think the act preempts the tort field as to them. A revision of our statutory dram-shop law was traced in *Nelson*, 338 N.W.2d at 883–84. Under that revision, the legislature expressly kept licensees and permittees under the dram shop act. In doing so, it struck for them a balance: They would remain strictly liable under the act and would continue to be compelled to post financial responsibility. But, under the scheme, their liability was limited to serving persons "while he or she is intoxicated" or "to the point where he or she is intoxicated." The liability ended there.

Social policies might support the expanded liability suggested by the plaintiffs. But the legislature was not persuaded by them, and we are bound to adhere to the limitations of the legislative plan.

The trial court was correct in dismissing claims against the defendant which were grounded on common-law theories of negligence in providing intoxicants to a minor.

AFFIRMED.

All Justices concur except REYNOLDSON, C.J., and SCHULTZ, McCORMICK and LARSON, JJ., who dissent.

SCHULTZ, Justice (dissenting).

With the result reached with the majority opinion our case law involving tort action for damages caused by the illegal furnishing of intoxicants to minors is now in a quagmire. Without renouncing the action taken on our previous cases by the majority opinion, our holdings are inconsistent and not in tune with each other. Four months ago this court interpreted the legislative intent in enacting Iowa Code chapter 123 and held a social host civilly responsible under common law principles for damages for a statutory violation of this chapter. *Clark v. Mincks*, 364 N.W.2d 226, 228–31 (Iowa 1985). Today, the majority opinion excuses one who profits from an illegal sale from civil liability to a third party for damages caused by this illegal act, again relying on legislative intent in the enactment of chapter 123. This interpretation is totally at odds with the public policy declared by the legislature:

This chapter ... shall be deemed an exercise of the police power of the state, for the protection of the welfare, health, peace, morals, and safety of the people of the state, and all *its provisions shall be liberally construed for the accomplishment of that purpose*, and it is declared to be public policy that the traffic in alcoholic liquors is so affected with a public interest that it should be regulated to the extent of prohibiting all traffic in them, except as provided in this chapter.

(emphasis added). The interpretation of section 123.92 to preempt tort actions brought on grounds outside of the section is a concept in the narrowest sense that does not square with the stated policy of the legislature and places tavern owners who violate the law by selling to minors in a position of immunity not enjoyed by any

CASE—*Continued*

834 Iowa   371 **NORTH WESTERN REPORTER, 2d SERIES**

other citizen of this state. I cannot and will not ascribe this intent to the legislature. Rather, I believe that we must confess that the inconsistency is ours.

The majority opinion simply indicates the writer thinks that section 123.92 preempts the tort field to licensees and permittees. Not one word in this section expresses that thought, however. Consequently, to arrive at such a result the majority must imply a legislative intent to excuse licensees from liability for a tort that is not remedied by section 123.92 despite the fact that other citizens incur this liability. The only reason the majority advances for preemption of licensees from liability is a so-called trade-off when the licensees assumed strict liability in instances where they are liable under the act and post financial responsibility. This was not a trade-off for avoiding other tort liability under the common law. At the time and until *Lewis v. State*, 256 N.W.2d 181, 191–92 (Iowa 1977), the common law of this state as announced by this court did not recognize anyone's liability grounded on the illegal furnishing of intoxicants. I would not ascribe to the legislature an intent to do a useless act. Consequently, I conclude it could not have been thinking in terms of preempting common law liability when it did not exist under our case law. Rather, I ascribe to the legislature an intent more consistent with positive terms. The purpose of section 123.92 is to provide injured parties a remedy against those who profit in the liquor industry for wrongs caused under the narrow terms of this section. I cannot ascribe to the legislature an intent to provide a higher protection to profiteers than we would to a social host.

The majority declines to discuss the history of our decisions as it would be "repetitious." I find the retracing of our case law not only instructive, but conclude that these cases patently point out the error of the majority.

Until 1977 we held that at common law a person injured by an intoxicated person was not entitled to recover from the party who wrongfully furnished the intoxicants

to the intoxicated person. This principle was based on the theory that the proximate cause of the injury was the consumption of the intoxicants and not the sale. *Cowman v. Hansen*, 250 Iowa 358, 373, 92 N.W.2d 682, 690 (1958). To alleviate the hardship caused by our position on common law liability, our legislature has prescribed a statutory remedy since 1862. *See* 1862 Iowa Acts ch. 47, § 2. The 1862 statute has been modified, and other statutes have been enacted to provide various remedies against various parties. *See generally,* Comment, *Beyond the Dram Shop Act: Imposition of Common-Law Liability on Purveyors of Liquor*, 63 Iowa L.Rev. 1282, 1298–99 (1978).

The common law non-liability rule was abrogated when, in *Lewis*, 256 N.W.2d at 191–92, we held than an actionable, common law negligence claim could be predicated on the violation of a statute prohibiting the sale of liquor to a minor. We reviewed the statute prohibiting sales or gifts of intoxicants to a minor, a predecessor to our present section 123.47, and determined it set a minimum standard of care for the purpose of common law negligence. *Id.* at 187–89. Abandoning the position expressed in *Cowman*, we held that the illegal sale of intoxicants "may well be the proximate cause of injuries sustained as a result of an intoxicated individual's tortious conduct and liability may thus be imposed upon the violators in favor of the injured, innocent third party. The question of proximate cause under such facts and circumstances would be for the trier of fact." *Id.* at 191–92.

In *Snyder v. Davenport*, 323 N.W.2d 225, 227 (Iowa 1982), we held that the common law negligence action provided in *Lewis* was unavailable in an action against a licensee grounded on violation of Iowa Code section 123.49(1) which prohibits the providing of intoxicants to an intoxicated person. We reasoned that the legislature preempted this particular theory of recovery when it enacted section 123.92. *Id.* Thus, we held that section 123.92 provides the exclusive remedy against a licensee for

Continued

CASE—*Continued*

CONNOLLY v. CONLAN   Iowa   **835**
Cite as 371 N.W.2d 832 (Iowa 1985)

the illegal sale of intoxicants to an intoxicated person. *Id.* at 226.

At the time of *Lewis* there were two dram shop statutes. Iowa Code section 123.92 (1966) provided an action against a licensee and was a predecessor of our present section 123.92, and Iowa Code section 129.2 (1966) provided an action against "any person who shall by selling or giving to another contrary to the provisions of this title any intoxicating liquors, cause the intoxication of such person." We did not discuss the issue of preemption in *Lewis*. In *Snyder*, however, we carefully differentiated between section 129.2, which had been in effect at the inception of *Lewis*, and section 123.92. 323 N.W.2d at 226–27. We determined that the explicit statutory scheme of section 123.92 directed against a licensee for selling liquor to an intoxicated person preempted any common law action for this identical statutory violation. *Id.* We expressly reserved the issue of whether a common law action could be maintained in cases to which section 123.92 is not applicable. *Id.* at 228 n. 2.

Since *Snyder* we have decided other cases concerning the actionability of common law negligence arising from the illegal provision of intoxicants. In *Haafke v. Mitchell*, 347 N.W.2d 381 (Iowa 1984), in addition to deciding the issue regarding the liability of the licensee under common law negligence, we held that the licensee's employees would be liable to an injured person under the common law. *Id.* at 388. In *Haafke* we were equally divided on the issue of the common law liability of a licensee for acts falling outside the parameters of section 123.92. Resultantly, the trial court ruling dismissing an injured party's common law claim against a licensee, grounded on an illegal sale of intoxicants to a minor which caused plaintiff's injury, was affirmed by operation of law.

We extended our *Lewis* and *Haafke* decisions by allowing recovery under the common law against a social host who provided intoxicants in violation of our beer and liquor statutes. *Clark*, 364 N.W.2d at 228–31. More recently, we held that section

123.92 does not preempt actions against licensees based on negligent failure to provide safe premises for patrons or on assault and battery by an employee under a theory of respondeat superior. *Golden v. O'Neill*, 366 N.W.2d 178, 179 (Iowa 1985).

Our ruling concerning preemption in *Snyder* is readily distinguishable. In *Snyder* we reasoned that the statutory scheme of section 123.92 and the fact its enactment created a liability unknown at common law and a specific method by which liability could be ascertained required that we hold the statutory remedy be exclusive. 323 N.W.2d at 226–28. The remedy of section 123.92 is prescribed for a specific wrong, the sale or gift of intoxicants to an intoxicated person. The remedy of section 123.-92 does not cover the wrong claimed here, the provision of intoxicants to a minor. Although the statutory remedy to enforce a new right or liability is generally exclusive, it is exclusive only to the extent that it is coextensive with the right. 1 C.J.S. *Actions* § 6(e) (1936). The statutory remedy "ordinarily will not be permitted to restrict the right or to preclude a resort to other remedies in cases or under circumstances other than those for which the remedy is given." *Id.* Section 123.92 does not provide a remedy for the wrong caused by the illegal sale or gift of intoxicants to a minor.

Reason supports a conclusion that the legislature did not intend preemption of all common law theories of recovery against a licensee by the enactment of section 123.92. Preemption of all common law liability would relieve the licensee from civil responsibility for the sale of kegs and cases of beer or other intoxicants to sober minors, who do the predictable thing—drink to the point of intoxication and then drive vehicles on the streets and highways. Under these facts the licensee would fare better than the liquor store employee in *Lewis*, the employee in *Haafke* and the social host in *Mincks*. I do not attribute such intent to the legislature. We stated in *Golden:*

CASE—*Continued*

836 Iowa   **371 NORTH WESTERN REPORTER, 2d SERIES**

In adopting the dram shop civil liability statute the legislature has not immunized licensees from liability for intentional torts and negligence not based on the sale or gift of intoxicating beverages to an intoxicated person. Jim's [licensee] reliance on *Snyder* to bolster his claim that section 123.92, when applicable, preempts all other claims is misplaced. 366 N.W.2d at 180.

Allowing a common law action that does not coincide with the dram shop statute, section 123.92, would be consistent with our position on other strict liability actions. We indicated that a statute imposing strict liability on a dog owner for injury from a dog bite did not limit the right of an injured party to institute a common law action and seek punitive damages that were not recoverable in the statutory action. *Dougherty v. Reckler*, 191 Iowa 1195, 1198, 184 N.W. 304, 305 (1921). We allowed an action grounded on negligence for failing to fence in an animal in violation of the Iowa Code section 188.2 and indicated a theory of strict liability pursuant to section 188.3 for unlawful trespass was also available to plaintiff. *Wenndt v. Latare*, 200 N.W.2d 862, 869 (Iowa 1972). Also, we have held that where the common law provides a strict liability action in tort, it does not preclude an alternate remedy based on negligence. *Hawkeye-Security Insurance Co. v. Ford Motor Co.*, 174 N.W.2d 672, 685 (Iowa 1970); *see Franken v. City of Sioux Center*, 272 N.W.2d 422, 426-27 (Iowa 1978).

In summary, I would hold that section 123.92 only preempts those common law actions that arise from a claim that the licensee negligently sold or gave intoxicants to an intoxicated person or served a person to the point of intoxication. I would hold that a common law action exists against a licensee for illegally providing intoxicants to a minor.

REYNOLDSON, C.J., and McCORMICK and LARSON, JJ., join this dissent.

In re the MARRIAGE OF Bruce GRAVATT and Sandra Sue Gravatt, Upon the Petition of Bruce Gravatt, Petitioner-Appellant,

and

Concerning Sandra Sue Gravatt, Respondent-Appellee.

No. 84–369.

Court of Appeals of Iowa.

May 10, 1985.

Proceeding was instituted on application of father to modify provision of desolution decree giving custody of parties' children to mother. The District Court, Linn County, Thomas L. Koehler, J., denied application, and father appealed. After remand, 365 N.W.2d 48, the Court of Appeals, Sackett, J., held that custody provision of dissolution decree should have been modified to provide for a change in custody of minor children to father with visitation for mother, in interest of children, where children were shown by a specialist in pediatric endocrinology to have developed a condition known as phychosocial dwarfism while living in mother's home since date of decree and, though there were no assurances that living with father would alleviate condition, short term effects on children after spending time with father were very promising.

Reversed and remanded.

Hayden, J., dissented and filed opinion.

1. Divorce ⟨key⟩303(7)

Father, seeking modification of custody provision of dissolution decree, was required to show by a preponderance of evidence that there had been a substantial change in circumstances, since date of dis-

CASE

CAMPBELL v. CARPENTER

Cite as, Or., 566 P.2d 893

Or. **893**

These citations appear to harm plaintiff's position rather than to help it. Gift subscriptions paid for by others are paid subscriptions.

Plaintiff also contends that a person to whom a paper is sent without his consent is not a subscriber but cites no postal regulation in this regard. Instead, plaintiff cites *Ashton v. Stoy*, 96 Iowa 197, 64 N.W. 804, 805 (1895), to the effect that a subscriber must be one who gives his consent. However, in issue was the definition of a "subscriber" under a section of the Iowa Code concerning newspapers eligible to publish official county reports.

[2] Because plaintiff indicated he particularly relied upon the report made to the United States Postal Service regarding the number of subscriptions, the regulations concerning who is entitled to be included upon a subscription list in such a report would appear to be particularly appropriate. Plaintiff has called to our attention the above-quoted regulation 132.463 which says that "[a] minor portion of the subscription list may consist of persons whose subscriptions were paid for as gifts," which is the situation here. It says nothing about having to have the consent of the person to whom the subscription is given. No information is given to us as to what percentage constitutes a "minor portion" and we cannot say, as a matter of law, that 500 out of the number here is not a minor portion.

[3] Plaintiff also points out that a considerable number of the requests for subscriptions came to defendants with no money enclosed, and that these subscriptions were from persons who had filled out and mailed a printed request form for a subscription which the paper had published. He claims these were not legitimate subscriptions. There is no copy of the request form in evidence. However, defendants treated a completed request form as a promise to pay for the subscription and plaintiff has not produced proof that it was improper to treat it so.

The decree of the trial court is affirmed.

279 Or. 237

Joy A. **CAMPBELL**, personal representative of the Estate of Marie M. Scheie, Deceased, Respondent,

v.

Keith **CARPENTER** and Mary Carpenter, Individually and dba Mary Jo's Inn, Appellants,

and

Betty Jean Pierce, Respondent.

Paul D. **SCHEIE**, personal representative of the Estate of Arnold Scheie, Deceased, Respondent,

v.

Keith **CARPENTER** and Mary Carpenter, Individually and dba Mary Jo's Inn, Appellants,

and

Betty Jean Pierce, Respondent.

Supreme Court of Oregon, Department 2.

Argued and Submitted May 9, 1977.

Decided July 20, 1977.

Actions were brought for death of persons killed by automobile whose driver had become intoxicated at defendant's tavern. The Circuit Court, Multnomah County, William M. Dale, J., entered judgments against driver of automobile and against owners of tavern and owners appealed. The Supreme Court, Tongue, J., held that evidence would support findings that bartenders had continued to serve beer to customer after she was visibly intoxicated and that at time of serving drinks to customer tavern owners had reason to know that upon leaving the tavern she would probably drive away in her automobile.

Affirmed.

CASE—*Continued*

1. Appeal and Error ⊕934(1)

In appeal from judgment in favor of plaintiff, court would view evidence in light most favorable to the plaintiff in the event of any conflicts in the evidence and would accord to the plaintiff the benefit of all reasonable inferences that the jury could have drawn from the evidence.

2. Intoxicating Liquors ⊕310

Evidence in action against owners of tavern where driver became intoxicated before she was involved in accident resulting in death of plaintiffs' decedents would support finding that bartenders had continued to serve beer to driver after she was "visibly" intoxicated and that at time of serving the drinks the tavern owners had reason to know that upon leaving the tavern driver would probably drive away in her automobile. ORS 471.410(3), 472.310(3); N.J.S.A. 33:1–77.

3. Intoxicating Liquors ⊕285

A tavern keeper is negligent if, at the time of serving drinks to a customer, that customer is "visibly" intoxicated because at that time it is reasonably foreseeable that when such a customer leaves the tavern he or she will drive an automobile. ORS 471.-410(3).

———————

Francis F. Yunker, Portland, argued the cause for appellants Carpenter. With him on the brief was Mary J. Vershum, Portland.

Elden M. Rosenthal, Portland, argued the cause for respondents Campbell and Scheie. With him on the brief was Charles Paulson, P. C., Portland.

No appearance for respondent Pierce.

Before DENECKE, C. J., and TONGUE, BRYSON and TOMPKINS, JJ.

TONGUE, Justice.

These are two consolidated actions for wrongful death against the owners and operators of a tavern. Both decedents were

killed by an automobile whose driver had become intoxicated at the tavern. The cases were tried before the court, without a jury. Judgments were entered against both the driver, defendant Pierce, and against the owners of the tavern, defendants Carpenter. Only defendants Carpenter appeal.

The principal allegation of the complaint is that defendants Carpenter sold and continued to sell alcoholic beverages to defendant Pierce "after she had become perceptibly under the influence of intoxicating liquors" when they knew or should have known that she would "leave the premises" by "operating a motor vehicle and constitute an unreasonable hazard and risk of harm to other persons on the public highway." Defendants Carpenter do not contend that these allegations fail to state a cause of action, but contend that the evidence was insufficient to prove this allegation.[1]

Despite the fact that defendants do not challenge the sufficiency of the allegations of the complaint, it should be noted that this is the first case in Oregon in which this particular question has been presented. In *Wiener v. Gamma Phi, ATO Frat.*, 258 Or. 632, 485 P.2d 18 (1971), a case involving the serving of liquor to minors who were later involved in an automobile accident, we said (at 639, 485 P.2d at 21):

> "*   *   * Ordinarily, a host who makes available intoxicating liquors to an adult guest is not liable for injuries to third persons resulting from the guest's intoxication. There might be circumstances in which the host would have a duty to deny his guest further access to alcohol. This would be the case where the host 'has reason to know that he is dealing with persons whose characteristics make it especially likely that they will do unreasonable things.' *Such persons could include those already severely intoxicated,* or those whose behavior the host knows to be unusually affected by alcohol.   *   *   *" (Emphasis added)

1. The complaint also alleged that defendants Carpenter were negligent in permitting defend-

ant Pierce to leave the premises when they knew that she would be driving.

CASE—*Continued*

CAMPBELL v. CARPENTER   Or. **895**
Cite as, Or., 566 P.2d 893

As authority for that statement we cited, among other authorities, *Rappaport v. Nichols*, 31 N.J. 188, 156 A.2d 1, 9, 75 A.L.R.2d 821 (1959). That case involved facts more similar to those involved in this case. In affirming a judgment for the plaintiff, and on a theory of common law negligence, that court stated the following rules (156 A.2d at 8–9), which defendants Carpenter apparently do not question and which we approve:

"* * * Negligence is tested by whether the reasonably prudent person at the time and place should recognize and foresee an unreasonable risk or likelihood of harm or danger to others. * * *

"The negligence may consist in the creation of a situation which involves unreasonable risk because of the expectable action of another. See *Brody v. Albert Lifson & Sons*, 17 N.J. 383, 389, 111 A.2d 504 (1955). *Where a tavern keeper sells alcoholic beverages to a person who is visibly intoxicated or to a person he knows or should know from the circumstances to be a minor, he ought to recognize and foresee the unreasonable risk of harm to others through action of the intoxicated person or the minor.* * * *

"When alcoholic beverages are sold by a tavern keeper to a minor or to an intoxicated person, the unreasonable risk of harm not only to the minor or the intoxicated person but also to members of the traveling public may readily be recognized and foreseen; this is particularly

evident in current times when traveling by car to and from the tavern is so commonplace and accidents resulting from drinking are so frequent. * * *

"The defendants contend that, assuming their conduct was unlawful and negligent as charged in the complaint, it was nevertheless not the proximate cause of the injuries suffered. But a tortfeasor is generally held answerable for the injuries which result in the ordinary course of events from his negligence and it is generally sufficient if his negligent conduct was a substantial factor in bringing about the injuries. * * *"[2] (Emphasis added)

[1] The question remains, however, to determine whether the evidence in this case was sufficient to satisfy the requirements as stated in *Rappaport*. As usual in an appeal from a judgment in favor of a plaintiff, we must view the evidence in the light most favorable to the plaintiff in the event of any conflicts in the evidence and also accord to the plaintiff the benefit of all reasonable inferences that the jury could have drawn from the evidence. See *Geer v. Farquhar*, 270 Or. 642, 644, 528 P.2d 1335 (1974).

In considering that question it is important to bear in mind that the question is not whether there was sufficient evidence from which the trial court could have properly found that Mrs. Pierce was "visibly" intoxicated at the time she left the tavern owned

---

2. To the same effect, *see Waynick v. Chicago's Last Department Store*, 269 F.2d 322 (7th Cir. 1959); *Jardine v. Upper Darby Lodge No. 1973, Inc.*, 413 Pa. 626, 198 A.2d 550 (1964); *Vesely v. Sager*, 5 Cal.3d 153, 95 Cal.Rptr. 623, 486 P.2d 151 (1971); *Mitchell v. Ketner*, 54 Tenn. App. 656, 393 S.W.2d 755 (1964), among other cases. *See also generally* Annot., 75 A.L.R.2d 833 (1961).

It is also to be noted that in Oregon, as in New Jersey, state law prohibits the serving of intoxicating beverages to persons who are "visibly" or "apparently" intoxicated. *See* ORS 471.410(3) and ORS 472.310(3), and Oregon Liquor Control Regulations No. 10–065(2). *Cf.* R.S. 33:1–77, N.J.S.A. and Regulation No. 20, Rule 1, Division of Alcoholic Beverage Control, as discussed in *Rappaport v. Nichols*, 31 N.J. 188, 156 A.2d 1, 8, 75 A.L.R.2d 821 (1959).

We also note that in *Stachniewicz v. Mar-Cam Corporation*, 259 Or. 583, 586–87, 488 P.2d 436 (1971), we not only commented upon these statutes and regulations, but also commented upon the difficulty of determining whether a third party's injuries would have been caused by an already intoxicated person. Although we still consider that observation to have been appropriate under the quite different facts of that case, we accept and adopt the reasoning of the New Jersey court, as quoted above, as applied to cases involving facts such as those involved in this case. We do so not based upon or because of ORS 471.410(3), but as a matter of common law negligence, as did the New Jersey court.

CASE—*Continued*

by defendants Carpenter, but whether there was substantial evidence from which the trial court, as the trier of the facts could properly have found that at the time Mrs. Pierce was served the last (or any) drink prior to leaving the tavern she was "visibly" intoxicated.

There was testimony that Mrs. Pierce went to the tavern at about 4 p. m. and left about 6:30 p. m.; that during that interval she was served as many as eight beers; that before leaving the tavern she got into an argument with a man she met at the tavern, her ex-husband; that she was then asked by the bartender to leave and called the bartender a "bitch."

In addition, there was testimony that immediately upon leaving the tavern Mrs. Pierce drove her car in an exceedingly erratic manner, "screaming" up a street where children were playing, lurching around the next corner, "burning rubber" in doing so, swerving into the opposite lane of traffic so as to nearly hit oncoming cars head on; going through a "red light" at the next intersection, and then accelerating up a hill, passing four cars, at a speed of from 75 to 80 miles per hour, all immediately prior to the fatal accident in which the two decedents were killed.

Blood samples taken after the accident with the consent of Mrs. Pierce at 8:30 p. m., approximately two hours after leaving the tavern, showed a blood alcohol content of .24 percent. A professor of toxicology testified, that, in his opinion, such a blood alcohol content at that time for a woman of her weight, would indicate that if she stopped drinking at 6 p. m. she would still probably be showing "outward symptoms of intoxication" at 6:50 p. m., the time of the accident, but that he "would not say" whether she would be showing such symptoms at 5:30 p. m. (an hour before she left the tavern, according to at least some witnesses).

[2] He also testified, however, that even five and one-fourth beers would "build up" a blood alcohol level of .24 percent in a woman of her size and that at that level such a person would be "under the influence" and would probably show "outward symptoms" of intoxication. As previously noted, there was testimony from which the trial court could have found that the serving of beer to Mrs. Pierce continued until she had up to eight beers in a period of approximately two hours.[3]

We believe that the trial court could have properly found from this evidence that defendants' bartenders had continued to serve beer to Mrs. Pierce after she was "visibly" intoxicated.

We also hold that the trial judge, as the finder of the facts in this case, could have properly found from this evidence that at the time of serving such drinks to Mrs. Pierce defendants Carpenter had reason to know that upon leaving the tavern she would probably drive away in her automobile. It is also our opinion that the trial judge, in making that finding, could properly take notice of the fact that "in current times * * * traveling by car to and from the tavern is so commonplace" (as also observed in *Rappaport v. Nichols, supra*, 156 A.2d at 8) and that this includes visits to taverns by single women.

It is true that at some time after the drinks had been served to Mrs. Pierce, she left the tavern with her ex-husband. If a proper test of the negligence of a tavern keeper in such cases is that of negligence in allowing an intoxicated customer to drive an automobile upon leaving a tavern (as also alleged in plaintiffs' complaint), it might be contended that defendants Carpenter had no reason to know, at the time when Mrs. Pierce left the tavern, that she would try to drive her automobile because it was just as likely, if not more likely, that her ex-husband would be the driver.

---

3. There was also some evidence that Mrs. Pierce took valium, a tranquilizer, while at the tavern. The trial court was not required to believe that evidence. There was also some

testimony that after leaving the tavern Mrs. Pierce stopped elsewhere for another drink but that was contradicted by other witnesses.

Continued

CASE—*Continued*

FISHERMEN'S MARKETING ASS'N v. WILSON   Or.   **897**
Cite as, Or., 566 P.2d 897

[3] Under the rule of *Rappaport*, however, which we now adopt for application in such cases, a tavern keeper is negligent if, at the time of serving drinks to a customer, that customer is "visibly" intoxicated because at that time it is reasonably foreseeable that when such a customer leaves the tavern he or she will drive an automobile. As previously stated, we believe that there was sufficient evidence to support a finding in this case that at the time of serving the drinks to Mrs. Pierce, it was reasonably foreseeable to the defendants Carpenter that when she left the tavern she would be the driver of her own car, rather than that her estranged husband would be the driver.

Concluding, as we do, that there was substantial evidence to support the findings of fact by the trial court, its judgment in this case is affirmed.

279 Or. 259

**FISHERMEN'S MARKETING ASSOCIA-
TION, INCORPORATED, a California
Corporation, dba Fishermen's Marketing
Association of California, Incorporated,
Appellant,**

v.

**Walter WILSON, aka "Roy
Wilson", Respondent.**

Supreme Court of Oregon,
In Banc.

Argued and Submitted May 5, 1977.

Decided July 20, 1977.

Nonprofit cooperative association, which was engaged in marketing fish for its members, brought action against a member to collect liquidated damages and attorney fees on basis of contention that he delivered a catch of fish to a nondesignated dealer in violation of association's bylaws and membership agreement. The Circuit Court,
Douglas County, Don H. Sanders, J., refused to enforce liquidated damages provisions, and association appealed. The Supreme Court, Linde, J., held that: (1) fact that association did not produce actual membership agreement signed by member for purpose of proving terms of his membership did not preclude recovery against member, and (2) provision for $1,000 liquidated damages was enforceable against member, though it was found that the actual damages could be ascertained.

Reversed and remanded.

1. **Appeal and Error** ⟨⊷⟩719(6)
In action by nonprofit cooperative association, which was engaged in marketing fish, to collect liquidated damages and attorney fees against member on basis of contention that he delivered catch of fish to nondesignated dealer in violation of association's bylaws and membership agreement, fact that association did not produce actual membership agreement signed by member for purposes of proving terms of his membership did not preclude recovery against member, in light of fact that he did not challenge finding that membership agreement provided for liquidated damages and attorney fees. ORS 41.610.

2. **Damages** ⟨⊷⟩76
Liquidated damages provisions in cooperative bylaws and membership agreements are enforceable if they relate broadly to the assumptions which led to their authorization by statute, including the assumption that marketing cooperatives have a greater stake in each member's adherence to his agreement for the term of his membership than only the monetary loss resulting from a particular sale by the member outside the marketing agreement. ORS 62.355, 62.-355(2).

3. **Damages** ⟨⊷⟩79(1)
Mere fact that monetary loss from a breach of a cooperative association's membership agreement is ascertainable does not relieve a member from an otherwise valid provision for liquidated damages, nor does

CASE

ATLANTIC REPORTER

VOLUME 156, SECOND SERIES

31 N.J. 188

Selma RAPPAPORT, etc., Plaintiff-
Appellant,

v.

Robert NICHOLS et al., Defendants,

and

Hub Bar, Inc., a New Jersey corporation,
et al., Defendants-Respondents.

No. A–22.

Supreme Court of New Jersey.

Argued Oct. 14, 1959.

Decided Nov. 23, 1959.

Action for the death of decedent and damages to the automobile of plaintiff received in an automobile accident. Plaintiff appealed to the Appellate Division from a judgment entered in the Law Division in favor of the defendants and the Supreme Court certified the matter on its own motion. The Supreme Court, Jacobs, J., held that if defendant tavern keepers unlawfully and negligently sold alcoholic beverages to minor causing his intoxication which in turn caused or contributed to his negligent operation of motor vehicle at time of fatal accident, a jury could find that the plaintiff's injuries resulted in the ordinary course of events from the defendants' negligence and that such negligence was the substantial factor in bringing them about and that the minor's negligent operation of the motor vehicle after leaving the defendants' taverns was a normal incident of the risk they created or an event which they could reasonably have foreseen and hence the question of proxi-

156 A.2d—1

mate causal relation between the defendants' unlawful negligent conduct and the plaintiff's injuries would be a question for the jury.

Reversed and remanded for trial.

1. Pleading ⬅34(1, 3)

In dealing with the legal sufficiency of a complaint, plaintiff is entitled to a liberal interpretation of its contents and to the benefits of all of his allegations and most favorable inferences which may reasonably be drawn from them.

2. Intoxicating Liquors ⬅283

Where during prohibition days, New Jersey had a Civil Damage Law imposing strict liability for damages upon unlawful sellers of alcoholic beverages and the law was repealed in 1934, in light of abandonment of prohibition and its replacement by the Alcoholic Beverage Control Act, the repealer left unimpaired the fundamental negligence principles prevailing in New Jersey. L.1934, c. 32; R.S. 33:1–1 et seq., N.J.S.A.

3. Negligence ⬅4, 10

Negligence is tested by whether the reasonably prudent person at the time and place should recognize and foresee an unreasonable risk or likelihood of harm or danger to others and the standard of care is the conduct of the reasonable person of ordinary prudence under the circumstances.

4. Negligence ⬅10

Negligence may consist in the creation of a situation which involves unreasonable

1

Continued

CASE—*Continued*

risk because of the expectable action of another.

5. Intoxicating Liquors ⬅286

Where a tavern keeper sells alcoholic beverages to a person who is visibly intoxicated or to a person he knows or should know to be a minor, he ought to recognize and foresee the unreasonable risk of harm to others through action of the intoxicated person or the minor.

6. Intoxicating Liquors ⬅159(1), 161

Regulation of the Division of Alcoholic Beverage Control that no licensee shall permit any minor to be served or consume alcoholic beverages and prohibiting service to or consumption by any person "actually or apparently intoxicated" was not intended to benefit minors and intoxicated persons alone but was intended for the protection of members of the general public as well. R.S. 33:1–77, N.J.S.A.

7. Intoxicating Liquors ⬅286

If the patron of a tavern keeper is a minor or is intoxicated when served the keeper's sale to him is unlawful and if the circumstances are such that the keeper knows or should know that the patron is a minor or is intoxicated his service to the minor may constitute common-law negligence.

8. Intoxicating Liquors ⬅293

While plaintiff injured by negligence of intoxicated minor to whom defendants sold intoxicating liquors may introduce evidence that defendants knew or should have known that the minor was a minor, intoxicated when served, and could avail herself of the violations of the Alcoholic Beverage Control Law and regulations as evidence of the defendant's negligence, each defendant could assert that it did not know or have reason to believe that its patron was a minor or intoxicated when served and that it acted as a reasonably prudent person would have acted at the time and under the circumstances. R.S. 33:1–77, N.J.S.A.

9. Negligence ⬅10, 56(1.9), 62(1)

A tort-feasor is generally held answerable for the injuries resulting in the ordinary course of events from his negligence, and it is generally sufficient if his negligent conduct was a substantial factor in bringing about the injuries, and the fact that there were also intervening causes which were foreseeable or were normal incidents of the risk created would not relieve the tort-feasor of liability.

10. Negligence ⬅136(25)

Ordinarily questions of proximate and intervening cause are left to the jury for its factual determination.

11. Intoxicating Liquors ⬅316

If defendant tavern keepers unlawfully and negligently sold alcoholic beverages to minor causing his intoxication which in turn caused or contributed to his negligent operation of motor vehicle at time of fatal accident, a jury could find that the plaintiff's injuries resulted in the ordinary course of events from the defendants' negligence and that such negligence was the substantial factor in bringing them about, and that the minor's negligent operation of the motor vehicle after leaving the defendants' taverns was a normal incident of the risk they created or an event which they could reasonably have foreseen and hence the question of proximate causal relation between the defendants' unlawful negligent conduct and the plaintiff's injuries would be a question for the jury.

12. Negligence ⬅1, 56(1.14)

Policy considerations and the balancing of conflicting interests are vital factors in the molding and application of common-law principles of negligence and proximate causation.

13. Intoxicating Liquors ⬅159(1), 161

Liquor licensees who operate their businesses by way of privilege rather than as of right are under strict obligation not to serve minors and intoxicated persons.

CASE—*Continued*

RAPPAPORT v. NICHOLS   N. J.   **3**

Cite as 156 A.2d 1

Seymour B. Jacobs, Newark, for plaintiff-appellant (Fred Freeman, Newark, attorney).

Sheldon Schachter, Newark, for defendants-respondents (Joseph A. D'Alessio, Newark, attorney for defendants-respondents Nathan Sweet and Solomon Lustig, t/a Nate's Tavern; Leon Sachs, Newark, attorney for defendant-respondent Hub Bar, Inc.; Morris Barr, Newark, attorney for defendant-respondent Murphy's Tavern, Inc.).

The opinion of the Court was delivered by

JACOBS, J.

The plaintiff-appellant appealed to the Appellate Division from a judgment entered in the Law Division in favor of the defendants-respondents. We certified the matter on our own motion.

The plaintiff's complaint alleges that during the night of November 14 or the early morning of November 15, 1957 Robert Nichols, who was then about 18 years of age, was "wrongfully and negligently sold and served alcoholic beverages" at the tavern premises of the defendants Hub Bar, Inc., 146 Mulberry Street, Newark, Murphy's Tavern, Inc., 135 Mulberry Street, Newark, Nathan Sweet and Solomon Lustig, trading as Nate's Tavern, 116 Mulberry Street, Newark and El Morocco Cocktail Bar, Inc., 1011 Broad Street, Newark; that the alcoholic beverages were sold and served under circumstances which constituted "notice or knowledge" by the tavern operators that Nichols was a minor who could not lawfully be served by them; that during his visits to Murphy's Tavern and the El Morocco Cocktail Bar, Nichols was accompanied by the defendant Leonard Britton, an adult, who paid for the alcoholic beverages under circumstances which constituted notice or knowledge that Nichols should not be served because of "his age and apparent condition"; that by reason of the "negligence and wrongful

conduct" of the defendants, Nichols was rendered "under the influence of alcoholic beverages and unfit and incompetent to safely and reasonably operate" the motor vehicle entrusted to him by his mother, the defendant Mary Nichols; that he nevertheless drove it along the public highway at Washington and Academy Streets in Newark in a careless manner, resulting in a collision with a car operated by Arthur Rappaport and owned by the plaintiff; that Arthur Rappaport died as the result of injuries received in the collision and the plaintiff was appointed as general administratrix and administratrix *ad prosequendum* and seeks damages as the representative of his estate and in her individual capacity as owner of the car. Upon the basis of the limited record before us we may, for present purposes, infer that Nichols had just attained his eighteenth birthday, that he was served with intoxicating beverages at each of the four named taverns, that he left the last of the taverns at about 2 a. m., that he was intoxicated and negligently drove the motor vehicle and collided with the plaintiff's car between 2:15 and 2:20 a. m., and that his negligent operation of the motor vehicle was the result of his intoxication.

[1] The tavern operators moved for summary judgment on the ground that the complaint "fails to state a cause of action and that as a matter of law" they are entitled to judgment. On March 20, 1959 the Law Division judge granted the motion in a letter opinion which stated that "while in some other jurisdictions outside New Jersey one may be held responsible for the actions of another to whom he has served intoxicating liquors, such is not the present law in New Jersey and to apply the doctrine of foreseeability to the facts in the case would stretch the intent of the doctrine too far". On April 20, 1959 a formal order for summary judgment was entered; it contained a provision staying proceedings against the remaining defendants until the plaintiff's rights are finally determined on appeal as against the tavern

Continued

CASE—*Continued*

keepers. Cf. R.R. 4:55–2. Notice of appeal was filed by the plaintiff and her supporting brief as well as the brief in opposition by the tavern keepers addresses itself entirely to the issue of whether the plaintiff's complaint against the tavern keepers sets forth a common law cause of action grounded on negligence. We shall do the same, bearing in mind that in dealing with the legal sufficiency of the complaint the plaintiff is entitled to a liberal interpretation of its contents and to the benefits of all of its allegations and the most favorable inferences which may be reasonably drawn from them. See Puccio v. Cuthbertson, 21 N.J.Super. 544, 548, 91 A.2d 424 (App.Div.1952); Mianulli v. Gunagan, 32 N.J.Super. 212, 215, 108 A.2d 200, (App.Div.1954); Di Cristofaro v. Laurel Grove Memorial Park, 43 N.J. Super. 244, 248, 128 A.2d 281 (App.Div. 1957). At oral argument, counsel for the plaintiff indicated that the complaint was intended to charge not only that the tavern keepers unlawfully and negligently sold and served alcoholic beverages to Nichols under circumstances which constituted notice or knowledge that he was a minor but also that the sale and service by one or more of the tavern keepers was at a time when Nichols' intoxicated condition was apparent. Despite its vague phraseology we shall assume that the complaint embodies such charge; in any event an amendment to that end would readily be allowed. See Schierstead v. City of Brigantine, 29 N.J. 220, 234, 148 A.2d 591 (1959).

Judges elsewhere have dealt with the issue of whether tavern keepers who unlawfully sell alcoholic beverages to persons who are already intoxicated or to minors who become intoxicated may properly be subjected to common law claims grounded on negligence where the intoxicated persons leave the taverns, carelessly drive their cars and injure others. Most of them, while acknowledging the justness of the common law principles which generally result in the imposition of liability for negligent conduct which causes injury to others, have rejected such claims. See Fleckner v. Dionne, 94 Cal.App.2d 246, 210 P.2d 530 (Dist.Ct.App.1949); State for Use of Joyce v. Hatfield, 197 Md. 249, 78 A.2d 754 (Ct.App.1951); Cowman v. Hansen, 92 N.W.2d 682 (Iowa Sup.Ct.1958); 30 Am.Jur. Intoxicating Liquors § 520 (1958); Annotation 130 A.L.R. 352 (1941); cf. Cole v. Rush, 45 Cal.2d 345, 289 P.2d 450, 54 A.L.R.2d 1137 (Sup.Ct.1955). In the Fleckner case a divided court sustained the dismissal of a count in the complaint which charged that the defendant tavern keeper had unlawfully and negligently sold liquor to a minor while he was actually intoxicated and that the plaintiffs were injured when the minor left the tavern, negligently drove his car while intoxicated and collided with the plaintiffs' car causing their injuries. The majority took the position that the sale of the liquor was not the "proximate cause" of the plaintiffs' injuries and cited earlier cases which sought to separate and insulate the selling of the liquor from its consumption, suggesting that the latter and not the former was the proximate cause. In his dissenting opinion, Justice Dooling indicated that he was not at all impressed by this highly legalistic type of reasoning; he considered that the plaintiffs' claim came well within fundamental common law negligence principles which are recognized in his state as well as elsewhere throughout the country; and he placed analogical reliance on the many decisions which impose common law liability on car owners who negligently loan their cars to intoxicated persons who then negligently injure innocent third parties. See Deck v. Sherlock, 162 Neb. 86, 75 N.W.2d 99 (Sup.Ct.1956); Mitchell v. Churches, 119 Wash. 547, 206 P. 6, 36 A.L.R. 1132 (Sup.Ct.1922).

In State for Use of Joyce v. Hatfield, supra, the court sustained a dismissal of a common law claim against the defendant tavern keeper on the ground that, as a matter of law, the sale to the intoxicated minor could not be considered the proximate cause of the later collision; the court

CASE—*Continued*

RAPPAPORT v. NICHOLS   N. J.   5
Cite as 156 A.2d 1

stressed the fact that while many other states had done so, Maryland had never adopted a so-called Civil Damage Law or Dram Shop Act imposing strict liability upon tavern keepers for injuries resulting from sales of alcoholic beverages. See Appleman, "Civil Liability under Illinois Dramshop Act," 34 Ill.L.Rev. 30 (1939); Note, "Liability under the New York Dram Shop Act," 8 Syracuse L.Rev. 252 (1957). In Cowman v. Hansen, supra, the Iowa Supreme Court rejected the plaintiff's common law claim on the ground that the sale of the alcoholic beverage was "too remote" to be considered the proximate cause of the injury; in the course of its opinion it discussed Pratt v. Daly, 55 Ariz. 535, 104 P.2d 147, 130 A.L.R. 341 (Sup.Ct.1940) where the court, citing many supporting cases involving habit forming drugs, held that a wife could properly assert a common law negligence claim against a tavern keeper for the loss resulting to her from the tavern keeper's continued service of alcoholic beverages to her husband, an habitual drunkard. See Moberg v. Scott, 38 S.D. 422, 161 N.W. 998, L.R.A.1917D, 732 (Sup. Ct.1917); cf. Nally v. Blandford, 291 S.W. 2d 832 (Ky.Ct.App.1956); Riden v. Gremm, 97 Tenn. 220, 36 S.W. 1097, 35 L.R.A. 587 (Sup.Ct.1896); Dunlap v. Wagner, 85 Ind. 529, 44 Am.Rep. 42 (Sup.Ct. 1882); Skinner v. Hughes, 13 Mo. 440 (Sup.Ct.1850). The Iowa court sought to distinguish Pratt v. Daly, on the rather unconvincing ground that while "it may be foreseen" or it may be "a natural result" of furnishing an alcoholic beverage to an intoxicated person "that he himself will get hurt" it is "not at all clear that he will naturally assault someone, drive a car and injure or kill another, or do some other tortious act". [92 N.W.2d 686.]

The reasoning in cases such as Cowman v. Hansen, supra, has in effect been rejected in decisions under Civil Damage Laws which have sustained findings that the ensuing collisions were the proximate consequences of the liquor sales. In Manning v. Yokas, 389 Pa. 136, 132 A.2d 198, 199,

(Sup.Ct.1957) the plaintiffs were injured when their car was struck by a car driven by Kordowski who was intoxicated. Kordowski was a minor and had been served alcoholic beverages at the defendant's premises. The plaintiffs claimed damages from the defendant under the Pennsylvania statute of 1854, Act May 8, 1854, P.L. 663, which provided, in part, that any person who wrongfully furnishes alcoholic beverages "to a minor" shall be held civilly responsible for any injuries "in consequence of such furnishing". The trial court, in setting aside a verdict by the jury for the plaintiffs, found that while the defendant's conduct was negligent, the later injury was not remediable under the statute; this finding was reversed by the Pennsylvania Supreme Court which had this to say:

"If a drunken minor staggered from a saloon and fell over a child, it could not be argued that his fall was not the consequence of the furnishing of the liquor. So far as liability is concerned, there can be no difference between an injury caused through one's falling body and an injury inflicted by one's automobile under his management and control. If an innkeeper plied a minor with whiskey to a degree that the minor became offensively aggressive and, while under the influence of the liquor, injured another with a knife, it could not be doubted that the innkeeper, under the Act of 1854, would be liable for those injuries. An automobile when handled recklessly by its driver can be a weapon no less damaging and no less fatal than a knife. That the negligent operation of the automobile by Kordowski caused the accident is unquestioned in this appeal. But Kordowski's negligence was the result of his imbibing intoxicating liquor supplied by Yokas. Yokas thus, under the Act, became as much responsible for the accident as if he had stripped the gears of the car or had damaged the steering wheel, which defects in the operation of the

Continued

CASE—*Continued*

car were directly responsible for the uncontrollability which caused the collision." (132 A.2d at pages 199–200)

In McKinney v. Foster, 391 Pa. 221, 137 A.2d 502 (Sup.Ct.1958), the defendant wrongfully served beer to a minor who left the defendant's premises, drove his car while under the influence of intoxicants and ran into the decedent who was walking along the edge of the public highway. In an action brought by the decedent's administrator under the 1854 statute the jury found for the plaintiff but the trial court set aside its verdict and granted judgment for the defendant on the ground the defendant could not have foreseen that the minor would become intoxicated, drive an automobile and become involved in a fatal accident. In reversing the trial court's action, the Pennsylvania Supreme Court pointed out that implicit in its earlier holding in Manning v. Yokas, supra, was the common knowledge that great numbers of minors as well as adults drive automobiles "and that it was well within the realm of foreseeability that one illegally served with intoxicants might negligently drive an automobile and cause injury to persons or property".

Although the actions in Manning v. Yokas, supra and McKinney v. Foster, supra, were grounded on the Pennsylvania statute of 1854, a later Pennsylvania case rests entirely on common law principles. See Schelin v. Goldberg, 188 Pa.Super. 341, 146 A.2d 648 (Super.Ct.1958), leave to appeal denied by the Pennsylvania Supreme Court on February 27, 1959. There the plaintiff visited a series of taverns, the last of which was operated by the defendant. Although visibly intoxicated he was served alcoholic beverages in the defendant's taproom. While leaving the taproom the plaintiff was assaulted by another patron whom he had apparently offended; he sued the defendant and received a favorable verdict from the jury. The 1854 statute had been repealed before the assault but the court nevertheless held that the plaintiff could maintain his action on principles of negli-

gence. In directing the entry of judgment for the plaintiff on the jury's verdict, the Pennsylvania Superior Court, in an opinion by Judge Woodside, expressed the view that the defendant's unlawful sale of alcoholic beverages to the plaintiff while he was intoxicated constituted common law negligence and that the defendant could be held liable for the proximate consequences of his negligence including the assault on the plaintiff by the other patron. Cf. Reilly v. 180 Club, Inc., 14 N.J.Super. 420, 82 A.2d 210, (App.Div.1951).

In Waynick v. Chicago's Last Department Store, 269 F.2d 322 (7 Cir. 1959), the complaint charged that the defendants had unlawfully sold alcoholic beverages in Illinois to Sims and Owens while they were intoxicated and that Sims, the owner, and Owens, the driver, then took their car to Michigan where they were in a collision which caused the death and injuries described in the plaintiffs' complaint. The court assumed that the Dram Shop Acts of Illinois and Michigan were inapplicable but sustained the complaint as properly setting forth a common law action grounded on negligence. In the course of his opinion, Circuit Judge Schnackenberg first referred to the fundamental common law principles which generally result in the imposition of liability on those whose negligent acts cause injury to others and to the broad public purposes of the statutory prohibition against the sale of alcoholic beverages to intoxicated persons; he then said:

"In applying the common law to the situation presented in this case, we must consider the law of tort liability, even though the chain of events, which started when the defendant tavern keepers unlawfully sold intoxicating liquor to two drunken men, crossed state boundary lines and culminated in the tragic collision in Michigan. We hold that, under the facts appearing in the complaint, the tavern keepers are liable in tort for the damages and injuries sustained by plaintiffs, as a

CASE—*Continued*

RAPPAPORT v. NICHOLS   N. J.   **7**
Cite as 156 A.2d 1

proximate result of the unlawful acts of the former." (269 F.2d at page 326)

The result in Waynick finds support in many comparable situations where the courts have imposed liability on persons whose unlawful and negligent conduct contributed with the negligent conduct of other tortfeasors in injuring innocent third parties. In Anderson v. Settergren, 100 Minn. 294, 111 N.W. 279 (Sup.Ct.1907), the defendant unlawfully sold cartridges and loaned a .22 caliber rifle to a minor who negligently fired the rifle and injured the plaintiff; in sustaining a common law complaint by the plaintiff grounded on negligence, the Minnesota Supreme Court pointed out that the statute which prohibited the possession of firearms by minors was for the benefit of members of the public generally as well as the minors themselves and that the firing of the gun by the minor did not constitute an efficient intervening cause which broke the legal chain of causation. Similarly in Semeniuk v. Chentis, 1 Ill.App.2d 508, 117 N.E.2d 883 (App.Ct. 1954), the defendant sold an air rifle for use by a child who negligently fired it, injuring the plaintiff. The plaintiff filed a complaint sounding in negligence and charging that the sale was in violation of a local ordinance and that the defendant knew that the child was inexperienced and lacking in judgment and discretion and would probably injure some member of the public; in sustaining the complaint, the court rejected the defendant's contentions that the sale of the rifle was not the proximate cause of the injury and that the child's intervening act in firing the rifle was a superseding cause. See Mazzilli v. Selger, 13 N.J. 296, 99 A.2d 417 (1953), c.c. Mazzilli v. Accident & Casualty Ins. Co., etc., 26 N.J. 307, 139 A.2d 741 (1958); Driesse v. Verblaauw, 9 N.J.Misc. 173, 153 A. 388 (Sup.Ct.1931); cf. Dixon v. Bell, 5 M & S 198, 105 Eng.Rep. 1023 (K.B.1816); Yachuk v. Oliver Blais Co. [1949] A.C. 386, 2 All Eng.Rep. 150, 20 A.L.R.2d 111 (H.L.1949); Zamora v. J. Korber & Co., 59 N.M. 33, 278 P.2d 569 (Sup.Ct.1955).

In Ney v. Yellow Cab Company, 2 Ill.2d 74, 117 N.E.2d 74, 76, 51 A.L.R.2d 624 (Sup.Ct.1954), the defendant left his taxicab unattended with the key in the ignition lock in violation of a statute. It was stolen and while being operated by the thief it struck the plaintiff's car. The plaintiff filed a complaint grounded on negligence and the defendant contended that his conduct was neither negligent nor the proximate cause of the injury. In sustaining the complaint the court took the position that the statute was "a public safety measure", that its violation was *"prima facie* evidence of negligence"*, that if the intervention of the theft might reasonably have been foreseen it would not break the chain of causation (see Brower v. New York Cent. & H. R. R. Co., 91 N.J.L. 190, 193, 103 A. 166, 1 A.L.R. 734 (E. & A. 1918)) and that it could not be said, as a matter of law, that the negligent act was not the proximate cause of the injury suffered by the plaintiff. Similarly in Ross v. Hartman, 78 U.S.App.D.C. 217, 139 F.2d 14, 158 A.L.R. 1370 (C.A.D.C. 1943), certiorari denied 321 U.S. 790, 64 S.Ct. 790, 88 L.Ed. 1080 (1944), the court reversed a lower court finding that a plaintiff could not maintain a common law negligence action against a defendant whose truck had been stolen and had injured the plaintiff while it was being driven by the thief. The truck had been left unlocked and unattended with the key in the ignition in violation of an ordinance of the District of Columbia. See Kinsley v. Von Atzingen, 20 N.J.Super. 378, 381, 90 A.2d 37 (App.Div.1952). The court expressed the view that the ordinance was a safety measure and that its violation constituted negligence which proximately resulted in the harm to the plaintiff; in practical support of its determination it pointed out that the defendant had created the risk and that it was "fairer to hold him responsible for the harm than to deny a remedy to the innocent victim".

Continued

CASE—*Continued*

[2, 3] During prohibition days, New Jersey had a Civil Damage Law which imposed strict liability for compensatory and punitive damages upon unlawful sellers of alcoholic beverages. See L.1921, c. 103, p. 184; L.1922, c. 257, p. 628. The law was repealed in 1934 (L.1934, c. 32, p. 104) along with other miscellaneous liquor enactments in the light of the abandonment of prohibition and its replacement by the Alcoholic Beverage Control Act. L.1933, c. 436, p. 1180; R.S. 33:1–1 et seq., N.J.S.A. The repealer left unimpaired the fundamental negligence principles which admittedly prevail in New Jersey and upon which the plaintiff grounds his common law claim. See Schelin v. Goldberg, supra; cf. Evers v. Davis, 86 N.J.L. 196, 90 A. 677 (E. & A. 1914); 1 Sutherland, Statutory Construction § 2043 (3d ed. 1943). Negligence is tested by whether the reasonably prudent person at the time and place should recognize and foresee an unreasonable risk or likelihood of harm or danger to others. See Gaulkin, J. in Schaublin v. Leber, 50 N.J.Super. 506, 510, 142 A.2d 910 (App. Div.1958); cf. Martin v. Bengue, Inc., 25 N.J. 359, 371, 136 A.2d 626 (1957); Harpell v. Public Service Coordinated Transport, 20 N.J. 309, 316, 120 A.2d 43 (1956); Bohn v. Hudson & Manhattan R. Co., 16 N.J. 180, 186, 108 A.2d 5 (1954). And, correspondingly, the standard of care is the conduct of the reasonable person of ordinary prudence under the circumstances. See Ambrose v. Cyphers, 29 N.J. 138, 144, 148 A.2d 465 (1959).

[4–6] The negligence may consist in the creation of a situation which involves unreasonable risk because of the expectable action of another. See Brody v. Albert Lifson & Sons, 17 N.J. 383, 389, 111 A.2d 504 (1955). Where a tavern keeper sells alcoholic beverages to a person who is visibly intoxicated or to a person he knows or should know from the circumstances to be a minor, he ought to recognize and foresee the unreasonable risk of harm to others through action of the intoxicated person or the minor. The Legislature has in explicit terms prohibited sales to minors as a class because it recognizes their very special susceptibilities and the intensification of the otherwise inherent dangers when persons lacking in maturity and responsibility partake of alcoholic beverages; insofar as minors are concerned the sale of the first drink which does "its share of the work" (Taylor v. Wright, 126 Pa. 617, 621, 17 A. 677, 678 (1889)) and which generally leads to the others is unequivocally forbidden. See R.S. 33:1–77, N.J.S.A. In furtherance of the legislative policy, the Division of Alcoholic Beverage Control has by its Regulation No. 20, Rule 1, provided that no licensee shall permit any minor to be served or consume any alcoholic beverages; and the same regulation contains a provision against service to or consumption by any person "actually or apparently intoxicated". It seems clear to us that these broadly expressed restrictions were not narrowly intended to benefit the minors and intoxicated persons alone but were wisely intended for the protection of members of the general public as well. See State v. Dahnke, 244 Iowa 599, 603, 57 N.W.2d 553, 556 (Sup.Ct.1953); Waynick v. Chicago's Last Department Store, supra, 269 F.2d at page 325; cf. Essex Holding Corp. v. Hock, 136 N.J.L. 28, 54 A.2d 209 (Sup.Ct.1947); Sportsman 300 v. Board of Com'rs of Town of Nutley, 42 N.J.Super. 488, 127 A.2d 208 (App.Div. 1956).

[7, 8] When alcoholic beverages are sold by a tavern keeper to a minor or to an intoxicated person, the unreasonable risk of harm not only to the minor or the intoxicated person but also to members of the traveling public may readily be recognized and foreseen; this is particularly evident in current times when traveling by car to and from the tavern is so commonplace and accidents resulting from drinking are so frequent. See National Safety Council, Accident Facts, p. 49 (1959 ed.); cf. Resume of Annual Reports of the Chief Medical Examiner of the County of Middlesex, State of New Jersey (1933–1958),

CASE—*Continued*

RAPPAPORT v. NICHOLS   N. J.   **9**
Cite as 156 A.2d 1

p. 9 (1959); Study No. 885.A13 Minnesota Department of Highways, The Relationship of Drinking & Speeding to Accident Severity, p. 5 (1959). If the patron is a minor or is intoxicated when served, the tavern keeper's sale to him is unlawful; and if the circumstances are such that the tavern keeper knows or should know that the patron is a minor or is intoxicated, his service to him may also constitute common law negligence. In view of the standard of conduct prescribed by the statute and the regulations, a tavern keeper's sale of alcoholic beverages when he knows or should know that the patron is a minor or intoxicated may readily be found by the jury to be imprudent conduct. While the plaintiff here may introduce evidence that the defendants knew or should have known that Nichols was a minor, or intoxicated when served, and may avail herself of the violations of the statute and the regulations as evidence of the defendants' negligence, each of the defendants is at liberty to assert that it did not know or have reason to believe that its patron was a minor, or intoxicated when served, and that it acted as a reasonably prudent person would have acted at the time and under the circumstances. See Evers v. Davis, supra; cf. Carlo v. Okonite-Callender Cable Co., 3 N.J. 253, 264, 69 A.2d 734 (1949); Moore's Trucking Co. v. Gulf Tire & Supply Co., 18 N.J.Super. 467, 472, 87 A.2d 441 (App. Div.1952), certification denied 10 N.J. 22, 89 A.2d 306 (1952).

[9–11] The defendants contend that, assuming their conduct was unlawful and negligent as charged in the complaint, it was nevertheless not the proximate cause of the injuries suffered. But a tortfeasor is generally held answerable for the injuries which result in the ordinary course of events from his negligence and it is generally sufficient if his negligent conduct was a substantial factor in bringing about the injuries. See Francis, J., in Lutz v. Westwood Transportation Co., 31 N.J.Super. 285, 289, 106 A.2d 329 (App.Div.1954), certification denied 16 N.J. 205, 108 A.2d

156 A.2d—1½

120 (1954); cf. Hartman v. City of Brigantine, 42 N.J.Super. 247, 261, 126 A.2d 224 (App.Div.1956), affirmed 23 N.J. 530, 129 A.2d 876 (1957); Melone v. Jersey Central Power & Light Co., 30 N.J.Super. 95, 105, 103 A.2d 615 (App.Div.1954), affirmed 18 N.J. 163, 113 A.2d 13 (1955). The fact that there were also intervening causes which were foreseeable or were normal incidents of the risk created would not relieve the tortfeasor of liability. See Prosser, Torts § 49 (2d ed. 1955); cf. Menth v. Breeze Corporation, Inc., 4 N.J. 428, 442, 73 A.2d 183, 18 A.L.R.2d 1071 (1950); Andreoli v. Natural Gas Company, 57 N.J. Super. 356, 366, 154 A.2d 726 (App.Div. 1959). Ordinarily these questions of proximate and intervening cause are left to the jury for its factual determination. See Martin v. Bengue, Inc., supra, 25 N.J. at page 374, 136 A.2d at page 634; Brower v. New York Cent. & H. R. R. Co., supra, 91 N.J.L. at page 191, 103 A. at page 166. If, as we must assume at this stage of the proceeding, the defendant tavern keepers unlawfully and negligently sold alcoholic beverages to Nichols causing his intoxication, which in turn caused or contributed to his negligent operation of the motor vehicle at the time of the fatal accident, then a jury could reasonably find that the plaintiff's injuries resulted in the ordinary course of events from the defendants' negligence and that such negligence was, in fact, a substantial factor in bringing them about. And a jury could also reasonably find that Nichols' negligent operation of his motor vehicle after leaving the defendants' taverns was a normal incident of the risk they created, or an event which they could reasonably have foreseen, and that consequently there was no effective breach in the chain of causation. In the light of the foregoing, we are in no position to hold that as a matter of law there could have been no proximate causal relation between the defendants' unlawful and negligent conduct and the plaintiff's injuries. See Menth v. Breeze Corporation, Inc., supra; Martin v. Bengue, Inc., supra; Andreoli v. Natural Gas Company, supra.

Continued

CASE—*Continued*

In the Menth case, supra, the plaintiffs alleged that the defendant had negligently stored combustible materials in a shed and that the materials had become ignited and had burned the plaintiffs' household furnishings in a nearby apartment house; this court held that the questions of negligence and proximate cause were for the jury and in answer to the contention that there may have been an intervening cause which had ignited the materials, it had this to say:

"There may be any number of causes and effects intervening between the first wrongful act and the final injurious occurrence and if they are such as might, with reasonable diligence, have been foreseen, the last result as well as the first, and every intermediate result, is to be considered in law as the proximate result of the first wrongful cause. A tort-feasor is not relieved from liability for his negligence by the intervention of the acts of third persons, including the act of a child, if those acts were reasonably foreseeable. The theory being that the original negligence continues and operates contemporaneously with an intervening act which might reasonably have been anticipated so that the negligence can be regarded as a concurrent cause of the injury inflicted. One who negligently creates a dangerous condition cannot escape liability for the natural and probable consequences thereof although the act of a third person may have contributed to the final result. The law of negligence recognizes that there may be two or more concurrent and directly cooperative and efficient proximate causes of an injury. Davenport v. McClellan, 88 N.J.L. 653, 96 A. 921; (E. & A. 1915); Daniel v. Gielty Trucking Co., 116 N.J.L. 172, 182 A. 638 (E. & A. 1935); 38 Am.Jur. (Negligence), § 63, p. 715; Ibid., § 70, pp. 726–727." (4 N.J. at pages 441–442, 73 A.2d at page 189.)

[12, 13] Although it is evident that the strict civil liability prevailing by statute in many of the states is a much heavier responsibility, the defendants urge that the sustaining of the plaintiff's complaint will place an "inconceivable" burden on them. We are fully mindful that policy considerations and the balancing of the conflicting interests are the truly vital factors in the molding and application of the common law principles of negligence and proximate causation. But we are convinced that recognition of the plaintiff's claim will afford a fairer measure of justice to innocent third parties whose injuries are brought about by the unlawful and negligent sale of alcoholic beverages to minors and intoxicated persons, will strengthen and give greater force to the enlightened statutory and regulatory precautions against such sales and their frightening consequences, and will not place any unjustifiable burdens upon defendants who can always discharge their civil responsibilities by the exercise of due care. It must be borne in mind that the plaintiff's complaint has no relation to service by persons not engaged in the liquor business or to lawful sales and service by liquor licensees, or to sales by reasonably prudent licensees who do not know or have reason to believe that the patron is a minor or is intoxicated when served; the allegations of the complaint are expressly confined to tavern keepers' sales and service which are unlawful and negligent. Liquor licensees, who operate their businesses by way of privilege rather than as of right, have long been under strict obligation not to serve minors and intoxicated persons and if, as is likely, the result we have reached in the conscientious exercise of our traditional judicial function substantially increases their diligence in honoring that obligation then the public interest will indeed be very well served.

The judgment entered in the Law Division is reversed and the cause is remanded for trial.

CASE—*Continued*

HAYES v. AMBASSADOR COURT, INC. N. J. 11
Cite as 156 A.2d 11

For reversal: Chief Justice WEIN-TRAUB and Justices BURLING, JACOBS, FRANCIS, PROCTOR, HALL and SCHETTINO—7.

For affirmance: None.

58 N.J.Super. 215

Hubert HAYES, Petitioner-Respondent,

v.

AMBASSADOR COURT, INC., Respondent-Appellant.

No. A–707.

Superior Court of New Jersey

Appellate Division.

Argued Oct. 27, 1959.

Decided Nov. 24, 1959.

Proceeding wherein apartment building superintendent sought to recover workmen's compensation from employer-landlord for injuries which he sustained when he fell while attempting to free paint-locked window in a tenant's apartment when superintendent was engaged in washing windows at tenant's request. The Deputy Director dismissed petition for compensation, deciding that injury did not arise out of and in course of employment. The County Court reversed and awarded compensation. The employer appealed. The Superior Court, Appellate Division, Gaulkin, J. A. D., held that employer's evidence was insufficient to show that superintendent was forbidden to wash windows in the apartment or was told not to fix stuck windows and that even if superintendent was not in scope of his employment, for purposes of workmen's compensation, while he was washing windows in occupied apartment, he stepped back into scope of employ-

ment when he undertook to release a paint-locked window.

Judgment affirmed.

1. Workmen's Compensation ⊂787

Whether employee's activities were outside the scope and did not arise in the course of employment because employee was acting in violation of employer's rule depends on employee's understanding of the rule and not upon employer's understanding of it.

2. Workmen's Compensation ⊂1675

In proceeding by apartment building superintendent to recover compensation for injuries which he sustained when he fell while attempting to pry open paint-locked window in furnished apartment, when he was in course of washing windows at tenant's request, assertedly after he had been instructed by employer to wash windows in furnished apartments, though employer's president testified that superintendent was supposed to do nothing for tenants, evidence was insufficient to show that he was forbidden to wash windows in furnished apartments or to fix stuck windows.

3. Workmen's Compensation ⊂670

Even if apartment building superintendent was not in scope of his employment, for purposes of workmen's compensation, while he was washing windows in occupied apartment, he stepped back into scope of employment when he undertook to release a paint-locked window and was entitled to compensation for injuries sustained when he fell while attempting to release the window.

4. Workmen's Compensation ⊂661

Even if apartment building superintendent's act in freeing paint-locked window was part and parcel of operation of washing windows at tenant's request and even if superintendent was performing such services for tenant in order to receive a tip, as landlord benefited from superintendent's activities in freeing window, act was within

10

DRAFTING BRIEFS

In Chapter 8 we discussed "briefing cases," the process of extracting the meat from a judicial opinion and writing a concise and objective summary of its facts, holding, and rationale. That is one sort of "brief." In this chapter, we shall discuss a second kind.

BRIEFS

Briefs are formal, written, adversarial arguments. They are presented to the court to persuade the judge or judges to rule in a way favorable to the writer's client. Commonly, the opposing party then submits a brief in response, which attempts to defeat the other side's argument and persuade the court to rule for its client.

Briefs are an essential advocacy tool. Because a brief gives an attorney the chance to state the client's argument without objection by opposing counsel or questions from the bench, it must be well written and carefully researched. Everything in a brief has but two purposes: to educate and persuade the court.

> Lawyers make the mistake of assuming that the judge knows all the law which . . . is a violent assumption. It should be remembered that a judge sitting in a trial term must necessarily often decide questions of law on the spur of the moment and without the thoughtful and careful consideration which an appellate tribunal has an opportunity to give to its decisions.
>
> Moscowitz, *Glimpses of Federal Trials and Procedure,* 4 F.R.D. 216, 223 (1946).

Remember from Chapter 8 that case briefs are an *objective and unbiased* summary of a case. The briefs discussed in this chapter are *adversarial,* that is, argumentative in your client's favor. Every part of the brief is written to present your client's position in the most favorable light. As you will see, it is permissible to write the brief so that it emphasizes the facts favorable to your client and minimizes those that are not.

Sometimes briefs are supplemented by oral argument before the court; sometimes they are not. Especially in the appellate arena, the enormous press of business has forced the courts to restrict the time for oral argument or abolish it altogether.

PRACTICE TIP

The purposes of a brief are to educate and persuade the court.

brief
Formal written, adversarial arguments presented to the court to educate and persuade it to rule in favor of the writer's client.

PRACTICE TIP

It is never permissible to submit a brief with facts so slanted and biased that it distorts or misrepresents the case to the court. But you may argue whatever reasonable inferences you believe the facts support.

Hence, the importance of power and precision in writing briefs is greater than ever. Your brief may be the only chance you have of educating and persuading the court.

You must persuade in *one reading*, and your writing must be clear beyond question. It is not uncommon for many state trial court judges to have only one law clerk, or none at all, to help them wade through the mass of paper they must negotiate each day. Judges and their clerks simply do not have time to slog through a complex, murky brief to ferret out the point buried in a mass of meandering verbiage. The court wants to know what the problem is—the issue presented for decision—and the legal considerations and authority controlling that decision.

If you do not tell the court clearly and concisely what the issues, facts, and authorities are, the court will turn to the other side's brief for enlightenment. That, of course, is precisely what you do *not* want. You want the court to learn about the case from your persuasive argument and reasoning, not the opponent's.

Although in writing briefs, as in all things, you will follow the orders of your supervising attorney, the procedures of your office, and the court rules, we can offer one word of general advice. If you have the chance to submit a brief on some point, but are not required to, *do it*, even if your boss will argue the matter in person. The reasons for this are quite practical.

A great many legal questions are not decided on the spot. A judge often wishes to mull over a decision, and will "take the matter under advisement." That means he or she wants to think it over some more before deciding how to rule, in chambers (the judge's office) or at home. When the judge does that thinking-over, you want your written argument close at hand, so that the judge may consult it again before ruling.

Court Rules

court rules
Rules promulgated and adopted by courts that have the force of law and govern practice and procedure.

local court rules
Rules adopted by an individual court to supplement the Rules of Civil Procedure applicable to that court.

The **court rules** determine the format you will use to prepare your brief, e.g., cover sheets, table of contents, and table of authorities. Generally, the **local court rules** supply the most information about a court's requirements for briefs. Local rules tell you things such as which motions require supporting briefs, or whether the court has a limit on the number of pages. Follow the rules *exactly*. Do not put your attorney in the position of asking leave to file a brief that is on the wrong size paper, too long, or out of time. You handicap your attorney and your client by trying to file a brief that may be disregarded by the court because it fails to follow the court rules.

Each jurisdiction has its own set of local rules, and the requirements for briefs may change from one court to another. It is not unusual for a brief to be governed by two sets of rules (the court rules and local court rules) at the same time. Unless you are familiar with all the requirements for each brief, it is easy to overlook something.

To avoid that problem, we suggest that you create a "brief cheat sheet" for all of the court rules affecting briefs for each jurisdiction in which your supervising attorney practices. You will find an example of one for courts in central Oklahoma at Appendix F.

Notice that our sample brief cheat sheet not only tells you what rules control various aspects of the brief, but includes sample formats for two types of cover sheets, tables of contents, and tables of authorities. We have found that these sample forms are especially helpful for secretaries who are unfamiliar with court rules and preparing briefs.

The sample we have provided should not be followed unless you are preparing a brief to be filed in those jurisdictions. Use our sample brief cheat sheet at Appendix F as a model to create one that meets your own needs.

Brief Banks

It may be helpful in developing your expertise to study briefs that your attorney or others in the law firm have written. You may wish to create a **brief bank**, if your firm does not already have one, to use as a reference tool. A brief bank is like a form file in which briefs may be filed by types (i.e., a brief accompanying a motion for summary judgment), or filed by the area of law to which it applies. Use the brief bank as "forms" to help you with phrasing and repetitious language. A well-organized brief bank can also be an effective research tool. It is also a good idea to read the bar journals and add to your brief bank copies of cases that either clarify or redefine the areas of law in which you work.

brief bank
A Form file and research tool in which briefs are filed and categorized for easy retrieval.

■ TRIAL BRIEFS

As the name implies, a brief is generally filed in support of, or opposition to, some question that arises in connection with litigation, present or pending. In some jurisdictions, trial briefs are called memorandums of points and authorities, or simply memorandums of law. A **trial brief** may be filed before, during, or just after trial, and addresses one or several of a broad range of questions connected with the trial.

trial brief
A written statement and arguments prepared by counsel on the issues to be decided before, during, or after trial.

Distinguish trial briefs from briefs filed on appeal, after a case has been decided in the trial court. These are, logically, called appellate briefs, and are quite formal in tone. They tend to be longer and more complex than trial briefs, and even more closely controlled by court rules. We will discuss them later in this chapter.

Related to the trial brief, but not quite the same, are briefs filed in support of motions made at other stages of the litigation, such as a brief in support of a motion to compel the opponent to answer discovery. Briefs such as these, filed contemporaneously with a motion as "support" for that motion, are referred to simply as **supporting briefs**. We discuss these briefs in Chapter 12, together with the motions they support.

supporting briefs
Briefs filed contemporaneously with a motion that states the facts, arguments, and authorities which support that motion.

When the court allows, we strongly suggest submitting a trial brief to help you and your attorney prepare for trial, if for no other reason. The trial brief will help to formulate a clear concept of the facts and inform your attorney on anticipated points of law to be argued at trial, as shown by the example given below by a federal district court judge:

> A case comes to mind in which plaintiff's attorney argued a point of law without preparing himself on the subject-matter. I asked him if he had any authorities to sustain his contention, to which he replied, "Well, your honor, this is elementary." I stated, "It may be elementary, counselor, but not to me. I would appreciate it very much if you would go to the library to-night and check on this law which you regard as so elementary." The following morning he came into my chambers a little bit crestfallen with his adversary and admitted that the decisions revealed him in error. . . . [H]e was wiser for having had the experience of learning what the preparation of a trial brief would have accomplished.

> Moscowitz, *Glimpses of Federal Trials and Procedure*, 4 F.R.D. 216, 223 (1946).

Scheduling Conference and Order

In most instances, it is the court, rather than the attorneys, that decides whether a trial brief will be filed. The court has the discretion, pursuant to Rule 16 of the Federal Rules of Civil Procedure, to hold a **scheduling conference** with counsel for each of the parties. From that conference, a **scheduling order** is issued by the court. We have provided a sample scheduling order in Exhibit 10.1 (p. 230).

scheduling conference
A conference held by the judge and counsel for all parties in the lawsuit to determine the deadlines for the various stages of the litigation.

scheduling order
An order issued by the court that sets the deadlines for many stages of the litigation.

EXHIBIT 10.1   *Scheduling Order Form (Federal Court)*

IN THE UNITED STATES DISTRICT COURT FOR THE
WESTERN DISTRICT OF OKLAHOMA

_____ Plaintiff,	)))	
vs.	)))	Case No. _____
_____ Defendant.	)))	TRACK: _____

SCHEDULING ORDER

Date _____   Time _____   To _____

Judge _____   Clerk _____   Total _____

JURY TRIAL DEMANDED _____   **NONJURY TRIAL** _____   Trial Docket _____

Appearing for Plaintiff: _____

Appearing for Defendant: _____

THE FOLLOWING DEADLINES ARE SET BY THE COURT
(May not be extended except by Court order pursuant to Local Court Rule 14)

1. Motions to join additional parties to be filed by _____

2. Motions to amend pleadings to be filed by _____

3. (a) Plaintiff to submit to defendant list of **expert witness(es)** by _____

   (b) Plaintiff to submit to defendant **final** list of **witnesses** in chief, including expert witnesses, together with addresses and brief summary of expected testimony where witness has not already been deposed*_____

4. (a) Defendant to submit to plaintiff list of **expert witness(es)** by _____

   (b) Defendant to submit to plaintiff **final** list of **witnesses** in chief, including expert witnesses, together with addresses and brief summary of expected testimony where witness has not already been

   deposed*_____

5. Plaintiff to submit to defendant final **exhibit** list and any exhibits not previously submitted.* _____

6. Defendant to submit to plaintiff final **exhibit** list and any exhibits not previously submitted*_____

7. Discovery to be completed by _____

8. Plaintiff's final contentions to be submitted to defendant's counsel by _____

9. Defendant's final contentions to be submitted to plaintiff's counsel by _____

10. All dispositive motions to be filed by _____

11. All stipulations to be filed by _____

Continued

EXHIBIT 10.1 —*Continued*

12. Motions in limine to be filed by
_____

13. Requested jury instructions to be submitted on or before
_____

14. Joint Statement of case to be submitted on or before
_____

15. Requested voir dire to be submitted by: _____

16. Trial Briefs to be filed by
_____

17. NON JURY CASES ONLY: Proposed findings and conclusions of law to be submitted no later than
_____

18. Any objections to the above trial submissions to be filed 5 days thereafter.

19. Final pretrial order approved by all counsel to be submitted to the Court by _____

20. Plaintiff's counsel is directed to initiate settlement discussions with defendant
_____
and report status of such discussions to the Court no later than _____

21. Supplemental Status Conference to be set _____

22. Final Pretrial to be set
_____

23. This case is hereby assigned to the **Special Management Track.** ☐

A **Joint Specialized Case Management Plan** shall be filed by _____ and include the following topics:

> (1) Identification of lead and liaison counsel and the responsibilities of each; (2) suggestions for maintaining confidentiality; (3) a description of, and the sequence of, discovery to be had under relevant provisions of the Federal Rules of Civil Procedure; (4) in class action cases, a proposed timetable for class issue discovery, briefing, and hearing; (5) a timetable for the filing and service of dispositive motions under Fed.R.Civ.P. 12 and/or Fed.R.Civ.P. 56; (6) proposals relating to the addition of parties, bifurcation, and special needs concerning service of process; and (7) subjects bearing upon the administration of the case, including consideration of the appointment of a special master to administer discovery, resolving initial discovery disputes, identifying a custodian of exhibits, and serving notices and court orders to multiple parties when necessary.

24. This case is referred to Mandatory Arbitration under Local Rule 43 ☐.

This case is referred to Consensual Arbitration under Local Rule 43 ☐.

The proposed Arbitration Hearing date is _____.

The Court exempts the case from Arbitration ☐.

Continued

EXHIBIT 10.1 —*Continued*

25. This case is referred to Mediation under Local Rule 46 ☐.

A Mediation Session will be held between _____ and

_____ .

26. The parties consent to trial by a magistrate judge. ☐

27. IT IS ORDERED that all exhibits intended to be offered herein be
premarked at least _____ days before the commencement of the trial. The
Clerk will supply labels for this purpose.

28. Other: _____

_____

                                   BY ORDER OF THE COURT
                                   ROBERT D. DENNIS, CLERK

                                   By: _____
                                                      Deputy Clerk

NOTICE: READ CAREFULLY

* All provisions of Local Rule 17, as amended, all other applicable
local rules and the provisions of the Court's Civil Justice Expense and
Delay Reduction Plan apply. The parties are admonished to comply with
the requirements concerning the physical exchange of exhibits. The
exchange of witnesses required by numbers 3 and 4 above shall be by
letter with two copies of the letter of transmittal to be submitted to
the Clerk of this Court for filing. Except for good cause shown, no
witness shall be permitted to testify in chief for any party unless
such witness' name was listed in the letter of transmittal. The
exchange of exhibits required by numbers 5 and 6 above shall also be
accomplished by **ACTUAL PHYSICAL EXCHANGE, OR BY MAKING SUCH EXHIBITS
AVAILABLE FOR VIEWING AND EXAMINATION BEFORE THE SPECIFIED DATE.** If
upon completion of such exchange of exhibits a party does not make
written objection thereto within five (5) days, all objections to said
exhibit or exhibits are deemed waived. If written objection is so
filed, the basis of same shall be spelled out in detail by way of
brief. Further, in the event of objection both sides shall, in the
pretrial order, state the rule or rules upon which they rely.

The scheduling order sets the deadlines for many stages of the litigation, such as amending the pleadings, joining other parties, filing motions, completing discovery, and filing witness and exhibit lists. Among the numerous filing deadlines set by the scheduling order are dates for filing all of the pretrial documents, such as requested jury instructions, voir dire, motions in limine, and trial briefs. The scheduling order may also set dates for other events, such as a final pretrial conference or trial.

The deadlines set by the scheduling order, including any deadline for a trial brief, cannot be changed by the parties without **leave of court**, that is, without first getting the court's permission by filing a motion formally requesting the change. The court will not grant the motion unless the party requesting the change has a sufficient reason for the court to do so. Be warned that courts rarely, if ever, feel compelled to accommodate counsel for reasons such as the "press of business" or vacation trips.

leave of court
Permission from the court to take a particular action that is otherwise prohibited without the court's consent.

Pretrial Conference and Final Pretrial Order

If the scheduling order does not mention whether trial briefs will be allowed or required, the issue may be addressed by yet another document filed before trial, called the **pretrial order**.

At the **pretrial conference**, the court and counsel for the parties meet as close to the time of trial as reasonable to set the stage for trial. At least one of the attorneys who will conduct the trial for each of the parties must attend the conference. There, the court and the parties formulate a plan for trial and attempt to simplify the issues to be tried, obtain stipulations to facts or the authenticity of documents, and identify the witnesses and exhibits to be introduced by each party and objections to the same. After the pretrial conference, a pretrial order, such as the sample form at Exhibit 10.2 (p. 234), is entered reciting the action taken at the conference. The pretrial order controls the course of action taken by the parties from that point forward and at trial. In some courts, the pretrial order also states whether a trial brief will be required by the court and, if so, the deadline for filing it.

pretrial order
An order jointly prepared by counsel for all parties that controls the future course of action at trial.

pretrial conference
Meeting of counsel for all parties and the judge before the trial.

The trial brief's length depends on the complexity of the issues to be decided at trial and the number of pages allowed by the court rules. Some trial briefs are quite short, especially if they address a single issue.

Brevity is a special virtue in a trial brief, since you are writing for a busy judge who does not have time for long, complex submissions. Whatever its length, the trial brief *always* contains **citations of authority** and applications of that authority to the question or questions to be decided by the court at or before trial.

Often, in addition to the discussion of authority contained in the brief itself, wise legal professionals will, where the court permits, append photocopies of one or two decisive cases. If the judge wants to read the whole case in addition to your discussion of it, he or she will appreciate not having to look elsewhere to dig it out. Many judges would rather not break their concentration to go and to find a case, or have

citations of authority
Statutes, case law, regulations, or treatises cited in support of a legal argument.

PRACTICE TIP

If neither the scheduling order nor the pretrial order address whether a trial brief will be allowed, a party may request permission from the court to file a trial brief if it thinks one is necessary.

■ PRACTICE TIP

The *pretrial order* controls the future course of action at trial and lists, among other things, the allegations and defenses of the parties, the witnesses and exhibits each party plans to introduce at trial and the other side's objections to that evidence, the chances of settlement, the anticipated length of trial, and whether a trial brief is to be submitted.

| EXHIBIT 10.2 | *Final Pretrial Order Form* |

IN THE DISTRICT COURT, JUDICIAL DISTRICT.
_____ COUNTY, STATE OF

_____)
　　　　　　　　　　　　　　　　)
_____Plaintiff,)
　　　　　　　　　　　　　　　　)
v.　　　　　　　　　　　　　　　) No._____
　　　　　　　　　　　　　　　　)
_____)
　　　　　　　　　　　　　　　　)
_____Defendant.)

PRE-TRIAL CONFERENCE ORDER

1. *Appearances:*

_____ for the _____
_____
_____ for the _____
_____
_____ for the _____
_____
_____ for the _____
_____

2. *General Statement of Facts:*
   a. **What:**_____
   b. **Where:**_____
   c. **When:**_____
   d. **Who:**_____
   e. **Other:**_____

3. *Plaintiff's Contentions:*

Grounds for Recovery	Applicable Statute, Ordinance, Common Law Rule
a. _____	_____
b. _____	_____
c. _____	_____
d. _____	_____
e. _____	_____
f. _____	_____
g. _____	_____

Continued

EXHIBIT 10.2   —*Continued*

4. *Damages or Relief Sought*   **Amount**
   a. Personal injuries:
      (Permanent_____ Temporary_____)   _____
      Describe:_____
   b. Pain and suffering: (Past_____ Future_____)   _____
   c. Medical and hospital expense:
      (Past_____ Estimated Future_____)   _____
   d. Loss of earnings and impairment of earning
      capacity:
      (Period_____ Rate_____ Employer_____)   _____
   e. Property loss: (Repairable_____
      Not Repairable_____)   _____
   f. Other:_____   _____
                                          TOTAL   _____

5. *Defenses:*

   | | **Applicable Statute,** |
Grounds for Defense	**Ordinance, Common Law Rule**
a. _____	_____
b. _____	_____
c. _____	_____
d. _____	_____
e. _____	_____
f. _____	_____
g. _____	_____

6. *Cross Petition (or Counterclaim or Set-off):*

   | | **Applicable Statute,** |
Grounds for Recovery	**Ordinance, Common Law Rule**
a. _____	_____
b. _____	_____
c. _____	_____
d. _____	_____

Damages or Relief Sought	**Amount**
a. _____	_____
b. _____	_____
c. _____	_____
d. _____	_____
	TOTAL _____

7. *Reply:*
   Filed: Yes_____ No_____

Continued

EXHIBIT 10.2 —*Continued*

8. *Miscellaneous:*
   a. Jury waived: Yes_____ No_____
   b. Objection to jurisdiction of court: Yes_____ No_____
      Why:_____
   c. Are parties proper and correctly named or identified:
      Yes_____ No_____
      Objections:_____
   d. Need for guardian ad litem: Yes_____ No_____
   e. Are all city ordinances, relied on by all parties, plead in full:
      Yes_____ No_____ N/A_____
   f. Are allegations of agency denied under oath: Yes_____
      No_____ N/A_____
      Or admitted by _____
   g. Is discovery complete: Yes_____ No_____
      Comment:_____
      _____
   h. Any amendments to pleadings: Yes_____ No_____
      Order of Court:_____
      _____
   i. Trial brief required by Court: Yes_____ No_____ Due by_____
   j. What legal issues to be resolved:_____
      _____
      _____
      _____
   k. Any novel or unusual points of law involved:_____
      What are the points:_____
      _____
      _____
      _____
      When will they be presented:_____
      Are briefs desirable:_____
      Time:_____
   l. What fact issues remain to be resolved:_____
      _____
      _____
   m. Will a view of the scene be requested or advisable:
      Yes_____ No_____

9. *Plaintiff's Exhibits:*

Number	Title	Objection	Authority Relied Upon
_____	_____	_____	_____
_____	_____	_____	_____
_____	_____	_____	_____
_____	_____	_____	_____

Continued

EXHIBIT 10.2 —*Continued*

10. *Defendant's Exhibits:*

Number	Title	Objection	Authority Relied Upon
_____	_____	_____	_____
_____	_____	_____	_____
_____	_____	_____	_____
_____	_____	_____	_____
_____	_____	_____	_____

11. *Maps or diagrams:*
Plaintiff: _____ Defendant _____

12. *Requested Instructions: Numbers of   UJI-CIV:*
Subjects of Modified Requested Instructions:
(a) _____
(b) _____
(c) _____
(d) _____
Time: _____

13. *Plaintiff's Witnesses:*

Name	Address	Proposed Testimony
_____	_____	_____
_____	_____	_____
_____	_____	_____
_____	_____	_____
_____	_____	_____
_____	_____	_____
_____	_____	_____

14. *Defendant's Witnesses:*

Name	Address	Proposed Testimony
_____	_____	_____
_____	_____	_____
_____	_____	_____
_____	_____	_____
_____	_____	_____
_____	_____	_____

15. *Estimated Trial Time:* _____

Continued

EXHIBIT 10.2   —*Continued*

16. *Stipulations:*
    a. Ordinances pled are correctly set forth and were in force at time
       and place of incident involved: Yes_____ No_____ N/A_____
    b. Life Expectancy:_____
       Exhibits: (Failure to object to specific exhibits in this
                   Order will result in a waiver of such objection.)
    c. Identification waived of:
       Pltfs. Exhibits Numbered:_____
       Defts. Exhibits Numbered:_____
    d. Identification waived, medical bills:_____
    e. Identification waived, repair bills:_____
    f. Identification waived, photographs:_____
    g. Other:_____

17. *Settlement:* Anticipated_____ Possible_____ Not Possible_____

18. *Other Matters:*_____
    _____
    _____
    _____
    _____
    _____
    _____

19. *Trial Date Set:*_____ _____.M., _____, 19_____

20. Dated this _____ day of _____, 19_____.

                          _____
                          Trial Judge
                          Approved:

                          _____

                          _____
                                       Attorney for Plaintiff

                          _____

                          _____
                                       Attorney for Defendant

                          _____

                          Attorney for

                          _____

                          _____

                          Attorney for

their clerk (if any) do it. Hence, photocopy *anything* critical, especially if it is probably not in the judge's library yet, or at all. We think it is an especially good idea to attach copies of *any* case that may not be found in the judge's library, such as recent cases that have yet to appear in the bound reporter or advance sheets that are available only on WESTLAW or LEXIS.

In some courts, counsel may thoughtfully highlight or underline the decisive parts of the opinion. In other courts, this practice may be considered too informal. Be guided by local custom, your supervising attorney's preference, and court rules.

Components of the Trial Brief

The parts generally required in briefs are often specified in the court rules and local court rules, which differ from jurisdiction to jurisdiction. Before writing any brief, you should always check the applicable court rules. They may tell you the format for your brief, as well as other requirements, such as how long the brief may be and whether a cover page, table of contents, or table of authorities is required.

Suppose your attorney is representing a defendant in a criminal matter. Your client, Jones, has killed a man named Slivovitz in a barroom fight. Slivovitz was a big man, but unarmed. Your client, somewhat smaller, was being beaten when he grabbed a beer bottle and hit his antagonist over the head with it. Jones hit Slivovitz too hard, and has been charged with second-degree murder.

You have learned that Slivovitz was a real hoodlum whose hobby seems to have been beating people up whenever he got a few drinks inside him. He had quite a history of this behavior. If you can get this evidence before the jury, you have every chance of an acquittal.

Assume that the law in your jurisdiction permits such evidence on the issue of who was the aggressor (who began the fight). But the law requires that to get the evidence in, you must show a substantial pattern of violent behavior by Slivovitz, a pattern extending over time to a point reasonably close to the time of his death. The prosecution will object to the introduction of Slivovitz's violent history. Your task is to persuade the judge, through a motion in limine and supporting brief, that the evidence should come in. The court has called for briefs from both sides.

Cover Page. Your jurisdiction will have a format for papers filed in civil and criminal lawsuits. As we noted above, the format may be just a customary way of preparing briefs for the trial court, or it may be controlled in part or entirely by court rules.

In either case, depending on the court rules, your brief may have a **cover page**, which you will produce according to that format. The cover usually sets out the case number, the style of the case, the title of the brief, the name, address, and telephone number of the attorney filing the brief and which party that attorney represents, and the date the brief was filed. Appellate brief covers may also include the name of the trial judge and the jurisdiction from which the case came.

The cover is made from slightly heavier paper stock, a little like the cover of a softbound book. Often the court has requirements about the color of the cover stock. If there are no rules governing the color, we suggest that you use either off-white, tan, navy, light blue, or red. Avoid pastels or "neon" colors; they look unprofessional.

Even when a cover is not required, we think it a good idea; it adds formality to your brief. We have provided two samples in Appendix F. Another, taken from a criminal case in a state district court, is shown in Exhibit 10.3 (p. 240).

PRACTICE TIP

A trial brief *always* contains citations of authority and application of that authority to the question or questions to be decided by the court at or before trial.

cover page
A brief's first page that usually sets out the case number, the style of the case, the title of the brief, the name, address, and telephone number of the attorney filing the brief and which party that attorney represents, and the date the brief was filed. Appellate brief covers may also include the name of the trial judge and the jurisdiction from which the case came.

EXHIBIT 10.3 *Cover Page for a Trial Brief*
Case No. CRF–92–877W
IN THE DISTRICT COURT OF CLEVELAND COUNTY STATE OF OKLAHOMA
THE STATE OF OKLAHOMA, Plaintiff, -vs- ROBERT THOMAS JONES, Defendant.
TRIAL BRIEF OF DEFENDANT ROBERT THOMAS JONES
Name of Attorney Firm Name Street Address City, State, ZIP Code Telephone Number [Fax Number—Optional] Attorneys for Defendant Robert Thomas Jones [Date of Filing]

Table of Contents
An index of a brief's headings and subheadings which indicates the page number where each is found within the body of the brief.

Table of Authorities or Table of Cases
An index of the citations for all of the authorities in the brief grouped by type of authority, e.g. case law, statutes, etc., which also indicates the page number(s) where each is cited within the body of the brief.

PRACTICE TIP

Do *not* include in the Table of Authorities any citation found within a quotation used in the text of the brief; it is not the citation on which you base your argument.

Because the caption or style of the case is the first information the court will read, it must be correct. Be sure that the parties' names are correctly spelled and listed. Also, *always proofread the case number.* A transposed number could easily cause your brief to be misfiled by the court clerk.

Table of Contents and Table of Authorities. Depending on court rules and local custom, the next section of the trial brief is often an index of the headings and subheadings within the body of the brief, called a **Table of Contents**. Look at the example given in Appendix F and Exhibit 10.4 to see how a typical Table of Contents might look.

The next section will normally be a **Table of Authorities**, sometimes called a **Table of Cases**. The applicable court rules will tell you whether a Table of Authorities is required. If it is, the rules will also prescribe its format.

The order for citing legal authorities in a Table of Authorities is (1) case law (in alphabetical order, regardless of jurisdiction or reporter); (2) constitutional law (in sequential order, beginning with the smallest number to the largest); (3) statutes (federal statutes first if your case is in federal court; state statutes first if your case is in state court;) (4) court rules; and (5) other authorities. Several examples are provided for you in Appendix F.

EXHIBIT 10.4 *Trial Brief Table of Contents*

<u>TABLE OF CONTENTS</u>

Cases are always listed in alphabetical order, regardless of their jurisdiction or reporter. When listing each case, include the number of the volume of the reporter and the page on which the case begins, but not pages within the case used as spot cites throughout the brief.

Incorrect: *Anderson v. United Finance Co.,*
666 F.2d 1274, **1278** (9th Cir. 1982) 14, 15, 16

Correct: *Anderson v. United Finance Co.,*
666 F.2d 1274 (9th Cir. 1982) 14, 15, 16

Also, a citation found *within* a quote is *never* listed in the Table of Authorities, because it is not the citation upon which your argument is based. Exhibit 10.5 is an example.

In Exhibit 10.5, only *Daughtery v. Elmwood* would be listed in the Table of Authorities.

EXHIBIT 10.5 *Citations within a Quotation*

In *Daughtery v. Elmwood,* 597 F.Supp. 749, 750 (D. Mass. 1994), the court stated:

> To succeed in her claim, plaintiff must prove the four elements of common law negligence: duty, breach, proximate cause, and damages. *See, e.g., Bennett v. Eaglebrook Country Store, Inc.,* 408 Mass. 355, 358 (1990). [Defendant] argues that the court's analysis should begin and end with the issue of duty. "There can be negligence only where there is a duty to be careful." *Yakubowicz v. Paramount Pictures Corp.,* 404 Mass. 624, 629 (1989). (Citation omitted). Whether [defendant] owed a duty of care to the plaintiff is a question of law for the court. *O'Gorman v. Anotonio Rubinaccio & Sons, Inc.,* 408 Mass 758, 760 (1990) (citing *Monadnock Display Fireworks, Inc. v. Andover,* 388 Mass. 153, 156 (1983)).

Constitutional law, statutes, and court rules should be listed in their separate categories in sequential order, from the smallest number to the largest. An example of what we mean is shown in the Table of Authorities found at Exhibit 10.6.

EXHIBIT 10.6 *Trial Brief Table of Authorities*

<u>TABLE OF AUTHORITIES</u>

Cases: **Page**

Aspen v. State, 73 Okla. Crim 244,
221 P.2d 665 (1941) 3

Cameron v. State, 561 P.2d 211
(Okla. Crim. App. 1978) 4

Marshall v. State, 680 P.2d 827
(Okla. Crim. App. 1981) 5

Sciani v. State, 762 P.2d 4
(Okla. Crim. App. 1990) 2, 5

Statutes:

21 Okla. Stat. 384 (Supp. 1992) 3, 4, 6

21 Okla. Stat. 386 (Supp. 1993) 5

–ii–

The *Aspen* citation in Exhibit 10.6 differs from the others because *Aspen* was decided before Oklahoma stopped publishing its official reporter. Remember that when you cite a state case in a court of that state, you must include both official and unofficial citations if the case was reported in both.

Introduction
An optional section at the beginning of a brief used to tell the court who sued whom and why and what the author wants the court to do.

Introduction. The **Introduction** to your brief is short, but nevertheless important. It is never a required component of any brief, but it can be a useful way of "introducing" the lawsuit to the judge who may not recall anything at all about it. By clearly stating these points at the beginning of your brief, you have set the stage for a logical explanation and argument by which the judge will consider your brief and request.

Also, use the Introduction to familiarize the court with the parties and specific things, such as the contract that is the subject of the lawsuit. Designate names using the suggestions we gave you in Chapter 9 to help the court identify each of the important players, events, or things, and use those designations consistently throughout the brief.

▪ PRACTICE TIP

Use an Introduction to inform the court of:
1. The nature of the case
2. The purpose of your brief
3. The specific relief you want

Tell the court who sued whom, why, and what you want the court to do. The judge now knows what the case is about and what you want.

■ PRACTICE TIP

Be sure that you have included all of the facts upon which you will base your propositions and argument. For instance, do not suddenly refer to "Mrs. Bates' knife" in the middle of your argument if you have not already set the stage in the Statement of Facts.

Statement of the Case.   Usually a **Statement of the Case** includes both facts and a procedural history of the case, when that history is important. A procedural history is required in appellate briefs. It may be unimportant in a trial brief, and local rules may not require that it be mentioned at all.

Statement of the Facts.   The **Statement of Facts** relates for the court those facts necessary to decide whatever-it-is. The judge relies on the parties' briefs to present the facts of the case as succinctly and clearly as possible. Use the Statement of Facts as one more way to further educate the court about why your client should prevail.

As in any legal writing, the facts are all-important. Remember that the court may not attach the same importance to a piece of testimony that you did. The judge may even have forgotten it, even though most judges have prodigious memories for the evidence presented in a case. In either event, you must remind the court of the facts it will use to decide your question. You need not rehearse all the facts in the case, just those that affect the decision of the question you are arguing.

Because you want the brief to be as persuasive as possible, narrow your facts—without distorting or misrepresenting the entire picture—to those that lead into your legal analysis. Do not include dates, legal descriptions, or other details unless they are pertinent to the issues.

You can, and should, state your case to emphasize the facts in your client's favor and minimize those that are not. There is nothing to gain by concealing or ignoring damaging facts. Instead, *confront* them, and then explain them. Although you may slant the facts to fit your argument and stated purpose, *be ethical.* Misstated court decisions and exaggerated factual statements only hurt your cause.

Your Statement of the Facts should be clear, concise, and interesting. Tell the facts in such a way that the reader is intrigued and acquires an interest and sympathetic curiosity about what will be said next. Your Statement of the Facts should persuade the reader *without appearing to do so.* If you want to emphasize a word or phrase, put it at the end of the sentence and make sure that the sentence is in the active voice. To deemphasize something, put it at the middle of the sentence and use the passive voice.

In our imaginary case, *State v. Jones,* our fact statement in Exhibit 10.7 (p. 244) is stated in the nature of an **offer of proof**. That is, we are going to set out those things we expect to prove, showing the court the pattern the law requires to admit the whole history of Slivovitz's violent past.

Notice something important about the Statement of Facts in Exhibit 10.7. The language used, like the language in any good trial brief, is terse, plain, and simple. Remember, you must both illuminate and convince in one reading, without confusion. In Exhibit 10.7, the sentences and paragraphs are short. We used strong verbs and ordinary nouns, and avoided adjectives and adverbs. Short and simple is always best.

Statement of the Case
The section of a brief that includes both facts and a procedural history of the case.

Statement of Facts
The section of a brief containing a narrative of the pertinent facts needed to understand the issues discussed in the brief.

PRACTICE TIP

If you want to emphasize a word or phrase, put it at the end of the sentence and make sure that the sentence is in the active voice. To deemphasize something, put it at the middle of the sentence and use the passive voice.

offer of proof
Telling the court what evidence a party proposes to present in order to obtain a ruling on admissibility.

> EXHIBIT 10.7   *Trial Brief Statement of Facts*
>
> <u>STATEMENT OF FACTS</u>
>
> Through testimony and records of conviction, the defense will show the extensive criminal history of Bernard Slivovitz. In particular, the defense will show that Slivovitz committed violent assaults at these times and places:
>
> 1. At Muskogee, Oklahoma, on June 15, 1988, he assaulted John Kerrigan without provocation, breaking Kerrigan's nose and two ribs. He was not tried for this offense because he reached a private settlement with Kerrigan.
>
> 2. At Weatherford, Oklahoma, on December 11, 1989, he struck Arthur Running Deer with a chair, fracturing Running Deer's skull. Slivovitz was convicted of aggravated assault for this offense, and served six months in the county jail as a result.
>
> 3. At Oklahoma City, Oklahoma, on . . . .

Even so, pay attention to the language you use and how you designate your client and the opposing party. In Exhibit 10.7, the dead man is designated as simply "Slivovitz." You could call him the "victim," as the prosecution will. But that term may arouse sympathy, and certainly mischaracterizes the dead man: after all, your point is that Slivovitz, not your client, is the villain of the piece. We also used the term violent assault. Strictly speaking, there is some sort of real or threatened violence in any assault, so perhaps violent is redundant. Even so, we used the word to reinforce the impression of Slivovitz's lawlessness and brutality.

Argument and Authorities
The section of a brief that argues the issues and states the sources relied upon for that legal argument.

Proposition
A succinct statement, normally a single sentence or sentence fragment in heading form, that states the question or issue to be discussed and answered in the discussion that follows.

Argument and Authorities.   The **Argument and Authorities** is the body of your trial brief. It normally follows your Statement of Facts.

Proposition.   Within the Argument and Authorities section, the discussion of each of your arguments and subarguments is preceded, in outline form, by a heading known as a Proposition. The **Proposition** is simply a trenchant statement of the argument to follow, terse and hard-hitting. It is stated positively and argumentatively, flatly asserting the law as you believe it is or ought to be. The tone of the Proposition is partisan, although each argument must be reasonable to have any chance of acceptance by the court.

Think of it as a heading, normally a single sentence, that tells the court what the question is. Generally the judge who reads the brief knows the problem already; often he or she has called for briefs on it from both sides. Nevertheless, you should begin with the Proposition; it reminds the judge of what the precise question is, and it does so affirmatively and plainly, putting your best argument forward.

Sometimes the matter you have briefed is decided by a judge who knows nothing about the matter except what you tell her. This happens in jurisdictions where the matter is decided by a "law and motion" judge, one who hears all manner of preliminary questions from dozens of different cases.

The first Proposition stated should be the best and strongest of all the Propositions in your brief. It may be followed by subheadings, or subpropositions if you prefer, some of which will also have subheadings. Each of the subheadings should flow from the major premise of the Proposition, and each should logically follow the last. If the Proposition is written correctly, it should be possible to follow your argument easily by reading the Propositions and subpropositions in order as they appear in the Table of Contents.

Insert a new Proposition or subproposition where you begin a distinctly new and important point. Avoid inserting a heading or subheading when the discussion of that point lasts only a paragraph or two. Still, it is better to use too many than to use too few, and thereby misplace the force and logic of your argument in an unbroken river of words. The best briefs have an inexorable quality about them, flowing steadily and logically toward their writer's goal, carrying the reader along. Headings will help this flow.

Note that the Proposition in Exhibit 10.8 is stated affirmatively—as if it were absolutely so—not as a question. You are telling the court what you think the law is and requires. There is no rule against stating the question the court will decide *as* a question; however, your brief is much stronger and more persuasive if you put the Proposition positively, as a fact.

EXHIBIT 10.8   *Trial Brief Proposition*

I. EVIDENCE OF THE DEAD MAN'S HISTORY OF ASSAULTS IS ADMISSIBLE BECAUSE IT SHOWS A PATTERN OF AGGRESSION LEADING UP TO THE OFFENSE CHARGED.

As any useful Proposition should, this one states positively not only what the court ought to do with the question, but *why*: "*because* it shows a pattern of aggression." The proposition can take two forms: "X should happen because of Y" (the pattern we used above) or, "because of Y, X should happen." Use whichever form seems smoothest and most persuasive, but always make the proposition say *why* the court should rule as you want.

Using the example of our homicide case, let us suppose that your client (the defendant) has taken the position that Slivovitz was killed in self-defense. In your trial brief, you want to take the position that your client's self-defense theory is fairly raised by the evidence, and you want the court to instruct the jury on that issue. How do you state your Proposition?

> I. DEFENDANT IS ENTITLED TO A JURY INSTRUCTION ON SELF-DEFENSE.

Blah. The issue is stated, but it is so broad and drab that it neither informs nor arouses. Try again.

> I. A DEFENDANT MAY SHOOT AN UNARMED MAN IN SELF-DEFENSE.

No better, and a little worse. The issue is more specific, but it is still dreary and sounds as if the other side wrote it.

> I. DEFENDANT, THREATENED BY AN ANGRY, LARGER MAN, HAD THE RIGHT TO DEFEND HIMSELF.

Much improved, but maybe we can still do better.

> I. A SMALL MAN, THREATENED WITH SERIOUS INJURY BY AN AGGRESSIVE LARGER MAN, MAY KILL TO DEFEND HIMSELF.

Ah! Now this is a fair summary of the question, but it states the case from your client's perspective. If you can, you want to state the Proposition not only fairly, but in such a way that persons reading it will answer instantly as you wish them to.

Here is another example. Your supervising attorney represents a municipality in a civil appeal by a criminal defendant who was convicted on his own confession. The defendant filed the case below, alleging that his constitutional rights were violated because he was not warned of his right to say nothing to the police. When the defendant was first interviewed by the police, a police detective asked his name and address. He gave both and gratuitously added, "I did it."

You could state the Proposition something like this:

> I. THE POLICE MUST GIVE A MIRANDA WARNING TO THE ACCUSED BEFORE ASKING ANY QUESTIONS OF HIM.

Stated like this, the Proposition is vague, divorced from the facts of the case, and does not begin to state your theory. Start over.

> I. A DEFENDANT MUST BE WARNED BEFORE ANYTHING HE SAYS MAY BE USED AS EVIDENCE AGAINST HIM.

Nothing. Same old flat Proposition, restated. Try one more time.

> I. A CRIMINAL DEFENDANT'S VOLUNTEERED CONFESSION MUST BE ADMITTED, WHERE THE POLICE DID NOT WARN HIM, BUT ONLY ASKED HIS NAME AND ADDRESS.

Now you have something more useful. It fairly states the question, but it states it in your words.

Now a word of caution: Keep the length of your Proposition to four or six single-spaced lines. More than that, and your Proposition becomes intimidating rather than persuasive. Delete all *unnecessary* words that do nothing to convey the meaning of what you are trying to say. If you feel that you simply cannot state the Proposition adequately within this limit, it may be a signal that subheadings are necessary.

To make the Proposition in our last example really strong, you could write it like this:

> I. THERE IS NO REASON TO EXCLUDE A VOLUNTEERED, UNWARNED CONFESSION WHEN ALL THE POLICE ASKED WAS THE DEFENDANT'S NAME AND ADDRESS.

PRACTICE TIP
Always be scrupulously fair when stating any Proposition.

Remember, always be scrupulously fair when stating any Proposition. The court will lose confidence in your brief if it appears that you are slanting the issues or embroidering on the basic question or issues before the court.

Summary of the Argument. If your trial brief is lengthy, you may wish to precede the argument with a special, short section, a "Summary of the Argument." Even where this section is not required, it is a powerful addition to your brief.

The Summary of the Argument is a short, hard-hitting capsule of your argument, a blunt summation of what your client wants and why the law says he or she should have it. The Summary of Argument is short and simple, a page or less, usually written after the Argument and Authorities section has been completed. It omits all citations, and simply states your major arguments briefly, succinctly, and powerfully: "We win *because*." But, if you have a statute or case that unquestionably requires the result you seek, by all means say so here. The Summary of Argument is discussed in greater detail under "Appellate Briefs," later in this chapter.

The Argument.   Remember that the reader gives the most emphasis to statements that appear at the beginning of a sentence or at the end. The same is true for paragraphs; and a strong, clear quote often impresses the reader more than the same information in narrative form.

Your argument begins with your Proposition—or your first Proposition, if there are more than one. Then you must "argue" the point made in your Proposition by answering the question raised and explaining why it must be so. Do *not* save the best for last—lead with your best arguments and your best authorities. First impressions here will be important.

Start with your **controlling authority**. If it is a statute, discuss it first, and then any case law, beginning with your best case first, that interprets it. It is not necessary to cite every case that interprets your controlling authority. "A few good cases on point with sufficient discussion of their facts to show that they are relevant are much to be preferred over a profusion of citations." *Practitioner's Guide, to the United States Court of Appeals for the Tenth Circuit.*

Lead your discussion with your most compelling authority, analyze it, and apply it to your own facts. Discuss cases *in the order of their importance*. Once again, remember to whom you are writing. The judge or clerk who picks up your brief will be in a hurry and may not read the entire argument to get to the "heart of the matter." This is not the time to wax eloquent—be clear, concise, and persuasive.

Look at Exhibit 10.9 to see how the argument might begin in our hypothetical homicide.

Summary of the Argument
A short, blunt summation of what the client wants and why the law says he should have it which immediately precedes the Argument and Authorities section.

controlling authority
Any law (predominately case law) in your case's jurisdiction, dealing with the same issue as yours, on which the court could rely in reaching its decision.

EXHIBIT 10.9   *Trial Brief Proposition I*

I. EVIDENCE OF THE DEAD MAN'S HISTORY OF ASSAULTS IS ADMISSIBLE BECAUSE IT SHOWS A PATTERN OF AGGRESSION LEADING UP TO THE OFFENSE CHARGED.

In *Sciani v. State*, 762 P.2d 4 (Okla. Crim. App. 1990), the defendant killed a man who attacked him without provocation. The attacker beat the defendant with his fists. The defendant then picked up a piece of scrap lumber and struck the attacker, killing him.

The dead man in *Sciani* had a history of unprovoked assaults, just as Slivovitz did in the case at bar. The court held that evidence of the dead man's penchant for violence was admissible on the issue of who the aggressor was. *Sciani* at 4. The court reasoned that a demonstrated propensity for violence is relevant to establish who started the fight that led to the killing. The court stated that such a propensity "[s]urely makes it more probable than not that the dead man began the affray." *Id.* at 5.

Continued

EXHIBIT 10.9 *—Continued*

Specific incidents of violence are admissible so long as (1) they form a pattern of physical aggression; and (2) the last incident in the pattern occurred "reasonably near" the time of the killing being tried. *Id.* at 6–7.

In *Sciani*, the defense offered to prove five separate incidents of aggressive violence by the dead man. The last of these took place about six months prior to his death at the hands of the defendant. The pattern in the case at bar is even more pronounced than the pattern in *Sciani*—six incidents of unprovoked assault in as many years.

The last of these occurred only four months before Mr. Jones defended himself by killing Slivovitz. An attack occurring six months before the killing satisfied the "reasonably near" requirement in *Sciani*. *Id.* at 5. It follows that Slivovitz's attack only <u>four</u> months before assaulting Mr. Jones surely meets the "reasonably near" requirement with ease.

Sciani is only the most recent in a substantial line of well-reasoned cases supporting admission of a pattern of aggressive conduct by the dead man in a homicide case. The seminal case in this long-established line of cases is *State v. Aspen*, 73 Okla. Crim. 244, 221 P.2d 665 (1941). In *Aspen*, the court held that . . . .

You get the idea. Note that the whole tone of the brief is partisan and argumentative. It is not the impartial analysis you make when you write memorandums of law for your attorney. This is a strong statement of what result the court ought to reach, and an explanation—based on case law and other legal authority—of why the law compels that result.

Remember that in writing a brief, just as in writing a memorandum of law, you must furnish your reader with certain information about each case on which you rely. The reader must have enough facts to know why the case is similar to the case at bar, and therefore persuasive. You must also give your reader the **holding** in the authority case, and the **rationale** (or **reasoning**) of the court. Then, you must *apply* the case, that is, reason from its rationale to the facts of your case, the **case at bar.**

When discussing each case:

1. State the facts and holding in the case.
2. Then give the court's rationale—its reasoning—for its holding.
3. Then compare the facts of that case to your own case situation.

Never forget that your brief is written to *educate and persuade the court.* Just as you learned when writing a legal memorandum, lead your reader (the court) through the brief's arguments in a logical progression of thought and reason. Any jumps in logic from one point to another result in confusion and frustration for the reader and disaster for your client.

holding
In an opinion, the court's resolution of the legal issue before it.

rationale or reasoning
In an opinion, the court's application of the law to the facts to solve the question before the court and the court's explanation of why it decided an issue as it did.

case at bar
The case now before the court and under its consideration.

■ PRACTICE TIP

Keep the reader with you at all times. Your points must be made in a logical sequence, supported by solid authorities and reasoning.

First, *tell* the court the facts of the case, that court's holding, and its reasoning. Then *show* why the case is relevant to the question presented. Then *explain* the similarities or the differences between the cited case and your client's situation. Remember that your goal is to have the reader subconsciously nodding his or her head in agreement with your analysis at the end of your discussion.

As we did in Chapter 9, once again we urge you to *keep the reader with you* at all times. Make your points logically, *step by step*, and back them up with solid authorities and reasoning so that you and the reader reach the same conclusion.

Use the technique for discussing case law that you learned in Chapter 9. Do not merely say that "In *Tennessee v. Garner*, the court held that . . . ." First, *tell* the court about the facts of the case, that court's holding, and then the court's reasoning. Second, *show* the court *why* this case is relevant to the question presented in the Proposition. Then, third, *explain* the similarities or the differences between the cited case and your client's situation.

Develop your most persuasive cases, starting with the best of them. Once you have fully explained and applied three or four of them (if you have that many) you may **string-cite** three or four other persuasive cases, including for each a short **parenthetical** summary of its facts and holding. We describe string-citing in detail in Chapter 7, "Citation Form."

Frequently, a statute affects the outcome of your problem. When a statute is substantially involved in your case, it is good practice to include it *verbatim* someplace in your brief, just as you do in writing a memo. If you have a pertinent statute no more than a couple of lines long, you can include it at the bottom of your index, or add a section just before or just after the facts called **Pertinent Statutes.**

Do not, however, *quote a statute of any length up front.* Remember, the first part of your argument is liable to have the greatest effect on the court. You do not want to interrupt that persuasive effect by giving the court a long statutory quotation to read. Therefore, any statute more than a few lines long ought to be put in an annex at the end of your brief. It will be available to the reader there, but it will not interfere with the flow of your argument.

Avoid using footnotes—or worse, endnotes—in a brief. For that matter, avoid using them anyplace in legal writing unless you are writing an article for a scholarly journal. Nothing breaks a train of thought and interferes with comprehension like a plague of footnotes. If you have material—such as a verbatim statute—that needs to be included but is not essential to understanding the argument, put it at the back of the brief.

Dealing with Negative Authority.   Often, the pertinent authority is not entirely on your side. Some very strong cases may reach a conclusion opposite to the one you seek. Like bad meat, hostile authority gets no better with age. You cannot ignore it; you cannot afford to let the first mention of it be by the other side.

Therefore, one of your jobs is to attack the authority the other side relies on, and show why it should not be followed. Normally, you deal with hostile cases by **distinguishing** them—showing that they are not persuasive. Usually you do this by showing that they are so different on their facts from your own case that they need not be applied.

Be careful. You cannot simply dismiss an antagonistic case from your own state by saying it was "badly decided" or "inequitable." That may be so, and the trial judge may agree with you. Even so, he or she must follow the law laid down in that case, if it was decided by a court in the same jurisdiction and superior in rank.

For this reason, you must concentrate on showing the judge that, *factually*, the other side's case is different enough from your case (the case at bar) that it need not be followed. An exception to this rule is the case that just does not fit the holdings in other cases by the same court or in other courts of equal or greater rank. A case like that can sometimes be written off as "an aberration," or "a maverick case," or a case that has been implicitly overruled, if you have no other means of getting around it.

PRACTICE TIP

Any statute more than a few lines long ought to be put in an annex at the end of your brief as an exhibit or appendix.

string cite
A series of citations separated by semicolons which are often preceded by a signal and used to support a statement or legal argument.

parenthetical
An abbreviated summary of the case's facts, holding, or reasoning.

Pertinent Statutes
Those statutes that control the issues to be discussed.

distinguish
When discussing case law, to point out an essential difference or to prove a case cited as applicable or inapplicable.

Even here, however, it is best to distinguish on the grounds of factual dissimilarity, if you can.

Conclusion. The **Conclusion** is short, no more than a medium-sized paragraph for each proposition. This summary should review—briefly—each major point of your argument. It is simply a restatement, with few or no citations, of what your client wants and why he or she ought to get it. Finally, tell the court what you want in the request for specific relief. If necessary, ask for alternative relief.

Just as it does for any brief, the Conclusion closes—and closes the body of the brief—with the **prayer**, a formal request for relief. In Exhibit 10.10, we have shown how you might write the Conclusion for our hypothetical homicide case.

conclusion
In memorandum or brief writing, the summary of each major point made in the argument or discussion.

prayer
A formal request to the court made as the final closing paragraph of a legal document which asks for specific relief, damages, or process.

EXHIBIT 10.10   *Trial Brief Conclusion*

<u>CONCLUSION</u>

Our evidence will show that Slivovitz assaulted other people regularly over the last eight years. The last assault occurred only four months before the attack on Mr. Jones. These assaults form a clear pattern of calculated brutality, culminating in the attack on Mr. Jones. Under *Sciani* and the other cases cited, this evidence is admissible on the issue of who was the aggressor.

For the reasons and arguments given above, Defendant Robert Thomas Jones requests that this court admit evidence at trial of Mr. Slivovitz's violent history to show a pattern of aggression leading up to the offense charged.

Usually the Conclusion is followed by a boilerplate line such as "Respectfully submitted," and the **signature block** of the lawyer or firm representing the client, something like what is shown in Exhibit 10.11.

signature block
At the end of the text of a legal document, the section containing the signature line for the counsel of record, the attorney or law firm's address, and telephone number.

EXHIBIT 10.11   *Signature Block of a Trial Brief*

Respectfully submitted,

NAME OF LAW FIRM

By: _____
　　Attorney's Name
　　Law Firm's Address
　　City, State, and ZIP Code
　　Telephone Number
　　Fax Number [optional]

　　ATTORNEYS FOR DEFENDANT
　　ROBERT THOMAS JONES

A brief is signed by the attorney preparing it. Because you are a legal assistant and not an attorney, you will never sign a brief, even though you might have done most of the work on it. Your supervising attorney will designate which lawyer's name will appear on the "by" line.

■ APPELLATE BRIEFS

Many of the same considerations that influence trial briefs apply to **appellate briefs**. They are, however, very different sorts of documents.

Most obviously, the appellate brief is written only after a matter has been disposed of by a trial court. This means that the appellate court is deciding matters of *law*, not fact. Appellate judges do not second-guess a decision made on the facts by the trial judge or jury, unless there was no competent evidence on which the trier of fact could have decided as it did. In the normal case, that is a very hard thing to show. Therefore, it seldom does any good to complain on appeal that the jury or judge decided wrongly on the facts.

The questions on appeal are therefore questions of law, for instance, whether the court gave legally correct instructions to the jury, whether evidentiary rulings were legally correct, or whether some procedural rule was correctly followed.

Having said all that, let us also say that, on appeal, *the facts are still critical*. The appellate court knows absolutely nothing about the facts of the case except what it is told by counsel, or whatever its clerks can dig out of the record. Therefore, you must pay particular attention to telling the court the facts clearly, fully, and succinctly.

More on this later. For now, note what a veteran Supreme Court Justice had to say about the importance of the facts:

> The main purpose of a hearing is that the court may learn what it does not know, and it knows least about the facts. It may seem paradoxical but *most legal contentions are won or lost on the facts.*
>
> Robert H. Jackson, *Advocacy Before the Supreme Court*, 37 A.B.A.J. 801 (1951) (reprinted by permission) (Emphasis supplied).

While this is not the place for a treatise on the appellate process, it is important to know that appeals are controlled rather strictly by statutes, court rules, or both. Not everything that happens in the trial court is appealable. Sometimes certain "fundamental" errors can be appealed without being raised in the trial court. Generally, however, little can be appealed that was not "saved" at trial as part of the record, usually by appropriate objection.

Other rules prescribe the time within which an appeal may be taken, and the prerequisites to filing one. Suffice it to say here that the time to prepare for an appeal is *immediately* after trial. Formal notice of intention to appeal is not always required, but other things must often be done at once, such as designating portions of the record of the trial proceedings to be transcribed.

Know the appellate court rules. Appellate rules and statutes prescribe not only time periods and other requirements or limitations, but often such things as format and even citation form. For example, Rule 32(a) of the Federal Rules of Appellate Procedure requires that the cover page of an appellate brief contain:

> (1) The name of the court and the number of the case; (2) the title of the case (see Rule 12 (a)); (3) the nature of the proceeding in the court (*e.g.*, Appeal, Petition for Review) and the name of the court, agency or board below; (4) the title of the document . . . and (5) the names and addresses of counsel representing the party on whose behalf the document is filed.

See Appendix F, "Brief Cheat Sheet," for a sample cover page for the United States Court of Appeals for the Tenth Circuit.

---

appellate brief
A brief prepared by counsel for filing with an appellate court after a case has been decided in the trial court.

PRACTICE TIP

An appellate court decides matters of *law*, not fact.

PRACTICE TIP

Know the appellate court rules, and follow them to the letter.

PRACTICE TIP

Appellate rules and statutes prescribe not only time periods and other requirements or limitations, but also format and even citation form.

EXHIBIT 10.12   *Cover Page of Amicus Curiae Brief*

FILED
SUPREME COURT
STATE OF OKLAHOMA

No. 78293

JUL 2 0 1992

JAMES W. FATTERSON
CLERK

In the Supreme Court of Oklahoma

MURRAY STATE COLLEGE OF TISHOMINGO, APPELLANT

v.

WILLIAM P. BROWN, APPELLEE

BRIEF FOR THE AMERICAN ASSOCIATION OF UNIVERSITY PROFESSORS, THE OKLAHOMA CONFERENCE OF THE AMERICAN ASSOCIATION OF UNIVERSITY PROFESSORS, THE FACULTY SENATE OF THE UNIVERSITY OF OKLAHOMA, AND THE FACULTY COUNCIL OF OKLAHOMA STATE UNIVERSITY, AS AMICI CURIAE.

HARRY F. TEPKER, JR.
OKLA. BAR ASSN. NO. 010984
University of Oklahoma Law Center
Norman, Oklahoma 73019-0271
(405) 325-4832
Counsel for Amici Curiae

ANN H. FRANKE
Counsel, American Association of University Professors
1012 14th Street, N.W., Suite 500
Washington, D.C. 20005
Of Counsel

JULY 20, 1992

Remember that the rules differ from jurisdiction to jurisdiction, and you must know those that apply to you.

The Parts of the Appellate Brief

We shall discuss the components of an appellate brief in the order in which they generally appear in the brief.

◼ PRACTICE TIP

The party bringing the appeal is the *appellant,* regardless of whether that party was the plaintiff or defendant in the district, or trial, court. The *appellee* is the party against whom an appeal is brought; the appellee could have been either the defendant or the plaintiff in the lower court.

If the appellant was the defendant in the lawsuit below, make the distinction by changing the cover sheet caption to "Appellant/Defendant."

Cover Page.   The rules for covers and cover pages vary a little from one jurisdiction to another. With minor differences, however, a brief cover looks something like the examples provided in Appendix F and the sample provided in Exhibit 10.12.

Just as with any other document filed with the court, this is the first information the court reads. It must be correct. Incorrect captions seem to be a particular problem of appellate briefs rather than trial briefs.

The style of the case remains the same when the lawsuit is appealed. It is the designation of the parties that changes. The party bringing the appeal is the **appellant**, regardless of whether that party was the plaintiff or defendant in the district, or trial, court. The party against whom the appeal was filed is the **appellee**, again regardless of whether that party was the defendant or plaintiff below. If the appellant was the defendant in the lawsuit below, make the distinction by changing the cover sheet caption to "Appellant/Defendant." The court will appreciate your attention to detail.

A word of explanation. In Exhibits 10.12 and 10.13, you may notice references to **amici curiae** and **amici**. These expressions are Latin for "friends of the court." They refer to persons or legal entities who are not actual parties to the lawsuit, but who have shown some vital interest in the outcome. Because of this, the court has allowed them to file briefs—and perhaps to make oral arguments—as "friends of the court."

appellant
The person or party who brings the appeal.

appellee
The person or party against whom an appeal is brought.

amicus curiae, amici
Latin meaning "friends of the court" used to refer to persons or legal entities who are not actual parties to the lawsuit but who have shown some vital interest in its outcome.

Table of Contents.   The appellate brief requires a Table of Contents, while the trial brief may or may not. The Table of Contents may or may not include your propositions, but it always lists the beginning page for all sections of the brief. Examples are shown in Appendix F and Exhibit 10.13.

EXHIBIT 10.13 *Appellate Brief Table of Contents*

Continued

EXHIBIT 10.13   *—Continued*

Table of Authorities.   The Table of Authorities is an index, showing all the cases, statutes, and other authority you cited in your brief. All authority is listed by full formal citation, according to the rules of the court to which you are appealing. Generally, all citations should be in *Bluebook* form, but some local rules require special citation for particular authorities as shown in Appendix F. Some rules may require that your propositions - your arguments - be shown in the Table of Authorities, followed by the authority in support of each proposition.

Some jurisdictions may require that you list United States Supreme Court cases first, followed by other federal cases and then state cases. Within each subdivision of case law, it is customary to alphabetize the cases by first litigant's name. Cases are followed by statutes, then by secondary authority such as legal periodicals and treatises.

passim
A Latin word meaning simply "dispersed," that is, "here and there" used when an authority is cited on many pages.

Show the pages on which each authority appears, just as you did in the index to the trial brief. If the court rules allow, you may substitute ***passim*** in place of multiple page numbers where an authority is cited on many pages, although this is not a common practice.

Appendix F includes an example of a Table of Authorities taken from a brief filed in the Supreme Court of Oklahoma. Note in Appendix F how that Table of Contents and Authorities is different from the Table of Authorities for the Tenth Circuit, State District Courts, and Federal District Courts because of the Oklahoma Supreme Court's rules for its briefs. In the Oklahoma Supreme Court Table of Contents and Authorities, the authorities are listed under each proposition or subproposition as they appear in the brief, rather than being listed together alphabetically in a separate Table of Authorities.

Exhibit 10.14 is another example of a Table of Authorities.

EXHIBIT 10.14   *Appellate Brief Table of Authorities*

TABLE OF AUTHORITIES

Cases: *Page*

Beitzell v. Jeffrey,
    643 F.2d 870 (1st Cir. 1981). 8, 9

Hamburger v. Cornell University,
    240 N.Y. 328 148 N.E. 539 (N.Y. 1925). 5, 8

King v. University of Minnesota,
    774 F.2d 224 (8th Cir. 1985). 6, 10, 11

Levin v. Harleston,
    770 F.Supp. 895 (S.D.N.Y. 1991),
    aff'd in part, vacated in part on
    other grounds, 96-6 F.2d 85,
    1992 WL 122106 (2nd Cir. 1992) 6, 10, 11

Oliver v. Xavier University,
    553 So.2d 1004 (La. Ct. App. 1989). 8, 12

Price v. Oklahoma College of Osteopathic
    Medicine & Surgery, 733 P.2d 1357
    (Okla. Ct. App. 1986). 7, 8

Thorne v. Monroe City School Board,
    542 So.2d 490 (La. 1989). 8, 9, 11

Other Authorities:

William Van Alstyne, *Tenure: A Summary,*
    Explanation and "Defense,"
    AAUP Bull. 328 (1971). 6, 7

AAUP, *General Report of the Committee on*
    Academic Freedom and Tenure (1915) 7

FACULTY TENURE: A REPORT & RECOMMENDATION
    BY THE COMMISSION ON ACADEMIC TENURE
    IN HIGHER EDUCATION 256 (1973) 7

---

spot cites
The second page number given in a full citation to a legal authority or a short form citation that gives the number of the page where the statement or quotation can be found in the cited original source.

subsequent history
The appellate court's treatment of the cited case after the date of the cited case.

affirmed
A declaration by an appellate court that the judgment of a lower court is valid and must stand as rendered.

vacated
To cancel or rescind a decision, or part of a decision, judgment, or decree.

In Exhibit 10.14, note that the citations include only the number of the volume of the reporter and the first page on which the case appears. The pages of the opinion used as **spot cites** throughout the brief are not included as part of the citation for the Table of Contents. The pages on which that case appears in the brief are shown on the righthand side of the page.

Also, let us discuss at a few points about *Levin v. Harleston* in Exhibit 10.14. First, notice how the **subsequent history** of the case is shown. The phrase "*aff'd in part, vacated in part on other grounds*" tells us that the appellate court **affirmed** a portion of the decision made by the court below in *Levin* and **vacated** another part of that same decision.

If we are citing *Levin* as an example of how we think our court should decide our case, then seeing *affirmed* is good news. But note that the *Levin* decision was vacated in part on appeal. *Vacated* means the decision, or a part of it, was annulled or set

■ PRACTICE TIP

Never cite a case with negative history, such as vacated, reversed, limited, superseded, overruled, criticized, or modified, without first thoroughly reading the case and determining that the negative treatment does not affect the point of law for which you are using the case.

negative history
The subsequent history of a cited case indicating that the case has been vacated, reversed, overruled, limited, superseded, criticized, modified, distinguished, or questioned.

reversed
To reverse a judgment or opinion is to overthrow it by contrary decision.

limited
A later opinion restricts the decision of the cited case in duration, extent, or scope.

superseded
When an appellate court suspended, canceled, or replaced a prior opinion or decision of a lower court.

overruled
A later decision, rendered by the same court by a superior court, or expressing a judgment on the same question of law directly opposite to that which was given before, thereby depriving the earlier opinion of all authority as a precedent.

criticized
The soundness of reasoning in the cited case is criticized by subsequent opinions.

modified
The amendment or adjustment of a lower court's decision by an appellate court.

Question Presented
A terse, clear statement of the legal question or questions that the legal memorandum or the brief is intended to address.

aside. Never cite a case with **negative history**, such as vacated, **reversed, limited, superseded, overruled, criticized,** or **modified,** without first thoroughly reading the case and determining that the negative treatment does not affect the point of law for which you are using the case.

In Exhibit 10.14, we could have said "*aff'd in part, vacated in part,*" and left it at that. But if we add "*vacated on other grounds,*" we tell the reader that yes, a portion of the court's decision was vacated, but not on the same issues for which *Levin* is used in our brief.

Questions Presented.   The **Questions Presented** is a short section, not always formally required but quite important. Required or not, we recommend that this section always be included.

Just as with the trial brief, you will argue one or more propositions—argumentative, partisan statements of the law as you believe it to be and as you want the court to decide it is. These will lead off each major topic raised in the body of your brief and may also, if required by the court's rule, appear in your Table of Authorities.

The Questions Presented section, however, is something different. It is simply a statement of the questions the court must answer on appeal, stated as the court might state them for itself, impartially and without bias. It helps the court to ascertain precisely what problems it is called upon to solve.

Appellate judges will tell you that what lawyers do least well is isolate and define the legal issues to be decided on appeal. These issues are, along with the facts, the most important things the court wishes to know. A United States appellate judge put it this way:

> The most aggravating brief is the one which is unfocused. Counsel should strive to state and define the issues with as much precision as possible.

One appellate judge told the story of handing a lawyer friend three sets of briefs, and asking him to define the issues in the cases. The lawyer could not, because the brief-writers had not clearly said exactly what everybody wanted the court to decide. The lawyers who wrote those briefs failed to fully serve either the court or their clients.

Remember that telling the court what the question is does more than just help the court. Because the reader now knows the problem to be solved, your argument becomes more intelligible and convincing than it would otherwise be.

Now, of course, your supervising attorney selects the issues, or approves the ones you select. But once you gain experience and prove your ability, your attorney may depend on you to draft and polish an appellate brief. One of the most important things you will do is state the issue or issues so that the court can learn precisely what the dispute is about.

Issues are generally stated in a single sentence, beginning with *whether.* Remember, they must be as specific as possible and tied to the facts of your case. Let us consider a few.

"Whether the court's instructions were erroneous." This is the sort of amorphous issue-statement about which the judge complained in the quotation just given. This may be the question, surely, but it is stated in so general and non-specific a fashion that it does not help the court.

In Exhibit 10.15, we have provided the statements of three issues as they appeared in a real-world brief. If you define all your issues as carefully as those in Exhibit 10.15, you will not only help the court, but you will enhance your chances of success. Your brief will strike the court as highly professional, and everything else you say will be read with all the more attention and respect.

EXHIBIT 10.15   *Appellate Brief Questions Presented*

QUESTIONS PRESENTED

I

Whether faculty who have earned tenure at Oklahoma's public colleges and universities enjoy tenure protection as customarily defined by colleges and universities through the United States.

II

Whether the contract rights of tenured faculty serving in Oklahoma's public colleges and universities are abrogated, nullified, or impaired because of the balanced budget provisions of the Constitution of the State of Oklahoma. Okla. Const., art. 10, § 23.

III

Whether a faculty member who is dismissed in violation of tenure rights by a public college or university in Oklahoma is entitled to a remedy that protects his or her expectation interest in performance of the contract.

Statement of the Case.   The Statement of the Case section tells the court what has happened in the case so far. Normally it recites when the case was tried, the result, and the steps taken (including dates) to perfect the appeal. It presents the procedural history in chronological order.

Sometimes, you may elect to combine this section with the next one—the Statement of Facts—and call both the Statement of the Case. You will ordinarily choose to do this when your Statement of Facts is reasonably short. Even when you combine the two sections, you may wish to separate the history of prior proceedings from the facts with short subheadings.

Statement of the Facts.   In the Statement of the Facts, set out, as concisely as you can, the facts that the court needs to render its decision. You must assume that the court knows *nothing* of the facts of the matter on appeal except what you tell it. The court has a right to expect, and will expect, a fair statement of the facts for both sides, not a one-sided rendering of those facts that favor only your side.

Many judges call the Statement of Facts the most important part of the brief. Remember the quotation we gave you earlier from Justice Jackson and the *Practitioners' Guide to the United States Court of Appeals for the Tenth Circuit*? As you state the facts, you must tell the court where the facts can be found in the **record** of

> **PRACTICE TIP**
> Many judges call the Statement of Facts the most important part of the brief.

record
The official collection of pleadings, transcripts, exhibits, and so on, designated by the parties which constitutes the written memorial of all the acts and proceedings in an action or lawsuit in a court of record.

transcript
A word-for-word record
of everything that was
said at a hearing, depo-
sition, or trial, commonly
taken in shorthand form
by a court reporter who
transcribes it into a
typed transcript.

trial, like this: (R.119). This is a citation to page 119 of the **transcript** of what actually went on at trial.

In the Statement of Facts—as everywhere else in the brief—keep your sentences and paragraphs short and crisp, your subjects and verbs close together, your language plain. Exhibit 10.16 shows part of the Statement of Facts from a brief in a state supreme court. This exhibit also shows how the Statement of the Case may be combined with the Statement of Facts into a single clear, succinct section.

EXHIBIT 10.16   *Appellate Brief Statement of the Case*

STATEMENT OF THE CASE

William P. Brown ("Professor Brown") served as Chair of the Horse Management and Training Program at Murray State College (the "College") from January, 1982, until his termination in 1989. As conceded by the College, "[p]laintiff [Brown] had tenure." Defendant Murray State College's Trial Brief ("College's Trial Brief"), page 1.

Professor Brown was forced to resign without a hearing in 1989. In January 1989, the College's Director of Occupational Education notified Professor Brown that a female colleague had filed a written complaint against Professor Brown. The Director asked for Professor Brown's resignation. The Director added that, if Brown did not resign by defined deadlines, Brown's employment would be on a probationary basis. Also, if Professor Brown did not resign, the Director said the President of the College would initiate an investigation of the allegations, which could lead to Professor Brown's dismissal. In subsequent correspondence, the President of the College reaffirmed the College's position.

Initially, Professor Brown denied the allegations, demanded a hearing, and refused to resign. However, six days later, Professor Brown sent a memorandum submitting his resignation effective as of June 30, 1989. The President accepted the resignation on behalf of the Board of Regents.

Two months after the President accepted Professor Brown's resignation, Professor Brown made a formal request to rescind his resignation. The request was denied, and the Board of Regents terminated Professor Brown's employment on June 30, 1989.

Professor Brown sued the College and several individual defendants, alleging that his resignation was the result of duress and coercion. Professor Brown's claims against the College for breach of contract and tortious breach of contract were tried to a jury, which rendered a verdict for Plaintiff, Professor Brown, and awarded damages in the total amount of $100,000. The trial court entered judgment for the full amount plus attorneys' fees and post-judgment interest. Both the College and Professor Brown filed cross-appeals in this Court.

There are no references to the record in Exhibit 10.16. This is because the form of the verdict at trial in this case framed the issue on appeal without requiring reference to the trial transcript.

Summary of the Argument.   A Summary of Argument section, quite a short one, is normally not required by any rules of court. Next to the Statement of Facts, however, we think it the most important part of any brief, and strongly encourage you to include it if your attorney concurs.

The Summary of Argument is simply a concise, hard-hitting statement of why your client ought to win. It is especially useful in a case in which the argument itself—the body of the brief—is relatively long and complex. The Summary should normally be no more than two pages long, preferably a single page. It should not discuss any authority, unless you are convinced that a single case or statute compels the result you want; in that case, your Summary will urge that case or statute as the decisive factor in the appeal.

The great value of the Summary of Argument is that a judge or her clerk, before reading the body of your brief, gets a strong, simple statement of what your client wants and why he ought to get it. It can be read again just before deciding the case, or just before your attorney goes before the court for oral argument, or both.

It is a good practice to write your Summary of Argument only after you have finished writing the rest of your argument. Since your summary is your argument condensed to a fine essence, you must have a tight grasp on your theory of the case before your summary can approach the perfection of clarity and force it needs to carry the day. Avoid the tendency of many legal professionals to simply regurgitate the headings and subheadings contained within the body of the brief. This is not only boring, but wastes an additional opportunity to restate your theory of the case in a fresh and interesting manner.

This restatement may include a complete resequencing of the points contained within the body of your argument. Don't be afraid to do that. All judges understand that an argument made within one or two pages of a brief may, by necessity, be structured differently from an argument made within the following twenty to thirty pages.

The requirement that you make your argument quickly and concisely does not mean that you must simply restate in the same manner the extended argument you make in your brief. It is important that you use this opportunity to its fullest extent. Even if you do decide to draft your summary before your argument is in final form, at least return to it later to edit and polish.

Argument and Authorities.   The Argument and Authorities is the body of the brief. Here you apply the law to the facts, and show the court why your client ought to prevail. As shown in Exhibit 10.17, it begins with your Proposition, the argumentative

---

EXHIBIT 10.17   *Appellate Brief Argument and Authorities*

ARGUMENT AND AUTHORITIES

I.   **OKLAHOMA'S LAW RECOGNIZES TENURE RIGHTS AS CUSTOMARILY DEFINED BY COLLEGES AND UNIVERSITIES THROUGHOUT THE UNITED STATES.**

A.   *Colleges and universities make express offers and guarantees of tenure to attract faculty of quality with promises of economic security and academic freedom.*

Academic tenure is a "status granted, usually after a probationary period, which protects a teacher from dismissal except for serious misconduct, incompetence, financial exigency, or change in institutional programs." *Price v. Oklahoma College of Osteopathic Medicine & Surgery*, 733 P.2d 1357, 1358 n.1 (Okla. Ct. App. 1986).

Continued

EXHIBIT 10.17   —*Continued*

Though tenure is often perceived as a commitment to employ a professor until death or retirement, the commitment is not absolute in any sense. "Tenure . . . lays no claim whatever to a guarantee of lifetime employment." William Van Alstyne, *Tenure: A Summary, Explanation and "Defense,"* AAUP Bull. 328 (1971)(emphasis in original). Instead, academic tenure is appropriately and precisely defined as "an arrangement under which faculty appointments in an institution of higher education are continued until retirement . . . subject to dismissal for adequate cause." *FACULTY TENURE: A REPORT & RECOMMENDATION BY THE COMMISSION ON ACADEMIC TENURE IN HIGHER EDUCATION* 256 (1973).

---

statement we discussed earlier. Next comes a subheading (subproposition), if appropriate, and the argument itself.

More often than not, you will see citations to case law appear as the reference to *Price* does in Exhibit 10.17: a statement of what the case held, followed by a *Bluebook*-style citation. But when the case you are discussing is a powerful one for your side, we recommend you discuss it in some depth before applying it to your facts.

First, tell the court what the case held, much as the writer did for *Price* in Exhibit 10.17. Then give enough of the case's facts that the reader can see the important similarities—or differences—between that case and the case at bar. Next, tell your reader what the court's rationale was (see Exhibit 10.18).

EXHIBIT 10.18   *Appellate Brief Discussion of Case*

In *United States v. Pretzinger*, 542 F.2d 517 (9th Cir. 1976), the court held that the warrantless installation of a "beeper" on an airplane was not a search because the owner of the airplane had consented to the installation the day before the airplane was sold to the defendant. Consequently, the *Pretzinger* court concluded that no warrant is needed to justify installing a beeper unless Fourth Amendment rights would . . . have to be violated in the initial installation. *Id.* at 522.

Note in Exhibit 10.18 that we have eliminated all facts save those essential to understanding and applying the case. We know that a beeper was installed on an aircraft and that the owner of the plane had consented to that installation before selling the craft to the defendant. For these reasons, said the court, there was no "search" in the Constitutional sense. Obviously there were more facts involved in the case, including much procedural maneuvering. Nevertheless, we gave the court what it needed to decide this question—whether the beeper installation in this case was, under these particular circumstances, a "search."

Your next step is to *apply* the authority to the facts of your own case. You might use *United States v. Pretzinger,* as we did in Exhibit 10.19. As you read through Exhibits 10.18 and 10.19, you will catch the flow of the text, leading the reader through the law to what seems an inevitable conclusion. The style makes compre-

---

EXHIBIT 10.19   *Appellate Brief Application of Authority to Facts*

The rationale of the *Pretzinger* court in rejecting monitoring as a Fourth Amendment search was that one flying an airplane has no reasonable expectation of privacy in his movements. *Id.* at 522. Since aircraft are already tracked on radar, the aircraft has no Constitutional protection against affixing a "beeper" to it.

However, the reasoning of *Pretzinger* compels a different result in the case at bar. Here the vehicle was an ordinary automobile, a vehicle not ordinarily tracked by the government or anybody else. Therefore it should have, unlike an aircraft, Constitutional protection from warrantless searches.

---

hension easy by using plain language and simple structure. It also helps understanding by careful use of headings and subheadings.

Choosing Authorities for Your Brief.   How many cases do you use? Sometimes there will be dozens of useful cases, sometimes dozens on both sides. Which ones do you choose, and how many? There is no court-imposed requirement to use some magic number of authorities. Sometimes many are available; sometimes very few. Here are some guidelines:

- *Which cases to use.* The guidelines are much like those we mentioned in talking about the trial brief. Choose cases from the highest court of your own jurisdiction whenever possible. Choose cases dealing with the question of law raised in your case, and choose cases with facts as close as possible to those of the case at bar.
- *How many cases to use.*   You do not need a lot of cases if you choose the best ones. The courts believe that quality outweighs quantity in choosing cases, but judges also want a brief to give enough facts to show why those cases should persuade the court.

We think that three or four good cases should be enough to prove any legal point. Choose them according to these guidelines. Try to find suitable cases decided as recently as possible. Include, whenever there is one, the **seminal case**, the well-known case that subsequent decisions regularly cite for the proposition you are discussing in your brief.

After you have fully discussed and applied your major cases, you are free to string-cite a few other good cases, if you choose. Do as we told you earlier, giving the proposition for which they stand, their full citation, and a parenthetical (an abbreviated sentence telling your reader something about each case's facts and rationale).

Treat hostile authority exactly as we discussed under the subject of trial briefs. Do not lead off with an attack on the other side's authority; if you do that, you overemphasize its importance. Rather, start with your own affirmative argument, put as powerfully as possible. Only after you have made your own points fully should you distinguish dangerous authority on the other side. Here is an example of how it is done:

> In *United States v. Hufford*, 539 F.2d 32 (9th Cir. 1976), the court held . . . . However, the facts of *Hufford* are inapposite here. A warrant had already been issued for the installation of a "beeper" on the defendant's truck. Moreover, the . . . installation had been consented to by the owner. . . .

seminal case
A well-known case that subsequent cases regularly cite for the same issues you are discussing in your brief.

As we discussed under "Trial Briefs," the best way to nullify an opposing case is to show that it is so different on the facts from the case at bar that it does not apply, or at best is unpersuasive. The example we just gave does exactly that, stating that *Hufford* is hostile authority, but arguing that it does not apply because it was decided on very different facts.

It is well to remember that no appellate court likes to overrule a prior case, even when it does not want to follow the case. The court would far rather decide that the case simply does not apply because it is factually different from the case at bar.

We have already mentioned appellate rules. They are not merely guidelines that are nice to follow; *they are requirements.* Most appellate rules limit the number of pages allowed for briefs. Courts do not take kindly to litigants trying to circumvent these limitations by hiding argument in annexes and appendixes. Put your argument up in the body of the brief, where it belongs, and obey the court's strictures on the length of briefs.

Even better, say what you have to say as succinctly as possible, and shut up. Busy judges are grateful for a brief whose writer does not feel compelled to use up every allowable page. If your page limitation is forty pages, and you can say powerfully what you have to say in fifteen, then use your fifteen pages and stop.

Conclusion.   **The Conclusion** is short. It may include a very short summary of the heart of your argument, no more than a medium-sized paragraph for each proposition. Just as it does for any brief, the Conclusion closes—and closes the body of the brief—with the prayer, a formal request for relief. A typical prayer might look something like this:

> For the reasons set out above, Plaintiff respectfully requests that the judgment of the trial court be reversed, and that the motions to suppress the evidence and to issue an order dismissing the second count of the indictment be granted.

In the alternative, the Conclusion may be simply an invitation to the court to grant the relief asked for, without a formal prayer:

> This Court should vacate the judgment and remand the case with instructions for the trial court to fashion a remedy that will vindicate Plaintiff's expectation interest in the performance of the tenure contract.

Conclusion
In memorandum or brief writing, the summary of each major point made in the argument or discussion.

◼ FINALIZING AND PREPARING A BRIEF FOR FILING

We include here a checklist of steps to take, after the brief is written, to finalize and prepare it for filing with the court clerk. Space-saving tips follow the checklist.

Checklist for Finalizing and Filing a Brief

✓ **Shepardize** and **cite-check** every citation. Look up every statute to be sure that (1) it is the correct reference for that point of law, and (2) the numbers have not been transposed.

✓ Proofread all quotations. Double-check citations to quotations. Every quotation should have a cite showing the page number where it appears in the opinion.

shepardize
To use the volumes of *Shepard's* to collect the research references provided for that item, such as the subsequent history of a particular case and how subsequent cases have cited or interpreted a particular case.

cite-check
The process of proofreading every legal authority in a legal document to check it for accuracy and correct citation form.

✓ Proofread the brief for sense, typographical mistakes, or grammatical errors; check for internal consistency such as:

- Appendix ("App. _____.")
- Record ("R. _____.")
- Exhibit ("Ex. _____.")
- Short form/abbreviated references to parties or name of motion—the name designated at the beginning of the brief
- Propositions/subpropositions
- Any dates given (i.e., dates of contracts or dates a pleading or other paper was filed with the court)
- All references to exhibits, transcripts, depositions, and appendixes.

✓ Review the appropriate court rules. Here are some examples of points to check:

- Does the brief comply with any page-number limit?
- Does the brief need a Table of Contents or Table of Authorities?
- Should the brief be bound and, if so, is a specific color required for the outside cover stock?
- Is the brief in the proper format as required by all of the rules applicable to that court?

✓ Prepare the cover page, Table of Contents, and Table of Authorities in the format set out in the applicable court rules. Check to be sure that each document is arranged properly according to the rules.

✓ Return a revised draft to the supervising attorney for final approval.

✓ Determine the number of copies to be filed with the court and to be mailed to counsel of record (listed on the Certificate of Service).

✓ Proofread the completed draft to be sure that all changes have been accurately made.

✓ Have the appropriate color of cover stock printed or copied for the cover page, and have the necessary number of copies of the brief bound according to the applicable court rules.

✓ Arrange for the brief to be filed with the court clerk and mailed to the counsel of record as shown on the Certificate of Mailing. (Be sure that the date and time for any hearing on the motion is shown on the copies mailed to counsel of record.)

✓ Note on the file copy that copies of the brief were mailed to counsel as shown on the Certificate of Mailing (cc: all counsel of record, the date, and your initials).

✓ Docket the response or reply dates or the date and time set for the hearing on the motion.

Tips for Saving Space

What do you do when the court rules allow only fifteen pages for a brief and your brief takes sixteen and a half? Other than cutting text, "here are" a few helpful hints to try whenever your brief is too long:

- Delete any double-spacing between paragraphs.
- Shorten proposition headings.

- Narrow the width of the margins (if you can without violating a court rule).
- Make the Statement of Facts an exhibit rather than part of the text of the brief.

CHAPTER SUMMARY

This chapter cannot be more than a simple, shallow treatment of the science of brief writing. There are many fine books on the subject, and frequent opportunities to attend continuing legal education classes on the art of writing briefs. Take advantage of both.

This chapter introduces you to the basics. You cannot go far wrong in writing a brief if you carefully follow the elementary guidelines we have set out, in particular:

- Write simply in short phrases, short sentences, and short paragraphs.
- Use plain language, keep your subject and verb very close together, and avoid legalese.
- Understand and follow all court rules pertaining to briefs and motions.
- Pay close attention to detail, including your citation form, Table of Contents, and Table of Authority, if any.
- Include in your brief all the facts necessary to decide the question briefed. Always assume your reader knows nothing about the matter except what you relate in your brief.
- Briefs are *argumentative*. You are no longer unbiased, but are now an advocate, limited only by honesty and the Canons of Ethics.
- In an appellate brief, give the court a short, unslanted statement of the issues, separate from your propositions.
- Get to the point. Remember, you must convince the court in just one reading. Being long-winded increases the chance that the court will quickly turn to the opposition's brief.
- Include a Summary of Argument whenever your brief is long or complex.
- Choose two or (at most) three good issues, and lead off with your strongest argument and most powerful authority.
- Use headings and subheadings whenever possible.
- Keep your propositions short, concise, and hard-hitting.
- Lead with your most important proposition.
- Start the discussion of each proposition with your most powerful authority.
- *Apply* your authority to the facts of the case at bar.
- Carefully select three or four of your best cases, explain them clearly, and apply them to the facts of the case at bar.
- If you string-cite, use parentheticals.
- Spot cite whenever you discuss the holding or rationale of the court in a case you cite.
- Quote sparingly, and only for *how* something is said.
- Distinguish the opposition's best cases showing why it is unpersuasive and should not be followed, but only after you have powerfully made your own argument.
- Proofread once, twice, and again; and have somebody else do it too, preferably somebody not acquainted with the case at all.
- Use the steps for finalizing and preparing a brief for filing as a checklist to ensure accuracy and quality.

KEY WORDS AND PHRASES

affirmed	cover page	prayer	Statement of Facts
amicus curiae, amici	criticized	pretrial conference	string cite
appellant	distinguish	pretrial order	subsequent history
appellate briefs	holding	Proposition	Summary of the Argument
appellee	introduction	Questions Presented	superseded
Argument and Authorities	leave of court	rationale	supporting briefs
brief	limited	record	Table of Authorities
brief bank	local court rules	reversed	Table of Cases
case at bar	modified	scheduling conference	Table of Contents
citations of authority	negative history	scheduling order	transcript
cite-check	offer of proof	seminal case	trial brief
Conclusion	overruled	shepardize	vacated
controlling authority	parenthetical	signature block	
court rules	*passim*	spot cites	
	Pertinent Statutes	Statement of the Case	

EXERCISES

Chapter Review

You have learned about several types of briefs, each with its own purpose in the legal process. This exercise will help you assess your understanding of the purposes and distinguishing characteristics of each. Answer the following questions.

1. What is another name for a memorandum of law submitted to courts in support of, or in opposition to, motions that have arisen in the present or pending litigation?

2. Of the two types of legal briefs, which is the longer and more complex document, usually written in a more formal tone?

3. As you draft the trial brief, you consider providing a list of the legal authorities upon which your arguments are based. You are not sure whether a Table of Authorities is permitted. Where would you look to find out?

4. This section of the brief usually provides an index of the headings and subheadings found within the body of the brief. What is it?

5. What is the primary purpose of both trial briefs and appellate briefs?

6. In both trial briefs and appellate briefs, a well-written proposition accomplishes two things. What are they?

7. In the body of a trial brief, you will fully discuss each of your authority cases. What are the four elements of your discussion of each case?

8. This section precedes the body of the appellate brief, and provides a hard-hitting capsule of the argument.

9. Assume that your argument relies on a lengthy statute. What is the guiding rule on the use of statutes in a brief?

10. Your research has produced a case that you are certain could help Mr. Raymond's position. How should you deal with this hostile case?

11. When attempting to minimize the impact of an antagonistic case from an appellate court in your jurisdiction, it is best to emphasize the factual distinctions between the problem case and the case at bar. Why should you not point out that the case is based on poor reasoning?

12. In appellate briefs, as in trial briefs, it is best to use your own affirmative arguments before distinguishing cases that are hostile to your position. Why?

Table of Authorities and Citation Form

1. Here is a list of cases and statutes, such as those you will use in your trial brief for the case against Mr. Allegretti. Using the sample Table of Authorities in Appendix F as your guide for format, construct a Table of Authorities for your brief. This is your opportunity to apply what you have learned about case names, citation form, and order of authorities. If you do this exercise properly, you will give your *Bluebook* a workout.

   - *United States v. Pandozzi,* a 1989 First Circuit case, found in volume 878 of the second series of the Federal Reporter on page 1526.
   - *United States of America v. Bay,* another Federal Reporter case, second series, volume 762, page 1314, decided by the Ninth Circuit in 1984.
   - *United States v. Garza,* a 5th Circuit case from 1985, found at page 1202 of the 754th volume of the second series of the Federal Reporter.
   - *Campbell v. Greer,* a 1987 Seventh Circuit case, found on page 700 of volume 831 of the second series of the Federal Reporter.

   - A case involving Charles H. Lenz as the plaintiff-appellee, and Chris Chalamidas as the defendant-appellant, in the Supreme Court of New Mexico, decided on November 1, 1989. The case is found in the second series of the Pacific Reporter, volume 782, on page 85. It is also located in volume 109, page 113 of the New Mexico Reporter.
   - A New York statute, found in Chapter 11–A, Part one, Title D, Article 60, section 40, entitled "Rules of evidence; proof of previous conviction; when allowed." Assume that the law was most recently approved on August 16, 1994.
   - A case reported by the Fourth District of the Appellate Court of Illinois, with the People of the State of Illinois as the plaintiff-appellee, and John Lewis Kunze as the defendant-appellee. The case is reported in three publications: In the third edition of the Illinois Appellate Court Reporter, page 708 of the 193rd volume; in the Northeast second series Reporter, volume 550 at page 284; and in Illinois Decisions, volume 140, page 648. It was a 1990 case and a rehearing was also denied in 1990.
   - A statute from the California Evidence Code, Division 6, Chapter 6, Article 2, Section 787, titled "Specific instances of conduct." Assume this is a 1993 statute, with a 1994 supplement.

2. Correct the Table of Authorities given below by cite-checking the cases and correcting the citations and format where needed. The first page for each of these cases can be found after the exercises in this chapter. For purposes of this exercise, you must assume that the page numbers given on the righthand side of the Table of Authorities accurately depict the pages where that particular authority is found within the brief.

TABLE OF AUTHORITIES

Affanato v. Merrill Bros, Inc.
547 F.2d 138 at 140 (1st Cir. 1977) 14

Anderson v. Liberty Lobby, Inc., 477 U.S. 242, 255,
91 L.ed.2d 202, 216 (1986) 15, 16

Baden v. Craig-Hallum, Inc., 115 F.R.D. 582 (Minn. 1987) 8

Writing Propositions

As you know, propositions of law in any brief create the skeleton around which you form your legal argument. Remember, a proposition uses a persuasive tone to tell the court what the law is and why. The following are improper and ineffective drafts of propositions. Some may not accurately tell the court what the law is; some may need styling changes. Assume that these propositions will be used in Ms. Healy's case, and edit each where necessary.

Allegretti wants Charles Raymond to testify, but the attorney has moved the court to exclude evidence of Mr. Raymond's prior drunk-driving convictions. Remember, the convictions occurred in 1986 and 1990, and each had a sentence of 60 days.

To help you convey the proper meaning of each proposition, we have provided the rules of law from *Lenz v. Chalamidas*, 782 P.2d 85 (N.M. 1989), upon which each of the propositions is based.

Propositions 1 through 4 are based on the following rule:

Under rule allowing admission of prior criminal convictions of witness for purpose of attacking credibility of witness, trial court must admit evidence in criminal prosecution if crime was punishable by imprisonment in excess of one year and court determines probative value of admitting evidence outweighs prejudicial effect to defendant or crime was an offense, felony or misdemeanor, involving dishonesty or false statement.

1. IF MR. RAYMOND TESTIFIES, EVIDENCE OF HIS DRUNK-DRIVING CONVICTIONS IS INADMISSIBLE AS PROOF THAT HE WOULD LIE ON THE WITNESS STAND.

2. EVIDENCE OF MR. RAYMOND'S DRUNK-DRIVING OFFENSES PROBABLY WILL NOT BE ADMISSIBLE TO ATTACK HIS CREDIBILITY BECAUSE THE CONVICTIONS ARE TOO OLD.

3. IF THE JURY HEARS THAT MR. RAYMOND WAS CONVICTED OF DRUNK DRIVING, THEY WILL ASSUME HE IS A BAD PERSON AND WILL NOT PROPERLY WEIGH THE EVIDENCE.

4. MINOR OFFENSES ARE ADMISSIBLE ONLY IF THE OFFENSES ARE RELATED TO TRUTH-FULNESS.

Propositions 5 through 8 are based on the following rule:

Requirement of rule, which provides for admission of prior criminal convictions for purpose of attacking credibility of witness, that court must determine that probative value of admitting evidence outweighs prejudicial effect, does not apply in civil cases but only in criminal cases.

5. THE COURT MAY NOT ADMIT EVIDENCE OF CHARLES RAYMOND'S PRIOR DRUNK-DRIVING CONVICTIONS BECAUSE THIS IS A CIVIL CASE.
6. IN THE CASE AT BAR IT DOES NOT MATTER WHETHER THE PROBATIVE VALUE OF THE DRUNK-DRIVING OFFENSES OUTWEIGHS THE PREJUDICIAL EFFECT.
7. CHARLES RAYMOND'S PRIOR CONVICTIONS ARE NOT ADMISSIBLE.
8. PRIOR CRIMINAL CONVICTIONS CAN BE ADMITTED FOR PURPOSE OF ATTACKING CREDIBILITY OF WITNESS.

Writing a Trial Brief

You are now ready to write a trial brief. Recall that this is a document submitted to the court by the party's counsel. It is intended to persuade the judge to rule in favor of that party.

The following exercises address each section of a brief separately, so that you can master one part before proceeding to another. At the end of these exercises, you will have written an entire trial brief, one section at a time.

Use the following scenario for this assignment.

FACT SCENARIO

You work for a district attorney who asks you to write a trial brief defending two deputy sheriffs, Robert Scott and Susan Thomas. (Although district attorneys normally prosecute criminals, they also represent county employees, such as deputy sheriffs, in civil lawsuits.)

On January 4, 1995, the Sheriff's office received a call from Diane Klein. She was frantic. She said that her husband, David, was loading his shotgun and preparing to go the home of their next-door neighbors, the Gearys, to shoot the Gearys' Rottweiler dogs.

Mrs. Klein explained that the dogs had been chasing the Kleins' horses and cattle for the last two to three weeks. The Kleins had mentioned the problem to Mr. Geary at least twice, and Mr. Geary had always refused to believe that his dogs were the culprits in spite of the Kleins' positive identification.

Then, that day, for no reason, the dogs went after Mr. Klein as he was walking from his barn to the house. Mr. Klein ran toward the house, yelling for his wife to be ready to slam the door behind him. He made it inside the house before the dogs reached him, just barely escaping serious injury. Now her husband was loading the shotgun, shouting that he was "sick and tired of it" and intended to "fix the _____ problem once and for all."

The Sheriff, Jeb Samuelson, spoke with Mr. Klein on the phone. After a lengthy discussion, Sheriff Samuelson was able to convince Mr. Klein to abandon his plan by promising to send two deputies to the Gearys' home to check things out. Deputies Scott and Thomas were sent to talk to the Kleins and the Gearys, and then make their report.

When the deputies arrived at the Kleins' home, Mr. Klein told them that he and his wife had been having a lot of trouble lately with the Gearys' dogs. The Gearys' dogs had chased the Kleins' dogs and livestock for several weeks. Then, that day, the Gearys' dogs went after Mr. Klein. The Kleins felt that their safety and that of their livestock and pets were at stake. They were tired of dealing with this constant problem and wanted it stopped.

After talking with both Mr. and Mrs. Klein, the deputies went next door to the Gearys'. As the deputies approached the Gearys' mobile home, they saw two Rottweiler dogs lying beside the front door. The dogs did not react in any way to the deputies' presence and did not seem to be aware of the deputies' presence.

The deputies retreated to their car and radioed their position to the Sheriff's office. Then, they just sat there for about thirty seconds trying to decide what to do. Since no one had come to the door of the mobile home during that time, the deputies decided to approach the mobile home once more.

As the two deputies got out of their car and began to approach the front porch, a third Rottweiler they had not seen before that moment came running at full speed from behind a nearby parked car, snarling and barking ferociously and charging directly at Deputy Scott. When the dog was within ten feet of Deputy Scott, Deputy Scott pulled his firearm and shot the dog, killing it instantly.

The sounds of gunfire, the deputies' yelling, and the dog's barking awakened the other two Rottweilers, who also began to run snarling and barking toward the deputies. Deputy Thomas hurriedly shot at both of the dogs, wounding one and missing the other. Frightened by the gunshots, both dogs stopped, then ran under the mobile home out of sight. The wounded dog, which was pregnant, later died, as did her four unborn puppies.

The Gearys have sued the Sheriff's Department and the two deputies for $3,008.25 in actual damages and $3,000 for mental anguish. The deputies claim that they shot the animals in self-defense and, therefore, are not liable.

Your research has discovered these cases: *Grizzle v. State*, 707 P.2d 1210 (Okl. Crim. App. 1985); *State v. Simmons*, 36 N.C. App. 354, 244 S.E.2d 168 (1978); and *Smith v. Palace Transportation Co.*, 142 Misc. Rep. 93, 253 N.Y.S. 87 (1931). These cases are provided at the end of this chapter, starting on page 290, for your use in this assignment. For purposes of this assignment, you are to assume that these three cases are *all* of the pertinent cases that exist. Unless your instructor directs you otherwise, *do not add any research other than the cases provided.*

The Gearys have cited to these cases: *Fleck v. Russell*, 269 P. 883 (Or. 1928) and *Laporte v. Associated Independents*, 163 So.2d 267 (Fla. 1964).

In their brief, plaintiffs contended that their dogs did nothing to provoke the deputies' use of deadly force against them. The plaintiffs further argued that, even if their dogs attacked the deputies, which they deny, the dogs were only protecting the Gearys' home from intruders. The plaintiffs also contended that the deputies used unreasonable deadly force against their dogs, and that the deputies' actions were retribution for the dogs' past acts (chasing the Kleins and their livestock).

1. **The Introduction.**   You are ready to begin writing the brief. For now, skip drafting the cover page, Table of Contents, and Table of Authorities. Write an Introduction for your brief that tells the court about this case.
2. **The Statement of the Facts.**   Now write a Statement of the Facts that presents the facts in a light most favorable to your client, the deputies.
3. **The Propositions.**   Read the cases provided as your research for this assignment. Review the plaintiffs' contentions. Decide how many Propositions your brief will contain. Remember that you should respond to every claim made by the plaintiffs. Your brief should refute the arguments made by the plaintiffs' brief and also give reasons why the defendant deputies should win at trial based on the facts and the law. Decide on the order in which you will present your Propositions, and then draft each Proposition.
4. **The Argument and Authorities.**   Now, under each Proposition that you drafted for exercise 3, write the argument for each Proposition using the research provided for this assignment.
5. **The Conclusion.**   Now write the Conclusion for your brief.
6. **The Finishing Touches—Cover Page, Table of Contents, and Table of Authorities**   Congratulations! Your brief is almost finished. Compile everything you have written for exercises 1 through 5 into one document. Now prepare a cover page, Table of Contents, and Table of Authorities using the format provided in Appendix F for federal district court briefs.

CASE

138   **547 FEDERAL REPORTER, 2d SERIES**

§ 501 might otherwise have been ignored. It is true that plaintiff alleges that defendants dealt with him (and Local 259) as an adverse party and held a pecuniary or personal interest in conflict with his and the Local's interests; but when the complaint is read as a whole it fails to reveal anything more than dissatisfaction on plaintiff's part with the pension plan which was obtained by the union as his collective bargaining agent. Moreover, it is clear from the pleadings that the alleged conflict of interest arises only from the fact that defendants do not belong to the same pension plan as does plaintiff. Of itself, however, this fact is insufficient to state a cause of action claiming conflict of interest or breach of a fiduciary relationship.

[5, 6] Plaintiff also alleges that defendants breached their § 501 fiduciary duty by failing to obtain a more favorable pension plan through the collective bargaining process. We have considerable doubt whether, in view of the other avenues of relief available under the Labor-Management Relations Act of 1947, *see* § 301, 29 U.S.C. § 185; *Vaca v. Sipes*, 386 U.S. 171, 87 S.Ct. 903, 17 L.Ed.2d 842 (1967), Congress intended that § 501 be a means of monitoring the results of collective bargaining. Even assuming, however, that § 501 reaches conduct during the collective bargaining process, we do not think that the fiduciary duty imposed by it is violated in a case where nothing more is alleged than poor performance as a collective bargaining agent. *See Aikens v. Abel*, 373 F.Supp. 425, 433 (W.D.Pa.1974). While § 501 surely imposes obligations in addition to "the punctilio of an honor the most sensitive," *Meinhard v. Salmon*, 249 N.Y. 458, 464, 164 N.E. 545, 546 (1928) (Cardozo, C. J.), on those to whom it is addressed, we do not believe that it permits a cause of action to be stated whenever a union member is dissatisfied with the results of the collective bargaining process. Although a fiduciary relationship implies certain affirmative as well as negative obligations, *cf. O'Brien v. Dwight*, 363 Mass. 256, 294–95, 294 N.E.2d 363, 385 (1973); *Berry v. Kyes*, 304 Mass. 56, 58–59, 22 N.E.2d 622, 624 (1939), it does not require that collective bargaining

agents necessarily obtain what hindsight reveals to be *optimal* results. *Cf. O'Brien v. Dwight, supra*, 363 Mass. at 295, 294 N.E.2d at 386. The collective bargaining process is, by definition, too complex and too adversarial in nature to subject the participants in it to liability for every failure fully to satisfy their constituency.

We express no view as to whether plaintiff might be able to state a claim under some other jurisdictional heading.

Affirmed.

Harold AFFANATO, Plaintiff, Appellee,

v.

MERRILL BROTHERS and Cianbro Corporation, Defendants.

Appeal of CIANBRO CORPORATION.

No. 76–1296.

United States Court of Appeals, First Circuit.

Argued Oct. 7, 1976.

Decided Jan. 11, 1977.

In tort action, after entry of default judgment, the United States District Court for the District of Massachusetts, Frank H. Freedman, J., awarded plaintiff damages, and defendant appealed. The Court of Appeals, McEntee, Circuit Judge, held that district court did not abuse its discretion in defaulting defendant after repeated orders of the court with respect to answers to interrogatories and other discovery had been ignored.

Affirmed.

CASE

U.S. SUPREME COURT REPORTS   91 L Ed 2d

[477 US 242]

JACK ANDERSON, et al., Petitioners

v

LIBERTY LOBBY, INC. and WILLIS A. CARTO

477 US 242, 91 L Ed 2d 202, 106 S Ct 2505

[No. 84-1602]

Argued December 3, 1985. Decided June 25, 1986.

Decision: Court, in ruling on motion for summary judgment in public-figure libel action, held required to consider clear and convincing evidence standard in determining whether there is genuine issue of actual malice.

SUMMARY

Plaintiffs, a lobbying corporation and its founder, filed a diversity libel action in the United States District Court for the District of Columbia against the publishers of a magazine which had allegedly libelled the plaintiffs by printing three articles which portrayed them as neo-Nazi, anti-Semitic, racist, and fascist. The author of two of the articles, on which the third had been based, stated in an affidavit that he had engaged in extensive research and had derived his facts from several sources. Relying on that affidavit, the publishers moved for summary judgment, asserting that the plaintiffs were required under the First Amendment to show that the publishers had acted with "actual malice," that is, with deliberate or reckless disregard for the truth, and that such malice was absent in this case as a matter of law; but the plaintiffs contended that several of the author's sources were patently unreliable, and that this raised an issue as to actual malice. The District Court granted summary judgment in favor of the publishers, holding (1) that the plaintiffs were limited-purpose public figures; (2) that the actual malice rule was therefore applicable; and (3) that the author's stated conduct precluded a finding of such malice. The United States Court of Appeals for the District of Columbia Circuit affirmed as to some of the allegedly libellous statements and reversed and remanded as to others, holding that, in such actions, the constitutional requirements of "clear and convincing" proof and independent judicial determination of the ultimate issue of actual malice are not to be applied on a motion for

Briefs of Counsel, p 643, infra.

CASE

582   **115 FEDERAL RULES DECISIONS**

which suggests a different conclusion. *See, Casualty Indemnity Exchange v. Village of Crete,* 731 F.2d 457, 461–462 (7th Cir.1984); *Tillman v. City of Milwaukee,* 715 F.2d 354, 357–360 (7th Cir.1983); *Pasco,* 637 F.2d at 500–506; *LeBeau v. Libby-Owens-Ford Co.,* 484 F.2d 798, 800–802 (7th Cir.1973); *Filippini,* 110 F.R.D. at 134–136; *Alkot Industries, Inc. v. Takara Co., Ltd.,* 106 F.R.D. 373, 376–377 (N.D.Ill. 1985); *William Chris Trucks v. First Canadian Bank,* 98 F.R.D. 584 (N.D.Ill.1983). The facts of this case analyzed under Rule 19 do not require or permit joinder of the third-party defendants as defendants under the plaintiffs' complaint.

[3] Sprayrite also argues for permissive joinder under Rule 20. The principle thrust of the defendants' argument is that they will be forced to pursue multiple lawsuits and piecemeal litigation if joinder is not permitted. However, under the facts and circumstances of this case "joinder of a nondiverse party could only occur when the party is indispensable." *Filippini,* 110 F.R.D. at 137.

Accordingly, and for all the above reasons, it is the ORDER of the Court that the defendant/third-party plaintiff's Sprayrite Manufacturing Company, Motion for Joinder be, and is hereby, DENIED. SO ORDERED.

Lois M. BADEN, Plaintiff,

v.

CRAIG–HALLUM, INC. and DeWayne Derksen, Defendants.

Civ. No. 4–86–565.

United States District Court,
D. Minnesota,
Fourth Division.

May 11, 1987.

In securities action, one defendant moved for dismissal on ground that he was not timely served. The District Court, MacLaughlin, J., held that plaintiff had demonstrated good cause for failure to effect service within 120–day period prescribed by rule.

Motion denied.

1. Federal Civil Procedure ⚖417

Plaintiff may move for extension of time either before or after expiration of 120–day period for service of summons and complaint, but motions to extend prior to expiration of that period are to be liberally permitted, while if party delays until after period has expired or raises motion as a defense to motion to dismiss, the time limits are strictly construed, mitigated by the "good cause" time allowances. Fed.Rules Civ.Proc.Rules 1, 4(j), 6(b), 28 U.S.C.A.

2. Federal Civil Procedure ⚖417

Whether a motion for extension of time for service of summons and complaint is made before or after expiration of the normal 120–day time period, burden is on party by whom service is required to show "good cause" why service was not effected within the prescribed 120–day period. Fed. Rules Civ.Proc.Rules 4(j), 6(b), (b)(2), 28 U.S.C.A.

3. Federal Civil Procedure ⚖417, 852

Amendment of complaint does not justify delay in service of original complaint unless amended complaint names a new party defendant, and then a new 120–day period begins to run as to the added defendant, but amendment does not toll the 120–day period as to defendants already named; appropriate course is to amend original complaint after serving it on the original defendants. Fed.Rules Civ.Proc. Rules 4(j), 15(a), 28 U.S.C.A.

4. Federal Civil Procedure ⚖402

Neither fact that defendant has received actual notice of pending action nor fact that defendant has not been prejudiced

CASE

fusals to deal are predominantly anticompetitive.

Northwest Wholesale Stationers, Inc. v. Pacific Stationery Printing Co., 472 U.S. 284, 298, 105 S.Ct. 2613, 2621, 86 L.Ed.2d 202 (1985); *see also Bhan v. NME Hosps., Inc.*, 929 F.2d 1404, 1412 (9th Cir.1991) ("the per se rule should be invoked for a group boycott when the challenged activity would almost always tend to be predominantly anticompetitive"). Denying staff privileges to a physician through peer review on the basis that the physician's conduct is unprofessional and inappropriate is not an activity "likely to have predominantly anticompetitive effects" such that *per se* treatment is necessary.[19]

[19, 20] The district court went on to apply the rule of reason analysis. In doing so, the court correctly noted that the first question is whether plaintiffs proved there was joint action sufficient to satisfy the requirement that there be a contract, combination or conspiracy. *See McKenzie v. Mercy Hosp. of Independence*, 854 F.2d 365, 367 (10th Cir.1988). In this case, the court specifically found that there was "no evidence, apart from the peer review process, that a conspiracy existed." District Court Findings of Fact and Conclusions of Law at 33. After noting that existing precedents do not completely answer the question of whether peer review by itself provides the requisite joint action or whether a hospital can conspire with its medical staff, the court held that, even assuming *arguendo* that joint action was established, plaintiffs once again simply failed to establish the required impact upon *competition*. Plaintiffs' failure to prove adequately the relevant markets within which competition was allegedly affected, and their failure to prove that Dr. Tarabishi's inability to use

the facilities at the Hospital affected competition, as opposed to Dr. Tarabishi himself as a competitor, doomed plaintiffs' section one claims to failure.[20] We affirm. While plaintiffs might wish us to assume or infer an impact on competition based on the denial of Dr. Tarabishi's staff privileges, and the failure of his TMD center, the reality is that it is plaintiffs' burden to *prove* such an impact, and plaintiffs simply failed to do so here.

CONCLUSION

For the foregoing reasons, the judgment of the district court dismissing plaintiffs' claims is AFFIRMED.

COLORADO PUBLIC UTILITIES COMMISSION and State of Colorado, Plaintiffs–Appellees,

v.

Lawrence HARMON and United States Department of Energy, Defendants–Appellants,

Wisconsin Electric Power Company, Virginia Power Company, TU Electric Company, Rochester Gas and Electric Corporation, Public Service Electric & Gas Company, Pennsylvania Power & Light Company, Northern States Power Company, Northeast Utilities, New York Power Authority, Georgia Power Company, Florida Power & Light Company, Duquesne Light Company, Commonwealth Edison Company, Carolina

---

19. The district court similarly rejected *per se* treatment of plaintiffs' conspiracy to stabilize prices claim. We affirm, and we further affirm the district court's conclusion that there was "no evidence of such a price stabilization conspiracy, whether directly or through the effect of the peer review proceedings." District Court Findings of Fact and Conclusions of Law at 40.

20. The district court noted that "the only impact upon *competition*, as distinguished from plain-

tiffs, is based upon the speculation that TMD would ultimately become a hospital. The Court finds this speculation to be tenuous." District Court Findings of Fact and Conclusions of Law at 39. While it is true that there was an area—the provision of out-patient surgery—in which the Hospital arguably did compete with TMD, plaintiffs never quantified the impact on competition in that market.

CASE

**CHARLTON L. DAVIS & COMPANY, P.
C., Plaintiff-Appellee,**

v.

**FEDDER DATA CENTER, INC.,
Defendant,**

**Financial Computer Corporation,
Defendant-Appellant.**

**No. 77–1313
Summary Calendar.***

United States Court of Appeals,
Fifth Circuit.

July 22, 1977.

A motion to set aside a default judgment was denied by the United States District Court for the Middle District of Georgia at Valdosta, J. Robert Elliott, Chief Judge, and the moving defendant appealed. The Court of Appeals, Roney, Circuit Judge, held that where a defendant asserted that it had a meritorious defense, where it did not appear that time was of the essence, and where, when it was discovered that no answer to the complaint had been filed, an extension of time had been requested of plaintiff's attorney and the latter said he would consult his client but later plaintiff obtained default judgment alleging no appearance had been made by defendant, relief from the default judgment should have been granted under the rule.

Vacated and remanded.

1. Federal Civil Procedure ⬅2411

Judgments by default are a drastic remedy and should be resorted to only in extreme situations. Fed.Rules Civ.Proc. rules 55(b)(2), 60(b), 28 U.S.C.A.

2. Federal Civil Procedure ⬅2418

Under rule requiring notice to party who has appeared in action but against whom judgment by default is sought, "ap-

pearance" required by the rule is not limited to formal court appearance. Fed.Rules Civ.Proc. rules 55(b)(2), 60(b), 28 U.S.C.A.

3. Federal Civil Procedure ⬅2450

Where defendant asserted that it had meritorious defense, where it did not appear that time was of essence, and where, when it was discovered that no answer to complaint had been filed, extension of time had been requested of plaintiff's attorney and latter said he would consult his client but later plaintiff obtained default judgment alleging no appearance had been made by defendant, relief from default judgment should have been granted under rule. Fed.Rules Civ.Proc. rules 55, 55(b)(2), (c), 60(b), (b)(6), 28 U.S.C.A.

Ed G. Barham, Willis L. Miller, III, Valdosta, Ga., for defendant-appellant.

H. Arthur McLane, Valdosta, Ga., for plaintiff-appellee.

Appeal from the United States District Court for the Middle District of Georgia.

Before THORNBERRY, RONEY and HILL, Circuit Judges.

RONEY, Circuit Judge:

The district court entered a $20,500 default judgment against two defendants, one of which was Financial Computer Corporation. Financial moved to set aside the judgment because the plaintiff failed to give the three-day notice required by Fed. R.Civ.P. 55(b)(2). The district court denied the motion. We reverse, deciding that Financial made a sufficient "appearance" to be entitled to Rule 55(b)(2) notice, and that adequate grounds exist for setting the judgment aside under Fed.R.Civ.P. 60(b).

Plaintiff filed this suit in the Middle District of Georgia on July 9, 1976. Following service on July 27, 1976, Financial's president forwarded the papers to his Maryland attorney. Because of a misunderstanding

---

* Rule 18, 5 Cir., see *Isbell Enterprises, Inc. v. Citizens Casualty Co. of New York et al.*, 5 Cir., 1970, 431 F.2d 409, Part I.

CASE

474   60 **FEDERAL RULES DECISIONS**

proceeded independently from their inception in 1969 until they were consolidated for trial by Chief Judge Lord in July of 1971. We believe that the defendant was required to pursue discovery independently, including the taking of the plaintiffs' depositions at different times and responding to requests for admissions of fact in each case. Not until their consolidation two years and two months after the filing of these actions was the defendant able to treat this matter as a single consolidated case. Under these circumstances, we believe that the defendant is entitled to a separate docket fee in each case, and accordingly, we reverse the decision of the Clerk on this point, and we will tax each plaintiff $20.00 costs for the attorney's docket fee.

Finally, we find that the plaintiffs' claim that the defendant's cross-appeal was untimely filed is without merit, and the plaintiffs' motion to dismiss the defendant's cross-appeal is denied.

Therefore, the Clerk's taxation of costs is affirmed in part and reversed in part, and the Court will enter the following Order and Civil Judgment.

ORDER AND CIVIL JUDGMENT

And now, to wit, this 3rd day of August, 1973, it is Ordered that the Clerk of Court's judgment entered in the amount of $228.00 in favor of the defendant, Hellenic Sea Transports, Ltd. and against the plaintiff, Rogers Lockett, in Civil Action No. 69–1026, and also the judgment entered in favor of the defendant, Hellenic Sea Transports, Ltd. and against the plaintiff, Perry Ford, in the amount of $228.00 in Civil Action No. 69–1050, be and the same is hereby vacated.

It is further Ordered that judgment be and the same is hereby entered in favor of the defendant, Hellenic Sea Transports, Ltd., and against the plaintiff, Rogers Lockett, in Civil Action No. 69–1026, in the amount of $338.30. It is further Ordered that judgment be and

the same is hereby entered in favor of the defendant, Hellenic Sea Transports, Ltd., and against the plaintiff, Perry Ford, in Civil Action No. 69–1050, in the amount of $338.30.

And it is so ordered.

John N. FLOOD, M.D., Plaintiff,

v.

John MARGIS, Jr., et al., Defendants.

No. 70–C–110.

United States District Court,
E. D. Wisconsin.

Feb. 13, 1973.

Complaint alleging arbitrariness in relation to raising of license fees and refusal to renew plaintiff's license to operate a mobile home park. On the making of various motions for, inter alia, default judgment and to strike certain paragraphs of complaint, the District Court, Myron L. Gordon, J., held that plaintiff was not required to file an amended complaint, that motion to strike certain paragraphs of complaint would be granted, and that controverted portions of two paragraphs of answer were relevant to plaintiff's claims and would not be stricken.

Order accordingly.

1. Federal Civil Procedure ⇐2411

Default judgments are not favored by the courts.

2. Federal Civil Procedure ⇐839

Defendant would be required to defend against complaint, and plaintiff would not be required to file an amended complaint, where the Court of Appeals had determined that the complaint stated a cause of action.

CASE

Citation	Rank (R)	Database	Mode
849 F.2d 605 (Table)	R 1 OF 1	ALLFEDS	Page

UNPUBLISHED DISPOSITION
(CITE AS: 849 F.2D 605, 1988 WL 60618 (4TH CIR. (MD.)))

NOTICE: Fourth Circuit I.O.P. 36.6 states that citation
of unpublished dispositions is disfavored except for
establishing res judicata, estoppel, or the law of the
case and requires service of copies of cited unpublished
dispositions of the Fourth Circuit.

(The decision of the Court is referenced in a "Table of
Decisions Without Reported Opinions" appearing in the
Federal Reporter.)

GNB, INCORPORATED, Plaintiff-Appellee,
v.
TROPEX, INC; Best Battery Company, Inc.; Arthur R. Best;
Roland C. Best,
Defendants-Appellants,
and
Best-West, Inc.; Rolart, Inc., Defendants.
No. 87-1637.
United States Court of Appeals, Fourth Circuit.
Argued: March 11, 1988.
Decided: June 3, 1988.
Copr. (C) West 1995 No Claim to orig. U.S. govt. works

CASE

U.S. SUPREME COURT REPORTS   73 L Ed 2d

[457 US 800]

BRYCE N. HARLOW and ALEXANDER P. BUTTERFIELD, Petitioners

v

A. ERNEST FITZGERALD

457 US 800, 73 L Ed 2d 396, 102 S Ct 2727

[No. 80–945]

Argued November 30, 1981. Decided June 24, 1982.

Decision: Senior aides and advisers of President of United States, held entitled to qualified immunity from civil damages suits insofar as their conduct does not violate rights of which reasonable person would have known.

SUMMARY

A civilian employee of the Department of the Air Force was terminated from his position. He instituted a suit for civil damages in the United States District Court for the District of Columbia against two senior aides and advisers of the President of the United States, alleging that they participated in a conspiracy to violate his constitutional and statutory rights, and entered the conspiracy in their official capacities, to effect his unlawful discharge. At the conclusion of discovery, the supporting evidence remained inferential, whereupon the aides moved for summary judgment. In denying their motion, the District Court also ruled that the aides were not entitled to absolute immunity. The aides appealed the denial of their immunity defense to the United States Court of Appeals for the District of Columbia, which dismissed the appeal.

On certiorari, the United States Supreme Court vacated and remanded. In an opinion by POWELL, J., joined by BRENNAN, WHITE, MARSHALL, BLACKMUN, REHNQUIST, STEVENS, and O'CONNOR, JJ., it was held that, in a suit for civil damages based upon their official acts, senior aides and advisers of the President of the United States are not entitled to a blanket protection of absolute immunity as an incident of their offices as Presidential aides either derivatively from the President's absolute immunity or from their special functions as Presidential aides, but are entitled to application of the qualified immunity standard that would permit the defeat of insubstantial claims

Briefs of Counsel, p 1463, infra.

396

CASE

HIBERNIA NAT. BK. v. ADMIN. CENT. SOC. ANONIMA 1277
Cite as 776 F.2d 1277 (1985)

HIBERNIA NATIONAL BANK,
Plaintiff-Appellee,

v.

ADMINISTRACION CENTRAL
SOCIEDAD ANONIMA, et al.,
Defendants,

Jorge Raoul Garcia Granados de
Garay, Defendant-Appellant.

No. 85–3078.

United States Court of Appeals,
Fifth Circuit.

Nov. 20, 1985.

Bank brought debt action against endorser/guarantor of instrument in Louisiana state court, and case was removed on grounds of diversity of citizenship. The United States District Court for the Eastern District of Louisiana, Adrian G. Duplantier, J., granted bank's motion for summary judgment, and endorser/guarantor appealed. The Court of Appeals, Clark, Chief Judge, held that trial court erred in granting summary judgment without considering merits of defense.

Reversed and remanded.

1. Federal Civil Procedure ⟐2544

Motion for summary judgment cannot be granted simply because there is no opposition, even if failure to oppose violates local rule. Fed.Rules Civ.Proc.Rule 56(e), 28 U.S.C.A.

2. Federal Civil Procedure ⟐2544

Movant for summary judgment has burden of establishing absence of genuine issue of material fact and, unless movant has done so, court may not grant motion regardless of whether any response is filed. Fed.Rules Civ.Proc.Rule 56(e), 28 U.S.C.A.

3. Federal Civil Procedure ⟐2544

District court's decision to grant summary judgment, if in fact based solely on nonmovant's default in filing responsive pleading, was reversible error. Fed.Rules Civ.Proc.Rule 56(e), 28 U.S.C.A.

4. Federal Civil Procedure ⟐2535

Even if district court did not err in granting summary judgment because judgment was based on the merits rather than on nonmovant's default in filing timely responsive pleading, district court erred in failing to consider merits of nonmovant's defense as reflected in its belated response. Fed.Rules Civ.Proc.Rules 56(e), 60(b)(1), 28 U.S.C.A.

5. Federal Civil Procedure ⟐2646

Civil Rule 60(b)(1), providing for relief from judgment in cases of mistake, surprise, or excusable neglect, is to be liberally construed so that doubtful cases may be resolved upon the merits, and decision to grant or deny relief is within trial court's sound discretion. Fed.Rules Civ.Proc.Rule 60(b)(1), 28 U.S.C.A.

6. Federal Civil Procedure ⟐2444

In ruling on motion to set aside default judgment for mistake, surprise, or excusable neglect under Civil Rule 60(b)(1), courts generally look at three factors: extent of prejudice to plaintiff, merits of defendant's asserted defense, and culpability of defendant's conduct. Fed.Rules Civ.Proc.Rule 60(b)(1), 28 U.S.C.A.

7. Federal Civil Procedure ⟐2656

Mere possibility of prejudice from delay, which is inherent in every case, is insufficient to require denial of motion for relief from judgment for mistake, surprise, or excusable neglect. Fed.Rules Civ.Proc. Rule 60(b)(1), 28 U.S.C.A.

8. Federal Civil Procedure ⟐2533

Attorney's neglect in following local rule on filing of responsive pleadings to motions for summary judgment should have been excused where district judge's notice of filing deadline did not reach attorney until day after deadline had passed and attorney had already prepared responsive pleadings and moved with all possible speed to secure leave of court for late filing. Fed.Rules Civ.Proc.Rule 60(b)(1), 28

CASE

is his client. Moreover, Frost concedes that Benn's operations were "unethical," though he testified that he did not discover this until a few weeks after he had purchased the notes. And, for some largely unaccountable reason, Frost would not take an assignment of the notes in his own name because he did not wish his name associated with the notes. And he purchased the notes at a considerable discount, a fact which, of itself, would not impugn the good faith of the assignment, but is a fact that can properly be considered in connection with all the other facts in the case, including the unique form in which payment was made by Frost to Benn.[14] It must be borne in mind that the notes, in default as they were, carried "suspicion" on their face. It is of interest that the assignment to Frost's nominee came after the District Court had begun its consideration of the ownership of the Florida property and after Morrison had given notice, by his motion for leave to file a counterclaim, of his claim to the property or its proceeds. We are by no means as certain as apparently the District Court was that Frost could, even under the normal rules applicable to non-negotiable instruments, have qualified as a bona fide purchaser for value without notice. This is, of course, aside from the real issues in the case, which turn on the proper application of the Uniform Commercial Code for resolution.

Reversed and remanded with directions.

Henry Clayton **JONES and Royal Globe Insurance Company, Plaintiffs-Appellants,**

v.

Joy E. NELSON and Robert M. Nelson, Defendants-Appellees.

No. 72–1891.

United States Court of Appeals,
Tenth Circuit.

Argued and Submitted May 25, 1973.

Decided Aug. 31, 1973.

The driver of a truck and his insurer brought diversity action for damages for personal injuries sustained when the vehicle of defendants, while passing the truck or shortly thereafter, suffered a blowout and collided with the truck. The United States District Court for the Western District of Oklahoma, D. C., No. CIV 72–372, Stephen S. Chandler, J., entered summary judgment for defendants, and plaintiffs appealed. The Court of Appeals, Hill, Circuit Judge, held that, although plaintiffs had improperly denominated their appeal as being taken from denial of their motion for a new trial, the appeal would be considered as one from the entry of summary judgment, and that such summary judgment had been improperly entered because the record revealed disputed issues as to material facts.

Judgment set aside and case remanded.

1. Federal Civil Procedure ⬗**2462**
Summary judgment is not substitute for trial, and its very purpose is to

---

14. *See*, City of New Port Richey v. Fidelity & Deposit Co. (5th Cir. 1939) 105 F.2d 348, 353, 123 A.L.R. 1352.

Frost claims he gave Benn five cashier's checks payable to Southgate Associates (one of Benn's corporate *alter egos*) for $18,000 each, his personal check for $5,000, payable to Southgate Associates, and $5,000 in cash. The balance of the purchase price of the notes in question, secured as they were by property worth, by Frost's own appraisal,

$200,000, was in the form of a $50,000 credit on an attorney's fee due Frost by Benn. All in all, it must not be forgotten, though, that for a long time after this transaction, Benn and/or his corporate *alter ego* was representing the notes as "under pledge" and, as late as 1971 the District Court was still uncertain whether the notes were "under pledge," as its opinion of May, 1971 demonstrates.

CASE

RASMUSSEN v. W. E. HUTTON & CO.

Cite as 68 F.R.D. 231 (1975)

231

basis of the record presently before the Court. It should be noted, however, that with a similar record before it, including many of the same depositions that were filed here, the Commission concluded that for the purposes of 19 U.S.C. § 1337, the patent in suit had no validity because the Cecil gloves were offered for sale in the United States more than one year before the date of the patent application. *See Report of March 13, 1975, supra* at pages 5, 6 and 22.

IV

For the reasons stated, plaintiff's motion for summary judgment is granted. Counsel should prepare and submit an appropriate Order.

V. C. RASMUSSEN and Edna L. Rasmussen, Plaintiffs,

v.

W. E. HUTTON & CO. and Roland G. Strid, Defendants.

Civ. A. No. C 74–1464 A.

United States District Court, N. D. Georgia, Atlanta Division.

Jan. 29, 1975.

The plaintiffs alleged violations of the Commodities Exchange Act, the Securities Act of 1933, the Securities Exchange Act of 1934, and the Georgia commercial gambling law, and filed a motion to enter default judgment, individual defendant filed a motion to quash return of service or application for relief under federal rule, and corporate defendant applied for relief under federal rule. The United States District Court for the Northern District of Georgia, Atlanta Division, James C. Hill, J., held, inter alia, that the district court may up-

on showing of good cause set aside an entry of default; that certain factors must be considered in determining whether default should be set aside; that the entry of default against defendants would be set aside; and that plaintiffs' motion to require posting of a security bond would be denied.

Order in accordance with opinion.

1. Federal Civil Procedure ⊙=2443

Determination of whether good cause exists to set aside an entry of default depends upon the court's applying its discretion with proper regard to the peculiar circumstances surrounding the case before it. Fed.Rules Civ.Proc. rule 55(c), 28 U.S.C.A.

2. Federal Civil Procedure ⊙=2411

Judgments by default are not generally favored, and hence, generally, any doubts should be resolved in favor of permitting a hearing on the merits. Fed.Rules Civ.Proc. rule 55(c), 28 U.S.C.A.

3. Federal Civil Procedure ⊙=2444

A distinction exists between removal of a party from default and setting aside default judgment; a motion to vacate default judgment is subject to the strictness of Federal Rule 60(b), whereas Federal Rule 55(c) permits setting aside an entry of default upon showing of good cause. Fed.Rules Civ.Proc. rules 55(c), 60(b), 28 U.S.C.A.

4. Federal Civil Procedure ⊙=2444

Among factors to be considered in determining whether good cause exists to set aside an entry of default are: a requirement that the party in default must have a meritorious defense; the promptness with which defaulting party acts; the reason for the default; and the possible prejudice to the nondefaulting party. Fed.Rules Civ.Proc. rule 55(c), 28 U.S.C.A.

5. Federal Civil Procedure ⊙=2450

In considering plaintiffs' motion for entry of default judgment in their ac-

CASE

1162   **565 FEDERAL REPORTER, 2d SERIES**

"veil piercing" in the same manner as are corporations in general. However, a bankruptcy court, as a court of equity, has not merely the power but the duty to disregard the fiction of separate legal entities when the ends of justice so require, even though one of the entities was ostensibly formed in the public interest. *Macfadden v. Macfadden*, 46 N.J.Super. 242, 134 A.2d 531 (Ch. 1957), *aff'd.*, 49 N.J.Super. 356, 139 A.2d 774 (App.Div.1958), *cert. denied*, 27 N.J. 155, 141 A.2d 828 (1958).

The order of the district court is affirmed.

Bertha M. RUTHERFORD,
Plaintiff-Appellee,

v.

AMERICAN BANK OF COMMERCE,
Defendant-Appellant.

No. 76–1467.

United States Court of Appeals,
Tenth Circuit.

Argued and Submitted July 21, 1977.

Decided Nov. 21, 1977.

Plaintiff brought a discriminatory employment action against defendant as her former employer. The United States District Court for the District of New Mexico, Edwin L. Mechem, J., entered judgment in favor of plaintiff, and defendant appealed. The Court of Appeals, McWilliams, Circuit Judge, held that: (1) act of defendant as plaintiff's former employer in advising a prospective employer of fact that plaintiff had filed a sex discrimination charge against defendant was a retaliatory act and, as such, was a form of discrimination and an unlawful employment practice; (2) circumstances of case permitted an inference that, as result of information parted

by defendant to prospective employer, plaintiff lost her employment opportunity with prospective employer, and (3) applicable statute could not be read literally to preclude defendant from being held liable for retaliatory act just because plaintiff had voluntarily terminated her employment several months prior thereto, and hence, was no longer employed by defendant.

Affirmed.

1. Civil Rights ⟷9.10

Act of defendant, plaintiff's former employer, in advising a prospective employer of fact that plaintiff had filed a sex discrimination charge against defendant was an act of retaliation and, as such, a violation of statutory provision making it an "unlawful employment practice" for an employer to discriminate against an employee for making a discriminatory employment charge where, before plaintiff filed charge, defendant's vice-president had given plaintiff a glowing letter of recommendation. Civil Rights Act of 1964, § 704(a) as amended 42 U.S.C.A. § 2000e–3(a).

   See publication Words and Phrases for other judicial constructions and definitions.

2. Evidence ⟷595

Inferences from circumstantial facts may frequently amount to full proof of a given theory and may on occasion even be strong enough to overcome effect of direct testimony to contrary.

3. Civil Rights ⟷43

Circumstances indicating that a representative of prospective employer was sufficiently interested in plaintiff that he made contact with defendant as plaintiff's former employer and did not advise plaintiff until after such contact that she had no chance of employment with prospective employer were such as to permit an inference that, as result of information imparted by defendant to prospective employer concerning act of plaintiff in filing a sex discrimination charge against defendant, plaintiff lost her employment opportunity with prospective

CASE

242   **189 FEDERAL REPORTER, 2d SERIES**

relied upon the very passage quoted by this Court at 177 F.2d 917, from Linville v. Nissen, 162 N.C. 95, 101, 77 S.E. 1096, 1099, as holding that the doctrine respondeat superior did not apply in the Eleazer case, viz.: "This doctrine applies only when the relation of master and servant is shown 'to exist between the wrongdoer and the person sought to be charged for the result of wrong at the time and in respect to the very transaction out of which the injury arose.'"

For the reasons stated, the judgment below will be reversed and the cause will be remanded with direction to enter judgment for the United States.

Reversed.

TOZER et al. v. CHARLES A. KRAUSE MILLING CO.

No. 10342.

United States Court of Appeals, Third Circuit.

Argued Feb. 8, 1951.

Decided May 7, 1951.

Action by William St. John Tozer and Dominick Cordiano, as trustees of Italian Cook Oil Corporation against Charles A. Krause Milling Co., for breach of an implied warranty of quality of crude corn oil sold by defendant corporation to plaintiff. The United States District Court for the Eastern District of Pennsylvania rendered judgment for plaintiff by default and thereafter denied defendant's motion to set aside the default judgment and defendant appealed. The Court of Appeals, Staley, Circuit Judge, held that allegations of defendant's answer, if established on trial, to effect that defendant expressly negatived any implied warranties of quality would constitute a complete defense to action and as defendant corporation alleged that it had never received notice of the action prior to the entry of default judgment, denial of defendant's motion to set aside the default judgment was an abuse of discretion.

Order reversed and cause remanded.

1. Courts ☞406.5(12)
Federal civil procedure ☞2443

A motion to set aside a default judgment is addressed to sound discretion of court, and should not be disturbed on review unless there has been abuse of such discretion. Fed. Rules Civ. Proc. rules 55 (b) (1), 60(b) (1, 6), 28 U.S.C.A.

2. Federal civil procedure ☞2450

Where plaintiff obtained default judgment against defendant for an alleged breach of an implied warranty of crude corn oil sold to plaintiff and defendant, on its motion to vacate judgment on ground that it had received no notice of filing of complaint or of entry of judgment, alleged that it expressly negatived any express or implied warranties of quality, allegations of answer, if established on trial, would have constituted a complete defense to action and denial of defendant's motion to have judgment set aside was an abuse of discretion. Fed. Rules Civ. Proc. rules 55(b) (1), 60(b) (1, 6), 28 U.S.C.A.

3. Federal civil procedure ☞2450

Question whether defendant presents a wholly meritorious defense is always an important factor in consideration of a motion to set aside a default judgment. Fed. Rules Civ. Proc. rules 55(b) (1), 60(b) (1, 6), 28 U.S.C.A.

4. Federal civil procedure ☞2641

Federal Rule providing that on motion, and on such terms as are just, court may relieve a party or his legal representative from a final judgment, order or proceeding for mistake, inadvertence, surprise or excusable neglect or any other reason justifying relief from operation of judgment, must be given a liberal construction. Fed. Rules Civ. Proc. rule 60(b) (1, 6), 28 U.S.C.A.

5. Federal civil procedure ☞2412, 2452

Matters involving large sums should not be determined by default judgments if it can reasonably be avoided and any doubt should be resolved in favor of petition to set aside judgment so that cases may be decided on their merits. Fed. Rules Civ. Proc. rules 55(b) (1), 60(b) (1, 6), 28 U.S. C.A.

CASE

LENZ v. CHALAMIDAS   N. M. **85**
Cite as 782 P.2d 85 (N.M. 1989)

109 N.M. 113

Charles H. LENZ, Plaintiff–Appellee,

v.

**Chris CHALAMIDAS,
Defendant–Appellant.**

No. 17973.

Supreme Court of New Mexico.

Nov. 1, 1989.

General contractor brought action against homeowner to recover damages resulting from alleged breach of oral agreement and to foreclose on residence pursuant to materialman's lien. The District Court, Bernalillo County, Richard B. Traub, J., entered judgment in favor of general contractor. Homeowner appealed. The Supreme Court, Larrabee, J., held that: (1) homeowner's prior commercial gambling convictions were admissible to impeach his credibility, and (2) remand was required for additional findings on issue of attorney fees.

Affirmed in part and remanded in part.

1. Witnesses ⚖=345(1)

Under rule allowing admission of prior criminal convictions of witness for purpose of attacking credibility of witness, trial court must admit evidence in criminal prosecution if crime was punishable by imprisonment in excess of one year and court determines probative value of admitting evidence outweighs prejudicial effect to defendant or crime was an offense, felony or misdemeanor, involving dishonesty or false statement. SCRA 1986, Rule 11–609.

2. Witnesses ⚖=345(1)

Requirement of rule, which provides for admission of prior criminal convictions for purpose of attacking credibility of witness, that court must determine that probative value of admitting evidence outweighs prejudicial effect does not apply in civil cases but only in criminal cases. SCRA 1986, Rule 11–609, subds. A, A(1, 2).

3. Evidence ⚖=146

Party opposing use of evidence under rule, which provides that relevant evidence may be excluded if its probative value is substantially outweighed by danger of unfair prejudice, has burden of persuading trial judge to exclude evidence, whereas under rule, allowing admission of prior criminal conviction for purpose of attacking credibility of witness, party seeking use of evidence has burden of persuasion. SCRA 1986, Rules 11–403, 11–609.

4. Witnesses ⚖=345(1)

Rule allowing for admission of prior criminal convictions for purpose of attacking credibility of witness if crime was punishable by imprisonment in excess of one year is always subject to possible exclusion under rule which provides for exclusion of relevant evidence if its probative value is substantially outweighed by danger of unfair prejudice, among other things. SCRA 1986, Rules 11–403, 11–609, subd. A(1).

5. Witnesses ⚖=336

Defendant homeowner's prior commercial gambling convictions were admissible to attack defendant's credibility in general contractor's breach of contract action; convictions were punishable by imprisonment in excess of one year and probative value of evidence was not outweighed by its prejudicial effect. SCRA 1986, Rules 11–403, 11–609, subd. A(1).

6. Mechanics' Liens ⚖=310(3)

Under attorney fee section of legislation on materialmen's liens, allowance of attorney fees is discretionary, but exercise of discretion must be reasonable when measured against objective standards and criteria. NMSA 1978, § 48–2–14.

7. Mechanics' Liens ⚖=310(3)

Reasonableness of attorney fees awarded materialmen from owner must be closely scrutinized if amount is based on defense of counterclaims and other questions collateral to enforcement of lien. NMSA 1978, § 48–2–14.

8. Costs ⚖=208

In setting attorney fee awards, trial court must make findings of fact on those

Continued

CASE—*Continued*

factors on which parties have presented evidence; without findings of fact and conclusions of law, Supreme Court cannot properly perform its reviewing function.

9. Appeal and Error ⚖⎓1177(8)

Failure of trial court to make findings of fact and conclusions of law on issue of attorney fees in action brought by materialman against owner necessitated remand of case. NMSA 1978, § 48–2–14.

Carl J. Schmidt, Albuquerque, for defendant-appellant.

Kemp, Smith, Duncan & Hammond, P.C., Mary Catherine McCulloch, John P. Eastham, Albuquerque, for plaintiff-appellee.

OPINION

LARRABEE, Justice.

This is an appeal from a jury verdict in the amount of $13,364.82 in favor of plaintiff-appellee, Charles H. Lenz, and from the trial court's award of attorney fees to plaintiff in the amount of $26,268.03. We affirm the jury verdict and remand to the district court for findings of fact and conclusions of law on the issue of attorney fees awarded at trial.

Lenz, a general contractor, filed this lawsuit to recover damages resulting from the breach of an oral agreement and to foreclose on the residence of defendant-appellant, Chris Chalamidas, pursuant to a materialman's lien. Evidence in support of the jury verdict is as follows: Lenz and Chalamidas entered into an oral "cost-plus 15%" agreement for certain construction work on Chalamidas' residence. The work began on August 1, 1986, and was completed December 20, 1986. Progress payments in the amount of $14,264.16 were made by Chalamidas. Upon completion, plaintiff submitted a final bill in the amount of $13,-364.82, which was not paid after demand was made by plaintiff. Lenz recorded a second amended claim of lien on January 19, 1987, in the amount of $13,364.82 plus costs and attorney fees.

During cross-examination of Chalamidas, plaintiff introduced into evidence, over de-fendant's objection, two prior criminal convictions for commercial gambling. The first conviction was a guilty plea entered on December 4, 1981, and the second a guilty plea entered on January 28, 1982. In ruling the evidence admissible, the trial court stated:

[I]t seems to me that his testimony * * * wasn't as believable as I thought it really should be. [Defendant] made some statements to the effect that he had never heard of the term "cost plus." That seems highly improbable. He made—commented he had never heard of getting a "ball park" figure. That's a rather common term that almost anybody in our society, I think, has heard of.

He also indicated to the jury lack of knowledge about construction contracts and construction work, and yet, in the same breath, he tells of having owned 10 homes that he has remodeled and sold. And it seems highly improbable that he was being completely honest and forthright in his testimony, and, therefore, you felt if this case comes down to an issue as to the credibility of Mr. Lenz, that it would be important for the Jury then to appreciate the character of the Defendant.

Thereafter the jury returned a verdict for plaintiff. On July 29, 1988, a hearing was held on plaintiff's motion for attorney fees. The trial court awarded plaintiff attorney fees in the amount of $26,268.03, prejudgment interest of $2,583.51 and costs of $681.13.

On appeal, Chalamidas argues (1) the district court erred in admitting evidence in a civil contract case on defendant's prior criminal gambling convictions; and (2) the court abused its discretion in awarding exorbitant and excessive attorney fees in an amount double the jury verdict.

1. *Admissibility of Prior Convictions in a Civil Case*

Defendant claims the prior conviction evidence is inadmissible under Evidence Rule 404, SCRA 1986, 11–404; Rule 609, SCRA 1986, 11–609; and Rule 403, SCRA 1986, 11–403. We need not address defendant's

CASE—*Continued*

LENZ v. CHALAMIDAS   N. M. **87**

Cite as 782 P.2d 85 (N.M. 1989)

argument that evidence of a person's prior criminal record under Rule 404 is inadmissible to prove the character of a person or that a person acted in conformity with such character, because the trial court ruled the prior convictions admissible under Rule 609 to impeach the credibility of Chalamidas, and not under Rule 404.

[1] Rule 609 provides for the admission of prior criminal convictions for the purpose of attacking the credibility of a witness, but with certain express limitations. A trial court must admit evidence of the conviction of a crime if the crime was (1) punishable by imprisonment in excess of one year and the court determines the probative value of admitting this evidence outweighs the prejudicial effect to the defendant, or (2) an offense, felony or misdemeanor, involving dishonesty or false statement.[1] *State v. Lucero,* 98 N.M. 311, 313, 648 P.2d 350, 352 (Ct.App.), *cert. denied,* 98 N.M. 336, 648 P.2d 794 (1982). The charges of commercial gambling to which Chalamidas pled guilty in 1981 and 1982 carry the potential imprisonment in excess of one year, thus implicating subparagraph (A)(1) of Rule 609.

It is unclear from the case law in New Mexico whether the balancing provision of subsection (A)(1), applicable in criminal cases, was intended to apply to evidence of prior convictions for purposes of impeachment in civil cases. It is the phrase "to the defendant" that is ambiguous with respect to its applicability in civil cases. A literal reading of the rule allows a defendant in a civil case, but not a plaintiff, to complain about the use of his or her criminal record to impeach.

[2] New Mexico's rule of evidence, Rule 609(A)(1) and (2), is essentially identical to Federal Rule of Evidence 609(a)(1) and (2). The Supreme Court has addressed this controversy in *Green v. Bock Laundry Mach.*

---

1. SCRA 1986, 11–609 reads:

   A. General rule. For the purpose of attacking the credibility of a witness, evidence that he has been convicted of a crime shall be admitted if elicited from him or established by public record during cross-examination but only if the crime

Co., —— U.S. ——, 109 S.Ct. 1981, 104 L.Ed.2d 557 (1989). The Court stated in *Green* that a literal interpretation of the rule "that would deny a civil plaintiff the same right to impeach an adversary's testimony that it grants to a civil defendant" is unacceptable and therefore the rule cannot mean what it appears to say as far as civil trials are concerned. After an exhaustive review of the legislative history of the rule, the Court concluded the ambiguity therein was a result of legislative oversight by an almost exclusive focus on criminal trials and criminal defendants when Congress drafted the rule. *See id.* at ——, 109 S.Ct. at 1990–92. That history, leading to the enactment of the rule as law, established that Congress intended only the defendant in a criminal case should be protected from unfair prejudice by the balancing requirement set out in Rule 609(a)(1). *Id.* at ——, 109 S.Ct. at 1992. Accordingly, the Court reasoned, in order to comport with the language, background and legislative history of the rule, the only witness who may demand a balancing of the prejudicial value of a prior conviction against its probative effect is the defendant in a criminal trial. *Id.* Thus, the Court held a judge must "permit impeachment of a civil witness with evidence of prior felony convictions regardless of ensuant unfair prejudice to the witness or the party offering the testimony." *Id.* at ——, 109 S.Ct. at 1993. We are persuaded by the reasoning of the Supreme Court and conclude that the balancing provision in Rule 609 subparagraph (A)(1) should not apply to civil cases in New Mexico.

[3] Another area of controversy with respect to prior conviction impeachment evidence in civil cases, also addressed in *Green,* focuses on the interrelationship between Rule 609 and Rule 403 and whether Rule 609 preempts Rule 403. Federal Rule

---

(1) was punishable by death or imprisonment in excess of one (1) year under the law under which he was convicted, and the court determines that the probative value of admitting this evidence outweighs its prejudicial effect to the defendant, or

(2) involved dishonesty or false statement, regardless of the punishment.

Continued

CASE—*Continued*

of Evidence 403 provides: "Although relevant, evidence may be excluded if its probative value is substantially outweighed by the danger of unfair prejudice, confusion of the issues or misleading the jury, or by considerations of undue delay, waste of time or needless presentation of cumulative evidence."[2] Rule 403 is less restrictive than Rule 609. Evidence may be excluded under Rule 403 only if its probative value is *substantially* outweighed by its prejudicial effect. Moreover, a comparison of the wording of the two rules shows the burden of persuasion differs under them. A party opposing the use of evidence under Rule 403 has the burden of persuading the trial judge to exclude the evidence, whereas under Rule 609 the party seeking the use the evidence has the burden of persuasion.

Several federal courts have used Rule 403 to weigh prejudice and probativeness of impeaching testimony in civil cases to exclude relevant evidence that may be substantially prejudicial to a party. *Donald v. Wilson,* 847 F.2d 1191 (6th Cir.1988); *Shows v. M/V Red Eagle,* 695 F.2d 114 (5th Cir.1983); *Tussel v. Witco Chem. Corp.,* 555 F.Supp. 979 (W.D.Pa.1983). These courts construe Rule 403 as an overriding provision that cuts across the rules of evidence to afford the trial judge a modicum of discretion to exclude a civil witness' unduly prejudicial felony conviction.

In *Green,* the Court concluded that since it is clear that Rule 403 does not modify the mandatory provisions of Rule 609(A)(2) involving crimes of dishonesty or false statement, it strains logic to view Rule 403 as modifying one subsection of Rule 609(A)(1), a specific subsection containing its own balancing provision, but not as modifying the other subsection. *Green,* —— U.S. at ——, 109 S.Ct. at 1992–93.

Rule 609(a) states that impeaching convictions evidence "shall be admitted." With regard to subpart (2), which governs impeachment by [crimes of dishonesty or false statement] it is widely agreed that this imperative coupled with the absence of any balancing language, bars exercise of judicial discretion pursu-

ant to Rule 403. Subpart (1), concerning felonies, is subject to the same mandatory language; accordingly, Rule 403 balancing should not pertain to this subsection either.

Id. at ——, 109 S.Ct. at 1993 (footnotes omitted); *accord Campbell v. Geer,* 831 F.2d 700, 705 (7th Cir.1987) (Rule 403 "was not meant to overlap, supplant, or contradict the policy premises of, more specific rules, such as Rule 609."). In other words, the discretion afforded by Rule 403 does not apply because Rule 609(a)(1) specifically addresses circumstances under which judicial discretion is permitted. The Court thus held that "Rule 609(a)(1)'s exclusion of civil witnesses from its weighing language is a specific command that impeachment of such witnesses be admitted, which overrides a judge's general discretionary authority under Rule 403. *Green,* —— U.S. at ——, 109 S.Ct. at 1993.

Research of New Mexico cases reveals one civil case dealing with evidence of prior convictions for attacking credibility, *Jaramillo v. Fisher Controls Co.,* 102 N.M. 614, 698 P.2d 887 (Ct.App.), *cert. denied,* 102 N.M. 613, 698 P.2d 886 (1985). On cross-examination in *Jaramillo,* plaintiff admitted he had pled guilty to shoplifting, a crime involving dishonesty. The evidence was allowed under Rule 609(A)(2). In affirming the trial court, the appellate court stated the evidence was "proper for the purpose of attacking the credibility of [defendant]," and a conviction of this type of crime bears on credibility. *Id.* at 622, 698 P.2d at 895. Plaintiff also challenged the prior conviction evidence under Rule 403 claiming "the probative nature of the conviction was outweighed by its prejudicial impact." *Id.* Following a brief analysis, the court said there was no abuse of discretion by the trial court to require exclusion of the evidence under Rule 403. *Id.* at 623, 698 P.2d at 896.

A case that is more insightful on whether Rule 609 preempts Rule 403 is *State v. Day,* 91 N.M. 570, 577 P.2d 878 (Ct.App.), *cert. denied,* 91 N.M. 491, 576 P.2d 297 (1978). Although a criminal case, *Day* dis-

---

2. New Mexico's rule of evidence, SCRA 1986,   11–403, is identical.

CASE—*Continued*

cusses generally the interrelationship of Rules 403 and 609. After examining Rule 609(A) as originally adopted in 1973, which lacked the specific balancing requirement in subparagraph (A)(1), the court stated that "Evidence Rule 403 gave the trial court discretion to exclude evidence 'if its probative value is substantially outweighed by the danger of unfair prejudice.'" *Id.* at 574, 577 P.2d at 882. The court thus reasoned Rule 403 was always applicable in deciding on the admissibility of evidence relevant to impeachment. "Evidence admissible under Evidence Rule 609 was subject to exclusion by the trial court under Evidence Rule 403." *Id.*

In 1976 Rule 609 was amended to include the specific reference to a balancing requirement in (A)(1), which conformed the New Mexico rule to the federal evidence rule. *Id.* at 574–75, 577 P.2d at 882–83. The court concluded that Rule 403, which applies to the admission of all evidence, continued to apply to impeachment evidence even with the amendment of Rule 609(A). *Id.* at 576, 577 P.2d at 884. In so concluding, the court opined:

> In resolving the interrelationship of Evidence Rules 403 and 609, the intent of Congress in adopting the federal rules of evidence is not controlling. New Mexico adopted rules of evidence before Congress approved the federal rules. In addition, the variations between the New Mexico and federal rules prevent us from stating that the federal intent was New Mexico's intent.
>
> In our opinion, New Mexico's intent is ascertained by considering *two* New Mexico evidentiary rules.
>
> Our rule, a general one, was that the trial court had discretion in the admission or exclusion of evidence. * * * [T]his general rule is not limited to criminal cases; it applies to any type of case, and all forms of evidence. This general rule of evidence is reflected in Evidence Rule 403.
>
> A second rule, which is a specific application of the general rule, applies to the cross-examination of a witness concerning prior convictions * * *. This specific application [the balancing provision] was

included by the amendment to Evidence Rule (a)(1).

> The amendment which brought the pre-existing specific rule into the rules of evidence cannot be considered as removing the applicability of the general rule [which] has been reaffirmed subsequent to adoption of the amendment. [Emphasis in original.]

Id. at 575–76, 577 P.2d at 883–84 (citations omitted).

[4] It is clear from *Day* that the balancing provision of Rule 403 continues to apply to Rule 609(A)(2). Since we have stated that, based on *Green*, the specific balancing provision in 609(A)(1) is applicable to criminal but not civil cases, we hold that 609(A)(1) evidence is always subject to possible exclusion under Rule 403. We agree with the position espoused in *Day* and decline to follow *Green* on Rule 403.

[5] Employing these principles in the present case, we conclude the prior convictions for purposes of attacking defendant's credibility were admissible. Commercial gambling is a crime punishable by imprisonment in excess of one year. Notwithstanding the admissibility of the prior convictions under Rule 609(A)(1), we must next determine whether the evidence is subject to exclusion under Rule 403. At the appellate level the only question we decide is whether the trial court abused its discretion in permitting this evidence. *Jaramillo*, 102 N.M. at 622, 698 P.2d at 895; *Lucero*, 98 N.M. at 314, 648 P.2d at 353. Abuse of discretion is defined "as a ruling clearly against the logic and effect of the facts and circumstances before the court." *Lucero*, 98 N.M. at 314, 648 P.2d at 353. Credibility of the parties was a key issue in this case. The trial court weighed the probative value of the evidence against its prejudicial effect and determined the evidence should not be excluded. There was no abuse of discretion.

2. *Attorney Fees*

The issue raised by defendant is that the trial court abused its discretion in awarding

Continued

CASE—*Continued*

attorney fees approximately double the amount of the jury verdict.

[6] It is well-settled that, absent statutory authority or rule of court, attorney fees are not recoverable as an item of damages. *Hiatt v. Keil,* 106 N.M. 3, 4, 738 P.2d 121, 122 (1987); *Riggs v. Gardikas,* 78 N.M. 5, 8, 427 P.2d 890, 893 (1967). The attorney's fee section of the legislation on materialmen's liens, NMSA 1978, Section 48–2–14 (Repl.Pamp.1987), provides that the court may allow a reasonable attorney's fee in an action to enforce the liens in the trial and appellate courts. Under this statute, the allowance of attorney fees is discretionary, but the exercise of that discretion must be reasonable when measured against objective standards and criteria. *Ulibarri v. Gee,* 106 N.M. 637, 639, 748 P.2d 10, 12 (1987). "The award of an attorney's fee, like the award of other costs of litigation, is not the same question as the determination of reasonableness of a fee as between the attorney and client * * *." *Id.* Factors that have been considered in determining the reasonableness of attorney fees as between attorney and client include: (1) the time and labor required—the novelty and difficulty of the questions involved and skill required; (2) the fee customarily charged in the locality for similar services; (3) the amount involved and the results obtained; (4) the time limitations imposed by the client or by the circumstances; and (5) the experience, reputation and ability of the lawyer or lawyers performing the services. *Thompson Drilling, Inc. v. Romig,* 105 N.M. 701, 705, 736 P.2d 979, 983 (1987); *see also* SCRA 1986, 16–105 (Repl.Pamp. 1988). We have also stated that time spent and quality of representation are not always dispositive of the amount of attorney fees to be awarded in the successful enforcement of liens. *Ulibarri,* 106 N.M. at 639, 748 P.2d at 12 (net cost to a plaintiff in enforcing a lien that is questionable in merit should be more than where the defense is frivolous); *Fryar v. Johnsen,* 93 N.M. 485, 487, 601 P.2d 718, 720 (1979). For example, when the plaintiff has sued for a small sum clearly owed, then a higher percentage of the award may be reasonable as an attorney's fee. When the sum is large and

the defense is meritorious, then a smaller percentage may be reasonable. *Ulibarri,* 106 N.M. at 639, 748 P.2d at 12.

[7] Under Section 48–2–14, the trial court permits recovery of a "reasonable attorney's fee" by the plaintiff-materialman from the owner. The reasonableness of the fee must be closely scrutinized if the amount is based on the defense of counterclaims and other questions collateral to the enforcement of the lien. *Id.; see Hiatt,* 106 N.M. at 4, 738 P.2d at 122.

[8] In setting attorney fee awards, a trial court must make findings of fact on those factors on which the parties have presented evidence. *Woodson v. Phillips Petroleum Co.,* 102 N.M. 333, 339, 695 P.2d 483, 489 (1985). Without findings of fact and conclusions of law, this court cannot properly perform its reviewing function. *Fryar,* 93 N.M. at 488, 601 P.2d at 721.

In the present case at the hearing on attorney fees, plaintiff's counsel submitted an affidavit and was questioned by defense counsel on the reasonableness of the fees. Defense counsel argues that this case does not involve novel or difficult issues, does not vindicate any important public policy and does not advance any legal principle of pervasive applicability to entitle plaintiff's counsel to a strict percentage fee. Instead, defendant maintains the affidavit is replete with documentation of only a few pleadings prepared, which were amended and edited on numerous occasions; is replete with memoranda done and redone, conferences held again and again; shows trial preparation of 109.5 hours for a fourteen-hour trial; and even seeks reimbursement for mileage from counsel's office two blocks away. Plaintiff's counsel claims that at the hearing defendant had a full opportunity to cross-examine; plaintiff was billed for the time spent on the case based on the firm's hourly rates; defendant had set forth six counterclaims in his answer, which were not dropped until the morning of trial; and the fees charged were reasonable in light of the difficulty of proving the case. The trial court concluded the case was difficult because the veracity of the

CASE—*Continued*

STATE v. MOORE   N. M. **91**
Cite as 782 P.2d 91 (N.M.App. 1989)

two parties involved was crucial. Further, the trial judge stated, "the law is very clear in materialmen's and mechanic's lien type cases, that costs and attorney fees are to be recovered in a case where you are successful, over and above the actual amount of damage principle."

For purposes of an appeal, defense counsel requested the court make findings of fact. In declining to do so, the court said: "Findings of fact and conclusions of law are inappropriate in a jury trial. The jury found the facts and the law is contained in the judgment."

[9] In light of the trial court's failure to make findings of fact and conclusions of law, we must determine if we can properly review the award without such findings or conclusions. While we are mindful that judicial economy is an important goal, especially because of the increase in litigation and appeals of attorney fees, we are hesitant to pick an arbitrary fee without findings and conclusions. Notwithstanding the trial judge's recent departure from the bench, we prefer to remand this case to the trial court to make these findings. We note that the time billed by plaintiff's attorney is not necessarily determinative of the reasonable amount of an award of attorney fees as costs. Moreover, the reasonableness of the fee awarded in this case must be closely scrutinized if based on the defense of the counterclaims. In *Ulibarri*, the award of over $30,000 in attorney fees was not substantiated by the evidence, but the evidence in the record did substantiate the reduced award of $10,000, which we did allow. Unlike *Ulibarri*, the record in the present case is insufficient for us to make the determination without findings and conclusions.

We affirm the jury verdict and remand the case to the district court for a rehearing based on the foregoing considerations. In light of SCRA 1986, 1–063, this rehearing will be a new trial on the issue of the amount of attorney fees to be awarded. *See Pritchard v. Halliburton*, 104 N.M. 102, 717 P.2d 78 (Ct.App.), *cert. denied*, 103 N.M. 798, 715 P.2d 7186216137 (1986). The

782 P.2d—4

parties will bear their own costs for this appeal.

IT IS SO ORDERED.

RANSOM and MONTGOMERY, JJ., concur.

109 N.M. 119

**STATE of New Mexico,
Plaintiff–Appellee,**

v.

**Charles Robert MOORE,
Defendant–Appellant.**

No. 10836.

Court of Appeals of New Mexico.

Aug. 29, 1989.

Certiorari Denied Oct. 18, 1989.

Defendant was convicted in District Court, Lea County, Patrick J. Francoeur, D.J., of aggravated burglary, armed robbery, and false imprisonment, and he appealed. The Court of Appeals, Minzner, J., held that: (1) admission of pistol seized by police and exculpatory statements defendant made to third person was proper; (2) admission of witnesses' in-court identification was proper; (3) remand was necessary to determine whether State's peremptory challenge of only black member of venire was racially motivated; (4) imposition of consecutive sentences of two counts of armed robbery and two counts of false imprisonment was proper; and (5) motion to amend docketing statement was timely.

Conditionally affirmed and remanded.

1. Criminal Law ⇐394.6(4)

Finding that tenant voluntarily disclosed location of pistol to police and voluntarily told them that defendant had given her gun and money which he said he obtained in robbery was supported by evi-

CASE

tion on improper prosecutorial comments only if "their combined effect was so prejudicial as to adversely affect the fundamental nature and impartiality of the proceedings." *Freeman v. State*, 681 P.2d 84, 85 (Okl.Cr.1984), quoting *Cobbs v. State*, 629 P.2d 368, 369 (Okl.Cr.1981). Although the comments by the prosecutor were improper, the error was not so fundamental as to require reversal or modification. This assignment of error is without merit.

We have also examined the various assignments of error contained in the appellant's *pro se* brief, and likewise find them to be without merit.

The judgment and sentence of the District Court is AFFIRMED.

BRETT and BUSSEY, JJ., concur.

Tommy Dean GRIZZLE, Sr. Appellant,

v.

STATE of Oklahoma, Appellee.

No. F–83–338.

Court of Criminal Appeals of Oklahoma.

Oct. 17, 1985.

Defendant was convicted in the District Court, Hughes County, Gordon R. Melson, J., of pointing a weapon at another and cruelty to animals, and he appealed. The Court of Criminal Appeals, Parks, P.J., held that: (1) one is privileged to destroy or injure an animal for purpose of defending himself or third persons against harm threatened by the animal if its actions led him to know or reasonably believe that animal would inflict such harm and destruction or injury was reasonable in view of the gravity of the harm threatened and the person reasonably believed that the harm could only be prevented by immediate destruction or injury of the animal; (2) the trial court's instructions on defense of another were confusing and thus deprived defendant of his instructions on his theory of defense; and (3) the defense opened the door to the State's cross-examination of the defendant on issues of prior fights and whether he had a loaded weapon in his truck.

Affirmed in part and reversed and remanded in part.

Bussey, J., concurred in part and dissented in part with statement.

1. Animals ⟜45

One is privileged to destroy or injure animal for purpose of defending himself or third persons against harm threatened by animal if its action led him to know or reasonably believe that animal would inflict such harm and destruction or injury was reasonable in view of gravity of harm threatened and person reasonably believed harm could be prevented only by immediate destruction or injury of animal. 21 O.S. 1981, § 1685.

2. Animals ⟜45

Kind and amount of force used to defend oneself or third persons against harm threatened by animal should be reasonably proportionate to kind and amount of danger presented by animal's attack for one to be privileged to destroy or injure animal and avoid criminal liability for cruelty to animal. 21 O.S.1981, § 1685.

3. Animals ⟜45

Trial court properly instructed jury on defendant's theory of defense that there was lawful cause for shooting dog by defining "lawful cause" to include killing or destroying of animal in defense of one's person or another person, or one's home or property. 21 O.S.1981, § 1685.

4. Animals ⟜45

Trial court's instructions concerning defense of others in prosecution for cruelty to animal were confusing and deprived defendant of his instructions on his theory of

CASE—Continued

GRIZZLE v. STATE
Okl. **1211**

Cite as 707 P.2d 1210 (Okl.Cr. 1985)

defense that he shot dog while dog was attacking his son. 21 O.S.1981, § 1685.

5. Animals ⚖45

Evidence raised jury issue as to whether defendant was guilty of cruelty to animals in connection with his shooting of dog while it allegedly was attacking defendant's son. 21 O.S.1981, § 1685.

6. Criminal Law ⚖1038.1(4, 5)

Instruction concerning requisite intent and its method of proof were not fundamentally erroneous in prosecution giving rise to conviction for pointing a weapon at another. 21 O.S.1981, § 1279.

7. Criminal Law ⚖728(2), 1037.1(1)

Allegedly erroneous remarks made by prosecutor during closing argument were waived by failure to object and did not constitute fundamental error.

8. Criminal Law ⚖1120(9)

Defendant waived assignment of error challenging admission of photographs of dead dogs into evidence in prosecution for cruelty to animals and pointing weapon at another where photographs were not supplied with appeal record.

9. Witnesses ⚖277(2)

Defendant opened door to cross-examination about whether defendant was carrying loaded firearm in his truck and about his propensity for "getting into fights" by defendant's son's testimony that he struck victim first in order to "settle an old score," and defendant and son both testified that they were at scene of incident giving rise to prosecution for pointing a weapon at another to test fire pistol, even if cross-examination involved commission of other crimes by defendant.

10. Criminal Law ⚖730(13)

Prosecutor's comments during cross-examination of defendant concerning defendant's son's previous conviction for public drunkenness were not prejudicial where defense counsel properly objected, objection was sustained and jury was admonished to disregard question and answer.

11. Criminal Law ⚖824(3)

Defendant waived assignment of error that trial court committed reversible error by failing to instruct on reckless conduct with a pistol as lesser included offense of feloniously pointing a firearm where defense counsel did not offer requested instructions on issues until after jury had been instructed and after closing arguments of prosecution.

An appeal from the District Court of Hughes County; Gordon R. Melson, District Judge.

Tommy Dean Grizzle, appellant, was convicted of Pointing a Weapon at Another and Cruelty to Animals, in the District Court of Hughes County, Case No. CRF-82-18, sentenced to a $500 fine on Count I, and to one (1) year in the county jail on Count II, and appeals. The conviction for the offense of Cruelty to Animals is REVERSED and REMANDED for a new trial, and the conviction for the offense of Pointing a Weapon at Another is AFFIRMED.

Mark H. Barrett, Sp. Counsel, Appellant Public Defender System, Norman, for appellant.

Michael C. Turpen, Atty. Gen., William H. Luker, Asst. Atty. Gen., Oklahoma City, for appellee.

OPINION

PARKS, Presiding Judge:

The appellant, Tommy Dean Grizzle, Sr., was tried in the District Court of Hughes County, Case No. CRF-82-18, for the offenses of Feloniously Pointing a Firearm, 21 O.S. 1981, § 1289.16, and Cruelty to Animals, 21 O.S.1981, § 1685. The jury found appellant guilty of the lesser included offense of Pointing a Weapon at Another, 21 O.S. 1981, § 1279, as well as guilty of Cruelty to Animals. Appellant was sentenced to imprisonment of one year in the county jail for each offense, the terms to run consecutively.

At approximately 1:30 p.m. on the afternoon of March 14, 1982, Everett Chronister

Continued

CASE—*Continued*

went to the Holdenville Lake to join his family and friends for a picnic. He brought along his eleven month old German Shepherd puppy. Though normally kept on a leash, the dog was allowed to run loose while at the lake.

Around 5:00 p.m., the group was unexpectedly joined by appellant and his son. Appellant was at the lake to test a new weapon, a .25 caliber automatic pistol, that he had just purchased. Appellant pulled into the area where the picnic was located because Robert Merriman, a friend and relative of Chronister, waved him over. After Chronister offered appellant's son a beer, the latter, for no apparent reason, hit Chronister on the side of the head. The two men began fighting. As the combatants wrestled on the ground, Chronister's dog came to the aid of its master, and began biting the leg of young Grizzle. At this point, appellant shot the dog four times with his .25 caliber pistol, killing it.

According to Chronister, appellant shot over the heads of the wrestling men, and never attempted to separate the dog from young Grizzle. Appellant testified that he tried repeatedly to keep the dog away and opened fire only after the dog continued to attack both him and his son.

Subsequent to the shooting, appellant allowed his son to beat Chronister, while pointing the weapon at him. Chronister was threatened if he tried to defend himself. Appellant asserts that he did not intentionally point the pistol at anyone, rather he only turned around while holstering the weapon. Appellant also claims that he did not make any threats on Chronister, but only wanted to make sure that there was a fair fight.

Tommy Grizzle, Jr. stated that the dog chewed through his socks at the ankle. However, he neither sought medical attention, nor reported the bites to the authorities until after the arrest of himself and his father two days later. It was only then that the Sheriff's office was made aware of the bites.

I.

Appellant's first three assignments of error deal with a question of first impression in our jurisdiction. The issue is to what extent is one entitled to defend oneself or another from the attack of an animal, so as to avoid criminal liability for Cruelty to Animals under 21 O.S. 1981, § 1685.

We agree with the appellant that the trial court's instructions were erroneous. Though portions of the instructions were proper, the instructions as a whole were confusing so as to deny appellant his fundamental right to instructions on his theory of defense. *Neal v. State,* 597 P.2d 334 (Okl.Cr.1979).

[1, 2] Oklahoma has no case law defining when a person may lawfully kill an animal and avoid criminal liability under 21 O.S.1981, § 1685. We hold today, therefore, that one is "privileged to destroy [or injure] an animal for the purpose of defending himself or third persons against harm threatened by the animal, (a) if its actions led him to know or reasonably believe that the animal would inflict such harm and (b) the destruction [or injury] was reasonable in view of the gravity of the harm threatened, and (c) the person reasonably believed the harm could only be prevented by immediate destruction [or injury] of the animal." *Devincenzi v. Faulkner,* 174 Cal. App.2d 250, 344 P.2d 322, 325 (1959). *See also State v. Wrobel,* 3 Conn.Cir. 57, 207 A.2d 280 (1964). The kind of and amount of force, however, should be reasonably proportionate to the kind and amount of danger presented by the animal's attack. *Accord State v. Wrobel, supra.* Appellant's theory of defense is based upon this rule. In essence, he asserts that if one is reasonably defending himself or another from the attack of an animal, the injury to the animal is not so cruel and malicious as to be within the scope of 21 O.S.1981, § 1685. Appellant contends that the shooting of this dog was not unreasonable under the circumstances.

[3] The trial court properly instructed the jury on appellant's theory of defense that there was lawful cause for shooting

CASE—*Continued*

GRIZZLE v. STATE   Okl. **1213**
Cite as 707 P.2d 1210 (Okl.Cr. 1985)

the dog. The trial court defined "lawful cause" in Jury Instruction No. 9 to include "the killing or destroying of an animal in defense of one's person, or another person, or one's home or property." It was noted further in Jury Instruction No. 10 that the appellant put on evidence that at the time of the alleged incident, he was acting in lawful defense of another.

[4] However, the trial court confused the jury when it rendered its instructions concerning the defense of others. The trial court in Jury Instructions No.'s 12–14, instructed the jury that the defense of another was not available to the defendant "when the person on whose behalf the defendant intervened was the aggressor, no matter how great the danger to personal security becomes during the altercation unless the right of defense of another is reestablished." The trial court then explained when the defense of another might be reestablished.

In its deliberations, the jury could construe the instructions to mean that though there was lawful cause for shooting the dog, the defense is still not available if the defendant could not come to the aid of another (person). This construction is not only incorrect, but it is also confusing in such manner to deprive the appellant of his instructions on his theory of defense. Even if it were assumed that there was no more a right to repel an attacking dog than to repel an attacking person, the instructions on defense of another were prejudicially erroneous because it would be impossible for the jury to determine whether the "aggressor" were to be determined as between Grizzle, Jr. and Chronister or as between the dog and Grizzle Jr. It is well established under Oklahoma Law that the trial court is under a duty to give instructions concerning the defendant's theory of defense when there is evidence in the record to support it, and that such instruction is a fundamental right. *Smith v. State*, 485 P.2d 771, 773–74, (Okl.Cr.1971).

See also Hall v. State, 316 P.2d 620 (Okl. Cr.1957). In the instant case, the appellant presented sufficient evidence to warrant instructions on his theory of defense, but was denied that right when the trial court gave confusing instructions. *Neal v. State, supra* at 338. We accordingly reverse the conviction for "cruelty to animals," and remand for a new trial.

[5] In this regard, appellant also has maintained that insufficient evidence was presented to show appellant guilty of Cruelty to Animals. We do not agree. Appellant shot Chronister's dog, and the evidence showed the killing was not accidental. A *prima facie* case was established by the prosecution. *See Stockbridge v. Territory*, 15 Okl. 167, 79 P. 753 (1905). Whether the appellant acted reasonably in killing the dog will be a question of fact for the jury to resolve on retrial. *See Renfro v. State*, 607 P.2d 703, 705 (Okl.Cr.1980). *See also Hunt v. State*, 601 P.2d 464 (Okl. Cr.1979) *cert. denied* 446 U.S. 969, 100 S.Ct. 2951, 64 L.Ed.2d 830 (1980).

II.

[6] Appellant raises three assignments of error concerning his conviction on Count I—Pointing a Weapon at Another. In proposition IV of his brief, appellant alleges that the trial court improperly instructed the jury concerning the requisite intent required and its method of proof. Review of the entire record before this Court discloses no evidence that appellant requested jury instructions, nor objected to those utilized by the trial court. We find that instructions were not fundamentally erroneous, and this assignment of error is without merit. *Maghe v. State*, 620 P.2d 433, 436 (Okl.Cr.1980); and *Kelsey v. State*, 569 P.2d 1028 (Okl.Cr.1977).

[7, 8] In his fifth assignment of error, appellant asserts that the prosecutor's conduct during closing argument was improper and warrants reversal.[1] This Court

---

1. Appellant makes this proposition of error applicable to both counts I and II of his conviction. Since we have reversed the conviction for

Cruelty to Animals on other grounds, we reach this issue only insofar as it relates to Count I, Pointing a Weapon at Another.

Continued

CASE—*Continued*

notes that at no time were any objections made to the prosecutor's comments during the course of closing arguments. It is well settled that erroneous remarks made by the prosecutor are waived if they are not objected to at the time that they are made, and do not constitute fundamental error. *See Tahdooahnippah v. State*, 610 P.2d 808, 810 (Okl.Cr.1980). Appellant contends further that photographs of the dead dog admitted into evidence were prejudicial because there was no issue for which they were relevant. Review of the original record and the transcripts discloses that these photographs have not been supplied to this Court with the rest of the appeal record. Counsel for the appellant has a duty to ensure that sufficient record is supplied to the Court to determine the issues raised. Failure to do so results in waiver of the error. *Ferguson v. State*, 645 P.2d 1021 (Okl.Cr.1982); *Martinez v. State*, 569 P.2d 497 (Okl.Cr.1977). Since the photographs in question have not been supplied to this Court, this assignment of error is waived.

[9] Appellant further asserts that the prosecutor's line of questioning on cross-examination of both himself and his son was improper and prejudicial. On cross-examination, the prosecutor inquired into whether or not appellant was carrying a loaded firearm in his truck, and whether he knew that such action was a felony. The defense counsel objected to the line of questioning, and the objection was sustained. The prosecutor also inquired into appellant's propensity for "getting into fights." An objection was made and overruled by the trial judge.

The subject of the prior fights and the carrying of the pistol in the truck had been brought up on direct examination by the appellant. Appellant's son testified that he struck Chronister first, in order to settle an old score. Appellant testified, as did his son, that they went to the lake to test fire appellant's .25 caliber pistol, which he acquired a few days previously.

We therefore hold that the defense opened the door to the State's cross-examination on the issues of prior fights and the .25 caliber pistol. Where the prosecutor's remarks or questions are on matters initially raised by the defense, they will generally not be grounds for reversal. *Wacoche v. State*, 644 P.2d 568, 573 (Okl. Cr.1982). *See* 12 O.S. 1981, § 2611(C). Counsel may generally cross-examine a witness on all matters covered during direct examination. Where the appellant, as in this case, voluntarily takes the witness stand in his own defense, the prosecuting attorney has the right to cross-examine him with the same latitude as any other witness. This rule also applies when the subject matter of cross-examination involves the commission of other crimes by the appellant. *Fite v. State*, 526 P.2d 956, 959 (Okl.Cr.1974). *See Maynard v. State*, 625 P.2d 111, 113 (Okl.Cr.1981).

[10] The prosecution also made comments on cross-examination concerning the younger Grizzle's previous conviction for public drunk. Defense counsel properly objected, and the objection was sustained. The trial judge admonished the jury to disregard the question and answer. Though such comment may not have been proper, there is no apparent prejudice to the appellant. Therefore, this assignment is without merit.

[11] In his seventh assignment of error, appellant contends the trial court committed reversible error by failing to instruct, as to Count I, on the lesser included offense of Reckless Conduct with a Pistol. Close scrutiny of the trial record and transcript reveal that defense counsel did not timely offer a requested instruction on these issues, nor object to the State's offerings. Any objections to the trial judge's instructions and any requested instructions should be made to the trial court prior to the time they are read to the jury. *Wyatt v. State*, 491 P.2d 1098, 1104 (Okl.Cr.1971) (modified on other grounds). In the instant case, however, counsel for the defense offered the requested instruction following the reading of the instructions to the jury, and the closing arguments of the prosecution. Consequently, appellant's request for

CASE—*Continued*

ROWLAND v. STATE   Okl. **1215**

Cite as 707 P.2d 1215 (Okl.Cr. 1985)

the instruction in question was not timely, and therefore this assignment of error has been waived.

Accordingly, the conviction for the offense of Cruelty to Animals is REVERSED and REMANDED for a new trial consistent with this opinion. The conviction for the offense of Pointing a Weapon is hereby AFFIRMED.

BRETT, J., concurs.

BUSSEY, J., concurs in part, dissents in part.

BUSSEY, Judge, concurring in part, dissenting in part.

While I agree that the judgment and sentence for the offense of Feloniously Pointing a Firearm should be affirmed, I am of the opinion that the instructions given concerning the offense of Cruelty to Animals were not so erroneous and confusing as to require a reversal of the conviction of that crime.

Cleatius Wilson ROWLAND, Appellant,

v.

STATE of Oklahoma, Appellee.

No. F–82–749.

Court of Criminal Appeals of Oklahoma.

Oct. 22, 1985.

Defendant was convicted in the District Court, Mayes County, Jess B. Clanton, Jr., Associate Judge, of knowingly permitting cultivation of marijuana, and he appealed. The Court of Criminal Appeals, Brett, J., held that punishment arrived at by jury was the result of a quotient verdict necessitating new trial.

Reversed and remanded.

Bussey, J., dissented.

Criminal Law ⟜866, 1175

Punishment in prosecution for knowingly and feloniously permitting cultivation and production of wild growing of marijuana was the result of improper quotient verdict necessitating reversal for new trial where jurors put down on piece of paper the time that each juror felt defendant should be given, added those figures together, and divided them to get an average. 22 O.S.1981, § 952; 63 O.S.1981, § 2–509.

An appeal from the District Court of Mayes County; Jess B. Clanton, Jr., Associate District Judge.

CLEATIUS WILSON ROWLAND, appellant, was convicted of Knowingly Permitting the Cultivation of Marijuana, in the District Court of Mayes County, Case No. CRF–81–115, was sentenced to a $1,000 fine and two years' imprisonment, and he appeals. REVERSED and REMANDED for a New Trial.

Thomas G. Smith, Jr., Asst. Appellate Public Defender, Norman, for appellant.

Michael C. Turpen, Atty. Gen., Thomas J. Spencer, Asst. Atty. Gen., Oklahoma City, for appellee.

OPINION

BRETT, Judge:

The appellant, Cleatius Wilson Rowland, was charged with Knowingly and Feloniously Permitting the Cultivation, Production of Wild Growing of Marijuana in violation of 63 O.S.1981, § 2–509, in Mayes County District Court, Case No. CRF–81–115. The jury returned a verdict of guilty and set punishment at two years' imprisonment plus a $1,000 fine. The trial court suspended the fine because of the appellant's indigency and set the sentence in accordance with the jury's verdict. From this judgment and sentence, the appellant appeals.

As the case was submitted to the jury by the trial court, the jury was instructed not to arrive at a quotient verdict: "You must

CASE

168 N.C.   **244 SOUTH EASTERN REPORTER, 2d SERIES**

36 N.C.App. 354

STATE of North Carolina

v.

Charles SIMMONS.

No. 7713SC926.

Court of Appeals of North Carolina.

May 16, 1978.

Defendant was convicted in Superior Court, Columbus County, Donald L. Smith, J., of unlawfully, willfully, and wantonly killing a dog, and he appealed. The Court of Appeals, Morris, J., held that defendant was not entitled to an instruction with respect to self-defense where there was no evidence in the record that the dog was attacking defendant or even threatening to attack or doing anything which would make a reasonable person think he was about to attack, where defendant did not testify that he thought the dog was going to attack, and where the only evidence with respect to the nature of the dog was that he was gentle and had never bitten anyone.

No error.

Animals ⊂⟩45

In prosecution for unlawfully, willfully, and wantonly killing dog, defendant was not entitled to instruction on self-defense where only evidence with respect to nature of dog was that he was gentle and had never bitten anyone, where there was no evidence that defendant thought dog was vicious, that dog was attacking defendant or even threatening to attack, or doing anything which would make reasonable person think he was about to attack, and where defendant did not testify that he thought dog was going to attack.

———

Defendant was tried in District Court under a warrant charging that he "unlawfully, willfully, and wantonly did cruelly overdrive, mutilate and kill a dog, the property of Tylon V. Mills". He was convicted in District Court and appealed to Superior

Court. There he was convicted by the jury and appeals from the judgment entered on the verdict.

His only argument on appeal is that the court failed to instruct the jury with respect to self-defense. Such facts as are necessary for decision are set out in the opinion.

Atty. Gen. Rufus L. Edmisten by Asst. Atty. Gen. Archie W. Anders, Raleigh, for the State.

Ray H. Walton, Southport, for defendant-appellant.

MORRIS, Judge.

The statute under which defendant was charged is G.S. 14–360 which provides, in pertinent part:

"If any person shall willfully . . . kill . . . ., any useful beast, fowl or animal, every such offender shall for every such offense be guilty of a misdemeanor punishable by a fine not to exceed five hundred dollars ($500.00), imprisonment for not more than six months, or both. . . . "

The killing of a dog, the property of another, without justification, has long been a criminal offense in this State. *See State v. Latham,* 35 N.C. 33 (1851). In *State v. Smith,* 156 N.C. 628, 72 S.E. 321 (1911), the Court had before it on appeal a conviction for willfully killing a dog, the property of the prosecutor. The statute was substantially the same. The Court said: It would be vain and unprofitable to discuss, for the purpose of deciding, that a dog is a living creature within the meaning of Revisal, sec. 3299 [now G.S. 14–360] under which the indictment was drawn and presented to the grand jury." *Id.* at 629, 72 S.E. at 321. The Court discussed cases decided prior to the statute which had recognized that a dog is property and said:

"The right to slay him cannot be justified merely by the baseness of his nature, but it is founded upon the natural right to

CASE—*Continued*

STATE v. SIMMONS   N. C. **169**

Cite as 244 S.E.2d 168

protect person or property. He has the good-will of mankind because of his friendship and loyalty, which are such marked traits of his character that they have been touchingly portrayed both in song and story. Why, then, should he be declared an outlaw and a nuisance, and forfeit his life without any sufficient cause? This was never the law. Neither at the common law nor since the passage of our present statute prohibiting cruelty to animals can a dog be killed for the commission of any slight or trival [sic] offense (*S. v. Neal,* 120 N.C. 613, 614, 27 S.E. 81); nor to redress past grievances (*Morse v. Nixon, supra* [51 N.C. 293]). As said by *Chief Justice Pearson* in the last cited case: 'It may be the killing will be justified by proving that the danger was imminent making it necessary "then and there" to kill the hog in order to save the life of the chicken, or prevent great bodily harm.' " *Id.* at 631, 72 S.E. at 322.

And the Court concluded:

"It is not the dog's predatory habits, nor his past transgressions, nor his reputation, however bad, but the doctrine of self-defense, whether of person or property, that gives the right to kill." *Id.* at 635, 72 S.E. at 324.

When these principles are applied to the case before us, it becomes necessary to determine from the evidence whether the issue of self-defense should have been presented to the jury.

There is no dispute about the fact that the prosecuting witness and defendant's brother were having a dispute over some land and, on the day in question, the two were fighting at a point on the land in dispute. Defendant, according to his testimony, was asked to go "down there" by his sister-in-law, wife of the person who was fighting with the prosecuting witness at the time of the shooting. The State's evidence was that when he saw defendant, he, the prosecuting witness was on the ground, and defendant's brother was beating and kicking him. Defendant exited from a vehicle carrying a "long-type" firearm and was running in the direction of the fight. De-

fendant stopped and pointed the firearm in the direction of prosecuting witness. His brother then stopped the beating and hollered to defendant to "kill them dogs". Defendant was then "some 50 yards plus" from where prosecuting witness was. Defendant called the dogs, and they started toward him. When they got some distance from him, they turned and started circling away from him, and as they turned, defendant shot and killed the dog named Silver. The dog got no closer to defendant than 40 yards.

Defendant testified that when he got to the point where he could see around the hedgerow, he saw two men in the northeast corner of the field. One was on his knees and appeared to have his hands on the ground. The other one "seemed to have his hand up on his head and his right arm holding it up in the air." He never, on that day, got any closer to that corner of the field than approximately 150 yards. He did not shoot the dog. "There is a difference in shooting and shooting at. I shot to turn the dogs off of me. I said I shot to turn the dogs off of me." At that time he was from 200 to 250 yards from the two men. The dogs were coming up beside the hedgerow from down in the southeast corner of the field. There were two "big old" dogs. He had never seen them before and did not know whose they were. He shot four times. "As to whether those dogs got anywhere near me, they were just about like from here to that deputy sheriff standing over there and were coming right at me. That was as close as they got to me because I shot at them. I did not shoot right at them. I shot in front of them in the ground."

The court had placed in the record the following statement:

"In the instructions to the jury the court is not going to charge on the defendant's right to kill a dog in protecting himself, there being no evidence that the defendant was under attack, but rather, the only evidence is that the dogs were proceeding in his direction."

Continued

CASE—*Continued*

We agree with the court. There is no evidence in the record that the dogs, or either of them, were attacking defendant or even threatening to attack, or doing anything which would make a reasonable person think they were about to attack. Nor does defendant testify that he thought they were going to attack. There is absolutely no evidence that the dogs were ferocious or vicious or that either of them had ever caused any trouble whatever. The only evidence with respect to the nature of the dog which was killed was that he was gentle and had never bitten anyone. There is no evidence that the defendant thought the dog was vicious. He said he had never seen the dogs before and did not know to whom they belonged.

The court instructed the jury that the State would have to prove, beyond a reasonable doubt, that the defendant shot a dog belonging to the prosecuting witness; that, in so doing, the defendant acted willfully and needlessly; that "the shot, if any, proximately caused the dog's death"; and the jury would have to find all these elements before they could find the defendant guilty. Under the evidence in this case, defendant was not entitled to more.

No error.

MARTIN and ARNOLD, JJ., concur.

36 N.C.App. 358

STATE of North Carolina

v.

John Leslie HEISER, Sr.

No. 7714SC1030.

Court of Appeals of North Carolina.

May 16, 1978.

Defendant was convicted in Superior Court, Durham County, Henry A. McKin-non, Jr., J., of child abuse, and he appealed. The Court of Appeals, Hedrick, J., held that: (1) where doctor at child care center who was familiar with medical records testified that entries in such records were made by physician as child was examined and that he recognized handwriting of physician who prepared record, there was sufficient basis for admission of medical record prepared during examination of defendant's son; (2) where there was inconsistency in testimony of defendant's wife as to approximate date when child fell from bed and judge intervened in cross-examination of witness to ask her if fall was few weeks or 3½ months prior to alleged child abuse incident, judge's questioning was for purpose of clarifying testimony and was not improper expression of opinion, and (3) when trial court's instruction to jury that it was not essential for State to prove exact date of incidents of alleged child abuse was taken in conjunction with sustaining of objection with respect to dates in complaint in earlier civil action for custody of minor children, the court had not put itself in position of not allowing defendant to cross-examine witness with respect to date of alleged child abuse occurrences.

No error.

1. Criminal Law ☞444

Proper foundation for admission of hospital and medical records under business records exception to hearsay rule consists of testimony by witness familiar with records and system under which they were made that the record is authentic and that it was prepared at or near to the time of the event recorded by a person having personal knowledge of the event.

2. Criminal Law ☞444

Testimony of child care center physician, who was familiar with medical records, that entries in such records were made by physician as child was examined and that he recognized handwriting of physician who prepared record constituted sufficient basis, in prosecution for child abuse, for

CASE

SMITH v. PALACE TRANSP. CO.   87
253 N.Y.S.   **Mun. Ct.**

(142 Misc. Rep. 93)

SMITH v. PALACE TRANSP. CO., Inc.

Municipal Court of City of New York, Borough of Manhattan, Seventh District.

Oct. 19, 1931.

1. Automobiles ☞214.

To release young dog from leash or muzzle on street is not in itself negligence, as respects owner's right to recover for killing of dog by automobile.

2. Animals ☞44.

Ordinance requiring leashing and muzzling of dogs on streets was adopted to protect public from attack by dogs, not to protect dogs from assault by public.

3. Automobiles ☞214.

As respects owner's right to recover for killing of dog by automobile, standard of prudence marking conduct of average careful creature cannot be exacted.

4. Animals ☞1.

A live dog is personal property.

5. Animals ☞44.

As respects damages for killing of dog, its value is governed by type, traits, and pedigree, but owner's feeling therefor cannot be recognized as element.

In this connection, what one pays for property is of import in appraising its value, though not necessarily controlling.

Action by William Smith against the Palace Transportation Company, Inc.

Judgment for plaintiff.

A. Spencer Feld, of New York City (Samuel J. S. Feld, of New York City, of counsel), for plaintiff.

A. Bertram Samuels, of New York City (David F. Pisik, of New York City, of counsel), for defendant.

DAVID C. LEWIS, J.

Man's attachment for the dog is of old standing.

☞For other cases see same topic & KEY-NUMBER in all Key-Numbered Digests & Indexes

Continued

CASE—*Continued*

88   253 NEW YORK SUPPLEMENT
Mun. Ct.

The auto has driven the horse from the highway, but even in this mechanical age the dog is no stranger on our streets.

Plaintiff was the owner of a five months old fox terrier. One day his wife brought the pup to the streets. The dog ran or romped to the children, and then, while in the 179th street roadway, close to the north curb, a taxi south-bound on Pinehurst avenue, after making a left turn, lay the little dog lifeless on the highway.

At this locality (179th street and Pinehurst avenue), the cross-street was not then a much-traveled thoroughfare. The construction of the George Washington Bridge had cut off south-bound traffic on Pinehurst avenue, below 179th street; and obstructions in the highway had narrowed the lane of traffic going east. These facts and features in themselves called for cautious driving.

[1, 2] To take a pup from the household to the highway is a legitimate errand. To release it of its leash or muzzle is not in itself negligence. The ordinances requiring these precautions manifestly were adopted to protect the public from attack by the dog, not to protect the dog from assault by the public. New York Code of Ordinances, c. 17, art. 1, § 16; c. 20, art. 2, § 17.

[3] Naturally, one cannot exact or expect of a dumb animal that standard of prudence that marks the conduct of the average careful creature.

Aside from the question of negligence and contributory negligence, there is presented the question of damages.

[4, 5] A live dog is personal property. Its value is governed by the type and traits and pedigree of the dog. What one pays for property is of import in appraising its value, though not necessarily controlling.. While one's feelings for a dog constitute a sentiment which we are inclined to value, it is not recognized as an element of damage.

Judgment for the plaintiff for $75. Ten days' stay.

CASE

FLECK v. RUSSELL   (Or.)   883
(269 P.)

FLECK v. RUSSELL.

Supreme Court of Oregon. July 31, 1928.

**1. Animals ⚖═52—Statute authorizes game
warden to kill dog only when chasing game
animal; "at such time" (Laws 1921, p. 267,
§ 14).**

Laws 1921, p. 267, § 14. providing that a
dog running game animals may be killed "at
such time" by a game warden, authorizes the
killing of the dog only at the time of its offense.

[Ed. Note.—For other definitions, see Words
and Phrases, Second Series, At Such Time.]

**2. Animals ⚖═52—Statute held not to author-
ize killing of unlicensed dog chasing game,
in view of its age at last time for taking out
license (Laws 1921, p. 267, § 14; Laws 1925,
p. 462, § 1, amending Or. L. § 9367).**

Laws 1921, p. 267, § 14, providing that a
dog running game animals, if not wearing a
collar with license number thereon in compliance with Or. L. § 9367, may be killed by a
game warden, in view of Laws 1925, p. 462, § 1,
amending said section 9367, *held* not to authorize killing a dog which, by reason of being less
than eight months old on March 1st of the year
of its offense, did not require a license for that
year.

Department 1.

Appeal from Circuit Court, Tillamook
County; Geo. R. Bagley, Judge.

Action by Charles Fleck against George
Russell. Judgment for plaintiff, and defendant appeals. Affirmed.

September 6, 1926, the plaintiff owned a
dog, which his complaint alleges was worth
$500. On that day the defendant, who was
a deputy game warden, shot and killed it. The
answer in justification of defendant's act alleges that September 5, 1926, one S. R. Pollock discovered this dog "running, chasing,
and following upon the tracks of a deer in
the fields, woodlands, and bush lands" of this
state; that Pollock communicated with the
defendant, and the latter instructed his informant to take the dog into custody and
hold it for the defendant. The answer alleges
that Pollock complied with this request, and
that the following day the defendant called
for the dog and received it; later in that day
the defendant shot and killed it. The plaintiff demurred to this new matter; the demurrer was sustained. Upon the trial, the
defendant made an offer to prove these allegations; the offer was rejected. From a
judgment for the plaintiff in the sum of $250,
the defendant appeals.

J. B. Hosford, of Salem (I. H. Van Winkle,
of Salem, and L. F. Callahan, of Yakima,
Wash., on the brief), for appellant.
Geo. P. Winslow, of Tillamook (Botts &
Winslow, of Tillamook, on the brief), for re-
spondent.

ROSSMAN, J. (after stating the facts as
above). Chapter 153, § 14, 1921 Session Laws,
provides:

"Any dog or dogs running deer or other game
animals in any of the fields, woodland, brush
land or other territory inhabited by deer. or
following upon the track of any game animals
of the state, are hereby declared a public nuisance if such dog or dogs are not wearing a
leather collar with a license number thereon in
compliance with section 9367, Oregon Laws,
and may be killed at such time by any game
warden or other person intrusted with the enforcement of the game laws of Oregon."

[1] The plaintiff contends that the words,
"may be killed at such time by any game
warden," imply that the game warden must
have seen the dog offend in the prohibited
manner, and that his execution shall then
take place. The defendant submits that these
words do not limit his authority to the time
of the offense, but empower him to execute
upon information imparted to him by others.

The dog days seem to be here; gradually
this faithful friend of man has won his way
upwards. In the early days of the common
law, he experienced difficulty in convincing
the courts that he possessed the capacity of
being property; but, when he won this victory, he was not content, but insisted that he
was capable of becoming the subject-matter
of a larceny charge; many statutes to-day so
recognize. But the dog's victory has now become so complete that we find in the reports
of the appellate courts many decisions affirming the convictions of those who needlessly
took the life of a dog. The words of the statute before us seem clear; to hold that the
game warden's authority is limited to "such
time" as the offense occurs does not suspend
these words upon the bare legislative fiat and
deprive them of the support of reason. The
Legislature very properly may have believed
that a dog's life should depend upon something more substantial than the hearsay information gathered by a deputy game warden,
perhaps at a time when the informant's recollection suffered by the passage of time.
Since there is substantial reason to support
the plain words of the statute, there is no
occasion for construction; we accept the
statute as we find it.

[2] It will be observed from the portion of
the act which we have quoted that the game
warden is authorized to deal with unlicensed
dogs only in this summary manner. Chapter
254, 1925 Session Laws (section 1, amending
Or. L. § 9367) provides:

"Every person owning or keeping any dog
over the age of eight months within the state
of Oregon shall, not later than March 1 of each
year * * * procure from the county clerk
* * * a license for such dog. * * *"

The court received evidence that the dog
was not quite a year old when the defendant

⚖═For other cases see same topic and KEY-NUMBER in all Key-Numbered Digests and Indexes

Continued

CASE—*Continued*

884   (Or.)   **269 PACIFIC REPORTER**

killed it, and that its birth occurred September 19, 1925. The answer alleged on information and belief that the dog was about two years old; the defendant made on offer of proof to this effect, which was rejected. This was followed by some discussion between the judge and counsel, and finally in the instructions to the jury we find:

"It is uncontradicted in this case that the dog was twelve months old on September 19, 1926, and therefore it was not necessary for plaintiff to have procured a license for such dog between January 1, and March 1, 1926, or for the year 1926 at all."

No exception was taken to this instruction. Such being the case, the defendant took the life of a dog whose death the statute had not decreed. Further, the statute, as we have seen, authorized the defendant to kill dogs only at the time of their offenses; hence the defendant's alleged justification was insufficient.

Finding no error in the record, the judgment of the circuit court is affirmed.

RAND, C. J., and COSHOW and Mc-BRIDE, JJ., concur.

STATE v. BRAZELL.

Supreme Court of Oregon.   July 31, 1928.

1. Infants ⬅20—Adult male, who practices masturbation on person of boy, commits act of sexual perversity (Or. L. § 2099).

Male person over 21, who practices masturbation on person of boy, is guilty of sexual perversity, within meaning of Or. L. § 2099.

2. Criminal law ⬅511(3)—Evidence corroborating testimony of accomplice may be circumstantial (Or. L. § 1540).

Evidence necessary to corroborate testimony of accomplice, under Or. L. § 1540, need not be direct and positive, but may be circumstantial in character.

3. Criminal law ⬅753(2)—Question of law arises on motion for directed verdict of acquittal only where there is no evidence tending to show defendant's guilt.

Question of law arises on motion for directed verdict of acquittal only where there is no evidence tending to connect defendant with commission of the crime.

4. Criminal law ⬅511(3)—Testimony of accomplice held sufficiently corroborated in prosecution for sexual perversity by performing masturbation on boy (Or. L. §§ 1540, 2099).

In prosecution under Or. L. § 2099, for sexual perversity, alleged to have been committed by performing masturbation on boy, testimony of accomplice *held* sufficiently corroborated, under section 1540, by testimony that defendant and boy with whom he was intimate slept together, and testimony as to squeaking of bed.

In Bank.

Appeal from Circuit Court, Multnomah County; Arlie G. Walker, Judge.

Clarence Brazell was convicted of having committed an act of sexual perversity, and he appeals. Affirmed.

Wm. G. Smith and E. F. Bernard, both of Portland (Collier, Collier & Bernard, of Portland, on the brief), for appellant.

George Mowry and Leon Behrman, Deputy Dist. Attys., both of Portland (Stanley Myers, Dist. Atty., and John Mowry, Deputy Dist. Atty., both of Portland, on the brief), for the State.

BELT, J. [1] Defendant was convicted, under section 2099, Or. L., of having committed an act of sexual perversity. The indictment, so far as material, is as follows:

"The said Clarence Brazell, on the 3d day of January, A. D. 1928, in the county of Multnomah and state of Oregon, then and there being, did then and there unlawfully and feloniously commit an act of sexual perversity with one Gordon Erickson, also known as Gordon Franks, who was then and there a male person over the age of 14 years and under the age of 18 years, by then and there willfully, knowingly, and intentionally placing the hands of him, the said Clarence Brazell, who was then and there a male person over the age of 21 years, upon the private parts of the said Gordon Erickson, also known as Gordon Franks, and by then and there willfully, knowingly, and intentionally performing, practicing, and completing an act of masturbation upon the said private parts of the said Gordon Erickson, also known as Gordon Franks."

There is no merit in the contention that the indictment is vulnerable to demurrer. It was certainly within the power of the Legislature to declare acts of sexual perversity criminal. Practicing masturbation by a man upon a boy is an act of sexual perversity, within the ordinary meaning and acceptation of the words.

[2-4] The serious question on appeal is whether the defendant was convicted on the uncorroborated testimony of an accomplice. We inquire whether there was any evidence, independent of that of the accomplice, which, in the language of section 1540, Or. L., tends to connect the defendant with the commission of the crime alleged in the indictment. It need not be direct and positive, but may be circumstantial in character. Such crimes are ordinarily not committed where they can be observed. The jury is permitted to draw reasonable inferences from facts proven. The weight of the corroborating evidence is, of course, for the jury. It is only when there is no evidence tending to connect the defend-

⬅For other cases see same topic and KEY-NUMBER in all Key-Numbered Digests and Indexes

CASE

When subjected to this analysis the decision of the District Court does not collide with our prior decisions. Hence, no jurisdictional conflict arises.

The writ is discharged.

It is so ordered.

THOMAS, Acting C. J., and ROBERTS, O'CONNELL and CALDWELL, JJ., concur.

Phyllis LA PORTE, Petitioner,

v.

ASSOCIATED INDEPENDENTS, INC., a Florida corporation, Respondent.

No. 33167.

Supreme Court of Florida.

April 3, 1964.

Rehearing Denied May 13, 1964.

Action against an employer for malicious killing of plaintiff's pet dog through the wrongful act of its employee, a garbage collector. The Court of Record for Broward County, Raymond J. Hare, J., entered judgment for plaintiff and employer appealed. The District Court of Appeal, Kanner, Acting C. J., 158 So.2d 557, reversed and remanded for new trial on issue of damages, and certiorari was granted. The Supreme Court, Thomas, J., held that element of owner's mental suffering as the result of the malicious destruction of her dog was properly submitted to the jury for their consideration in assessing damages.

Writ of certiorari granted; judgment of the District Court of Appeal quashed with directions to order judgment of the trial court reinstated

Damages ⊕208(6)

Element of owner's mental suffering as the result of the malicious destruction of her dog was properly submitted to the jury for their consideration in assessing damages.

———◆———

Morgan, Carratt & O'Connor, Fort Lauderdale, for petitioner.

Gotthardt, Christie & Shepard, Miami, for respondent.

THOMAS, Justice.

An action for damages was brought by the petitioner, then plaintiff, against the defendant, now respondent, based on facts we will presently, briefly relate. The plaintiff, was awarded a verdict of $2000. compensatory damages and $1000. punitive damages. The subsequent judgment was appealed to the District Court of Appeal, Second District, and there reversed for reconsideration not of "the issue of liability, but for determination only of compensatory and punitive damages."

The appellate court observed that appellant was contending error had been committed by the trial judge when he charged the jury that the plaintiff could recover for alleged mental suffering. The question here is simplified by the apparent concession on the part of the respondent that under the evidence the jury could believe the petitioner was entitled to recover both compensatory and punitive damages, which have been allowed, however, the respondent complains that the element of mental suffering was injected improperly by the judge's instruction.

The respondent is a corporation engaged in the business of collecting garbage. Among its customers was the petitioner. Early one morning, while the petitioner was occupied in the preparation of breakfast, a garbage collector came for the refuse. The petitioner had tethered her pet, a miniature dachshund, Heidi, outside the

Continued

CASE—*Continued*

268 Fla.   163 **SOUTHERN REPORTER, 2d SERIES**

house and beyond reach of the garbage can. Heidi was pedigreed and had been purchased two years before. She saw the garbage man empty the can and hurl it in the direction of the dog. Upon hearing her pet yelp, the petitioner went outside to find Heidi injured. The collector laughed and left. Heidi expired from the blow.

In the afternoon petitioner consulted a physician who later testified that she was upset to the point of marked hysteria and in such a plight that she could not recount the experience coherently. The doctor testified also that he had been treating her for nervousness for the past two years. But there is no need to pursue the matter of the effect of Heidi's demise upon her nervous system.

The narrow point for decision is whether or not the element of mental suffering was properly submitted to the jury for their consideration in assessing damages. It is humanly impossible, of course, to extract from the record whether or not the jury was influenced by that feature or, if so, to what extent. In these circumstances if no such factor should have been considered the opinion of the District Court of Appeal should not be disturbed so that upon re-trial the instruction on the point might be eliminated. If such damages are recoverable then the judgment of the trial court should prevail.

The petition for review here was based on an alleged conflict between the decision of the District Court of Appeal in the instant case and decisions of the Supreme Court in Kirksey v. Jernigan, 45 So.2d 188, 17 A.L.R.2d 766; Crane v. Loftin, 70 So.2d 574, and Slocum v. Food Fair Stores of Florida, 100 So.2d 396.

In the first of these cases it was shown that an undertaker had possessed and embalmed the body of a child without authority of the parent and had refused to surrender the body until a fee for the embalming was paid. The action of the parent for compensatory and punitive damages was dismissed in the trial court. The

Supreme Court reversed the judgment and undertook to distinguish cases involving mental suffering from intentional or malicious torts and those in which mental suffering may have resulted from negligent acts. This court acknowledged its commitment to the rule that there could be no recovery for mental pain unconnected with physical hurt in an action arising from "negligent breach of a contract [when] simple negligence [was] involved."

The court then remarked that the rule would not, however, be extended to cases purely in tort "where the wrongful act is such as * * * reasonably [to] imply malice," or when from "great indifference to the persons, property, or rights of others, such malice will be imputed as would justify the assessment of exemplary or punitive damages."

It is to us obvious from the facts we have related that the act performed by the representative of the respondent was malicious and demonstrated an extreme indifference to the rights of the petitioner. Having this view we think there was no prohibition of punitive damages under the rule just cited relative to awarding compensation for mental pain, as would be the case if there had been physical injury resulting only from simple negligence. There must have been no dispute before the District Court of Appeal about the propriety of punitive damages for that court observed in the opinion: "Appellant [respondent] acknowledges that, under the version of the evidence which the jury must have accepted, appellee [petitioner] was entitled to recover both compensatory and punitive damages," leaving, as we have already written, the sole question whether or not in setting the amount of damages mental suffering could be considered as the trial court had charged.

The District Court of Appeal held that *generally* in the case of injury to, or destruction of, a dog only the market value of the animal or some special or pecuniary value could establish the amount of the

CASE—*Continued*

loss. Then the court concluded with the flat statement: "It is improper to include an allowance for sentimental value of the dog to its owner." The restriction of the loss of a pet to its intrinsic value in circumstances such as the ones before us is a principle we cannot accept. Without indulging in a discussion of the affinity between "sentimental value" and "mental suffering", we feel that the affection of a master for his dog is a very real thing and that the malicious destruction of the pet provides an element of damage for which the owner should recover, irrespective of the value of the animal because of its special training such as a Seeing Eye dog or sheep dog.

The respondent tries to distinguish between the Kirksey case, supra, and the instant one on two bases, namely, that in the former the body of a child was involved and in the latter a dog; that in the former there was a personal transaction between the undertaker and complainant while in the latter there was none since the garbage gatherer "did not even know the plaintiff was anywhere within sight, nor had he ever met her or seen the dog previously." As to the first of these we hasten to say that the anguish resulting from the mishandling of the body of a child cannot be equated to the grief from the loss of a dog but that does not imply that mental suffering from the loss of a pet dog, even one less an aristocrat than Heidi, is nothing at all. As for the matter of contact between the miscreant and the injured person, the attempted distinction is just too fine for us to accept.

We think upon serious consideration that the opinion of the District Court of Appeal sufficiently collides with our opinion in the cited case to justify our assuming jurisdiction and in such event, as we have often held, we extend our power to determination of the merits.

Before closing, we state that the other two cases with which conflict is claimed have been examined and found irrelevant

because in Crane v. Loftin, supra, it was simply held that there could be no recovery for mental anguish suffered by the plaintiff when she fled her car as the defendant's train bore down upon her at a crossing since it was not established that the allegations about the operation of the train were sufficient to imply malice, entire want of care, wantonness, or great indifference to the rights of others.

In the third case the facts were so dissimilar as not to indicate a genuine conflict with the instant legal problem.

For the reasons given, the writ of certiorari is granted and the judgment of the District Court of Appeal is quashed with directions to order the judgment of the trial court reinstated.

DREW, C. J., and O'CONNELL, CALDWELL and ERVIN, JJ., concur.

The **GULF FERTILIZER COMPANY**, a Florida corporation, Petitioner-Appellant,

v.

R. R. WALDEN, as Tax Assessor of Hillsborough County, et al., Respondents-Appellees.

Nos. 32668, 32676.

Supreme Court of Florida.

April 22, 1964.

Action for refund of intangible personal property taxes paid by corporation as agent for its stockholders on its outstanding capital stock, on ground that statute providing formula for assessment and levy of the taxes is unconstitutional. The Circuit Court for Hillsborough County, Harry N. Sandler, J., treated defendants' motion to strike significant allegations of the complaint as a motion to dismiss, held the stat-

11

PLEADINGS

FEDERAL COURTS

The American court system has two levels: (1) the **trial court,** sometimes called the lower court, and (2) the **appellate,** or higher, **court,** which reviews the decisions made by the trial court.

There are three different federal courts in the federal system: (1) the United States District Court (the **district court** or trial level), sometimes called the **court of original jurisdiction;** (2) the United States Court of Appeals, the first level of appellate review (commonly called **circuit courts,** e.g., Fifth Circuit Court of Appeals, or just Fifth Circuit); and (3) the United States Supreme Court, the second and last level of appellate review.

The United States has been divided into separate "jurisdictional" districts, and none of these districts contains more than one state. The number of federal district courts in each state depends on the state's population. For example, Alabama has three federal district courts while California has four. Each state, regardless of its population, has at least one.

RULES OF CIVIL PROCEDURE

Civil procedure rules are created by the Congress, with assistance and input from the judiciary, and then are adopted as statutes. These rules are most commonly referred to as the **Rules of Civil Procedure.** These **court rules** define the issues and control how the parties may present factual and legal arguments to support their case, especially during the pretrial process. These rules apply to the federal trial and appellate courts. However, the **Federal Rules of Civil Procedure,** as well as the **Federal Rules of Evidence,** have been adopted in whole or in part by most states.

In addition, local district courts, both state and federal, may promulgate their own rules of civil procedure, known as **local court rules .** Local court rules apply *only* to the court the creates them. For example, each federal district court may

trial court, district court
The court of original jurisdiction where all evidence is first received and considered.

appellate court
A court having jurisdiction of appeal and review of decisions made by a lower court.

circuit court
Federal courts that review decisions made by the United States District Courts.

Rules of Civil Procedure
Procedural rules that govern civil actions in district courts.

court rules
Regulations with the force of law governing practice and procedure in various courts.

Federal Rules of Civil Procedure
Rules that govern procedure in the United States federal courts in all civil lawsuits.

Federal Rules of Evidence
Court rules that govern the admissibility of evidence at trials and hearings.

local court rules
Rules promulgated by individual local district courts, both state and federal, which apply only to the court that creates them and supplement the Rules of Civil Procedure.

307

PRACTICE TIP

When drafting
pleadings, follow
the Federal Rules of
Civil Procedure, as
well as any local
rules, that apply to
your document.

promulgate its own local rules. These local rules do not supersede the Federal Rules of Civil Procedure, but rather supplement them. Local rules usually address technical details, such as the number of copies to be filed with the court, paper size and type, document formats, and bindings allowed. You can obtain a copy of any court's local rules of civil procedure by contacting its court clerk's office.

You will refer constantly to the rules of civil procedure when drafting pleadings, motions, discovery documents, briefs, and every other document filed with the court. Each year, West Publishing Company publishes soft-bound handbooks that contain the rules of civil procedure for each state and the federal courts, as well as the rules of evidence and appellate court rules. If you do not already have a copy of your state's civil procedure rules and a copy of the *Federal Civil Judicial Procedure and Rules* published by West, we urge you to invest in them.

We cannot overemphasize how important it is to know the federal, state, and local rules of civil procedure for all of the courts in which your law firm practices, as well as those in your geographical area (i.e., the federal district court (the United States District Court for the _____ District of _____), the federal appellate (circuit) court (United States Court of the Appeals for the _____ Circuit), the county district court (the District Court for _____ County, State of _____), and state appellate court (the Supreme Court for the State of _____).

The rules of civil procedure govern all of the steps in the pretrial process, the trial proceedings, post-trial matters, and how an appeal is made. In litigation, every move made by you or your attorney should be checked against the rules of civil procedure. Failure to do so may result in the loss of some right your client would otherwise be able to claim.

PRACTICE TIP

In federal court, the
purpose of plead-
ings is limited to the
notice of claims
and defenses.

pleadings
A legal term of art used
to describe the docu-
ments filed with the court
that contain parties'
claims and defenses.

claim
Also called a cause of
action, a legally accept-
ed reason to sue and
the facts that give a person the right to judicial
relief.

defense
The allegations of fact or
legal theories offered to
offset or defeat a plain-
tiff's claims or demands.

complaint
Sometimes called a
"Petition" or "Bill of
Particulars," the first
step, and pleading, in
any lawsuit that gives
the opposing party, the
defendant, notice of the
grounds for the plaintiff's
claim.

PLEADINGS

In litigation, the word **pleadings** is a legal term of art used to describe the documents containing **claims** and **defenses** that are filed by the parties with the court. In other words, pleadings set out the issues to be tried.

Years ago, pleadings were used to discover facts, narrow the issues, and dispose of frivolous claims, things now addressed in discovery or through motions. Today, in federal court, the purpose of pleadings is limited to the notice of claims and defenses. The word *pleading* should not be used to describe any other documents filed with the court, such as motions or applications, briefs, or discovery documents.

Throughout this chapter, we will discuss choosing legal theories of recovery, jurisdiction, and venue. These are complex issues, and our discussion of them here only scrapes the surface. This chapter was designed to note these legal considerations in broad, general terms. You and your attorney have a responsibility to research any legal issues thoroughly before filing any pleading.

Types of Pleadings

Rule 7 of the Federal Rules of Civil Procedure states what pleadings are allowed:

- *Complaint (sometimes called a "Petition" or "Bill of Particulars" in state courts).* The first step in any lawsuit is when the plaintiff files the Complaint with the court. The **Complaint** gives the opposing party, the defendant, notice of the grounds for the plaintiff's claim.

- *Answer.*   An **Answer** is filed by a defendant in response to the claims made by the plaintiff in the Complaint.
- *Counterclaim.*   A **Counterclaim** is a cause of action or claim for relief by one or more defendants asserted against one or more plaintiffs in the same lawsuit.
- *Cross-Claim.*   A **Cross-Claim** is a cause of action or claim for relief by one or more defendants asserted against one or more co-defendants in the same law-suit.
- *Third-Party Complaint.*   A **Third-Party Complaint** is filed by a defendant against someone who is not presently a party to the lawsuit. That defendant then also becomes the **third-party plaintiff.**
- *Third-Party Answer.*   A **Third-Party Answer** is filed by the **third-party defendant** in response to the claims made by the defendant/third-party plaintiff.

Further, under Rule 7, courts may allow a **Reply** to an Answer (this is required by some states) or a Reply to a Third-Party Answer. Some states, such as California, do not use the same terminology we have here, and may refer to counterclaims, cross-claims, and third-party complaints as simply cross-complaints. Regardless of its name, *each of the pleadings described briefly here asks the court for some kind of relief—* that is the key element to remember. The name of the pleading merely shows *which* party is making the claim.

In Exhibit 11.1, the triangle represents the relationship between parties whenever there is a counterclaim, cross-claim, or third-party claim. Notice that we have used a *pi* (π) symbol to represent our imaginary plaintiff and a *delta* (Δ) symbol to represent imaginary defendants, adding a number next to the symbol to show that each is a separate person or entity. If our example showed multiple plaintiffs, we would have designated the first plaintiff as π_1 and the second plaintiff as π_2, and so on.

If one of the defendants should assert a claim against the plaintiff, that pleading is called a counterclaim. If one defendant asserts a claim against a co-defendant, that is called a cross-claim, meaning that one defendant has sued another defendant.

Answer
The pleading filed by a defendant in response to the Complaint.

Counterclaim
Sometimes called a Cross-Complaint, a cause of action or claim for relief by one or more defendants asserted against one or more plaintiffs in the same lawsuit.

Cross-Claim
A cause of action or claim for relief by one or more defendants assert-ed against one or more co-defendants in the same lawsuit.

Third-Party Complaint
A Complaint filed by a defendant against someone who is not presently a party to the lawsuit.

third-party plaintiff
When a defendant files a Third-Party Complaint, the defendant then also becomes the third-party plaintiff to signify that party's adversarial rela-tionship against the third-party defendant.

Third-Party Answer
Pleading filed by the third-party defendant in response to the claims made by the defendant/third-party plaintiff.

third-party defendant
The party against whom a Third-Party Complaint is filed by a defendant/third-party plaintiff.

Reply
The plaintiff's response to the defendant's Answer.

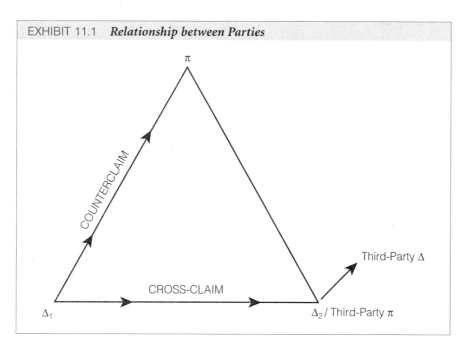

EXHIBIT 11.1   *Relationship between Parties*

Whenever a defendant makes a claim against someone who is not already included in the lawsuit, that is called a third-party claim. The defendant who brought the third-party claim is known as the third-party plaintiff. The person against whom the claim is asserted is called the third-party defendant.

Here is a brief example of how each of the pleadings we just described would be used in a civil lawsuit. Paul Brown buys a widget from Buy From Us, a local discount store, which purchased the widget from Better Widgets for America, Inc., a manufacturer in another state. The widget is defective. When Paul Brown uses the defective widget, he is injured.

Paul Brown (plaintiff) files a Complaint stating his claim against Buy From Us (defendant) and Better Widgets for America, Inc. (defendant). Both defendants are served with a copy of the Complaint and a **summons.** (In federal court, the filing of the Complaint commences the lawsuit; in most state courts, a lawsuit does not commence until the Complaint, or Petition, is served on the defendant(s) with a summons.) Each defendant then files its Answer in response to the allegations made in the Complaint. The plaintiff or either defendant, all of whom are parties to the lawsuit, will file motions, briefs, and discovery during the lawsuit.

Fact Pleadings and Notice Pleadings

There are two types of pleadings. **Fact pleadings** require that the party allege the facts necessary to allege a **cause of action.** In this type of pleading, the party must allege all of the facts for each claim that must be proved to win the lawsuit. **Notice pleadings** require only a short statement of the grounds upon which the party bases each claim. Notice pleadings have been incorporated into the Federal Rules of Civil Procedure, which stress that all pleadings should be written with brevity and conciseness.

◼ PRACTICE TIP

A pleading must contain:
1. A short, plain statement of the grounds upon which the court's jurisdiction depends
2. A short, plain statement of the claim showing that the pleader is entitled to relief
3. A demand for judgment for the relief the pleader seeks

Rule 8 of the Federal Rules of Civil Procedure says that a pleading need only contain these three things:

1. A short and plain statement of the grounds upon which the court's jurisdiction depends
2. A short and plain statement of the claim showing that the pleader is entitled to relief
3. A demand for judgment for the relief the pleader seeks[1]

A notice pleading need only state sufficient information to notify opposing parties of the nature of the claim against them. It does not require a statement of facts or conclusions of law to establish the elements of a cause of action.

---

[1] Samples of legally sufficient pleadings can be found in Forms 2 through 23, in the Appendix of Forms to West's *Federal Rules of Civil Procedure.*

summons
A means of acquiring jurisdiction over a party which notifies defendants that a lawsuit has been commenced against them.

fact pleadings
Formal allegations by the parties to the lawsuit that require identification of all facts which must be proved to allege a valid cause of action.

cause of action
Also called a claim, the legally accepted reason for suing and the facts that give a person the right to juridical relief against another.

notice pleadings
Formal allegations by the parties to a lawsuit of their respective claims and defenses to provide notice of what is to be expected at trial.

■ PRACTICE TIP

A person or entity should be named as a party in the lawsuit if any of the following applies:

- That party's presence is required to grant complete relief to the claimant.
- The party has some type of interest in the lawsuit so that its presence is necessary for it to protect its interest.
- If the party's absence may expose other parties to multiple or inconsistent liabilities.

Lawsuits are brought by and against parties who have a legal capacity to sue or be sued. Rule 17(a) of the Federal Rules of Civil Procedure requires that an action be brought in the name of the **real party in interest,** meaning the one who, under applicable substantive law, has the right that the lawsuit seeks to enforce.

real party in interest
The one who, under applicable substantive law, has the right that the lawsuit seeks to enforce.

For an individual, the capacity to sue is determined by the state law of the individual's domicile. For corporations, the capacity to sue is determined by the law of the state of incorporation. In other types of lawsuits, the law of the forum state is controlling.

A person or entity should be named as a party in the lawsuit if: (1) that party's presence is required to grant complete relief to the claimant; or (2) the party has some type of interest in the lawsuit so that its presence is necessary for it to protect its interest; or (3) if the party's absence may expose other parties to multiple or inconsistent liabilities. Generally, a plaintiff should include any potentially liable party unless that party cannot be served with process, or if naming the party as part of the lawsuit would defeat subject-matter jurisdiction.

Boilerplate Pleadings

In many of these chapters, we caution you on the pitfalls of using **boilerplate forms.** Most form books provide samples of pleadings for the most commonly used legal theories. Even more useful are specialized form books that often include detailed checklists on how the lawsuit should be commenced, what the Complaint should contain, and how to conduct discovery and prepare for trial. These books also often contain legal research pointers and a synopsis of relevant law.

boilerplate forms
Forms that include standard language and, if used in a particular document, retain the same specific meaning from form to form.

If you should use this type of book, *never* rely totally on whatever legal research and or relevant law the book provides. Use them only as guides. They should never be copied or adopted blindly without thorough editing and proofreading. Whenever you use a sample form from any source, *be sure to revise the form to suit your specific cause of action.*

We suggest that you create your own **form files** from copies of documents you or others draft in your office. Your form file or **form bank** may also contain pertinent research in particular areas, articles that address drafting a specific document or

form files, form bank
Samples of pleadings and other documents.

■ PRACTICE TIP

Use form books or boilerplate forms only as guides. Never copy a form without thoroughly proofreading and editing it. Never rely totally on the legal research or relevant law found in form books or other forms. If you should use that research, shepardize it to make sure that it is still good law.

PRACTICE TIP

Rule 17 of the Federal Rules of Civil Procedure requires that every action must be brought in the name of the "real party in interest." Use this rule to determine whether (a) each party has the capacity to be sued and (b) the proper person has been designated as a party.

"how to" navigate through the many procedural rules that affect almost every legal document you will draft. Before long, you will have developed a substantial library of forms from which to draw when drafting future documents.

GENERAL FORMAT FOR PLEADINGS

The format for all pleadings is set out by the Rules of Civil Procedure and any local court rules. Before drafting any pleading, you should review both. Generally, each pleading will contain

- a style or caption of the case
- the title of the pleading
- the body of the pleading
- an introductory sentence or paragraph
- a statement of jurisdiction and venue
- the party's claims and/or defenses
- the prayer for relief
- attorney's signature block
- a certificate of service or mailing

Caption or Style of the Case

caption or style of the case
The beginning of a pleading, motion, deposition, or other legal instrument which indicates the names of the parties, the name of the court, and the docket or case number.

case number
The number assigned to a lawsuit by the court clerk which is used on all subsequent documents in that lawsuit to distinguish it from other cases.

The **style** or **caption of the case** contains the name of the court in which the case is being filed, the names of the party or parties and which side each party is on (plaintiff or defendant), and the **case number** assigned to it by the court. Note the format in Exhibit 11.2.

EXHIBIT 11.2 *Style or Caption of the Case*
IN THE UNITED STATES DISTRICT COURT FOR THE WESTERN DISTRICT OF OKLAHOMA

JANE HEALY,   )
)
Plaintiff,   )
)
v.   )   Case No. _____
)
CHARLES RAYMOND, an   )
individual,   )
)
Defendant.   )

In Exhibit 11.2, the name of the court is centered in all capital letters at the top of the document. Note also that a closed-parentheses symbol is used down the middle of the caption to separate the name and designation of the parties from the case number. The name of each party is typed in all capital letters with the legal description of the party in lowercase letters.

The caption or style is treated as a complete thought. Always put a comma after the word *Plaintiff* (or *Plaintiffs*) and a period after the word *Defendant* (or *Defendants*). When there are multiple plaintiffs and/or defendants, you should always list each one when drafting any complaint or petition. This is not necessary, however, in subsequent pleadings or other documents. Instead, you may list the *first* plaintiff and the *first* defendant only, and refer to the missing plaintiffs and/or defendants as **et al.,** which literally means "and others." Note the example in Exhibit 11.3.

et al.
A Latin phrase, literally meaning "and others."

EXHIBIT 11.3   *Style of the Case—Multiple Parties*

```
            IN THE UNITED STATES DISTRICT COURT
           FOR THE WESTERN DISTRICT OF OKLAHOMA

JANE HEALY,                      )
                                 )
    Plaintiff,                   )
                                 )
    v.                           )         Case No. CIV–96–1798
                                 )
CHARLES RAYMOND et al.,          )
                                 )
                                 )
    Defendants.                  )
```

You have probably noticed that the case number is only a blank line in exhibit 11.2. In Exhibit 11.3, we made up a case number to show you what one normally looks like. The reason for the blank line in the first example is simple. No one but the court clerk may assign a case number.

When the Complaint is filed with the court clerk, the clerk will assign a number to that lawsuit by stamping that number on the complaint. The first two digits of the number are the year the Complaint is filed. The remaining numbers and/or letters are assigned by the court clerk. This number must appear on all subsequent pleadings, motions, briefs, or discovery documents—in other words, on everything.

Title of the Pleading

The **title** of the pleading is exactly what it sounds like, that is, Complaint, Answer, etc. The title should be single-spaced and underlined, and all of the letters should be capitalized. For a pleading like the Complaint, the name of the pleading itself is sufficient. The reader automatically knows that the plaintiff is the author of that pleading. But for each of the subsequent pleadings, motions, and other documents, we suggest that you include the name of the party within the title, like this:

title
The name of the document, i.e., Complaint, Answer, etc.

DEFENDANT CHARLES RAYMOND'S ANSWER

Or:

ANSWER OF DEFENDANT CHARLES RAYMOND

This is particularly important when there are multiple plaintiffs and defendants, each of whom is represented by separate counsel.

Sometimes the plaintiff needs to add or change something in the original Complaint. The plaintiff would then file an **Amended Complaint** including those changes or additions. Any later additions or changes to the Amended Complaint would be called the "Second Amended Complaint," then "Third Amended

Amended Complaint
A modified or corrected Complaint filed after service of the original Complaint.

Complaint," and so on. Therefore, the defendant's answer to each of these Complaints should specify which Complaint the Answer is addressing, like this:

<u>DEFENDANT CHARLES RAYMONDS' ANSWER</u>
<u>TO PLAINTIFF'S SECOND AMENDED COMPLAINT</u>

Body of the Pleading

As we stated earlier, a pleading must state a claim of relief and contain:

1. A short and plain statement of the grounds upon which the court's jurisdiction depends
2. A short and plain statement of the claim showing that the pleader is entitled to relief
3. A demand for judgment for the relief sought by the pleader

The body of the pleading should also include:

✓ the names of the parties involved;

✓ the date and place of the transaction or event upon which the lawsuit is based;

✓ the legal wrong alleged by one party against another party;

✓ the nature and extent of the harm suffered because of that legal wrong; and

✓ the defenses raised to refute the allegations made by one party against another.

You should also always check the procedural rules, statutes, and case law to determine the following information:

✓ Who has the burden to plead the claim or defense.

✓ Whether the pleading must contain particular allegations to state a claim.

✓ Which claims or defenses can be joined.

✓ Who should, and can, be named as a party.

✓ Whether the court has subject-matter jurisdiction over the claims and personal jurisdiction over the parties.

✓ Whether venue is proper.

✓ What time deadlines are involved, such as the statute of limitations.

✓ What the format requirements are for that pleading.

Rule 11
Court rule regarding the attorneys' and litigants' obligation to the court for their conduct which provides sanctions for violation of the rule.

Rule 11.   All pleadings are subject to the provisions of **Rule 11** of the Federal Rules of Civil Procedure. Rule 11 requires that all pleadings shall be signed by at least one attorney of record in the attorney's individual name. If the party is not represented by an attorney, the motion shall be signed by the party. Each pleading shall also state the signer's address and telephone number.

Rule 11(b) states, in pertinent part, that:

By presenting to the court (whether by signing, filing, submitting, or later advocating) a pleading, written motion, or other paper, an attorney or unrepresented party is certifying that to the best of the person's knowledge, information, and belief, formed after an inquiry reasonable under the circumstances,

(1) it is not being presented for any improper purpose, such as to harass or to cause unnecessary delay or needless increase in the cost of litigation;

(2) the claims, defenses, and other legal contentions therein are warranted by existing law or by a nonfrivolous argument for the extension, modification, or reversal of existing law or the establishment of new law;

(3) the allegations and other factual contentions have evidentiary support or, if specifically so identified, are likely to have evidentiary support after a reasonable opportunity for further investigation or discovery; and

(4) the denials of factual contentions are warranted on the evidence or, if specifically so identified, are reasonably based on a lack of information or belief.

Should the court determine that Rule 11(b) has been violated, the court may impose an appropriate **sanction** upon the attorneys, law firms, or parties who have violated Rule 11(b) or who are responsible for the violation. Sanctions awarded by the court usually consist of the payment by the violator of opposing counsel's attorney's fees and costs. Sanctions may also be nonmonetary.

Introductory Paragraph or Sentence. The body of most pleadings begins with an **introductory paragraph** or **sentence.** This should be a concise statement containing the name of the party, the party's designation, and the character of the pleading, something like this:

> Plaintiff, Jane Healy ("Healy"), for her Complaint against Defendant Charles Raymond ("Raymond"), alleges as follows:

Notice that the **designation** assigned to each party is within parentheses and quotation marks. Make designations short and clear labels that identify each party. Use part of the parties' names as we did, or use their real role in the lawsuit. For the remainder of the pleading, you will refer to each party by its designation until you reach the **prayer**, the request for relief or damages. At that time, you will return to using the full name for each party (e.g., Plaintiff Jane Healy, rather than Healy). For a more detailed discussion of how to use designations, see Chapter 9.

Never use antiquated language, such as "Comes Now the Plaintiff in the above-styled and numbered cause," or "premises considered," when drafting pleadings or any other legal document. Although some lawyers still cling to this outdated legalese, *avoid it like the plague.* It adds nothing to the legal meaning of the pleading other than to make it more confusing.

George Hathaway, Chair of the Plain English Committee of the State Bar of Michigan, made this astute observation about legal professionals who refuse to abandon legalese:

> [L]awyers and legal secretaries [and legal assistants] would be ridiculed if they admitted that they used legalese for prestige and client control. Therefore, they make up the following four rationales or excuses for using legalese: 1) legalese is used because it is more precise than plain English, 2) some legal topics must be written in legalese because they are too complex for plain English, 3) legalese is often required by case precedent, and 4) legalese is often required by statutes.
>
> These four excuses are false. Lawyers use legalese—especially the archaic words—because they want to use legalese, not because they don't know any better or because of precision, complexity, case precedent, or statute.[2]

PRACTICE TIP
Sanctions awarded by the court usually consist of the payment by the violator of opposing counsel's attorney's fees and costs.

sanctions
Penalties awarded by the court upon the attorneys, or parties who have violated Rule 11(b) or who are responsible for the violation.

introductory paragraph or sentence
A concise statement at the beginning of a pleading or other document containing the name of the party, the party's designation, and the character of the pleading.

designation
Abbreviation or short, clear names, for each of the parties or other actors, or for some other important event, document, or thing.

prayer
Also called a "demand for relief" or "wherefore clause," a requisite element of a pleading in a civil lawsuit that states the specific type of relief sought, costs, interest, attorney's fees, and any type of special damages to which the pleader deems him- or herself entitled.

---

[2] George Hathaway, *An Overview of the Plain English Movement for Lawyers . . . Ten Years Later,* Michigan Bar Journal, Vol. 73, No. 1, pp. 26, 30 (Jan. 1994).

PRACTICE TIP

When you are attempting to wean lawyers away from legalese, we recommend subtleness and patience rather than the blunt, hit-them-over-the-head-with-it approach.

jurisdiction
The power of a court to hear and determine a case.

in personam jurisdiction
The power a court has over the defendant himself, that enables the court to issue an *in personam* judgment, in contrast to the court's power over the defendant's interest in property (quasi in rem) or power over the property (in rem).

in rem jurisdiction
Refers to an action taken directly against the defendant's property, or the power by a court over a thing which allows it to seize and hold the object for some legal purpose.

subject-matter jurisdiction
The court's power to hear and deal with the subject matter involved in the lawsuit.

diversity of citizenship
Jurisdiction of federal courts extending to cases between citizens of different states or between a citizen of a state and an alien, for which a requisite jurisdictional amount must also be met.

venue
The geographical area in which a court with jurisdiction may hear and determine a case.

forum
The court to which the litigation is brought.

Another way to make your pleading less confusing and cumbersome to read is to omit needless words or phrases, such as *said, to wit, same, and/or, hereby, herein, whereas, thereof, in the premises, would show,* and *be it remembered.* Delete tautologies, such as *each and every, save and except, past history, mutual agreement, wrongful conversion,* and *total sum.*

Now, after all of these admonitions against using legalese when drafting pleadings, we give you some words of warning. Your supervising attorney, not you, decides the type of language to be used in that pleading. If your supervising attorney still clings to these outdated, overused, and redundant words and phrases, and insists that you do so as well, you must obey.

Jurisdiction and Venue.   The first requirement of a pleading is a statement of the court's **jurisdiction.** In one sense, a court's jurisdiction is the geographical territory or domain over which a particular court has authority. In another more legal sense, a court's jurisdiction means the power of a court to hear and determine a case. **In personam jurisdiction** refers to the power of a court over an individual. **In rem jurisdiction** refers to the power of a court over property. **Subject-matter jurisdiction** refers to the power of a court to hear particular matters. Knowing which jurisdiction's substantive law applies to your case will assist you in determining which claims, defenses, and relief or damages to raise in your pleadings.

For example, federal courts have limited jurisdiction. To "invoke a federal court's jurisdiction," a party must affirmatively plead and show the court that it has proper subject-matter jurisdiction. If the court does not have subject-matter jurisdiction, the lawsuit must be dismissed.

Generally, statements about jurisdiction identify whatever statutes apply to facts about the parties and their claims or defenses. If no particular statute establishes the basis for jurisdiction, you may cite applicable general jurisdictional statutes. In federal court, a common jurisdictional statute, 28 U.S.C. § 1332, relates to **diversity of citizenship** or to the dollar amount of the controversy:

(a) The district courts shall have original jurisdiction of all civil actions where the matter in controversy exceeds the sum or value of $50,000, exclusive of interest and costs, and is between—
(1) citizens of different States;
(2) citizens of a State and citizens or subjects of a foreign state;
(3) citizens of different States and in which citizens or subjects of a foreign state are additional parties; and
(4) a foreign state, defined in section 1603(a) of this title, as plaintiff and citizens of a State or different States.
28 U.S.C. § 1332(a).

Venue is the geographical area in which a court with jurisdiction may hear and determine a case. Venue statutes control where a plaintiff files its initial complaint and were designed to protect a defendant from being forced to litigate in an "unfair" **forum.** It is not unusual for a plaintiff to have more than one venue available in which to file the lawsuit.

When choosing the appropriate venue, you should consider several things, such as:

- Convenience and cost to your client
- Location of key witnesses
- Applicable statutes of limitations
- Necessary elements to prove your client's claim(s) and allowable damages

- Choice of judges
- Prospective jury pools
- Length of time until trial

Exhibit 11.4 shows what the paragraphs for jurisdiction and venue commonly look like.

EXHIBIT 11.4   *Jurisdiction and Venue*

1. Plaintiff *[name]* is a citizen of the State of Oklahoma residing at *[address, city]*, Oklahoma *[ZIP code]*.

2. Defendant *[name]* is an individual and citizen of the State of Oklahoma residing at *[address]*, *[city]*, Oklahoma *[ZIP code]*.

3. Defendant *[name]* is a corporation organized and existing under the laws of a state other than the State of Oklahoma with its principal place of business in *[city and state]*.

4. Defendant *[name]* is a corporation organized and existing under the laws of a state other than the State of Oklahoma with its principal place of business in *[city and state]*.

5. Jurisdiction of this court is based on diversity of citizenship, 28 U.S.C. § 1332, and the amount in controversy exceeds the sum of $50,000, exclusive of interest and costs.

Researching Claims and Defenses.   When your supervising attorney agreed to represent your client, he or she had already determined that a **prima facie** case could be proven on at least one theory of recovery. It is likely that the client has provided some type of admissible proof for the necessary elements of that theory. If not, then your supervising attorney has a reasonable basis for believing that the required proof can be obtained during discovery. Regardless, it is critical that you and your supervising attorney take whatever time is necessary to develop a persuasive and rational theory of the case.

Once you have identified all of the possible claims or defenses, make sure that you have also identified each of the elements necessary to prove that claim or defense. One of the best ways to check whether you have addressed all of the necessary elements for each claim is to review the applicable jurisdiction's standard **jury instructions.** You should have no trouble finding **uniform jury instructions** for the most common claims and defenses.

These jury instructions usually itemize the necessary elements to support a prima facie case. Do not rely on jury instructions alone, however. Do additional research if necessary to assure yourself and your supervising attorney that all the bases have been covered.

You will be tempted to assert every conceivable claim, remedy, or defense that meets the Rule 11(b) requirements. But, the more claims you add to a lawsuit, the more complex the lawsuit becomes. The more complex the lawsuit, the more time-consuming it is for you and your attorney, and the more expensive it is for your client.

This is not to say that you should forego adding claims at the expense of your client's interests. You should protect your client's interests by asserting essential claims and adding other claims only after considering the costs and disadvantages of litigating every claim against every possible proper party.

PRACTICE TIP

Statements of jurisdiction identify whatever statutes apply to facts about the parties and their claims or defenses.

prima facie
A Latin term meaning "on the face of it," pertaining to a fact that is presumed to be true unless disproved by some evidence to the contrary.

jury instructions
Instructions given by the trial judge to the jury, concerning the law of the case that they will need to know in order to reach a verdict.

uniform jury instructions
Model or pattern jury instructions that are required to be used, or substantially followed, by the trial judge.

PRACTICE TIP

Another factor to consider when deciding the legal theory of the lawsuit is the impact those claims have on your discovery strategy. If your pleadings are complex, it broadens the scope of your discovery, thereby creating more expense to your client.

punitive damages
Damages on an increased scale awarded to the plaintiff over and above what will compensate for his or her property loss, where the wrong was aggravated by violence, oppression, malice, fraud, or wanton conduct of the defendant.

allegation
A statement of fact that one expects to prove.

count
The statement of a cause of action, or a separate and independent claim, involving a single theory of recovery even though each is based on the same transaction or event.

Before drafting any pleading, research the legal theory or theories and remedies or defenses to be claimed by your client, and determine the elements necessary to prove each theory, remedy, or defense. One or several may need to be proven for your client to prevail. The elements to prove each theory or defense may be quite simple or complex, depending upon the legal theory you wish to prove. You can then determine what claims or defenses to make when drafting the pleading.

A party can state as many separate claims, remedies, or defenses as it has regardless of consistency or whether those claims or defenses are based on legal, equitable, or maritime grounds. This is when a form book's checklist of potential theories for claims, remedies, and defenses can be extremely useful.

For example, assume that the law firm for which you work has been hired by Jane Healy, the plaintiff in our scenario in Chapter 1. Your supervising attorney wants to file a personal injury lawsuit on Ms. Healy's behalf. Think about what claims could be alleged in the Complaint, and who should be named as parties in the lawsuit. What about a negligence claim and a claim based on violating the "rules of the road" against Charles Raymond, the driver of the vehicle that struck Ms. Healy's car?

What other facts might give rise to a claim? What about the fact that Charles Raymond had been drinking before the accident? Is there any liability on the part of Charles Raymond' employer? What about a claim against the manufacturer of Ms. Healy's car because her seat belt broke, thus causing her to have more serious injuries than she would have had if it had operated properly? Our scenario has been purposely drafted in such a way as to support numerous legal theories. These are only a sample of the parties who should be included in the lawsuit and the types of claims that could be alleged. What others can you think of?

In our scenario, Jane Healy could consider whether to plead a claim for **punitive damages** against Charles Raymond and his employer. If your supervising attorney decided to seek punitive damages on Ms. Healy's behalf, you would want to discover the safety history and financial information for those defendants. If there is little likelihood of getting punitive damages against these defendants, should you and your attorney aggressively pursue a claim for punitive damages? How these questions are answered will make a significant difference in how the lawsuit is conducted by each of the parties.

Drafting the Claims and Defenses.   The claims and defenses are the heart of any pleading. Think of pleadings as the means for bringing the theory of the lawsuit to the court. A party's claims, usually referred to as the **allegations,** create its cause of action. Each cause of action is based upon a particular legal theory that gives the party making the claim a right to some type of judicial relief, remedy, or damages.

Cause of Action.   The allegations are drafted as separate, consecutively numbered paragraphs. Each numbered paragraph should contain only one sentence that focuses on one idea or point. Each paragraph builds on the other to establish the necessary elements of just one of the claims to be asserted against the other party. The group of paragraphs for each claim are called a *cause of action.*

Usually, each cause of action, sometimes called a separate **count,** or claim, involves a single theory of recovery even though each is based on the same transaction or event. Each cause of action, and there may be several or only one, should be set out separately and titled as the "First Cause of Action," "Second Cause of Action," and so on.

Usually each subsequent cause of action requires the restatement of some of the allegations stated as separate paragraphs in the First Cause of Action. Rather than repeating these paragraphs in their totality in the subsequent causes of action, it is more concise to adopt those paragraphs at the beginning of the subsequent cause of action, as we did in Exhibit 11.5. Then you would begin the next paragraph of the second cause of action as number 7.

EXHIBIT 11.5   *Second Cause of Action*

SECOND CAUSE OF ACTION

6. The allegations contained in paragraphs 1 through 5 of the First Cause of Action are incorporated as part of the Second Cause of Action as though they were stated in full.

When you are drafting the body of a pleading, remind yourself that you are telling the reader a story—your client's story. Not only do you want the reader to understand it, you want the reader to see it from your client's point of view.

Tell the reader what happened, how, to whom, and when. Use as many facts as necessary to personalize the pleading to create empathy for your client, to implicate the opposing party (whether plaintiff or defendant), and to tell your client's story. If needed to understand the reason for the lawsuit, describe the history of the parties' relationship to each other. Give a detailed chronology of the incident in question and the events leading up to it.

Intertwine a combination of facts, law, and empathy for your client. As when drafting briefs, it is acceptable to slant the language in a pleading to be sympathetic to your client. But you must never exaggerate, embellish, or misstate the facts. The court will not tolerate it.

Exhibits.   If there are documents that support the claims or allegations made in the pleading, those documents should be attached as **exhibits** and referred to in the body of the pleading, as shown in Exhibit 11.6.

EXHIBIT 11.6   *Pleading Exhibit*

1. On May 17, 1993, Plaintiff Acme Construction ("Builder") entered into a contract (the "Contract") with Phillips Management, Inc. ("Owner") to construct an office building at the corner of Main Street and Rockwell Boulevard. A copy of the Contract is attached as Exhibit "A."

In certain types of lawsuits, such as those involving contracts, any documents that form that basis for a claim should always be attached to the pleading as an exhibit.

Prayer.   The prayer for relief, also called the "wherefore clause" or just "prayer," is the final paragraph of the pleading before the signature block for the attorney. This paragraph sets out exactly what you want from the court. There are two types of **relief—legal** (a remedy available, under the particular circumstances of the case, in a court of law) and **equitable** (relief sought from a court with equity powers, such as specific performance on a contract or an injunction or restitution). Procedurally, the distinction between equitable and legal relief is no longer generally relevant, because,

exhibit
A paper, document, chart, or other thing that is shown to a judge, jury, etc., or attached to a brief, pleading, or other document.

legal relief
A remedy available, under the particular circumstances of the case, in a court of law.

equitable relief
Relief sought from a court with equity powers, such as in the case of one seeking an injunction or specific performance instead of money damages.

civil action
An action to enforce private rights.

under the Rules of Civil Procedure, there is only one form of action—known as a **civil action.**

Most state courts have specific requirements for the manner in which the amount of damages sought by the party is stated. Check the court rules to determine what requirements, if any, apply to your pleading. Rule 8(a) of the Federal Rules of Civil Procedure requires only that the pleading contain a demand for judgment for the relief sought and that relief "in the alternative" or of several different types may be demanded.

In federal court, be especially careful when drafting the prayer, for two reasons. First, the prayer should be drafted either to ensure the right to a jury trial or to forego it, because the remedy sought is often controlled by the question of the right to a **jury trial.** Second, the method by which a **default judgment,** which is always a possibility in any lawsuit, may be obtained is determined by the type of relief sought in the prayer.

jury trial
The trial of a matter before a judge and jury as opposed to a trial solely before a judge.

default judgment
A judgment rendered against a party who has failed to defend against a claim that has been brought by another party.

The prayer should state the specific type of relief sought, costs, interest, attorney's fees, and any specific type of special damages. The prayer should look something like the one in Exhibit 11.7. If, once you have drafted the prayer, you notice that it has become rather complex, we suggest that you break it down into itemized and numbered subparagraphs for clarity.

PRACTICE TIP

Many federal jurisdictions, such as the United States District Court for the District of Arizona, are specific about where and how jury demands are made in pleadings, so check your applicable court and local rules.

EXHIBIT 11.7   *Prayer for Relief*

WHEREFORE, Plaintiff Jane Healy prays for judgment against Defendant Charles Raymond in an amount exceeding $10,000 for actual damages, as well as punitive damages in an amount exceeding $10,000, together with interest, costs, attorney's fees, and any further relief to which Plaintiff Jane Healy may be entitled.

According to Fed.R.Civ.P. 38(c), any party may serve upon all other parties a demand for jury trial on any issue *not later than 10 days after service* of the last pleading directed to that issue. If the party filing the pleading intends to demand a jury trial on any claim triable by right before a jury, the party customarily adds a statement to that effect—simply **JURY TRIAL DEMANDED**—somewhere on the pleading, such as under the case number in the style of the case or before or after the attorney signature block.

Jury Trial Demanded
A statement made by a party filing the pleading demanding a jury trial on any claim triable by right before a jury to prevent the waiver of that right.

To ensure your client's right to a trial by jury, check all applicable court and local rules to determine whether you have met all of the requirements for making a demand for a jury trial. *Failure to demand a jury trial can result in a waiver of that right.*

Signature Block

According to Rule 11, the attorney who prepares a pleading is required to certify by his or her signature that he or she has read it and has made a reasonable inquiry that the allegations or claims made in it are well grounded in fact, warranted by existing law, and not filed for harassment.

signature block
The final section of the pleading containing the signature line, name, address, and telephone of the attorney of record or the pro se litigant, which also serves to meet the requirements of Rule 11.

As a practical matter, the attorney's **signature block** can be prepared in several formats. Essentially, it contains a blank line for the attorney of record's signature, the name of the attorney typewritten beneath the blank line, and often the attorney's bar number as well. It then reflects the name of the law firm, its complete address, and its telephone number. Below that appears "Attorney for Plaintiff" or "Attorney for Defendant," and then the name of the plaintiff or defendant, all of which are single-spaced. Exhibits 11.8 and 11.9 show two examples of what the signature block should look like.

A legal assistant may *never* sign any pleading or other document—except correspondence, and then only if the correspondence does not set fees or give legal advice.

Legal assistants who do not observe this cardinal rule risk being prosecuted for the **unauthorized practice of law.**

unauthorized practice of law
When a non-lawyer performs acts that only a lawyer in good standing may perform.

EXHIBIT 11.8   *Signature Block*

Marcia Wilmington, OBA #14500
WILMINGTON & ASSOCIATES, P.C.
170 Park Avenue, Suite 200
Oklahoma City, Oklahoma 73102
Telephone: 405/232–0311

ATTORNEY FOR DEFENDANT CHARLES RAYMOND

EXHIBIT 11.9   *Alternate Signature Block*

WILMINGTON & ASSOCIATES, P.C.

BY: _____

Marcia Wilmington, OBA #14500
170 Park Avenue, Suite 200
Oklahoma City, Oklahoma 73102
Telephone: 405/232–0311

ATTORNEY FOR DEFENDANT CHARLES RAYMOND

◼ PRACTICE TIP

Rule 5 of the Federal Rules of Civil Procedure, in pertinent part, requires that:

> [E]very order required by its terms to be served, every pleading subsequent to the original complaint unless the court otherwise orders because of numerous defendants, every paper relating to discovery required to be served upon a party unless the court otherwise orders, every written motion other than one which may be heard ex parte, and every written notice, appearance, demand, offer of judgment, designation of record on appeal, and similar paper shall be served upon each of the parties. No service need be made on parties in default for failure to appear except that pleadings asserting new or additional claims for relief against them shall be served upon them in the manner provided for service of summons in Rule 4.

Certificate of Service

The next part of your pleading is the **Certificate of Service,** also known as the **Certificate of Mailing.** Rule 5 allows service upon the attorney (when the party is represented by counsel) or upon a party (when the party is *not* represented by counsel) by delivering a copy to the attorney or party or by mailing it to the attorney or party at that person's last known address. Service by mail is considered complete upon the *actual mailing* of the document.

Rule 5 is specific as to what *delivery* means. The document must be handed to the attorney or the party. In the alternative, the document may be left with the attorney's or party's office with a clerk or other person in charge. If no one is in charge, then it

Certificate of Service, Certificate of Mailing
Written assurance that a copy of the document upon which the Certificate appears has been served upon counsel for all parties or pro se litigants in the lawsuit, commonly made in accordance with the Rules of Civil Procedure.

may be left in a conspicuous place. If the office is closed or the person has no office, then the document should be left at the person's residence with a person of "suitable age and discretion" who also resides there.

Usually, service is effected by mailing a file-stamped copy of the document to the party's attorney. If the party is not represented by an attorney, then the individual or entity must be served personally or by one of the permitted methods. Check the applicable court rules for the requirements on Certificates of Service and the ways in which service should be made.

Although there are some exceptions, any document that is served on the parties must be filed with the court clerk either before service or within a reasonable time after service. Usually, after the original document has been prepared and signed, the appropriate number of copies is made and the original document and the copies are taken to the court clerk's office for filing. The court clerk will file and stamp the original with that day's date, keep the original, and file-stamp any copies that you have. Be sure that you have retained a file-stamped copy of any document filed with the court clerk for your file.

Basically, a Certificate of Service is a statement that indicates when and how service of the document was made and to whom. It includes a signature of the attorney "certifying" that the statement is true. In some states, it is permissible for a legal assistant or legal secretary to sign the Certificate of Service. Before you do so, we suggest checking with your state's bar association about the propriety of a legal assistant signing a Certificate of Service.

The Certificate of Service looks something like that shown in Exhibit 11.10.

> **PRACTICE TIP**
>
> Before you sign a Certificate of Service, we suggest that you check with your state's bar association about the propriety of doing so.

> **PRACTICE TIP**
>
> A Certificate of Service states when and how service of the document was made and to whom. The attorney's signature "certifies" that the statement is true.

EXHIBIT 11.10 *Certificate of Service*

<u>CERTIFICATE OF SERVICE</u>

This is to certify that on the _____ day of _____, 199___, a correct copy of Defendant Charles Raymond's Answer was mailed, postage prepaid, to Marcia Wilmington, Wilmington & Associates, P.C., 170 Park Avenue, Suite 200, Oklahoma City, Oklahoma 73102, Attorney for Plaintiff Jane Healy.

_____
[name of attorney typed here]

Proofread the Final Draft.   Now that the pleading has been completely drafted, read it over carefully. Have you included each critical document as an exhibit, and are all exhibits consecutively numbered or lettered? Is there any way that the pleading can be attacked because of some technical insufficiency? Have all unnecessary words and legalese been deleted? Once those questions have been satisfied, double-check all dates, the spelling of names, and internal consistency (e.g., that designations assigned to the parties were used the same consistently throughout the document, and that all headings and subheadings are consecutively numbered or lettered).

■ SERVICE OF PROCESS

service of process
The delivery or communication of writs, summonses, etc.

We have mentioned several times that pleadings give notice of parties' claims and defenses. **Service of process** is the delivery of this formal notice. It is the means by which the parties have assured the court that the pleading or other document was delivered and received by the other parties in the lawsuit. Rule 4 of the Rules of Civil Procedure describes what service of process is, how it is effected, and the court's requirements.

In a civil lawsuit, a summons is used to notify the defendants that a lawsuit has been commenced against them, and commands the defendants to appear so that they may answer the plaintiff's claims. A **subpoena ad testificandum,** commonly just called a **subpoena,** is used to command someone who is *not* a party to the lawsuit to appear and testify in court or at a deposition. The federal court clerk office in your district provides blank forms for summonses and subpoenas. Exhibits 11.11 (p. 324, 325) and 11.12 (p. 326, 327) are sample blank forms of a federal summons and subpoena.

    To fill out a blank summons, type the name of the court, the style of the case, the name and address of a single defendant, and the name, address, and telephone number of the attorney(s) for the plaintiff, if any. Prepare a separate summons for each defendant. When the Complaint is filed with the court clerk, the clerk will issue the summons by signing it and stamping it with the clerk's seal. Then the court clerk returns the issued summons(es) and filed copies of the Complaint to the plaintiff's attorney. The plaintiff's attorney now is responsible for promptly serving the summons, with a copy of the filed Complaint, on each defendant.

    A summons and Complaint can be served personally by a **process server** or by first-class mail, postage prepaid, or by certified mail, return receipt requested. If the summons and Complaint are served by first-class mail, Rule 4(C)(ii) requires that a document called a *Notice and Acknowledgement of Receipt of Summons and Complaint* also be served on the defendant. The defendant is then required to sign the Notice and Acknowledgement and return it within twenty days.

    To simplify this procedure, use certified mail, return receipt requested, instead of first-class mail. Certified mail is more expensive than first-class mail, but less expensive than the cost of a process server. Noting "return receipt requested" on the post office's green certified mail card ensures that the green card is returned to you; and on it will be the signature of the person who received the summons and Complaint, and the date they were delivered by the postal service.

    The person serving the summons and Complaint also has the responsibility of making the **proof of service.** A form for making the proof of service, regardless of whether service was made personally or by mail, can be found on the back of the summons and subpoena form. The form should be filled out and then filed with the court clerk to prove that service of the summons and Complaint was made on each defendant.

subpoena ad testificandum
Commonly called a subpoena, used to command someone who is not a party to the lawsuit to appear and testify in court or at a deposition.

process server
A person authorized by law, such as a sheriff, to serve process papers.

proof of service
Also known as "return of service," the evidence submitted by a process server that he or she has made service on a party or others.

▉ DRAFTING SPECIFIC PLEADINGS

Up to this point, we have discussed the general requirements for pleadings. The following sections address the specifics that you need to know for drafting each type of pleading.

Drafting the Complaint

According to Rule 8 of the Federal Rules of Civil Procedure, a Complaint should state:

1. The names of the persons involved (the parties)
2. The date and place of the transaction or event

▉ PRACTICE TIP

Caveat: Always check the local district court rules where the Complaint will be filed. Its rules may differ slightly from Rule 4 of the Federal Rules of Civil Procedure, and its forms or procedures may be different from those we have used as examples in this chapter.

EXHIBIT 11.11   *Federal Summons*

AO 440 (Rev. 5/85)   Summons in a Civil Action

United States District Court

———————————————————— DISTRICT OF ————————————————————

SUMMONS IN A CIVIL ACTION

V.   CASE NUMBER:

TO: (Name and Address of Defendant)

YOU ARE HEREBY SUMMONED and required to file with the Clerk of this Court and serve upon

PLAINTIFF'S ATTORNEY (name and address)

an answer to the complaint which is herewith served upon you, within _____ days after service of this summons upon you, exclusive of the day of service. If you fail to do so, judgment by default will be taken against you for the relief demanded in the complaint.

CLERK   DATE

BY DEPUTY CLERK

Continued

EXHIBIT 11.11 —*Continued*

AO 440 (Rev. 5/85) Summons in a Civil Action

RETURN OF SERVICE

Service of the Summons and Complaint was made by me[1]	DATE
NAME OF SERVER	TITLE

Check one box below to indicate appropriate method of service

☐ Served personally upon the defendant. Place where served : _____

_____

☐ Left copies thereof at the defendant's dwelling house or usual place of abode with a person of suitable age and discretion then residing therein.
Name of person with whom the summons and complaint were left: _____

☐ Returned unexecuted: _____

_____

_____

☐ Other (specify): _____

_____

_____

STATEMENT OF SERVICE FEES

TRAVEL	SERVICES	TOTAL

DECLARATION OF SERVER

I declare under penalty of perjury under the laws of the United States of America that the foregoing information contained in the Return of Service and Statement of Service Fees is true and correct.

Executed on_____ _____
　　　　　　　　Date　　　　　　　　　　*Signature of Server*

_____
Address of Server

1) As to who may serve a summons see Rule 4 of the Federal Rules of Civil Procedure.

EXHIBIT 11.12   *Federal Subpoena*

. AO 88 (11/91) Subpoena in a Civil Case

United States District Court

_____ **DISTRICT OF** _____

V.   **SUBPOENA IN A CIVIL CASE**

                                                              CASE NUMBER:

TO:

☐ YOU ARE COMMANDED to appear in the United States District Court at the place, date, and time specified below to testify in the above case.

PLACE OF TESTIMONY	COURTROOM
	DATE AND TIME

☐ YOU ARE COMMANDED to appear at the place, date, and time specified below to testify at the taking of a deposition in the above case.

PLACE OF DEPOSITION	DATE AND TIME

☐ YOU ARE COMMANDED to produce and permit inspection and copying of the following documents or objects at the place, date, and time specified below (list documents or objects):

PLACE	DATE AND TIME

☐ YOU ARE COMMANDED to permit inspection of the following premises at the date and time specified below.

PREMISES	DATE AND TIME

    Any organization not a party to this suit that is subpoenaed for the taking of a deposition shall designate one or more officers, directors, or managing agents, or other persons who consent to testify on its behalf, and may set forth, for each person designated, the matters on which the person will testify. Federal Rules of Civil Procedure, 30(b) (6).

ISSUING OFFICER SIGNATURE AND TITLE (INDICATE IF ATTORNEY FOR PLAINTIFF OR DEFENDANT)	DATE
ISSUING OFFICER'S NAME, ADDRESS AND PHONE NUMBER	

(See Rule 45, Federal Rules of Civil Procedure, Parts C & D on Reverse)

Continued

EXHIBIT 11.12   —*Continued*

AO 88 (11/91) Subpoena in a Civil Case

PROOF OF SERVICE

	DATE	PLACE
SERVED		

SERVED ON (PRINT NAME)	MANNER OF SERVICE

SERVED BY (PRINT NAME)	TITLE

DECLARATION OF SERVER

I declare under penalty of perjury under the laws of the United States of America that the foregoing information contained in the Proof of Service is true and correct.

Executed on _____
DATE

_____
SIGNATURE OF SERVER

_____
ADDRESS OF SERVER

_____

Rule 45, Federal Rules of Civil Procedure, Parts C & D:

(c) PROTECTION OF PERSONS SUBJECT TO SUBPOENAS.

(1) A party or an attorney responsible for the issuance and service of a subpoena shall take reasonable steps to avoid imposing undue burden or expense on a person subject to that subpoena. The court on behalf of which the subpoena was issued shall enforce this duty and impose upon the party or attorney in breach of this duty an appropriate sanction, which may include, but is not limited to, lost earnings and a reasonable attorney's fee.

(2)(A) A person commanded to produce and permit inspection and copying of designated books, papers, documents or tangible things, or inspection of premises need not appear in person at the place of production or inspection unless commanded to appear for deposition, hearing or trial.

(B) Subject to paragraph (d)(2) of this rule, a person commanded to produce and permit inspection and copying may, within 14 days after service of the subpoena or before the time specified for compliance if such time is less than 14 days after service, serve upon the party or attorney designated in the subpoena written objection to inspection or copying of any or all of the designated materials or of the premises. If objection is made, the party serving the subpoena shall not be entitled to inspect and copy the materials or inspect the premises except pursuant to an order of the court by which the subpoena was issued. If objection has been made, the party serving the subpoena may, upon notice to the person commanded to produce, move at any time for an order to compel the production. Such an order to compel production shall protect any person who is not a party or an officer of a party from significant expense resulting from the inspection and copying commanded.

(3) (A) On timely motion, the court by which a subpoena was issued shall quash or modify the subpoena if it

(i) fails to allow reasonable time for compliance;

(ii) requires a person who is not a party or an officer of a party to travel to a place more than 100 miles from the place where that person resides, is employed or regularly transacts business in person, except that, subject to the provisions of clause (c)(3)(B)(iii) of this rule, such a person may in order to attend trial be commanded to travel from any such place within the state in which the trial is held, or

(iii) requires disclosure of privileged or other protected matter and no exception or waiver applies, or

(iv) subjects a person to undue burden.

(B) If a subpoena

(i) requires disclosure of a trade secret or other confidential research, development, or commercial information, or

(ii) requires disclosure of an unretained expert's opinion or information not describing specific events or occurrences in dispute and resulting from the expert's study made not at the request of any party, or

(iii) requires a person who is not a party or an officer of a party to incur substantial expense to travel more than 100 miles to attend trial, the court may, to protect a person subject to or affected by the subpoena, quash or modify the subpoena or, if the party in whose behalf the subpoena is issued shows a substantial need for the testimony or material that cannot be otherwise met without undue hardship and assures that the person to whom the subpoena is addressed will be reasonably compensated, the court may order appearance or production only upon specified conditions.

(d) DUTIES IN RESPONDING TO SUBPOENA.

(1) A person responding to a subpoena to produce documents shall produce them as they are kept in the usual course of business or shall organize and label them to correspond with the categories in the demand.

(2) When information subject to a subpoena is withheld on a claim that it is privileged or subject to protection as trial preparation materials, the claim shall be made expressly and shall be supported by a description of the nature of the documents, communications, or things not produced that is sufficient to enable the demanding party to contest the claim.

3. The legal wrong alleged by the plaintiff against the defendant (what the plaintiff claims the defendant did that was wrong)
4. The type and extent of the harm (losses or injuries) suffered by the plaintiff because of the defendant's wrong
5. A demand for the amount of compensation or relief requested, commonly referred to as the "prayer for relief" or "prayer." Relief "in the alternative" or of several different types may be demanded

Although your legal research for drafting the Complaint will include case law, you never cite case law within the Complaint. You should, however, include any citations to statutes or regulations on which you rely for any claim.

Rule 10(b), Fed.R.Civ.P., requires that all statements of a claim must be made in sequentially numbered paragraphs. The statement in each paragraph should be limited as far as practicable to a statement of a *single set of circumstances*. Each paragraph may be referred to by number in subsequent pleadings. Each claim founded upon separate transactions or occurrences must be set out in a separate count whenever that separation helps to present the issue more clearly.

Normally, most Complaints state each claim involving a separate theory of recovery in a separate count or cause of action. This is generally true even when all of the claims are based on the same event or occurrence. If you are not sure whether something belongs in a separate paragraph, remember it is better to have too many paragraphs than too few.

Keep in mind that, when the defendant is drafting his Answer to the Complaint, he will respond to each paragraph. If there is more than one point or claim in a paragraph—or if your paragraph is a long, rambling narrative—you increase the possibility for error, confusion, and ambiguity. For example, if there is more than one allegation in a paragraph, the defendant may admit to a portion of the paragraph but deny the remainder, making it difficult to determine specifically what the defendant's answer really is.

Before you begin drafting the Complaint, organize your thoughts. Make an outline or checklist of the claims to be included in the Complaint, then write the necessary elements to prove each claim. State the events and facts in logical and chronological order.

Avoid the temptation to include multiple theories and facts from which the trier of fact is to select the most favorable option for your client. Simplicity breeds credibility. Too many theories may only confuse the judge or jury and create a loss of credibility for your attorney or your client.

Before you spend hours drafting the Complaint, ask your supervising attorney if she or he has a form that would be useful. If so, pay particular attention to determine what portions of the form should be adopted and what should be discarded. Never copy a form blindly or without editing it to meet the current assignment.

Pleading "Special Matters."   One exception to the "notice" pleading format requirements is when it is necessary to plead **special matters.** Under Rule 9, Fed.R.Civ.P., some allegations (such as fraud, mistake, subject-matter jurisdiction, and special damages) must be pleaded "specifically" and "with particularity." This means that, when drafting the portion of the pleading dealing with these issues, you must give enough details and facts to describe the fraud, mistake, etc., and how the defendant's alleged conduct produced it.

PRACTICE TIP

All of the statements within one claim must be made in sequentially numbered paragraphs. The statement in each paragraph should be limited as far as practicable to a statement of a single set of circumstances.

PRACTICE TIP

Simplicity breeds credibility. Too many theories may only confuse the judge or jury and create a loss of credibility for your attorney or your client.

special matters
The one exception to notice pleading format requirements, which requires that some allegations, such as fraud, mistake, subject-matter jurisdiction, and special damages, must be pleaded "specifically" and "with particularity."

Exhibit 11.13 is an example of what facts and details are necessary to plead fraud as a special matter.

EXHIBIT 11.13 *Pleading Special Matters*

1. On June 1, 1994, Plaintiff Susan Jones ("Buyer") and Defendant Mark Smith ("Seller") entered into a contract (the "Contract"), a copy of which is attached as Exhibit "A."

2. Under the Contract, Buyer agreed to pay Seller $15,000 for 10 acres in Norman, Oklahoma. The legal description for the 10 acres is set out in the Contract attached as Exhibit "1."

3. Before the Contract was signed by the parties, Seller represented to Buyer that he had legal title to the 10 acres and that the 10 acres was free of any encumbrances.

4. Before the Contract was executed, Seller also represented to Buyer that the 10 acres would be rezoned to an R–1 zoning upon Buyer's application for rezoning to the City of Norman.

5. The representations made by Seller in paragraphs three and four above were false and fraudulent, and Seller willfully and knowingly made those representations to Buyer to induce Buyer to enter into the Contract.

6. Buyer relied upon Seller's false and fraudulent representations, and was damaged.

Verification.   In some jurisdictions, court rules or statutes require that a **verification** be attached to the Complaint. A verification is simply a sworn statement by the party that he or she has read the Complaint, and that all of the allegations contained in the Complaint are true to the best of his or her knowledge or belief, such as the one in Exhibit 11.14. Verifications are commonly required for a Complaint and responses to discovery requests.

verification
A sworn statement by the party that he or she has read the document and that all of the allegations, statements, and answers in it are true and correct to the best of his or her knowledge or belief.

EXHIBIT 11.14 *Verification*

VERIFICATION

STATE OF _____   )
)   SS.
COUNTY OF _____   )

I, [name of plaintiff], of lawful age, being first duly sworn upon my oath, state:
    1. That I am the Plaintiff in this lawsuit;
    2. That I have read the Complaint and am familiar with its contents;
    3. That the statements and facts contained in the Complaint are true and correct to the best of my knowledge and belief.

                                _____
                                    [Name of Plaintiff]

Subscribed and sworn to before me this ___ day of _____, 199__.

                                _____
                                  Notary Public

My Commission Expires:
[Seal]
_____

civil cover sheet
A form sometimes required by federal courts to be filed with the Complaint.

praecipe
A document signed by the plaintiff or plaintiff's attorney requesting the court clerk to issue a summons to a defendant.

filing fee
The fee assessed by the court clerk for filing any Complaint or Petition and other documents or for issuing a summons or subpoena, regardless of whether the document is filed with, or issued from, a state or federal court.

Civil Cover Sheet.   Federal courts require that a **civil cover sheet** be prepared, signed by the attorney of record, and filed with the Complaint. Most district courts use a form similar to the one shown at Exhibit 11.15. As you can see from Exhibit 11.15, the civil cover sheet basically asks for the type of information that will assist the court clerk's office in identifying what type of case it is and in compiling other statistical data.

The civil cover sheet is not difficult to fill out. Most, if not all, of the information it requires can be found within the Complaint. It is not necessary to serve this form with the Complaint and summons on the defendants. It is merely filed with the court clerk's office.

Praecipe.   In some federal jurisdictions a praecipe, like the one shown in Exhibit 11.16, p. 333, is also required. A **praecipe** is basically a request (in writing) to the court clerk to issue a summons to a defendant, and it is signed by the plaintiff or plaintiff's attorney who wants a summons issued. The praecipe gives the name and address of the person to be served or, if the defendant is a corporation, the corporation's service agent or officer to be served. The praecipe also states how service will be effected, whether by certified mail or private process server. If you are not sure whether a praecipe is required, a quick check of the court's local rules or a call to the court clerk's office should provide the answer

Filing Fees

There will be a **filing fee** for filing any Complaint or Petition, whether filed in state or federal court. There may also be additional fees for each summons issued by the court clerk. If you are unsure about the amount for these fees, call the court clerk's office. Determine exactly what filing fees will be necessary *before* the Complaint leaves your office to be filed with the court clerk.

Most court clerk offices publish a list of all filing fees and the number of copies required when filing various documents, and will provide the list to anyone who asks for it. Commonly this list is also published in the state bar journal at least once a year. Keep a copy close at hand so that you may refer to it as necessary.

Filing the Complaint

Before the Complaint is taken to the court clerk's office for filing, check to be sure that all of the necessary documents have been prepared, meaning an original and copies of the complaint, the civil cover sheet (if any is required), the original and copies of the summons (together with a praecipe, if required) for each defendant, and a check that will cover all required filing fees.

If the Complaint and accompanying documents will be hand-delivered to the court clerk's office for filing, no cover letter to the court clerk is necessary. But if you are mailing the documents to the court clerk for filing, we suggest that you include a cover letter to the court clerk's office that says something like the one in Exhibit 11.17 (p.333).

If the court clerk's office is in another city or state, you may wish to enlist a private process service to help you. There are several books listing private process offices all over the country. If you do not have access to such a book, then call that court clerk's office, and ask them to recommend several reliable private process servers. Call the process server and explain what you want to file. The process server should be able to tell you how many copies are required, what documents, such as the civil

EXHIBIT 11.15 *Federal Civil Cover Sheet*

JS 44
(Rev. 07/89)

CIVIL COVER SHEET

The JS-44 civil cover sheet and the information contained herein neither replace nor supplement the filing and service of pleadings or other papers as required by law, except as provided by local rules of court. This form, approved by the Judicial Conference of the United States in September 1974, is required for the use of the Clerk of Court for the purpose of initiating the civil docket sheet. **(SEE INSTRUCTIONS ON THE REVERSE OF THE FORM.)**

I (a) PLAINTIFFS

DEFENDANTS

(b) COUNTY OF RESIDENCE OF FIRST LISTED PLAINTIFF _____
(EXCEPT IN U.S. PLAINTIFF CASES)

COUNTY OF RESIDENCE OF FIRST LISTED DEFENDANT _____
(IN U.S. PLAINTIFF CASES ONLY)
NOTE: IN LAND CONDEMNATION CASES, USE THE LOCATION OF THE
TRACT OF LAND INVOLVED

(c) ATTORNEYS (FIRM NAME, ADDRESS, AND TELEPHONE NUMBER)

ATTORNEYS (IF KNOWN)

II. BASIS OF JURISDICTION (PLACE AN × IN ONE BOX ONLY)

☐ 1 U.S. Government
    Plaintiff

☐ 2 U.S. Government
    Defendant

☐ 3 Federal Question
    (U.S. Government Not a Party)

☐ 4 Diversity
    (Indicate Citizenship of
    Parties in Item III)

III. CITIZENSHIP OF PRINCIPAL PARTIES (PLACE AN × IN ONE BOX
(For Diversity Cases Only) FOR PLAINTIFF AND ONE BOX FOR DEFENDANT)

	PTF	DEF		PTF	DEF
Citizen of This State	☐ 1	☐ 1	Incorporated or Principal Place of Business in This State	☐ 4	☐ 4
Citizen of Another State	☐ 2	☐ 2	Incorporated and Principal Place of Business in Another State	☐ 5	☐ 5
Citizen or Subject of a Foreign Country	☐ 3	☐ 3	Foreign Nation	☐ 6	☐ 6

IV. CAUSE OF ACTION (CITE THE U.S. CIVIL STATUTE UNDER WHICH YOU ARE FILING AND WRITE A BRIEF STATEMENT OF CAUSE.

DO NOT CITE JURISDICTIONAL STATUTES UNLESS DIVERSITY.)

V. NATURE OF SUIT (PLACE AN × IN ONE BOX ONLY)

CONTRACT	TORTS		FORFEITURE/PENALTY	BANKRUPTCY	OTHER STATUTES
☐ 110 Insurance	**PERSONAL INJURY**	**PERSONAL INJURY**	☐ 610 Agriculture	☐ 422 Appeal 28 USC 158	☐ 400 State Reapportionment
☐ 120 Marine	☐ 310 Airplane	☐ 362 Personal Injury— Med Malpractice	☐ 620 Other Food & Drug		☐ 410 Antitrust
☐ 130 Miller Act	☐ 315 Airplane Product Liability		☐ 625 Drug Related Seizure of Property 21 USC 881	☐ 423 Withdrawal 28 USC 157	☐ 430 Banks and Banking
☐ 140 Negotiable Instrument	☐ 320 Assault, Libel & Slander	☐ 365 Personal Injury— Product Liability	☐ 630 Liquor Laws		☐ 450 Commerce/ICC Rates/etc.
☐ 150 Recovery of Overpayment & Enforcement of Judgment	☐ 330 Federal Employers' Liability	☐ 368 Asbestos Personal Injury Product Liability	☐ 640 R.R & Truck	**PROPERTY RIGHTS**	☐ 460 Deportation
☐ 151 Medicare Act	☐ 340 Marine		☐ 650 Airline Regs	☐ 820 Copyrights	☐ 470 Racketeer Influenced and Corrupt Organizations
☐ 152 Recovery of Defaulted Student Loans (Excl. Veterans)	☐ 345 Marine Product Liability	**PERSONAL PROPERTY**	☐ 660 Occupational Safety/Health	☐ 830 Patent	☐ 810 Selective Service
☐ 153 Recovery of Overpayment of Veteran's Benefits	☐ 350 Motor Vehicle	☐ 370 Other Fraud	☐ 690 Other	☐ 840 Trademark	☐ 850 Securities/Commodities/ Exchange
☐ 160 Stockholders' Suits	☐ 355 Motor Vehicle Product Liability	☐ 371 Truth in Lending	**LABOR**	**SOCIAL SECURITY**	☐ 875 Customer Challenge 12 USC 3410
☐ 190 Other Contract	☐ 360 Other Personal Injury	☐ 380 Other Personal Property Damage	☐ 710 Fair Labor Standards Act	☐ 861 HIA (1395ff)	☐ 891 Agricultural Acts
☐ 195 Contract Product Liability		☐ 385 Property Damage Product Liability	☐ 720 Labor/Mgmt. Relations	☐ 862 Black Lung (923)	☐ 892 Economic Stabilization Act
REAL PROPERTY	**CIVIL RIGHTS**	**PRISONER PETITIONS**	☐ 730 Labor/Mgmt. Reporting & Disclosure Act	☐ 863 DIWC/DIWW (405(g))	☐ 893 Environmental Matters
☐ 210 Land Condemnation	☐ 441 Voting	☐ 510 Motions to Vacate Sentence		☐ 864 SSID Title XVI	☐ 894 Energy Allocation Act
☐ 220 Foreclosure	☐ 442 Employment	Habeas Corpus:	☐ 740 Railway Labor Act	☐ 865 RSI (405(g))	☐ 895 Freedom of Information Act
☐ 230 Rent Lease & Ejectment	☐ 443 Housing/ Accommodations	☐ 530 General	☐ 790 Other Labor Litigation	**FEDERAL TAX SUITS**	☐ 900 Appeal of Fee Determination Under Equal Access to Justice
☐ 240 Torts to Land	☐ 444 Welfare	☐ 535 Death Penalty	☐ 791 Empl. Ret. Inc. Security Act	☐ 870 Taxes (U.S. Plaintiff or Defendant)	
☐ 245 Tort Product Liability	☐ 440 Other Civil Rights	☐ 540 Mandamus & Other		☐ 871 IRS—Third Party 26 USC 7609	☐ 950 Constitutionality of State Statutes
☐ 290 All Other Real Property		☐ 550 Other			☐ 890 Other Statutory Actions

VI. ORIGIN (PLACE AN × IN ONE BOX ONLY)

☐ 1 Original
    Proceeding

☐ 2 Removed from
    State Court

☐ 3 Remanded from
    Appellate Court

☐ 4 Reinstated or
    Reopened

Transferred from
☐ 5 another district
    (specify)

☐ 6 Multidistrict
    Litigation

Appeal to District
☐ 7 Judge from
    Magistrate
    Judgment

VII. REQUESTED IN COMPLAINT:

CHECK IF THIS IS A **CLASS ACTION**
☐ UNDER F.R.C.P. 23

DEMAND $

Check YES only if demanded in complaint:
JURY DEMAND: ☐ YES   ☐ NO

VIII. RELATED CASE(S) IF ANY (See instructions):

JUDGE _____   DOCKET NUMBER _____

DATE

SIGNATURE OF ATTORNEY OF RECORD

UNITED STATES DISTRICT COURT

Continued

EXHIBIT 11.15 *—Continued*

INSTRUCTIONS FOR ATTORNEYS COMPLETING CIVIL COVER SHEET FORM JS-44

Authority For Civil Cover Sheet

The JS-44 civil cover sheet and the information contained herein neither replaces nor supplements the filings and service of pleading or other papers as required by law, except as provided by local rules of court. This form, approved by the Judicial Conference of the United States in September 1974, is required for the use of the Clerk of Court for the purpose of initiating the civil docket sheet. Consequently a civil cover sheet is submitted to the Clerk of Court for each civil complaint filed. The attorney filing a case should complete the form as follows:

I. (a) Plaintiffs - Defendants. Enter names (last, first, middle initial) of plaintiff and defendant. If the plaintiff or defendant is a government agency, use only the full name or standard abbreviations. If the plaintiff or defendant is an official within a government agency, identify first the agency and then the official, giving both name and title.

(b) County of Residence. For each civil case filed, except U.S. plaintiff cases, enter the name of the county where the first listed plaintiff resides at the time of filing. In U.S. plaintiff cases, enter the name of the county in which the first listed defendant resides at the time of filing. (NOTE: In land condemnation cases, the county of residence of the "defendant" is the location of the tract of land involved).

(c) Attorneys. Enter firm name, address, telephone number, and attorney or record. If there are several attorneys, list them on an attachment, noting in this section "(see attachment)".

II. Jurisdiction. The basis of jurisdiction is set forth under Rule 8 (a), F.R.C.P., which requires that jurisdictions be shown in pleadings. Place an "X" in one of the boxes. If there is more than one basis of jurisdiction, precedence is given in the order shown below.

United States plaintiff. (1) Jurisdiction is based on 28 U.S.C. 1345 and 1348. Suits by agencies and officers of the United States are included here.

United States defendant. (2) When the plaintiff is suing the United States, its officers or agencies, place an X in this box.

Federal question. (3) This refers to suits under 28 U.S.C. 1331, where jurisdiction arises under the Constitution of the United States, an amendment to the Constitution, an act of Congress or a treaty of the United States. In cases where the U.S. is a party, the U.S. plaintiff or defendant code takes precedence, and box 1 or 2 should be marked.

Diversity of citizenship. (4) This refers to suits under 28 U.S.C. 1332, where parties are citizens of different states. When Box 4 is checked, the citizenship of the different parties must be checked. (See Section III below; federal question actions take precedence over diversity cases.)

III. Residence (citizenship) of Principal Parties. This section of the JS-44 is to be completed if diversity of citizenship was indicated above. Mark this section for each principal party.

IV. Cause of Action. Report the civil statute directly related to the cause of action and give a brief description of the cause.

V. Nature of Suit. Place an "X" in the appropriate box. If the nature of suit cannot be determined, be sure the cause of action, in Section IV above, is sufficient to enable the deputy clerk or the statistical clerks in the Administrative Office to determine the nature of suit. If the cause fits more than one nature of suit, select the most definitive.

VI. Origin. Place an "X" in one of the seven boxes.

Original Proceedings. (1) Cases which originate in the United States district courts.

Removed from State Court. (2) Proceedings initiated in state courts may be removed to the district courts under Title 28 U.S.C., Section 1441. When the petition for removal is granted, check this box.

Remanded from Appellate Court. (3) Check this box for cases remanded to the district court for further action. Use the date of remand as the filing date.

Reinstated or Reopened. (4) Check this box for cases reinstated or reopened in the district court. Use the reopening date as the filing date.

Transferred from Another District. (5) For cases transferred under Title 28 U.S.C. Section 1404(a). Do not use this for within district transfers or multidistrict litigation transfers.

Multidistrict Litigation. (6) Check this box when a multidistrict case is transferred into the district under authority of Title 28 U.S.C. Section 1407. When this box is checked, do not check (5) above.

Appeal to District Judge from Magistrate Judgment. (7) Check this box for an appeal from a magistrate's decision.

VII. Requested in Complaint. Class Action. Place an "X" in this box if you are filing a class action under Rule 23, F.R.Cv.P.

Demand. In this space enter the dollar amount (in thousands of dollars) being demanded or indicate other demand such as a preliminary injunction.

Jury Demand. Check the appropriate box to indicate whether or not a jury is being demanded.

VIII. Related Cases. This section of the JS-44 is used to reference relating pending cases if any. If there are related pending cases, insert the docket numbers and the corresponding judge names for such cases.

Date and Attorney Signature. Date and sign the civil cover sheet.

(rev. 07/89)

EXHIBIT 11.16   *Federal Praecipe*

In The United States District Court For The
Western District of Oklahoma

	)	
_____	)	Case No._____
	)	
_____	)	
Plaintiff	)	
v.	)	
	)	PRAECIPE FOR SUMMONS
_____	)	(Required by Local Court Rule 7)
	)	
_____	)	
Defendant	)	
	)	

TO THE CLERK OF SAID COURT: YOU WILL PLEASE ISSUE SUMMONS IN THE ABOVE ENTITLED CAUSE FOR:

Name of Defendant(s)	Address	Serve	Service To Be Made by	Date to Answer

AND MAKE THE SAME RETURNABLE ACCORDING TO LAW

_____
Plaintiff or Attorney for Plaintiff (Please Type or Print)

_____
Attorney Signature

_____
Address of Attorney

_____
City & State   Zip

EXHIBIT 11.17   *Cover Letter to Court Clerk*

Dear Court Clerk:

   Enclosed are the original and seven copies of the Complaint, the original and two copies of the Civil Cover Sheet, and the original and two copies of the Praecipes and Summons for each defendant, and this firm's check for $_____ to cover the filing fees. Please file the Complaint and issue the Summons for each Defendant, then return file-stamped copies of the Complaint and the Summons to the undersigned in the self-addressed, stamped envelope. This office will serve the Summons and Complaint on each Defendant by certified mail.

   Thank you for your assistance. If you have any questions or require additional information, please do not hesitate to contact me at [telephone number].

■ PRACTICE TIP

Most court clerk offices publish a list of all filing fees and the number of copies required when filing various documents, and will provide the list to anyone who asks for it. Commonly this list is also published in the state bar journal at least once a year.

return of service
The evidence submitted that proper service has been made on a party or others.

cover sheet, are required by that court, the filing fees, and any other requirements that might have an impact on filing the document and having the summons issued. Then, once everything has been prepared, you can simply send everything to the process server who will file and serve the documents, make the **returns of service** with the court clerk, and return file-stamped copies to you.

Checklist for Drafting and Filing the Complaint

Once you have drafted the Complaint, proofread it as you would any other pleading. Satisfy yourself that a reasonable inquiry has been made, and that all facts stated in the Complaint are true. Also check that all prerequisites for filing the Complaint have been fulfilled, such as exhausting administrative remedies.

✓ Check the file for the correct names and addresses and/or service agents for each of the parties. Is each party's name spelled correctly?

✓ Is the lawsuit being filed in the proper court?

✓ Does the Complaint include the necessary jurisdictional paragraph, including any money amount, and any required paragraphs on venue?

When drafting the body of the Complaint, check for the following:

✓ Have you researched the necessary elements to prove each cause of action and made sure that these elements are included in your draft?

✓ Did you determine whether enough facts and details were stated to meet the minimum pleading requirements (does the court require fact or notice pleadings?) for the applicable court, and that facts were included to support each claim?

✓ Is each sequentially numbered paragraph limited to one idea?

✓ Did you remember not to state evidence or conclusions?

✓ Are the statements made brief and concise?

✓ Were you truthful? Did you make exaggerated statements about the facts? You may include allegations even though you are uncertain as to the facts if you have some information or belief to support a good-faith allegation.

✓ Do the statements in the body of the pleading follow a logical progression, as if you were telling the reader a story?

✓ Have any special matters been pleaded with sufficient particularity and detail?

✓ Does the prayer for relief (demand for judgment) meet the applicable court's requirements for how the amount of damages sought is stated?

✓ Is a demand for jury trial needed and, if so, has it been included?

✓ Does the pleading comply with all applicable rules, not only as to content but also as to size of paper, number of copies, etc.?

✓ Did you check all references to exhibits for internal consistency and check to be sure that each exhibit was designated, marked, and attached to the pleading?

✓ Is a Verification necessary? If so, has one been drafted and signed by the client, and has the client's signature been notarized? Make whatever arrangements are necessary to prepare this document and have it executed by the client *before* the deadline for filing the Complaint.

✓ Have you proofread the information in the signature block and certificate of service? Are all names spelled correctly? Is each attorney's address accurate?

Before filing the Complaint:

✓ Before copying the Complaint for filing, check to be sure that:

- All exhibits have been marked and attached.
- The Verification has been signed and notarized, and is attached.
- The Complaint and the Certificate of Service have been signed by the attorney of record.

✓ Before filing the Complaint and having the court clerk issue the summons for each defendant:

- Determine the amount of the necessary filing fees and arrange for a check to the court clerk for that amount.
- Prepare a summons for each defendant.
- Be sure that an adequate number of copies of the Complaint and each Summons has been made.
- Determine the method of service for each defendant.

✓ Once the Complaint has been filed and each summons has been issued by the court clerk, arrange for service of the Summons and Complaint on each defendant. Once service has been effected, prepare and/or arrange for the filing of each return of service with the court clerk.

✓ Docket the answer date for each defendant based on the *date of service.*

Drafting the Answer

Rule 12 of the Federal Rules of Civil Procedure requires a defendant to serve an Answer on the plaintiff within twenty days from the date of service of the complaint on the defendant. But when a defendant is served with the Complaint, filing an answer is not the only response allowed.

It is possible that there is some procedural reason that the court should not proceed with the lawsuit. If such a problem does exist, the defendant could file preliminary objections in the form of a motion to the content of the Complaint. These preliminary objections would be filed before an Answer or, in some instances, with the Answer. We will discuss these and other motions later in this chapter, and focus now only on drafting the Answer.

Rule Requirements.   Rule 10(b), Fed.R.Civ.P., requires that all statements of a claim or defense shall be made in numbered paragraphs. The statement in each paragraph

Answer
Defendant's formal, written response to the allegations in the plaintiff's Complaint.

PRACTICE TIP

An Answer may have three separate parts:
1. Responses to the Complaint's allegations
2. Affirmative defenses
3. Rule 12(b) defenses

should be limited as far as practicable to a statement of a *single set of circumstances.* Just as in the Complaint, each paragraph in the Answer is numbered sequentially and may be referred to by number in subsequent pleadings.

Each defense, other than a **denial,** must be stated in a separate count whenever that separation helps to present the issues more clearly. In short, each defense in the Answer is organized into numbered paragraphs and by counts or causes of action, just like the Complaint.

Rule 8(b) states that a party shall admit or deny the allegations (claims) made by the opponent (plaintiff), and state the defense to each claim asserted in short, plain terms. In other words, the defendant may simply prepare an Answer responsive to each of the allegations in the Complaint. The Answer should look something like the example in Exhibit 11.18.

denial

Defense in which the defendant denies one or more facts necessary to support the claim, often based upon a different view of the same rule of law raised by the opponent.

EXHIBIT 11.18 *Answer of Defendant Charles Raymond*

ANSWER OF DEFENDANT CHARLES RAYMOND

Defendant Charles Raymond states the following as his Answer to the Complaint:

1. Admitted;

2. Denied;
   and so on.

PRACTICE TIP

The defendant must respond in the Answer to each allegation made in the Complaint. Any allegations in the Complaint that are not denied by the defendant are deemed *admitted.*

During discovery, the plaintiff will have an opportunity to find out why the defendant answered as he did.

Situations may occur in which the defendant simply does not know the answer to the plaintiff's allegation. The plaintiff's allegation may assert facts or claims the defendant knows nothing about. When this happens, the defendant may state that he or she lacks the first-hand knowledge needed to form a belief about the truth of the plaintiff's allegations, as shown in Exhibit 11.19.

EXHIBIT 11.19 *Lack of Sufficient Information Clause*

5. Defendant is without knowledge or information sufficient to form a belief as to the truth of the allegations contained in paragraph 5 of Plaintiff's Complaint and, therefore, denies the same.

The type of statement found in Exhibit 11.19 has the same effect as a denial. Although a defendant is not required to assume the burden of an exhaustive search, a defendant may not make this statement without first making a good-faith attempt to ascertain that knowledge and information. This is particularly true when the information is easily determined within the 20-day time limit to answer the Complaint.

If the defendant can, in good faith, deny only a part of a statement made in the Complaint, the defendant may specify that only a portion of the statement is true and deny the rest, as we did in Exhibit 11.20.

EXHIBIT 11.20 *Partial Denial*

1. Defendant Charles Raymond admits a motor vehicle collision occurred on or about _____[date]_____ involving Plaintiff Jane Healy and Defendant Charles Raymond, but denies the remaining allegations contained in paragraph 1 of Plaintiff's Complaint.

Another safe way to deal with this situation is for the defendant to generally deny all averments or paragraphs except for those which the defendant expressly admits, as in Exhibit 11.21.

EXHIBIT 11.21   *General Denial*

ANSWER OF DEFENDANT CHARLES RAYMOND

As his Answer to Plaintiff's Complaint, Defendant Charles Raymond generally denies each allegation contained in Plaintiff's Complaint except for those specifically admitted, as follows:

1. Defendant Charles Raymond admits that he is a citizen of the State of Oklahoma as alleged in paragraph one of Plaintiff's Complaint.
2. Defendant Charles Raymond admits that, on or about the ___ day of _____, 199___, he and Plaintiff Jane Healy were involved in a motor vehicle accident.

Each allegation within the Complaint *must* be responded to by the defendant in the Answer. Any allegations made in the Complaint that are not denied by the defendant are deemed admitted.

In a Complaint where there are multiple defendants, it may not be necessary for each defendant to respond to every allegation in the Complaint. That is because not every allegation will be directed against each defendant. When this occurs, state that no answer is required because the allegation does not concern your defendant, as in Exhibit 11.22.

EXHIBIT 11.22   *Allegation Requiring No Answer*

5. The allegations contained in paragraph five of Plaintiff's Complaint are not directed against Defendant Charles Raymond and, therefore, no answer is required.

Affirmative Defenses.   Once the defendant has answered all of the allegations contained in the plaintiff's Complaint, the defendant can then state whatever **affirmative defenses** he or she has to the substance of the Complaint. An affirmative defense may raise an issue not found in the Complaint. An affirmative defense is valid regardless of whether the defendant has admitted the truth of all of the Complaint's allegations in his or her answer. For example, what if the statute of limitations had expired before the lawsuit was filed? Even if all of the allegations in the Complaint were true, this would still be a valid, and effective, defense.

Some affirmative defenses may, under Rule 12(b), be made by motion rather than as part of the defendant's Answer. Those affirmative defenses are as follows:

1. Lack of jurisdiction over the subject matter
2. Lack of jurisdiction over the person
3. Improper venue
4. Insufficiency of process
5. Insufficiency of service of process
6. Failure to state a claim upon which relief can be granted
7. Failure to join a party under Rule 19[3]

affirmative defenses
Matter asserted by defendant which, assuming the Complaint to be true, constitutes a defense to it.

PRACTICE TIP

A defendant may use affirmative defenses regardless of whether the allegations contained in the Complaint are true.

[3.] Rule 19, Fed.R.Civ.P., requires that a person who is subject to service of process and whose joinder will not deprive the court of jurisdiction over the subject matter *shall be joined as a party* if that person's absence somehow impedes the court from giving complete relief to the parties or all persons who may claim an interest relating to the lawsuit.

It is not required that these affirmative defenses be made solely by motion. But if any of these defenses are raised in the Answer, they should be stated in separate paragraphs and follow the language of Rule 12(b) as closely as possible. Exhibit 11.23 is an example.

EXHIBIT 11.23 *Affirmative Defenses*

AFFIRMATIVE DEFENSES OF DEFENDANT RAYMOND CHARLES

1. Plaintiff Jane Healy's Complaint fails to state a claim against Defendant Charles Raymond upon which relief can be granted.

Additionally, according to Rule 12(h)(1), Fed.R.Civ.P., a defense of lack of jurisdiction over the person, improper venue, insufficiency of process, or insufficiency of service of process is *deemed waived* if it is not made in either an Answer or a Rule 12 motion to dismiss.

entry of appearance
A document filed with the court stating that the attorney named is entering an appearance as counsel of record on behalf of a litigant.

In some jurisdictions, local court rules may require the counsel for all parties to file an **Entry of Appearance** whenever a party has entered the lawsuit. If that is the case, the entry of appearance must be filed with the court clerk before that party can file any other document with the court. A file-stamped copy of the entry of appearance should be mailed to all other parties in the lawsuit. It serves to notify the parties and the court of the name, address, and telephone number of that party's counsel of record. The entry of appearance shown in Exhibit 11.24 basically states that the attorney named in the document is entering an appearance on behalf of the defendant.

In some jurisdictions, filing an entry of appearance is an option for the defendant, not a requirement. In those instances, the entry of appearance is generally used to postpone the 30-day deadline for filing the defendant's Answer by another 20 days. If the court rules also allow the defendant filing the entry of appearance to reserve an additional 20 days to file his or her Answer, that language should be added to the entry of appearance, like this:

> Pursuant to Rule ___ of the Rules for the ___ Court, Defendant [name] reserves an additional 20 days from _____ [the date of service upon defendant], or until _____ [the date 50 days from the date of service upon defendant], to file his or her Answer to Plaintiff's Complaint.

One fatal flaw of filing an entry of appearance is that, according to Rule 12(R), certain defenses are automatically waived.

■ PRACTICE TIP

A list of other affirmative defenses is found in Rule 8(c), Fed.R.Civ.P.:
[A] party shall set forth affirmatively accord and satisfaction, arbitration and award, assumption of risk, contributory negligence, discharge in bankruptcy, duress, estoppel, failure of consideration, fraud, illegality, injury by fellow servant, laches, license, payment, release, res judicata, statute of frauds, statute of limitations, waiver, and any other matter constituting an avoidance or affirmative defense. When a party has mistakenly designated a defense as a counterclaim or a counterclaim as a defense, the court on terms, if justice so requires, shall treat the pleading as if there had been a proper designation.

EXHIBIT 11.24 *Entry of Appearance*

AO 458 (Rev. 5/85) Appearance

United States District Court

_____ DISTRICT OF _____

[Insert style of the case.]

APPEARANCE

CASE NUMBER: [Insert case number.]

To the Clerk of this court and all parties of record:

Enter my appearance as counsel in this case for Plaintiff [or Defendant] [name of party].

_____   _____
Date   *Signature* [attorney who is making the Appearance]

_____
Print Name

_____
Address [Address of Law Firm]

_____
City   *State*   *Zip Code*

_____
Phone Number

Look over the list of affirmative defenses set out earlier. What affirmative defenses might be raised by the defendants in our fact scenario in Chapter 1? Defendant Charles Raymond might raise the affirmative defense of contributory negligence, sometimes called comparative negligence in some jurisdictions. What affirmative defenses might be raised by the other defendants?

When an affirmative defense is raised in federal diversity cases, be aware that your defendant may also have to assume the burden of proof for that defense, depending upon state law. It is safer, however, to plead all available affirmative defenses under Rule 8(c) and assume the burden of proof, if required by state law, rather than risk waiving those defenses by failing to raise them.

Exhibit 11.25 (p. 340) gives some examples of affirmative defenses based on our fact scenario.

EXHIBIT 11.25 *Affirmative Defenses*

AFFIRMATIVE DEFENSES

1. If Defendant Charles Raymond should be found to be negligent as stated in paragraphs 3, 5, and 9 of Plaintiff's Complaint, which Defendant Charles Raymond specifically denies, then Plaintiff Jane Healy was contributorily negligent.

2. Plaintiff Jane Healy assumed the risk of the accident by remaining in the middle of the intersection after the light had changed from green to red.

Checklist for Drafting an Answer to the Complaint

Use the following checklist when you are drafting an Answer to a Complaint:

✓ Once the Complaint has been served on the defendant, determine the deadline for filing the Answer or Rule 12 motions according to the court rules, and docket that date on the firm's deadline tickler or docket calendar.

✓ Answer each allegation in the plaintiff's Complaint.

✓ If an allegation is admitted in part and denied in part in the Answer, clearly state the facts being admitted and clearly deny the remaining allegations.

✓ Identify all Rule 12 defenses and affirmative defenses that can be raised in good faith under Rule 11.

✓ Set out individually in separate paragraphs each of the Rule 12 defenses and affirmative defenses identified.

✓ If the plaintiff failed to demand a jury trial and a jury trial is in your client's best interests, be sure that the Answer states "JURY TRIAL DEMANDED" in accordance with applicable court rules.

✓ Determine if you should include a cross-claim against other defendants in the lawsuit and/or a counterclaim against the plaintiff.

Drafting the Counterclaim or Cross-Claim

counterclaim
Sometimes called a cross-complaint, a cause of action or claim for relief by one or more defendants asserted against one or more plaintiffs in the same lawsuit.

The principle of judicial economy requires that related claims should be disposed of in the same action whenever possible. When you draft an Answer to a Complaint, therefore, you must consider whether you should also draft a cross-claim or counterclaim.

permissive counterclaim
A counterclaim grounded in facts different from those in the main lawsuit, although the parties to both controversies are the same, not waived by failure to press them in the plaintiff's action, and may be filed as a separate lawsuit.

Counterclaim. A **Counterclaim** (sometimes called a **Cross-Complaint**) may be either *permissive* or *compulsory*. In federal practice, counterclaims are governed by Rule 13 of the Federal Rules of Civil Procedure. That rule defines which is which.

Permissive counterclaims are grounded in facts different from those in the main lawsuit, although the parties to both controversies are the same. Permissive counterclaims are not waived by failure to press them in the plaintiff's action. They may be included, or they may be filed as a separate lawsuit. If they are included, the plaintiff may move to sever the permissive counterclaim from the original action, if the counterclaim confuses the issues in the original action.

Consider this example of a permissive counterclaim. Suppose A, a bank, sues a creditor, B, on a debt owed the bank. B may file a permissive counterclaim, alleging that the bank owes B money in an entirely separate transaction. If the bank moves to sever B's counterclaim, the judge must decide whether the two matters will be tried together.

Compulsory counterclaims are those that are permanently waived if they are not included in the litigation. Compulsory counterclaims arise out of the same facts or the same transaction that gives rise to the plaintiff's Complaint. Requiring that such claims be made part of the action filed by the plaintiff conserves judicial resources: All controversies arising from the same set of facts are settled in one action.

Contrast this example of a compulsory counterclaim. A Bank sues B Creditor, alleging that B owes a past-due debt to A. B may respond that A fraudulently induced B to enter into the loan giving rise to the debt. The allegation of fraud may be more than a defense; it may be a complaint for damages as well. In that case, because it arises from the same facts as the plaintiff's allegations, it must be filed as a Counterclaim in Answer to the Bank's Complaint.

Here is another example, this time involving an automobile accident. A is the plaintiff, suing B after the two struck one another head-on on a dark country road. A alleges that B crossed the center line into his lane. B, the defendant, then counterclaims, alleging that A was driving at high speed and without lights. The Counterclaim is included in B's Answer to A's Complaint.

In Exhibit 11.26 the paragraph numbers of the Counterclaim follow in sequence the numbered paragraphs of the Answer.

compulsory counterclaim
A counterclaim arising out of the same facts or transaction which gives rise to the allegations in the plaintiff's Complaint. It is permanently waived if not included in the litigation.

EXHIBIT 11.26   *Compulsory Counterclaim*
<u>COUNTERCLAIM OF JANE DOE</u>

Counterclaimant [or defendant], Jane Doe, counterclaims against Plaintiff, Richard Roe.

12. At the time and place alleged in Plaintiff's Complaint, Counterclaimant was driving south on Interstate Drive in a lawful manner, keeping within the south-bound lane of travel.

13. At the same time and place, Plaintiff was negligently driving north on Interstate Drive at a high rate of speed and without lights, although it was night and the road was unlit.

14. Plaintiff negligently crossed the center line of Interstate Drive, driving north in the south-bound lane, and struck Counterclaimant's vehicle head-on, leaving Counterclaimant no opportunity to avoid the collision.

15. As a proximate result of Plaintiff's negligence, Counterclaimant suffered the following damage and injury: . . .

. . . .

WHEREFORE, Counterclaimant demands judgment as follows:

1. The dismissal of Plaintiff's Complaint;

2. Against Plaintiff for Counterclaimant's damage in the sum of two hundred fifty thousand dollars and costs; and

3. For such other and further relief to which Counterclaimant is justly entitled.

Cross-Claim. A Cross-Claim is generally made by one defendant in an action against another defendant in the same action. Theoretically, a cross-claim may also be brought by one plaintiff against another plaintiff, although this situation is rare. More often than not, a cross-claim is filed by one of two or more defendants connected by some business relationship. The subject matter of a cross-claim must relate to the subject matter of the plaintiff's original Complaint. A cross-claim is drafted just as you would draft the allegations in a Complaint.

For example, suppose a plaintiff is injured when he falls over a frayed carpet in an apartment. He may sue both tenant and landlord. In that case, the tenant will probably lodge a cross-claim against his co-defendant, the landlord.

Or, suppose that A's automobile is struck from behind at an intersection by B's car, knocking it into C's pickup, already in the intersection. A sues B for personal injury and damage to A's vehicle, alleging that B was following too closely. A also sues C, alleging C had violated his right-of-way. C then files a cross-claim against B, alleging that B's negligent driving was the sole cause of the accident, and therefore also responsible for C's injury and automobile damage.

As with all pleadings, you must pay close attention to the form required by state and local rules. Federal rules on cross-complaints and counterclaims are generally uniform. State rules, by contrast, are not. Even the terminology may vary. In California, for example, what the Federal Rules term a counterclaim is called a cross-complaint.

■ PRACTICE TIP

Some states have adopted the Federal Rules, in whole or in part. Some have not. Make certain you understand the rules before you begin to write. It is always best to pull out a counterclaim or cross-complaint filed by your firm in some earlier case in the same court. As with all forms, use it as a model, but never copy. Remember that each case is different from every other case.

Pleading Checklist

Use the following checklist when you are drafting any type of pleading:

✓ Make sure that each sequentially numbered paragraph is limited to one idea.

✓ Do not state evidence or conclusions.

✓ Make concise, brief statements.

✓ Be truthful; do not make exaggerated statements about the facts.

✓ Have any special matters been pleaded or answered with sufficient particularity and detail?

✓ Does the prayer for relief (demand for judgment) meet the applicable court's requirements for how the amount of damages sought is stated?

✓ Does the pleading comply with all applicable rules, not only as to content but also as to size of paper, number of copies, etc.?

✓ Are all references to exhibits internally consistent and in sequential order? Be sure that each exhibit has been designated, marked, and attached to the pleading.

✓ Proofread the information in the signature block and Certificate of Service. Be sure that all names are spelled correctly and that each attorney's address is accurate.

✓ Before copying the pleading for filing, check to be sure that (1) all exhibits have been marked and attached, and (2) the pleading and its Certificate of Service have been signed by the attorney of record.

✓ After the pleading has been filed with the court clerk, be sure that a file-stamped copy of the pleading is served upon opposing counsel of record in accordance with the Certificate of Service.

✓ Retain a file-stamped copy of all pleadings for the file.

CHAPTER SUMMARY

Here are brief highlights of the pertinent points made in this chapter:

- Know and follow the court rules applicable to your case, as well as any local court rules, when drafting pleadings, motions, supporting briefs, or other documents filed with the court. Keep a copy of these rules handy in your office so that you may refer to them often.
- A pleading is a legal term of art used to describe the documents that contain claims and defenses filed by the parties. A pleading asks the court for some kind of relief.
- In federal court, the purpose of pleadings is limited to the notice of claims and defenses.
- The Complaint gives the opposing party, the defendant, notice of the grounds for the plaintiff's claim.
- The Answer is the response filed by the defendant to the claims made in the Complaint.
- A Counterclaim is a claim for relief by one or more defendants asserted against one or more plaintiffs in the same lawsuit.
- A Cross-Claim is a cause of action or claim for relief by one or more defendants asserted against one or more co-defendants in the same lawsuit.
- A Third-Party Complaint is filed by a defendant (who then becomes the third-party plaintiff) against someone (the third-party defendant) who is not presently a party to the lawsuit.
- A Third-Party Answer is filed by a third-party defendant in response to the claims made by the defendant/third-party plaintiff.
- Fact pleadings require that the party allege all of the facts for each claim which must be proven to win the lawsuit; notice pleadings require only a short statement of the grounds upon which the party bases each claim.
- According to Fed.R.Civ.P. 8, a pleading *must* contain:
  −A short and plain statement of the grounds upon which the court's jurisdiction depends
  −A short and plain statement of the claim showing that the pleader is entitled to relief
  −A demand for judgment for the relief sought
- A real party in interest is one who, under applicable substantive law, has the right that the lawsuit seeks to enforce.
- A person or entity should be named as a party if any of the following conditions exist:

–That party's presence is required to grant complete relief to the claimant.

–The party has some type of interest in the lawsuit so that its presence is necessary for it to protect its interest.

–If the party's absence may expose other parties to multiple or inconsistent liabilities.

- Use form books or boilerplate forms only as guides. Never copy a form without thoroughly proofreading and editing it. Never rely totally on the legal research or relevant law found in form books or other forms. If you decide to use that research, always shepardize it to make sure it is still good law.
- Create a form file or form bank from copies of documents you or others draft in your office.
- The caption or style of the case contains the name of the court in which the case is filed, the names of the party or parties and which side each party is on, and the case number.
- Pleading titles should be single-spaced and underlined, and all of the letters should be capitalized. The title to all pleadings other than the Complaint should include the name of the party who is filing the document.
- Rule 11 of the Federal Rules of Civil Procedure requires, among other things, that all pleadings and other documents filed with the court be signed by the attorney of record, and include the signer's address and telephone number.
- Use introductory paragraphs or sentences to begin pleadings.
- Never use legalese when drafting pleadings. Omit needless words or phrases.
- *Jurisdiction* means "the power of a court to hear and determine a case." *In personam jurisdiction* refers to the power of a court over an individual. *In rem jurisdiction* refers to the power of a court over property. *Subject-matter jurisdiction* refers to the power of a court to hear particular matters.
- Venue is the geographical area in which a court with jurisdiction may hear and determine a case.
- You and your attorney must develop a persuasive and rational theory of the case. Identify all possible claims and defenses, and each of the elements necessary to prove that claim or defense.
- Notice pleadings do not require a statement of facts or conclusions of law to establish the elements of a cause of action.
- Allegations should be drafted as separate, consecutively numbered paragraphs, each containing only one sentence focusing on one idea or point. The group of paragraphs for each claim is called a *cause of action.*
- After the first cause of action, each subsequent cause of action requires the restatement of some of the allegations stated in the first cause of action. This is done by incorporating and adopting those allegations in the beginning paragraph of the subsequent cause of action.
- When drafting a pleading or any legal document, never forget that you are telling the reader a story. You want the reader not only to understand the story, but to see it from your client's point of view.
- It is acceptable to slant the language in a pleading to be sympathetic to your client, but you must never use exaggeration, embellishments, or misstatements of the facts.
- If there are documents supporting claims or allegations or statements made in a pleading, those documents should be attached as exhibits and referred to in the body of the pleading.
- The prayer for relief should state the specific type of relief sought, costs, interest, attorney fees, and any specific type of special damages.

- If the party filing the pleading intends to demand a jury trial on any claim triable by right before a jury, it should add a statement to that effect in accordance with the applicable court rules. Failure to demand a jury trial can result in the waiver of that right.
- A Certificate of Service or Certificate of Mailing is a statement that indicates when and how service of the document was made and to whom. It includes a signature of the attorney of record, or if allowed, the legal assistant or secretary, certifying that the statement is true.
- Service of process is the delivery of the formal notice of the parties' claims and defenses.
- A summons is used to notify the defendants of the lawsuit filed against them and commands them to appear so that they may answer the plaintiff's claims.
- A subpoena ad testificandum (or subpoena) is used to command someone who is not a party to the lawsuit to appear and testify in court or at a deposition.
- A Complaint should state (1) the names of the persons involved (the parties); (2) the date and place of the transaction or event; (3) the legal wrong alleged by the plaintiff against the defendant; (4) the type and extent of harm (losses or injuries) suffered by the plaintiff because of that wrong; and (5) a demand for the amount of compensation or relief requested.
- Before drafting the Complaint, draft an outline or checklist of the claims to be included with the necessary elements to prove each claim.
- Know which claims should be treated as "special matters" under Rule 9 of the Federal Rules of Civil Procedure and how they should be pled.
- A Verification is a sworn statement by a party that he or she has read the Complaint, and that all of the allegations contained in it are true to the best of his or her knowledge or belief.
- Be sure to include a civil cover sheet when filing a Complaint in federal district court.
- Become familiar with the filing fees required by the court clerk, and keep a copy of the fee schedule in your office.
- Before filing any pleading, proofread it and satisfy yourself that a reasonable inquiry has been made and that all of the facts stated in it are true. Also review the steps outlined in the various checklists provided in this chapter.
- The defendant's Answer is due 20 days after service of the Complaint. An Answer may have three separate parts:
  –Responses to the Complaint's allegations
  –Affirmative defenses
  –Rule 12(b) defenses
- The defendant must respond by either admitting or denying in his or her Answer to each allegation within the Complaint. If the defendant fails to do so, that allegation is deemed admitted.
- Once the defendant has answered all of the allegations in the Complaint, the defendant can then raise any affirmative defenses.
- Some affirmative defenses may, under Rule 12(b), be made by motion rather than as part of the defendant's Answer:
  –Lack of jurisdiction over the subject matter
  –Lack of jurisdiction over the person
  –Improper venue
  –Insufficiency of process
  –Insufficiency of service of process

–Failure to state a claim upon which relief can be granted

–Failure to join a party under Rule 19

Other affirmative defenses are found in Rule 8(c) of the Federal Rules of Civil Procedure.

- Compulsory counterclaims arise out of the same facts or same transaction that gives rise to the plaintiff's Complaint and are permanently waived if not included in the litigation.
- Permissive counterclaims are grounded in facts different from those in the main lawsuit, although the parties to both controversies are the same. They are not waived by failure to press them in the plaintiff's action, and may be included, or may be filed as a separate lawsuit.
- A cross-claim is made by one defendant in an action against another defendant in the same action. The subject matter must relate to the subject matter of the plaintiff's original Complaint.

KEY WORDS AND PHRASES

affirmative defenses

allegation

Amended Complaint

Answer

appellate court

boilerplate forms

caption or style of the case

case number

cause of action

Certificate of Mailing

Certificate of Service

circuit court

civil action

civil cover sheet

claim

Complaint

compulsory counter-claim

count

Counterclaim

court of original juris-diction

court rules

Cross-Claim

Cross-Complaint

default judgment

defense

denial

designation

district court

diversity of citizenship

entry of appearance

equitable relief

et al.

exhibit

fact pleadings

Federal Rules of Civil Procedure

Federal Rules of Evidence

filing fee

form files, form bank

forum

in personam jurisdiction

in rem jurisdiction

introductory paragraph or sentence

jurisdiction

jury instructions

jury trial

legal relief

local court rules

notice pleadings

permissive counterclaim

pleadings

praecipe

prima facie

process server

proof of service

punitive damages

real party in interest

Reply

return of service

Rules of Civil Procedure

Rule 11

sanctions

service of process

signature block

special matters

subject-matter jurisdic-tion

subpoena

subpoena ad testifican-dum

summons

Third-Party Answer

Third-Party Complaint

third-party defendant

third-party plaintiff

title

trial court

unauthorized practice of law

uniform jury instruc-tions

venue

verification

EXERCISES

Part I—Review of Chapter 11

___1. The first pleading filed in a civil lawsuit in federal district court is called the:
   a. Complaint
   b. Summons
   c. Third-Party Complaint
   d. Answer

___2. A _____ is filed by a defendant in response to the Complaint.
   a. Cross-Claim
   b. Counterclaim
   c. Reply
   d. Answer

___3. A notice pleading need contain only:
   a. statements of facts or conclusions of law to establish the elements of a cause of action
   b. short, plain statement of the grounds upon which the court's jurisdiction depends and of the claim showing that the pleader is entitled to relief, and a demand for judgment for the relief sought
   c. all of the facts for each claim which must be proven to win the lawsuit
   d. all of the facts necessary to allege a cause of action

___4. A _____ is a cause of action or claim for relief by one or more defendants asserted against one or more plaintiffs in the same lawsuit.
   a. Cross-Claim
   b. Counterclaim
   c. Reply
   d. Answer

___5. A real party in interest is:
   a. someone who has an interest in the real estate that is the subject of the lawsuit
   b. someone who, under applicable substantive law, has the right that the lawsuit seeks to enforce
   c. someone who is interested in the outcome of the lawsuit
   d. none of the above

___6. A _____ is filed by a third-party defendant in response to the claims made by the defendant/third-party plaintiff.
   a. Cross-Claim
   b. Counterclaim
   c. Third-Party Complaint
   d. Third-Party Answer

___7. A _____ is a cause of action or claim for relief by one or more defendants asserted against one or more co-defendants in the same lawsuit.
   a. Cross-Claim
   b. Counterclaim
   c. Reply
   d. Answer

___8. Which of the following are not part of the caption or style of the case?
   a. the names of the parties and their relationships in the lawsuit
   b. the attorney's signature block
   c. the case number
   d. the title of the document

___9. *In rem jurisdiction* refers to:
   a. the power of a court to hear particular matters
   b. the power of a court over an individual
   c. the power of a court over property
   d. a and c

___10. *In personam jurisdiction* refers to:
   a. the power of a court to hear particular matters
   b. the power of a court over an individual
   c. the power of a court over property

___11. *Subject-matter jurisdiction* refers to:
   a. the power of a court to hear particular matters
   b. the power of a court over an individual
   c. the power of a court over property

12. What three things determine whether a person or entity should be named as a party in the lawsuit?

   ▪ _____

   ▪ _____

   ▪ _____

13. Explain the purpose of an introductory sentence or paragraph in a pleading.

14. Explain diversity of citizenship in federal lawsuits.

15. What is a statement of jurisdiction at the beginning of a pleading, and what must it contain?

16. Explain the meaning of *venue* and the things that should be considered in choosing the appropriate venue for your client.

17. Should you include all possible claims that meet Rule 11 requirements in your pleadings? Explain why or why not.

18. What is a cause of action? Explain and give an example.

19. To find samples of pleadings for the most commonly used legal theories, where would you look?

20. What is the final paragraph of a pleading before the signature block, and what is its purpose?

21. An answer may have three parts. What are they?

22. Explain the difference between a compulsory counterclaim and a permissive counterclaim.

Part II—True or False

___1. A party can state as many separate claims, remedies, or defenses as it has regardless of consistency or whether those claims or defenses are based on legal, equitable, or maritime grounds.

___2. Pleadings are the means of bringing the theory of the lawsuit to the court.

___3. A party's claims are drafted in one or two lengthy paragraphs that include all applicable case law and statutes.

___4. If a party does not include all possible claims in its original complaint, it may not add other claims later in the lawsuit.

___5. Notice pleadings require a statement of facts or conclusions of law to establish the elements of a cause of action.

___6. Each cause of action should be based upon as many legal theories as possible to ensure that the party is entitled to some type of relief.

___7. An allegation made in a pleading does not have to be true; it just has to be possible.

___8. When stating the facts in a pleading, it is acceptable to characterize the facts in a way favorable to your client.

___9. The prayer for relief should state the specific type of relief sought, costs, interest, attorney fees, and any specific type of special damages.

Part III—Identifying Claims and Defenses

Review the discussion of claims and defenses in this chapter. Then, for each of the cases cited below, identify the claims and defenses for each of the parties. Remember that a cause of action is a legally acceptable reason for suing, which means that it is based on a rule of law that entitles the plaintiff to some kind of relief. Each cause of action is based upon a particular legal theory, such as the violation of a particular statute. There may be more than one claim raised by the plaintiff and more than one defense raised by the defendant.

Each of the cases cited below can be found at the end of these exercises.

1. *Morgan v. Rinehart*, 834 F. Supp. 233 (S.D. Ohio 1992).
2. *Miller v. Medical Center of Southwest Louisiana*, 22 F.3d 626 (5th Cir. 1994).
3. *Trevino v. Union Pacific Railroad Company*, 916 F.2d 1230 (7th Cir. 1990).

Part IV—Identification of Pleadings

Which of the following are pleadings? Answer "Y" for yes and "N" for no.

___1. Petition

___2. Notice to Take Deposition

___3. Cross-Claim

___4. Interrogatories

___5. Motion for Summary Judgment

___6. Answer

___7. Complaint

___8. Counterclaim

___9. Motion to Dismiss

___10. Brief

___11. Reply

___12. Subpoena Duces Tecum

Part V—Poorly Drafted Pleadings

1. Read the following Petition carefully. Identify and correct any errors.

IN THE DISTRICT COURT OF _____ COUNTY
STATE OF SOUTH CAROLINA

ANN HAFNER,	)	
	)	
Plaintiff,	)	
	)	
v.	)	Case No. _____
	)	
WE BUY WIDGETS, a	)	
South Carolina	)	
corporation, and	)	
CHAD SWAN,	)	
an individual,	)	
	)	
Defendants.	)	

PETITION

    1.   Plaintiff is an individual residing in _____ County, South Carolina.

    2.   Defendant WE BUY WIDGETS is a corporation incorporated under the laws of the State of South Carolina.

    3.   Defendant CHAD SWAN is an individual residing in the State of North Carolina who conducts business in the State of South Carolina.

COUNT I—BREACH OF CONTRACT

    4.   Paragraphs 1–3 are incorporated by reference.

    5.   On March 10, 19__, Plaintiff and Defendant WE BUY WIDGETS entered into a written contract to sell and purchase, respectively, widgets.

    6.   Under the terms of the contract, Plaintiff agreed to deliver the widgets to Defendant SWAN on April 9, 19__, and Defendant WE BUY WIDGETS agreed to pay Plaintiff $5,000 (5,000 widgets at $1 each). The contract is annexed hereto as Exhibit A.

    7.   On or about April 9, 19__, Plaintiff delivered the widgets to Defendant SWAN. All conditions precedent to performance by Defendant SWAN have been performed and have occurred.

    8.   Defendant SWAN has made no payment to Plaintiff for the widgets purchased.

COUNT II—FRAUD IN THE INDUCEMENT

    9.   On February 21, 19__, Defendant SWAN requested Plaintiff to enter into a contract with Defendant WE BUY WIDGETS for sale of 5,000 widgets. Defendant orally represented to Plaintiff that Defendant WE BUY WIDGETS was a viable ongoing business with the financial capacity to pay for the widgets and furnished to Plaintiff certain financial statements so reflecting. In fact, these representations and the financial statements were false. Defendant WE BUY WIDGETS had no assets and no ongoing business. Defendant CHAD SWAN knew the representations to be false and made them with the purpose of inducing

Continued

Plaintiff to deliver the widgets in reliance on the statements. Plaintiff in fact relied upon the representations and false financial statements and would not have delivered the widgets without them. Plaintiff has been damaged by delivering widgets of a value of $7,005 with no prospect of payment therefor.

Wherefore Plaintiff demands judgment against Defendant CHAD SWAN for the sum of $7,005, interest and costs including reasonable attorney fees.

Respectfully submitted,

_____

Brett Miller

Of the Firm Miller & Miller

Miller & Miller
111 Oak Tree Avenue
South Bend, South Carolina
(111) 555-5555
Bar No. 77777
Attorney for Plaintiff

ANN HAFNER

2. Read the following answer, which was drafted in response to the Petition in No. 1 above. Correct any errors that you find.

<u>ANSWER OF DEFENDANT WE BUY WIDGETS</u>

First Defense

1. Defendant admits the allegation of Paragraph 1, 3, 5, 6 and 8 of the petition.

2. Defendant is without knowledge or information sufficient to form a belief as to the truth of Paragraph 2 of the petition.

3. Paragraphs 4 and 9 require no further answer.

<u>Second Defense</u>

The right of action set forth in the petition did not accrue within ___ years next before the commencement of this action and is therefore barred because of the statute of limitations for actions on contracts in writing.

Respectfully submitted,

_____

Sharon Scott
Legal Assistant

Of the Firm Catwood & Catwood

Catwood & Catwood
333 Eagle Street
South Bend, South Carolina 88888
(111) 222-3333
Bar No. 00000
Attorney for Defendant

WE BUY WIDGETS

Part VI—Drafting Pleadings

For each of the following exercises below, use the Jane Healy scenario from Chapter 1.

1. Identify all of the possible parties who should be named by the plaintiff in her Complaint and identify the plaintiff's claim against each defendant you identify.

2. Now draft a Complaint against all of the defendants you listed in exercise 1 above.

3. Identify all of the possible defendants and the possible defenses for each defendant.

4. Contact the court clerk for the federal district court in your jurisdiction and:

   a. Determine the filing fees for filing a Complaint or for having a summons or subpoena issued by the court clerk.

   b. Determine how many copies are required when filing a Complaint or other documents with the court clerk.

   c. Determine whether a praecipe is required by the court clerk for a summons.

5. Assume that you are a legal assistant for the law firm that represents BMW. Draft an Answer for BMW to Jane Healy's Complaint (the one you wrote in exercise 3 above).

6. Assume you are a legal assistant for the firm that represents Charles Raymond. Draft an Answer and Counterclaim against Jane, alleging that she failed to yield the right of way.

7. Now draft a Cross-Claim on behalf of Charles Raymond against the bartender at Red's Tavern, alleging that the bartender should not have served Raymond so much alcohol in that short amount of time.

CASE

the Act. None of these amended counts states a claim under this section because the risks tobacco poses are commonly recognized.

The only remaining counts in the amended complaint are derivative claims for medical and funeral expenses (Count VIII), pain and suffering (Count IX), and loss of consortium (Count XI). Since all of Paugh's substantive counts as amended fail, these derivative claims fail as well.

VI.

Accordingly, this Court's prior marginal entry order granting Paugh leave to amend her complaint is vacated. Reynold's motion to dismiss Paugh's complaint is granted, and judgment is entered in favor of the defendant. This is a final and appealable order.

IT IS SO ORDERED.

John L. MORGAN, Plaintiff,

v.

Dana G. RINEHART, et al., Defendants.

No. C2–90–780.

United States District Court,
S.D. Ohio, E.D.

July 30, 1992.

Former city employee filed § 1983 action against city and various city officials, alleging that he was discharged for exercising his privilege against self-incrimination. City and city officials moved for summary judgment and employee moved for partial summary judgment. The District Court, Beckwith, J., held that: (1) employee waived his Fifth Amendment privilege against self-incrimination by failing to inform police internal affairs tribunal of his intention to claim privilege at time of interview about employee's work while employee had been

police officer, and (2) employee's privilege against self-incrimination was not violated by discharge of employee for refusal to answer any questions during internal affairs investigation, absent any discussion of employee's immunity from subsequent use of testimony in any criminal proceeding.

Dismissed.

Judgment affirmed, 7 F.3d 234 (Table).

1. Criminal Law ⟜393(1)

City employee waived his Fifth Amendment privilege against self-incrimination by failing to inform police internal affairs tribunal of his intention to claim privilege at time of interview about employee's involvement in surveillance operation while city employee had been police officer, regardless of any conversations that employee or his counsel had with other city officials who were not conducting investigation. U.S.C.A. Const. Amend. 5.

2. Officers and Public Employees ⟜66

Public employees can be discharged for refusing to answer questions concerning their employment activity if they are not required to waive their constitutional rights.

3. Criminal Law ⟜393(1)

City employee's Fifth Amendment privilege against self-incrimination was not violated by discharge of employee for refusal to answer any questions during police internal affairs investigation of employee's work while he had been police officer, absent any discussion of issue of immunity before internal affairs hearing; directive to employee to answer questions or be fired did not require employee to waive his constitutional immunity from use of answers at any subsequent criminal proceeding. U.S.C.A. Const.Amend. 5.

4. Civil Rights ⟜242(3)

Evidence established that city did not have policy, practice, or custom requiring employees to relinquish their Fifth Amendment rights if confronted with question's concerning employees' conduct, despite policies of individual city officials advocating or em-

CASE—*Continued*

phasizing that all employees should be open and forthcoming in any type of investigation. U.S.C.A. Const.Amend. 5.

5. Civil Rights ⟋146

Former city employee could not maintain § 1983 claim against mayor or city official, absent any causal link between mayor or city official and alleged deprivation of employee's civil rights concerning his discharge. 42 U.S.C.A. § 1983.

6. Civil Rights ⟋146

Former city employee could not maintain § 1983 claim against former supervisor who directed employee to answer any questions during police investigation that employee could answer without violating his rights or else employee would be discharged, absent causal link between supervisor's directive and any alleged deprivation of employee's civil rights concerning his discharge.

7. Federal Courts ⟋18

District courts should decline to exercise pendent jurisdiction over state law claims if federal issues are dismissed before trial.

Edna Marianne Gabel, Delaware, OH, Gunther Karl Lahm, Luper, Wolinetz, Sheriff & Neidenthal, Emily Jane Lewis, Columbus, OH, for plaintiff.

Glenn Brooks Redick, City Attorney's Office, Columbus, OH, for defendants.

MEMORANDUM and ORDER

BECKWITH, District Judge.

This matter is currently before the Court on the Defendants' motion for summary judgment and the Plaintiff's motion for partial summary judgment. This case arose when the Plaintiff, the former Deputy Development Director for the City of Columbus, filed suit against the City of Columbus, Dana G. Rinehart, the former Mayor of Columbus, Raymond Lorello, the former Director of Development for Columbus, and Jane Schoedinger, the current Director of Development.

On January 24, 1988, the Plaintiff was appointed the Deputy Development Director for the City of Columbus. At that time, Raymond Lorello was the Plaintiff's appoint-

ing authority and immediate superior while Dana Rinehart was the Mayor of Columbus and Mr. Lorello's immediate superior. By the time this case was filed, Jane Schoedinger was the Director of Development for the City of Columbus.

In October of 1988, while Plaintiff was serving as Deputy Development Director, and no longer a member of the Columbus Police Division, the Internal Affairs Bureau of the Columbus Police Division ("Internal Affairs Bureau") began a formal investigation into the Plaintiff's alleged 1983 surveillance of a Columbus family, the Pardues. In 1983, the Plaintiff was a Columbus police officer. The Pardues had alleged that Mr. Rinehart sexually molested their daughter, Vicki Pardue, while she was babysitting for the Rineharts.

The Internal Affairs Bureau was acting as an investigative arm of the City Solicitor's office pursuant to a City Council directive. The City Solicitor's office was not equipped to investigate the alleged 1983 surveillance, as requested by City Council. It, therefore, sought the assistance and expertise of the Internal Affairs Bureau, since the allegations implicated a former Columbus police officer and might have involved improper on-duty conduct.

Mr. Lorello ordered the Plaintiff to appear before the Internal Affairs Bureau on October 21, 1988, to answer questions relating to the alleged surveillance of the Pardue family. On October 21, 1988, the Plaintiff appeared before the Internal Affairs Bureau, read a prepared statement, and refused to answer questions. On October 25, 1988, the Plaintiff was discharged from his position as Deputy Development Director for insubordination. The Plaintiff has brought claims pursuant to 42 U.S.C. § 1983 for violation of his constitutional rights and pendent state law claims for breach of public policy, breach of contract, promissory estoppel and intentional infliction of emotional distress. Under § 1983, the Plaintiff claims that he was discharged for exercising his constitutional right against self-incrimination when he was subjected to questioning, without a grant of immunity, about his alleged surveillance of the Pardues.

Continued

MORGAN v. RINEHART
Cite as 834 F.Supp. 233 (S.D.Ohio 1992)

235

In their motion for summary judgment, the Defendants assert that no city policy led to the discharge of the Plaintiff. The Defendants also assert that public employees can be discharged for refusing to answer questions concerning their employment activity if they are not required to waive their constitutional rights. The Defendants further assert that the suit against the individual defendants in their official capacities is a suit against the City of Columbus and thus that the individual defendants should be dismissed. The Defendants also contend that the pendent state law claims should be dismissed if the Defendants prevail on their argument that no federal claim has been established.

Standard of Review

Rule 56(c) of the Federal Rules of Civil Procedure provides:

> [Summary judgment] ... shall be rendered forthwith if the pleadings, depositions, answers to interrogatories, and admissions on file, together with the affidavits, if any, show that there is no genuine issue as to any material fact and that the moving party is entitled to judgment as a matter of law.

The purpose of a summary judgment motion is not to resolve factual issues, but to determine if there are genuine issues of fact to be tried. *Lashlee v. Sumner*, 570 F.2d 107, 111 (6th Cir.1978).

In 1986, the United States Supreme Court issued three decisions which gave new life to Rule 56 as a mechanism for weeding out meritless claims at the summary judgment stage. *Anderson v. Liberty Lobby, Inc.*, 477 U.S. 242, 106 S.Ct. 2505, 91 L.Ed.2d 202 (1986); *Celotex Corp. v. Catrett*, 477 U.S. 317, 106 S.Ct. 2548, 91 L.Ed.2d 265 (1986); and *Matsushita Electric Industrial Co. v. Zenith Radio Corp.*, 475 U.S. 574, 106 S.Ct. 1348, 89 L.Ed.2d 538 (1986). It is well recognized that these cases brought about a "new era" in summary judgment practice. *Street v. J.C. Bradford & Co.*, 886 F.2d 1472, 1476 (6th Cir.1989). The three opinions by the Supreme Court reflect a return to the original purpose of the summary judgment motion. *Id.*

Accordingly, the summary judgment "standard provides that the mere existence of *some* alleged factual dispute between the parties will not defeat an otherwise properly supported motion for summary judgment; the requirement is that there be no *genuine* issue of *material* fact." *Anderson*, 477 U.S. at 247–8, 106 S.Ct. at 2509–10 (emphasis in original). Moreover, when a party cannot establish the existence of an element essential to that party's case on which the party will have the burden of proof at trial, the Court must enter summary judgment against that party, pursuant to Rule 56. *Celotex*, 477 U.S. at 322, 106 S.Ct. at 2552. Thus, in order to survive a motion for summary judgment, a Plaintiff "must come forward with more persuasive evidence to support their claims than would otherwise be necessary." *Matsushita*, 475 U.S. at 575, 106 S.Ct. at 1349.

Rule 56(e) of the Federal Rules of Civil Procedure provides:

> When a motion for summary judgment is made and supported as provided in this rule, an adverse party may not rest upon the mere allegations or denials of the adverse party's pleading, but the adverse party's response by affidavits or as otherwise provided in this rule, must set forth specific facts showing that there is a genuine issue for trial. If the adverse party does not so respond, summary judgment if appropriate, shall be entered against the adverse party.

Accordingly, mere allegations are not sufficient to defeat summary judgment. The Court can now apply this standard to the Defendants' motion for summary judgment.

Analysis

The Plaintiff asserts that the Defendants improperly discharged him for exercising his Fifth Amendment privilege against self-incrimination. The Fifth Amendment provides that: "[n]o person ... shall be compelled in any criminal case to be a witness against himself." The Fifth Amendment privilege "not only protects the individual against being involuntarily called as a witness against himself in a criminal prosecution but also

CASE—Continued

privileges him not to answer official questions put to him in any other proceeding, civil or criminal, formal or informal, where the answers might incriminate him in future criminal proceedings." *Lefkowitz v. Turley*, 414 U.S. 70, 77, 94 S.Ct. 316, 322, 38 L.Ed.2d 274 (1973). The Fifth Amendment privilege can be raised "in any proceeding, civil or criminal, administrative or judicial, investigatory or adjudicative." *Kastigar v. United States*, 406 U.S. 441, 444, 92 S.Ct. 1653, 1656, 32 L.Ed.2d 212 (1971); *In re Morganroth*, 718 F.2d 161 (6th Cir.1983). When an individual asserts the privilege, "he 'may not be required to answer a question if there is some rational basis for believing that it will incriminate him, at least without at that time being assured that neither it or its fruits may be used against him' in a subsequent criminal proceeding." *Minnesota v. Murphy*, 465 U.S. 420, 429, 104 S.Ct. 1136, 1143, 79 L.Ed.2d 409 (1984) (quoting *Maness v. Meyers*, 419 U.S. 449, 473, 95 S.Ct. 584, 598, 42 L.Ed.2d 574 (1975) (White, J. concurring in result)). It is well settled that the Fifth Amendment is applicable to the states through the Fourteenth Amendment. *Malloy v. Hogan*, 378 U.S. 1, 84 S.Ct. 1489, 12 L.Ed.2d 653 (1963).

The United States Supreme Court has held that the Fifth Amendment privilege against self-incrimination is not a self-executing mechanism. *Roberts v. United States*, 445 U.S. 552, 559, 100 S.Ct. 1358, 1363, 63 L.Ed.2d 622 (1980). The Supreme Court has also held that the privilege can be waived or lost by a claimant's failure to assert the privilege in a timely fashion. *Maness*, 419 U.S. at 466, 95 S.Ct. at 595. Previously, the Supreme Court stated that the privilege "must be deemed waived if not in some manner fairly brought to the attention of the tribunal which must pass upon it." *Vajtauer v. Commissioner of Immigration*, 273 U.S. 103, 113, 47 S.Ct. 302, 306, 71 L.Ed. 560 (1927).

In this case, the Plaintiff was called before the Internal Affairs Bureau on October 21, 1988. The interview was conducted by Sergeant William Smith. During the interview, the Plaintiff was represented by three attorneys, Lawrence Riehl, Gunther Lahm and Wallace Neidenthal. The Plaintiff is also an attorney. The following is a complete transcript of the interview:

Q: Mr. Morgan, would you please identify yourself?

A: John L. Morgan

Q: Mr. Morgan, are you aware that this interview is being tape recorded?

A: Yes, I am.

Q: Mr. Morgan, the purpose of this interview is to have you answer questions concerning the investigation that you conducted of the Pardue family during the 1983 campaign of Dana Rinehart. At this point are you willing to answer questions?

A: No, I am not.

Q: Do you want to make a statement?

A: At the Mayor's directive, I'm meeting with Internal Affairs relative to the allegations about a 1983 investigation of the Pardue family. This investigation was apparently initiated as a result of an interview I was directed by the Mayor and his staff to give to Gary Webb of the Cleveland Plain Dealer. Prior to giving this interview, I consulted with and obtained legal advice from the Columbus City Attorney. The Plain Dealer article which resulted from that interview was slanted, inaccurate, misleading and incomplete.

Since the publication of that article, apparently an uncertain number of investigations including those by the Columbus Division of Police, the Columbus Public Safety Department, the Columbus City Attorney's Office, the Columbus City Council and the Federal Bureau of Investigation have been initiated. Some of the very same offices that directed me and from whom I received legal advice have initiated or are now conducting the investigations. Furthermore, since the publication of the article, I have received numerous communications from the Mayor, several aides to the Mayor, Councilman John P. Kennedy, police officers involved in the investigation, police officers not involved in the investigation, representatives of the Fraternal Order of Police and others. All of this

Continued

CASE—*Continued*

MORGAN v. RINEHART   237
Cite as 834 F.Supp. 233 (S.D.Ohio 1992)

has led to an extremely confusing and contradictory situation that leaves me unable to respond to questions at this time. I appreciate the countless communications from friends and others throughout the community who know me and have given me their support. That is my statement in its entirety today.

Q: Mr. Morgan, would you be willing to turn over to us a copy of the tape recording that you had with Mr. Gary Webb of the Plain Dealer?

A: I have nothing further to say today.

Q: Thank you.

The Defendants argue that the Plaintiff did not indicate to the Internal Affairs Bureau that he was claiming a privilege under the Fifth Amendment. In his statement at the Internal Affairs Bureau interview, the Plaintiff stated that he was refusing to answer any questions due to the "confusing and contradictory situation." The Plaintiff never gave any indication at the interview that he was refusing to answer questions because he was afraid that he might incriminate himself. After thoroughly reviewing the Plaintiff's answers at the interview, the Court concludes as a matter of law that none of the Plaintiff's responses could be construed as an attempt to claim or invoke the Fifth Amendment privilege at the Internal Affairs Bureau interview.

[1] The Court finds that one who wishes to assert a Fifth Amendment privilege against self-incrimination must affirmatively assert the privilege to the appropriate tribunal at an appropriate time. Clearly, the Plaintiff did not inform the appropriate tribunal, the Internal Affairs Bureau, of his intention to claim a Fifth Amendment privilege at the appropriate time, his interview on October 21, 1988.

The Plaintiff, however, asserts that he, through his attorneys, invoked his privilege against self-incrimination prior to the October 21, 1988 interview with the Internal Affairs Bureau. The Plaintiff alleges that the Plaintiff's attorneys spoke with city attorneys and others in the city administration about the Plaintiff's fear of prosecution and thus invoked the privilege. The Defendants, how-

ever, argue that any such statements to other parties are irrelevant because the other parties were not conducting the investigation. The Defendants question why the Plaintiff and his attorneys did not also inform the Internal Affairs Bureau itself of the Plaintiff's intention to claim the Fifth Amendment privilege if they had already informed others in the city's administration of the Plaintiff's intention to claim the Fifth Amendment at the interview.

The Court finds that the other conversations which occurred outside the interview conducted by the Internal Affairs Bureau are irrelevant to the issue of whether the Plaintiff effectively invoked the Fifth Amendment privilege at the critical time and place. The Court agrees with the Defendants that these other individuals were not conducting the investigation and could not accept or reject a claim of privilege. In this case, the Internal Affairs Bureau was the appropriate tribunal where the Plaintiff should have raised the Fifth Amendment privilege if he intended to do so. Any conversations which the Plaintiff and his counsel had with city attorneys or officials outside of the Internal Affairs Bureau hearing are irrelevant to the question of whether the Plaintiff properly claimed the Fifth Amendment privilege at the critical time and place.

[2] The Defendants also argue that a public employee can be discharged for not obeying an order to answer questions concerning the employee's employment activity as long as the employee is not required to relinquish constitutional rights. Before reaching the merits of the Defendants' argument, the Court must review the applicable case law.

In 1967, the United States Supreme Court held that when police officers being investigated were given a choice either to incriminate themselves or to lose their jobs pursuant to a state law, and the officers chose to make confessions, such confessions were not voluntary but were coerced, and thus the Fourteenth Amendment precluded their usage in a subsequent criminal prosecution. *Garrity v. State of New Jersey*, 385 U.S. 493, 87 S.Ct. 616, 17 L.Ed.2d 562 (1967). In *Garrity*, the police officers had been asked to

CASE—*Continued*

testify in an Attorney General investigation which concerned the alleged fixing of traffic tickets. *Id.,* at 494, 87 S.Ct. at 617. Before the questioning, each officer was informed "(1) that anything he said might be used against him in any state criminal proceeding; (2) that he had the privilege to refuse to answer if the disclosure would tend to incriminate him; but (3) that if he refused to answer he would be subject to removal from office." *Id.* Although no immunity from prosecution was granted, the officers answered the questions at the investigation. *Id.* at 495, 87 S.Ct. at 617. Later, certain answers of the officers were used against the officers in prosecutions even though the officers objected. *Id.*

In delivering the opinion of the Court in *Garrity,* Justice Douglas wrote:

> [t]he choice given petitioners was either to forfeit their jobs or to incriminate themselves. The option to lose their means of livelihood or to pay the penalty of self-incrimination is the antithesis of free choice to speak out or to remain silent. That practice, like interrogation practices we reviewed in *Miranda v. State of Arizona,* ... is 'likely to exert such pressure upon an individual as to disable him from making a free and rational choice.' We think the statements were infected by the coercion inherent in this scheme of questioning and cannot be sustained as voluntary under our prior decisions.

Id. at 497–8, 87 S.Ct. at 618–19 (citation omitted) (footnote omitted). Justice Douglas concluded that pursuant to the protection of the individual under the Fourteenth Amendment, coerced statements obtained through a threat of removal from employment are prohibited from any usage in a subsequent criminal proceeding. *Id.* at 500, 87 S.Ct. at 620.

In 1968, the Supreme Court issued two other opinions which further illuminate this area. First, the Court held that a police officer was entitled to immunity when he was required to testify although the self-incrimination privilege would not bar a subsequent dismissal if the officer refused to answer questions specifically, directly, and narrowly relating to the performance of his official duties. *Gardner v. Broderick,* 392 U.S. 273,

88 S.Ct. 1913, 20 L.Ed.2d 1082 (1968). In *Gardner,* a policeman asserted that he had been unlawfully dismissed because he refused to waive his constitutional privilege against self-incrimination. *Id.* at 274, 88 S.Ct. at 1914. Pursuant to a subpoena, the policeman had appeared before a New York County grand jury that was investigating the alleged bribery and corruption of police officers in connection with unlawful gambling operations. *Id.* Although he was informed of his privilege against self-incrimination, the policeman was told that he would be fired if he did not sign a waiver of immunity. *Id.* After he refused to sign the waiver, the policeman was discharged solely for this refusal to sign under New York City Charter § 1123. *Id.* at 275, 88 S.Ct. at 1914.

In delivering the opinion of the Court in *Gardner,* Justice Fortas wrote:

> [i]f appellant, a policeman, had refused to answer questions specifically, directly, and narrowly relating to the performance of his official duties, without being required to waive his immunity with respect to the use of his answers or the fruits thereof in a criminal prosecution of himself, *Garrity v. State of New Jersey, supra,* the privilege against self-incrimination would not have been a bar to his dismissal.

Id. at 278, 88 S.Ct. at 1916. (footnote omitted). Unlike the case presently under consideration, the plaintiff in *Gardner* was discharged for his refusal to expressly waive a constitutional right and not for his refusal to answer relevant questions about his official duties.

In another case decided the same day as *Gardner,* the Supreme Court held that the constitutional privilege against self-incrimination was violated when city employees were discharged for invoking this privilege before an investigation commissioner who had advised them that their answers could be used against them in subsequent proceedings. *Uniformed Sanitation Men Ass'n. v. Commissioner of Sanitation,* 392 U.S. 280, 88 S.Ct. 1917, 20 L.Ed.2d 1089 (1968). In the *Uniformed Sanitation Men* case, fifteen sanitation workers were brought before a hearing conducted by a commissioner of investigations. *Id.* at 281, 88 S.Ct. at 1918. The

Continued

CASE—*Continued*

MORGAN v. RINEHART   239
Cite as 834 F.Supp. 233 (S.D.Ohio 1992)

commissioner was investigating charges that employees of the sanitation department were not charging certain fees for the use of certain city facilities and were keeping for themselves the fees which they did charge. *Id.*

The fifteen workers were each advised that if they refused to testify at the hearing on the grounds of self-incrimination, their employment with the city would end pursuant to a section of the New York City Charter. *Id.* at 281–2, 88 S.Ct. at 1918–19. After asserting the privilege against self-incrimination, twelve of the workers who refused to testify were dismissed by the city on the ground that they had refused to testify. *Id.* at 282, 88 S.Ct. at 1918–19. The other three workers answered questions at the hearing, but were suspended afterwards on the grounds of "information received from the Commissioner of Investigation concerning irregularities arising out of (their) employment in the Department of Sanitation." *Id.* Later, the three workers were asked to sign waivers of immunity in front of a grand jury and they refused. *Id.* The three workers were then discharged from their employment on the sole ground that they had violated the section of the City Charter by refusing to sign waivers of immunity. *Id.*

In *Uniformed Sanitation Men,* Justice Fortas, in delivering the opinion of the Court, noted first that the workers were not discharged for their refusal to account for their conduct as city employees. *Id.* at 283, 88 S.Ct. at 1919. Instead, Justice Fortas pointed out that the workers were discharged solely for invoking and refusing to waive their constitutional right against self-incrimination. *Id.* Justice Fortas wrote that:

> ... if New York had demanded that petitioners answer questions specifically, directly, and narrowly relating to the performance of their official duties on pain of dismissal from public employment without requiring relinquishment of the benefits of the constitutional privilege, and if they had refused to do so, this case would be entirely different. In such a case, the employee's right to immunity as a result of his compelled testimony would not be at stake. But here the precise and plain impact of the proceedings against petitioners as well

as of § 1123 of the New York Charter was to present them with a choice between surrendering their constitutional rights or their jobs. Petitioners as public employees are entitled, like all other persons, to the benefit of the Constitution, including the privilege against self-incrimination. At the same time, petitioners being public employees, subject themselves to dismissal if they refuse to account for their performance of their public trust, after proper proceedings, which do not involve an attempt to coerce them to relinquish their constitutional rights.

Id. at 284–85, 88 S.Ct. at 1920. (citations omitted).

In this case, the parties agreed previously to certain stipulations in a proffer of stipulated facts in a related case heard by Judge Patrick West of the Court of Common Pleas of Franklin County. The parties agreed that the investigation of the Internal Affairs Bureau was aimed at determining, among other things: (1) whether John Morgan violated any criminal laws or otherwise engaged in conduct which could result in civil liability; (2) whether John Morgan's activities were conducted off duty or on duty; and (3) whether police department personnel, or anyone else, knew of Mr. Morgan's investigation or assisted him in it. The parties further agreed that John Morgan met with investigators from the Internal Affairs Bureau on October 21, 1988 and refused to answer any questions. The parties also agreed that at no time either prior to or during Mr. Morgan's interview with the Internal Affairs Bureau did any administration official, city attorney, or Internal Affairs Bureau member offer use immunity to John Morgan. The parties also agreed that Dana Rinehart spoke with John Morgan and told him to answer the questions of the Internal Affairs Bureau investigators or he would be fired. The parties further agreed that John Morgan was terminated by the City on October 26, 1988.

In his deposition, Defendant Lorello related a conversation which he had with the Plaintiff the day before the Plaintiff's appearance before the Internal Affairs Bureau.

Question: And do you recall how the matter was left between you and John?

CASE—*Continued*

Answer: Very vividly. John knew fully what my policy was. He also knew the ramifications, and we left on that basis . . . I said, John, all I'm looking for is cooperation. *I'm not asking you to violate any of your actual rights,* but if you've got 10 to 12 questions and you can answer 7 of them by your own admission *without getting into the area of violating your rights,* then answer them. If you show no cooperation, I have no choice but to terminate. . . .

(emphasis added). The Defendants thus assert that the City took no action which required a relinquishing of the Plaintiff's constitutional rights.

[3] Upon review of the law in this area, the Court agrees with the Defendants that public employees can be discharged for refusing to answer questions concerning their employment activity if they are not required to waive their constitutional rights. In this case, the Court finds that the Plaintiff appeared before the Internal Affairs Bureau at a hearing on October 21, 1988 and refused to answer any questions whatsoever from the Internal Affairs Bureau. The Court thus finds that the Plaintiff was not required to waive any constitutional rights by being asked to respond to questions at the hearing.

The Court further finds that the Plaintiff did not ask the Internal Affairs Bureau or anyone else for immunity before the hearing and the parties also agree that no one offered the Plaintiff immunity. Since the question of granting the Plaintiff immunity never arose, the Plaintiff can not now argue that he was required to waive any immunity to testify at the hearing on October 21, 1988.

This case would have been entirely different if the Plaintiff had been required to sign a waiver of immunity like the policeman in *Gardner.* Here, however, the Plaintiff was not required or even asked to sign a waiver of immunity. Moreover, if the Plaintiff had testified at the hearing such statements would have been coerced under a threat of removal of employment and hence, any utilization of such statements in a subsequent criminal proceeding would be prohibited under *Garrity.* The Court, therefore, finds the Defendants' summary judgment motion to be meritorious. Although the Court finds that

it is not necessary to reach either the Plaintiff's or the Defendants' remaining arguments because it is granting the Defendants' motion for summary judgment for the reasons stated above, the Court will briefly address these other arguments.

[4] The Defendants assert that the Plaintiff has not alleged that the Plaintiff was terminated pursuant to some official policy, practice or procedure. The Defendants argue that the Plaintiff has simply set forth that the Plaintiff was terminated from his employment and that there is no evidence that the City of Columbus has any such custom or practice of terminating employees who refuse to waive their constitutional rights. Thus, the Defendants argue that the Plaintiff has not established a claim for relief for a violation of 42 U.S.C. § 1983.

Section 1983 provides:

Every person who, under color of any statute, ordinance, regulation, custom, or usage of any state or Territory, subjects, or causes to be subjected, any citizen of the United States or other person within the jurisdiction thereof to the deprivation of any rights, privileges or immunities secured by the Constitution and laws, shall be liable to the party injured in action at law, suit in equity, or other proper proceeding for redress.

The Supreme Court recently noted that the first inquiry in a Section 1983 case is "whether there is a direct causal link between a municipal policy or custom, and the alleged constitutional deprivation." *Canton v. Harris,* 489 U.S. 378, 385, 109 S.Ct. 1197, 1203, 103 L.Ed.2d 412 (1989). The Court further noted that a municipality may only be held liable under Section 1983 if the " 'execution of the government's policy or custom . . . inflicts the injury.' " *Id.* at 385, 109 S.Ct. at 1203 (quoting *Springfield v. Kibbe,* 480 U.S. 257, 267, 107 S.Ct. 1114, 1119, 94 L.Ed.2d 293 (1987) (O'Conner, J., dissenting).

The Plaintiff argues that the official city policy was that an employee was absolutely required to answer any questions concerning the employee's conduct as posed by the Internal Affairs Bureau. The Plaintiff argues that this official city policy did not recognize

Continued

CASE—*Continued*

MORGAN v. RINEHART 241
Cite as 834 F.Supp. 233 (S.D.Ohio 1992)

any Fifth Amendment considerations of the employees. The Defendants, however, argue that the Plaintiff has offered no evidence that the City of Columbus had such a policy. The Defendants also argue that the City of Columbus did not have such a policy. The Court agrees with the Defendants that there is no evidence before the Court that the City of Columbus had such a policy.

There is evidence before the Court that some of the individual Defendants had individual policies advocating or emphasizing that all employees should be open and forthcoming in any type of investigation. There is, however, no evidence that these individual policies mandated that employees forfeit their Fifth Amendment rights when confronted with an investigation. The Court thus finds that the City of Columbus did not have a policy, practice, or custom of requiring employees to relinquish their Fifth Amendment rights when confronted with questions concerning the employee's conduct.

Furthermore, as the Court has already determined that the Plaintiff never properly invoked his Fifth Amendment privilege at the Internal Affairs Bureau hearing, the issue of whether the city had such a policy is irrelevant in this case.

[5] Regarding the liability of the individual Defendants, the Court notes that according to the evidence presented by the parties, Defendant Rinehart did not actually terminate the Plaintiff. Defendant Rinehart also had no authority to reinstate the Plaintiff to his former position. The Court notes that Defendant Schoedinger apparently played no part in either the termination of the Plaintiff or the events which led up to the Plaintiff's termination. Accordingly, the Court finds that because there is no causal link between these two individual Defendants and the actions complained of, that the Plaintiff can not maintain a claim against Defendant Rinehart or Defendant Schoedinger.

[6] As regards Defendant Lorello, the Court finds the uncontroverted evidence shows that he directed Plaintiff to answer such questions as he could … "without getting into the area of violating your rights." Clearly, he did not require or even suggest

that Plaintiff waive his Fifth Amendment privilege against self-incrimination. Consequently, there is no factual predicate for this Defendant's liability. Likewise, therefore, the Court finds no causal link between the actions of this individual Defendant and any alleged violation of Plaintiff's constitutional rights. Plaintiff was terminated by Defendant Lorello for refusing to answer any questions at the Internal Affairs Bureau interview. Since Plaintiff refused to answer any questions at the interview, the Court need not, indeed cannot, reach the issue of whether the questions which might have been asked were directly and narrowly related to Plaintiff's performance of his official duties. The Plaintiff cannot maintain a claim against Defendant Lorello.

The Plaintiff's State Law Claims

[7] The Plaintiff's amended complaint also alleges several state law causes of action. Where federal issues are dismissed before trial, district courts should decline to exercise pendent jurisdiction over state law claims. *Gaff v. Federal Deposit Insurance Corp.*, 814 F.2d 311, 319 (6th Cir.1987) (citing *United Mine Workers v. Gibbs*, 383 U.S. 715, 86 S.Ct. 1130, 16 L.Ed.2d 218 (1966)). Accordingly, because the Court has granted summary judgment on the Plaintiff's federal claim, the Court declines to exercise pendent jurisdiction over the Plaintiff's state law claims.

Conclusion

For the above reasons, this Court finds that the Defendants' motion for summary judgment is **GRANTED** on the Plaintiff's federal claim alleging a violation of 42 U.S.C. § 1983, and the Plaintiff's claims alleging state law violations are **DISMISSED WITHOUT PREJUDICE.** This action is hereby **DISMISSED** in its entirety.

IT IS SO ORDERED.

CASE

breach of fiduciary duty. We conclude and hold that this constituted error. The issue was raised in the court-approved Joint Pretrial Order which supplanted all previous pleadings and controlled all subsequent action in the litigation.[4] The evidence adduced at trial suggested both a fiduciary relationship and a breach. While we are mindful that the issue before the trial court was not an easy one, the seventh amendment preserves the right of parties to a jury trial unless there is "no legally sufficient evidentiary basis for a reasonable jury to find for [the] party on th[e] issue."[5] Viewing the evidence in the light most favorable to Pendleton, and drawing all inferences in its favor, we must conclude that the evidence did not point so strongly and overwhelmingly in favor of Lloyd and McCormack that reasonable jurors could not find a breach of fiduciary duty under Texas law.[6] We further conclude that the failure to instruct the jury with regard to the fiduciary duty issue may have tainted its answers to the questions posed. We therefore must VACATE the judgment of the trial court and REMAND for a new trial on all issues.

Roger Dale MILLER, Individually and o/b/o Nick Miller, et al., Plaintiffs–Appellants,

v.

MEDICAL CENTER OF SOUTHWEST LOUISIANA, et al., Defendants–Appellees.

No. 93–5123.

United States Court of Appeals, Fifth Circuit.

June 14, 1994.

Parents of injured child brought action against hospital, alleging that hospital had refused to treat child after automobile accident in violation of Emergency Medical Treatment and Active Labor Act (EMTALA). The United States District Court for the Western District of Louisiana, Richard T. Haik, J., dismissed, and plaintiffs appealed. The Court of Appeals, Johnson, Circuit Judge, held that child did not "come to" emergency department at hospital, which allegedly instructed doctor over telephone not to send child to hospital, precluding imposition of liability on hospital under EMTALA.

Affirmed.

1. Federal Courts ⟨key⟩794

On review of dismissal for failure to state claim on which relief could be granted, Court of Appeals must accept all well-pleaded facts as true and view them in light most favorable to nonmovant. Fed.Rules Civ. Proc.Rule 12(b)(6), 28 U.S.C.A.

2. Hospitals ⟨key⟩7

Hospitals covered by Emergency Medical Treatment and Active Labor Act (EMTALA) are hospitals with emergency department that execute Medicare provider agreements with federal government. Social Security Act, §§ 1866, 1867, as amended, 42 U.S.C.A. §§ 1395cc, 1395dd.

3. Hospitals ⟨key⟩7

Statutory precondition for triggering hospital's duties under Emergency Medical Treatment and Active Labor Act (EMTALA) are conjunctive, requiring both that individual come to emergency department, and that request for examination or treatment be made. Social Security Act, § 1867, as amended, 42 U.S.C.A. § 1395dd.

4. Hospitals ⟨key⟩7

Injured, uninsured child did not "come to" emergency department at hospital which

---

4. Fed.R.Civ.P. 16(e); *United States v. Shanbaum,* 10 F.3d 305 (5th Cir.1994); *Syrie v. Knoll Int'l,* 748 F.2d 304 (5th Cir.1984).

5. Fed.R.Civ.P. 50(a)(1); *see also Kirby Lumber Corp. v. White,* 288 F.2d 566, 573 (5th Cir.1961).

6. *See Omnitech Int'l, Inc. v. Clorox Co.,* 11 F.3d 1316 (5th Cir.1994); *see also, Gaines v. Hamman,* 163 Tex. 618, 358 S.W.2d 557 (1962) (reversing summary judgment on facts similar to those presented in this case).

Continued

CASE—*Continued*

MILLER v. MEDICAL CENTER OF SOUTHWEST LOUISIANA   627
Cite as 22 F.3d 626 (5th Cir. 1994)

allegedly instructed doctor over telephone not to send child to hospital, precluding imposition of liability on hospital under Emergency Medical Treatment and Active Labor Act (EMTALA).   Social Security Act, § 1867, as amended, 42 U.S.C.A. § 1395dd.

> See publication Words and Phrases for other judicial constructions and definitions.

5. Statutes ☞189

In rare cases where application of literal terms of statute will produce result that is demonstrably at odds with intention of its drafters, those intentions must be controlling.

6. Hospitals ☞7

Individual must "come to" emergency department in order to trigger hospital's duty under Emergency Medical Treatment and Active Labor Act (EMTALA).   Social Security Act, § 1867, as amended, 42 U.S.C.A. § 1395dd.

Patrick D. McArdle, Laura E. Fahy, New Orleans, LA, for appellants.

Daniel A. Reed, Ronald A. Seale, Seale Smith, Zuber & Barnette, Baton Rouge, LA, for appellees.

Appeal from the United States District Court for the Western District of Louisiana.

Before JOHNSON, BARKSDALE, and DeMOSS, Circuit Judges.

JOHNSON, Circuit Judge:

Roger Dale Miller and Andrea Miller (Plaintiffs), individually and on behalf of their minor son Nick, brought this action against Hamilton Medical Center, Inc., d/b/a Medical Center of Southwest Louisiana (Hamilton), alleging that Hamilton had refused to treat Nick after an automobile accident in violation of the Emergency Medical Treatment and Active Labor Act (EMTALA), 42 U.S.C. § 1395dd.[1]   The district court, however, found that Nick had never "come to" Hamil-

ton within the meaning of the statute.   Accordingly, the district court granted Hamilton's Fed.R.Civ.P. 12(b)(6) motion to dismiss for failure to state a claim on which relief could be granted.   Plaintiff appeals and we affirm.

FACTS AND PROCEDURAL HISTORY

On March 29, 1992, nine-year-old Nick Miller suffered serious injuries in an automobile accident when his leg became pinned in between two colliding cars.   A passerby rushed Nick to nearby Acadia–St. Landry Hospital (Acadia)[2] in Church Point, Louisiana.   Once there, Dr. Williams, the general practitioner on duty at Acadia, determined that Nick needed the care of an orthopedist and a surgical facility for debridement of the wound.   Unable to provide such treatment, Dr. Williams called Dr. Olivier, an orthopedist at Hamilton some thirty minutes away in Lafayette.

Plaintiffs contend that Dr. Olivier agreed to treat Nick and preparations were made to transport Nick to Hamilton.   However, before Nick left Acadia, Plaintiffs allege that an administrator from Hamilton called back and, after determining that Nick had no insurance, instructed Dr. Williams not to send Nick to Hamilton.

Following this, Dr. Williams called several other hospitals seeking to find a facility that could treat Nick.   Eventually, Charity Hospital in New Orleans agreed to treat Nick and he was flown there by helicopter.   Once at Charity, Nick's leg was immediately surgically debrided.   The delay caused by this sequence of events was approximately seven hours and Plaintiffs allege that, on account of this delay, Nick's injuries materially worsened.

On March 22, 1993, Plaintiffs filed suit against Hamilton alleging that Hamilton's refusal to treat Nick was in violation of EMTALA, 42 U.S.C. § 1395dd.   Hamilton responded with a motion to dismiss pursuant to Fed.R.Civ.P. 12(b)(6) arguing that Plaintiffs

---

1.   § 1395dd was enacted as a part of COBRA—the Consolidated Omnibus Budget Reconciliation Act of 1986.   Pub.L. No. 99–272, § 9121, 100 Stat. 82, 164–67 (1986).

2.   This facility is a small, country clinic where only two family doctors practice.

CASE—*Continued*

failed to state a claim on which relief could be granted because they did not allege that Nick "came to" the emergency department at Hamilton. Further, Hamilton argued that it was a transferee hospital and, as such, it could only be liable under EMTALA if it had agreed to a transfer which it had not. The district court granted the motion to dismiss, apparently because the court believed that under the facts alleged, Nick never "came to" the emergency department at Hamilton within the meaning of the statute. Plaintiffs now appeal.

1. STANDARD OF REVIEW

[1] In review of a dismissal under Fed. R.Civ.P. 12(b)(6) for failure to state a claim on which relief could be granted, we must accept all well-pleaded facts as true and view them in a light most favorable to the non-movant. *McCartney v. First City Bank,* 970 F.2d 45, 47 (5th Cir.1992). "We will not go outside the pleadings and we cannot uphold the dismissal 'unless it appears beyond doubt that the plaintiff can prove no set of facts in support of his claim which would entitle him to relief.'" *Rankin v. Wichita Falls,* 762 F.2d 444, 446 (5th Cir.1985) (quoting *Conley v. Gibson,* 355 U.S. 41, 44–45, 78 S.Ct. 99, 102, 2 L.Ed.2d 80 (1957).

2. EMTALA

[2] The sole issue before this Court is whether the plaintiffs have stated a claim under EMTALA, 42 U.S.C. § 1395dd.[3] This

statute is also known as the "anti-dumping" statute and it was passed in 1986 in response to a growing concern that hospitals were dumping patients who could not pay by either turning them away from their emergency rooms or transferring them before their emergency conditions were stabilized. *Brooks v. Maryland Gen. Hosp., Inc.,* 996 F.2d 708, 710 (4th Cir.1993). Accordingly, this statute mandates that a hospital[4] must conduct appropriate screening examinations for any individual who presents to its emergency department. Further, if an emergency condition is found to exist, the hospital must either provide sufficient treatment to stabilize the patient or transfer the patient in accordance with the strictures of the statute. *Green v. Touro Infirmary,* 992 F.2d 537, 539 (5th Cir.1993); 42 U.S.C. § 1395dd.

[3] Under the terms of the statute, however, these duties are only triggered when an individual "*comes to* the emergency department *and a request is made* on the individual's behalf for examination or treatment...." 42 U.S.C. § 1395dd (emphasis added). These two preconditions are conjunctive requiring both that an individual 1) comes to the emergency department and 2) that a request be made. In the instant case, it is the first requirement that is problematic.

[4] It is undisputed that Nick Miller never physically came to the emergency department at Hamilton. There was only a request over a telephone. Nevertheless, the Plain-

---

3. In pertinent part, this statute provides as follows:

(a) Medical screening requirement

In the case of a hospital that has a hospital emergency department, if any individual ... comes to the emergency department and a request is made on the individual's behalf for examination or treatment for a medical condition, the hospital must provide for an appropriate medical screening examination within the capability of the hospital's emergency department, including ancillary services routinely available to the emergency department, to determine whether or not an emergency medical condition (within the meaning of subsection (e)(1) of this section) exists.

(b) Necessary stabilizing treatment for emergency medical conditions and labor

(1) In general

If any individual (whether or not eligible for benefits under this subchapter) comes to a

hospital and the hospital determines that the individual has an emergency medical condition, the hospital must provide either—

(A) within the staff and facilities available at the hospital, for such further medical examination and such treatment as may be required to stabilize the medical condition, or

(B) for transfer of the individual to another medical facility in accordance with subsection (c) of this section.

42 U.S.C. § 1395dd.

4. The hospitals covered by this statute are hospitals with emergency room departments that execute Medicare provider agreements with the federal government pursuant to 42 U.S.C. § 1395cc. *Burditt v. U.S. Dept. of Health and Human Services,* 934 F.2d 1362, 1366 (5th Cir.1991). It is undisputed that Hamilton has entered into a Medicare provider agreement.

Continued

CASE—*Continued*

MILLER v. MEDICAL CENTER OF SOUTHWEST LOUISIANA   **629**
Cite as 22 F.3d 626 (5th Cir. 1994)

tiffs argue that we should not construe this statute to require physical presence at the emergency room. Instead, the Plaintiffs contend that Congress intended that the statute would extend the hospital's duty to any individual in need of emergency care who requests treatment at the hospital's emergency department.[5] In essence, the Plaintiffs are asking this Court to excise the "comes to" clause out of the statute by construing it so as to make it redundant with the "request is made" clause.

[5] We reject this argument for two reasons. First, the language of the statute unambiguously describes the individuals covered by section 1395dd as those who come to the emergency department. *Brooker v. Desert Hospital Corp.*, 947 F.2d 412, 414 (9th Cir.1991); 42 U.S.C. § 1395dd. Except in rare and exceptional circumstances, when "'we find the terms ... unambiguous, judicial inquiry is complete....'" *Pavelic & LeFlore v. Marvel Entertainment Group*, 493 U.S. 120, 123, 110 S.Ct. 456, 458, 107

L.Ed.2d 438 (1989) (quoting *Rubin v. United States*, 449 U.S. 424, 430, 101 S.Ct. 698, 701, 66 L.Ed.2d 633 (1981). No such exceptional circumstances exist in this case.[6]

[6] Second, such an interpretation would render the "comes to" clause a nullity. This would be contrary to "the elementary canon of construction that a statute should be interpreted so as not to render one part inoperative...." *Mountain States Tel. & Tel. Co. v. Pueblo of Santa Ana*, 472 U.S. 237, 249, 105 S.Ct. 2587, 2594, 86 L.Ed.2d 168 (1985) (quoting *Colautti v. Franklin*, 439 U.S. 379, 392, 99 S.Ct. 675, 684, 58 L.Ed.2d 596 (1979)); *In re Dyke*, 943 F.2d 1435, 1443 (5th Cir.1991). Accordingly, we hold Congress to its words when it said that an individual must "come to" the emergency department to trigger a hospital's duty under EMTALA.

Moreover, we find support for our conclusion in the case law construing the statute. While this precise issue has seldom been in controversy, most courts have implicitly recognized that the individual must come to the

---

5. In support of this argument, the Plaintiffs cite two cases in which a patient came to a hospital, but did not enter the emergency department. *Thornton v. Southwest Detroit Hospital*, 895 F.2d 1131 (6th Cir.1990); *McIntyre v. Schick*, 795 F.Supp. 777 (E.D.Va.1992). Even though § 1395dd(a) states that a patient must come to the "emergency department," these courts took a broader view of the statutory language and still found EMTALA liability. *Thornton*, 895 F.2d at 1135; *McIntyre*, 795 F.Supp. at 781. The basis for this holding was the belief that the "antidumping statute is not based upon the door of the hospital through which a patient enters, but rather upon the notion of proper medical care for those persons suffering medical emergencies, whenever such emergencies occur at a participating hospital." *McIntyre*, 795 F.Supp. at 781.

As these courts did not require physical presence at the emergency department, the Plaintiffs herein argue that we should not require physical presence at Hamilton's emergency department. We do not face the issue that those courts faced and we make no comment on the soundness of those decisions. However, we do note that while the plaintiffs in *Thornton* and *McIntyre* did not enter the emergency department, they did reach the hospital and the emergencies did occur at a participating hospital. This is very different from someone who never came within thirty miles of the building and, in fact, never even began the journey there.

6. In rare cases where application of the literal terms of the statute will produce a result that is

"demonstrably at odds with the intentions of its drafters," those intentions must be controlling. *Griffin v. Oceanic Contractors, Inc.*, 458 U.S. 564, 571, 102 S.Ct. 3245, 3250, 73 L.Ed.2d 973 (1982). Such a situation is not present in this case.

The legislative history of EMTALA is replete with general statements about the munificent purpose of its drafters to prevent hospitals with emergency departments from dumping patients who have no insurance. *See* H.R.Rep. No. 241, 99th Cong., 1st Sess. pt. 1, at 27 (1985) U.S.Code Cong. & Admin.News pp. 42, 605; *Gatewood v. Washington Healthcare Corp.*, 933 F.2d 1037, 1039 (D.C.Cir.1991). However, there is nothing in the legislative history that specifically deals with whether, in order to trigger the hospital's duty under EMTALA, an individual must be physically present at the emergency department.

The statute, as written and as we construe it, does serve the drafters' purpose of ensuring that hospitals do not turn away anyone who shows up at the their emergency room doorstep in an emergency condition. The Plaintiffs, however, would have us extend the hospital's duty to require it to accept for emergency treatment any individual who can communicate a request to the emergency department. We see nothing demonstrably at odds with the purpose of the drafters, though, in limiting that duty, in accordance with the unambiguous terms of the statute, to those individuals who come to the emergency department as opposed to any individual who can get to a telephone.

CASE—*Continued*

emergency room.[7] Additionally, in devising judicial tests for violation of this statute, courts have most often listed as the first element that the individual come to the emergency department.[8]

Finally, this was the conclusion of the only case to have dealt with this issue directly. *Johnson v. University of Chicago Hosp.*, 982 F.2d 230, 233 (7th Cir.1992). In *Johnson,* the University of Chicago Hospitals (UCH) was operating a telemetry system to direct paramedics transporting emergency patients to the appropriate hospital in the system. During this time, paramedics were dispatched on an emergency call to aid a one-month-old infant who had stopped breathing. On arriving at the scene, the paramedics contacted the telemetry operator from UCH. The paramedics informed the nurse that they were only five blocks from UCH, but the nurse instructed the paramedics to transport the infant to a more distant hospital. *Id.* at 231.

The baby died sometime after arriving at the other hospital and the mother of the child brought suit against UCH for, inter alia, a violation of EMTALA. *Id.* The Seventh Circuit upheld the dismissal of this claim, however, because of its conclusion that, under the plain meaning of the statute, the infant never came to UCH or its emergency department. *Id.* at 233. In explaining its

decision, the court stated that the baby "simply never 'came to' UCH for medical assistance, and thus never crossed the threshold of [EMTALA] liability." *Id.* at 233 n. 7.

As did the court in *Johnson,* we find that, from the facts alleged in the complaint, Nick Miller never "came to" the emergency department at Hamilton as required by EMTALA. Accordingly, the Plaintiffs have failed to state a claim on which relief could be granted and the district court correctly granted Hamilton's motion to dismiss under Fed.R.Civ.P. 12(b)(6).[9]

CONCLUSION

For the foregoing reasons, the district court's dismissal pursuant to Fed.R.Civ.P. 12(b)(6) is AFFIRMED.

---

7. *See e.g. Green,* 992 F.2d at 537 ("individuals who enter their emergency rooms requesting care"); *Baber v. Hospital Corporation of America,* 977 F.2d 872, 884 (4th Cir.1992); *Collins v. DePaul Hospital,* 963 F.2d 303, 305 (10th Cir. 1992) ("if 'any individual' comes, or is brought, to such emergency department and requests"); *Burditt,* 934 F.2d at 1366 (Hospitals "must treat all human beings who enter their emergency departments in accordance with [EMTALA]"); *Cleland v. Bronson Health Care Group, Inc.,* 917 F.2d 266, 269 (6th Cir.1990) ("The benefits and rights of the statutes extend 'to any individual' who arrives at the hospital"); *Deberry v. Sherman Hospital Ass'n,* 741 F.Supp. 1302, 1305 (N.D.Ill.1990) ("Once it is established that the plaintiff showed up at the hospital's emergency room"); *Owens v. Nacogdoches County Hospital Dist.,* 741 F.Supp. 1269, 1273 (E.D.Tex.1990) ("an emergency room must provide a medical screening examination to any patient who appears complaining of an emergency medical condition").

8. The usual formulation of the test for a violation of EMTALA labels the elements as follows:

    1) the individual went to the defendant's emergency room

    2) with an emergency medical condition, and the defendant hospital either

    3) did not adequately screen him to determine whether he had an emergency medical condition, or

    4) discharged him before the emergency condition was stabilized.

Ruiz v. Kepler, 832 F.Supp. 1444, 1447 (D.N.M. 1993); *Huckaby v. East Ala. Medical Ctr.,* 830 F.Supp. 1399, 1402 (M.D.Ala.1993); *Deberry,* 741 F.Supp. at 1305. *See also, Stevison v. Enid Health Systems, Inc.,* 920 F.2d 710, 712 (10th Cir.1990) (setting forth a slightly different test).

9. As we decide this case on the failure to allege that Nick Miller "came to" the emergency department at Hamilton, we do not address Hamilton's argument that it had no liability as a transferee hospital.

CASE

jury apparently transposed on the special verdict form the amount for punitive damages and the sum for compensatory damages. In cumulating the damages allegedly flowing from Martin's "misrepresentations" listed in the jury instructions paragraphs e) through i), we note that the total equals exactly $70,025.79, the amount the jury awarded as *punitive* damages. On the other hand, the jury awarded $50,000 as compensatory damages against Martin in favor of Sylvester. Such an apparent mechanical error in transposing compensatory and punitive damages is not fatal to the verdict. See, e.g., *Big John, B.V. v. Indian Head Grain Co.*, 718 F.2d 143, 150 (5th Cir.1983). In any event, the compensatory damages awarded for Martin's intentional deceit misrepresentations and for conversion, and the amount awarded as punitive damages, all find a reasonable basis in the record.

III.

For the reasons stated, the order of the district court is

AFFIRMED.

Ricardo TREVINO, Plaintiff–Appellant,

v.

UNION PACIFIC RAILROAD COMPANY and Missouri Pacific Railroad Company, Defendants–Appellees.

No. 89–3402.

United States Court of Appeals, Seventh Circuit.

Argued Sept. 14, 1990.

Decided Oct. 22, 1990.

Automobile passenger injured when automobile struck standing train at crossing brought action against railroads for personal injuries. The United States District Court, Northern District of Illinois, Charles P. Kocoras, J., granted judgment on pleadings against passenger. Passenger appealed. The Court of Appeals, Posner, Circuit Judge, held that: (1) there was potential that passenger could establish existence of special circumstances coming under exception to Illinois' standing-car rule, under which railroad generally has no duty to warn of railroad car standing in crossing, and (2) record did not warrant holding that disused railroad crossing was "crossing" within meaning of Illinois standing-car rule.

Reversed and remanded.

1. Railroads ⟷307(3)

Until right-of-way beneath railroad crossing is sold or otherwise transferred, railroad remains owner, and like other landowners is under under common-law duty to avoid using its land so as to cause injury to persons using public roadway at crossing; duty can be fulfilled in variety of ways, including warning such persons of hazards and removing hazards.

2. Federal Civil Procedure ⟷673

Federal rules do not require plaintiff to allege sufficient facts to establish right to judgment, but rather, rules generally require only nonlegalistic, nonjargonistic statement of what claim is. Fed.Rules Civ. Proc.Rules 8(a)(2), 84, 28 U.S.C.A.; Fed. Rules Civ.Proc.Form 9, 28 U.S.C.A.

3. Pleading ⟷345(1.4)

Complaint would have stated claim under Illinois law sufficient to avoid judgment on pleadings had it alleged only that plaintiff was passenger in car on date in question at railroad crossing in question, that car collided with train operated by defendant railroads, that collision was due to negligence on part of defendants, and that passenger had been injured in collision. Fed.Rules Civ.Proc.Rules 8(a)(2), 84, 28 U.S.C.A.; Fed.Rules Civ.Proc.Form 9, 28 U.S.C.A.

CASE—*Continued*

4. Federal Civil Procedure ⟜630

Plaintiff can plead himself out of court by unnecessarily alleging facts which demonstrate that he has no legal claim.

5. Railroads ⟜307(3)

Illinois rule that railroad has no duty to warn of railroad car standing in crossing contains exception for special circumstances, and determination of whether circumstances of accident are special will usually require going beyond pleadings.

6. Railroads ⟜307(3)

Illinois' standing-car rule, under which railroad, absent special circumstances, has no duty to warn of railroad car standing in crossing, is not rule of contributory negligence, and is complete bar to liability regardless of degree of plaintiff's negligence.

7. Federal Civil Procedure ⟜1067

Illinois' standing-car rule, under which railroad, absent special circumstances, has no duty to warn of railroad car standing in crossing, is appropriately enforced by means of judgment on pleadings, as existence of duty is question of law for court to determine. Fed.Rules Civ.Proc.Rule 12(c), 28 U.S.C.A.

8. Railroads ⟜314

Either snow or fog can create "special circumstances" placing on railroad a duty to warn under exception to Illinois' standing-car rule, under which railroad generally has no duty to warn of railroad car standing in crossing.

See publication Words and Phrases for other judicial constructions and definitions.

9. Railroads ⟜332

While Illinois' standing-car rule, under which railroad, absent special circumstances, has no duty to warn of railroad car standing in crossing, is not rule of contributory negligence, contributory negligence remains possible defense in case in which rule does not apply because of special circumstances.

10. Federal Civil Procedure ⟜1067

Allegations that automobile passenger was injured when automobile struck standing train car at "crossing" did not necessarily fall within Illinois rule that railroad generally has no duty to warn of railroad car standing in crossing, so as to warrant judgment on pleadings against passenger, in light of potential that passenger could establish existence of special circumstances coming under exception to rule, including fact that crossing was abandoned and that fence had been put across track at one side of crossing.

11. Railroads ⟜307(3)

Record did not warrant holding that disused railroad crossing was "crossing" within meaning of Illinois' standing-car rule, under which railroad has no duty to warn of railroad car standing in crossing in absence of special circumstances.

See publication Words and Phrases for other judicial constructions and definitions.

12. Railroads ⟜307(3)

Illinois' standing-car rule, under which railroad has no duty to warn of railroad car standing in "crossing" in absence of special circumstances, is applicable only to accidents at live crossings.

13. Federal Civil Procedure ⟜1067

It would have been unduly harsh to presume, on railroad's motion for judgment on pleadings, that injured automobile passenger's description of accident site as "crossing," without qualifications of "disused" or "abandoned," was intended as legal, rather than factual, description, so as to bring case within scope of Illinois rule under which railroad has no duty to warn of railroad car standing in crossing in absence of special circumstances.

14. Federal Courts ⟜617

By arguing that Illinois case, under which railroad has no duty to warn of railroad car standing in crossing in absence of special circumstances, did not apply, automobile passenger injured when automobile struck train sufficiently preserved argument that one reason case did not apply was that accident did not occur at kind

Continued

CASE—*Continued*

of crossing to which standing-car rule applied.

15. Federal Civil Procedure ⟜1838

Plaintiff challenging dismissal of his complaint or suit for failure to state claim is free to show, with reference to facts as yet hypothetical, that he may be able to establish set of facts, consistent with though not necessarily enumerated in his complaint, that would entitle him to judgment. Fed.Rules Civ.Proc.Rule 12(c), 28 U.S.C.A.

16. Railroads ⟜304, 308

Illinois statutes regulating railroad crossings had no application to standing-car collisions as statutes did not have purpose of protecting traveler from hitting train and, thus, any failure of railroad to comply with statutes would not render it liable to automobile passenger injured when automobile struck standing train car at crossing; statutes prohibited trains from stopping at crossings for more than ten minutes and required particular warning signals at crossings.

17. Railroads ⟜304, 308

Illinois statutes regulating railroad crossings were designed for live crossings and, thus, were not applicable in action by automobile passenger injured when automobile struck standing train at crossing which passenger claimed had been abandoned; statutes prohibited trains from stopping at crossings for more than ten minutes and required particular warning signals at crossings.

Saul I. Ruman, David M. Hamacher, William H. Tobin, Alan Faulkner, Ruman, Clements & Tobin, Hammond, Ind., for plaintiff-appellant.

Robert L. Landess, Raymond H. Groble, III, Daniel P. Hogan, Ross & Hardies, Chicago, Ill., Jack Friedlander, Calumet City, Ill., for defendants-appellees.

Before CUDAHY, POSNER, and FLAUM, Circuit Judges.

POSNER, Circuit Judge.

This is a diversity suit for personal injuries, brought by Ricardo Trevino against the Union Pacific Railroad and its subsidiary, the Missouri Pacific. The subsidiary was the injurer, and why the parent was also sued is a mystery but one unnecessary to dispel in order to decide this appeal. The parties agree that Illinois law governs the substantive issues.

The complaint alleges that on February 8, 1987, the defendants "owned, operated, maintained and controlled a certain train of cars which was left standing across Joe Orr Road [in Chicago Heights, Illinois] and which then and there blocked travel" on the road; that Trevino was a passenger in an automobile being driven west on Joe Orr Road; that the automobile "came into contact with the train of cars" blocking the road, and Trevino was injured in the collision; and that the cause of the accident was the defendants' violation of their common law and statutory duties to maintain a safe crossing, and, most important, of their common law duty to warn that the crossing was occupied. The defendants, having answered the complaint, moved for judgment on the pleadings. Fed.R.Civ.P. 12(c). Their ground was *Dunn v. Baltimore & Ohio R.R.*, 127 Ill.2d 350, 130 Ill.Dec. 409, 537 N.E.2d 738 (1989), which holds that "a train stopped at a crossing is generally held to be adequate notice and warning of its presence to any traveler who is in the exercise of ordinary care for his own safety, and the railroad is under no duty to give additional signs, signals or warnings.... The exception to the general rule is that more warnings may be required if 'special circumstances' are present. There is no fixed rule as to what constitutes special circumstances." 127 Ill.2d at 357, 130 Ill. Dec. at 412, 537 N.E.2d at 741.

Responding to the defendants' motion the plaintiff argued that the Federal Rules of Civil Procedure did not require him to plead the existence of special circumstances, but that if the court disagreed he would like permission to file an amended complaint setting forth the following additional facts, some drawn from depositions

CASE—Continued

given in the companion case brought by the driver of the car (the plaintiff's brother) in an Illinois state court: "The railroad car that the automobile in which the plaintiff was riding collided with was a flat bed car which was dark in color. The crossing was unlit, and there were no street lights on the road approaching the crossing. The track that Joe Orr Road crossed was rusted and unused, and the driver of plaintiff's car had traveled that crossing many times before, and had never encountered a train.... [T]he cars were only on the crossing because the defendants had negligently bumped the cars through a holding fence onto the crossing." The district court granted the motion for judgment on the pleadings and denied the plaintiff permission to amend his complaint, holding that the facts that the plaintiff wanted to allege would not bring the case within the "special circumstances" exception to the "standing-car" rule. That rule, by the way, including its exception for special circumstances, is not an esoteric Illinois doctrine. It is the position of most states. Annot., *Liability of Railroad for Injury Due to Road Vehicle Running Into Train or Car Standing on Highway Crossing,* 84 A.L.R.2d 813 (1962). For illustrative decisions, see *Clark v. Columbus & Greenville Ry.,* 473 So.2d 947 (Miss.1985); *Davis v. Burlington Northern, Inc.,* 663 F.2d 1028 (10th Cir.1981); *Owens v. International Paper Co.,* 528 F.2d 606 (5th Cir.1976); *Pennsylvania R.R. v. Goldenbaum,* 269 A.2d 229, 233–34 (Del.1970); *Union Pacific R.R. v. Cogburn,* 136 Colo. 184, 315 P.2d 209 (1957). A few states have rejected the rule. *Terranova v. Southern Pacific Transportation Co.,* 158 Ariz. 125, 761 P.2d 1029 (Ariz.1988); *McLaughlin v. Chicago, Milwaukee, St. Paul & Pacific Ry.,* 31 Wis.2d 378, 143 N.W.2d 32 (1966).

By failing to submit the amended complaint with his motion, the plaintiff left the district judge substantially in the dark concerning the plaintiff's ability actually to cure the deficiencies that the judge had found in the original complaint. Whether this deficiency alone justified the district judge in denying the motion is an interesting question, on which see *Clayton v.*

White Hall School District, 778 F.2d 457, 460 (8th Cir.1985); *Bownes v. City of Gary,* 112 F.R.D. 424 (N.D.Ind.1986); cf. *Mortell v. Mortell Co.,* 887 F.2d 1322, 1327 (7th Cir.1989), but not one we need decide. The original complaint was sufficient, as we shall see.

A fuller picture of the accident, at least as the plaintiff believes it occurred, emerges from the briefs and argument in this court. The accident occurred late at night in an unlit rural area. The railroad track at the point where it crosses Joe Orr Road had not been used for a decade, and was rusty and overgrown with weeds. To one side of the disused crossing a fence had been built across the track, and on the night of the accident the cars had crashed through the fence and come to rest on the abandoned crossing. The cars were not part of a live train; no live train used this track. The track was used to store cars, and for some reason the cars rolled down the track and through the fence. The flatbed car which came to rest on the disused crossing and into which the Trevino brothers' car drove was very low—even lower than a regular flatcar, though exactly how far it stood off the track no one could tell us at argument; and it was the same dark color as the surrounding vegetation. There was no gate or electrical signal at the crossing and indeed, so far as appears, no signal of any kind—not even a cross-arms signal.

[1] There may seem to be a fatal tension between Trevino's claim that the railroads failed to maintain a safe crossing and his claim that they failed to warn him of the train that was occupying the crossing. The second claim is premised in significant part on the assertion that it was an *abandoned* crossing, and if a crossing is abandoned one might suppose that there would no longer be a duty to maintain it. But this is not entirely correct. Until the right of way beneath the crossing is sold or otherwise transferred, the railroad remains the owner, and like other landowners is under a common law duty to avoid using its land in such a way as to cause injury to persons lawfully on (or for that matter off)

Continued

CASE—*Continued*

the land, such as persons using the public roadway at the crossing. *In re Chicago, Rock Island & Pacific R.R.*, 756 F.2d 517, 520–22 (7th Cir.1985); *Justice v. CSX Transportation, Inc.*, 908 F.2d 119, 123 (7th Cir.1990); *Hoffman v. Vernon Township*, 97 Ill.App.3d 721, 53 Ill.Dec. 135, 423 N.E.2d 519 (1981); *Hynes v. New York Central R. Co.*, 231 N.Y. 229, 131 N.E. 898 (1921) (Cardozo, J.); *Alamo National Bank v. Kraus*, 616 S.W.2d 908 (Tex.1981); Prosser and Keeton on the Law of Torts § 57, at pp. 387–89 (5th ed. 1984). It can fulfill this duty in a variety of ways, and only one of them is by warning those persons of hazards (another would be by removing the hazards), although that is the way emphasized by Trevino.

[2–4] This suit may in the end fail, but we think the district judge jumped the gun in dismissing it on the pleadings. The federal rules do not require a plaintiff to allege sufficient facts to establish his right to a judgment. All it requires, with certain exceptions enumerated in Rule 9, none of which is applicable to this case, is a "short and plain"—which is to say, nonlegalistic, nonjargonistic—statement of what his claim is. Fed.R.Civ.P. 8(a)(2), 84; Fed.R. Civ.P.App., Form 9, ¶ 2; *American Nurses' Ass'n v. Illinois*, 783 F.2d 716, 723 (7th Cir.1986). It would have been enough if the complaint had alleged that Trevino had been a passenger in a car that on February 8, 1987, at the railroad crossing on Joe Orr Road in Chicago Heights, collided with a train operated by the defendants; that the collision was due to negligence on the part of the defendants; and that he had been injured in the collision. In fact the complaint contains very little more than this. It contains some more, though, and a plaintiff can plead himself out of court by unnecessarily alleging facts which, all unwittingly on his part, demonstrate that he has no legal claim. *Id.* at 724; *Stewart v. RCA Corp.*, 790 F.2d 624, 632 (7th Cir.1986); *Orthmann v. Apple River Campground, Inc.*, 757 F.2d 909, 915 (7th Cir.1985); 5A Wright & Miller, Federal Practice and Procedure § 1357, at pp. 348–59 (2d ed. 1990). Not only does Trevino's complaint allege that the car in which he was riding hit the train, rather than vice versa, but in listing the duties that the defendants violated it describes the accident as having occurred at a "crossing," and there is nothing about the crossing being disused or abandoned. By pleading in this fashion Trevino created an opening for the defendants to move to dismiss the suit on the basis of the standing-car rule that the Supreme Court of Illinois had reaffirmed recently in *Dunn*.

[5] If this rule were that a railroad has no duty to warn of a railroad car standing in a crossing (because the car itself is warning enough), period, then Trevino's characterization of the accident as having occurred at a crossing might be fatal and might therefore justify the district court's action (though we think not, as will appear). But the rule is not that flat. It contains an exception for special circumstances. Whether the circumstances of an accident with a standing car are special cannot be determined until those circumstances are known, and in the usual case that will require going beyond the pleadings.

Whether this is the usual case depends on the precise contours of the standing-car rule. The statement of the rule in *Dunn* is authoritative, but not clear. After the passage we quoted earlier the court notes that circumstances that have been recognized as special in reported cases include "a blinding snowstorm" and "malfunctioning warning lights which erroneously indicated that the crossing was clear." But "darkness, heavy fog and poor visibility do not constitute special circumstances." 127 Ill.2d at 357, 130 Ill.Dec. at 412, 537 N.E.2d at 741, citing *Petricek v. Elgin, Joliet & Eastern Ry.*, 21 Ill.App.2d 60, 157 N.E.2d 421 (1959) (snowstorm); *Langston v. Chicago & N.W. Ry.*, 398 Ill. 248, 75 N.E.2d 363 (1947) (warning lights), and *Bachman v. Illinois Central R.R.*, 132 Ill.App.2d 277, 268 N.E.2d 42 (1971) (fog). All a blinding snowstorm does is reduce visibility, and a heavy fog can reduce it just as much. Generalizing from the blinding snowstorm, the court in *Dunn* then remarks "that if the train is not perceptible to one exercising ordinary care, the railroad may be liable."

CASE—*Continued*

127 Ill.2d at 358, 130 Ill.Dec. at 412, 537 N.E.2d at 741. But heavy fog could bring about an equal invisibility; so why is it treated differently from a blinding snowstorm? *Dunn* does not explain. Turning to the facts before it the court remarks that the following are alleged as special circumstances: "darkness; the presence of vehicular traffic at the crossing; the absence of lighting at the crossing; the grade of the crossing; and unnecessary distractions in the vicinity of the crossing." 127 Ill.2d at 360, 130 Ill.Dec. at 413, 537 N.E.2d at 742. These are held to be insufficient, as a matter of law, to avoid the standing-car rule; the existence of a "common law duty to construct and maintain the crossing in such a way as to promote visibility of standing trains" is rejected. Later we learn that the crossing in *Dunn* was steeper than allowed by Illinois regulations governing the safe operation of railroads. Dunn argued that as a result the headlight of his motorcycle shone not on the railroad car that he collided with, but under it. But this violation is held to be immaterial because the regulation that was violated was not intended to protect travelers from standing cars. 127 Ill.2d at 368–71, 130 Ill.Dec. at 417–18, 537 N.E.2d at 746–47.

[6, 7] One might have thought that the standing-car rule was a rule of contributory negligence and hence would not be a complete bar to liability under the regime of comparative negligence which Illinois had adopted before *Dunn*. Not so. There is no duty to warn of a standing car, and "unless a duty is owed, there is no negligence"; hence the plaintiff's negligence, slight or great, is irrelevant. 127 Ill. 2d at 365, 130 Ill.Dec. at 415, 537 N.E.2d at 744. Since, moreover, "the existence of a duty is a question of law for the court to determine," the standing-car rule is appropriately enforced by means of judgment on the pleadings.

The most puzzling suggestion in *Dunn* is that the standing-car rule has nothing to do with negligence by the plaintiff. The suggestion is potentially critical to this case. Trevino (our Trevino—not the brother) was a passenger in the car that hit the train. There is no suggestion that *he* was negligent, as Dunn, who drove a motorcycle into a train, may well have been. If the standing-car rule is a rule of contributory negligence, it would have no application to this case, since the contributory negligence of a driver is not imputed to his passenger, *Bauer v. Johnson*, 79 Ill.2d 324, 38 Ill.Dec. 149, 403 N.E.2d 237 (1980), and there is no suggestion that passenger Trevino may have contributed to the accident by being negligent, like the passenger in *Scruggs v. Baltimore & O.R. Co.*, 287 Ill.App. 310, 4 N.E.2d 878 (1936).

Yet it is difficult not to think of the standing-car rule in terms of contributory negligence. The rule allocates the burden of preventing crossing accidents between railroad and traveler, and in this it closely resembles Holmes's rejected "stop, look, and listen" rule, *Baltimore & Ohio R.R. v. Goodman*, 275 U.S. 66, 48 S.Ct. 24, 72 L.Ed. 167 (1927), overruled in *Pokora v. Wabash Ry.*, 292 U.S. 98, 54 S.Ct. 580, 78 L.Ed. 1149 (1934) (Cardozo, J.), which is a rule of contributory negligence per se. Under Holmes's approach the railroad has no liability to a traveler at a crossing who fails to stop, and under the standing-car rule it has no liability to a traveler who collides with a railroad car that is at rest in the crossing. In both cases the burden of prevention rests wholly on the traveler; if the accident occurs, he is solely at fault for having failed to prevent it. Both rules buck the twentieth-century trend—as strong in Illinois as anywhere, *Brenton v. Sloan's United Storage & Van Co.*, 315 Ill.App. 278, 284, 42 N.E.2d 945, 948 (1942); *Shea v. LaCost*, 16 Ill.App.2d 454, 148 N.E.2d 484 (1958); *Graves v. North Shore Gas Co.*, 98 Ill.App.3d 964, 968–69, 54 Ill. Dec. 376, 380, 424 N.E.2d 1279, 1283 (1981) —toward leaving questions of care to the jury to be decided under the broad, unelaborated standard of negligence. Prosser and Keeton on the Law of Torts, *supra*, § 35. Both rules also buck the trend, one that is also prominent in Illinois, toward making the victim's negligence a partial rather than a complete bar to damages. *Alvis v. Ribar*, 85 Ill.2d 1, 52 Ill.Dec. 23,

Continued

CASE—*Continued*

421 N.E.2d 886 (1981); Ill.Rev.Stat. ch. 110, ¶ 2–1116. Harmonizing *Dunn* with the overall thrust of Illinois negligence law is not easy; and the standing-car rule, as stated in *Dunn* anyway, even lacks internal coherence, because of the different treatment of snow and of fog.

We can begin to make sense of the rule by bringing to the surface the reciprocal relationship between an injurer's duty of care and a victim's duty of care. Even if contributory negligence were no defense at all—even a partial defense—to a claim of negligence, there would be cases in which it got the defendant off the hook. A reasonable person acts with reference to the likely behavior of the people with whom he interacts. The crew of a train that is stopped at a crossing will not think it necessary to toot the train's whistle at every automobile approaching the crossing, because it will assume, quite reasonably, that approaching autos will see the train and stop. So, if there is a collision, the railroad will not be deemed negligent; it violated no duty of care. This was the reasoning in the first case to apply the standing-car rule in Illinois, *Coleman v. Chicago, B. & Q.R. Co.*, 287 Ill.App. 483, 5 N.E.2d 103 (1936), as it had been in the cases from other states, such as *Gage v. Boston & M.R.R.*, 77 N.H. 289, 90 Atl. 855 (1913), that created the rule in the first place. Under this approach it makes no difference whether the suit is by a driver or by a passenger; the railroad just is not negligent for failing to take steps to prevent so improbable an accident. Therefore, Trevino's status as a passenger, which distinguishes him from the plaintiff in *Dunn*, does not take him outside the orbit of that decision.

The standing-car rule is analogous to the rule that excuses a potential injurer from having to warn of an obvious danger, *Pomer v. Schoolman*, 875 F.2d 1262, 1268 (7th Cir.1989); *Stone v. Guthrie*, 14 Ill.App.2d 137, 148–51, 144 N.E.2d 165, 170–71 (1957), both rules being instances of the larger principle that a person is entitled to assume that the people with whom he deals exercise reasonable care. That principle has been understood to imply, and rightly so, in our view, that if the accident is the sort that reasonable care by potential victims (other than a purely passive victim, such as a passenger) would always avoid, the potential injurer has no duty of care. *LeRoy Fibre Co. v. Chicago, Milwaukee & St. Paul Ry.*, 232 U.S. 340, 352, 34 S.Ct. 415, 418, 58 L.Ed. 631 (1914) (Holmes, J., concurring); *McCarty v. Pheasant Run, Inc.*, 826 F.2d 1554, 1557–58 (7th Cir.1987); *Davis v. Consolidated Rail Corp.*, 788 F.2d 1260, 1265 (7th Cir.1986); *Stark v. D & F Paving Co.*, 55 Ill.App.3d 921, 925, 13 Ill.Dec. 598, 601, 371 N.E.2d 315, 318 (1977); *Phillips v. Croy*, 173 Ind.App. 401, 405, 363 N.E.2d 1283, 1285 (1977). The type of railroad car in *Dunn* does not appear from the opinion, but the briefs in the case indicate that it was a tank car, not a low-slung flatcar, and the accident occurred at an active, rather than at an abandoned, crossing. If the motorcyclist in *Dunn* simply drove into a large railroad car of full height standing in an active crossing on a clear night, the inference of a high degree of negligence on his part would be pretty compelling, even if the grade was steep (though against this is the fact, again mentioned in the briefs but not in the opinion in *Dunn*, that the car was painted a flat black). And if *only* a negligent driver would drive into a train in this setting, this would be a powerful reason for concluding that the railroad had no duty to warn of the train.

The situation is different in the present case, as it is different in the *Goodman–Pokora* setting. Just as a careful person might be hit by a train at a crossing—which is why Holmes's "stop, look, and listen" rule really was a rule of contributory negligence, and not a rule about the railroad's duty of care—so in special circumstances a careful person might drive into a standing car at a crossing. The intermediate case, unnecessary to discuss, is where the driver hits a moving, not a standing, train which he could not have seen in time to avoid the collision.

The fact that in this case the driver drove into a flatcar rather than a tall car is relevant, though not decisive, on the question of special circumstances. *Owens v.*

CASE—Continued

TREVINO v. UNION PACIFIC R. CO.   1237
Cite as 916 F.2d 1230 (7th Cir. 1990)

International Paper Co., supra, 528 F.2d at 610. Far more important is the fact that the crossing was abandoned and that a fence had actually been put across the track at one side of the crossing. The analogy to those malfunctioning warning signals that *Dunn* cited as an example of special circumstances is close. A defendant's conduct can lull the plaintiff into ignoring what, but for that conduct, would be an obvious danger most easily averted by the plaintiff himself. The railroad in the well-known case of *Erie R. Co. v. Stewart,* 40 F.2d 855 (6th Cir.1930), employed a watchman at one of its crossings to warn of approaching trains. Unbeknownst to the driver of the truck in which the plaintiff was riding, the watchman failed to warn of an approaching train, which then struck the truck. The railroad had no duty to station a watchman at this crossing, but having done so and thereby induced reliance on the practice by travelers it could not discontinue the service without notice; it could not assume that a reasonably careful plaintiff could protect himself. Of course that was not a standing-car case; courts that follow the standing-car rule regard the car as warning enough. But that is in the absence of special circumstances, one of which could be the creation of an impression that the crossing was no longer in use and therefore drivers should not expect to encounter a train in their path. (There has been such a case, as we shall see, though not in Illinois.) It was on this ground that *Langston,* after citing with approval the principle that we illustrated with reference to the *Stewart* case, found the malfunctioning warning signal to be a special circumstance. 398 Ill. at 255, 75 N.E.2d at 366. The same misleading impression was created here by the placing of a fence across the track. No one would suppose that a track was in use when to use it a train would have to plow through a fence. Even the fact that a track is used rarely has been held to constitute a special circumstance, because of the tendency to lull the traveler into a false sense of security. *Broberg v. Northern Pacific Ry.,* 120 Mont. 280, 293, 182 P.2d 851, 858 (1947).

Against this it can be argued that a careful driver can be expected to scan the road ahead of him for obstacles whether or not he is approaching a crossing. We asked the defendants' lawyer whether it would have made a difference if there had never been a crossing where the accident occurred but the flatcar had simply been derailed (through the defendants' negligence) and rolled into the middle of Joe Orr Road. Consistent with the argument that we have just sketched, the lawyer said no, it would make no difference, unless of course there was a blinding snowstorm. We are skeptical. The same argument could be made in a case in which an electrical warning signal malfunctioned, indicating that the coast was clear when in fact a train was sitting on the track; yet *Dunn* said that that was a special circumstance, even though the train was visible. Taken to its logical extreme the argument implies—what no one believes—that you can, without any risk of liability, abandon your car in the middle of a highway at night, without lights, counting on the other users of the highway to see the car in their headlights and avoid crashing into it. *Montgomery v. National Convoy & Trucking Co.,* 186 S.C. 167, 195 S.E. 247 (1938).

[8, 9] The remaining mystery is reconciling fog with snow, and is quickly cleared up by an examination of the *Petricek* and *Bachman* cases. In *Petricek,* the snow case, the plaintiff stopped his car right before he reached the track, opened his window, and looked out; in other words he was careful. In *Bachman,* the fog case, the plaintiff zipped through heavy fog at 45 m.p.h., smack into the train. The difference between the cases is not, then, the difference between snow and fog; either can create a special circumstance placing on the railroad a duty to warn; the difference is that in one case (*Bachman*) the plaintiff was barred by contributory negligence, and in the other (*Petricek*) not. The standing-car rule, as we have seen, is not a rule of contributory negligence; but contributory negligence remains a possible defense in a case in which, the rule not applying because of special circumstances,

Continued

CASE—*Continued*

the railroad needs a defense. Cf. *Scruggs v. Baltimore & O.R. Co., supra.* Nowadays of course contributory negligence is not a complete defense, but it was when *Bachman* was decided.

[10] Construing the facts favorably to the plaintiff in our case, as we must do when a case is dismissed on the pleadings, we have here a situation in which a driver at night, having every reason to believe that a railroad car would be about as likely to be found in the middle of the road as an escaped circus elephant, drives into the car because the car is low to the ground and is of the same dark color as the surrounding vegetation, so that it does not reflect his headlights clearly. This seems if anything a stronger case than that of the blinding snowstorm, since the snowstorm is a warning to the driver to slow down and drive with utmost care, and there was no such warning here. Considering that there has been no pretrial discovery, so that for all one knows there are still other facts tending to bring this case within the special-circumstances exception to the standing-car rule, we are not prepared to say that the case is governed by *Dunn.*

[11, 12] And this for a separate reason as well. It is unclear that this case is within the scope of the standing-car rule at all. As described in *Dunn* and the other cases, it is a rule about crossings. For a good reason: a crossing is by definition the only place where a railroad line intersects a road. But what is a crossing? Is the intersection of an abandoned line with a road a crossing until the tracks are pulled up? Cf. *In re Chicago, Rock Island & Pacific R.R., supra.* Once a crossing, always a crossing? Possibly yes, for reasons stated earlier, if we are speaking of the railroad's liability to users of the road, at least until the railroad ceases to own the right of way. Probably no, if we are speaking of the application of the standing-car rule. The rationale of that rule is related to the expectations that a traveler brings to a crossing and hence to the expectations that the railroad can reasonably entertain about the traveler's behavior at the crossing. The traveler knows it to be a place that may be occupied by a train blocking his right of way, and this knowledge imposes a duty of vigilance. But if the railroad has taken steps to remove any expectation that a train might be encountered—which, it can be argued, the defendants did here, most dramatically by running a fence across the track next to the crossing—the traveler's duty of vigilance is less and the railroad is correspondingly less entitled to assume that it need take no measures to prevent an accident. On the scanty record that is all we have before us, we are not prepared to hold that this disused crossing was a crossing within the meaning of the standing-car rule, which, contrary to the defendants, we believe to be applicable only to accidents at live crossings.

[13, 14] Although this is the first case we have discovered dealing with an abandoned crossing—which is no surprise, since how likely is a railroad car to be found on a stretch of abandoned track?—we have found a case where the *appearance* that the crossing had been abandoned was held to be a special circumstance on the lulling rationale that we discussed in connection with the *Stewart* case. *Atlantic Coast Line R.R. v. Kammerer,* 239 F.2d 115, 118–19 (5th Cir.1956). It hardly matters whether the standing-car rule does not apply to abandoned crossings, or abandonment is a special circumstance because it causes the traveler to lower his guard. And because it does not matter, we need not spend too much time deciding whether Trevino has waived the argument that the accident did not occur at a crossing within the meaning of the standing-car rule. His complaint and other submissions describe the place of the accident as a "crossing," and do not qualify it with "disused" or "abandoned." But it would be unduly harsh to presume at this early stage of the litigation that he intended this as a legal as distinct from a factual description. Of course in a literal sense the accident occurred at a place where the track "crossed" the road, but for reasons we have just explained it does not follow that this place was a "crossing" within the meaning of

CASE—*Continued*

WILSON v. HUMPHREYS (CAYMAN) LTD., 1239
Cite as 916 F.2d 1239 (7th Cir. 1990)

Dunn. By arguing that *Dunn* does not apply to this case, Trevino has sufficiently preserved the argument that one reason it does not apply is that the accident did not occur at the *kind* of crossing to which the standing-car rule applies.

[15] And speaking of a scanty record, the facts that Trevino's counsel presented to the district judge in his opposition to the defendants' motion for judgment on the pleadings and to us in his brief and argument in this court are not part of the evidentiary record, and for all we know are untrue or incomplete. It makes no difference to our disposition of this appeal. As we explained in *Orthmann v. Apple River Campground, Inc., supra,* 757 F.2d at 914–15, a plaintiff challenging dismissal of his complaint (or indeed his suit) for failure to state a claim is free to show, with reference to facts as yet hypothetical, that he may be able to establish a set of facts, consistent with though not necessarily enumerated in his complaint, that would entitle him to a judgment. Whether he *can* establish them is a separate question, not answerable at the pleadings stage of the lawsuit.

[16, 17] We think it worth adding, however, that insofar as the complaint alleges, not a duty to warn, but a duty to comply with certain Illinois statutes regulating railroad crossings, it fails to state a claim. *Dunn* holds that statutes which forbid trains to stop at crossings for more than ten minutes (this is the statute on which Trevino places the greatest weight), or which require particular warning signals at crossings, have no application to standing-car collisions. The purpose of these statutes is to prevent tying up traffic (the purpose of the ten-minute rule) or to protect the traveler from being hit by a train (the purpose of requiring warning signals); in neither case is the purpose to protect a traveler from hitting a train. 127 Ill.2d at 368–71, 130 Ill.Dec. at 417–18, 537 N.E.2d at 746–47. Such statutes are doubly inapplicable here, because they are statutes designed for live crossings and an important strut beneath the plaintiff's case is

that the crossing at which he was injured had been abandoned.

Nevertheless the case was dismissed prematurely and must be returned to the district court for further proceedings consistent with this opinion.

Reversed and Remanded.

Dorothy A. WILSON and Louis P.
Wilson, Plaintiffs–Appellees,

v.

HUMPHREYS (CAYMAN) LIMITED, a
corporation, and Holiday Inns, Inc., a
corporation, Defendants–Appellants.

Nos. 88–2495, 88–2496.

United States Court of Appeals,
Seventh Circuit.

Argued Oct. 31, 1989.

Decided Oct. 24, 1990.

Rehearing Denied Nov. 21, 1990.

Participant of tour that originated in Indiana filed diversity action against operator of Cayman Islands hotel where she was assaulted, and its licensor. The United States District Court for the Southern District of Indiana, Indianapolis Division, Larry J. McKinney, J., denied motions to dismiss for lack of subject matter and personal jurisdiction and on forum non conveniens grounds, but certified questions for interlocutory appeal. The Court of Appeals, Ripple, Circuit Judge, held that: (1) policies supporting alienage jurisdiction permitted United States district court to assume subject matter jurisdiction over corporate citizen of Cayman Islands; (2) Indiana federal district court had specific personal jurisdiction over hotel operator; (3) remand was warranted for further inquiry into licensor's Indiana contacts and conduct, for purposes of determining whether general personal jurisdiction existed over licensor; and (4) trial court did not abuse its discre-

12

MOTIONS AND SUPPORTING BRIEFS

Motions are requests to the court that either ask the court to order something to be done or attack the pleadings. Motions that ask the court to order something to be done generally deal with housekeeping matters, such as requests for an extension of time to meet a court-scheduled deadline or motions relating to discovery. Motions that attack the pleadings, such as a motion to dismiss or motion for summary judgment, are called **dispositive motions.**

Increasingly, most lawsuits are resolved in one way or another before they get to trial. Because of this, motions and their supporting briefs have come to play a pivotal role in the outcome of cases. They are golden opportunities to secure the court's attention and persuade it in your client's favor.

Generally, motions are used for one of the following reasons:

- To control information (to obtain, suppress, or include evidence)
- To control the final outcome (as in a motion to dismiss, motion for summary judgment, motion for directed verdict, motion to vacate judgment, etc.)
- To control the procedure (as in a motion for change of venue, motion for leave to file reply, motion for extension of time, etc.)
- To control the parties (as in a motion to compel discovery, motion for restraining order, etc.)

Before drafting a motion, first think about the motion's purpose and the desired goal. When is the proper time to file the motion or a scheduling order? When would it have the greatest strategic impact on the case? Do court rules prescribe a certain deadline for filing the motion or responding to it? Consider also how the motion's outcome, both positive and negative, will influence your client's case. Once you have considered all of these factors, you can then concentrate on drafting the motion itself.

motion
An application made to a court to obtain a favorable action or decision.

dispositive motion
A motion that attacks the pleadings which, when ruled upon by the court, resolves the entire lawsuit or a portion of it.

PRACTICE TIP
Motions are different from pleadings in that a pleading makes an assertion while a motion makes a request.

◼ COURT RULES

Although motions do not require any technical form, Rule 7(b) of the Federal Rules of Civil Procedure ("Fed.R.Civ.P.") gives three basic requirements for every motion.

local court rules
Rules promulgated by
individual courts, both
state and federal, which
apply only to the court
that creates them and
supplement the Rules of
Civil Procedure.

court rules
Regulations with the
force of law governing
practice and procedure
in various courts.

caption, style of the case
The beginning of a
pleading, motion, depo-
sition, or other legal
instrument which indi-
cates the names of the
parties, the name of the
court, and the docket or
case number.

title
The name of the docu-
ment that should also
include the exact reason
for the motion (e.g.,
Defendant's Motion for
Extension of Time to
Answer).

signature block
The section of the
motion after the
Conclusion containing
the signature line, name,
address, and telephone
of the attorney of record
or the pro se litigant,
which also serves to
meet the requirements
of Rule 11.

Certificate of Service, Certificate of Mailing
Written assurance that a
copy of the document
upon which the
Certificate appears has
been served upon the
counsel for all parties or
the pro se litigants in the
lawsuit.

Some jurisdictions' local rules may have additional requirements for any motion filed in that jurisdiction. Most **local court rules** determine the format, if any, for motions (such as a motion for summary judgment) and other requirements (such as the page number limit and format). Local rules tell you which motions require an accompanying supporting brief. **Court rules** relating to format, page number limit, requirements for service, attached exhibits, and deadlines for filing the motion apply to any motion filed with that court.

Requirements for Drafting Motions

Rule 7(b) requires that every motion or application for an order of the court conform to these specifications:

1. Must be made in writing, unless the motion is made during a trial or hearing
2. Must state "with particularity" the ground upon which it relies; that is, on what authority (such as court rule or statute) the movant is asking the court for the order
3. Must state the relief or order requested

The format for motions is basically the same as that for pleadings:

1. A **caption** or **style of the case** that includes the name of the court, the names of the parties, and the case number
2. The **title** of the motion
3. A **signature block** for the attorney of record or unrepresented party
4. A **Certificate of Service**

Facts that support the motion can be made as statements within the motion, with an exhibit supporting them attached to the motion. Facts can also be presented to the court as an affidavit attached to the motion. Any affidavits or exhibits accompanying or supporting the motion are attached to the motion or its supporting brief when the motion is filed. This supporting documentation should be attached to the original motion and any copies, and served on all parties.

Setting the Motion for Hearing and Giving Notice to Opposing Counsel

The motion is set for a hearing before a judge or magistrate by the court clerk when the motion is filed. The Rule 7(b)(1) requirement that all motions shall be made in writing is fulfilled if the motion also states the time and date of the hearing.

Here is how this normally works in most courts. The original and copies of the motion and proposed order are taken or mailed to the court clerk for filing. The court clerk stamps the original and copies with that day's date. The clerk then keeps the original (and sometimes one or more copies, depending on the local rules).

Usually the court clerk then sets the motion for hearing according to the assigned judge's docket for that case. The date, time, and assigned judge may be indicated in a note handwritten by the clerk at the top of the front page of the motion. This information may also be inserted by hand into a standard form that is commonly found at the end of a motion *after* the Certificate of Service, as shown in Exhibit 12.1.

EXHIBIT 12.1 *Notice of Hearing*

<u>NOTICE OF HEARING</u>

This motion has been scheduled for hearing before the Honorable
_____in courtroom_____on the _____day of _____, 199__.

PRACTICE TIP

Be sure to docket any hearing date and advise the attorney who will be arguing the motion of the hearing's date, time, and assigned judge.

Sometimes the **notice of hearing** also includes the number of the courtroom or the exact location of the hearing. Most judges normally have assigned courtrooms. Therefore, by stating which judge will be hearing the motion, you have effectively advised opposing counsel where the hearing will be held.

notice of hearing
Written notice of the date, time, and location of any motion set to be heard before the court which must be served on every party in the lawsuit at least five days before the date of the hearing.

◼ PRACTICE TIP

Before setting a motion for hearing, your supervising attorney may wish to contact opposing counsel to ask for preferred dates and times for the hearing, depending on the court's docket and schedule. However, this is a matter of professional courtesy only and is not required unless the court's rules make it so.

Rule 6(d) requires that notice of each motion and hearing must be served on every party in the lawsuit *at least five days before the date of the hearing.* Local rules may require a longer or shorter notice period.

Rule 11

Like pleadings, all motions are subject to the provisions of **Rule 11** of the **Federal Rules of Civil Procedure.** All motions must be signed by *at least* one attorney of record in the attorney's individual name or, if the party is not represented by an attorney, a motion *must* be signed by the party. Each motion must also state the signer's address and telephone number. Rules 11(a) through (c) do not apply to motions that are subject to the provisions of Rules 26 through 37 (rules on discovery).

Rule 11, Federal Rules of Civil Procedure
A court rule regarding the attorneys' and litigants' obligation to the court for their conduct which provides for sanctions for violation of the rule.

◼ DRAFTING THE BODY OF THE MOTION

A simple procedural motion states (1) the nature of the request, (2) the authority upon which the movant relies in making the request (usually a statute or court rule), and (3) the relief sought. The motion should also include a notice of hearing that indicates the date, time, and courtroom for the motion to be heard by the court.

◼ PRACTICE TIP

A simple procedural motion states (1) the nature of the request, (2) the authority upon which the movant relies in making the request, and (3) the relief sought. It should also include a notice of hearing that establishes the date, time, and courtroom for the motion to be heard by the court.

PRACTICE TIP

It is not unusual for a housekeeping-type motion to rely solely on one statute or rule.

Tell the court up front the reason for the motion. A good place to start is with the title. If you are asking the court for an extension of time for some reason, say so in the title, like this:

<u>DEFENDANT'S MOTION FOR EXTENSION OF TIME</u>

When stating the nature of the request, do so in plain English. Combine into one sentence the request, the authority upon which you rely in making the request, and the relief sought.

Say, for instance, that you and your supervising attorney have written a brief in support of a motion for summary judgment that is thirty pages long. But the local court rules prohibit briefs longer than twenty-five pages. Despite your best concerted efforts, the two of you find that the case is simply too complex to present the matter to the court in fewer pages. If five pages were cut from the brief, it would certainly suffer in persuasiveness and coherency.

So what do you do? The same local rules should provide a solution. Another local rule says that you can file a brief in excess of twenty-five pages, but you must first ask permission from the court.

You ask the court's permission by filing a motion requesting that the court permit you to file a brief in excess of twenty-five pages. The motion should cite the local rule that gives the court the authority to grant your request, as shown in Exhibit 12.2. It is not necessary to cite case law for this type of motion; the rule by itself is sufficient authority.

The motion in Exhibit 12.2 is an example of a motion that requires no supporting brief and relies on a single court rule as its authority. This type of motion is com-

---

EXHIBIT 12.2 *Motion for Leave to File Oversized Brief*

**DEFENDANT CHARLES RAYMOND'S MOTION FOR PERMISSION
TO FILE BRIEF IN EXCESS OF TWENTY-FIVE PAGES**

Pursuant to Local Rule _____, Defendant Charles Raymond requests permission to file a brief in support of his Motion for Summary Judgment which is thirty pages in length. In support of this Motion, Defendant Charles Raymond states:

1. This is a lawsuit involving personal injury, product liability, respondeat superior, and employment law issues.

2. In her Complaint and Reply to this Defendant's Answer, Plaintiff has alleged numerous factual issues that must be addressed in Defendant's Motion for Summary Judgment and Brief in Support.

3. Because of the complexity of this lawsuit and the numerous factual issues raised by Plaintiff in the pleadings, Defendant Charles Raymond cannot adequately address each factual issue or cite to the authorities upon which he relies within the twenty-five page number limit required by Local Rule—.

4. Defendant Charles Raymond's Brief in Support of his Motion for Summary Judgment, a copy of which is attached to this Motion, is thirty pages.

5. Although not required to do so by this court, counsel for Defendant Charles Raymond has conferred with Plaintiff's counsel and is authorized to state that Plaintiff's counsel has no objection to the filing of Defendant's thirty-page brief.

Continued

EXHIBIT 12.2 —*Continued*

6. Further, Defendant Charles Raymond has no objection to this court granting permission to Plaintiff to file a thirty-page brief in response to his Motion for Summary Judgment and Brief in Support should Plaintiff make such a request.

WHEREFORE, pursuant to Local Rule ____, Defendant Charles Raymond requests permission from this court to file a brief thirty pages in length in support of his Motion for Summary Judgment.

■ PRACTICE TIP

In any type of motion or supporting brief, you must always *tell the court what you want and then give the court the means to do what you ask of it.* Any motion that tells the court what you want and then fails to cite the proper authority that gives the court the power to do what you request is doomed to failure.

---

monly used for procedural matters. Generally, this type of procedural motion needs no exhibits or supporting brief, and cites one or two authorities at most, commonly court rules or local rules.

One of the most common procedural motions is a **motion for extension of time.** Most courts have promulgated local rules that have certain requirements for making such a request of the court. When requesting an extension of time from the court, the local court rules commonly require the movant to show:

- The reason for the extension
- Whether the movant has contacted opposing counsel, and whether opposing counsel objects to the extension or
- Whether granting the extension will adversely affect any of the parties or other deadlines already set by the court

We provide an example motion for extension of time in Exhibit 12.3, but it is only an example, as any form should be. Check your jurisdiction's court rules to determine whether it has different requirements for this type of motion.

motion for extension of time
A procedural motion in which the movant asks the court for additional time to file a document with the court or otherwise respond to an opposing party.

EXHIBIT 12.3 *Motion for Extension of Time*

DEFENDANT CHARLES RAYMOND'S
MOTION FOR AN EXTENSION OF TIME TO
ANSWER PLAINTIFF'S DISCOVERY REQUESTS

Pursuant to Rule ____, Defendant Charles Raymond moves this Court for a ten-day extension of time, or until June 1, 1995, to respond to Plaintiff's discovery requests. In support of this Motion, Defendant Charles Raymond states that:

1. Defendant's responses to Plaintiff's discovery requests are currently due May 21, 1995;

2. Counsel for Defendant has conferred with counsel for Plaintiff and is authorized to state that counsel for Plaintiff has no objection to this extension of time;

Continued

EXHIBIT 12.3   *—Continued*

3. Defendant has not requested any previous extensions of time;

4. This extension of time would not negatively affect any party or any deadline currently set by this Court's Scheduling Order; and

5. Defendant requests a ten-day extension because he has not had sufficient time to conduct an adequate factual or legal investigation necessary to respond to all of Plaintiff's discovery requests.

WHEREFORE, pursuant to Rule ____, Defendant Charles Raymond moves this Court for a ten-day extension of time, or until June 1, 1995, to respond to Plaintiff's discovery requests.

---

proposed order
An order that is submitted with a motion for the court's execution to save the court from drafting the order itself.

Most court rules require that a **proposed order** be attached to any motion filed with the court. It is still a good idea to attach a proposed order even when the court rules do not require it, because it gives the movant the opportunity to suggest specific language to the court for the order. In Exhibit 12.4, we give you an example of a proposed order for the Motion for Extension of Time found in Exhibit 12.3.

EXHIBIT 12.4   *Proposed Order*

<u>**ORDER**</u>

On motion of Defendant Charles Raymond, without objection by Plaintiff, and for good cause shown, the Court finds that Defendant Charles Raymond's Motion for an extension of time should be granted.

IT IS ORDERED that Defendant Charles Raymond is granted an additional ten days, or until June 1, 1995, within which to respond to Plaintiff's discovery requests.

DATED THIS ____day of_____, 1995.

_____
JUDGE OF THE DISTRICT COURT

APPROVED:

_____
Marcia Wilmington, OBA #14500
170 Park Avenue, Suite 200
Oklahoma City, Oklahoma 73102
Telephone: 405/232-0311

ATTORNEY FOR DEFENDANT CHARLES RAYMOND

---

supporting brief
The written legal arguments and authorities supporting a specific motion, or objection to another party's motion, which states the party's grounds for bringing the motion, or objecting to it, and the reasons why the motion should be granted or denied.

motion in limine
A motion filed with the court, made before or after the beginning of a jury trial, for a protective order against the potential use of prejudicial statements, evidence, or questions by the other side.

motion to assess attorney fees
A motion filed with the court requesting an award of attorney fees to be given to the prevailing party (the movant).

▣ MOTIONS THAT REQUIRE SUPPORTING BRIEFS

Some motions require **supporting briefs.** The brief in support of a motion states the party's legal arguments and legal citations supporting those arguments. The court rules specify whether a supporting brief is required. Generally, supporting briefs are provided for motions that raise questions of substantive law, such as a motion to dismiss, motion for summary judgment, **motion in limine,** motion to compel discovery, or **motion to assess attorney fees.**

The motion and supporting brief may be filed as two separate documents or joined together as one. When the supporting brief is somewhat lengthy or contains a table of contents and table of authorities, it is usually written and filed as a separate document.

When drafting the motion and supporting brief together as one document, simply make a statement of the reason for the motion, the authority upon which the movant relies in bringing the motion, and the relief sought. The next statement should say something like, "In support of this motion, Defendant Charles Raymond submits the following brief."

Motion to Compel Discovery

In Exhibit 12.5, the combined motion and supporting brief use only one authority to support the argument to the court, but are sufficient in this instance to accomplish the desired result.

EXHIBIT 12.5 *Motion to Compel and Supporting Brief*

DEFENDANT CHARLES RAYMOND'S MOTION
TO COMPEL DISCOVERY AND BRIEF IN SUPPORT

Defendant Charles Raymond, pursuant to Rule 37 of the Federal Rules of Civil Procedure, moves the Court to compel Plaintiff Jane Healy to respond to Defendant Charles Raymond's First Set of Interrogatories to Plaintiff ("Defendant's Interrogatories"), and for his attorney fees and costs in procuring this order.

In support of this Motion, Defendant Charles Raymond states:

1. Defendant Charles Raymond served Defendant's Interrogatories on counsel for Plaintiff Jane Healy on December 12, 1995, by certified mail, return receipt requested. A copy of Defendant's Interrogatories is attached as Exhibit "A."

2. Plaintiff's response to Defendant's Interrogatories was due January 11, 1995. A copy of the return receipt signed by counsel for Plaintiff is attached as Exhibit "B."

3. On January 13, 1995, counsel for Defendant Charles Raymond requested a response to Defendant's Interrogatories from counsel for Plaintiff. A copy of that letter is attached as Exhibit "C."

4. In compliance with Local Rule 14(e) of the Rules of the United States District Court for the Western District of Oklahoma, Defendant Charles Raymond's counsel attempted to contact counsel for Plaintiff by telephone to discuss and resolve the emerging dispute over the delinquent responses to Defendant's Interrogatories. On or about January 17, 1995, after repeated telephone calls, counsel for Defendant Charles Raymond reached counsel for Plaintiff Jane Healy, who agreed to forward responses to Defendant's Interrogatories within one week. A copy of the January 17, 1995 letter sent from counsel for Defendant Charles Raymond to counsel for Plaintiff confirming this agreement is attached as Exhibit "D."

5. Plaintiff Jane Healy failed to submit her responses to Defendant's Interrogatories within the agreed time and has yet to submit responses or explain the reason for her delay.

Continued

EXHIBIT 12.5 *—Continued*

6. Counsel for Defendant Charles Raymond has attempted in good faith to resolve the discovery dispute between the parties in compliance with Rule 14(e) of the Local Rules but, after reasonable attempts made by counsel for Defendant Charles Raymond, the dispute remains unresolved.

7. Defendant Charles Raymond is entitled to the information requested by Defendant's Interrogatories. Plaintiff, by her failure to respond, has waived any objection she may have to providing the information requested.

BRIEF IN SUPPORT

On August 19, 1990, Plaintiff Jane Healy instituted this action in the United States District Court for the Western District of Oklahoma. Defendant Charles Raymond denied Plaintiff's allegations, and began discovery to determine the basis of Plaintiff's claim. Defendant Charles Raymond twice proceeded to prepare for jury trial of this action. However, in each instance, Plaintiff sought and received new scheduling deadlines in which to complete preparation of her claims.

On October 3, 1992, at the pretrial of this action, Plaintiff sought leave to amend her Complaint. After Plaintiff's written motion to amend the Complaint and Defendant Charles Raymond's and other defendants' objections, the Court granted Plaintiff leave to amend the Complaint and established scheduled deadlines for the future proceedings in this action.

The discovery deadline is now February 15, 1995, less than one month away. Plaintiff, by her failure to respond timely to Defendant Charles Raymond's discovery requests, has impaired this Defendant's ability to conduct further discovery before that deadline. Specifically, Defendant Charles Raymond will be unable to propound additional discovery requests based on Plaintiff's responses and has been thus extremely prejudiced by Plaintiff's conduct.

Rule 37 of the Federal Rules of Civil Procedure provides in pertinent part:

> (a)(2)(B) If . . . a party fails to answer an interrogatory submitted under Rule 33, . . ., the discovering party may move for an order compelling an answer, . . . in accordance with the request.
>
> ******
>
> (b)(4)(A) If a party . . . fails . . . (2) to serve answers or objections to interrogatories submitted under Rule 33, . . ., the court . . . on motion may make such orders in regard to the failure as are just, and among others it may take any action authorized under subparagraphs (A), (B), and (C) of subdivision (b)(2) of this rule. . . . In lieu of any order or in addition thereto, the court shall require the party failing to act or the attorney advising that party or both to pay the reasonable expenses, including attorney's fees. . . .

CONCLUSION

Plaintiff Jane Healy has wholly failed to respond to Defendant's discovery requests. Defendant Charles Raymond has incurred attorney fees and costs in pursuing this order to compel Plaintiff Jane Healy to respond to his proper discovery requests.

WHEREFORE, pursuant to Rule 37, Defendant Charles Raymond requests that this Court compel Plaintiff Jane Healy to respond to Defendant's Interrogatories and award Defendant Charles Raymond his attorney fees and costs in pursuing this order.

■ PRACTICE TIP

In Exhibit 12.5, one authority—a court rule—was sufficient. However, it would have been acceptable if we had also included a few citations to case law that supported the movant's position in the supporting brief.

■ PRACTICE TIP

Rule 26(c) of the Federal Rules of Civil Procedure:
> Upon motion by a party or by the person from whom discovery is sought, accompanied by a certification that the movant has in good faith conferred or attempted to confer with other affected parties in an effort to resolve the dispute without court action, and for good cause shown, the court in which the action is pending or alternatively, on matters relating to a deposition, the court in the district where the deposition is to be taken may make any order which justice requires to protect a party or person from annoyance, embarrassment, oppression, or undue burden or expense, including one or more of the following:
> (1) that the disclosure or discovery not be had;
> (2) that the disclosure or discovery may be had only on specified terms and conditions, including a designation of time or place;
> (3) that the discovery may be had only by a method of discovery other than that selected by the party seeking discovery;
> (4) that certain matters not be inquired into, or that the scope of the disclosure or discovery be limited to certain matters;
> (5) that discovery be conducted with no one present except persons designated by the court;
> (6) that a deposition, after being sealed, be opened only by order of the court;
> (7) that a trade secret or other confidential research, development, or commercial information not be revealed or be revealed only in a designated way; and
> (8) that the parties simultaneously file specified documents or information enclosed in sealed envelopes to be opened as directed by the court.
> If the motion for protective order is denied in whole or in part, the court may, on such terms and conditions as are just, order that any party or other person provide or permit discovery. The provisions of Rule 37(a)(4) apply to the award of expenses incurred in relation to the motion.

Of course, in Exhibit 12.5, the attorney's signature block, Certificate of Mailing, and Notice of Hearing would complete this discovery motion. If you were responsible for preparing this document for filing with the court clerk, you would double-check that all exhibits referred to within the motion were attached to it before it was copied and filed. The date and time of the hearing should be noted on the file-stamped copy of the motion that is sent to opposing counsel.

The motion in Exhibit 12.5 is a **discovery motion,** that is, a motion dealing solely with discovery issues. Motions to compel responses to discovery are filed when the parties in a lawsuit reach an impasse on a discovery issue.

discovery motion
A motion filed with the court that deals solely with discovery issues.

Here is a situation from a real-life lawsuit involving another type of discovery motion. In this case, the plaintiffs were former management employees of a nationwide corporation like General Motors or Kerr McGee. Plaintiffs were fired from Defendant XYZ Corporation for violations of corporate policies and for fraud. Plaintiffs have sued Defendant XYZ Corporation for wrongful termination of employment.

motion to compel
A motion filed with the court requesting the court to order the opposing party to respond to discovery requests.

motion for protective order
A motion filed with the court requesting the court to enter a protective order to protect one party from abusive service of process or discovery by the opposing party or to order a party to cease some act or harassment, or to keep certain privileged documents or information confidential.

Introduction
The short, clear section at the beginning of a pleading, motion, or brief that identifies the parties and sets the stage for the remainder of the document.

affidavit
A written declaration of facts made voluntarily and under oath before a person authorized to administer oaths, such as a notary public.

proposition
A heading or subheading which consists of a succinct statement—normally a single sentence or sentence fragment—that tells the court the question or issue to be discussed and answered in the proposition.

sheperdize
The process of determining the subsequent history of a particular case and how subsequent cases have cited or interpreted a particular case.

As part of their discovery, Plaintiffs insisted on taking the depositions of numerous corporate witnesses, each of whom was an employee of Defendant XYZ Corporation. The witnesses were scattered all over the United States. To reduce their costs, Plaintiffs wanted Defendant XYZ Corporation to agree to hold all of the depositions in one location which, not surprisingly, was the same city where Plaintiffs' lawyer's office was located.

As you might imagine, Defendant XYZ Corporation strenuously opposed this plan. Plaintiffs filed a **Motion to Compel,** designed to force Defendant XYZ Corporation to produce all of the corporate witnesses at one location. In response to the Plaintiffs' Motion to Compel, Defendant XYZ filed an "Objection to Plaintiffs' Motion to Compel and Defendant's **Motion for Protective Order,**" which is provided as Appendix H.

In this example, the defendant believes that the plaintiffs have overstepped the boundaries of the discovery rules. To counter the plaintiffs' motion to compel, the defendant is seeking a protective order from the court to prevent the plaintiffs from forcing it to comply with their demands. Protective orders are governed by Rule 26(c) of the Federal Rules of Civil Procedure.

Motion for Protective Order

In Appendix H, the Motion for Protective Order argues that the plaintiffs' chosen "designated" site for all depositions of the corporate defendant's witnesses was inappropriate. Protective orders can also be used to keep confidential certain privileged documents or information, such as trade secrets. In some instances, a protective order may be used to order the destruction at the end of the litigation of specific documents produced under that protective order.

The document in Appendix H is a little more complex than the Motion to Compel in Exhibit 12.5. For one thing, it combines a response to a motion to compel with a motion for protective order and supporting brief together as one document. It also uses an **Introduction** to rebut statements made by the opposing party and to state facts in a light favorable to the client. Notice that, although quotations from several cases and court rules were used, the quotations themselves are short, never more than two or three sentences at most.

This document also has two affidavits as exhibits. An **affidavit** is a written declaration of facts made voluntarily and under oath before a person authorized to administer oaths, such as a notary public. Both of these exhibits were used to support statements of fact made by the defendant corporation.

Although you have not read the Plaintiffs' Motion to Compel referred to in Appendix H, what can you determine from reading the Defendant's response? Look at the first **proposition.** What can you determine about the quality of research that was put into the Plaintiffs' motion and supporting brief?

For one thing, it appears that at least one of the key cases relied upon by the Plaintiffs—*Terry v. Modern Woodmen of America*—was not carefully **sheperdized** or

■ PRACTICE TIP

Always cite-check every authority relied upon by opposing counsel before drafting your response. Even if none of the opposing party's cases have been overruled, you may still find cases that criticize or distinguish those cases. Any negative treatment of the opposing party's cases will help you develop a convincing argument to counterattack your opponent's position.

cite-checked. Perhaps the researcher did discover that *Terry* was no longer the prevailing authority, and chose to use it anyway. But it is difficult to imagine that someone would discover that a case had been **overruled** and then use it as a cornerstone of his or her argument.

The supporting brief in Appendix H is organized in an **issue-by-issue approach.** Each proposition states the issue to be discussed in that proposition. The reader is led in a logical, methodical way to the conclusion. The motion asks the court to enter a protective order. The supporting brief explains why such an order is needed and cites authorities that give the court the power to enter that order.

Remember what we said in Chapter 10 about leading with your controlling authority? The prevailing law for this court's jurisdiction—*General Leasing Co. v. Lawrence Photo-Graphic Supply, Inc.*—is cited in the first proposition. Other important authorities, such as court rules, case law, and to a lesser extent, treatises, are used throughout the propositions to add weight and support to the argument.

Now look at the Conclusion in Appendix H. The first paragraph of the Conclusion succinctly sums up the arguments made throughout the brief in three sentences. The following paragraph is the prayer for relief—what the moving party wants the court to do.

Motion for Sanctions

A **motion for sanctions** is another discovery motion. This motion, which relies on Rule 37, Fed.R.Civ.P., may be filed when one party has deliberately failed to respond to discovery or comply with discovery orders. In the example in Exhibit 12.6, the motion for sanctions and its supporting brief rely on Rule 37 as authority. Motions for sanctions may also be filed under Rule 11 of the Federal Rules of Civil Procedure to impose sanctions on attorneys for other types of improper conduct.

EXHIBIT 12.6 *Motion for Sanctions and Supporting Brief*

PLAINTIFF'S MOTION FOR SANCTIONS AND BRIEF IN SUPPORT

Plaintiff Jane Healy moves the Court, pursuant to Rule 37 of the Federal Rules of Civil Procedure, for sanctions against Defendant Charles Raymond on the ground that Defendant Charles Raymond has failed and refused to respond adequately to Plaintiff's discovery requests. In support of this Motion, Plaintiff states:

1. On September 30, 1994, Plaintiff propounded Interrogatories to Defendant Charles Raymond seeking the facts upon which Defendant Charles Raymond based his Answer to Plaintiff's Petition.

2. Defendant Charles Raymond's Answers to Plaintiff's Interrogatories were due on October 30, 1994.

3. On October 30, 1994, Defendant Charles Raymond requested additional time to respond to Plaintiff's Interrogatories. On June 12, 1995, eight months later, Defendant Charles Raymond submitted his answers which purport to respond to Plaintiff's Interrogatories. Defendant Charles Raymond's Answers to Plaintiff's Interrogatories, attached as Exhibit "A," are incomplete and evasive and, therefore, unresponsive to Plaintiff's discovery request.

Continued

---

cite-check
The process of proofreading citations and verifying that the authority cited is still "good" law.

overruled
An opinion is overruled when a later decision, rendered by the same court or by a superior court, expresses a judgment on the same question of law directly opposite to that which was given before, thereby depriving the earlier opinion of all authority as a precedent.

issue-by-issue approach
A specialized format for motions using individual propositions to state the issues through which the reader is led in a logical, methodical way to the conclusion.

motion for sanctions
A motion filed with the court requesting that Rule 11 sanctions or penalties be awarded by the court upon the attorneys, law firms, or parties who have violated Rule 11(b) or who are responsible for the violation, which usually consist of the payment by the violator of opposing counsel's attorney's fees and costs.

PRACTICE TIP

Regardless of the reason, sanctions against a party or that party's attorney are considered a severe penalty. Such a motion should never be filed without a careful review of the facts and the applicable court rules.

EXHIBIT 12.6 —*Continued*

4. On May 13, 1995, Plaintiff filed a Motion to Compel Answers to Interrogatories.

5. On June 16, 1995, Plaintiff requested that Defendant Charles Raymond supplement his responses to Plaintiff's Interrogatories. Plaintiff's June 16, 1995 letter to counsel for Defendant Raymond is attached as Exhibit "B." To date, no supplemental answers to Plaintiff's Interrogatories have been received from Defendant Raymond.

6. Counsel for Defendant Charles Raymond has represented to Plaintiff's counsel that he has insufficient facts to respond adequately to Plaintiff's Interrogatories, and that further investigation by Defendant Raymond is required before he can respond fully to Plaintiff's discovery.

7. On December 29, 1995, Defendant Charles Raymond filed his Response to Plaintiff's Motion for Summary Judgment. On December 30, 1995, Defendant Charles Raymond filed his Amended Response to Plaintiff's Motion for Summary Judgment. Attached to Defendant Raymond's Amended Response is the Affidavit of Joe West, which states facts upon which Defendant Raymond's defenses to Plaintiff's Petition and Counterclaim are based. A copy of Joe West's Affidavit is attached as Exhibit "C."

8. Defendant Charles Raymond has never provided this information to Plaintiff pursuant to Plaintiff's discovery requests. The discovery cut-off deadline has now expired. Therefore, Plaintiff is unable to conduct further discovery to explore these newly revealed factual allegations. The statements of Joe West are inadmissible at trial pursuant to Rule 37(c)(1) because Defendant Charles Raymond has failed to list witnesses pursuant to this Court's Scheduling Order.

BRIEF IN SUPPORT OF
PLAINTIFF'S MOTION FOR SANCTIONS

Rule 37(a) of the Federal Rules of Civil Procedure provides that certain sanctions may be imposed on the failure of a party to comply with a court's order on discovery. Those sanctions include, among others, the court's refusal to allow the disobedient party to support or oppose designated claims or defenses, or prohibiting that party from introducing designated matters in evidence. Defendant Charles Raymond has offered facts, through the Affidavit of Joe West, to support his defenses to Plaintiff's Complaint and his claims against Plaintiff in his Counterclaim. Yet Defendant Charles Raymond has failed or willfully refused to provide those facts in response to Plaintiff's discovery requests.

The discovery deadline has now passed, and no further discovery is permitted by the Court. Plaintiff has, therefore, been severely prejudiced by Defendant Charles Raymond's withholding of facts. Accordingly, sanctions should be imposed against Defendant Charles Raymond.

WHEREFORE, Plaintiff Jane Healy requests the Court, pursuant to Rule 37 of the Federal Rules of Civil Procedure, to impose sanctions against Defendant Charles Raymond for his failure and refusal to respond to discovery and to supplement dis-

Continued

EXHIBIT 12.6 *—Continued*

covery with facts in his possession, and for Plaintiff's costs and attorney fees incurred because of Defendant's conduct.

Respectfully submitted,

_____

Amelia Pepper
101 Park Avenue
Suite 100
River City, Oklahoma 73102
405/282-9918
Attorney for Plaintiff
Jane Healy

CERTIFICATE OF MAILING

This is to certify that on the _____day of January, 1996, a file-stamped copy of Plaintiff's Motion for Sanctions and Brief in Support was mailed, postage prepaid, to James B. Baxter, Baxter & Associates, 200 North Robinson, Suite 1700, River City, Oklahoma 73012.

_____

Amelia Pepper

As you can see in Exhibit 12.6, this motion for sanctions was based on a party's failure to respond to interrogatories. Sanctions might also be imposed under Rule 37 based on a party's failure to appear for a duly noticed deposition when that party made no objection to the deposition or said nothing about his or her intention not to attend. This is one reason to encourage your attorney to prepare and file a Notice to Take Deposition as evidence that the party was notified of deposition's date, time, and location.

Motion to Dismiss

There are two types of dismissals: voluntary and involuntary. The first part of this section will address voluntary dismissals.

Voluntary Dismissal. In a **voluntary dismissal,** the plaintiff decides to withdraw the lawsuit. In that instance, the plaintiff could file a **motion to dismiss,** bringing the lawsuit to an end without incurring any penalties. Even when the parties have settled the lawsuit, the plaintiff must still file a motion to dismiss to bring the lawsuit to a close. The plaintiff and defendant may also file a **joint stipulation for dismissal** or **joint motion to dismiss.** But a plaintiff may not attempt to dismiss a case in which a defendant has already filed a counterclaim against the plaintiff.

The wording of a motion and order for dismissal is relatively simple: "Plaintiff requests that its cause of action against Defendant be dismissed with prejudice." But the last three words are the critical language. Any motion or order for dismissal must always indicate whether the dismissal is **with prejudice** or **without prejudice.**

With prejudice means that the dismissal order is conclusive of the rights of the parties. It has the same effect as a final adjudication and bars the plaintiff's right to bring a lawsuit later on the same cause of action. *Without prejudice* means that no rights or privileges are waived or lost by dismissing the lawsuit. A dismissal without prejudice allows a new lawsuit to be brought later on the same cause of action (see Exhibit 12.7, p. 390).

voluntary dismissal
Under rules practice, a voluntary dismissal may be accomplished by the plaintiff without leave of court if filed before the defendant's Answer or by stipulation signed by all of the parties after the defendant's Answer is filed.

motion to dismiss, demurrer
A motion usually made before trial begins that requests the court to dismiss the case because the pleadings of the other side are insufficient or because the Complaint does not state a claim for which the law provides a remedy.

joint stipulation for dismissal, joint motion to dismiss
When both the plaintiff and defendant decide to dismiss the lawsuit.

dismissal with prejudice
Conclusive of the rights of the parties having the same effect as a final adjudication and bars the plaintiff's right to bring a lawsuit later on the same cause of action.

dismissal without prejudice
No rights or privileges are waived or lost by dismissing the lawsuit, and the plaintiff is not barred from bringing a new lawsuit later on the same cause of action.

PRACTICE TIP

A motion to dismiss can apply to the entire lawsuit or to only one or more of the counts or claims. Also, when there are multiple defendants, a motion to dismiss may dismiss one defendant while retaining the lawsuit against the other defendants.

PRACTICE TIP

A motion to dismiss asks a court to dismiss the plaintiff's Complaint either because it does not state a claim for which the law provides a remedy or because it is legally insufficient in some other way.

EXHIBIT 12.7 *Plaintiff's Motion to Dismiss*

PLAINTIFF'S MOTION TO DISMISS

Plaintiff Gatewood Investments, Inc. dismisses without prejudice its cause of action against Defendant Blair Alwyn Brently.

WHEREFORE, Plaintiff Gatewood Investments, Inc. moves this Court to dismiss without prejudice its cause of action against Defendant Blair Alwyn Brently.

Respectfully submitted,

_____

Sherman H. Thompson
101 First Avenue, Suite 40
Orlando, Florida 32751
Telephone: 407/690-0076

ATTORNEY FOR PLAINTIFF

Normally, the plaintiff would also attach a proposed order of dismissal to this motion, such as the one in Exhibit 12.8.

EXHIBIT 12.8 *Proposed Dismissal Order*

ORDER

On this date, upon consideration of Plaintiff's Motion to Dismiss, the Court finds that Plaintiff's Motion should be granted.

IT IS THEREFORE ORDERED by the Court that all of Plaintiff's causes of action against Defendant Blair Alwyn Brently are dismissed without prejudice.

DATED THIS _____day of _____, 199__.

_____

JUDGE OF THE DISTRICT COURT

APPROVED:

_____

Sherman H. Thompson
101 First Avenue, Suite 404
Orlando, Florida 32751
Telephone: 407/690-0076

ATTORNEY FOR PLAINTIFF

---

involuntary dismissal Under rules practice, may be accomplished on court's own motion for lack of prosecution or on motion of defendant for lack of prosecution or failure to introduce evidence of facts on which relief may be granted, and disposes of all of the party's rights, and is a "final" order which can be appealed.

Involuntary Dismissal. In the first part of this section, we discussed voluntary dismissals. The remainder of this section deals with **involuntary dismissals.** As mentioned earlier in this chapter, an Answer is not the only response available to a defendant when he, she, or it is served with the Complaint. There may be some procedural reason that the court should not proceed with the lawsuit.

The defendant may choose instead to file a dispositive motion, such as a motion to dismiss under Rule 12(b) of the Federal Rules of Civil Procedure. A motion to dismiss, also sometimes called a **demurrer,** asks a court to dismiss the plaintiff's Complaint because it does not state a claim for which the law provides a remedy or is legally insufficient in some other way. In this way, defective or meritless complaints can be dealt with in the early stages of the lawsuit. This type of dismissal is involuntary.

Under Rule 12(b) of the Federal Rules of Civil Procedure, the following defenses can be made by filing a motion to dismiss rather than by filing an Answer:

1. Lack of jurisdiction over the subject matter (subject-matter jurisdiction)
2. Lack of jurisdiction over the person (in personam jurisdiction)
3. Improper venue
4. Insufficiency of **process**
5. Insufficiency of **service of process**
6. Failure to state a claim upon which relief can be granted
7. Failure to join a party under Rule 19[1]

When drafting a motion to dismiss based on Rule 12(b), you must include *all* of the available Rule 12(b) defenses. Otherwise, some defenses may be waived. The idea is to prevent piecemeal attacks on the pleadings.

The exception to the rule is lack of subject-matter jurisdiction, which can be raised at any time. The defenses listed here as numbers 2, 3, and 4 are waived if not consolidated into one motion or included in the Answer. Failure to state a claim upon which relief can be granted and failure to join a party under Rule 19 can be raised in the Answer, Motion for Summary Judgment, or at trial.

As you might suspect, knowing which elements of Rule 12 must be consolidated in one document, and which elements could be waived if not pleaded, is more than a little complicated. This type of motion to dismiss is often complex and generally requires a lengthy supporting brief. Read Rule 12 carefully and follow it exactly. Failure to do so could cause some of your client's defenses to be permanently waived. As always, look to your supervising attorney for guidance if you are in doubt as to how to proceed.

Involuntary dismissals can be entered by the court for other reasons than Rule 12, such as the plaintiff's failure to prosecute a claim. "Failure to prosecute a claim" can mean that the plaintiff failed to appear at hearings or respond to motions, or can refer to other delaying actions by plaintiff (as shown in Exhibits 12.5, 12.6, 12.9, and 12.10). The court also has the power to dismiss the lawsuit where the plaintiff fails to follow court rules or procedure, although this is considered an extreme sanction. The court can also dismiss the lawsuit during a bench trial after the plaintiff has rested his or her case in chief when the plaintiff's evidence fails to show that plaintiff is entitled to relief.

---

1. Rule 19 states that a person who is subject to service of process and whose joinder will not deprive the court of jurisdiction over the subject matter of the action shall be joined as a party in the action if: (1) in the person's absence complete relief cannot be accorded among those already parties; or (2) the person claims an interest relating to the subject of the action and is so situated that the disposition of the action in the person's absence may, as a practical matter, impair or impede the person's ability to protect that interest or leave any of the parties subject to substantial risk of incurring double, multiple, or otherwise inconsistent obligations by reason of the claimed interest.

process
The means used by a court to acquire or exercise its jurisdiction over a person or over specific property.

service of process
The delivery or communication of writs, summonses, etc., or formal notice of parties' claims and defenses.

PRACTICE TIP

Involuntary dismissals are "with prejudice," meaning that they dispose of all of the party's rights, and are "final" orders that can be appealed.

EXHIBIT 12.9 *Motion to Dismiss for Failure to Prosecute*

**DEFENDANT'S MOTION TO
DISMISS FOR FAILURE TO PROSECUTE**

Pursuant to Rule 41(b) of the Federal Rules of Civil Procedure, Defendant moves this Court to dismiss Plaintiff's lawsuit on the grounds that Plaintiff has failed to prosecute his claims and to comply with the Court's Scheduling Order. Defendant's Brief in Support of this Motion is filed simultaneously with this Motion.

Continued

EXHIBIT 12.9   —*Continued*

In support of this Motion, Defendant states:

1. Plaintiff filed this lawsuit on August 19, 1994 in state court claiming that Defendant had failed to abide by the terms of the Contract entered into between Plaintiff and Defendant.

2. On September 8, 1994, Defendant removed this lawsuit to federal court. On September 10, 1994, Defendant answered Plaintiff's Petition and denied liability to Plaintiff.

3. On October 30, 1994, Defendant propounded Interrogatories to Plaintiff seeking the facts upon which Plaintiff based his claims against Defendant.

4. On February 10, 1995, the Court issued a Scheduling Order establishing deadlines for the prosecution of this lawsuit. As part of its Scheduling Order, the Court required the parties to exchange witness lists on November 2, 1995.

5. On May 13, 1995, Defendant filed a Motion to Compel Answers to Interrogatories propounded to Plaintiff on October 30, 1994.

6. On June 12, 1995, Plaintiff submitted "Plaintiff's Answers to Defendant's Interrogatories to Plaintiff," which purport to answer Defendant's Interrogatories. Plaintiff's Answers, however, are incomplete, evasive, and unresponsive to Defendant's discovery requests.

7. On June 16, 1995, Defendant requested by letter that Plaintiff supplement his responses to Defendant's Interrogatories. No supplemental answers have ever been received from Plaintiff.

8. On November 2, 1995, Defendant filed its witness list pursuant to the Court's Scheduling Order and mailed a copy of that list to Plaintiff. Plaintiff has failed to submit a witness list as required by the Court's Scheduling Order and is therefore barred from calling any witnesses at trial.

9. Defendant has been unable to investigate Plaintiff's claim because of Plaintiff's failure to provide responsive answers to discovery. Further, Plaintiff's failure to file a witness list on the mandated deadline prevents Defendant from continuing discovery.

WHEREFORE, Defendant requests the Court, pursuant to Rule 41(b) of the Federal Rules of Civil Procedure, to dismiss Plaintiff's lawsuit due to his failure to prosecute his claims and his failure to comply with the Court's Scheduling Order.

EXHIBIT 12.10   *Brief in Support of Motion to Dismiss for Failure to Prosecute*

BRIEF IN SUPPORT OF DEFENDANT'S
<u>MOTION TO DISMISS FOR FAILURE TO PROSECUTE</u>

Defendant submits the following Brief in Support of its Motion to Dismiss for Failure to Prosecute filed simultaneously with this Brief.

<u>STATEMENT OF THE CASE</u>

Plaintiff filed this lawsuit seeking an unspecified amount of damages for the "failure to abide by the terms of the Contract between Defendant and Plaintiff." Plaintiff alleges that Defendant failed to deliver certain machine parts to the purchaser for

Continued

EXHIBIT 12.10 *—Continued*

the credit of Plaintiff and failed to account to Plaintiff. Defendant has denied these general allegations.

Defendant propounded Interrogatories on October 30, 1994, seeking the facts upon which Plaintiff's claims are based. After Defendant filed its Motion to Compel on May 13, 1995, Plaintiff submitted his Answers to Defendant's discovery requests. Plaintiff's Answers were unresponsive, and Defendant requested that Plaintiff provide supplemental answers to its discovery. To date, no answers have been received by Defendant.

On February 10, 1995, the Court issued its Scheduling Order establishing deadlines for the completion of discovery and other proceedings in this action. The parties' witness lists were due on November 2, 1995.

Defendant timely filed its witness list. Plaintiff has failed to file a list of witnesses as required by the Court's Scheduling Order. Defendant cannot complete its discovery due to Plaintiff's continued failure to comply with discovery and to identify his witnesses for trial.

ARGUMENTS AND AUTHORITIES

Rule 41(b) of the Federal Rules of Civil Procedure provides in pertinent part:
> "For failure of the plaintiff to prosecute or to comply with these rules or any order of court, a defendant may move for dismissal of an action or of any claim against the defendant."

Rule 41(b) specifically addresses the present situation. Defendant, in its Motion to Dismiss, has set forth the chronology of events upon which its Motion is based. This chronology places the burden upon Plaintiff to explain the delay in prosecuting this action. *Campbell v. Plavchak,* 21 F.R.D. 41, 42 (E.D. Pa. 1957). Plaintiff did not, and cannot, justify his total failure to comply with the Court's Scheduling Order or the lack of prosecution of his claim.

In *Stanley v. Continental Oil Co.,* 536 F.2d 914 (10th Cir. 1976), the court examined a dismissal of a plaintiff's claim for failure to prosecute. In *Stanley,* the defendant in a racial discrimination class action filed detailed briefs in support of various motions to dismiss. At the hearing, plaintiff's counsel conceded that the defendant's motions were well taken. The court advised plaintiff's counsel that, because there were no uncontroverted facts, summary judgment would be granted on behalf of the defendant. Plaintiff contended that one controverted fact remained, a statement made in one of the defendant's affidavits that plaintiff had been offered the job and had turned it down. *Id.* at 915. .

The court ordered the plaintiff to file controverting affidavits "[s]o as to test the existence of genuine issue of material fact requiring trial." *Id.* at 915. The court stated that "[t]he party opposing a motion for summary judgment supported by affidavits cannot rest on mere allegations of his pleadings or affidavits which do not set forth specific facts showing the existence of genuine issues of material fact for trial." *Id.* at 916. When the plaintiff repeatedly failed to file any affidavits, the court dismissed the plaintiff's claim pursuant to Rule 41(b) of the Federal Rules of Civil Procedure. *Id.*

On appeal, the plaintiff argued that he had substantially complied with the court's order. The appellate court disagreed and found that the record reflected

Continued

sua sponte
A Latin phrase meaning "of his or its own will or motion" or "without prompting or suggestion."

motion for summary judgment
A dispositive motion filed with the court requesting it to conclude that there is no genuine issue as to any material fact and to render a judgment without the need for a trial.

motion for judgment on the pleadings
A dispositive motion filed with the court requesting it to make a decision on the pleadings alone without a trial, on the ground that the material facts are not in dispute and only questions of law remain.

final, appealable order or judgment
An order that disposes of issues and parties in the case and leaves nothing for further determination.

EXHIBIT 12.10   *—Continued*

"dilatory and unjustifiable conduct in [plaintiff's] failure to prosecute and to comply with the court's order." *Id.* at 917. The court noted that:

> "[T]he authority of a court to dismiss **sua sponte** for lack of prosecution has generally been considered an 'inherent power' governed not by rule or statute but by the control necessarily vested in courts to manage their own affairs so as to achieve the orderly and expeditious disposition of cases."

Id. at 917.

The district court's dismissal of plaintiff's claim pursuant to Rule 41(b) and its inherent power was affirmed.

In the present case, Plaintiff has failed to prosecute his action and to comply with the Court's Scheduling Order or identify witnesses. These actions have prejudiced Defendant by making it impossible for it to prepare its defense to Plaintiff's claim. "If trials are to be secured within a reasonable period from the date of the commencement of the action the calendars should not be clogged with cases where no serious effort is being made to prosecute them." *Tubman v. Olympia Oil Corp.*, 276 F.2d 581, 583 (2d Cir. 1960). Plaintiff's failure to comply with the Court's Scheduling Order, together with the inadequate responses to Defendant's discovery requests, justify dismissal of Plaintiff's case.

CONCLUSION

Plaintiff has taken little or no action in this case to respond to discovery or to permit Defendant to discern the basis of his claim. There is no serious effort here to prosecute this claim by Plaintiff, and it should therefore be dismissed.

▨ PRACTICE TIP

A judgment is considered final, and thus appealable, only if it determines the rights of the parties and disposes of all issues involved so that no future action by the court will be necessary to settle and determine the entire controversy except execute judgment.

PRACTICE TIP

The moving party is entitled to summary judgment only "if there is no genuine issue as to any material fact" and "the moving party is entitled to a judgment as a matter of law."

Rule 56(c), Federal Rules of Civil Procedure.

Motion for Summary Judgment

A **motion for summary judgment** is a dispositive motion governed by Rule 56 of the Federal Rules of Civil Procedure. It was designed to prevent useless trials on issues that cannot be supported by facts. Unlike other motions, since summary judgment is a determination of the merits of the lawsuit, further litigation of the case is barred if the summary judgment motion is granted.

Do not confuse a motion for summary judgment with a **motion for judgment on the pleadings,** which is a device for disposing of cases when the material facts are not in dispute and only questions of law remain. A motion for summary judgment also differs from a motion to dismiss in that it raises only issues addressing the merits of the lawsuit, not issues such as jurisdiction or venue. Likewise, an order sustaining summary judgment is different from an order sustaining a demurrer to a pleading because the latter is not a **final, appealable order.**

The moving party is entitled to summary judgment only "if the pleadings, depositions, answers to interrogatories, and admissions on file, together with the affidavits, if any, show that there *is no genuine issue as to any material fact*" and "*the mov-*

ing party is entitled to a judgment as a matter of law." Fed.R.Civ.P. 56(c). [Emphasis added.] Motions for partial summary judgment, disposing of only a part of the lawsuit, are also allowed by Rule 56.

In a summary judgment motion, *the moving party has the burden of showing that there is no genuine issue of fact.* In doing so, the moving party must point out what parts of the pleadings, depositions, answers to interrogatories and admissions, together with affidavits, if any, demonstrate the absence of a genuine issue of material fact. If the material facts of a lawsuit are not disputed, then there is no reason to go to trial.

The court decides whether any material facts are at issue, and whether the body of substantive law entitles the movant to summary judgment. This does not mean that the court determines which facts are true and which are not. Instead, the court looks at the pleadings, discovery, and affidavits attached in support of the motion and response to determine whether the material facts relevant to each claim are *in dispute*.

At the beginning of the lawsuit, each parties' pleadings allege a number of disputed facts. During the course of the lawsuit, a clearer picture of the facts emerges. After discovery, evidence supporting or disproving facts alleged by the parties should be apparent. If a pleading indicates that a material fact is still in dispute, but the evidence—the discovery and affidavits from witnesses—proves that no dispute exists, the court should grant the motion. Any doubt the court has about any disputed material fact must be resolved in favor of the moving party.

PRACTICE TIP

An issue is "genuine" if a reasonable jury could return a verdict for the nonmoving party.
A fact is "material" if, as identified by the substantive law, it might affect the outcome of the case.

Significant Summary Judgment Cases from the United States Supreme Court. We cannot include a discussion on summary judgment without at least mentioning three 1986 cases by the United States Supreme Court:

- *Anderson v. Liberty Lobby, Inc.,* 477 U.S. 242, 106 S. Ct. 2505, 91 L. Ed. 2d 202 (1986)
- *Celotex Corp. v. Catrett,* 477 U.S. 317, 106 S. Ct. 2548, 91 L. Ed. 2d 265 (1986)
- *Matsushita Electric Industrial Co. v. Zenith Radio Corp.,* 475 U.S. 574, 106 S. Ct. 1348, 89 L. Ed. 2d 528 (1986)

Each of these cases involved a different substantive law claim. In each case, the district court granted the defendant's motion for summary judgment based on the showing that the plaintiff was unable to prove one of the facts essential to recovery. Summary judgment was appealed in each case to the court of appeals (the circuit courts), where each district court decision was reversed. The United States Supreme Court reversed each of the court of appeal's opinions, and reinstated the summary judgment of the district courts. As a result, these three cases have had a tremendous influence on summary judgment practice in federal court.

Here is a brief overview of the holdings of these three cases. This, of course, is no substitute for studying these cases on your own, which we strenuously urge you to do.

- *Celotex* is the most important case from a "nuts and bolts" perspective. We have already mentioned that the moving party has the responsibility of identifying the portion of the record that shows an absence of issues of material fact. *Celotex* says that the movant *may,* but is not *required* to by Rule 56, support its motion with affidavits or other evidence from the record. *Celotex, supra,* 477 U.S. at 323, 91 L. Ed. 2d at 274. This requires the nonmoving party to go beyond the pleadings and, by its own affidavits, or by "depositions, answers to interrogatories, and admissions on file," designate "specific facts showing that there is a genuine issue for trial." *Celotex, supra,* 477 U.S. at 324, 91 L. Ed. 2d at 274.

- *Anderson* is significant because the court had to determine motive and intent in a summary judgment context. *Anderson* held that, even though the trial court does not have to weigh the evidence presented or determine the credibility of witnesses, it must "bear in mind the actual quantum and quality of proof necessary to support liability. . . . " *Anderson, supra,* 477 U.S. at 254, 91 L. Ed. 2d at 215. *Anderson* describes how and under what standard ("clear and convincing" rather than a "preponderance of the evidence") a district court should evaluate evidence submitted in support of a motion for summary judgment. *Anderson, supra,* 477 U.S. at 252–254, 257, 91 L. Ed. 2d at 214–215, 217.
- In *Zenith Radio,* the Supreme Court tackled the question of what standard should be used by a district court to decide summary judgment in a complex antitrust conspiracy case. *Zenith* is significant because it addresses the use of expert evidence and two issues that had been avoided on summary judgment—motive and conspiracy.

Because these cases have had such an impact on federal summary judgment practice, you should be familiar with them. The majority of all federal summary judgment briefs will cite at least one, if not all three, of these cases.

Timing of a Motion for Summary Judgment. A claimant (plaintiff) may move for summary judgment within 20 days from the commencement of the lawsuit, or after the opposing party has moved for summary judgment. The defending party (defendant) may file this motion at any time during the lawsuit. Regardless, the motion must be served on all of the parties at least 10 days before the hearing on the motion.

A motion for summary judgment is usually not filed until after most, if not all, of the discovery has been completed. Setting the stage for a successful motion for summary judgment should be part of any discovery strategy. You and your supervising attorney should determine what facts must be proven for your client to prevail, and then what evidence is needed to prove those facts.

◼ PRACTICE TIP

According to Rule 56(c) of the Federal Rules of Civil Procedure, a motion for summary judgment must be served on all of the parties *at least* 10 days before the hearing on the motion. Check the applicable local rules for other deadlines or requirements.

Scheduling Order
Issued by the court to set the deadlines for many stages of the litigation.

Unless the court's **Scheduling Order** states otherwise, there is no prohibition to filing a motion for summary judgment just before trial. We do not recommend it, however. Instead, we suggest that you and your attorney try to file a motion for summary judgment after discovery but before the trial date is set.

Drafting a Motion for Summary Judgment. Local court rules vary from jurisdiction to jurisdiction as to the specific format for a motion and/or brief for summary judgment or partial summary judgment. Most court rules, however, require a concise written statement of the material facts as to which the movant contends no genuine issue exists and the reasons why summary judgment should be granted. The facts should be numbered and refer specifically to the portion of the record or evidence upon which the moving party relies. If you use deposition transcript excerpts, references must be made to the pages and/or lines of the depositions to which you refer. Copies of deposition excerpts, discovery responses, affidavits, or any other document referred to by the motion or brief must be attached as exhibits to support the assertions made by the movant.

The moving and responding parties usually submit a supporting brief of arguments and authorities for the motion. In fact, in some jurisdictions, a brief or memorandum of law is a required component of any motion for summary judgment filed with the court.

■ PRACTICE TIP

Before the trial stage, frequently the only contact a district court judge has with the case, other than the court file, is a motion for summary judgment and the parties' briefs in support of or in response to the motion.

When drafting the brief in support of a motion for summary judgment, first and foremost, think about who your audience is. Judges, like everybody else, are confused and irritated by briefs that plunge the reader headfirst into the middle of a lengthy and rambling discourse.

Get the judge's attention at the very beginning of the brief with a simple, short, and clear Introduction. Use the Introduction to set the stage and identify the important actors. Then, begin the **Statement of Uncontroverted Facts,** but write them in a logical and chronological sequence.

Never assume that because you are familiar with the facts of the case, the judge is also. With the huge number of cases on each judge's docket, count yourself fortunate if your case looks vaguely familiar to the judge and his or her staff. It is unrealistic to expect the court to be as well acquainted with the facts and intricacies of your case as you are. Therefore, write the facts so that the first one logically leads the reader to the next fact, and so on, just as if you were telling a story.

Remember that the moving party has the responsibility of identifying the portion of the record that shows an absence of issues of material fact. Be sure to support each fact with documentary evidence in the form of an exhibit, affidavit, or deposition excerpt.

Statement of Uncontroverted Facts
The section of a motion for summary judgment or brief in support stating the material facts that are not in dispute in which each fact is supported by documentary evidence in the form of an exhibit, affidavit, or deposition excerpt.

■ PRACTICE TIP

When preparing deposition transcript excerpts as exhibits to any motion or supporting brief, always copy the first page of the deposition—the page with the style, the name of the deponent, and the date of the depostition. Place that page before the copied excerpt pages for that depostiion to complete the exhibit.

When drafting the **Argument and Authorities** section of your brief, keep the reader with you by writing in a logical progression. Start your discussion with your strongest authority. Always cite-check any authorities you use in the supporting brief. Make sure that all cited cases are still "good" law. Use authorities from that court's jurisdiction, if possible.

In the **Conclusion,** briefly sum up the primary points. Then, restate your request for summary judgment against the opposing party, and cite the applicable court rule. Finally, be sure that all exhibits, affidavits, and deposition excerpts referred to within the motion and brief are appropriately marked and attached to the motion and brief.

In Exhibit 12.11 (p. 398), we have provided a Motion for Summary Judgment and Supporting Brief. This example is rather simple and straightforward, and needs only

Argument and Authorities
The section of a brief that states the party's legal arguments and the authorities to support those arguments.

Conclusion
The closing section of a brief that provides a brief summary of the key points in the brief and restates the request for relief.

> EXHIBIT 12.11 *Motion for Summary Judgment and Supporting Brief*
>
> IN THE DISTRICT COURT FOR OKLAHOMA COUNTY
> STATE OF OKLAHOMA
>
> | | | |
> |---|---|---|
> | Beatrice Lillie, |) | |
> | |) | |
> | Plaintiff, |) | |
> | v. |) | Case No. FD–91–001 |
> | Joseph Lillie, |) | |
> | |) | |
> | Defendant. |) | |
>
> ### PLAINTIFF'S MOTION FOR SUMMARY JUDGMENT
> ### AND BRIEF IN SUPPORT
>
> Plaintiff, Beatrice Lillie ("Plaintiff"), moves this Court to grant summary judgment against defendant, Joseph Lillie ("Defendant"), pursuant to Rule 13, Rules of the District Courts, for the reason that there is no substantial controversy as to any material fact and that Plaintiff is entitled to judgment against Defendant as a matter of law.
>
> ### Statement of Material Facts Not in Controversy
>
> 1. The Court entered its Journal Entry of Judgment and Order for Support Payments on September 23, 1986. A copy of that document is attached as Exhibit "A."
>
> 2. On February 1, 1990, Defendant filed his Motion to Modify which, in part, requested the Court to provide for regularly scheduled visitation between Defendant and the parties' minor child, Joseph Bart Lillie, Jr. ("Joe Jr."). A copy of Defendant's Motion to Modify Visitation is attached as Exhibit "B."
>
> 3. On October 1, 1990, an Agreed Modification of Journal Entry of Judgment was filed, which awarded regularly scheduled visitation between Defendant and Joe Jr. A copy of this document is attached as Exhibit "C."
>
> 4. Upon Defendant's October 30, 1990 motion, this Court issued a Contempt Citation to Plaintiff for her alleged failure to comply with the Court's August 1, 1990 Order, which ordered visitation between Defendant and Joe Jr. A copy of Defendant's Motion and the Contempt Citation are attached as Exhibits "D" and "E," respectively.
>
> 5. On September 1, 1990, Joe Jr. was treated by his physician, Cynthia Hines, M.D., for a viral throat infection. Because the infection aggravated the child's asthma and made breathing difficult, Dr. Hines instructed Plaintiff to restrict the child's activity and administer prescribed medication. The Affidavit of Cynthia Hines, M.D., is attached as Exhibit "F."
>
> 6. As shown by Plaintiff's Affidavit, Plaintiff attempted, without success, to contact Defendant to advise him of Joe Jr.'s illness and to arrange an alternative time for visitation. Plaintiff finally left messages on Defendant's telephone answering machine; Defendant failed to return any of Plaintiff's telephone calls. In a further attempt to advise Defendant of his son's illness, Plaintiff contacted Defendant's parents requesting that, if they were able to contact Defendant, they would forward the information about Joe Jr.'s illness and the need to cancel Defendant's scheduled visitation. Plaintiff's Affidavit is attached as Exhibit "G."
>
> 7. Plaintiff was not contacted by Defendant until September 30, 1990, nearly a month after the scheduled visitation was to have occurred. At that time, Plaintiff offered Defendant additional visitation with Joe Jr. as recompense for the visitation canceled due to Joe Jr.'s illness. Defendant refused. *See* Exhibit "G."

Continued

> ### EXHIBIT 12.11 —*Continued*
>
> 8. Any alleged non-compliance by Plaintiff of the Court's August 1, 1990 Order was due to circumstances outside Plaintiff's control, and was not related to, or caused by, Plaintiff. *See* Exhibits "F" and "G."
>
> #### BRIEF IN SUPPORT OF MOTION FOR SUMMARY JUDGMENT
>
> #### ARGUMENT AND AUTHORITIES
>
> Summary judgment is appropriate only when it appears that there is no substantial controversy as to any material fact, and one of the parties is entitled to judgment as a matter of law. 12 O.S. Supp. 1984, Ch. 2, App., Rule 13(3), Rules of the District Courts. As shown by the pleadings on file with the Court and by the affidavits attached in support of this Motion, the issue here is whether Plaintiff willfully and knowingly violated this Court's August 1, 1990 Order by refusing to allow Joe Jr.'s regularly scheduled visitation with Defendant. The uncontroverted facts show that Defendant's visitation with Joe Jr. was interrupted due to the child's illness and for no other reason. *See* Exhibits "F" and "G."
>
> In *Davis v. Davis,* 739 P.2d 1029 (Okla. Ct. App. 1987), the court held that an alleged contemner has a defense to a charge of contempt if the contemner's non-compliance with the court's order occurred through no fault of the contemner. Here, through no fault of Plaintiff's, the parties' minor child became extremely ill. The child's doctor instructed Plaintiff to restrict his activities and to administer prescribed medication. The Affidavits of Cynthia Hines, M.D., and Plaintiff demonstrate Plaintiff's complete lack of willfulness to violate the Court's order. *See* Exhibits "F" and "G."
>
> The purpose of summary judgment is to avoid unnecessary trials. *Flanders v. Crane,* 693 P.2d 602, 605 (Okla. 1984); *Flick v. Crouch,* 434 P.2d 256, 262 (Okla. 1967). As shown above, the present matter contains no disputed material facts which must be submitted to a trier of fact. Thus, Plaintiff is entitled to summary judgment against Defendant as a matter of law.
>
> #### CONCLUSION
>
> For the reasons and arguments stated above, Plaintiff Beatrice Lillie should be granted summary judgment against Defendant Joseph Lillie, together with costs of this action, reasonable attorney's fees, and any other relief which the Court deems proper.
>
>
>
> SMITH AND ASSOCIATES, P.C.
>
> _____
>
> Richard C. Smith, OBA #8397
> 200 West Walker Tower
> Oklahoma City, Oklahoma 73102
> Telephone: 405/255-2525
>
> Attorney for Plaintiff
>
>
>
> #### CERTIFICATE OF MAILING
>
> I certify that a true and correct copy of Plaintiff's Motion for Summary Judgment and Brief in Support was mailed by regular mail, postage prepaid, on the _____ day of September, 1991, to Phillip Brent, 416 East Main Street, Oklahoma City, Oklahoma 73102, counsel for Defendant.
>
>
>
> _____
>
> Richard C. Smith
>
>

a few legal authorities to support its argument. However, many motions for summary judgment and their supporting briefs are lengthy and complex documents because of the number of facts and issues in the lawsuit.

Supporting Affidavits and Other Exhibits. The single most common error in summary judgment briefs is the failure to support statements of fact with references to admissible evidence. Each statement made by the movant or respondent of a material fact not in controversy must be evidenced by *at least* one supporting **exhibit.** The supporting exhibits consist of witnesses' affidavits, deposition testimony, answers to interrogatories or requests for production, or answers to requests for admissions.

exhibit
A paper, document, or thing referred to and made a part of an affidavit, pleading, or other document, and also an item of physical/tangible evidence which is to be or has been offered to the court.

◼ PRACTICE TIP

Affidavits used in support of a motion for summary judgment must be made by a person who has personal knowledge of the facts stated in the affidavit, and the statements asserted in the affidavit must contain facts that would be admissible as evidence at trial.

affadavit
A written declaration of facts made voluntarily and under oath before a person authorized to administer oaths, such as a notary public.

rules of evidence
Rules of court which govern the admisibility of evidence at trials and hearings.

An **affidavit** is a sworn statement by a witness. Rule 56(c) requires that affidavits used in support of a motion for summary judgment be made by a person competent to testify about the content of his or her affidavit. In other words, the person must have personal knowledge of the facts stated in the affidavit. The facts and statements asserted in the affidavit must comply with the **Rules of Evidence,** meaning that the affidavit must contain facts that would be admissible as evidence at trial. Statements such as, "I believe," or "upon information and belief," are not sufficient for this strict standard.

Affidavits are usually brief and straightforward. The affiant should identify himself and show that the facts set out in the affidavit are based on his personal knowledge. Usually the affidavit is designed to support some specific point to be made in the motion or supporting brief.

◼ PRACTICE TIP

Rule 56(e) states:
Supporting and opposing affidavits shall be made on personal knowledge, shall set forth such facts as would be admissible in evidence, and shall show affirmatively that the affiant is competent to testify to the matters stated therein. Sworn or certified copies of all papers or parts thereof referred to in an affidavit shall be attached thereto or served therewith. *The court may permit affidavits to be supplemented or opposed by depositions, answers to interrogatories, or further affidavits.* When a motion for summary judgment is made and supported as provided by this rule, an adverse party may not rest upon the mere allegations or denials of the adverse party's pleading, but the adverse party's response, by affidavits or as otherwise provided in this rule, must set forth specific facts showing that there is a genuine issue for trial. If the adverse party does not so respond, summary judgment, if appropriate, shall be entered against the adverse party. [Emphasis added.]

You and your attorney will decide whose affidavit will be necessary and the pertinent information the affidavit must set out. Once the affidavit has been drafted in final form, the legal assistant should take responsibility for contacting the affiant to arrange for the affidavit to be signed. Examples of affidavits can be found as exhibits in Appendix H. Note how each affidavit was sworn to before a notary public, a person competent to administer oaths.

■ PRACTICE TIP

> Each statement made by the movant or respondent of a material fact not in controversy *must* be evidenced by *at least* one supporting exhibit or affidavit. Remember that the single most common error in summary judgment briefs is the *failure to support statements of fact with references to admissible evidence.*

Designate short forms or abbreviations for references to exhibits, such as "Ex. A" for Exhibit A. Then be sure that you use them consistently throughout the document. Any deposition excerpts should include a copy of the beginning page of the deposition—the one that shows the style of the case, the name of the deponent, and the date the deposition was taken.

Because affidavits are a somewhat easy and painless way to support statements made in a motion for summary judgment, there is a certain temptation to misuse them. Rule 56(g) is already ahead of you. If at any time it appears to the court that an affidavit is submitted in bad faith or for delay, Rule 56(g) states that:

> [T]he court shall forthwith order the party employing [the affidavit] to pay to the other party the amount of the reasonable expenses which the filing of the affidavits caused the other party to incur, including reasonable attorney's fees, and any offending party or attorney may be adjudged guilty of contempt.

A motion for summary judgment is a search for *pleaded fact issues* not in genuine controversy. Undisputed facts do not entitle the movant to summary judgment on those facts. The movant must show the court that the undisputed facts are supported by evidence for each undisputed fact. The **record**—what the court considers in determining whether to grant or deny summary judgment—is confined to the evidentiary materials (the exhibits) offered in support of or opposition to a motion for summary judgment.

Drafting Responses to a Motion for Summary Judgment. Although there is no requirement to respond to a motion for summary judgment, we believe it is *always* good practice to do so. All material facts in the moving party's statement are deemed admitted for summary judgment purposes unless specifically controverted by the opposing party's statement. Even though you and your attorney believe that the opposing party's motion lacks the necessary elements to prevail, go ahead and file a response. Do not leave your client's side of the story untold—or worse, told by the opposing party.

The opposing brief should begin with a section containing a concise statement of material facts as to which the party contends no genuine issue exists. Each fact in dispute should be numbered and should refer with particularity to any portion of the record upon which the opposing party relies. Where appropriate, the opposing party should state the number of the moving party's fact that is disputed.

PRACTICE TIP

An affidavit's primary value is to authenticate documentary exhibits offered in support of or opposition to a motion for summary judgment.

PRACTICE TIP

Rule for Abbreviations: If it is not mentioned twice or more, do not abbreviate it.

record
A written memorial of acts or proceedings in an action or lawsuit in a court of record.

PRACTICE TIP

All material facts in the moving party's statement are deemed admitted for summary judgment purposes unless specifically controverted by the opposing party's statement.

■ CHECKLIST FOR COMPLETING MOTIONS AND SUPPORTING BRIEFS

We have already provided you with similar checklists at the end of other chapters. Still, some of these items merit repetition and apply not only to motions and supporting briefs, but to any document filed with the court. Use these checklists to help you write persuasive and well-written motions and supporting briefs.

✓ **Always check the appropriate rules for form and procedure for preparing and filing the motion and supporting brief,** such as page number limits, requirements for cover pages and Tables of Contents and Authorities, and deadlines for filing.

✓ **Proofread for typographical and grammatical errors.** Because your attorney is concentrating on the legal argument when writing a brief, he or she may inadvertently commit grammatical errors. Pencil in any corrections or styling suggestions for the attorney's review before the document is completed.

✓ **Check for internal consistency and cross-references.** All citations to the exhibits and references to the record must be consistent. Headings and subheadings must also be consistent in their numbering or lettering. Make sure that each time an authority is cited, it is cited correctly and consistently throughout the document.

If the document has gone through several drafts (and most do), citations and references to the record and exhibits may need revisions. Page numbers change if extensive revisions or additions are made, and that affects any cross-references in the document.

If footnotes are used, check to see that, for every reference in the text to a footnote, there is a corresponding footnote. Most word processors renumber footnotes automatically during revisions. Still, you should watch for mechanical errors, such as dropped or repeated lines.

■ PRACTICE TIP

To avoid the need for double-checking the cross-references after extensive revisions, purposely leave those references blank until the draft is near completion. It is also helpful to cite to section numbers or propositions rather than to page numbers.

PRACTICE TIP

Each case citation must be checked for accuracy as to the case name and case citation (the volume and page of the reporter, as well as the court and year the decision was handed down).

✓ **Check and shepardize the citations.** Check and shepardize all legal citations, either manually or by using computerized legal research such as WESTLAW or LEXIS. Each case citation must be checked for accuracy as to the case name and case citation (the volume and page of the reporter, as well as the court and year the decision was handed down). If the court has specific requirements, the court rules should tell you which citation forms may be used.

WESTLAW and LEXIS are excellent tools for checking and shepardizing citations. Some legal assistant programs offer classes in both. However, training opportunities for attorneys and their legal assistants are available from WESTLAW and LEXIS representatives, and often the training is held in the law firm's offices. Cite checking and shepardizing can be done more quickly and accurately with WESTLAW and LEXIS than by the conventional method. Although some smaller law firms may find the cost of computerized legal research prohibitive, more law firms find that it is well worth the expense.

✓ **Check any quotations word for word against the text of the original source.** As we have mentioned before, any quotation must also have a citation to the page of the reporter where the quotation appears. Even a misplaced or omitted comma can make the difference in the meaning of a sentence. Use the *Bluebook* as a guide to formatting quotations, using an ellipsis or brackets, or underlining words for emphasis.

✓ **Supervise the preparation of exhibits to be attached to the brief.** References to the record and the exhibits are made throughout the brief. You should take the responsibility of assembling, preparing, and marking all references to the record and exhibits to be attached to the motion or supporting brief. Check everything one last time before copies are made.

Exhibit dividers are useful in separating the exhibits, and we think they add a professional touch. These dividers can be purchased from any office supply store or produced in-house by the legal secretary. If you have retained a copying service to copy the motion, supporting brief, and their exhibits, you may be expected to provide the exhibit dividers (depending on the quality of the copying service).

✓ **Oversee the binding and copying of the motion and brief.** You should take the responsibility to determine whether the brief needs to be bound and, if so, whether a specific color or a particular format is required for the cover page. Most cover pages consist of the style of the case, the title of the document, the name of the attorney of record with the firm's name, address, and telephone number, and the date of filing.

The motion and brief can be sent to almost any copying service to be copied and bound. The number of copies required depends on how many copies must be provided for the court, for the counsel of all other parties, for your client, and for the file.

✓ **Supervise these steps: filing the document, mailing it to opposing counsel and the client, and docketing the response or reply deadline or the date and time of the hearing on the motion.**

> **PRACTICE TIP**
> The court rules and the court clerk can tell you how many copies must be provided for the court.

CHAPTER SUMMARY

Here are the key points to remember.

- Motions are requests to the court that either ask the court to order something to be done or attack the pleadings. In that respect, motions are different from pleadings in that a pleading makes an assertion where a motion makes a request.
- Motions are used for one of the following reasons:
  - To control information (to obtain, suppress, or include evidence)
  - To control the final outcome (as in a motion to dismiss, motion for summary judgment, motion for directed verdict, motion to vacate judgment, etc.)
  - To control the procedure (as in a motion for change of venue, motion for leave to file reply, motion for extension of time, etc.)
  - To control the parties (as in a motion to compel discovery, motion for restraining order, etc.)
- When drafting motions, check and follow all applicable court and local rules.
- Rule 7(b) requires that every motion or application for an order of the court must follow these specifications:
  - Be made in writing, unless the motion is made during a trial or hearing
  - State with particularity the ground upon which it relies; that is, on what authority (such as court rule or statute) the movant is asking the court for the order

–State the relief or order requested

- Facts that support the motion can be made as statements within the motion with an affidavit or exhibit supporting the statements attached to the motion.
- When the motion is filed, it is set for hearing by the court clerk. Notice of the date and time for the hearing should be written on the motion and served on all opposing counsel.
- Procedural "housekeeping" motions often rely solely on one statute or rule.
- In any type of motion or supporting brief, you must always tell the court what you want, and then give the court the means to do what you ask of it.
- Most court rules require that a proposed order be attached to any motion filed with the court. It also gives the movant an opportunity to suggest specific language to the court for the order.
- Supporting briefs are provided for motions that raise questions of substantive law, and state the party's legal arguments and legal citations that support those arguments.
- Discovery motions—motions to compel, motions for protective orders, or motions for sanctions—deal solely with discovery issues.
- Always cite-check every authority relied upon by opposing counsel before drafting the response. Even if none of the opposing party's cases have been overruled, you may still find cases that criticize or distinguish those cases.
- An affidavit is a written declaration of facts made voluntarily and under oath before a person authorized to administer oaths, such as a notary public.
- When drafting any supporting brief, lead the reader in a logical, methodical way through each proposition to the conclusion.
- A motion to dismiss can apply to the entire lawsuit or to only one or more counts or claims. This motion asks the court to dismiss the plaintiff's complaint because it does not state a claim for which the law provides a remedy or is legally insufficient in some other way.
- Dismissals are either voluntary or involuntary.
- Any motion or order for dismissal must indicate whether the dismissal is "with prejudice" or "without prejudice." *With prejudice* means that the dismissal order is conclusive of the rights of the parties, and bars the plaintiff's right to bring a lawsuit later on the same cause of action. *Without prejudice* means that no rights or privileges are waived or lost by dismissing the lawsuit, and that a new lawsuit may be brought later on the same cause of action.
- When drafting a Rule 12(b) motion to dismiss, all available Rule 12(b) defenses must be included or else they may be waived. There are exceptions to this rule.
- Involuntary dismissals are with prejudice, meaning that they dispose of all of the party's rights and are "final" orders which can be appealed.
- According to Rule 56 of the Federal Rules of Civil Procedure, the movant is entitled to summary judgment only "if there is no genuine issue as to any material fact" and "the moving party is entitled to judgment as a matter of law."
- In ruling on a motion for summary judgment, the court looks at the pleadings, discovery, and affidavits attached in support of the motion and response to determine whether the material facts relevant to each claim are in dispute.
- If a pleading indicates that a material fact is still in dispute, but the evidence (the discovery, etc.) proves that no dispute exists, the court should grant a motion for summary judgment.
- In a motion for summary judgment, each statement made by the movant or respondent of a material fact not in controversy must be evidenced by at least

one supporting exhibit. The single most common error in summary judgment briefs is the failure to support statements of fact with references to admissible evidence.

- A motion for summary judgment may be filed within 20 days from the commencement of the lawsuit, or after the opposing party has moved for summary judgment. A motion for summary judgment must be served on all parties at least 10 days before the hearing on the motion.

- Most court rules require a concise written statement of the material facts as to which the movant contends no genuine issue exists and the reasons why summary judgment should be granted.

- A motion for judgment on the pleadings is a device for disposing of cases when the material facts are not in dispute and only questions of law remain.

- A final appealable order or judgment is one that disposes of *all issues and all parties* in the case and leaves nothing for further determination. A judgment is considered final, and thus appealable, only if it determines the rights of the parties and disposes of all issues involved so that no future action by the court will be necessary to settle and determine the entire controversy except execute judgment.

- Three United States Supreme Court cases have tremendously influenced summary judgment practice in federal court: *Anderson v. Liberty Lobby, Inc.,* 477 U.S. 242, 106 S. Ct. 2505, 91 L. Ed. 2d 202 (1986); *Celotex Corp. v. Catrett,* 477 U.S. 317, 106 S. Ct. 2548, 91 L. Ed. 2d 265 (1986); and *Matsushita Electric Industrial Co. v. Zenith Radio Corp.,* 475 U.S. 574, 106 S. Ct. 1348, 89 L. Ed. 2d 528 (1986). Since almost all briefs supporting motions for summary judgment filed in federal district court cite one or all of these cases, you should be familiar with the court's reasoning and holdings in each of these cases.

- Copies of deposition excerpts, discovery responses, affidavits, or any other document referred to by the motion for summary judgment or supporting brief must be attached as exhibits to support the assertions made by the movant. If deposition transcript excerpts are used, references must be made to specific pages and lines of the depositions.

- Affidavits used in support of a motion for summary judgment must be made by a person competent to testify about the content of his or her affidavit. The facts and statements asserted in the affidavit must comply with the Rules of Evidence. The affiant should identify himself and show that the facts set out in the affidavit are based on his personal knowledge. Usually the affidavit is designed to support some specific point to be made in the motion or supporting brief.

- All material facts in the moving party's statement are deemed admitted for summary judgment purposes unless specifically controverted by the opposing party's statement.

- The opposing brief to a motion for summary judgment should begin with concise statements of material facts regarding which the party contends a genuine issue exists. Each fact in dispute should be numbered and should refer with particularity to any portion of the record upon which the opposing party relies. Where appropriate, the opposing party should state the number of the moving party's fact that is disputed.

- Always check the appropriate rules for form and procedure for preparing and filing the motion and supporting brief, such as page number limits; requirements for cover pages, Tables of Contents, and Tables of Authorities; and deadlines for filing.

- Proofread for typographical and grammatical errors, and check for internal consistency and cross-references.
- Cite check and shepardize the citations to any authorities used in a motion or supporting brief.
- Check any quotations word for word against the text of the original source.
- Supervise the preparation of exhibits to be attached to the brief, and take the responsibility for assembling, preparing, and marking all references to the record and exhibits to be attached to the motion or supporting brief.
- Oversee the binding (if any is required by court rules) and copying of the motion and brief.
- Supervise these steps: filing the document, mailing it to opposing counsel and the client, and docketing the response or reply deadline or the date and time of the hearing on the motion.

KEY WORDS AND PHRASES

affidavit
Argument and
   Authorities
caption, style of the case
Certificate of Mailing
Certificate of Service
cite-check
conclusion
court rules
demurrer
discovery motion
dismissal without preju-
   dice
dismissal with prejudice
dispositive motion

exhibit
final, appealable order
   or judgment
introduction
involuntary dismissal
issue-by-issue approach
joint motion to dismiss
joint stipulation for dismissal
local court rules
motion
motion for extension of
   time
motion for judgment on
   the pleadings

motion for protective
   order
motion for sanctions
motion for summary
   judgment
motion in limine
motion to assess attor-
   ney fees
motion to compel
motion to dismiss
notice of hearing
overruled
process
proposed order
proposition

record
Rules of Evidence
Rule 11, Federal Rules of
   Civil Procedure
scheduling order
service of process
shepardize
signature block
Statement of
   Uncontroverted Facts
sua sponte
supporting brief
title
voluntary dismissal

EXERCISES

Part I—Review of Chapter 12

___1. Which of the following is not required by Rule 7(b) of the Federal Rules of Civil Procedure?

   a. Motions must state with particularity the ground or authority on which they rely.

   b. Motions must state with particularity the party's legal arguments and theories for recovery.

   c. Motions must be in writing (unless made during the trial or a hearing.)

   d. Motions must state the relief or order requested.

___2. Motions that attack the pleadings are called:

   a. discovery motions

   b. dispositive motions

   c. housekeeping motions

   d. procedural motions

   e. none of the above

   f. all of the above

___3. Motions are used for different reasons. Which of the following is not something a motion would be used for?

a. to control information

b. to control the final outcome of the litigation

c. to control the procedure

d. to control the parties

e. none of the above

f. all of the above

___4 Which of the following motions could bring the lawsuit to an end?

a. motion to compel

b. motion to dismiss

c. motion to assess attorney fees

d. motion in limine

e. motion for summary judgment

f. c and b

g. b and e

h. d and e

___5. Which of the following would mean that the plaintiff is barred from bringing a lawsuit at a later time on the same causes of action?

a. joint stipulation for dismissal

b. dismissal with prejudice

c. dismissal without prejudice

d. a and c

e. b and c

f. a and b

g. none of the above

___6. Which of the following would mean that no rights or privileges had been waived by dismissing the lawsuit, and that a new lawsuit could be brought at a later time on the same causes of action?

a. joint stipulation for dismissal

b. dismissal with prejudice

c. dismissal without prejudice

d. a and c

e. b and c

f. a and b

g. none of the above

___7. A Rule 12(b)(6) Motion to Dismiss is a/an _____ type of dismissal.

a. voluntary

b. involuntary

c. neither a nor b

___8. A joint motion to dismiss is a/an _____ type of dismissal.

a. voluntary

b. involuntary

c. neither a nor b

9. How are motions different from pleadings?

10. State the three requirements for every motion or application for an order of the court.

a._____

b._____

c._____

11. A motion _____ is a determination of the merits of the lawsuit, and further litigation of the case is barred if this motion is granted by the court.

12. According to the Federal Rules of Civil Procedure, notice of each motion and hearing must be served on every party in the lawsuit _____ before the date of the hearing.

13. In any type of motion and supporting brief, what is the fatal flaw that will prevent the court from granting your motion?

14. What is a final, appealable order of the court?

15. A _____ was designed to prevent useless trials on issues that cannot be supported by facts.

16. In a motion for summary judgment, what is the moving party's burden, and how does the moving party meet that burden?

17. Explain what determines whether an issue is "genuine" in a motion for summary judgment.

18. Explain what determines whether a fact is "material" in a motion for summary judgment.

Part II—Practice Drafting Motions

1. To do this writing assignment, refer to the poorly drafted Petition found at Part V, number 1, of the exercises for Chapter 11. Draft a Rule 12(b)(6) Motion to Dismiss for failure to state a claim upon which relief can be granted in response to Count II of the Petition for the reason that the statute of limitations has expired.

   To complete this exercise, you will need to do your own legal research to determine the statute of limitations in either your own federal or state jurisdiction.

13

DRAFTING DISCOVERY DOCUMENTS

◼ DISCOVERY

In a civil lawsuit, **discovery** is how both parties gather information and evidence to determine the facts of a lawsuit. Discovery can begin at the instant a lawsuit is filed. The purpose of discovery is to allow a case to be decided on its merits rather than the attorneys' forensic skill. It also eliminates the element of surprise at trial. Discovery helps the parties to define and clarify issues and allows a party to prepare and present its case or defense at trial.

discovery
Pretrial devices that can be used by a party to obtain information about a lawsuit from the other side to assist in preparing for trial.

Discovery Narrows the Issues

The major purpose of discovery is to narrow and sharpen the lawsuit's issues. An **issue** is a single, certain point of fact or law disputed between the parties to the lawsuit. It is usually an affirmative assertion by one side (as in the plaintiff's Complaint or Petition) and a denial by the other (as in the defendant's Answer).

issue
A single, certain point of fact or law disputed between the parties to the lawsuit.

What Else Does Discovery Do?

Discovery is the best, and sometimes only way, to force disclosure of **evidence** by an opposing party. Evidence may be testimony, expert opinions, or tangible things such as documents or objects. The information obtained during discovery should:

evidence
Any kind of proof offered to establish the existence or nonexistence of a fact in dispute.

- Assist in determining the merit of your client's claim or lawsuit
- Preserve testimony and/or evidence
- Assist in evaluating settlement of the lawsuit
- Assist in determining whether any basis exists for summary judgment

Court Rules for Discovery

A variety of statutes and court rules apply to discovery. Each federal district has rules set out by federal statute and by its own local court rules. This is also true for the many state trial courts. State law for discovery procedures is not applicable in federal civil cases, because those cases are governed solely by the **Federal Rules of Civil Procedure**.

Federal Rules of Civil Procedure
Procedural rules that govern civil actions in district courts.

409

There are many references in this chapter to the Federal Rules of Civil Procedure, not only because they control in all federal courts but also because many states have adopted those rules either in their entirety or in part. Unless otherwise stated, any reference to discovery rules is to the Federal Rules of Civil Procedure.

What Is Discoverable?

By asking what is discoverable, we are really asking, "How far can we go?" The courts use a broad yardstick when measuring what parties can obtain through discovery. Rule 26(b) of the Federal Rules of Civil Procedure allows discovery to inquire about *any relevant matter* "[w]hether it relates to the claim or defense of the party seeking discovery or to the claim or defense of any other party, including the existence, description, nature, custody, condition, and location of any books, documents, or other tangible things and the identity and location of persons having knowledge of any discoverable matter." This allows a defendant to ask the plaintiff questions about anything in the plaintiff's Complaint that the defendant does not understand or would like augmented. The parties use discovery to learn what proof each has to support the allegations, or claims, and defenses made in the pleadings.

Court rules give the courts broad power to regulate discovery, even though the information requested is within the rule's scope. The court may limit, or even prohibit, discovery if it determines that:

- The discovery sought is unreasonably cumulative or duplicative, or can be obtained in another way that is more convenient, less burdensome, or less expensive.
- The party seeking discovery has had ample opportunity to obtain the information sought.
- The discovery sought is unduly burdensome or expensive, taking into account the needs of the case, amount in controversy, limitations on parties' resources, and importance of the issues.
- The discovery sought violates some type of privilege.

Relevance

Rule 26 and other corresponding state rules provide that parties may obtain discovery of anything that is not *privileged* which is relevant to the *subject matter* of the law-

---

Rule 26 of the Federal Rules of Civil Procedure, which is substantially the same as most state discovery statutes and rules, sets the guidelines for what is discoverable:

> Parties may obtain discovery regarding *any matter, not privileged, which is relevant to the subject matter involved in the pending action,* whether it relates to the claim or defense of the party seeking discovery or to the claim or defense of any other party, *including the existence, description, nature, custody, condition and location of any books, documents, or other tangible things and the identity and location of persons having knowledge of any discoverable matter.*

Rule 26(b) (1), Fed.R.Civ.P. [Emphasis added.]

suit. **Relevance** may also affect whether discovery is limited to fact-oriented issues unrelated to the merits of the case (e.g., jurisdiction and venue). Unless the information sought clearly has no possible bearing on the subject matter of the lawsuit, discovery is usually allowed under the **relevancy standard.**

Relevance means any matter that bears on, or could reasonably be connected or lead to evidence that could bear on, any issue presented or introduced in the case. More often than not, this broad definition of what is discoverable is at the heart of every discovery dispute in which one side accuses the other of "going on a fishing expedition."

Other states that have adopted different rules of discovery may require discoverable information to be *material and pertinent to the issues in the case.* Of the two, the relevancy standard is more liberal and considered broader than the **materiality test.**

If relevancy is contested, it is the discovering party's burden to show that the requested information is relevant to the lawsuit. When opposing a party's discovery requests, it is not enough for the opposing party's lawyer to file an affidavit stating that, to the best of his or her belief, a person upon whom discovery was served (or whose deposition is sought) possesses no relevant evidence. Only the court has authority to decide the relevancy of the requested discovery.

Privilege

Privilege is the second yardstick used to determine whether information will be discoverable. Rule 26(b) (1) states that privileged information is non-discoverable. Privilege in discovery is the same as that defined by the **Rules of Evidence.** Privilege may be voluntarily waived during discovery.

The claim of privilege can successfully delay or prevent discovery. If the party claiming the privilege voluntarily discloses information to a non-privileged source, the protected communication loses its privileged status. Even partial disclosure may constitute a waiver of the *entire* communication. The court has discretion under Rule 26(c) to prevent or limit disclosure of privileged information. (Such an order by the court is referred to as a **protective order.** Protective orders are discussed more fully in Chapter 11.) Trade secrets or personnel records are often protected in this way.

■ PRACTICE TIP

The party requesting the information is not compelled to allege that the material is not privileged; *it is the burden of the party objecting on the basis of privilege to establish the existence of that privilege, and the objecting party must raise the objection in the first place.*

Discovery Strategy

As discussed earlier, discovery allows you to gather and present the evidence necessary to prove your client's claim or defense. You and your attorney should develop a strategic discovery plan at the beginning of the lawsuit. First, identify the legal theory(ies) for your client's problem (or the client's defenses, if any), such as a statute of limitations. Then, second, determine whatever facts are needed to prove your client's case (i.e., to support each element of proof, claim, or defense).

---

relevance
Applicability to the matter in question and having a logical tendency to prove or disprove a material fact.

relevancy standard
Testimony is *relevant* if reasonable inferences can be drawn it from regarding, or if any light is shed upon, a contested matter; evidence is *relevant* not only when it tends to prove or disprove a precise fact in the issue, but when it tends to establish facts from which existence or non-existence of facts in issue can be directly inferred.

materiality test
Used to test evidence essential to the case, without which it could not be supported or evidence that tends to establish any of the issues raised by the lawsuit.

privilege
A special benefit or immunity enjoyed by a person, company, or class beyond the common advantages of other citizens.

Rules of Evidence
Rules that govern the admissibility of evidence at trials and hearings applicable in trial courts.

protective order
A court order designed to protect one party from abusive service of process or discovery by the opposing party or to order a party to cease some act or harassment, or to keep certain privileged documents or information confidential.

PRACTICE TIP

As a rule of thumb, if the information sought is relevant to the subject matter of the lawsuit, it is discoverable *unless* it is privileged.

Answering the following questions will help you to develop a discovery plan for each case:

1. What facts are needed to prove my client's allegations against the other side (or defeat the other side's claims against my client)?
2. What information am I missing in question 1 above?
3. Which discovery methods would be best to get the information and evidence I have determined that I need from questions 1 and 2?
4. What facts or witnesses (that are already known) need to be obtained through formal discovery to be used as evidence? Formal discovery will "nail down" in usable form those facts already known to you and help to fix the other side's position.
5. How much can the client pay for discovery? (This will determine which discovery methods will be used.)
6. In what order should the various discovery methods be used?

Think about these questions in relation to Jane Healy's lawsuit as you read about the different types of discovery we discuss in this chapter, and note the limitations and advantages of each method.

■ TYPES OF DISCOVERY

There are five types of discovery:

- Interrogatories
- Requests for Production of Documents (and tangible things such as access to land or other property)
- Oral and written depositions
- Requests for Physical and Mental Examinations
- Requests for Admissions

These five methods are not exclusive or restrictive of one another; instead, they complement each other. Various kinds of discovery can be used together in any way you want and in any sequence, provided that you always have some strategy or goal in mind. Each type of discovery is especially designed to obtain certain kinds of information:

Interrogatories—Rule 33, Fed.R.Civ.P.

interrogatories
Written questions about the lawsuit from one party to another to be answered under oath.

Interrogatories are written questions about the lawsuit submitted to one party by another. They are the most efficient and least costly way of getting *basic facts,* such as the identity of proper parties, witnesses, and experts, and the identity and location of documents or other evidence. Interrogatories are *not* effective in obtaining detailed facts, impressions, various versions of events, or demeanor of witnesses. Answers to

■ PRACTICE TIP

Interrogatories are the most efficient and least costly means of getting *basic facts,* such as the identity of proper parties, witnesses, and experts, and the identity and location of documents or other evidence. They are *not* effective to obtain detailed facts, impressions, various versions of events, or the demeanor of witnesses.

interrogatories are almost always drafted by opposing counsel and are, therefore, considered "sanitized," meaning that the party's attorney has written the answers in a way that reveals as little information as possible.

Requests for Production of Documents (or Tangible Things)—Rule 34, Fed.R.Civ.P.

Requests for Production of Documents and Things are written requests for documents or other tangible evidence relative to the lawsuit submitted by one party to another. They are the most effective means of obtaining copies of documents or other evidence for inspection, analyzing, or testing. They also permit a party to enter another party's property to inspect, photograph, or analyze things on it. Since the requesting party must pay its own copying costs, this kind of discovery can be expensive depending on the amount of documents requested. Keep in mind that the time spent researching and reviewing the documents may also be an added expense to your client.

Request for Production of Documents and Things
A discovery tool through which a party requests another party to disclose documents or things which are in that party's exclusive knowledge or possession and necessary to the party seeking discovery as evidence to prove that party's allegations or defenses.

■ PRACTICE TIP

Requests for Production are the most effective means of obtaining copies of documents or other evidence for inspection, analyzing, or testing. But since the requesting party must pay its own copying costs, this kind of discovery can be expensive depending on the number of documents requested.

Depositions—Rules 27, 28, 30, 31, and 32, Fed.R.Civ.P.

Depositions are oral questions asked by a party to another party or witness whose sworn verbal answers are given in the presence of a court reporter. The court reporter then prepares a transcript of the questions and answers. A deposition is the only discovery device that can (a) be used *both on a party or a non-party witness* and (b) *preserve testimony* if the witness becomes unavailable for trial.

Depositions are the best way to pin down parties and witnesses on details, find out what they know, and assess their credibility. Opposing counsel cannot control and "sanitize" a deponent's responses to questions, as is often done with interrogatories.

Depositions are usually the most expensive type of discovery. Costs include attorney time, witness fees, court reporter fees, and transcript costs. Further costs to the client will most likely include legal assistant time in summarizing the deposition transcript.

Deposition
A discovery device by which one party questions another party or a witness whose answers are given under oath in the presence of a stenographer or court reporter who transcribes what is said.

Request for Physical or Mental Examination—Rule 35, Fed.R.Civ.P.

Requests for Physical or Mental Examinations are written requests submitted by one party to another. These are usually used in personal injury or product liability cases where the physical or mental condition of a party is at issue. While you would

Request for Physical or Mental Examinations
Used when the physical or mental condition of a party or person in the custody or legal control of a party is in controversy to determine the genuineness of that condition, its extent and causes, and its prognosis.

■ PRACTICE TIP

Depositions are the only discovery device that (a) can be used *both on a party or a witness who is not a party* and (b) can *preserve testimony* if the witness becomes unavailable for trial. Depositions are the best way to pin down parties and witnesses on details, find out what they know, and assess their credibility.

■ PRACTICE TIP

Requests for Physical or Mental Examination are usually used in personal injury or product liability cases where the physical or mental condition of a party is at issue. While you would use a Request for Production of Documents to obtain *past* medical records, use a Request for Physical or Mental Examination to obtain an evaluation of the person's *present* condition.

use a Request for Production of Documents to obtain *past* medical records, use a Request for Physical or Mental Examination to obtain an evaluation of the person's *present* condition. This is an excellent way to evaluate the issue of damages (extent of the injury, permanence, etc.).

Request for Admissions—Rule 36, Fed.R.Civ.P.

Request for Admissions
Written statements of fact submitted to an adverse party, which that party is required to admit or deny.

Requests for Admissions are written statements of facts relating to the lawsuit submitted by one party to another who must admit or deny them. Anything "admitted" here does not have to be proven at trial. Requests for Admissions are used to force the other side to admit or deny facts, such as the genuineness of a document. This type of discovery is the most effective when asking for simple facts, such as the date of hire or resignation of an employee. Conversely, it is the least effective when you are trying to obtain opinions or answers that call for an evaluation of information or admissions of liability.

■ PRACTICE TIP

Requests for Admissions are used to force the other side to admit or deny facts, such as the genuineness of a document. It is the most effective when asking for simple facts, such as the date of hire or resignation of an employee. Conversely, it is the least effective when you are trying to obtain opinions or answers that call for an evaluation of information or admissions of liability.

■ APPLYING DISCOVERY STRATEGY

The best application of several discovery devices is to combine them and use each when its particular benefits apply. Ordinarily, discovery is used in this order:

1. Interrogatories
2. Requests for Production of Documents
3. Depositions
4. Requests for Physical or Mental Examination
5. Requests for Admissions

PRACTICE TIP

Always consider the costs of discovery to the client. Not every lawsuit calls for costly, or even extensive, discovery.

In the discovery strategy outlined earlier, first you would serve interrogatories on the opposing party to identify documents you may wish to obtain and to lay a foundation for questions to be asked at depositions. Next, using a Request for Production of Documents, you would obtain the documents identified by the answers to interrogatories. Once those documents had been received and digested, additional questions relating to those documents should be formed to be asked at deposition. Once depositions have been taken, you can use a Request for Admission to pin down disputed facts.

As an example, in a lawsuit that has numerous documented transactions, interrogatories may be used to identify the key players and acquire a list of relevant documents. Then, using a Request for Production of Documents, you could request the documents identified by the interrogatories. Finally, using the names of key persons you have already identified, together with the pertinent documents, you could depose those individuals to discover other valuable information, such as an explanation of the documents you had already requested and obtained.

As a general rule, when you want to serve an adverse party with interrogatories and to take his deposition, it is better to take the deposition *after* the answers to interrogatories are received. Because answers to interrogatories are sometimes prepared by counsel with limited interaction with the client, facts recalled by that client at his deposition might deviate from the answers given to interrogatories. Even if opposing counsel are smart enough to prepare their client for the deposition by giving the client the interrogatory answers to study beforehand, his oral answers could differ significantly because he cannot refer to his written interrogatory answers at the deposition. This means that your attorney can frame her questions at the deposition to exploit any weaknesses in the deponent's answers and to follow up on those leads.

Here is a quick exercise on how to use discovery to your best advantage. In the scenario given in Exhibit 13.1, how would you use all five types of discovery in this lawsuit?

PRACTICE TIP

As a general rule, when you want to serve an adverse party with interrogatories and to take his deposition, it is better to take the deposition *after* his answers to interrogatories are received.

EXHIBIT 13.1 *Discussion Exercise on How to Use Discovery*

Your client, Defendant Linda Werner, claims that the plaintiff, Jack Levi, drove his car across the center line into the path of Linda's car, causing the collision. You know there was a passenger in Jack's car. You already have photographs taken at the scene of the accident showing the position of the vehicles in relation to the road.

How would you use all five types of discovery in this lawsuit?

Our suggested answer is to first submit interrogatories to Jack Levi (making sure to ask for the identity of his passenger). Second, in a Request for Production of Tangible Things for Inspection, demand access to Jack's car in order to check it for the location and extent of damage. Third, by order of the court, require that Jack have a physical examination by any doctor you may choose. Fourth, in a Request for Admissions, send to Jack's counsel copies of your photos, together with a request for authenticity, determining the photo to be a fair and accurate representation of the accident scene. (The Request for Admissions could be sent simultaneously with the Interrogatories. If counsel refuses to verify the photographs, ask why at Jack's deposition.) Last, but not least, using the information gathered during the discovery just described, take the deposition of Jack and his passenger.

▨ INTERROGATORIES

Interrogatories (written questions requiring written answers given under oath) are an inexpensive but effective discovery device, whether used alone or with other forms of discovery. Interrogatories are most commonly used to obtain these facts:

- The names and opinions of expert witnesses who will testify at trial and the identity of documents or facts upon which the expert bases his or her opinions
- The names of other witnesses, their addresses, telephone numbers, and anticipated testimony at trial
- Measurements, including accurate answers or estimates of distance, time, speed, location, etc.
- Business or corporate information, such as the principal place of business, initial date of incorporation, state of incorporation, and state of domestication or licensing
- The existence, limits, and provisions of insurance (but only if the subject of insurance is discoverable; it is not in some jurisdictions)
- The existence and description of exhibits in the control or possession, or within the knowledge of the opposing party or others
- The facts obtained from a witness who either has not given a written statement or is now unavailable, or both
- The identification and location of documents supporting the answers given in response to the interrogatories

Interrogatories May Be Served Only upon Parties

One of the most important limitations of interrogatories is that interrogatories may be served only upon parties to the lawsuit, not on *non-party* witnesses. The word *party* here does not necessarily mean an *adverse* party; it can be a third party, *co-party,* etc. In some states, interrogatories are only available against an adverse party.

It is usually not difficult to determine who are the parties in a lawsuit—their names are listed in the style of the case. Note also that parties can be added to a lawsuit after the Complaint has been filed. If that happens, then those persons or entities are fair game for this type of discovery.

Drafting and Responding to Interrogatories

The problem with interrogatories is self-evident. The lawyer and legal assistant prepare the answers to interrogatories submitted to the client. Normally, while composing the answers for the client's signature and verification, the attorney and legal assistant do their best to sanitize their client's answers and give as little information as possible. Still, interrogatories are useful in obtaining detailed, although relatively undisputed, information. If properly drafted, interrogatories can extract specific information that cannot be clouded by a lawyer's linguistic acrobatics.

Even so, answers to interrogatories have at least one clear disadvantage: *they contain screened information that has been written in the least damaging terms possible.* If any juicy admissions were made by the answering party, you can bet that opposing counsel will water down that evidence as much as possible.

To overcome this disadvantage, *draft interrogatories so that they cannot be answered by a mere yes or no.* Phrase your questions so that a thorough and complete response cannot be avoided. Exhibit 13.2 is an example of what we mean.

EXHIBIT 13.2 *Interrogatory*

INTERROGATORY NO. 1: Has Plaintiff ever been convicted of a felony or a criminal charge of moral turpitude and, if so, specify in your answer to this Interrogatory the date, nature, and place of such conviction.

You will be tempted at first to draft interrogatories that ask for every conceivable bit of information that might be out there. But be careful how far you go. Interrogatories that are extensive in their scope are not always good strategy. By forcing your opponent to respond to exhaustive interrogatories, opposing counsel might stumble onto information that he or she might otherwise have overlooked or neglected. Lawyers may be too busy with other lawsuits to prepare thoroughly for each case, especially when the lawsuit may settle out of court.

If you are the one sending this exhaustive set of interrogatories, the thought of opposing counsel slaving away to draft responses might cause you to chortle with unrestrained glee. But if you are receiving this onerous discovery, your attitude will be quite different, particularly if you are assigned the task of answering these interrogatories (as legal assistants often are).

Never fear; there is a light at the end of this tunnel. The court rules have saved those of us whose response requires a compilation of reams of documents. When an answer to interrogatories may be extracted from the business records of the party upon whom the interrogatories are served, the answering party may simply specify the records from which the answer may be obtained, and give the party requesting the information an opportunity to examine, inspect, and copy those records.

At first glance, it may appear that the responding party has gotten off too easily. But take a closer look in this hypothetical situation. You propound interrogatories asking for information found in the other side's business records. The other side's business records consist of fifty boxes of various records and files.

Opposing counsel does not have to search through each of the fifty boxes to find the answer himself, but rather can say to you and your attorney, "They're in here somewhere, so help yourself—the coin-operated copier is down the hall to the left." Although this means you must conduct a time-consuming search, it also means that, after going through those documents, *you know more about your opponent's evidence than he does.*

Many courts have begun to limit this "blunderbuss" method of answering interrogatories by requiring the responding party to identify the documents that are responsive to a particular interrogatory (i.e., a note saying that the information in this stack answers Interrogatory No. 4.) Check the court rules to determine how this problem is addressed in your lawsuit's jurisdiction.

■ PRACTICE TIP

A comprehensive set of interrogatories forces the opposing party to collect facts he or she may not already have and to take steps that would otherwise be deferred until the eve of trial (i.e., obtaining a statement from a client about liabilities or injuries, examining of the scene of the incident, or obtaining and reviewing wage-loss records, medical reports, or hospital records).

Guidelines for Drafting Interrogatories

Interrogatories should be simple and concise, and concern matters reasonably expected to be within the answering party's knowledge. *Poorly drafted, vague, or overly broad interrogatories inevitably produce poor responses.* In other words, ask a silly question and you invariably get a silly answer. Interrogatories that make sweeping demands are probably too broad in scope and will evoke legitimate objections by the

PRACTICE TIP

Poorly drafted, vague, or overly broad interrogatories inevitably produce poor responses. Those that ask for *specific* information, such as names, dates, or documents, will obtain better answers than general questions.

respondents. Interrogatories that ask for *specific* information, such as names, dates, or documents, will obtain better answers than general questions.

Make interrogatories readable and understandable. It is easy, at times, to get carried away with technical or formal language and legalese when drafting interrogatories. If you must use formal or technical language because of the nature of the lawsuit, make your interrogatories more readable by applying a shortened version to the technical name. (Review the ways to designate names for persons or things discussed in Chapter 9.)

Before drafting interrogatories, *study the pleadings and the file(s) for that case.* You should be totally familiar with the claims and defenses made by each party in the pleadings. Use them as a checklist to devise interrogatories that seek facts or evidence supporting each claim and defense.

Here is an example of what we mean. In our scenario, Jane Healy may allege that she is without fault, and that her injuries and other damages from the collision were directly and proximately caused by and are due to Charles Raymond's negligence. In Defendant Charles Raymond's Answer to Ms. Healy's Complaint, he may deny each allegation contained in the Plaintiff's Complaint as his defense and may further claim, as an affirmative defense, that Ms. Healy was **contributorily negligent.**

If your attorney represents the plaintiff, Jane Healy, your interrogatories should seek to discover these facts:

> **contributory negligence**
> An act or omission amounting to want of ordinary care on the part of the complaining party which, concurring with defendant's negligence, is the proximate cause of the injury.

- The identity of any witnesses or expert witnesses
- Personal information about Charles Raymond (his address, social security number, date of birth, employment history, and education history)
- Whether Charles Raymond was acting within the **course and scope of his employment** at the time of the collision
- Whether Charles Raymond has made a statement or has obtained statements from any witnesses, and so on

> **course and scope of employment**
> Activities of an employee that fairly and reasonably may be said to be incident to his or her employment or logically and naturally connected with it.

In particular, you would want to find out what evidence Raymond has to support his contention that Jane Healy was contributorily negligent.

When drafting interrogatories, keep these things in mind:

- *Always* assume that any facts known to you are incomplete.
- *Always* assume that there are different versions of the truth or facts; ask who, what, where, when, and why questions to get the *full* picture.
- Avoid drafting a question that violates a privilege.
- Do not ask questions that can be answered with a yes or no.
- Ask questions that obtain *definite information,* such as dates, names, addresses, telephone numbers, exact amounts, and the identity and location of documents or other evidence.
- Last but not least, ask that the documents (or other tangible evidence) be attached to the responding party's answers to your interrogatories. (Sometimes this last request is reserved for inclusion in a separate Request for Production of Documents.)

Then, after you have made your initial rough draft, read the interrogatories again and ask yourself these questions:

✓ Can each interrogatory be redrafted in a simpler way?

✓ Will the answer to each interrogatory provide the information you want? How?

✓ Can some interrogatories be eliminated or consolidated?

✓ Is there a way that responses to your interrogatories could be dodged? If so, redraft the questions and narrow your request to avoid any incomplete answers.

Limitation on the Number of Interrogatories

Rule 33 allows not more than twenty-five interrogatories, including all discrete **subparts.** If a party wishes to propound more than twenty-five, that party must obtain **leave of court,** the court's permission, to do so. Many districts also have local court rules limiting the number of interrogatories that may be asked without leave of court. These same local court rules may control the use of subparts to interrogatories.

In Exhibit 13.3, subparagraphs (a), (b), and (c) would be considered subparts to this one interrogatory. So, instead of counting as only one interrogatory, it counts as three. You may ask as many interrogatories as you like—unless, of course, the court limits the number of interrogatories, or the number of interrogatories is restricted because they are unduly burdensome or oppressive.

> **interrogatory subparts**
> Subparagraphs to an interrogatory that, depending on the applicable court rules, may be counted as separate interrogatories.
>
> **leave of court**
> Permission from the court to take a particular action otherwise prohibited without the court's consent.

EXHIBIT 13.3 *Interrogatory Subparts*

INTERROGATORY NO. 1: Identify all witnesses who may be called at trial by stating:

    (a) each witness' full name, residence address, and telephone number;

    (b) each witness' business address and telephone number; and

    (c) the anticipated testimony for each witness identified by this interrogatory.

If the court rules do impose a limit on the number of interrogatories that can be asked, you may file a motion with the court requesting leave to ask more upon a showing of **good cause** or with the consent of opposing counsel. The court rules will tell you what requirements are needed. If you must ask leave of the court, be sure to include those necessary components in your motion and proposed order.

Do not try to bamboozle the court with ritualistic recitations of good cause, like the "presence of multiple issues" or "the complex nature" of the case. (Here's a hint: judges have heard these before.) Good cause is established by showing that the proposed additional interrogatories are reasonably calculated to advance the orderly pretrial development of the lawsuit.

Here are some ways to deal with court rule limitations on the number of interrogatories that can be propounded:

> **PRACTICE TIP**
>
> *Good cause* is established by showing that the proposed additional interrogatories are reasonably calculated to advance the orderly pretrial development of the lawsuit.
>
> **good cause**
> A legally sufficient ground or reason.

- Be certain that you know what the applicable local court rule counts as a separate interrogatory (i.e., whether subparts are counted separately, and if so, how a subpart is defined).
- Lawyers representing more than one party may, instead of serving one set of interrogatories from all parties represented, serve an individual set from each party, each of which inquires in different areas.
- Ask a question that calls for multiple answers (i.e., "Identify all members of the auditing staff by name and position.").

One "trick" to get around the number limitation is to use **Instructions** and **Definitions,** such as the ones in Exhibits 13.6 (pp. 421, 422) and 13.7 (pp. 423, 424)

> **Instructions**
> Used as reminders to the answering party of the rules pertaining specifically to that type of discovery.
>
> **Definitions**
> Used to define the terms within that discovery so that the language is as comprehensive and unambiguous as possible.

at the beginning of your interrogatories. Instructions and Definitions are exactly what they sound like. They can be used to define words such as *identify* to mean that the answer must state the name of the person or entity, the home address and telephone, and business address and telephone. We discuss how to draft Instructions and Definitions more fully later in this chapter.

■ PRACTICE TIP

Using Instructions and Definitions is one way to expand the amount of information you net with only one interrogatory. Be cautioned, however. No one is fooled by using this old trick, and some courts take a rather dim view of interrogatories that are obviously onerous.

Ladder or Branching Interrogatories

ladder, branching interrogatories
interrogatories that first ask a broad question, followed by specific questions relating to one or more possible responses.

One technique used in drafting interrogatories is called the **ladder** or **branching** method. These interrogatories first ask a broad question, followed by specific questions relating to one or more possible responses, as shown in Exhibit 13.4.

EXHIBIT 13.4 *Ladder or Branching Interrogatories*

INTERROGATORY NO. 8: With respect to the allegation in the Affirmative Defenses of your Answer to Plaintiff's Complaint, "[t]he contract upon which Plaintiff relies was rightfully terminated pursuant to the terms of the contract:"

    (a) Describe fully every fact supporting your contention that Plaintiff's contract was rightfully terminated pursuant to the terms of the contract;

    (b) Identify every person with knowledge or information about the facts requested by this Interrogatory, specifying the facts of which each person has knowledge; and

    (c) Identify all documents that relate to or reflect facts requested by this Interrogatory.

We do not recommend this technique, especially in jurisdictions that limit the number of interrogatories. A better way to get the same information is to ask specific questions, such as, "Identify all persons who have knowledge of facts alleged in paragraph 4 of your Complaint."

The Basic Structure of Interrogatories

caption, style
The heading of a pleading, motion, or other legal document which indicates the name of the parties, name of the court, and the docket or case number.

The Caption or Style of the Case.   To begin your interrogatories, use the same **caption** or **style of the case** as set out on all of the other legal papers for that lawsuit. The caption recites the names of the plaintiff and defendant, the court that has jurisdiction over the case, and the case number assigned to the lawsuit by the court clerk. It is important that the names of the parties are (1) always capitalized; (2) stated consistently in the same order; and (3) spelled correctly.

title
The name of the document, which should also identify the party to whom the document belongs.

The Title.   In the **title,** state as clearly as possible who is submitting interrogatories to whom, and which set of interrogatories is being submitted (i.e., Plaintiff's First Set of Interrogatories to Defendant). Give sufficient information to avoid confusion among the parties. In the case of multiple plaintiffs or defendants, incorporate the parties' names in the title:

PLAINTIFF JAMES SMITH'S FIRST SET OF
INTERROGATORIES TO THE DEFENDANT BETTY SMITH

The Notice Paragraph. The **notice paragraph** appears immediately after the title of the interrogatories. It states specifically to whom the interrogatory is directed. It should include references to Rules 33 and 26 of the Rules of Civil Procedure, or whatever rules apply to interrogatories for your lawsuit (Exhibit 13.5).

notice paragraph
A paragraph at the beginning of certain types of discovery that states to whom the discovery is directed.

EXHIBIT 13.5 *Notice Paragraph*

TO: Plaintiff Jane Healy
        c/o Amelia Pepper, Esq.
        [*Lawyer's street or mailing address*]
        [*City or Town, State, and ZIP Code*]

    Pursuant to Rules 26 and 33 of the Federal Rules of Civil Procedure [or insert applicable state or federal statute or court rules], Defendant Charles Raymond submits the following Interrogatories to Plaintiff Jane Healy. You are required to answer each Interrogatory separately and in the fullest detail possible, under oath and in writing, according to the Definitions and Instructions below. The answers to these Interrogatories should be signed by the person making them or by her attorney, and a copy of the answers, together with your objections, if any, shall be served upon counsel for Defendant Charles Raymond within thirty days after service of these Interrogatories.

Instructions and Definitions. Instructions and Definitions may be included in every set of interrogatories propounded to an opposing party. They may also be used in Requests for Production of Documents and Requests for Admissions. Instructions and Definitions are usually located immediately after the notice paragraph.

- *Instructions.* Instructions commonly are reminders to the answering party about rules that pertain specifically to interrogatories, such as the time in which the answering party must respond. Instructions often state that the interrogatories are "deemed to be continuing," meaning that the answering party is obligated to supply supplemental information as it becomes aware of its existence. Another common instruction asks that, where an interrogatory cannot be answered completely, the responding party answer to the best of its ability and as completely as possible.

Be judicious in writing Instructions. An overzealous Instruction will certainly provoke an objection from the answering party, and justifiably so. The example provided in Exhibit 13.6 is as comprehensive as possible without being burdensome.

EXHIBIT 13.6 *Instructions*

INSTRUCTIONS

    These Instructions address all information that is known or available to you, whether known or available to you as an individual, or through your employees,

---

Continued

EXHIBIT 13.6 — *Continued*

agents, or attorneys, including anything in records and documents in your custody and control, or available to you upon a reasonable inquiry. Where any interrogatory cannot be completely answered, you shall answer it as completely as possible. Incomplete answers shall be accompanied by the specific reason(s) for the answer's incompleteness and whatever knowledge, information, or belief you possess as to each unanswered or incompletely answered interrogatory. Each interrogatory is to be considered as having been asked individually of *[responding party's name]*, and *[responding party]* shall file separate answers, first giving the question, following by *[responding party's]* response.

If you cannot completely answer a particular interrogatory after exercising due diligence to obtain the requested information, answer to the extent possible by specifying and explaining your inability to answer the remainder. State in as complete detail as possible whatever information or knowledge you can about the unanswered portion.

Each interrogatory is deemed to be continuing pursuant to *[applicable rule or statute]*. If, after serving an answer to any interrogatory, you obtain or become aware of any further information about that interrogatory, you should serve a supplemental answer giving such information. Further, you are required to amend your answers if you acquire information which informs you that an answer was incorrect when made or, although correct when made, is no longer true. Such supplemental answers shall be served seasonably, but not later than thirty days after such information is received by you.

As to any interrogatory that is not answered by you in whole or in part on the ground that the requested information involves a document or oral communication you contend is privileged or otherwise protected from disclosure, state in detail:

(a) the part of the interrogatory to which the response is claimed to be privileged;

(b) the document's identification;

(c) the general subject matter of that document or communication;

(d) the author and each recipient(s) of the document in question, and the persons who were part of the subject communication(s);

(e) the identity of any person(s) who have knowledge of the document or communication involved;

(f) the nature of the privilege you are claiming; and

(g) each fact upon which the claim of privilege, or the claim that the information need not be disclosed, is based.

PRACTICE TIP

Overzealous Instructions whose demands become onerous or burdensome may provoke objections from the answering party.

- *Definitions.* Definitions define the terms used within the interrogatories so that the language is as comprehensive and unambiguous as possible. The sample in Exhibit 13.7 is fairly comprehensive in scope. The same caution we gave you earlier about drafting Instructions applies to drafting Definitions as well. Avoid getting carried away. Definitions may arguably be so comprehensive as to become interrogatory subparts, which might possibly cause you to go over the limit for the number of interrogatories that may be served.

EXHIBIT 13.7 *Definitions*

PRACTICE TIP

In Exhibit 13.10, we used the ladder or branching method. How could we have asked the same questions, but without as many subparts?

DEFINITIONS

1. "Person" shall mean any natural person, firm, association, partnership, corporation, or any other form of legal business entity.

2. "You" and "your" refers to *[responding party]* and each of its subsidiaries, divisions, and/or affiliated entities, whether wholly owned, past and/or present, together with their officers, directors, agents, employees, investigators or other representatives.

3. "Identify," "identity," or "identification" shall mean:

   (a) when referring to a natural person, that you shall state his or her full name, residential and business address, residential and business telephone numbers, and present business affiliation, date of birth, and social security number;

   (b) when referring to a corporation or other business entity, that you shall state its full name and any names under which it does business, its state of incorporation, and address of its principal place of business *[and the addresses of all its offices];*

   (c) when referring to a written document, that you describe it in a manner sufficient for a subpoena duces tecum or request for production. Also, you shall provide the document(s)' present location or custodian. If any such writing was, but no longer is, in your possession or control, state what disposition was made of it, the date such disposition was made, the person responsible for making the decision about such disposition, and the person responsible for carrying out such disposition;

   (d) when referring to a meeting or conference, that you shall state the date and place it was held, the full name and present or last known position, business affiliation, and residential address of each person who attended;

   (e) when referring to a telephone conversation, you shall state the full name, business affiliation, and business address at the time, present or last known position, business affiliation, and residential address of each party to the conversation, the location of each party at the time the conversation took place, which of the parties initiated the conversation, and when the conversation took place;

   (f) when referring to all other oral conversations, you shall state when and where the conversation took place, the full name and present or last known position, business affiliation, and residential address of each party to the conversation.

4. "Communication" shall mean any oral or written statement, of any nature whatsoever, by and to whomsoever made including, but not limited to, correspondence, oral communications of any kind, consultations, agreements, or any other understanding between two or more persons and/or entities.

5. "Document" or "documentation" shall mean any medium or physical representation or recording of communication or data upon which information can be recorded or retrieved, whether in graphic form for visual inspection or in machine-readable form and includes, without limitation, the original and every copy, regardless of origin and location, or every kind of written, printed, typed or graphic matter including film, microfilm and magnetic or other visual or

Continued

EXHIBIT 13.7   —*Continued*

sound recording, however produced or reproduced, as well as any book, pamphlet, periodical, letter, memorandum, invoice, bill, order form, receipt, financial statement, accounting entries, diary, calendar, telex, telegram, cable, report, record, contract, agreement, study, handwritten note(s), work papers, laboratory records, photographs, graphs, which is in your possession, custody, or control or which was, but is no longer, in your possession, custody, or control, as well as its present location and custodian.

When a document refers to a particular meeting, conference, conversation or other communication, these terms require that you state the date and time of such communication, the identification of each person involved, and the location of the communication.

At your option, complete and legible copies of any document may be attached to your answers to these interrogatories. Those documents should be appropriately labeled to correspond to the interrogatory to which they refer.

6. The word "or" should not be construed as eliminating any part of an interrogatory but, whenever applicable, shall have the same meaning and use as the word "and."

7. The word "occurrence" or "incident" shall mean the *[give date and brief description of event giving rise to the cause of action]*.

8. The word "Agreement" or "Contract" shall mean the agreement *[or contract]* executed by plaintiff and defendant *[use names of the parties if necessary for clarification]* on *[date]*.

PRACTICE TIP

Define only those words that, if not adequately construed, would cause confusion and ambiguity.

boilerplate

Forms for various court documents that include standard language which, if used in a particular document, retain the same specific meaning from form to form.

Boilerplate Interrogatories

Form books, photocopies, and word processors have encouraged the frequent use of large numbers of standardized or **boilerplate** interrogatories. When properly used, they can be an efficient and economical way to draft interrogatories; if not used correctly, however, they are ineffective and embarrassing.

Ask your supervising attorney if he or she has a set of interrogatories from another case to use as a sample form or guide. Attorneys and law firms often develop their own style or manner of writing. By using a set of interrogatories that your attorney has "blessed," you eliminate guesswork about format and writing style.

Your law firm may have a form file or computer database that includes sample interrogatories. Before you "reinvent the wheel," ask around. If your client's lawsuit is a type that is often done in your law office, chances are a standard set of interrogatories has already been drafted and perfected.

If you should use these form interrogatories, be selective with these generic questions. Examine each form closely to ensure that it is applicable to your case. Once you have made a rough draft, proofread your final product carefully and edit language that obviously does not belong. Keep editing until the language is crisp and clear. *The most common error when using boilerplate forms is failing to edit and proofread.* Not only do these kinds of errors cause embarrassment, but they give the impression that no one is paying proper attention to the case.

How to Find Out the Identity of Documents and Witnesses

The first interrogatories served by either side are usually questions about the identification of **fact** and **expert witnesses** and documents. Rule 26(b) (1) allows discovery of the identity and location of persons who have *knowledge of discoverable matter* and gives the parties equal access to relevant facts. Discovery about witnesses usually includes their identity, opinions, and facts known about them. It may include background information as to the basis of opinions or any other factors relating to what the witness knows.

A common interrogatory is to request the identity of witnesses that the responding party may call at trial. In some jurisdictions, a party cannot be compelled to name its witnesses or expert witnesses until shortly before trial. In most federal jurisdictions, a Scheduling Order sets the deadline for exchanging witness and expert witness lists, as well as exhibit lists and the like. That being the case, some attorneys feel that they should not have to divulge the identity of the witnesses they intend to call at trial until such time as the court requires them to.

When you are using the various sample form interrogatories given in Exhibit 13.8, we suggest that you define the word *identity* to mean the name, home and business addresses and telephone numbers, business title, and social security number. Include date of birth and social security number if asking about individuals. That way, you use only one interrogatory to get all the information needed to find that person.

fact witness
A person who testifies to what he or she has seen, heard, or otherwise observed.

PRACTICE TIP

Always ask for the identity of the persons who helped or participated in preparing the interrogatories' answers; they are likely prospects for depositions.

expert witness
A witness who is retained or specially employed to provide expert testimony in the lawsuit.

EXHIBIT 13.8 *Interrogatory to Find the Identity of Witnesses*

INTERROGATORY NO. 1: Identify each person who has knowledge of the facts alleged in Plaintiff's Complaint, and provide a brief statement describing the relevant knowledge of each such person.

INTERROGATORY NO. 2: Identify every person who answered, contributed, and/or was consulted in answering these interrogatories.

INTERROGATORY NO. 3: Identify all documents that were used or relied upon in answering these interrogatories, and identify the location and custodian of such documents.

INTERROGATORY NO. 4: Identify the informed spokesperson for XYZ Corporation including that person's official capacity and title in XYZ Corporation.

INTERROGATORY NO. 5: Identify the personal representative of the Estate of the named decedent to this cause of action, as well as the date of appointment of same and the court of appointment.

INTERROGATORY NO. 6: Identify the deceased, and give the age and occupation of the deceased at the time of the deceased's death.

INTERROGATORY NO. 7: Identify all of the deceased's surviving next of kin.

INTERROGATORY NO. 8: Identify all persons on whose behalf this action is brought, stating all the next of kin of plaintiff's decedent and the relationship of each to plaintiff's decedent.

■ PRACTICE TIP

Request the name and address of persons (1) who were present when the accident or incident occurred, (2) who have knowledge of the accident or incident, or (3) who have given an oral or written statement relating to the accident or incident.

PRACTICE TIP

Remember to define the term "identify" or "identity" to mean full name and business and home addresses with both business and home telephone numbers.

PRACTICE TIP

The bracketed language is to prevent the responding party from giving an incomplete or "non-answer" answer.

In Exhibit 13.9, the responding party is asked to identify all witnesses or expert witnesses who *may* be called at trial, not for those who *will* be called at trial. Opposing party's counsel probably has no idea at this point who will be called to testify at trial. By asking who may be called, you can find everyone who may potentially be a witness.

EXHIBIT 13.9   *Witnesses Who May Be Called at Trial*

INTERROGATORY NO. 1:   Identify any witnesses who may be called to testify at trial. [Note: In answering this interrogatory, it is not sufficient to merely state that you have not yet determined who will be called as a witness at trial. This interrogatory is intended to identify all persons whom you reasonably anticipate may be called as witnesses on your behalf, even though you have not made a final determination as to which witnesses will be called.]

INTERROGATORY NO. 2:   If you, or anyone on your behalf, have taken or obtained a written or recorded statement of anyone purporting to have knowledge of the incident that is the basis of this lawsuit, state the date and time of such statement, the place such statement was given, the identity of the person whose statement was taken, the identity of the individual taking the statement, the form in which the statement was taken, and the content and facts of the statement. [Note: In answering this interrogatory, it is not sufficient to merely claim the statement is privileged under attorney work product. If you intend to claim the work product privilege, explain why the statement is work product.]

INTERROGATORY NO. 3:   State the identity of any witness(es) from whom an oral, but no written, statement has been taken, the identity of the individual taking the statement, the date of such statement, and the place where such statement was taken; identify the form in which the statement was taken; and identify the content and facts contained in the statement. [Note: In answering this interrogatory, it is not sufficient to merely claim the statement is privileged under attorney work product. If you intend to claim the work product privilege, state why the statement is work product.]

INTERROGATORY NO. 4:   State the identity of anyone who has been interviewed by you in the course of trial preparation, the identity of the individual interviewing such person, the date and place of such interview, and the facts and content given at such interview. [Note: In answering this interrogatory, it is not sufficient to merely claim the statement is privileged under attorney work product. If you intend to claim the work product privilege, state why the statement is work product.]

Expert Witnesses

Rule 26(b) (4) defines who is an expert witness, what can be discovered and under what circumstances, and how such discovery can be obtained. There are two kinds of expert witnesses: (1) those a party expects to call as a witness at trial and (2) those specially employed in anticipation of litigation. Interrogatories seeking the identity of expert witnesses should contain questions about the expert's identity, the subject matter of the proposed testimony, facts and opinions, and grounds for the opinions offered.

Once the identity of an expert witness has been learned, that witness may be deposed to learn more detailed information about what the witness knows or saw. Although the interrogatories suggested in Exhibit 13.10 could be used to obtain that information, depositions would be a more useful discovery tool for this type of inquiry.

EXHIBIT 13.10 *Expert Witnesses*

INTERROGATORY NO. 1:   Identify any expert witnesses whom you have hired or may hire, or who may be called to testify at trial.

INTERROGATORY NO. 2:   Identify any expert witness who has been retained, although not formally consulted.

INTERROGATORY NO. 3:   As to each expert witness listed in your answer to Interrogatory Nos. 1 and 2, please give a full description of the following:
  a) the name and address of each school attended;
  b) the dates of attendance;
  c) the name of each professional association by which the school was or is accredited;
  d) the course of study undertaken;
  e) each degree or honor received; and
  f) the date of graduation, if any.

INTERROGATORY NO. 4:   As to each expert witness listed in your answer to Interrogatory Nos. 1 and 2, describe fully each position of professional employment held by each expert, including:
  a) the name and address of employer;
  b) the dates of employment;
  c) the position or title held;
  d) a description of duties and responsibilities;
  e) where applicable, the reason why the person left the position; and
  f) whether the person was ever reprimanded or censured in any way at any position held by him or her.

INTERROGATORY NO. 5:   As to each expert witness listed in your answer to Interrogatory Nos. 1 and 2, describe fully each situation or case that person has handled or examined during the person's professional career that is similar to the present case.

INTERROGATORY NO. 6:   As to each expert witness listed in your answer to Interrogatory Nos. 1 and 2, list all scholarly or professional articles written by that person, including for each such article:
  a) the date and title of the publication in which such article was published;
  b) the nature and scope of such article; and
  c) the title of such article.

INTERROGATORY NO. 7:   As to each expert witness listed in your answer to Interrogatory Nos. 1 and 2, fully describe all appearances made by that person as an expert witness including:
  a) the number of appearances made on behalf of a plaintiff in the last ten years;
  b) the number of appearances made on behalf of a defendant in the last ten years;
  c) the caption of each case, including docket number, state and county, if known; and
  d) the subject matter of that person's testimony for each case.

INTERROGATORY NO. 8:   As to each expert witness listed in your answer to Interrogatory Nos. 1 and 2, state the percentage of each expert's gross income derived from providing expert testimony or consultation in the last ten years.

PRACTICE TIP

In Exhibit 13.10, we used the ladder or branching method. How could we have asked the same questions, but without as many subparts?

PRACTICE TIP

Issues of pure law
(i.e., legal issues
unrelated to the
facts of the case)
and pure legal con-
clusions are pro-
tected by privilege
under the "attorney
work product doc-
trine."

■ PRACTICE TIP

There are two types of witnesses: fact witnesses and expert witnesses. A *fact witness* is someone who can testify about the facts of the incident—what he or she
has seen, heard, or observed. An *expert witness* is someone who, by reason of
education or specialized experience, has superior knowledge on a subject about
which persons of no particular training are incapable of forming an accurate
opinion or deducing correct conclusions.

**contention interroga-
tory**
An interrogatory that
inquires of the opinions
and contentions of an
adverse party.

legal conclusions
A statement of legal duty
without stating facts from
which the duty arises.

legal opinion
A document or state-
ment in which an attor-
ney renders his or her
understanding of the law
as applied to the
assumed facts.

issues of pure law
An issue of law arises
where evidence is
undisputed and only one
conclusion can be
drawn from it.

Contention Interrogatories

Sometimes discovery inquires into issues of a case before they have been fully developed. When this happens, that discovery is often objected to as an inquiry of the
opinions and contentions of the adverse party. Although **contention interrogatories**
are not invalid merely because an answer pertains to an opinion or contention, it is
extremely difficult to define the issues of a case without referring to the opinions and
contentions relating to the facts of the case or the application of law to fact.

Still, a defendant is entitled to know the factual basis of the plaintiff's allegations,
especially if those allegations are broad, vague, or all-inclusive. Furthermore, the plaintiff may not object on the ground that the inquiry calls for **legal conclusions.** Likewise,
it is proper for a plaintiff to determine the factual basis of a defendant's defense. But
there is a fine line between an interrogatory that seeks to narrow the issues and one that
calls for **legal opinions,** conclusions, or contentions. Although there are still forbidden
subjects, such as **issues of pure law,** that may not be reached in interrogatories to narrow the issues, factual conclusions are proper targets for discovery. This means that one
party can properly ask another party in detail how an accident occurred.

In complex litigation, opinion-seeking interrogatories are valuable because they
narrow the legal issues and lessen the amount of preparation. For example, a defendant in a personal injury or wrongful death lawsuit uses interrogatories to make the
plaintiff particularize his general allegations of negligence. The plaintiff may retali-
ate by asking interrogatories of the defendant to specify what the defendant contends
was the cause of the accident, like this:

> **INTERROGATORY NO. 1:**   As to the accident on May 17, 1989, identify any witness(es)
> who support your affirmative defense that the deceased's negligence was the sole proxi-
> mate cause of her injuries or that her negligence was greater than the negligence of the
> defendant, and state all facts upon which you base this contention.

When drafting interrogatories that call for conclusions or opinions of law, try to
determine the possibility of prejudice put on the answering party. Determine
whether an interrogatory is directed to a discoverable opinion or conclusion applying law to fact or to an impermissible inquiry into a pure question of law. Facts supporting a party's contentions are discoverable so long as the discovery of information
narrows or clarifies the issues.

Until now, we have discussed the most obvious information interrogatories can
provide. But the well of valuable information has barely been tapped. If you get
stuck, ask yourself what information you need now to prepare a foundation for later
discovery to develop that information more completely. Here are the general topics
usually covered in interrogatories:

- The identity of witnesses
- The identity of documents or tangible things

- The identity of expert witnesses, facts, and opinions
- Details and sequences of events or transactions
- Information about damages and a party's ability to pay
- The identity of the persons who prepared the answers and the sources they used
- Positions on issues and opinions of fact

Once the interrogatories have been drafted, proofread, and completed, they are signed by the party's attorney. Interrogatories, just like all discovery papers, *must be served on each party*. In some jurisdictions, you must also file interrogatories with the court. Use a common Certificate of Mailing to show that a copy of the interrogatories has been mailed to each party in the lawsuit.

■ PRACTICE TIP

We suggest that if any discovery is sent by mail, you should use *certified mail*. That gives you written proof of when the responding party was served. Knowing the exact date the responding party was served also allows you to accurately calculate the deadline for the response.

Answers to Interrogatories

Most court rules require that interrogatories must be answered within thirty days from the date of service. As a legal assistant, you will commonly be asked to forward a copy of the interrogatories to the client and request that the client's answers be returned in time for you to draft the actual answers.

As a practical matter, the answers are drafted in the following format. Repeat the interrogatory identically as it is written. Then, provide your answer. It should look something like this:

INTERROGATORY NO. 1: State the name and address of every person whom Plaintiff intends to call as an expert witness at trial, and the subject matter on which such expert is to testify, the substance of the facts and opinions, including a summary of the grounds for each opinion to which the expert is expected to testify.

ANSWER TO INTERROGATORY NO 1: Plaintiff has not yet consulted or retained an expert witness in this case. The information requested by this interrogatory will be supplemented when this information becomes available.

When responding to interrogatories, you have two choices: to answer or to **object.** If your response is to object, state your **objection** as the answer to that interrogatory. We have discussed the two criteria for all discovery earlier in this chapter: relevance and privilege. If an interrogatory seeks information that is privileged, you can, and should, object as shown in Exhibit 13.11. You can also object if the information requested is unduly burdensome, oppressive, or expensive.

object, objection
Argument or reason contending that the matter objected to is improper or illegal which is used to call the court's attention to improper evidence or procedure.

EXHIBIT 13.11 *Objection*

INTERROGATORY NO. 10: Identify all conversations between Plaintiff and Plaintiff's corporate counsel between January 1, 1990, and December 31, 1991.

ANSWER TO INTERROGATORY NO. 10: Plaintiff objects to Interrogatory No. 10 on the ground of attorney-client privilege.

PRACTICE TIP

Once the answers are completed, the legal assistant is often responsible for sending a copy of the completed answers, together with the original Verification, to the client for the client's final approval and signature.

Verification
A sworn statement by the party that he or she has read the document and that all of the allegations, statements, or answers contained in it are true and correct.

In this chapter, we do not include a detailed list of each possible objection that might be available to you. Even so, be aware that there are other reasons why an objection to some interrogatories would be called for. If you should choose to object to an interrogatory, be sure your objection has a valid basis.

Signature, Verification, and Certificate of Mailing

If your court requires it, file the answers to interrogatories with the court clerk. The answers to interrogatories must be signed and sworn to by the person answering them. This is normally achieved by attaching a one- to two-page document, called a **Verification** (like the one shown in Exhibit 13.12). We recommend that you always put the Verification on a separate page behind the Certificate of Mailing.

EXHIBIT 13.12 *Verification*

<u>VERIFICATION</u>

State of _____   )
) ss.
County of _____   )

Aaron Pilkington, President of Pilkington's Sales & Service, Inc., after being first duly sworn, states that he has prepared these answers to Plaintiff's First Set of Interrogatories with the assistance of counsel, that these answers are based either on his personal knowledge or on information obtained from his records and that of Pilkington's Sales & Sevice, Inc., and that the information in these interrogatory answers is true to the best of his knowledge, information, and belief.

_____
Aaron Pilkington

Signed and sworn to before me on this _____ day of _____, 199__.

_____
Notary Public

My Commission Expires:
[Seal]

_____

We also recommend that you send any answers to discovery to opposing counsel by *certified mail, return receipt requested,* and indicate the same in the Certificate of Mailing. We are unaware of any court rules that require discovery to be mailed by certified mail. But using certified mail is the most economical and efficient way to prove that your discovery or responses were received by the other side. This can be especially important if the timeliness of discovery responses becomes an issue between the parties.

■ REQUESTS FOR PRODUCTION OF DOCUMENTS OR THINGS

In our discovery strategy plan, we decided to use interrogatories first to identify what documents or things we needed and to identify the location and custodian of that information. Once we have the answers to interrogatories, we are ready for the next step—a Request for Production of Documents or Things.

Under Rule 34, requests for production of documents or things can be used to obtain (1) documents; (2) tangible things; and (3) entry upon land or property for inspection, copying, or testing. *Requests for production may be served only on another party.* Remember that the standards for relevance and privilege apply to all discovery. Check the applicable court rules for any limitation on the number of requests allowed.

PRACTICE TIP

Requests for production may be served only on another party.

Guidelines for Drafting Requests for Production

Begin as you did with interrogatories, by starting with the caption or style of the case. Add the appropriate title. Again, make sure the title tells the reader who is making the request to whom.

Next, add a notice paragraph referring to Rule 34 or any other applicable court rules. Any request for production should indicate a date and manner for production or inspection. Usually, the notice paragraph instructs the opposing party to produce the requested documents or things to be available for inspection or copying within thirty days, the time allowed by the federal court rules. It is common for the parties to communicate either by telephone or correspondence to schedule a specific day, time, and place.

Definitions and Instructions

The same Definitions and Instructions we suggested earlier for interrogatories can also be used for requests for production. In requests for production, it is especially important to define words such as *document, incident, transaction,* or *contract,* and specify the date of an incident. Use the Definitions and Instructions to make your request for production as clear and understandable as possible (Exhibit 13.13). Your goal is to acquire this information, not to give the other side a reason to refuse because your request is confusing or unduly burdensome.

EXHIBIT 13.13 *Definitions and Instructions*

DEFINITIONS AND INSTRUCTIONS

1. If a document has been prepared and several copies or additional copies have been made that are non-identical (or are no longer identical because of subsequent additions, notations, or modifications), each non-identical copy shall be construed as a "separate" document.

2. Whenever a document over which you have any present or future right to custody or control cannot be produced because it is in the possession of another person or entity, you must separately identify each such document, indicating its date, its subject matter, to whom it was sent, who originated the document, others who received the original or a copy of that document, and the name and address of the person currently in possession of the document.

3. If you should refuse to produce any document because of an alleged claim of privilege or for any other reason or objection, you must state the identity of the document, its author, to whom it is addressed, its subject matter, the privilege, a summary of the contents of the documents, and the objection or reason why the document is not being produced.

Continued

EXHIBIT 13.13 *—Continued*

4. You are to produce those documents that are in your possession, custody, or control, as well as all documents in the possession, custody, or control of your attorneys, agents, or representatives.

5. No demand made within this request for production is an explicit or implicit restriction of any other demand.

6. Each Request for Production is deemed to be continuing pursuant to *[applicable rule or statute]*.

Drafting the Requests for Production

Any request for production should specifically describe the requested document or thing. After reviewing your discovery plan and the answers to interrogatories, you should have a good idea of what information you need and where to get it. One of the best ways is to request production of all documents, etc., that were identified in the answers to Interrogatories and that were used in the preparation of the answers to Interrogatories, as we did in Exhibit 13.14.

EXHIBIT 13.14 *Request for Production*

DEFENDANT'S REQUEST FOR PRODUCTION
OF DOCUMENTS TO PLAINTIFF

Pursuant to Rule 34 of the Federal Rules of Civil Procedure, Plaintiff is requested to produce the following for inspection and copying within thirty days from the date of service of this request at the offices of *[name of attorney or law firm]*, located at *[address, city, and state]*.

[Insert Instructions and Definitions here]

REQUEST NO. 1:   Produce all documents, recordings, photographs, and/or statements identified in Plaintiff's Answers to Defendant's Interrogatories.

REQUEST NO. 2:   Produce all documents, recordings, photographs, and/or statements that were referred to in preparing Plaintiff's Answers to Defendant's Interrogatories.

REQUEST NO. 3:   Produce a curriculum vitae for each expert witness identified in Plaintiff's Answers to Defendant's Interrogatories, as well as any reports prepared by that expert relating to this lawsuit.

REQUEST NO. 4:   Produce all documents or other information that refutes the affirmative defenses in Defendant's Answer.

REQUEST NO. 5:   Produce any statements that have been taken relating to this lawsuit.

REQUEST NO. 6:   Produce any photographs and/or any audio or video recordings made relating to this lawsuit.

REQUEST NO. 7:   Produce any information supporting Plaintiff's allegation that Defendant was speeding at the time of the accident.

REQUEST NO. 8:   Produce any information supporting Plaintiff's allegation that the seatbelts in her car were negligently designed.

Responses to Requests for Production

Generally, responses to Requests for Production are due within thirty days of the date of service. The court rules will tell you how many days are allowed to respond.

The preparation for responding to Requests for Production is the same as that done for answers to Interrogatories. Forward the request to the client as soon as possible, with a cover letter that clearly tells the client what you want and when. If the request asks for voluminous documentation, it could take the client some time to compile it.

Be sure that your client has produced everything in his or her custody, possession, or control. If possible, assist the client in gathering the requested information. After the documents are compiled, you or your attorney should review them to determine whether they are relevant and responsive to the request. *This is the time to note and mark confidential documents for which your client claims some privilege and for which you will make an objection in the response.*

■ PRACTICE TIP

After the documents are compiled, you or your attorney should review them to determine whether they are relevant and responsive to the request. Then note and mark confidential documents for which your client claims some privilege and for which you will make an objection in the response.

Documents otherwise discoverable may be withheld from production if the responding party claims that the documents are privileged or subject to a protection as trial preparation materials. Rule 26(b)(5), Fed.R.Civ.P., requires the responding party to describe the documents or things not produced. The description of the documents must be detailed enough to allow the other parties to assess the applicability of the privilege or protection *without* revealing privileged or protected information. The easiest way to do this is by creating a *Privileged Document Log* that identifies each document by the date it was written, the author, the recipient(s), and a brief description of its subject.

If the document request is especially large, thirty days simply may not be enough time to compile and sort through the material. In that event, prepare an application to the court requesting additional time to produce the documents, giving the court detailed reasons why the extra time is needed. (When preparing such an application to the court, check your court rules for authority to make such a request.) Usually, opposing counsel will have no objection to such an application if the need is genuine.

Just like answers to Interrogatories, your responses to Requests for Production will be either an answer or an objection. Remember that a privilege may be deemed waived if an objection is not made in your response. Objections should be made on the ground of privilege or because the request is unduly burdensome, oppressive, embarrassing, or costly.

Requests for Production are not the only documents that legal assistants draft in a document production. Once the documents are obtained, legal assistants are often used to compile, organize, and review the documents, stamp them in numeric sequence, and then prepare an index. When needed, a legal assistant may also prepare an internal memorandum discussing specific documents and their contents, or an index of documents for which some privilege is claimed and for which a protective order has been issued.

PRACTICE TIP

Remember that a privilege may be deemed waived if an objection is not made in your response. Objections should be made on the ground of privilege or because the request is unduly burdensome, oppressive, embarrassing, or costly.

◼ DEPOSITIONS

In a deposition, a party's lawyer asks oral or written questions of an opposing party or a non-party witness, whose answers are given under oath. Of the two types, oral depositions are the most common. *Depositions are the only discovery that can be used by a party on a non-party witness and the only discovery in which opposing counsel cannot directly "sanitize" or control the answers given.*

Depositions are usually held at the offices of lawyers or court reporters. During an oral deposition, a **court reporter** administers the oath to the **deponent** and then takes down both the questions and answers using a shorthand machine, transcribing that information later into a **deposition transcript,** such as the one in Appendix I. If the deponent is a party to the lawsuit, that person's attorney is also present.

A deposition is also the only type of discovery in which the parties and their respective attorneys come face-to-face. A deposition allows counsel for the parties to observe and evaluate the opposing lawyer's strategy and competence and the deponent's demeanor and credibility. *Depositions are also an excellent means of finding out what the witness or party knows and pinning a party or witness down to a specific version of the facts.* Deposition testimony and exhibits are often used in summary judgment motions and briefs.

Depositions are usually taken after interrogatories and requests for production of documents have been submitted and answered. As we discussed earlier, you should use the information gathered by these other types of discovery to identify (1) whose deposition should be taken; (2) what matters should be covered during the deposition; and (3) specific questions to be asked. If you are defending, rather than taking, the deposition, you and your attorney would use the information obtained during discovery to prepare to defend the deposition.

Drafting Deposition Documents

Rule 30(b) (1), Fed.R.Civ.P., states that "[a] party desiring to take the deposition of any person upon oral examination shall give reasonable notice in writing to every other party to the action." This **Notice to Take Deposition** must state the time and place for taking the deposition and the name and address of each person to be examined. If the name of the person to be examined is unknown, then a general description sufficient to identify the person, such as "Custodian of Records," is necessary.

Court rules specify that notice of a deposition must be sent to each party. The Certificate of Mailing in a Notice to Take Deposition should list every party in the lawsuit. When you are sending the Notice to each of the parties in the lawsuit, regular mail is usually sufficient.

Whenever your supervising attorney decides to take someone's deposition, we recommend always filing a Notice to Take Deposition, like the one in Exhibit 13.15, with the court clerk. By doing so, your attorney makes a record that notice was given to all of the parties advising them of the date, time, and location of the deposition. If the opposing party fails to appear at the deposition after receiving notice, he or she may make the excuse that he or she did not know about the deposition. That excuse, however, is hardly credible if the Notice was filed with the court well in advance of the deposition. A party who fails to appear for a duly noticed deposition may be forced to pay the costs and expenses incurred for that deposition.

court reporter
A person who transcribes by shorthand, stenographically takes down, or electronically records testimony during court or trial related proceedings.

deponent
One who testifies in a deposition.

deposition transcript
An official copy of the deposition which is a word-for-word typing of everything that was said "on the record" during the deposition.

Notice to Take Deposition
A written document filed with the court by one party to notify all other parties that a deposition of a witness or party has been scheduled at a certain date, time, and location.

PRACTICE TIP

A deposition allows counsel for the parties to observe and evaluate the opposing lawyer's strategy and competence and the deponent's demeanor and credibility.

EXHIBIT 13.15 *Notice to Take Deposition*

<u>NOTICE TO TAKE DEPOSITION</u>

TO: ALL PARTIES OF RECORD *[if deponent is a non-party]*
[or]
TO: George Winston   *[defendant/deponent]*
    c/o Carol Brown   *[George Winston's attorney]*
    [attorney's address]
    [city, state, and zip code]

YOU ARE NOTIFIED that, pursuant to Rule 30(b) of the Federal Rules of Civil Procedure, *[insert name of party taking deposition]* will take the deposition upon oral examination of *[name of deponent].* This deposition will take place at the offices of Ad Infinitum Reporting, Inc., located at *[address, city, and state],* or such other place as may be agreed upon by the parties, beginning at *[time]* on *[day and date].* This deposition will be taken before an officer authorized by law to administer oaths and will continue from day to day until completed. All or a part of this deposition may be offered into evidence in this lawsuit.

YOU ARE INVITED TO ATTEND AND CROSS-EXAMINE.

DATED THIS _____ day of _____, 199__.

               [LAW FIRM NAME]

               By:_____
               [attorney for deposing party]
               [attorney's address]
               [city, state, and ZIP code]
               [area code and telephone number]

               Attorney for _____

[Certificate of Mailing]

Deposing Non-Party Witnesses

Rule 45, Fed.R.Civ.P., states that a **subpoena** is necessary to require a non-party to attend a deposition and requires that any non-party witness be paid a **witness fee** and mileage as provided by statute. Non-party witnesses are considered "strangers" to your lawsuit. Witness fees and mileage are paid to them for the inconvenience and imposition placed upon them by the lawsuit's discovery. Title 28 U.S.C. § 1821(b) states that "[a] witness shall be paid an attendance fee of $40 per day for each day's attendance." Title 28 U.S.C. § 1821 gives the rates for mileage allowances, parking, and tolls. If your lawsuit is in a state district court, you should pay the witness whatever fee and mileage is set out in the applicable state statute.

Rule 45 provides for two different types of subpoenas: a **subpoena ad testificandum,** commonly just called a subpoena, and **subpoena duces tecum.** A subpoena is used to require the deponent to appear and give testimony at his or her deposition. A subpoena duces tecum is used to require the deponent to bring certain documents or things to the deposition. Remember that Rule 34 allows service of a request for production only on a party, not on a *non-party* witness. A subpoena duces tecum is the *only way* to obtain documents or other tangible things from a non-party.

As mentioned earlier, you will prepare a deposition subpoena to be issued for any non-party witness whom you wish to depose. In Exhibits 13.16 and 13.17, you will see examples of a deposition subpoena and deposition subpoena duces tecum.

PRACTICE TIP

A subpoena duces tecum is the only way to obtain documents or other tangible things from a non-party.

witness fee
The statutory per diem fee that must be paid to any non-party witness who testifies at a deposition or at trial.

subpoena ad testificandum, subpoena
Used to command someone who is not a party to the lawsuit to appear and testify in court or at a deposition.

subpoena duces tecum
A court process, initiated by a party in a lawsuit, compelling the production of certain specific documents and other items that are material and relevant to facts in issue in the lawsuit which are in the custody and control of the person or entity served with process.

EXHIBIT 13.16 *Deposition Subpoena*

AO 88 (11/91) Subpoena in a Civil Case

United States District Court

Eastern _____ Arkansas, Western Division
                        DISTRICT OF _____

Jane Healy, Plaintiff

V.   **SUBPOENA IN A CIVIL CASE**

Charles Raymond, et al., Defendants   CASE NUMBER: CIV-94-1728

TO: [Name of Non-Party Witness]
         [Address]
         [City, State, Zip Code]

☐ YOU ARE COMMANDED to appear in the United States District Court at the place, date, and time specified below to testify in the above case.

PLACE OF TESTIMONY	COURTROOM
	DATE AND TIME

☒ YOU ARE COMMANDED to appear at the place, date, and time specified below to testify at the taking of a deposition in the above case.

PLACE OF DEPOSITION	DATE AND TIME
Ad Infinitum Reporting, Inc. 416 Elm N.W. Ft. Smith, Arkansas	June 27, 1995 9 a.m.

☐ YOU ARE COMMANDED to produce and permit inspection and copying of the following documents or objects at the place, date, and time specified below (list documents or objects):

PLACE	DATE AND TIME

☐ YOU ARE COMMANDED to permit inspection of the following premises at the date and time specified below.

PREMISES	DATE AND TIME

Any organization not a party to this suit that is subpoenaed for the taking of a deposition shall designate one or more officers, directors, or managing agents, or other persons who consent to testify on its behalf, and may set forth, for each person designated, the matters on which the person will testify. Federal Rules of Civil Procedure, 30(b)(6).

ISSUING OFFICER SIGNATURE AND TITLE (INDICATE IF ATTORNEY FOR PLAINTIFF OR DEFENDANT)	DATE
[Signature of Attorney]	June 27, 1995

ISSUING OFFICER'S NAME, ADDRESS AND PHONE NUMBER

[Attorney's name, address, and telephone number]

(See Rule 45, Federal Rules of Civil Procedure, Parts C & D on Reverse)

Continued

EXHIBIT 13.16 —*Continued*

AO 88 (11/91) Subpoena in a Civil Case

PROOF OF SERVICE

	DATE	PLACE
SERVED		

SERVED ON (PRINT NAME)	MANNER OF SERVICE

SERVED BY (PRINT NAME)	TITLE

DECLARATION OF SERVER

I declare under penalty of perjury under the laws of the United States of America that the foregoing information contained in the Proof of Service is true and correct.

Executed on _____
DATE

SIGNATURE OF SERVER

ADDRESS OF SERVER

Rule 45, Federal Rules of Civil Procedure, Parts C & D:

(c) PROTECTION OF PERSONS SUBJECT TO SUBPOENAS.

(1) A party or an attorney responsible for the issuance and service of a subpoena shall take reasonable steps to avoid imposing undue burden or expense on a person subject to that subpoena. The court on behalf of which the subpoena was issued shall enforce this duty and impose upon the party or attorney in breach of this duty an appropriate sanction, which may include, but is not limited to, lost earnings and a reasonable attorney's fee.

(2)(A) A person commanded to produce and permit inspection and copying of designated books, papers, documents or tangible things, or inspection of premises need not appear in person at the place of production or inspection unless commanded to appear for deposition, hearing or trial.

(B) Subject to paragraph (d)(2) of this rule, a person commanded to produce and permit inspection and copying may, within 14 days after service of the subpoena or before the time specified for compliance if such time is less than 14 days after service, serve upon the party or attorney designated in the subpoena written objection to inspection or copying of any or all of the designated materials or of the premises. If objection is made, the party serving the subpoena shall not be entitled to inspect and copy the materials or inspect the premises except pursuant to an order of the court by which the subpoena was issued. If objection has been made, the party serving the subpoena may, upon notice to the person commanded to produce, move at any time for an order to compel the production. Such an order to compel production shall protect any person who is not a party or an officer of a party from significant expense resulting from the inspection and copying commanded.

(3) (A) On timely motion, the court by which a subpoena was issued shall quash or modify the subpoena if it

(i) fails to allow reasonable time for compliance;

(ii) requires a person who is not a party or an officer of a party to travel to a place more than 100 miles from the place where that person resides, is employed or regularly transacts business in person, except that, subject to the provisions of clause (c)(3)(B)(iii) of this rule, such a person may in order to attend trial be commanded to travel from any such place within the state in which the trial is held, or

(iii) requires disclosure of privileged or other protected matter and no exception or waiver applies, or

(iv) subjects a person to undue burden.

(B) If a subpoena

(i) requires disclosure of a trade secret or other confidential research, development, or commercial information, or

(ii) requires disclosure of an unretained expert's opinion or information not describing specific events or occurrences in dispute and resulting from the expert's study made not at the request of any party, or

(iii) requires a person who is not a party or an officer of a party to incur substantial expense to travel more than 100 miles to attend trial, the court may, to protect a person subject to or affected by the subpoena, quash or modify the subpoena or, if the party in whose behalf the subpoena is issued shows a substantial need for the testimony or material that cannot be otherwise met without undue hardship and assures that the person to whom the subpoena is addressed will be reasonably compensated, the court may order appearance or production only upon specified conditions.

(d) DUTIES IN RESPONDING TO SUBPOENA.

(1) A person responding to a subpoena to produce documents shall produce them as they are kept in the usual course of business or shall organize and label them to correspond with the categories in the demand.

(2) When information subject to a subpoena is withheld on a claim that it is privileged or subject to protection as trial preparation materials, the claim shall be made expressly and shall be supported by a description of the nature of the documents, communications, or things not produced that is sufficient to enable the demanding party to contest the claim.

EXHIBIT 13.17   *Deposition Subpoena Duces Tecum*

.AO 88 (11/91) Subpoena in a Civil Case

United States District Court

_____ WESTERN _____ **DISTRICT OF** ___ OKLAHOMA ___

Plaintiff,	SUBPOENA DUCES TECUM
V.	**SUBPOENA IN A CIVIL CASE**
THE CITY OF OKLAHOMA CITY and OFFICER	
Defendants.	CASE NUMBER: CIV-92-980-H

TO: , Director of Budget and Finance
Oklahoma City Public Schools
900 North Klein, Oklahoma City, OK 73106

☐ YOU ARE COMMANDED to appear in the United States District Court at the place, date, and time specified below to testify in the above case.

PLACE OF TESTIMONY	COURTROOM
	DATE AND TIME

☐ YOU ARE COMMANDED to appear at the place, date, and time specified below to testify at the taking of a deposition in the above case.

PLACE OF DEPOSITION Office of the Municipal Counselor	DATE AND TIME
200 North Walker, Room 309	December 1, 1994, at 9 a.m.
Oklahoma City, OK 73102	

☒ YOU ARE COMMANDED to produce and permit inspection and copying of the following documents or objects at the place, date, and time specified below (list documents or objects): Paychecks made payable to
      ,   , and   for security services provided for
      High School at a basketball game played on Feb. 4, 1992, paid from funds from the
      High School athletic fund or other funds of the Oklahoma City Public Schools

PLACE	DATE AND TIME

☐ YOU ARE COMMANDED to permit inspection of the following premises at the date and time specified below.

PREMISES	DATE AND TIME

     Any organization not a party to this suit that is subpoenaed for the taking of a deposition shall designate one or more officers, directors, or managing agents, or other persons who consent to testify on its behalf, and may set forth, for each person designated, the matters on which the person will testify. Federal Rules of Civil Procedure, 30(b)(6).

ISSUING OFFICER SIGNATURE AND TITLE (INDICATE IF ATTORNEY FOR PLAINTIFF OR DEFENDANT)	DATE
Richard C. Smith	November 21, 1994

ISSUING OFFICER'S NAME, ADDRESS AND PHONE NUMBER
Richard C. Smith, Litigation Division Head, Assistant Municipal Counselor, 200 North Walker Room 309, Oklahoma City, Oklahoma 73102; 405/297-2555

(See Rule 45, Federal Rules of Civil Procedure, Parts C & D on Reverse)

As we have mentioned, a subpoena duces tecum is used when requesting documents from a non-party witness. But what about a situation in which you just want the documents and are not really interested in taking that person's deposition? Here is an example of what we mean. Suppose that your law firm represents the defendant in a personal injury lawsuit, and you want to obtain the plaintiff's medical records from a hospital.

First, you would prepare a Notice to Take Deposition of the "Custodian of Medical Records" for the hospital. You can find out that person's name with just one telephone call to the hospital. Attach a subpoena duces tecum to the notice that describes exactly what documents you want. Of course, you will also attach a **Medical Authorization or Release,** signed by the plaintiff, that grants your firm access to the plaintiff's medical records. Have the subpoena issued by the court clerk or by what other means the court rules allow. Mail the Notice to Take Deposition, subpoena duces tecum, and Medical Authorization to the records custodian with a cover letter like the one in Exhibit 13.18.

Medical Authorization or Release
A written statement by a patient manifesting his or her intention to discharge another from the duty of confidentiality between physician and patient and authorizing the production of his or her medical records to the requesting party.

EXHIBIT 13.18 *Cover Letter to Records Custodian*

[date]

Ms. Shelby Anderson
Custodian of Records
River City General Hospital
Room 1001 West
100 Hospital Circle
River City, [state and ZIP code]

Re: Jane Healy
 [Date of Birth]
 [Social Security Number]

Dear Ms. Anderson:

Enclosed is a Notice to Take Deposition, subpoena duces tecum, and Authorization for Medical Records signed by Jane Healy. At the present time, your deposition has been scheduled for _____ at ____ o'clock a.m. The subpoena requires that you bring all of Jane Healy's medical records to that deposition. Mr. Baxter, counsel for Defendant Charles Raymond, will agree to forgo your deposition if you will provide copies of all of the documents described in the subpoena duces tecum on or before _____.

If there is any copying or service charge necessary for the production of Ms. Healy's medical records, please advise me as soon as possible and arrangements will be made to promptly pay the same. If you have any questions or require additional information, please do not hesitate to contact me at [telephone number].

Sincerely,

Phillip E. Green
Legal Assistant

Enclosures

When giving an assignment to draft deposition documents, the supervising attorney should advise the legal assistant of these facts:

- The names and addresses of the person(s) to be deposed
- Whether the deponent should bring documents to the deposition and, if so, enough information about what documents are sought so that the legal assistant can phrase the deposition subpoena duces tecum with enough particularity to obtain the desired result
- A proposed schedule for the depositions or an approximate idea of how much time will be needed to depose each person
- Whether there is a particular court reporter or court reporting service to be retained for the deposition

With this information, the legal assistant can then prepare the necessary documents, such as the Notice to Take Deposition, deposition subpoena, or deposition subpoena duces tecum, have them served on the appropriate person or parties, and set up the deposition.

Several responsibilities are usually given to legal assistants once a deposition has been taken. We recommend that the legal assistant organize the depositions and their respective exhibits into files once they are received from the court reporter. We also recommend that the legal assistant handle payment of any costs associated with the deposition. By controlling all aspects of the costs associated with the lawsuit, the legal assistant can keep an accurate accounting and document the costs incurred. This becomes invaluable when preparing a **Motion for Attorney Fees** and **Bill of Costs.**

Summarizing Depositions

The most common responsibility given to legal assistants once the deposition has been taken is preparing a **deposition summary,** sometimes called a **deposition index.** There are many different ways to draft a deposition summary. The format depends upon the attorney's taste and how the attorney will use it.

Some attorneys prefer to use deposition summaries as signposts for direction to specific passages in the deposition. Others prefer more extensive summaries that are a digest of the testimony. Here are some suggestions to help you prepare the most effective summary possible.

1. *Before summarizing the deposition, review the file and the pleadings.* Review the pleadings, especially the Complaint and Answer, to become acquainted with the pertinent points. What are the facts and issues? What is the case about? What are the claims and defenses of the parties?
2. *Ask your attorney if there is anything specific that should be noted or disregarded.* Does the attorney want specific items relating to specific people or dates, and if so, who and which? For example, most witnesses are asked about their education and work experience. If these facts are not pertinent to the issues of the case, the legal assistant can merely note them as "education" and "work experience" at page _____, line _____. But if the deponent is an expert witness, his or her credentials and experience in that field become critical and more detail may be desired.
3. *Ask the attorney if he or she prefers a certain format to be used for the summary.* Should the legal assistant paraphrase testimony or quote from the deponent's own words? How should the deposition exhibits be designated (i.e., in a separate column, in bold or underline, or by a full description)? If it is not a general summary, should the summary be indexed by chronological date of occurrence, by subject matter, or in page sequence?

Motion for Attorney Fees
A motion filed with the court requesting an award of attorney fees to be given to the prevailing party (the movant).

Bill of Costs
A certified, itemized statement of the amount of costs incurred by one of the parties in a lawsuit.

deposition summary, index
A concise summary of a deposition transcript used for various purposes by attorneys throughout the course of litigation and in preparation for trial.

Most deposition summaries have a column on the left-hand margin showing the page-line and a second column for summarized testimony. Some attorneys prefer yet another column, known as the *issue* or *topic column,* that is literally a summary of the summary and consists of only a key word or phrase. If an attorney prefers a specific deposition summary style, the legal assistant should be given a copy of that summary style to use as a guide.

Here are the most common formats used for deposition summaries:

a. A **page-line deposition summary** is simply a page-by-page summary of the transcript, like the one shown in Exhibit 13.19.

page-line deposition summary
A page-by-page summary of a deposition transcript.

EXHIBIT 13.19   *Page-Line Summary*

SUMMARY OF DEPOSITION OF *[NAME]*
taken on [date]

Page-Line	Summary
5 10–20	Graduated from high school in 1975. Took welding classes at vo-tech school. Worked as welder from 1977 to present.
6 1–5	Wears glasses; can't see anything if more than ten feet away.

---

b. A **page-only deposition summary** (Exhibit 13.20) is often referred to as an "index" of the deposition. The summary itself is often less detailed than the page-line summary shown in Exhibit 13.19. Some attorneys use this type of summary because they find it easier to skim through to find the location of certain information within the transcript.

page-only deposition summary
A summary by page that is less detailed than other types of deposition summaries.

EXHIBIT 13.20   *Page-Only Summary*

SUMMARY OF DEPOSITION OF *[NAME]*
taken on [date]

Page	Summary
5	Education and work history.
6	Wears glasses; can't see if ten feet away.

---

c. A **page-line-topic deposition summary** (Exhibit 13.21), although time-consuming to prepare, can be extremely useful to an attorney. The added topic column gives an attorney the best of both summaries discussed earlier.

page-line-topic deposition summary
A summary that states the page and lines being summarized, then the actual summary, and then a condensed one-word "topic."

EXHIBIT 13.21   *Page-Line-Topic Summary*

SUMMARY OF DEPOSITION OF *[NAME]*
taken on [date]

Page-Line(s)	Summary	Topic
5 10–20	Graduated from high school in 1975. Took welding classes at vo-tech. Worked as welder from 1977 to present.	Education Work History
6 1–5	Wears glasses; can't see anything if more than ten feet away.	Eyesight

---

PRACTICE TIP

Write one page of summary for every ten pages of transcript. For example, if the deposition is one hundred pages long, the summary should be no more than ten pages.

**chronological deposi-
tion summary**
A summary broken
down by subject matter
and stated in chronolog-
ical order.

**subject-matter depo-
sition summary**
A summary which is bro-
ken down into particular
topics, sometimes given
in chronological order.

d. A **chronological** or **subject-matter deposition summary** (Exhibit 13.22) is broken up into particular topics. It allows the attorney to find everything the deponent said about a given topic by looking at one place on the summary.

EXHIBIT 13.22   *Chronological/Subject-Matter Summary*

SUMMARY OF DEPOSITION OF *[NAME]*
taken on [date]

Page-Line   Summary

Prior Driving Record

20   1–15   Received speeding ticket on 4/17/90.

21   5–10   Received ticket for failure to stop at stop sign.

Medical History

54   1–17   Had never been hospitalized until this accident.

54   20–25   Cannot recall anything that happened during the first week she was in the hospital. Her mother has told her what happened during that week.

Lost Wages

41   3–16   Isn't sure how many days she missed from work before she was terminated. Mr. Wagner in Personnel at her former job should be able to provide that information.

10% Rule
The rule that requires
any deposition or tran-
script summary or index
to be one tenth of the
actual deposition tran-
script.

4. *Decide how much detail should be included in the summary.* One of the most common complaints by attorneys about deposition summaries is that the summaries are almost as long as the depositions themselves. This problem can be avoided by good communication between you and your attorney and by using this simple rule of thumb, called the **10% Rule:** *Write one page of summary for every ten pages of transcript.* For example, if the deposition is one hundred pages long, the summary should be no more than ten pages.

A few depositions cannot be summarized in accordance with the 10% Rule. For instance, if a deposition is extremely short or if it is the deposition of an expert witness, it may be difficult to keep the summary within the 10% guideline. In spite of that, strive to keep each summary as brief as possible.

5. *Determine the deadline for summarizing the depositions.* Deposition summaries are not assigned just to give legal assistants something to do. The attorney uses the summary for many reasons, such as to prepare for other depositions or trial. When the attorney makes the assignment, ask him or her to set a deadline for when the summaries need to be finished. If more than one deposition is to be summarized, ask whose deposition should be done first, and so on. If the attorney needs the summary completed so that he or she may prepare for some other event, find out how the attorney plans to use the summary and when. By asking for a deadline, the legal assistant can be sure that the summary is ready when the attorney needs it.

Also, most legal assistants work for more than one attorney. Knowing what deadlines you are facing will help you to better structure your time and meet everyone's needs.

6. *Determine what information is necessary for litigation support.* Most court reporters put the deposition transcript on a computer disk, known as an

ASCII disk, which can be fed into a computer. The legal assistant can duplicate the deposition and create a "work" copy that can be revised and summarized on the screen. Further, the deposition can be scanned for specific information. For instance, you are taking the deposition of a witness whose name has been mentioned by several people whose depositions have already been taken and loaded into the computer. Instead of reading the depositions and/or the deposition summaries for all references to the witness, the depositions can be scanned in a matter of minutes for any references to that person.

In addition, there are many software programs designed especially with depositions and deposition summaries in mind. Most large law firms use this type of litigation support, as well as others. If your firm does have access to this type of technology, by all means *use it.* Create a database for each case that includes all of the depositions taken in that case. Familiarize yourself with the software's capabilities and its weaknesses.

■ REQUESTS FOR PHYSICAL OR MENTAL EXAMINATION

As mentioned earlier, Requests for Physical or Mental Examinations are used most often in personal injury or product liability lawsuits where the physical or mental condition of a party (usually the plaintiff) is at issue. Under Rule 35 of the Federal Rules of Civil Procedure, when the physical or mental condition of a party is *in controversy,* the court may require that party, or a person in the custody or under the legal control of a party, to submit to a physical or mental examination by a suitably licensed or certified examiner. *Schlagenhauf v. Holder,* 379 U.S. 104, 119, 85 S. Ct. 234, 243, 13 L. Ed. 2d 152 (1964), the leading case on this subject, explained the rationale behind Rule 35:

> A plaintiff in a negligence action who asserts mental or physical injury, . . . placed that mental or physical injury clearly *in controversy* and provides the defendant with *good cause* for an examination to determine the existence and extent of such asserted injury. This is not only true as to a plaintiff, but applies equally to a defendant who asserts his mental or physical condition as a defense to a claim . . . . [Emphasis added.]

If a party alleges that the acts of another party caused him or her physical or mental injury, the party against whom the allegation is made has the right to determine the genuineness of the condition, its extent and causes, and to develop a prognosis.

In practice, it is a more common procedure for the parties' attorneys to arrange such examinations by agreement. If the physical or mental examination is not informally arranged or if the parties cannot agree, then Rule 35 can be used to force the party to submit to such an examination. In those instances, the party seeking to have another party examined must, through a Motion to Compel Medical Examination, ask the court to order the examination of a party or a person in the custody or control of the party.

The Motion to Compel must fulfill two requirements: it must allege a *genuine controversy* as to the person's physical or mental condition and show *good cause* for requesting the physical or mental examination. "Good cause" is often demonstrated by an affidavit that states the facts showing a need for the relief sought. *Schlagenhauf* states that the trial judge has discretion to decide whether the party's mental or physical state is "in controversy" and whether "good cause" exists:

> This does not, of course, mean that the movant must prove his case on the merits in order to meet the requirements for a mental or physical examination. Nor does it mean that an

evidentiary hearing is required in all cases. This may be necessary in some cases, but in other cases the showing could be made by affidavits or other usual methods short of a hearing. *It does mean, though, that the movant must produce sufficient information, by whatever means, so that the district judge can fulfill his function mandated by the Rule.*

Id., 379 U.S. at 119, 85 S. Ct. at 243. [Emphasis added.]

Rule 35 also specifically requires that notice must be given to the person to be examined, to his or her attorney, and to all parties. The notice must specify the time, place, manner, conditions, and scope of the examination and designate the physician who will conduct the examination. Although there is no set time restraint on when Rule 35 examinations must be completed, we suggest that they be scheduled before the discovery cut-off.

Although the person being examined must pay for any expenses or loss of time incurred for coming to the examination, the moving party bears the cost of the examination itself. Also, the moving party must, upon request, produce a written report by the examining physician that states the findings, results of tests, diagnoses, and conclusions. The moving party can then, upon request, obtain any previous or future reports about the same person for the same condition.

◼ REQUESTS FOR ADMISSIONS

Requests for Admissions are written requests from one party to another that ask for admission or denial of these three categories:

- The truth of statements or opinions of fact
- The application of law to fact
- The authenticity of certain documents

Under Rule 36, Fed.R.Civ.P., any fact admitted in response to a Request for Admission is deemed *conclusively established*. Some courts consider admissions as equal to sworn testimony.

Think back to our discovery plan. Although Requests for Admission can be served at any time during the lawsuit, they are commonly the last type of discovery device used before the pretrial conference or motions for summary judgment. *The purpose of Requests for Admission is to take the specific matter admitted out of issue and make it incontrovertible at trial.* Requests for Admission are not used to learn new facts, but rather are an excellent way to determine which facts the opposing party will concede or contest at trial. They are also an easy way to establish the authenticity and genuineness of documents obtained through other types of discovery.

The scope allowed for Requests for Admission is the same as all other discovery: anything that is relevant but not privileged. In some state and federal courts, the number of requests for admission that may be served on an opposing party is limited. Check the relevant court rules to determine what number restrictions, if any, apply.

◼ PRACTICE TIP

Requests for Admission are not used to learn new facts, but rather to determine which facts the opposing party will concede or contest at trial. They are also an easy way to establish the authenticity and genuineness of documents obtained through other discovery.

PRACTICE TIP

Any request by the examined party for the report of the physician who examined him waives that party's doctor-patient privilege, not only as to that physician but to any other physician who has examined, or who may later examine that party for the same condition.

PRACTICE TIP

An admission to any request is limited only to the pending lawsuit, and cannot be used for any other purpose or against the respondent in any other lawsuit.

Drafting Requests for Admissions

To decide what to request, review your client's claims and note each fact necessary to prove each claim at trial. Then organize these fact elements into the three categories listed earlier. Next, review the pleadings and discovery to determine what has already been admitted by the opposing party.

When reviewing discovery, note in particular any fact that is admitted in answers to interrogatories or in a deposition. Even though a fact is admitted during discovery, it may still be denied at trial. For this reason, facts admitted in answers to interrogatories or a deposition are not considered "conclusively established" for purposes of the lawsuit. *Only admissions made in response to Requests for Admission are considered conclusive and absolute.*

Any "inconclusive" facts should be included in your requests for admission because, once an admission is made in the opposing party's response, it will be deemed conclusively established. Further, because an opposing party has already admitted the fact in previous discovery, it is unlikely that it will contradict itself when responding to your Requests for Admission.

■ PRACTICE TIP

If the admission sought is the authenticity or genuineness of a document, describe the document in detail (e.g., type of document, date, number of pages, author, and addressee), and attach a copy of the document to the Request.

The most important thing to remember when drafting Requests for Admission is to *keep it simple*. Keep in mind that you want to elicit a "yes" or "no" type of answer. You will get the best results with short, single statements for each fact. Requests that are clear and specific make it difficult to avoid giving the desired admission. Complicated or overly long requests are easy to dodge.

The format for drafting Requests for Admissions is much like that used for Interrogatories. Rule 36 requires that each statement for which an admission is requested must be set out separately (Exhibit 13.23).

EXHIBIT 13.23   *Requests for Admission*

PLAINTIFF'S REQUESTS FOR ADMISSIONS TO DEFENDANT
[or]
PLAINTIFF'S FIRST REQUEST
FOR ADMISSIONS TO DEFENDANT ALLEGRETTI & SONS

Plaintiff Jane Healy requests Defendant Allegretti & Sons to respond to the following Requests for Admissions within thirty days from the date of service of this request:

[Use "Instructions and Definitions" here if there is any possible confusion over the meaning of words or phrases that will be used. For example, in a product's liability case, you may choose to define words such as "manufacturer," "distributor," "contract," "guarantee," etc.]

REQUEST FOR ADMISSION NO 1:   Admit that, at the time of the incident, you were aware that Charles Raymond's driving license had been suspended in the past three years for driving while intoxicated.

When drafting, refrain from making statements with which opposing counsel will feel compelled to argue or object. For instance, do *not* write statements such as the one in Exhibit 13.24. Instead, break it down into bite-sized chunks (Exhibit 13.25).

EXHIBIT 13.24   *Poorly Drafted Request for Admission*

REQUEST FOR ADMISSION NO. 1:   Admit that XYZ Company (the party from whom you are seeking an admission) manufactured the bulletproof vest that Plaintiff's decedent was wearing on April 27, 1990, when he was stabbed through the heart by Joe Brown during a demonstration of XYZ Company's products.

EXHIBIT 13.25   *Request for Admission*

REQUEST FOR ADMISSION NO. 1:   Admit that Plaintiff's decedent was a distributor of XYZ Company (the party from whom you are seeking an admission).

REQUEST FOR ADMISSION NO. 2:   Admit that among the products distributed by Plaintiff's decedent were bulletproof vests manufactured by XYZ Company.

REQUEST FOR ADMISSION NO. 3:   Admit that, on April 27, 1990, Plaintiff's decedent was wearing Model No. BULLET-NO-GO-THROUGH in a demonstration of XYZ Company's line of products.

REQUEST FOR ADMISSION NO. 4:   Admit that the literature by XYZ Company regarding Model No. BULLET-NO-GO-THROUGH states that the material of that bulletproof vest is impenetrable by knives or other similarly sharp-edged objects.

REQUEST FOR ADMISSION NO. 5:   Admit that, at the time of this incident, you were aware that Model No. BULLET-NO-GO-THROUGH could be penetrated by knives or other similarly sharp-edged objects.

We also recommend that Requests for Admission be sent by certified mail, return receipt requested. We are unaware of any court rules that require this type discovery to be mailed by certified mail. But as we have already mentioned, this is the most economical and efficient way to prove that your discovery or responses were received by the other side. This can be especially important if the timeliness of discovery responses becomes an issue between the parties.

Drafting Responses to Requests for Admissions

Rule 36 requires that responses specifically admit, deny, or object to the admission. The response must specifically admit or deny the admission or state, in detail, why the answering party cannot truthfully admit or deny the matter. If no response is given within thirty days of service of the Requests, the admission is deemed admitted.

Rule 36 also states that the answering party may not give lack of information or knowledge as a reason for failing to admit or deny, unless that party has made a reasonable inquiry and the information known or readily obtainable by the party is insufficient to enable the party to admit or deny. Rule 36 also states which grounds for objections are, and are not, available to the answering party.

If you admit the request, then that matter is conclusively deemed admitted for purposes of the lawsuit. If you deny the request, then the denial must be made in "good faith." Rule 36 states that "when good faith requires that a party qualify an answer or

PRACTICE TIP

Basically, responses fall into these categories: (1) admissions; (2) denials; (3) qualified answers; and (4) objections or motions for protective order.

deny only a part of the matter of which an admission is requested, the party shall specify so much of it as is true and qualify or deny the remainder."

Sometimes, a response can neither admit nor deny the request. That type of response would look something like the one in Exhibit 13.26. Or more simply, like the one in Exhibit 13.27. Be warned, however, that Rule 36 does not allow such a response unless the responding party answers that (1) it has made a reasonable inquiry and (2) the information known, or readily obtainable, by the party is insufficient to enable the party to admit or deny.

EXHIBIT 13.26   *Response to Request for Admission*

REQUEST FOR ADMISSION NO. 1:   Admit that forty-seven crates of bananas were delivered to the loading dock of Mellow Yellow Company on March 15, 1990.

RESPONSE TO REQUEST FOR ADMISSION NO. 1:   Defendant has made reasonable inquiry and the information known or readily available to this Defendant is insufficient to enable this Defendant to admit or deny that forty-seven crates of bananas were delivered to the loading dock of Mellow Yellow Company on March 15, 1990.

EXHIBIT 13.27   *Response to Request for Admission*

RESPONSE TO REQUEST FOR ADMISSION NO. 1:   Defendant has made reasonable inquiry but lacks sufficient information or knowledge to admit or deny Request for Admission No. 1.

But what if the request asks for something you and your attorney consider to be a genuine issue for trial? Rule 36 states plainly that an objection to such a request is not allowed. But you can, subject to Rule 37(c), deny the matter or give your reasons for neither denying nor admitting the request.

Lastly, you may object to the request, but only if you state the grounds for your objection. An objection has the effect of a qualified denial. An objection is an appropriate response if the request asks for information that is privileged or irrelevant to the lawsuit, or if the request is ambiguous or incoherent.

CHAPTER SUMMARY

Discovery is meant to allow a case to be decided on its merits rather than the attorneys' forensic skill. As a legal assistant, you will be involved in all aspects of the discovery process. Here is a review of the key points in this chapter.

- Discovery eliminates the element of surprise at trial, helps the parties to define and clarify issues, and allows a party to prepare and present its case or defense at trial.
- An issue is a single and certain point of fact or law disputed between the parties to the lawsuit, usually an affirmative assertion on one side and a denial by the other.
- The evidence obtained during discovery should:
  –Assist in determining the merit of your client's claim or lawsuit

−Preserve testimony and/or evidence

−Assist in evaluating settlement of the lawsuit

−Assist in determining whether any basis exists for summary judgment

- Check the applicable court rules automatically, not only when drafting court documents, but also for all procedural and time requirements.
- Fed.R.Civ.P. 26 allows discovery to inquire about anything that is not privileged which is relevant to the subject matter of the lawsuit.
- Discovery can be limited or even prohibited if the court determines that:

−The discovery sought is unreasonably cumulative or duplicative, or can be obtained in another way that is more convenient, less burdensome, or less expensive.

−The party seeking discovery has had ample opportunity to obtain the information sought.

−The discovery sought is unduly burdensome or expensive, taking into account the needs of the case, amount in controversy, limitations on parties' resources, and importance of the issues.

−The discovery sought violates some type of privilege.

- Relevance means any matter that bears on, or could reasonably be connected with, or lead to evidence that could bear on, any issue or material fact presented or introduced in the case.
- If the party claiming the privilege voluntarily discloses information to a non-privileged source, the protected communication loses its privileged status.
- A privilege may be deemed waived if an objection is not made in the response to discovery requests.
- When developing a discovery strategy, identify the legal theories in the case, then determine whatever facts are necessary to prove your client's case.
- There are five types of discovery: Interrogatories; Requests for Production of Documents or Things; Requests for Physical and Mental Examinations; Depositions; and Requests for Admissions.
- Interrogatories are written questions about the lawsuit submitted to one party by another.
- Interrogatories are the most efficient and least costly means of getting basic facts.
- An interrogatory is proper and appropriate if it seeks opinions and conclusions that:

−Relate to an essential element, such as a prima facie element

−Seek an answer that would serve a substantial purpose, such as to enable the party to determine the extent of proof required or to narrow the issues

−Seek disclosures about issues the responding party has raised as a claim or defense

−Constitute a request for the factual basis supporting the responding party's conclusory claims

- Draft interrogatories so that they cannot be answered by a mere yes or no. Interrogatories that ask for specific information, such as names, dates, or documents, will obtain better answers than general questions.
- A comprehensive set of interrogatories forces the opposing party to collect facts he or she may not already have and to take steps that would otherwise be deferred until the eve of trial.
- When drafting interrogatories;:

−*Always* assume that any facts known to you are incomplete.

–*Always* assume that there are different versions of the truth or facts; ask who, what, where, when, and why questions to get the full picture.

–Avoid drafting a question that violates a privilege.

–Ask questions that obtain definite information, such as dates, names, addresses, telephone numbers, exact amounts, and the identity and location of documents or other evidence.

–Last but not least, ask that the documents (or other tangible evidence) be attached to the responding party's answers to your interrogatories. (Sometimes this last request is reserved for inclusion in a separate Request for Production of Documents.)

–Then, after you have made your initial rough draft, read the interrogatories again and ask yourself these questions. Can each interrogatory be redrafted in a simpler way? Will the answer to each interrogatory provide the information you want? How? Can some interrogatories be eliminated or consolidated? Is there a way that responses to your interrogatories could be dodged? If so, redraft the questions and narrow your request to avoid any incomplete answers.

- Ladder or branching interrogatories ask a broad question and then follow it with specific questions relating to one or more possible responses.

- Fed.R.Civ.P. 33 allows only twenty-five interrogatories, including all discrete subparts. A party must obtain leave of court if it wishes to propound more than twenty-five.

- Local court rules often limit the number of interrogatories that may be asked without leave of court and control the use of interrogatory subparts.

- The notice paragraph appears immediately after the title of the interrogatories; it states specifically to whom the interrogatory is directed and includes references to Rules 33 and 26 of the Rules of Civil Procedure, or whatever rules apply.

- Instructions and Definitions, usually located immediately after the notice paragraph, may be included in every set of Interrogatories, Requests for Production, or Requests for Admissions propounded to an opposing party.

- Instructions commonly are reminders to the answering party about rules that pertain specifically to that type of discovery, such as the time in which the answering party must respond.

- Definitions define the terms used within the document so that the language is as comprehensive and unambiguous as possible.

- Boilerplate or form interrogatories are an efficient and economical way to draft interrogatories if used correctly.

- Rule 26(b) (1) allows discovery of the identity and location of persons who have knowledge of discoverable matter and allows the parties equal access to relevant facts.

- Discovery about witnesses usually includes their identity, opinions, and facts known about them, and may include background information as to the basis of opinions or any other factors relating to what the witness knows.

- Rule 26(b) (4) defines who is an expert witness, what can be discovered and under what circumstances, and how such discovery can be obtained.

- There are two kinds of expert witnesses: (1) those a party expects to call as a witness at trial and (2) those specially employed in anticipation of litigation.

- Interrogatories seeking the identity of expert witnesses should contain questions about the expert's identity, the subject matter of the proposed testimony, facts and opinions, and grounds for the opinions offered.

- Before drafting any type of discovery, find out if your supervising attorney has a standard form already drafted and perfected.
- The most common error when using boilerplate forms is a failure to edit and proofread.
- Requests for Production are written requests for production of documents or other tangible evidence relative to the lawsuit submitted by one party to another.
- Requests for Production are the most effective way to obtain copies of documents or other evidence for inspection, analyzing, or testing; they also permit a party to enter another party's property to inspect, photograph, or analyze things on it.
- Depositions are oral questions asked by a party to another party or witness whose sworn verbal answers are given in the presence of a court reporter.
- Depositions are the only discovery device that can be used both on a party and on a witness who is not a party and can preserve testimony if the witness becomes unavailable for trial.
- Depositions are the best way to pin down parties and witnesses on details, find out what they know, and assess their credibility.
- During an oral deposition, a court reporter administers the oath to the deponent and then takes down both the questions and answers using a shorthand machine, transcribing that information later into a deposition transcript.
- A deposition allows counsel for the parties to observe and evaluate the opposing lawyer's strategy and competence and the deponent's demeanor and credibility.
- A Notice to Take Deposition must state the time and place for taking the deposition and the name and address of each person to be examined.
- The Notice to Take Deposition must be sent to each party; the Certificate of Mailing in a Notice to Take Deposition should list every party in the lawsuit.
- When you file a Notice to Take Deposition with the court clerk, it is a record that notice was given to all of the parties advising them of the date, time, and location of the deposition.
- A party who fails to appear for a duly noticed deposition may be forced to pay the costs and expenses incurred for that deposition.
- Fed.R.Civ.P. 45 states that a subpoena is necessary to require a non-party to attend a deposition and requires that any non-party witness be paid a witness fee and mileage as provided by statute.
- A subpoena is used to require the deponent to appear and give testimony at his or her deposition.
- A subpoena duces tecum is used to require the deponent to bring certain documents or things to the deposition and is the only way to obtain documents or other tangible things from a non-party.
- Requests for Physical or Mental Examination are usually used in personal injury or product liability cases where the physical or mental condition of a party is at issue.
- Requests for Admissions are the most effective when asking admission of simple facts, and are the least effective when trying to obtain opinions or answers that call for an evaluation of information.
- Requests for Admissions are written requests from one party to another that ask for admission or denial of:

–The truth of statements or opinions of fact

–The application of law to fact

–The authenticity of certain documents

- Any fact admitted in response to a Request for Admission is deemed conclusively established.
- Although Requests for Admission can be served at any time during the lawsuit, they are commonly the last type of discovery device used before the pretrial conference or motions for summary judgment.
- The purpose of Requests for Admission is to take the specific matter admitted out of issue and make it incontrovertible at trial.
- Requests for Admissions are not used to learn new facts, but rather are an excellent way to determine which facts the opposing party will concede or contest at trial and an easy way to establish the authenticity and genuineness of documents obtained through other types of discovery.
- When drafting Requests for Admission, keep it simple; you will get the best results with short, single statements for each fact that will elicit a yes or no type of answer.
- When drafting Requests for Admission, refrain from making statements with which opposing counsel will feel compelled to argue or object.
- Rule 36 requires that responses to Requests for Admissions must specifically admit, deny, or object to the admission or state, in detail, why the answering party cannot truthfully admit or deny the matter.
- If no response to Requests for Admission is given within thirty days of service of the Requests, the admissions are deemed admitted.
- Fed.R.Civ.P. 36 states that the party answering Requests for Admissions may not give lack of information or knowledge as a reason for failing to admit or deny, unless that party has made a reasonable inquiry and the information known or readily obtainable by the party is insufficient to enable the party to admit or deny.
- According to Fed.R.Civ.P. 36, when good faith requires that a party qualify an answer or deny only a part of the matter of which an admission is requested, the party shall specify so much of it as is true and qualify or deny the remainder.
- An objection to a Request for Admission must state the grounds for the objection.
- An objection to a Request for Admission has the effect of a qualified denial.
- An objection is an appropriate response to a Request for Admission if the request asks for information that is privileged or irrelevant to the lawsuit, or if the request is ambiguous or incoherent.
- Ordinarily, discovery will be used in this order:
  1. Interrogatories
  2. Requests for Production of Documents
  3. Depositions
  4. Requests for Physical or Mental Examination
  5. Requests for Admissions
- As a general rule, when you want to serve an adverse party with interrogatories and to take his deposition, it is better to take the deposition after his answers to interrogatories are received.
- All discovery documents begin using the same caption or style of the case as is set out on all of the other legal papers for that lawsuit.

- When drafting discovery documents, state as clearly as possible in the document's title who is submitting discovery to whom and which set of discovery documents is being submitted.
- Opinion-seeking, or contention, interrogatories are valuable because they narrow the legal issues and lessen the amount of preparation.
- Facts supporting a party's contentions are discoverable so long as the discovery of information narrows or clarifies the issues.
- Most court rules require that Interrogatories, Requests for Production, and Requests for Admissions be answered within thirty days from the date of service.
- When responding to interrogatories, you have two choices: to answer or to object. If your response is to object, state your objection as the answer to that interrogatory.
- Answers to Interrogatories must be signed and sworn to by the person answering them.
- Send discovery requests and answers to discovery to opposing counsel by certified mail, return receipt requested, and indicate the same in the Certificate of Mailing. Certified mail is the most economical and efficient way to prove that your discovery or responses were received by the other side.
- Requests for Production may be served only on another party.
- After the documents have been gathered in response to Requests for Production, you or your attorney should review them to determine whether they are relevant and responsive to the request, and then note and mark confidential documents for which your client claims some privilege and for which you will make an objection in the response.
- Objections should be made on the ground of privilege or because the request is unduly burdensome, oppressive, embarrassing, or costly.
- Before summarizing the deposition, review the file and the pleadings and ask your attorney if there is anything specific that should be noted or disregarded, or if he or she prefers a certain format to be used for the summary.
- Most deposition summaries have a column on the left-hand margin showing the page-line and a second column for summarized testimony, and some attorneys prefer the addition of an issue or topic column that is literally a summary of the summary and consists of only a key word or phrase.
- A page-line deposition summary is simply a page-by-page summary of the transcript.
- A page-only deposition summary is often referred to as an "index" of the deposition and is often less detailed than the page/line summary.
- A page-line-topic deposition summary, although time-consuming to prepare, can be extremely useful to an attorney.
- A chronological or subject-matter deposition summary is broken up into particular topics allowing the attorney to find everything the deponent said about a given topic by looking at one place on the summary.
- The 10% Rule means to write one page of summary for every ten pages of deposition transcript.
- Whenever you are given depositions to summarize, ask the attorney for a deadline of when the summaries need to be finished.
- Always consider the costs of discovery to the client.

KEY WORDS AND PHRASES

Bill of Costs

boilerplate

caption, style of the case

chronological deposition summary

contention interrogatory

contributory negligence

course and scope of employment

court reporter

Definitions

deponent

Deposition

deposition summary or index

deposition transcript

discovery

evidence

expert witness

fact witness

Federal Rules of Civil Procedure

good cause

Instructions

Interrogatories

interrogatory subparts

issue

issues of pure law

ladder or branching interrogatories

leave of court

legal conclusions

legal opinion

materiality test

Medical Authorization or Release

Motion for Attorney Fees

notice paragraph

Notice to Take Deposition

object, objection

page-line deposition summary

page-line-topic deposition summary

page-only deposition summary

privilege

protective order

Request for Physical or Mental Examinations

Request for Production of Documents and Things

relevance

relevancy standard

Rules of Evidence

subject-matter deposition summary

subpoena

subpoena ad testificandum

subpoena duces tecum

title

Verification

witness fee

10% Rule

EXERCISES

1. You are now in the discovery phase of Jane Healy's lawsuit. Ms. Pepper hands you the following list. Which types of discovery would be most appropriate for obtaining each piece of information?
   a. Whether Charles Raymond had auto insurance, and if so, how much?
   b. Whether Charles Raymond has prior drunk driving convictions.
   c. Whether Mr. Allegretti will agree that Mr. Raymond was hired on March 15, 1990.
   d. Whether Tony Simpson thought Mr. Raymond was drunk when Mr. Raymond left Red's Tavern.
   e. Whether Mr. Raymond had ever been confined to an alcohol treatment center.

2. Suppose Mr. Baxter, Mr. Raymond's attorney, wants to obtain the following pieces of information. What discovery tools should he use?
   a. The nature and extent of Jane Healy's injuries.
   b. Whether Jane Healy was employed at the time of the accident, and if so, how much she was earning.
   c. How Ms. Healy thinks the accident happened.
   d. Whether Ms. Healy had any preexisting medical conditions.
   e. Whether Ms. Healy will acknowledge that she was speeding before she entered the intersection where the accident occurred.

3. Ms. Pepper asks you and Fred Wickham, your co-worker, to come up with a discovery strategy. Fred recommends the following plan of action. Critique it. What changes, if any, would you make?

   a. First, depose all the defendants and all the witnesses. That way you will get everyone's statements while their memories are fresh.

   b. Second, go over the depositions and think about the statements everyone made. If you have more questions about what was said, send out interrogatories demanding further explanations.

   c. Third, send each of the defendants a list of your discovery requests. After the deposition and interrogatories, you will know what documents you need to have.

   d. Fourth, use a Request for Physical and Mental Examination for Charles Raymond and Tony Simpson. You want to know why Mr. Simpson was crazy enough to serve liquor to a drunk customer, and why Mr. Raymond was crazy enough to drive while intoxicated. Also, it should really shake Mr. Raymond up.

   e. Finally, use a Request for Admissions for Mr. Raymond. Ask him to admit that he was negligent and that the accident was his fault.

4. Fred Wickham drafted the following interrogatories for Charles Raymond. Unfortunately, there is something wrong with each one. Identify what the problem is with each question, and how Fred could correct it, if it can be corrected.

   - **INTERROGATORY NO. 1:** Was Jane Healy in a hurry at the time the accident occurred?

   - **INTERROGATORY NO. 2:** List all the alcoholic beverages you have drunk since January 1, 1994, and where you drank them.

   - **INTERROGATORY NO. 3:** Did you drink anything the day of the accident, and if so, what?

   - **INTERROGATORY NO. 4:** What liability coverage do you currently possess on the vehicle that you were operating on the day of the event in dispute that you are eligible to avail yourself of in the event that a court of law finds your conduct on the date of the accident culpable?

   - **INTERROGATORY NO. 5:** State everything your attorney has told you about denying your guilt.

5. Fred has drawn up some interrogatories to send to Roy Collins, a customer in Red's Tavern who saw Charles Raymond drinking right before the accident occurred. Do you foresee any problems with serving the interrogatories on Mr. Collins? Why or why not?

6. Ms. Pepper is thinking seriously about talking to Fred about a career change—namely, his. She cannot use the interrogatories he prepared for Allegretti & Sons. Ms. Pepper comes to you and asks you to draft the interrogatories instead. Draft the interrogatories and assume that your jurisdiction limits interrogatories to ten questions, including subparts.

7. Ms. Pepper has decided to depose Sergeant Harrison, the officer who talked to Mr. Raymond after the accident and took him down to the police station for a breathalyzer test. She wants to have him appear at the deposition and bring a copy of the results of Mr. Raymond's blood-alcohol test. What documents does she need to prepare in order to require Sergeant Adams to appear and to bring the test results? Is there any other legal means she can use to require Sergeant Adams to bring the test results?

8. Ms. Pepper has found out that Mr. and Mrs. Nicks, the witnesses to the car wreck, took photographs of the accident scene. She would like to acquire those photographs without having to depose Mr. and Mrs. Nicks. Is there any way Ms. Pepper can accomplish this? If so, how?

9. Ms. Pepper is now ready to draft Requests for Admission. Fred has prepared a list of proposed Requests for Admission for several of the defendants. Which requests should be used, and which should be rejected?

   a. Requests for Admission for Caroline Bingley, owner of Red's Tavern:

      1. Admit that Caroline Bingley owns Red's Tavern.

      2. Admit that Red's Tavern served alcohol to Charles Raymond on the day of the accident.

      3. Admit that Red's Tavern knowingly served alcohol to an intoxicated patron.

   b. Requests for Admission for Hans Weber, owner and manager of dealership where Ms. Healy bought her BMW:

1. Admit that Hans Weber Import Autos sells BMWs.
2. Admit that Ms. Healy's seatbelt was defective.
3. Admit that Ms. Healy was driving a BMW the day of her accident.

c. Requests for Admission for Ajax, Inc., Ms. Healy's former employer:
1. Admit that Ms. Healy was fired because she knew Mr. Forbes had been embezzling company funds.
2. Admit that Ms. Healy was hired full-time in 1989, and worked at Ajax until the time of the accident.
3. Admit that Ms. Healy had an excellent work history while she was employed there.

10. As mentioned in the sample Verification, once the final draft of the client's response to Interrogatories has been drafted, the client must sign the Verification attesting to the truth of his or her answers. Draft a letter to the client enclosing the final draft of a Response to Interrogatories. [The letter should include instructions about signing the Verification and having the signature notarized, as well as a deadline to return the original signed Verification.]

11. Using the Jane Healy scenario, prepare a list of all documents to be used when either Plaintiff or Defendants take the deposition of Marjorie Jones, a witness to the accident (who lives in the jurisdiction of the lawsuit).

12. Now do a summary of the deposition of Charles Raymond, found in Appendix I. Use the page/line/summary method.

APPENDIX A
Commonly Misspelled Words

accelerator
accessible
accessories
accommodate
accoutrements
achievement
adjudge
allege
allegation
allotted
all right
analysis
appellant
appellee
asinine
attorneys
auxiliary

benefited
bookkeeper
bureaucracy

capillary
centrifugal
certiorari
changeable
chaparral
Cincinnati
codicil
collander
commensurate
committed
concede
connoisseur
conscientious
consensus

counsel
counselor

deductible
defendant
deleterious
desiccate
desirable
desuetude
diaphragm
dilemma
diphtheria
discreet
discrete
dissatisfied
dudgeon

ecstasy
embarrass
enforceable
exaggerate
exchangeable
exhilarate
exorbitant
expectant
extraordinary

February
flaccid
forcible
foresee

grievance
guarantee
guaranty

habeas corpus
handicapped
heinous
hors d'oeuvre
hygiene

iconoclast
illegible
implacable
inadvertent
inchoate
indemnity
independent
indictment
indispensable
inoculate
intercede
interstice
irresistible

jeopardy
judgment (preferred)

liable
liqueur
livelihood

maintenance
maneuver
mediocre
Mediterranean
miniature
miscellaneous
mischievous
misspell
mortgage

negligible
niece
ninety
noticeable
nuclear

occasionally
occurred
omitted
optimistic

pamphlet
parallel
parliamentary
particularly
percolator
permissible
perseverance
persistence
petitioner
picnicked
plaintiff
pneumonia
precedence
preferred
privilege
procedural
proceeding
profited
psychoanalysis

quarantine
questionnaire

rarefy
receipt
reducible

referred
regrettable
relief
rendezvous
repetitious
respondent
rhythm

sacrilegious
seize

siege
sophomore
subsidiary
supersede
susceptible
syphilis

tragedy
transferred

truly
twelfth

unbelievable
unforeseen

vacuum
variation
variety
vilify
visible

Wednesday
weird

yield

zucchini

APPENDIX B
Which Preposition?

Many words are written correctly only with certain prepositions, and never with others. Here are some common words and their wedded prepositions.

consequent	to, on, upon	hanker	for, after
consonant	with	healed	of, by
contiguous	to	hinge	on, upon
derogate	from	hint	at
desirous	of	immigrate	to
despair	of	impatient	with, for, at, of
destructive	of, to	improve	on, upon
devolve	from, upon	inaccessible	to, from, by
dissent	from	incidental	to, upon
dissimilar	to	incongruous	with
emanate	from	incorporate	into, with
emigrate	from	inimical	to, toward,
enamored	of, with	innate	in
encroach	on, upon	inquire	about, into, after
engaged	in, upon	insensible	to, of
exonerate	of, from	insight	into
experienced	at, in	instill	into, in
expressive	of	intention	to, of
exude	from	introduce	to, into
fascinated	by (a person)	intrude	into, on, upon
	with (an object)	inure	to
fascination	for	lacking	in
feed	on, off	meddle	in, with
fondness	for	necessary	for, to
freedom	from, of, to	observant	of
frown	on, at, upon	originate	in, with
fruitful	in, of	parallel	to, with
grieve	at, for, after	part	from, with

B-1

peculiar	to	proficient	at, in
permeate	through, into	propitious	to, for
persevere	in	receptive	to, of
persuaded	to, of	redolent	of
piqued	at, by	regret	at, for
possessed	of, with, by	rejoice	at, in
precedence	over, of	repent	of
prerequisite (adjective)	to	replete	with
		resentment	at, against
prerequisite (noun)	of	responsibility	for
prevail	on, upon, against, over, with	satiate	with
		sensible	of, to
prodigal	of	solicitous	of, about, for
productive	of		

APPENDIX C
Unnecessary Verbiage and Stuffy Words

Here are some editing suggestions to delete unnecessary words.

Instead of this:	Write this:	Instead of this:	Write this:
adjacent to	near, close to, next to	cite (noun)	citation
advert to	refer to	cognizant	aware
advise	tell	commence	start, begin
take under *advisement*	consider	in *comparison* to	in comparison with
affirmative (negative)	yes (no)	complete stop	stop
afford	give	in *connection* with	about
allow for	allow	in *contrast* with	in contrast to
alongside of	alongside	conform with	conform to
ameliorate	improve	general *consensus*	consensus
anterior to	before	consensus of opinion	consensus
apprise	tell	take into *consideration*	consider
appropriate	proper, correct, right	contained in	in
arising from the fact that	because	contiguous with	contiguous to
		contrast to	contrast with
as of	starting, beginning	in *excess* of	more than
as regards	on, for, about	end result	result
as well as	and, also	every single one	all
as to whether, when, how, who	whether, when, etc.	expectorate	spit
		explicate	explain
at the end of	after	expound on	expound
the reason is *because*	the reason is that	despite the *fact* that	even though
be helpful	help	fair and just	fair, just
by means of	by	feel like (believe)	feel
by itself	alone	in the *field* of	in
by virtue of	by	file an action against	sue
in that *case*	then	fill up	fill
than is the *case* with	than with	finalize	finish, complete
in *cases* in which	if, when	first began (started)	started, began
of a strange *character*	strange	first of all	first

C-1

Instead of this:	Write this:	Instead of this:	Write this:
firstly	first	join together	join
for the purpose of	to	at that *juncture*	then
give an indication of	indicate	a *large* percentage of	many
hale and hearty	healthy, well	large-sized	large
half of all the	half of the	in *length*	long
have an effect on	affect	likely	probably, probable
have an impact on	affect	like for	want, wish
have got to	must	likewise	also
be *helpful* to	help	live audience	audience
by *herself, himself*	alone	located in (at)	in (at)
hopefully	I (we) (they) hope	made up out of	made of
if	whether	make an argument	argue
it is *imperative* that he	he must	make a choice of	choose
is of *importance*	is important	make a decision about	decide
impressed with	impressed by	make changes	change
located *in*	in	make an objection	object
in addition to	besides	many of these	many
in an effort to	to	by *means* of	by
in cases in which	if, when	in the *neighborhood* of	about
in case	if	a *number* of	some, many, several
in the case of *Bakke*	in *Bakke*	oblivious to	oblivious of
instances in which	if, when	obtain	get
in order to	to	off of	off, from
in (with) regard to	about	on a regular basis	regularly
in relation to	about	on an annual basis	annually (yearly, monthly, etc.)
in respect to	about		
inside of	inside	on the order of	about
in spite of the fact that	although	on the part of	by
in the event of	if	on the basis of	because of
in the field of	in	one and the same	the same
in the near future	soon	of an *order* of magnitude of	about
in the region (vicinity) of	near, about, close to	orientate	orient
in view of the fact that	because	outside of	outside
in width	wide	over and above	over, above
independent from	independent of	over and done with	finished
individual	person, man, women	owing to the fact that	because
initiate	start, begin	a large (small) *part* of	many (few)
instead of	rather than	party	person, man, woman
institute	start	a *percentage* of	part of
integral part	part	pertaining to	about
interpose an objection	object	pick and choose	choose
interpretate	interpret	posterior to	after, behind
was *instrumental* in	helped in	practically	nearly, almost
made an *investigation* into (of)	investigated	predicated on	based on
		preliminary to	before
irregardless (a nonword)	regardless	preparatory to	before
it is to be hoped that	I hope	preplan	plan

Instead of this:	Write this:	Instead of this:	Write this:
at *present*	now	remunerate, remun-	pay
presented in	in	eration	
preventative	preventive	as a result	because
previously	before, earlier, on Tuesday	secure	get
		since (except time)	because
have *previously* received, done, gone	have received, done, gone	situated in	in
		so as to	to
prior experience	experience	in spite of	despite
prioritize	set priorities	subsequent to	after
proceed	drive, walk, fly, etc.	subsequent	later
provided (providing) that	near	subsequently	later
		sum total	total
in close *proximity* to	near	until such time as	until
for the *purpose* of	to, for	the sum of $10	$10
the *question* of whether	whether	supposing (that)	if
quote (noun)	quotation	have a tendency to	tend
reach a conclusion	conclude	there exist	there are
the *reason* why	the reason (that)	thereby	by that, by it
was the recipient of	got, received	therefrom	from it
refers back to	refers to	therein	in it, there
in the *region* of	near, close to	thereof	of its, its
remand back	remand	various and sundry	various

APPENDIX D
SAMPLE CASE BRIEF

Here is a sample case brief for *Cruse v. Aden,* 20 N.E. 73 (Ill. 1889)

Cruse v. Aden,
20 N.E. 73 (Ill. 1889)

Facts

    Widow, whose husband was killed in a horse-riding accident while intoxicated, sued her husband's friend for serving two alcoholic drinks to the decedent. Widow alleged that respondent was responsible for her loss of financial support per Section 9 of the Illinois Dram Shop Act. The Act provides a penalty for:

A)   whoever
B)   shall sell (or give away)
C)   liquor
D)   to minors (or to persons intoxicated) (or to persons who are in the habit of getting intoxicated)

Section 9 of the Act further provides:

A)   a right of action
B)   to persons injured
C)   in person (or means of support)
D)   in consequence of intoxication
E)   against any persons
F)   who by selling (or giving)
G)   intoxicating liquors
H)   have caused the intoxication

Procedural History

    Judg. $800 for P by trial ct.; reversed by appellate ct. 4th dist.; P appeals to Ill. S. Ct. on cert.

Issue(s)

    Whether the dram shop act creates liability in a person, not in the business of selling alcohol, who serves intoxicants on social basis to a friend;

    Whether a cause of action existed at common law for persons injured by intoxicated state of strong and able-bodied man, against the party who provided the intoxicant.

Holding

Section 9 of the dram-shop act does not apply to persons who are not engaged in distributing liquor with the expectation of pecuniary gain.

There is no tort at common law for providing liquor to a strong and able-bodied man.

Judgment

Judgment of the appellate court is affirmed. (The effect of this judgment was to reverse trial court's award to the Widow.)

Reasoning

1) Cause of action is purely statutory;
2) Under common rules of construction, all other provisions of dram-shop act specifically refer to those dispensing liquor for profit;
3) Full title of the Act, "An act to provide for the licensing of and against the evils arising from the sale of intoxicating liquor," further suggests that the Act applies to businesses rather than to private hosts as real intended meaning;
4) Statute is "highly penal" and should be given strict construction;
5) Intent of the Act is not to penalize friends or social hosts who have no pecuniary gain from distribution of liquor.

APPENDIX E
Sample Legal Memorandum

M E M O R A N D U M

TO: Amelia Pepper
FROM: Chris Roberts
RE: *Healy v. XYZ Seat Belt Corporation*
DATE: March 4, 1995

INTRODUCTION

Our client, Jane Healy, was involved in an automobile accident nearly one year ago. She has retained this firm to represent and advise her in the anticipated litigation against the person or persons responsible for this accident and Ms. Healy's injuries. This memorandum will address the liability of XYZ Seat Belt Corporation, Ms. Healy's claims, and XYZ's possible defenses.

STATEMENT OF FACTS

Jane Healy was involved in an automobile accident almost twelve months ago, on February 25, 1994. That evening, around 6:30 p.m., Ms. Healy was hurriedly driving home in her 1988 BMW 325i on 14th Street in heavy traffic. She was late for an appointment with a friend. As she approached the intersection of 14th Street and Childs Street, which is approximately four blocks from her home, the intersection's traffic light turned yellow.

Even though the speed limit was twenty-five miles per hour, Ms. Healy accelerated to thirty-five m.p.h. to try to get through the 14th and Childs intersection before the light turned red. As she entered the intersection, the traffic in front of her stopped suddenly. Ms. Healy slammed on her brakes to avoid hitting the car in front of her and stopped in the middle of the intersection. When the light turned red, the traffic in front of Ms. Healy remained at a stand-still, leaving her stranded in the intersection.

Charles Raymond was traveling south on Childs Street, and was the first car to have stopped at the Childs Street traffic light at the intersection of 14th and Childs. Raymond, who had been drinking heavily immediately before this incident, was paying little or no attention to the traffic in and around the 14th and Childs intersection. When the Childs Street traffic signal turned green, Raymond floored his car's accelerator. His car roared into the intersection and smashed into the side of Ms. Healy's car before Raymond even realized that she was there. The force of Raymond's car striking Ms. Healy's car shoved her car into a steel streetlight pole on the southwest corner of the intersection.

At the moment of impact with the pole, Ms. Healy's seat belt, manufactured by XYZ Seat Belt Corporation, broke. Without the seat belt to restrain her, she pitched forward, smashing her head and face into the windshield of her car.

As a result of the accident, she suffered a fractured skull, three broken ribs, a punctured lung, and numerous deep facial cuts. Ms. Healy remained in the hospital for six weeks following the accident. Although she has undergone three plastic surgeries on her face and will undergo at least two more, Ms. Healy will have facial scars for the rest of her life.

Ms. Healy purchased her car two years ago. At the time she purchased the car, no mention was made of any possible or actual defect in the car's seat belts. In fact, Ms. Healy had never experienced any problems with the seat belts until this accident. The mechanic—the only person to have done any repairs to her car since she bought it—never noticed that the seat belts had any problems or defects of any kind.

Before this accident, Jane Healy was a successful public relations specialist at Mahaffey & Co. Her annual salary was $55,000, plus generous health and retirement benefits. She had been promised by the President of Mahaffey & Co. that she would receive a promotion to Assistant Vice-President within the next four months. With the promotion, her annual salary would have increased to $70,000. However, because of the accident, Jane cannot make public appearances, an integral part of her work. As a result, Mahaffey & Co. has fired Jane because she can no longer fulfill her job duties.

XYZ Seat Belt Corporation is headquartered and domiciled in Delaware. Ms. Healy purchased her car in Oklahoma. We will advise Ms. Healy to file her lawsuit in federal court, based upon diversity jurisdiction and the dollar amount of relief sought.

QUESTION PRESENTED

Can Jane Healy recover damages for the enhanced injuries she received as a result of the defective seat belt?

BRIEF ANSWER

Yes. In the absence of proof that Ms. Healy knew the seat belt was defective, she can recover from XYZ Seat Belt Corp., the manufacturer of the defective product, under a "second impact" theory for her enhanced injuries which she would not have sustained but for the defective seat belt.

STATUTE
41 ABC Stat. 1991 § 999

A manufacturer is liable for injury caused by a product, as well as damages, whether compensatory, special or punitive. The user of the defective product may have a cause of action, regardless of who purchased the product.

The injured person cannot recover damages from the manufacturer if the injured person knew of the dangers of the product and voluntarily assumed the risks of the product.

DISCUSSION

I. The Necessary Elements to Recover Against the Manufacturer of a Defective Product.

This is a case of first impression in this jurisdiction. This jurisdiction has not previously specified what the plaintiff must prove under 41 ABC Stat. § 999 to recover damages from the manufacturer of a defective product. However, in *Perez v. Ford Motor Company,* 497 F.2d 82 (5th Cir. 1974), the manufacturer product liability statute was similar to that in this jurisdiction. In *Perez,* the court outlined the elements which the plaintiff must prove in order to recover. *Perez* held that, where the plaintiff can prove the product was defective, the manufacturer is strictly liable to any person injured as a result of using the defective product. *Id.* at 86.

In *Perez,* the plaintiff and his wife were riding in a truck designed and manufactured by the defendant. When the plaintiff's truck collided with another vehicle, the truck's frame broke. The truck overturned, killing the plaintiff's wife.

The court found that to recover in a manufacturer product liability action, the plaintiff first must prove the manufacturer's product was defective and unreasonably dangerous. *Id.* A product is defective and unreasonably dangerous when a reasonable seller would not sell the product if the seller knew of the risks involved or if the risks are greater than a reasonable buyer would expect. *Id.* at 87. Second, the plaintiff must prove that the plaintiff's use of the product at the time of the accident was normal. *Id.* at 86. The accident itself is not proof that the plaintiff's use of the product was abnormal. *Id.* at 87. The fact that the product was involved in an accident or that the accident involved uncommon occurrences does not preclude the plaintiff's recovery. *Id.*

Ms. Healy will argue that the case at bar fulfills the requirements that *Perez* set out. First, the risks involved with XYZ's defective seat belt are greater than a reasonable buyer would expect. The intended purpose of a seat belt is to protect passengers from serious injury during accidents. Ms. Healy, as a reasonable buyer, expected the seat belt to restrain her from hitting her head and face on the windshield during an accident. Clearly, the seat belt did not operate as Ms. Healy expected.

Second, Ms. Healy's use of the seat belt at the time of the accident was normal. Therefore, because the defective seat belt was unreasonably dangerous when Ms. Healy used it normally, XYZ is strictly liable for Ms. Healy's injuries.

On the other hand, XYZ will argue that the seat belt was not unreasonably dangerous. Raymond hit Ms. Healy's car with such great force as to push her car across the intersection and into a streetlight pole. The seat belt broke only when her car was impacted on both sides. Because this sort of accident is not common, the seat belt breaking in this situation is also uncommon. During a more common accident, the seat belt would not have broken. Therefore, given the unlikelihood of such an accident, the seat belt was not unreasonably dangerous.

A. The Second Impact Theory

Some jurisdictions have expanded the manufacturer's liability to include injuries from a second impact. In *Higginbotham v. Ford Motor Company,* 540 F.2d 762, 766 (5th Cir. 1976), the court defined "second impact" injuries as "enhanced injuries," injuries a person inside a vehicle receives because of the product's reaction to the vehicle's collision. There, the court held that, where the manufacturer could have substantially lessened the "second impact" injuries, the manufacturer is liable for the enhanced injuries. *Id.* at 766.

In *Higginbotham,* the plaintiff's truck was involved in a collision with a third party's car. Upon impact, the wheel suspension in the plaintiff's car broke. The frame of the car bent, and the front section of the car crushed the passenger in the front seat. The passenger in the plaintiff's truck died. The defendant designed and manufactured the plaintiff's truck.

In *Higginbotham,* the court reasoned that, because the defendant's product enhanced the plaintiff's injuries, the defendant was liable for the damages relating to the enhancement. *Id.* at 774. Although the manufacturer's act combined with a third party's act to produce the plaintiff's injuries, if there is a basis on which to apportion damages, the defendant and the third party are separate tortfeasors. *Id.* The damages attributable to the manufacturer's liability equal the total amount of the plaintiff's injuries, less the amount of injuries the plaintiff would have sustained had there not been a second impact. *Id.*

Applying the *Higginbotham* holding to the case at bar, Ms. Healy can recover from XYZ in an action separate from her suit against Charles Raymond, the driver of the car which struck her BMW. An accident reconstruction specialist can project what would have been the movement of Ms. Healy's body inside her car had the seat belt operated properly.

The fact that the seat belt was not the cause of the first impact has no bearing upon Ms. Healy's suit against XYZ. *See Caiazzo v. Volkswagenwerk A.G.,* 647 F. 2d 241, 246 (2d Cir. 1981) (second impact doctrine applies where defect enhances plaintiff's first impact injuries caused by third party); *Spier v. Barker,* 323 N.E. 2d 164, 169 (N.Y. 1974) (if party can prove that seat belt would have lessened injuries, damages can be apportioned). From this calculation, the court can determined the enhancement of Ms. Healy's injuries attributable to XYZ's defective seat belt. Therefore, because Ms. Healy's injuries can be apportioned between the first impact and the second impact, Ms. Healy can recover damages from XYZ for her second impact injuries.

B. Ms. Healy's Injuries Can Be Rationally Apportioned.

XYZ will possibly argue that Ms. Healy's injuries cannot be rationally apportioned. Ms. Healy sustained a single, indivisible injury. Any calculation or test that can be done by a reconstruction expert will only be an educated guess. It is unlikely that any expert can make the calculation with a degree of certainty. Therefore, because there is no definite basis for apportioning Ms. Healy's injuries between the first impact and the second impact, Ms. Healy must sue XYZ and Raymond jointly.

II. The Manufacturer's Defenses.
A. Assumption of the Risk.

When determining the manufacturer's liability, the court must also evaluate the manufacturer's defenses. In *Melia v. Ford Motor Company,* 354 F. 2d 795 (8th Cir. 1976), the court defined the defenses available to the manufacturer. *Melia* held that, because the defective product created a foreseeable and unreasonable risk to the plaintiff, the manufacturer was strictly liable absent the plaintiff's assumption of risk. *Id.* at 802.

In *Melia,* when the plaintiff drove his car into an intersection, a third party hit the plaintiff's car. The plaintiff's left front door latch broke, and the plaintiff was thrown from the car. The plaintiff sued the manufacturer of the defective door latch.

The court in *Melia* reasoned that, while the manufacturer is not an insurer of the car's users in all circumstances, where the risk of injury increases, the manufacturer's liability also increases. A car's manufacturer is liable if the plaintiff can prove that (1) the defect caused the plaintiff a second injury, and (2) the plaintiff's risk of injury was foreseeable. *Id.* at 798. The court emphasized that the required foreseeability is of the "unreasonable risk of injury in the event of a collision" and not of the risk of collision. *Id.*

Further, the court in *Melia* differentiated between contributory negligence and assumption of risk. Contributory negligence, where the plaintiff failed to discover the defect, is not a defense to the manufacturer's strict liability. *Id.* at 801, *citing*

Restatement (Second) of Torts § 402A. However, assumption of risk, where the plaintiff voluntarily and unreasonably assumes a known danger, is a valid defense. *Id.*

Just as the car's defect enhanced the plaintiff's injuries in *Melia*, XYZ's defective seat belt enhanced Ms. Healy's injuries. A properly operating seat belt would have prevented Ms. Healy from smashing her face and head into the windshield. When the seat belt did not properly restrain Ms. Healy, she suffered a fractured skull and deep facial cuts that she would not have otherwise suffered had the seat belt been working properly. It is foreseeable that, when the plaintiff was in a serious automobile accident, the plaintiff would be injured if the seat belt did not operate properly. Therefore, because Ms. Healy sustained greater injuries than she would have had the seat belt been properly operating, Ms. Healy can recover from XYZ.

In addition, Ms. Healy will argue that her actions do not constitute assumption of risk. She did not voluntarily and unreasonably increase her risk of injury. Ms. Healy attempted to reduce the possibility of sustaining serious injury by buckling her seat belt. Therefore, because the defect in XYZ's seat belt enhanced Ms. Healy's injury from the collision's second impact and Ms. Healy did not assume the risk of the enhanced injuries, XYZ is liable for Ms. Healy's enhanced injuries.

B. By Failing to Yield to the Yellow Light at the Intersection, Ms. Healy Did Not Assume the Risks Associated With Entering The Intersection.

There is one important difference between the facts of *Melia* and the case at bar that could damage Ms. Healy's argument. Unlike the plaintiff in *Melia*, Ms. Healy purposely sped into the intersection to beat the red light. She remained stranded in the middle of the intersection after the light turned red. Arguably, if she had stopped at the light rather than assuming the risks of entering the intersection, Raymond's car would not have collided with Ms. Healy's car. Therefore, because Ms. Healy purposely entered the intersection, she assumed the risk of a possible accident in the intersection.

In *Holt v. Deere & Company*, 24 F. 3d 1289 (10th Cir. 1994), the court narrowed the application of the assumption of risk defense. In *Holt*, the court held that the plaintiff will not be barred from recovering merely because the plaintiff should have known of the dangerous defect. *Id.* at 1293.

In *Holt*, the plaintiff, a mechanic, attempted to repair a tractor designed and built by the defendant. Each time that the plaintiff started the tractor while making his repairs, he remained standing on the ground rather than climbing into the driver's seat. When the plaintiff started the tractor's engine, the tractor unexpectedly started in gear and rolled over the plaintiff. The plaintiff did not knowingly or purposely start the tractor in gear.

The *Holt* court found that, to use the assumption of risk defense, the manufacturer must prove that the plaintiff was subjectively aware of, and appreciated, the dangers in using the product in the manner the plaintiff was using it when the accident occurred. *Id.* The plaintiff's ignorance or false sense of security about the effectiveness of the product do not bar the plaintiff's recovery. *Id.* The manufacturer must show the plaintiff knew of an unreasonably dangerous defect and still voluntarily used the product. *Id.* at 1292.

Under *Holt*, the court cannot find that Ms. Healy assumed the risk of the enhanced injuries the defective seat belt caused. Even if Ms. Healy assumed the risk of an accident by entering the intersection, she did not enter the intersection knowing that her seat belt would break. *See also LaHue v. General Motors Corp.*, 716 F. Supp. 407, 414 (W.D. Mo. 1989) (failure to prevent contributory-fault accident is not an available assumption of risk defense). Ms. Healy had not previously had problems with her seat belt, and did not know that the seat belt would not properly restrain her in the event of an accident. Therefore, because Ms. Healy did not know of the seat belt's defect at the time of the accident, XYZ cannot use the assumption of risk defense to bar Ms. Healy's recovery.

C. A Manufacturer Has No Duty To Make A Product That Lasts Forever or Can Withstand Lack of Maintenance.

XYZ may argue that a manufacturer does not have a duty to make a product that will last forever or will withstand a lack of maintenance. *See Hurt v. General Motors Corp.,* 553 F. 2d 1181, 1184 (8th Cir. 1977) (manufacturer does not have to build seat belt for passenger autos that would prevent all injuries); *Larsen v. General Motors Corporation,* 391 F.2d 495, 502 n. 3 (8th Cir. 1968) (manufacturer's duty is not to design car that creates unreasonable risks of enhanced injury); *Anton v. Ford Motor Company,* 400 F. Supp. 1270, 1280 (S.D. Ohio 1975) (manufacturer's product does not have to be fool-proof, thus liability imposed only when unreasonable danger is created).

Ms. Healy cannot blindly use her car without checking its components. Ms. Healy put on her seat belt each time she sat in her car. If the defect from the seat belt was due to wear, Ms. Healy will have a difficult time convincing the court that she did not know of the dangerous condition. If XYZ can prove that the seat belt was in a dangerous condition prior to the accident and Ms. Healy knowingly used that seat belt, Ms. Healy may be barred from recovery based on her assumption of risk.

<u>CONCLUSION</u>

Title 41 ABC Stat. 1991 § 999 makes a manufacturer of a defective product strictly liable for the injuries the manufacturer's product causes. After Jane Healy's car collided with a street light pole, the seat belt manufactured by XYZ broke. Jane Healy's seat belt did not restrain her body from hitting the windshield of the car. Had the seat belt been operating properly, Jane Healy would not have sustained the severe injuries that kept her in the hospital and caused her to lose her job. Under the "second impact" theory, she is entitled to damages for the enhanced injuries that she would not have sustained but for the defective seat belt.

XYZ cannot bar Jane Healy's recovery based upon a contributory negligence defense. Contributory negligence is not a valid defense to a manufacturer's product liability claim. The only affirmative defense that XYZ may use to reduce its liability is assumption of risk. However, to invoke the assumption of risk defense, the manufacturer must prove that the plaintiff knew of the product's defect and used the product regardless of that defect.

In Ms. Healy's case, she did not know the seat belt was defective. She did not previously have problems with the seat belt and did not suspect that the seat belt would break during an accident. XYZ cannot bar Jane Healy's recovery based upon on assumption of risk defense.

APPENDIX F
Brief Cheat Sheet

This sample Brief Cheat Sheet is for state and federal courts in central Oklahoma. We recommend that you prepare your own for the courts in all of the jurisdictions in which your supervising attorney practices. Notice that our sample not only tells you what rules control various aspects of the brief but also includes sample formats for two types of cover sheets, tables of contents, and tables of authorities.

The sample we have provided should *not* be followed unless you are preparing a brief to be filed in those jurisdictions. Use this sample as a model to create one that meets your own needs.

BRIEF CHEAT SHEET

STATE DISTRICT COURT (Oklahoma)
Oklahoma County Courthouse (405/236-2727)

Number of Copies Filed:	Original filed with Court Clerk. A copy <u>must</u> be delivered to assigned trial judge **5** days before hearing **(Rule 37,** Local Rules, 7th Judicial District.)[1] *See also* Rule 11, 7th Judicial District (requires cert. of mailing and delivery to judge); 14th Judicial District[2], **Local Rule 26(b)** (copy of brief must be delivered to assigned judge when brief is filed) and **Local Rule 30** (copy of brief must be delivered to assigned judge at least 3 working days prior to hearing).
Page Number Limit:	30 pages **excluding** exhibits, unless court grants leave for more than 30 pages. Local Rule 37, 7th Judicial District. (Page numbers limited to 20 pages for opening and opposition briefs (reply briefs limited to 5 pages) per Rule 30, 14th Judicial District.
Bound:	Not required. If brief and/or exhibits are lengthy, recommend binding with cover page.
Cover Page:	Required for certain motions[3], *e.g.*, motion for summary judgment. **Not required for motions listed in footnote 3**, but recommended for lengthy or bound briefs. No color requirement for cover page.
Brief Required:	Required for all motions **except** those listed in footnote 3 per Rule 4(c), Rules for District Courts. *See* attached examples of Table of Contents and Table of Authorities.
Table of Contents/ Authorities:	Not required but recommended for lengthy (10 pages or more) or bound briefs as a courtesy to the court. Would also recommend including a Table of Contents/Authorities for briefs that contain numerous authorities regardless of length.
Other Rules:	Must contain: style and # of case; title describing brief; name, bar #, address and telephone # of attorney of record and law firm filing brief; and, certificate of service or mailing per Local Rule 1, 7th Judicial District. For 14th Judicial District, must contain: attorney's bar #, name, address, and telephone number; and title showing if opening, opposition, or reply brief, the particular proceeding or application to which it relates, and party or parties on whose behalf it is presented per Rules 22 and 30.

---

[1]References to 1995 District Court Rules, Oklahoma - Canadian Counties, Seventh Judicial District, are designated as "Local Rules for the 7th Judicial District."

[2]Fourteenth Judicial District is Tulsa County District Court; Seventh Judicial District is Oklahoma County District Court.

[3]Rule 4(c) states that neither a brief nor list of authorities is required for these motions: extension of time; to continue hearing, pretrial conference, or trial; to amend pleadings or file supplemental pleadings; to appoint guardian *ad litem*; for physical or mental examination; to add or substitute parties; to enter or vacate default judgment; to confirm sales; to stay proceedings; to enforce judgment; to shorten a prescribed time period; or to compel discovery.

OKLAHOMA SUPREME COURT[4]
Court Clerk (405/521-2163)
Referee (405/521-3849)
Room One, State Capitol Building
Oklahoma City, Oklahoma 73105

Number of Copies Filed:	Original and 15. Rule 17, Supreme Court Rules. **One copy must also be filed with the Clerk of the trial court concurrently with its filing in appellate court** per Rule 1.28(d), Rules of Appellate Procedure in Civil Cases.
Page Number Limit:	30 pages **excluding** tables and indices. Rule 19, Supreme Court Rules.
Bound:	Yes (on left-hand side with spiral binding so that it opens flat). Rules 18 and 19, Supreme Court Rules. No color requirement for cover stock.
Form of Typed Briefs:	Pica type (10 spaces per inch); double-spaced; 1-1/4" left margin; 1" right margin; 1" top and bottom margins. Rules 18 and 19, Supreme Court Rules.
Cover Page:	Yes (see attached example)(**must contain docket #, title of case, county and Court or forum from which appeal is taken, name of trial judge, name/ address of attorney for party filing brief, and nature of action**). Rule 13, Supreme Court Rules. *See also* Rules 18 and 19, Supreme Court Rules 18 (form of printed briefs) and 19 (format for typewritten briefs), Supreme Court Rules. *See* example attached.
Table of Contents and Authorities:	Yes. *See* Rule 14, Supreme Court Rules, and attached form for specific requirements and format.
Citation Form:	Citation of authorities shall be to the volume and page of the National Reporter System or some other selected case system, if practical. Rule 21, Supreme Court Rules.
Appendices for Exhibits:	**Not favored** by the court. *See* Rule 19, Supreme Court Rules.
Due Dates for Filing:	*See* Rule 1.28(a), Rules of Appellate Procedure. **Brief in Chief:** within 60 days from receipt of notice of completion of the record. **NOTE: Brief in Chief must have an "abstract of the record."** **Answer Brief:** within 40 days from date the appellant's brief in chief is filed. **Reply Brief:** within 20 days from date the appellee's answer brief is filed. **Cross-Appellant's Reply Brief** (to Answer Brief on Cross-Appeal): within 20 days from date of filing answer brief on cross-appeal by appellant.
Other Rules:	Except for copies of cases relied upon, materials not part of the appellate record may not be copied in, or attached to, the brief. Rule 19, Supreme Court Rules.

---

[4]NOTE: Check Rules 10, 13 through 19, and 21 through 24, Rules of the Supreme Court, for other requirements.

WESTERN DISTRICT OF OKLAHOMA
200 Northwest 4th Street
Oklahoma City, Oklahoma 73102
Court Clerk: 405/231-4792

<u>**Motions Not Requiring Briefs Pursuant to Local Rule 14(C)**</u>: extensions of time; to continue pretrial conference, hearing, motion or trial; to amend pleadings; to file supplemental pleadings; to appoint next friend or guardian *ad litem*; for substitution of parties; or motions to compel answers to **interrogatories**.

Number of Copies Filed:	Original and one copy. Local Rule 13(A).
Page Number Limit:	Not more than 25 pages with special leave of court per Local Rules 13(C) and 14(B). Reply and supplemental briefs, no more than 10 pages. Local Rules 13(B) and (C).
Bound:	Not required; if bound, Court Clerk prefers 2-hole punch at the top with an ACCO fastener. **Do not use spiral binding.**
Cover Page:	Not required, but improves the look of any lengthy brief. Can use bond paper for cover page. No color requirements for cover page.
Title:	Must show whether opening, opposition, reply, or supplemental, application or proceeding to which it relates, and part on whose behalf it is presented; briefs shall refer to previous briefs filed relating to the same matter. Local Rule 13(B).
Table of Contents/ Authorities:	**YES, IF BRIEF EXCEEDS 15 PAGES.** Local Rule 13(C). *See* attached example.
Citation Form:	When citing U.S. Supreme Court cases, use only U.S. Supreme Court Reports (U.S.) and Lawyers Edition (L.Ed.) Any city/governmental authority having the force of law shall also be cited and quoted in the brief. (Also applies to any statutes foreign to the court's jurisdiction.) Local Rule 13(E).
Summary Judgment Briefs:	*See* Local Rule 14(B). Brief in support of motion must begin with concise numbered statement of material facts to which no genuine issue exists and must have references to record supporting those facts. Brief opposing motion must begin with concise numbered statement of material facts to which genuine issue exists and must have references to record supporting those facts and the # of movant's fact that is disputed.
Other Rules:	Local Rule 14(D)(clerk shall not accept for filing any motion, etc., requiring a brief, unless accompanied by such brief, without permission of the Court.)

U.S. COURT OF APPEALS FOR THE TENTH CIRCUIT
Office of the Clerk
The Byron White U.S. Courthouse
1823 Stout Street
Denver, Colorado 80257
Court Clerk: (303) 844-3157
Opal Carter: (303) 844-5019

Number of
Copies Filed: Original and 7 copies. 10th Cir. R. 31.6. Carbon copies not accepted except by indigent pro se litigant.

Page Number
Limit: **Appellant**: 50 pages, not including index, Table of Contents and Authorities, and
(FRAP 28(g)   Certificate of Service.

     Appellee: 50 pages, not including index, Table of Contents and Authorities, and Certificate of Service.

     First and Second Cross-Appeal Briefs: 50 pages, not including index, Table of Contents and Authorities, and Certificate of Service.

     Reply: 25 pages, not including index, Table of Contents and Authorities, and Certificate of Service.

     **Court discourages motions to exceed page limits; if such motion is filed within 10 days of brief's due date, must show why earlier filing was not practicable. 10th Cir. R. 28.3.

Bound: Not required, but if cover stock is used, use these colors (FRAP 32(a)):
Appellant -- Blue.
Appellee -- Red.
Reply -- Gray.
Amicus or Intervenor -- Green.
Response to Reply (if Court grants leave to file) -- White.

Cover Page: Required by FRAP 32(a)(**must contain** name of court and case #, title of case (*see* Rule 12(a)), nature of proceeding (*e.g.*, Appeal), name of court below, title (*e.g.*, Brief of Appellant), and names/address of counsel of party on whose behalf brief is filed. **Must also state if oral argument is desired** and, if so, must include statement of reason after conclusion stating relief sought. 10th Cir. R. 28.2(f).

Table of Contents/
Authorities: Yes. *See* attached example. FRAP 28(a)(1). Table of Authorities to include cases (alphabetically arranged), statutes, and other authorities cited with references to pages in brief where cited. Must append list of prior appeals to Table of Authorities. If there are none, that must also be stated. *See* 10th Cir. R. 28.2.

Spacing: Must be double-spaced. Space and one-half will not be accepted. *See* 10th Cir. R. 32.1(a).

Appendix:	Required; must contain chronological excerpts of record sufficient for consideration and determination of issues on appeal. Copies of record must not be certified but should have district court's "filed" stamp. 10th Cir. R. 30.1, 30.1.1, 30.1.2, 30.1.3, 30.1.4, and 30.3 and FRAP 32.
Supplemental Appendix:	Appellee may file if Appellant's omits items which should have been included. Must be in same form as Appellant's Appendix. 10th Cir. R. 30.1.2 and 30.2 and FRAP 32.
References to Record:	References to Appendix: Aplt. App. at 27 or Aplee. Supp. App. at 14. References to record (where no appendix): Doc. 4 at 6; Tr. Vol. VII at 37 or Tr. 8/31/91 at 37. *See* FRAP 28(e) and 10th Cir. R. 28.1
Other Rules:	*Check* FRAP 28(a) through (h), 31, and 32; 10th Cir. R. 28.1, 28.2(a) through (f), 30.1.3, 30.1.4, 31.1 through 31.6, 32.1, and 34.1.9.

Cover Sheet—Oklahoma Supreme Court Format

No. 11, 111
District Court No. CJ-94-1111-XX

IN THE SUPREME COURT OF THE STATE OF OKLAHOMA

NAME(S) OF PLAINTIFF(S),

Plaintiff/Appellant,
(OR Plaintiff/Appellee,)

v.

NAME(S) OF DEFENDANT(S),

Defendant/Appellee.
(OR Defendant/Appellant.)

APPEAL FROM THE DISTRICT COURT OF _____ COUNTY

THE HONORABLE _____, PRESIDING

ACTION FOR NEGLIGENCE AND WRONGFUL DEATH

PLAINTIFF/APPELLANT'S BRIEF IN CHIEF

Name of Attorney, OBA#
Name of Law Firm
Address
City, State, Zip Code
Telephone Number

Attorney for
Plaintiff/Appellant

Date of Filing

Oklahoma Supreme Court Format	

TABLE OF CONTENTS AND AUTHORITIES

IN THE UNITED STATES DISTRICT COURT

FOR THE WESTERN DISTRICT OF OKLAHOMA

Case No. CIV-91-778-W

NANCY E. WHEELER,

Plaintiff,

v.

THE CITY OF OKLAHOMA CITY,

Defendant.

DEFENDANT CITY OF OKLAHOMA CITY'S BRIEF IN SUPPORT
OF ITS MOTION FOR SUMMARY JUDGMENT OR, IN THE ALTERNATIVE,
MOTION FOR SUMMARY JUDGMENT ON PLAINTIFF'S FEDERAL CLAIMS
AND MOTION TO DISMISS ON PLAINTIFF'S PENDENT STATE CLAIMS

ORAL ARGUMENT IS (NOT) DESIRED.

[This is necessary for 10th Cir. cover sheets only -- see 10th Cir. R. 28.2(f)]

James G. Hamill
Municipal Counselor
Richard C. Smith
Litigation Division Head
Assistant Municipal Counselor
200 North Walker
309 Municipal Building
Oklahoma City, Oklahoma 73102
Telephone: 405/297-2451

December 2, 1991

Attorneys for Defendant
City of Oklahoma City

Table of Contents Format—10th Circuit Court, State District Courts, and Federal District Courts

TABLE OF CONTENTS

Table of Authorities Format—10th Circuit Court, State District Courts, and Federal District Courts

TABLE OF AUTHORITIES

APPENDIX G
Sample Trial Brief

IN THE DISTRICT COURT OF CLEVELAND COUNTY
STATE OF OKLAHOMA

Jane Healy,   )
)
    Plaintiff,   )
)
v.   )   No. 94-1115
)
XYZ SEAT BELT, INC.   )
a Delaware Corporation,   )
)
    Defendant.   )

BRIEF OF PLAINTIFF

S.T. Associate (OBA#100000)
SMITH & ELWELL, L.L.P.
12345 Main Street
Norman, OK 73072
(405) 555-5555

ATTORNEY FOR PLAINTIFF

March 16, 1995

TABLE OF CONTENTS

TABLE OF AUTHORITIES

IN THE DISTRICT COURT OF CLEVELAND COUNTY
STATE OF OKLAHOMA

Jane Healy,	)	
	)	
Plaintiff,	)	
v.	)	No. 94-1115
	)	
XYZ SEAT BELT, INC.	)	
a Delaware Corporation,	)	
	)	
Defendant.	)	

BRIEF OF PLAINTIFF

STATEMENT OF FACTS

On March, 4, 1994, Ms. Healy was on her way home from work. As Ms. Healy drove through an intersection, traffic in front of her stopped suddenly. Ms. Healy slammed on her brakes to avoid hitting the car in front of her. When the light changed, Ms. Healy remained stranded in the intersection because the traffic in front of her remained at a stand-still. Charles Raymond, driving drunk, sped into the intersection and hit Ms. Healy's car broadside. Raymond's car smashed Ms. Healy's car into a steel power pole.

At the moment of impact with the pole, Ms. Healy's seat belt broke. The belt was designed, manufactured and installed by XYZ. Ms. Healy's face smashed through the car's front windshield. She suffered a fractured skull, three broken ribs, a punctured lung and very deep cuts on her face. To date, Ms. Healy has undergone three plastic surgeries on her face. However, her face will remain forever scarred.

Ms. Healy's car is only two years old. The seat belt that broke during the automobile accident was the seat belt originally installed in Ms. Healy's car. Prior to the accident, Ms. Healy had no problem with the seat belt, nor did she have any repairs or mechanical adjustments made to the seat belt.

Ms. Healy is a successful public relations specialist. Before the accident, she was told that she would become the head of her large public relations department when her boss retired within four months. However, because of the accident, Ms. Healy has been unable to fulfill her public relation duties for the past year. The public relations firm was forced to replace Ms. Healy. In her position, Ms. Healy earned $55,000 annually. With the expected promotion, her salary would have increased to $70,000.

> I.   BECAUSE THE SEAT BELT XYZ DESIGNED, MANUFACTURED AND INSTALLED IN MS. HEALY'S CAR WAS DEFECTIVE, MS. HEALY SUSTAINED INJURIES MORE SERIOUS THAN SHE WOULD HAVE SUFFERED HAD XYZ'S PRODUCT BEEN PROPERLY OPERATING; THEREFORE, XYZ IS STRICTLY LIABLE FOR MS. HEALY'S INJURIES
>
> > A.   Because the defective seat belt XYZ manufactured caused Ms. Healy to sustain additional injuries during an automobile accident, XYZ is strictly liable to plaintiff for her enhanced injuries under the manufacturer's product liability theory.

This is a case of first impression in this jurisdiction. Other jurisdictions have statutes similar to this jurisdiction's manufacturer's product liability statute.

Under the manufacturer's product liability statutes, a manufacturer that sells any defective product is strictly liable for the harm the defective product causes. In *Perez v. Ford Motor Company,* 497 F.2d 82 (5th Cir. 1974), which involves one such statute, the court outlined the elements a plaintiff must prove to recover under manufacturer's liability. In *Perez,* the court held that a manufacturer was strictly liable for the death of a woman who died when the truck cab in which she riding overturned upon impact with another vehicle. *Perez* at 86.

The *Perez* court held that the manufacturer is strictly liable for the injuries the manufacturer's product causes if the product was defective and unreasonably dangerous. *Id.* If the product defect is such that a reasonable seller would not sell the product if the seller knew of the risks involved or if the risks of injury are greater than a reasonable buyer would expect, the manufacturer is liable. *Id.* at 87.

The facts of the case at bar fulfill the requirements of *Perez.* A reasonable seller would not sell an automobile with a seat belt that would not operate properly during an accident. Safety during an accident is, after all, the primary purpose of seat belts. Therefore, because the risk of harm is so great that a reasonable seller would not sell a defective seat belt, XYZ is strictly liable for Ms. Healy's injuries.

In addition, the risks involved with XYZ's defective seat belt are greater than a reasonable buyer would expect. The intended purpose of a seat belt is to protect passengers from serious injury during accidents. A reasonable buyer would certainly expect a seat belt to restrain the user from crashing into the windshield during an accident. A reasonable buyer would not expect that the seat belt would break during an accident, when the driver needed the seat belt the most. Clearly, the defective seat belt did not operate as a reasonable buyer would expect. Therefore, because the seat belt allowed Ms. Healy to smash into the windshield of her car contrary to the expectations of a reasonable buyer, XYZ is strictly liable for Ms. Healy's injuries.

Ms. Healy is seeking damages only for her enhanced injuries attributable to the broken seat belt. Damages for injuries a person inside a vehicle receives because the manufacturer's product does not properly operate, are recoverable. *Higginbotham v. Ford Motor Company,* 540 F.2d 762, 766 (5th Cir. 1976).

In *Higginbotham* the court held that where the manufacturer could have substantially lessened the "second impact" injuries, the manufacturer is liable for the enhanced injuries. *Higginbotham* at 766. The *Higginbotham* court held that a truck manufacturer was liable when the truck's wheel suspension broke upon impact and crushed the passenger in the front seat of the truck. *Id.* The *Higginbotham* court reasoned that because the manufacturer's product enhanced the user's injuries, the manufacturer should be liable for the injuries the manufacturer could have prevented. *Id.* at 774. Where the court can apportion the damages between the tortfeasor responsible for the first impact and the manufacturer responsible for the increased injuries of the second impact, the injured person can sue the manufacturer in a separate action. *Id.*

Ms. Healy received additional and enhanced injuries during the automobile accident because the seat belt did not operate properly. If the seat belt had not broken, the seat belt would have protected Ms. Healy from hitting her face and head on the front windshield.

The fact that the seat belt was not the cause of the first impact is irrelevant. *See Caiazzo v. Volkwagen,* 647 F.2d 241, 246 (2d Cir. 1981) (liability exists under second impact doctrine where defect enhances plaintiff's first impact injuries caused by third party); *Spier v. Barker,* 323 N.E.2d 164, 169 (N.Y. 1974) (if party can prove seat belt would have lessened injuries, damages can be apportioned). Expert testimony can then compare the injuries Ms. Healy would have sustained with Ms. Healy's actual injuries. Therefore, because the enhancement of Ms. Healy's injuries attributable to XYZ's defective seat belt can be determined, XYZ is liable for Ms. Healy's second-impact injuries.

> B.   Because Ms. Healy did not know the seat belt was defective, assumption of
> risk is no defense to this action.

Contributory negligence is no defense to this action. In *Melia v. Ford Motor Company,* 354 F.2d 795 (8th Cir. 1976), the court discussed the defenses available to a manufacturer in a strict liability action.

The court held that regardless of the plaintiff's negligent driving, the car manufacturer was liable for the plaintiff's injuries when the plaintiff's door latch broke during an automobile accident and the plaintiff was thrown from his car. *Melia* at 802.

The *Melia* court held that the manufacturer cannot use a contributory negligence defense to bar the plaintiff's recovery. *Id.* at 801 (citing Restatement (Second) of Torts §402A). Only where the plaintiff knows of the unreasonable danger and assumes the risk of the danger can a manufacturer raise an assumption of risk defense. *Id.*

Even if Ms. Healy can be found contributorily negligent by entering into the intersection when the light was yellow, Ms. Healy's driving is irrelevant to her recovery. Ms. Healy did not know of the defect in the seat belt. She relied on the belt to reduce the possibility of serious second-impact injury. Therefore, because Ms. Healy did not know the seat belt was defective, XYZ cannot raise the assumption of risk doctrine to bar Ms. Healy's recovery for the second impact injuries.

Further, many courts have narrowed the application of the assumption of risk doctrine in strict liability actions. In *Holt v. Deere & Company*, 24 F.3d 1289, 1293 (10th Cir. 1994), the court stated that a plaintiff cannot be barred from recovery merely because the plaintiff was careless.

In *Holt* the manufacturer could not rely on assumption of risk to bar the plaintiff's recovery where the plaintiff was injured after he started a tractor while standing in front of one of the tractor's wheels. *Id.* The *Holt* court reasoned that the manufacturer could not invoke the assumption of risk doctrine where the plaintiff was not aware of the dangers in using the product in the manner in which the plaintiff used it. *Id.* The plaintiff's ignorance or false sense of security about the effectiveness of the product does not bar the plaintiff's recovery. *Id.* Ms. Healy did not have problems with her seat belt prior to the accident.

Drivers assume the seat belt will protect them during an accident. XYZ cannot be encouraged to continue to create defective products on the belief that XYZ will escape liability when the car is involved in an accident.

CONCLUSION

In this jurisdiction, a plaintiff can recover from the manufacturer of a defective product based upon a strict liability theory for injuries the manufacturer's product caused. XYZ designed, manufactured and installed in Jane Healy's car a defective seat belt. During an automobile accident, the seat belt that Jane Healy expected to protect her from serious injury failed. As a direct result, Jane Healy's head and face smashed into the car's front window.

Jane Healy claims damages only for the enhanced injuries she sustained as a result of the defective seat belt. Under Oklahoma's second-impact defect theory, Jane Healy is entitled to damages for the enhanced injuries she sustained because the seat belt failed.

Contributory negligence is not a defense to a manufacturer's product liability claim. Moreover, because Ms. Healy did not know that the seat belt was defective and would break during an automobile accident, XYZ cannot raise the assumption of risk doctrine to bar Ms. Healy's recovery.

Respectfully Submitted,

S.T. Richards, OBA#10000A
Smith & Elwell, L.L.P.
12345 Main Street
Norman, OK 73072
(405) 555-5555

ATTORNEY FOR PLAINTIFF

APPENDIX H

Motion for Protective Order and Supporting Brief

IN THE UNITED STATES DISTRICT COURT

FOR THE WESTERN DISTRICT OF MISSOURI

MARTHA G. BALLARD, ROBIN SUE   )
MARSHALL, MILO MAHAFFEY,   )
SAMUEL ANNIS, and HERMAN   )
BERNARD,   )
)
    Plaintiffs,   )
)
v.   )   Case No. CIV-95-0000
)
XYZ CORPORATION,   )
)
    Defendant.   )

DEFENDANT XYZ CORPORATION'S OBJECTION TO PLAINTIFF'S MOTION TO COMPEL AND DEFENDANT'S MOTION FOR PROTECTIVE ORDER AND BRIEF IN SUPPORT

Defendant XYZ Corporation ("Defendant") submits the following as its response to Plaintiffs' Motion to Compel Discovery filed on January 16, 1995. In their Motion, Plaintiffs, five managerial employees in the Defendant's Missouri branch headquarters, ask the Court to enter an order:

(1) directing Defendant to present designated corporate representatives for deposition pursuant to Fed.R.Civ.P. 30(b)(6); and

(2) designating Overland Park, Kansas, as the permanent site for all depositions of Defendant's corporate witnesses.

In addition to opposing Plaintiffs' Motion to Compel, Defendant contends that Plaintiffs have improperly sought the deposition testimony of certain fact witnesses who are not officers, directors, or managing agents of Defendant, contrary to the purpose of Rule 30(b)(6). Further, Defendant asserts that Plaintiffs have sought the production of documents in conjunction with these depositions without complying with Fed.R.Civ.P. 34. Accordingly, Defendant requests that Plaintiffs' Motion to Compel be denied, and further moves this Court for an appropriate Protective Order pursuant to Rule 26(c) to prevent Plaintiffs from improperly using Rule 30(b)(6) Notices to:

(1) require witnesses to leave their residences and come to Overland Park;

(2) obtain the deposition testimony of fact witnesses who are not officers, directors, or managing partners of Defendant XYZ Corporation; and

(3) require the production of documents in conjunction with such depositions without complying with Rule 34.

INTRODUCTION

In their third Motion to Enlarge Deadlines Set at Status Conference, filed contemporaneously with their Motion to Compel, Plaintiffs advised this Court that Defendant has produced over 20,000 documents to date and that over 50 potential witnesses had been identified. Plaintiffs stated that these witnesses, all of whom are Defendant's employees, are scattered throughout the country and additional time is needed to conduct their depositions.

Plaintiffs have already deposed ten witnesses, five in Overland Park, four in Topeka, Kansas, and one in Lincoln, Nebraska. Plaintiffs now ask this Court to designate Overland Park as the "permanent deposition site of corporate witnesses," evidently meaning any employee of Defendant's who is a potential witness. Plaintiffs also wish to require Defendant to bring such witnesses to Overland Park at Defendant's expense.

Plaintiffs are not asking Defendant to produce one, or even a limited number, of designated corporate representatives to testify about Defendant's position on certain issues and to provide the identities and locations of specific fact witnesses. Instead, Plaintiffs are attempting to use multiple Rule 30(b)(6) Notices to force a corporate defendant to bring a potentially large number of fact witnesses to their own doorstep.

In each of their Rule 30(b)(6) Notices, Plaintiffs carefully tailored the matters for inquiry to require designation of certain specific individuals who are the only persons who could testify about that information. Plaintiffs know the identity of these witnesses and their locations, but their Rule 30(b)(6) Notices carefully avoid identifying them by name. Instead, Plaintiffs state the factual matters to be inquired into in such a way as to force production of specific individuals possessing such factual knowledge.

For example, the Notice attached as Exhibit "A" to Plaintiffs' Motion to Compel called for Defendant's designated witness to appear on December 1, 1994 to testify about 15 detailed factual matters. As Plaintiffs are aware, there is only one person who possesses knowledge of these matters—Julius Nesbitt. The following day, Defendant received yet another Notice, Exhibit "B" to Plaintiffs' Motion, for the deposition of the witness designated by Defendant to appear for deposition and testify about an additional 10 detailed factual matters. Again, as Plaintiffs are aware, there is only person who possesses knowledge of those matters—Jefferson Kingsley.

In each of their Rule 30(b)(6) Notices, Plaintiffs have directed the designated witness to bring all documents available to the witness that relate "in any manner" to the listed areas of inquiry. In a discussion held on December 15, 1994, counsel for Defendant advised Plaintiffs' counsel that corporate documents would only be produced in response to requests in compliance with Rule 34. Defendant's counsel stated that the requested documents—approximately 20,000 to date—had already been produced. Plaintiffs' counsel responded that Plaintiffs wanted the designated witnesses to independently search for and bring those documents to their depositions, even if this duplicated previously produced documents.

ARGUMENT AND AUTHORITIES

I. DEFENDANT SHOULD NOT BE COMPELLED TO PRODUCE DESIGNATED CORPORATE REPRESENTATIVES FOR DEPOSITIONS IN OVERLAND PARK, KANSAS.

Plaintiff's Motion is grounded on two essential facts:

1. Plaintiffs are effectively indigent and unable to bear the expenses associated with depositions anywhere but Overland Park; and
2. Defendant's employees and prospective designees travel frequently to conduct business for Defendant and, therefore, it would not be burdensome to Defendant or those employees to travel to Overland Park.

Plaintiffs also argue that, if these depositions were held outside of Overland Park, they would be denied an opportunity to assist their counsel because they cannot afford travel and lodging and time away from their employment.

Such arguments are ludicrous. Plaintiffs seek in excess of $200 million in damages from Defendant. Plaintiffs have engaged the services of three law firms, one of which is in Nebraska and one in California. Plaintiffs have served numerous discovery requests upon Defendant, and in response, Defendant has produced in excess of 20,000 documents. Plaintiffs now ask this Court to shift their burden of discovery costs to Defendant simply on the ground that Defendant is better able to bear the expense. Interestingly enough, Plaintiffs cite no authorities in their Motion to Compel which supports this position.

Plaintiffs attached several Affidavits to their Motion to Compel which state that it would be a minor inconvenience to the deponents/employees of Defendant to come to Overland Park for their depositions. Further, these Affidavits claim that Defendant has "corporate jets" on standby to transport these deponents to and from Overland Park, thus avoiding inconvenient airline schedules.

Regardless of whether such statements are relevant, they are certainly not true. The one Lear jet owned by Defendant is fully scheduled. Even if it were available, it could hardly accommodate the number of deponents or the deposition schedule contemplated by Plaintiffs. The Affidavits of George N. Ketcherside and William R. Neatherlin attached as Exhibits "A" and "B," show that compliance with Plaintiffs' demands would actually cause real hardship, not the minor inconvenience claimed by Plaintiffs.

In support of their Motion to Compel, Plaintiffs cite no authorities from this judicial district or the Eighth Circuit Court of Appeals. It is a well-established rule of law in this jurisdiction that a plaintiff seeking the deposition of a non-resident defendant must take the deposition at the defendant's place of residence or employment. *General Leasing Co. v. Lawrence Photo-Graphic Supply, Inc.,* 84 F.R.D. 130, 131 (W.D. Mo. 1979). None of the cases cited by Plaintiffs are controlling in this case, and none of the 30(b)(6) Notices in those cases involved the overwhelming number of areas sought to be covered or the large number of corporate designees as in the instant case.

One of the cases relied upon by Plaintiffs, *Terry v. Modern Woodmen of America,* 57 F.R.D. 141 (W.D. Mo. 1972), is no longer the controlling law in this jurisdiction. In *Terry,* a local plaintiff was successful in requiring one employee of the non-resident corporate defendant to travel to the litigation forum to give a deposition. The plaintiff relied heavily on his unfortunate financial situation, vis-a-vis the corporate defendant.

However, in *General Leasing Co. v. Lawrence Photo-Graphic Supply, Inc.,* 84 F.R.D. 130 (W.D. Mo. 1979), this Court noted that the weight of authority and current local practice required departure from *Terry.* The Court enunciated the following as the prevailing law in this district:

In the absence of exceptional or unusual circumstances, when a deponent resides at a substantial distance from the deposing party's residence, the deposing party should be required to take the deposition at a location in the vicinity in which the deponent resides, even if the deponent is a party. *Id.* at 131, *quoting* Order filed August 15, 1979, in *Timmons v. PPG Industries, Inc.,* No. 76-CV-0652-W-6 (W.D. Mo.).

To date, *General Leasing,* which Plaintiffs failed to cite in their Motion to Compel, is the prevailing law on this issue.

II. RULE 30(b)(6) NOTICES MAY NOT BE USED TO COMPEL TESTIMONY OF SPECIFIC CORPORATE EMPLOYEES WHO ARE NOT OFFICERS, DIRECTORS, OR MANAGING AGENTS.

Rule 30(b)(6) allows a party to name a public or private corporation as a deponent and describe with reasonable particularity the matters on which such an examination is requested. The corporation then must designate "one or more officers, directors, or managing agents, or other persons who consent to testify on its behalf, and may set forth, for each person designated, the matters on which the person will testify." Fed.R.Civ.P. 30(b)(6).

In their 30(b)(6) Notices served on Defendant, Plaintiffs seek deposition testimony from various designated witnesses. These witnesses are not identified by name, but the Notices frame the matters so narrowly that specific individuals must be presented by Defendant for these depositions. Plaintiffs already know the identity and location of these employee-witnesses and could easily subpoena them by name.

In many instances, these witnesses are not officers, directors, or managing agents. They are merely corporate employees who may possess some factual information of the matters involved in this lawsuit. By using Rule 30(b)(6) Notices instead of deposition subpoenas for these witnesses, Plaintiffs are attempting to elevate them to the level of corporate spokespersons.

The contrast between witnesses who are corporate employees or corporate spokespersons is clearly defined in *Cleveland v. Palmby,* 75 F.R.D. 654, 656 (W.D. Okla. 1977):

A distinction must be drawn between a mere corporate employee and those who may be regarded as speaking for the corporation. Except where the employee has been designated by the corporation under Rule 30(b)(6), as a witness who consents to testify on behalf of the corporation, or is an officer, director, or managing agent of the corporation, an employee is treated in the same way as any other witness. His presence must be obtained by subpoena rather than by notice and sanctions cannot be imposed against the corporation if he fails to appear. (Citations omitted.)

See also 8 C. Wright & A. Miller, *Federal Practice and Procedure: Civil* § 2103 (1988). Thus, unless properly designated, corporate employees must be treated as non-parties. *W.R. Grace & Co. v. Pullman, Inc.,* 74 F.R.D. 80 (W.D. Okla. 1977).

Plaintiffs have not actually named the specific employee witnesses sought in the Notices. It is clear that to do so would be an improper use of the 30(b)(6) Notice. In *Cleveland v. Palmby, supra,* the court stated:

Rule 30(b)(6), *supra,* provides that a party who is unable to name the specific employee or agent of an organization that he wishes to depose, can simply name the organization as the deponent and describe with reasonable particularity the matters on which examination is requestion . . . . This Rule does not provide that a party can specifically name an employee of an organization and then require the organization to designate such employee as a witness to testify on behalf of the organization.

Cleveland v. Palmby, 75 F.R.D. at 657.

Plaintiffs have attempted to avoid this clear prohibition by artful wording of the matters for inquiry. Plaintiffs should not be allowed to do indirectly, by focusing on the areas of inquiry, that which they could not do directly by naming the only witnesses who have that information. To the extent necessary, this Court should, for good cause shown, enter a Protective Order pursuant to Fed.R.Civ.P. 26.

III. THE RULE 30(b)(6) NOTICES FILED BY PLAINTIFFS FAILED TO COMPLY WITH FED.R.CIV.P. 34.

Plaintiffs have attempted to circumvent the requirements of Rule 34, Fed.R.Civ.P., in seeking the production of numerous documents by witnesses to be designated by Defendant. Rule 30(b) (5), Fed.R.Civ.P., provides in pertinent part:

> The notice to the party deponent may be accompanied by a request made in compliance with Rule 34 for the production of documents and tangible things at the taking of the deposition. The procedure of Rule 34 shall apply to the request.

As noted in *Contardo v. Merrill Lynch, Pierce, Fenner & Smith,* 119 F.R.D. 622, 624 (D. Mass. 1988):

> While it is permissible pursuant to Rule 30(b) (5), F.R.Civ.P., to serve a request for production of documents to a party at the same time as a notice of deposition on that party is served and to seek production of the documents at the deposition, the request for production of documents must comply with the provisions of Rule 34, F.R.Civ.P.

Rule 34 provides that the party upon whom the request is served shall serve a written response within 30 days after service of the request. The Notices served by Plaintiffs do not allow for that 30-day period or for a written response. Accordingly, the Notices are improper and do not comply with Rule 34.

In addition, as noted above, Defendant has already produced in excess of 20,000 documents pursuant to Plaintiffs' numerous discovery requests. To require designated representatives of Defendant to search for and produce the same documents previously produced in conjunction with their depositions is duplicative, burdensome, and unreasonable. As a result, Defendant should not be required to produce any additional documents, and an appropriate Protective Order pursuant to Rule 26 should be entered by this Court.

CONCLUSION

The use of a Rule 30(b)(6) Notice rather than subpoenaing known fact witnesses in an attempt to make them corporate spokespersons is a misuse of the Rule, and should not be allowed by this Court. Even where Rule 30(b)(6) is properly used, designated representatives should not be required to leave their residence location and come to Overland Park for Plaintiffs' convenience. Finally, Plaintiffs' requests for documents in a Rule 30(b)(6) Notice must comply with Fed.R.Civ.P. 34.

Defendant requests this Court to deny Plaintiffs' Motion to Compel and to enter a Protective Order pursuant to Fed.R.Civ.P. 26(c) to prevent Plaintiffs from improperly using Fed.R.Civ.P. 30(b)(6) Notices to (1) require witnesses to leave their residences and come to Overland Park, (2) obtain the deposition testimony of fact witnesses who are not officers, directors, or managing partners of Defendant XYZ Corporation, and (3) require the production of documents in conjunction with such depositions without complying with Fed.R.Civ.P. 34. Defendant XYZ Corporation further requests the Court pursuant to Fed.R.Civ.P. 26(c) and 37(a)(4) to allow Defendant to recover its attorney fees and costs incurred in defending against Plaintiffs' Motion and prosecuting its own Motion for Protective Order.

Respectfully submitted,

NEELY, STIERWALT & CLEMENCEAU

_____

Jane St. Andrews
500 South University Boulevard
Suite 2400
Kansas City, Missouri
Telephone: 816/848-0674

ATTORNEYS FOR DEFENDANT XYZ
CORPORATION

<u>CERTIFICATE OF MAILING</u>

This is to certify that a true and correct copy of Defendant XYZ Corporation's Objection To Plaintiffs' Motion to Compel and Defendant'S Motion for Protective Order and Brief in Support was mailed, postage prepaid, on the ____day of January, 1995, to:

Candace Rombauer
Delton, Wren & Rombauer, P.C.
200 North Main, Suite 1700
Lincoln, Nebraska
David Cosmos
Cosmos and Weinberger, P.C.
416 Country Club Plaza
La Jolla, California 92037

Thomas C. Wolleson
Wolleson & Associates, P.C.
900 Frontage Road, Suite 203
Overland Park, Kansas

ATTORNEYS FOR PLAINTIFFS

_____

Jane St. Andrews

<u>AFFIDAVIT OF GEORGE N. KETCHERSIDE</u>

STATE OF NEW JERSEY   )
)   SS.
COUNTY OF SOMERSET   )

Affiant George N. Ketcherside, of lawful age and duly sworn upon his oath, deposes and states:

1. I have been employed by XYZ Corporation since May 11, 1985. In April 1994, I was promoted to Branch Manager and, in July 1994, I became the Area Manager for all of Northern New Jersey.

2. Several months ago, I was appointed President of a new subsidiary of XYZ Corporation, XYZ Enterprises, Inc., located in Basking Ridge, New Jersey.

3. XYZ Enterprises, Inc. is still in the organizational stages, and it is my responsibility as its President to acquire the necessary staff and set up this new facility.

4. My present office address is 614 Blackwell Court, Suite 700, Basking Ridge, New Jersey 07920. My duties as President of XYZ Enterprises, Inc., especially in these formative stages, require that I be present in New Jersey on a daily basis.

5. Because of the flight schedules between New Jersey and Kansas City, giving a deposition in Overland Park would take me away from new Jersey for at least three days, which would constitute an extreme hardship at this critical time for XYZ Enterprises, Inc.

6. None of my regular business travel takes me in proximity to Kansas or Missouri, and a special trip would be required if I were to give my deposition in Overland Park, Kansas.

FURTHER AFFIANT SAYETH NOT.
DATED THIS _____ day of February, 1995.

                                        _____
                                        George N. Ketcherside

STATE OF NEW JERSEY   )
)
COUNTY OF SOMERSET)   SS.

Subscribed and sworn to before me this _____ day of February, 1995.

                                        _____
                                        Notary Public

My Commission Expires:
[Seal]

_____

AFFIDAVIT OF WILLIAM R. NEATHERLIN

STATE OF TEXAS   )
)   SS.
COUNTY OF DALLAS   )

Affiant William R. Neatherlin, of lawful age and duly sworn upon his oath, deposes and states:

1. I have been employed by XYZ Corporation since October 12, 1980, and have been an Area Manager since January 1, 1988. I am in charge of operations for Northern Texas, Oklahoma, Kansas, and Western Missouri, and my office is located in Dallas, Texas.

2. The headquarters for XYZ Corporation is New York City, New York. I report directly to the Regional Vice President for the Southern Region in Raleigh, North Carolina, who in turn reports directly to corporate headquarters in New York City.

3. XYZ Corporation has less than one hundred employees in Kansas and Missouri combined. The branch offices in Kansas and Missouri have no relationship to any other state's branch offices, and are totally separate operations that report through me to Raleigh, and then to New York City as mentioned above.

4. There are no XYZ Corporation employees located outside of Kansas or Missouri who travel to or through Missouri or Kansas on a regular basis. Even though I have supervisory responsibility over the offices in Kansas and Missouri, I personally visit them infrequently.

5. Since January 1991, XYZ Corporation has had a company-wide policy to restrict business travel and expenses for cost reduction purposes. All business travel, for any reason, must be specifically approved in advance by a vice-president.

6. This severely restricted travel policy applies to all of XYZ Corporation's offices and subsidiaries, which now heavily rely on telecommunications, including teleconferencing for business meetings.

                 FURTHER AFFIANT SAYETH NOT.
                 DATED THIS _____ day of February, 1995.

                                      _____
                                      William R. Neatherlin

STATE OF TEXAS   )
)   SS.
COUNTY OF DALLAS   )

Subscribed and sworn to before me this ____ day of February, 1995.

                                        _____
                                      Notary Public

My Commission Expires:
[Seal]
_____

APPENDIX I
Deposition of Defendant

CHARLES LEE RAYMOND

1 IN THE UNITED STATES DISTRICT COURT FOR THE
   WESTERN DISTRICT OF OKLAHOMA
2

3 ELIZABETH JANE HEALY,   )
)
4   Plaintiff,   )
)
5 -vs-   )   No. CIV-94-1742-H
)
6 DANTE ALLEGRETTI, CHARLES LEE   )
   RAYMOND, AJAX, INC., BMW WORLD   )
7 MANUFACTURERS, INC., HANS GARTON   )
   IMPORT AUTOS, INC.,   )
8   )
            Defendants.   )
9

10

11
                        * * * * * *
12

13   DEPOSITION OF CHARLES LEE RAYMOND

14   TAKEN ON BEHALF OF THE PLAINTIFF

15   IN OKLAHOMA CITY, OKLAHOMA

16   ON AUGUST 10, 1994

                        * * * * * *
17

18

19

20

21

22

23

24 REPORTED BY: ELIZABETH J. CAMPBELL, CSR 162, CP, RPR
            228 ROBERT S. KERR, SUITE 110
25   OKLAHOMA CITY, OKLAHOMA 73102

CHARLES LEE RAYMOND

2

APPEARANCES

FOR THE PLAINTIFF:

        AMELIA PEPPER
        Attorney at Law
        Nowack & Buechner
        100 West Crown Street
        Oklahoma City, Oklahoma   73107

FOR THE DEFENDANTS:

        MATTHEW RODRIGUEZ
        Attorney at Law
        122 South Federal Avenue
        Oklahoma City, Oklahoma   73212

CONTENTS

PLAINTIFF EXHIBITS

*   *   *   *   *   *

CHARLES LEE RAYMOND

3

1 **S T I P U L A T I O N S**

2   IT IS HEREBY STIPULATED AND AGREED BY and between the

3 parties hereto, through their respective attorneys, that the

4 deposition of CHARLES LEE RAYMOND may be taken on behalf of

5 the Plaintiff, on August 10, 1995, in Oklahoma City,

6 Oklahoma, by Elizabeth J. Campbell, Certified Shorthand

7 Reporter for the State of Oklahoma, pursuant to agreement.

8   IT IS FURTHER STIPULATED AND AGREED BY and between

9 the parties hereto, through their respective attorneys, that

10 all objections, except as to the form of the question and

11 responsiveness of the answer, are reserved until the time of

12 trial, at which time they may be made with the same force

13 and effect as if made at the time of the taking of this

14 deposition.

15   * * * * * *

16

17

18

19

20

21

22

23

24

25

4

1   CHARLES LEE RAYMOND,

2 being first duly sworn, deposes and says in reply to the

3 questions propounded as follows:

4   DIRECT EXAMINATION

5 BY MS. PEPPER:

6   Q   Mr. Raymond, my name is Amelia Pepper. I'm

7 the attorney for Jane Healy, the plaintiff in this lawsuit.

8 The deposition that you are giving here today may be used as

9 evidence in the lawsuit that has been filed against you and

10 your employer.

11   Have you had a chance to talk to your attorney, Mr.

12 Rodriguez, about the purpose of depositions?

13   A   Yes.

14   Q   Do you understand that I get to ask you ques-

15 tions and that if you understand the question, any answer

16 you give me is what I will assume is the truth to that ques-

17 tion; is that correct?

18   A   Yes.

19   Q   Have you ever given your deposition before?

20   A   No.

21   Q   What is your full name?

22   A   Charles Lee Raymond.

23   Q   Do you understand that when I ask you ques-

24 tions, your answers will be made under oath?

25   A   Yeah.

CHARLES LEE RAYMOND

5

1   Q   Okay. Maybe I had better cover some ground

2 rules that might help both of us and the court reporter.

3 Because the court reporter can only take down verbal respons-

4 es, I'll ask that all of your replies be made verbally instead

5 of shaking or nodding your head, because she can't record that

6 you shook your head. So, no "huh-uhs" or "uh-huhs," or nod-

7 ding your head up and down or side to side. Okay?

8   A   Okay.

9   Q   And then, if you have a question or if you

10 want to stop at any time or need a break, there's no prob-

11 lem. Or if you need to talk with your attorney, just tell

12 us and we can break this at any time and give you that

13 opportunity. All right?

14   A   All right.

15   Q   Also, if I ask you a question and you don't

16 understand the question, will you please ask me to rephrase

17 it or repeat it until you do understand it?

18   A   You mean if I don't get what you're asking, I

19 should ask you what you mean?

20   Q   Exactly.

21   A   Okay. I can do that.

22   Q   Mr. Raymond, did you review anything, any doc-

23 uments, to prepare for your deposition today?

24   A   Mr. Rodriguez showed me a video about having

25 my deposition taken.

CHARLES LEE RAYMOND

6

1   MS. PEPPER: Is that just a standard deposition

2 videotape that you show your clients to prepare them for a

3 deposition?

4   MR. RODRIGUEZ: Right.   It's titled something like

5 "What Is A Deposition," or something like that.

6   Q   (BY MS. PEPPER)   Okay.   Did you look at any-

7 thing else to prepare for this deposition?

8   A   I looked over the questions you sent me, the

9 answers.

10   Q   The interrogatory answers?

11   A   Yeah.

12   Q   So you are familiar with the questions that

13 were given and the answers; is that correct?

14   A   Yes, ma'am.

15   Q   Okay.   Those are the interrogatories — let me

16 just show you.   In response to looking over these questions,

17 can you look at this document that I think is what you're

18 referring to?   Is that familiar to you as far as what you

19 reviewed today?

20   A   Yes.

21   Q   All right.   Then let me just get some back-

22 ground information from you.   What is your date of birth?

23   A   February 12, 1954.

24   Q   What is your address?

25   A   2408 North Riverview Drive in River City.

CHARLES LEE RAYMOND

7

1	Q	Is that a house or an apartment?
2	A	An apartment; I live in No. 412.
3	Q	How long have you lived there?
4	A	About three months.
5	Q	When did you move in?
6	A	The second week or so of June.
7	Q	Where did you live before that?
8	A	I lived at 219 Oaktree Court in River City.
9	Q	What that a house or an apartment?
10	A	House.
11	Q	Did you live with anyone else there?
12	A	Yes. I lived with my mom.
13	Q	How long did you live there?
14	A	About four years.
15	Q	So you lived there from when to when?
16	A	From about the end of July 1990 until June of
17	this year.	
18	Q	Did you pay rent?
19	A	No. My mom said I didn't have to.
20	Q	Where did you live before then?
21	A	I lived in — well, like a health resort.
22	Q	Health resort?
23	A	Sort of.
24	Q	What was the name of this place?
25	A	Whispering Hills.

CHARLES LEE RAYMOND

8

1	Q	Whispering Hills?
2	A	Yes.
3	Q	Is that a psychiatric hospital?
4	A	No, certainly not.

5   Q   Well, what health condition did you have that
6 led you to stay there?

7   A   I had a problem of sorts with an addictive
8 substance.

9   Q   "Of sorts." What kind of addiction did you
10 have?

11   A   I didn't have an addiction. I just was doing
12 a bit of drinking at the time. And I used marijuana occa-
13 sionally, not much. I wasn't really addicted to either,
14 really. But it seemed like a good idea to go there anyway.

15   Q   I see. How long were you in Whispering Hills?
16   A   Thirty days.
17   Q   How did you end up staying there?

18   A   Well, after my last — well, my mom and I
19 talked about things. She was worried about my health. She
20 worries really easy, you know, like all moms. And my dad
21 died from cirrhosis of the liver from drinking, so she kind
22 of overreacts any time anybody drinks alcohol. She wanted
23 me to check in somewhere and kind of get a grip on every-
24 thing, you know, so I did.

25   Q   Did you have insurance?

       A   No. My mother paid for it.

CHARLES LEE RAYMOND

9

1   Q   So you did not have any health insurance at

2   the time that would have paid for such a hospital stay?

3   A   No. My job didn't carry health insurance.

4   Q   Where did you live before you stayed at

5   Whispering Hills?

6   A   I lived with my girlfriend, Carla.

7   Q   Carla who?

8   A   Carla Mayer.

9   Q   Would you please spell that for me?

10   A   Sure. M-a-y-e-r.

11   Q   Where was this?

12   A   This was in Lexington, Oklahoma.

13   Q   What was your address?

14   A   619 Meadowlark Street.

15   Q   How long did you live at that address?

16   A   I lived there for about four months, from like

17   February of 1990 to late June of 1990.

18   Q   Did you pay rent then?

19   A   No. She owned the house.

20   Q   Now, let me get this straight. You lived with

21   Carla until the end of June 1990, and then you checked into

22   Whispering Hills in late July 1990.

23   Where did you live during July of 1990?

24   A   I think that was when I was in the county

25   jail. Yeah, it must have been right about that time.

CHARLES LEE RAYMOND

1	Q	You were in the county jail for what?
2	A	DUI.
3	Q	Was this your first?
4	A	No. It seems I had another one in 1986.
5	Q	So you've had two DUIs?
6	A	Yes, I think so.
7	Q	I don't want you to guess.
8		Do you know how many DUIs you've had, without
9	guessing?	
10	A	Yes, ma'am. I've had two, the one in 1990 and
11	the other one in 1986.	
12	Q	Any other convictions for drunk driving?
13	A	Convictions?
14	Q	Yes.
15	A	No.
16	Q	Any other arrests for drunk driving?
17	A	Arrests? You mean like a ticket or something?
18	Q	Yes.
19	A	Well, I got pulled over around last Christmas,
20	and the police took me in.	
21	Q	This was Christmas of last year? 1993?
22	A	Yes.
23	Q	Do you remember what you pled?
24	A	No, not really, because it got suspended.
25		MR. RODRIGUEZ: Counsel, I was his attorney for

CHARLES LEE RAYMOND

11

1 | both of those matters.

2 | Raymond, you pled guilty to reckless driving.

3 | Q   (BY MS. PEPPER)   So on any of those three

4 | occasions, was your license suspended?

5 | A   Yes.   They suspended it each time.

6 | Q   Did any of those incidents involve a car wreck?

7 | A   The first one didn't.   The police pulled me

8 | over because they said I was weaving back and forth all over

9 | the road, but I wasn't.   I don't know why they stopped me on

10 | that one.   On the second one, I just kinda bumped another

11 | car from behind.

12 | Q   You bumped someone from behind?

13 | A   Yeah.   I was coming up to a stop light and I

14 | braked, but the street was wet and I didn't quite stop in

15 | time.   I just kinda slipped and bumped the car in front of me.

16 | Q   Was anyone injured?

17 | A   Well, you know how people complain about

18 | whiplash and soft tissue injuries, you know, stuff like

19 | that?   Keeps all of you lawyers in business, don't it?

20 | Someone called an ambulance and it came to the accident, but

21 | there wasn't no need because the old guy was fine.

22 | Q   So you hit an elderly man from behind?

23 | A   No, I just bumped him.   I didn't hit him.   It

24 | was just a little bump because my car was sliding because

25 | the pavement was wet.

CHARLES LEE RAYMOND

12

1 Q And an ambulance came?

2 A Yes.

3 Q Why did the ambulance come if the man you hit
4 was all right?

5 A That's a good one. I don't know, I really don't.

6 Q Did you get sued?

7 A No. My insurance company was able to get it
8 settled out of court.

9 Q And you were arrested?

10 A Yes, which didn't make sense because the acci-
11 dent wouldn't have happened if the street hadn't been wet.
12 It wasn't my fault that the street was wet that day.

13 Q When did this accident happen?

14 A This was the one in 1990. That's when I spent
15 that month in the county jail.

16 Q After you got out of county jail, was that
17 when you went to Whispering Hills?

18 A Yes. Me and Carla had broke up before I got
19 out of jail, so it seemed like a good time for a move.

20 Q All right. Now, I want to change the subject
21 and ask you some questions about your employment.

22   Where are you working now?

23 A Allegretti & Sons.

24 Q What type of work do you do?

25 A I'm a transmission repair technician.

CHARLES LEE RAYMOND

13

1   Q   I see. And you work out of a shop, I assume?

2   A   Yes. Mr. Allegretti's shop is on Northwest

3 63rd in Oklahoma City.

4   Q   How long have you been working there?

5   A   Since March 1990.

6   Q   Does your job involve any driving?

7   A   It's not supposed to. I mean, that's not part

8 of my job. It's someone else's. But sometimes I deliver

9 rebuilt transmissions for Mr. Allegretti.

10   Q   About how often?

11   A   Not too often -- I mean, usually I work in the

12 shop and they send some kid out to make deliveries. But I

13 sometimes make deliveries if the kid calls in sick or some-

14 thing and someone needs the transmission like right away.

15   Q   When you applied for the job, did you have to

16 give Mr. Allegretti a copy of your driving record?

17   A   No, because deliveries aren't part of my job

18 description. I mean, transmissions are my specialty. It's

19 a waste of my expertise to send me out making deliveries.

20   Q   Well, does Mr. Allegretti know about your dri-

21 ving record?

22   A   Well, sure. Do you mean did I tell him about

23 my accidents?

24   Q   Yes, and the times that you've been stopped or

25 ticketed.

CHARLES LEE RAYMOND

14

1   A   Okay. I told Mr. Allegretti about the two

2 DUIs and my suspended license because I didn't want to be

3 driving all over town. I mean, that's not my job, making

4 deliveries. I told him, I said, "Hey, man, you make me

5 drive around town all the time, I'm gonna get a job with Pep

6 Boys. I don't do deliveries, I do transmissions."

7   Q   So you told Mr. Allegretti about your 1986 and

8 1990 DUIs, and about your suspended license in 1993 for

9 reckless driving?

10   A   Well, sure. Why not? I mean, it's no big

11 deal. People get stopped all the time for traffic tickets.

12 No one thinks anything about it. Me and Mr. Allegretti even

13 used to laugh about it all the time when we'd go out togeth-

14 er on Fridays after the shop closed.

15   He'd always say, "Look, Wild Man —" that's

16 what he calls me, Wild Man, "— you better let me drive. You

17 don't drive too good when you're schnockered." It was kind

18 of a joke between us.

19   MR. RODRIGUEZ: Excuse me, Counsel. Can we

20 take a quick break here for just a minute? I need to talk

21 with my client.

22   MS. PEPPER: Sure, no problem.

23   (Brief recess)

24   Q   (BY MS. PEPPER) Okay. Mr. Raymond, I believe

25 before the break that you mentioned that you and your boss,

CHARLES LEE RAYMOND

15

1 | Mr. Allegretti, have gone out together in the past.

2 | A   Yeah, just a couple of times.

3 | Q   So, when you and Mr. Allegretti went out, what

4 | did you do?

5 | A   What do you mean?

6 | Q   Well, did you go out to eat, go to a show, go

7 | play pool? What did you do?

8 | A   Oh. Well, we usually went to Red's Tavern and

9 | played some pool with the guys.

10 | Q   Is that all? Would either of you have any-

11 | thing to drink?

12 | A   Huh? Well, yeah. It's a bar, isn't it?

13 | Sure, we would each have a couple of beers.

14 | Q   About how often did you and Mr. Allegretti go

15 | drinking together?

16 | A   Oh, maybe once every few weeks or so. We get

17 | along real well.

18 | Q   Would you say Mr. Allegretti trusted you with

19 | his company car?

20 | A   Well, he let me take it out to deliver stuff

21 | so I would say that he trusted me with it.

22 | Q   And he let you do this even though he knew

23 | about your driving record?

24 | A   Once in a while, like I said.

25 | Q   So on the day of the accident, you had with Jane

CHARLES LEE RAYMOND

16

```
 1   Healy, you were making a delivery?

 2          A     Yes.  I was delivering some parts to this man

 3   in River City.

 4          Q     What kind of car were you driving?

 5          A     A 1985 Trans Am, black.

 6          Q     Is that your car or Mr. Allegretti's company car?

 7          A     It's mine.

 8          Q     And you stopped someplace on the way there?

 9          A     I stopped at Red's Tavern.

10          Q     Do you go there often?

11          A     No, not really; maybe a few times a week.

12          Q     How long were you at Red's Tavern?

13          A     Oh, I'd say about an hour, maybe less.

14          Q     Do you remember seeing anyone there that you knew?

15          A     Yes.  I saw this guy who's there all the time.

16   I can't remember his name.  Also, I saw Tony Simpson, the

17   bartender.

18          Q     What did you drink while you were there?

19          A     Let me think here a minute.  Hmm.  You know,

20   I'm not sure.  Maybe just a beer.

21          Q     You're not sure what you had to drink at Red's

22   that day?

23          A     No.  To tell the truth, I really don't remem-

24   ber if I had anything at all to drink.

25          Q     So if Mr. Simpson said in his deposition that
```

CHARLES LEE RAYMOND

17

1   you had several drinks at Red's that day, would he be lying?

2   A   Well, no, I wouldn't say that. I mean, that

3   was a long time ago. But I think I had a shot of something,

4   a couple of beers, maybe a margarita, and then another shot

5   of something or other.

6   MR. RODRIGUEZ: Raymond, don't guess. If you

7   don't know, just say so.

8   THE WITNESS: No, I'm pretty sure that's what

9   I drank that day. I mean, that's my usual. It wasn't much.

10   Q   (BY MS. PEPPER) So you had five drinks?

11   A   Yeah. I sure didn't have any more than those

12 five. Like I said, it wasn't much.

13   Q   Were you drunk at the time you left?

14   A   No, not a bit. I hold my liquor real well. I

15 can drink a lot more than that and not even feel it. You

16 wouldn't even know I had been drinking to be around me

17 because that's how well I handle it.

18   Q   You had five drinks in the space of an hour,

19 but you weren't drunk?

20   A   Well, I was feeling pretty good, but I wasn't

21 like ready to black out yet or anything, so I figured I was

22 fine. Didn't feel sick at all.

23   Q   Did Mr. Simpson or anyone else at Red's suggest

24 to you that you should take a taxi instead of driving yourself?

25   A   No, because I wasn't drunk. If I had been drunk,

CHARLES LEE RAYMOND

18

1   I would have known it. I don't need Tony or nobody to tell me.

2   Q   The other man you mentioned, the one whose

3   name you can't recall, he didn't say anything?

4   A   Like what?

5   Q   Well, did he say anything to you like perhaps

6   you shouldn't drive or someone should call you a cab?

7   A   No. He was drunk. He didn't care.

8   Q   So what happened then?

9   A   I went out to the parking lot, got in my car,

10   and started to drive on over to River City to drop off the

11   parts. I was going south on Childs Street and making pretty

12   good time, when the light turned red. So I waited for it to

13   turn green. When it did, I just started driving through the

14   intersection.

15   Next thing you know, wham. I hit this babe

16   who was blocking the intersection. I mean, she's right

17   smack dab in the middle of the street. She must have run a

18   red light or something. These women drivers ....

19   Q   So the light was green when you started

20   through the intersection?

21   A   Yes, it certainly was. I had the right of way.

22   Q   Did you look to see whether the intersection

23   was clear before you started across it?

24   A   Hell, no. The light was green, that means

25   traffic has to yield to me.

CHARLES LEE RAYMOND

19

1   Q   What kind of car was it that you hit?

2   A   I think it was a BMW or some yuppy kind of import.

3   Q   Was the car you hit moving at the time you hit

4 it?

5   A   How should I know? It was right in the middle

6 of the street. There was no way to miss it. I don't know if

7 it was moving — I guess it was. It sure did after I hit it.

8   Q   It did? When you hit Ms. Healy's car, it moved?

9   A   It sure did.

10   Q   Where did the car move to?

11   A   It slid over and the side of it hit up against

12 a utility pole on the southwest corner of the intersection.

13   Q   What did you do then?

14   A   Well, I had to stop. My car was wrecked. I

15 mean, totalled. You should have seen it.

16   Q   Okay. Can you draw a picture for me here of the

17 intersection where the accident happened? Then mark the streets.

18   A   Like this (indicating)?

19   Q   Yes, that's fine.

20   Now, take this red pen and mark where your car

21 was while you were waiting for the red light to turn green.

22 Just mark it with a red "X."

23   A   (Witness complies.)

24   Q   Now, would you mark where Ms. Austin's car was

25 when you first saw it?

CHARLES LEE RAYMOND

20

1   A   Huh? When? When I first saw it where?

2   Q   Just mark where Ms. Austin's car was when you

3 first noticed it, wherever that might be.

4   A   Well, I guess I didn't notice her until my car

5 hit hers.

6   Q   Okay. So where would that be? Just mark it

7 with an "X" with this blue pen.

8   A   Well, that would have to be right in the mid-

9 dle of the intersection where she's not supposed to be.

10   Q   Okay. Now, just one last thing. Please mark

11 where Ms. Austin's car ended up when it came to rest after

12 the two cars collided.

13   A   Well, let's see. She ran into this street

14 light that was sitting there.

15   Q   Okay. Why don't you mark the street light

16 with this green pen, just make a circle for the street light

17 pole, and then use the blue pen — here it is — to mark where

18 Ms. Austin's car came to rest.

19   A   Okay. The pole was here, I think. She ended

20 up somewhere next to it.

21   MS. PEPPER: Counsel, I'm marking this drawing

22 as Plaintiff's Exhibit No. 1 and offering it into evidence.

23   MR. RODRIGUEZ: No objection.

24   (Plaintiff's Exhibit No. 1 marked for

25   identification purposes)

CHARLES LEE RAYMOND

21

1   Q   (BY MS. PEPPER) Mr. Raymond, after the acci-

2   dent happened, did you get out of the car?

3   A   Well, yes. I mean, at first I was kinda

4   dazed, I guess from the force of the accident. Then, yes, I

5   got out of my car and asked someone, one of the people that

6   was just standing around, to call the police.

7   Q   Do you have any idea how fast you were going

8   when you hit Ms. Healy's car?

9   A   Well, I couldn't have been going very fast

10   because I had just stopped for the red light.

11   Q   Yes, but how fast were you going when your car

12   hit Ms. Healy's?

13   A   I don't know. Maybe five miles per hour. I

14   have no idea.

15   Q   Okay. I don't want you to guess. How fast

16   does your car go? I mean, it's a Firebird, isn't it?

17   A   Well, you know, a Firebird is a quick little car.

18   And mine, well, she was really something special. I had done a

19   little tuning on her myself and used to take her out to the

20   drag races. You know Thunder Alley? It's down by the river.

21   Q   So, you had done some drag racing in this car,

22   the same car that was in this accident?

23   A   You bet. That's why I was so mad about your

24   client wrecking it. That was one sweet car. I could go

25   zero to sixty miles per hour in no time at all.

CHARLES LEE RAYMOND

22

```
 1            MR. RODRIGUEZ:   Can we take a break?

 2            (Brief recess)

 3       Q       (BY MS. PEPPER)   Do you know what the speed

 4  limit is on Childs?

 5       A       Huh?   No.   I guess around 40 miles per hour.

 6       Q       I don't want you to guess.   Just if you know.

 7  Do you know what the speed limit is on Childs?

 8       A       Well, not exactly.

 9       Q       Okay.   How long was it from the time you got

10  out of your car until the first police officer came?

11       A       Gee, I don't know.   It's hard to gauge time.

12  Seems like things happened so fast.   Maybe five minutes or

13  so. That's about when the ambulance came, too.

14       Q       Did you have a chance to apply your brakes, do

15  you recall?

16       A       No, I didn't have time to do nothing.   There

17  was absolutely no way to avoid this accident.   I mean, she

18  was sitting right there in the middle of the intersection.

19  It seemed like I had only just put my foot on the accelera-

20  tor before, bam, I ran into her.   I had the right of way,

21  you know.   I mean, I was the one with the green light.

22  Traffic was supposed to yield to me.

23       Q       Okay.   Did you tell anyone at the scene that

24  you were okay?

25       A       Yes.
```

CHARLES LEE RAYMOND

23

1   Q   Would that have been the police officer or

2 would that have been other people?

3   A   Probably both.

4   Q   Do you have any restriction on your driver's

5 license as far as corrective lenses that you have to wear?

6   A   Yes.

7   Q   When you say "yes," you're required to wear —

8   A   Glasses or contact lenses.

9   Q   Did you have your glasses or contact lenses on

10 at the time of the accident?

11   A   Yes.

12   Q   Which do you normally wear?

13   A   Contacts.

14   Q   And that's what you would have been wearing at

15 the time of the accident?

16   A   Yes.

17   Q   Did you talk to the police about the accident?

18   A   Yes.

19   Q   Do you recall the name of the officer you

20 talked to?

21   A   Well, not really. Hinson, Harris — something

22 like that.

23   Q   What did you tell him?

24   A   I told him this babe, your client, ran a red light

25 and was in the intersection when I tried to go through it.

CHARLES LEE RAYMOND

24

1	Q	What did the police officer do then?
2	A	He took my statement.
3	Q	Did the officer ask if you had been drinking?
4	A	Yes. They always do, don't they? I mean,

5 when there's been an accident.

6   Q   So the officer asked you if you had been
7 drinking. What did you say?

8   A   I told him that I'd had a few drinks, but that
9 I wasn't drunk.

10   Q   What did he do then?

11   A   He asked me if I'd be willing to go down to
12 the station for a breathalyzer test.

13   Q   What did you say?

14   A   I said I'd be happy to. I knew I wasn't drunk.

15   Q   Did you go with the officer to the police sta-
16 tion then?

17   A   Yes, I did. This other officer said he would
18 take care of getting my car towed, because like I said, it
19 was totalled. I mean, there was no way I could have drove
20 it home like it was.

21   Q   All right. About what time did the accident
22 occur?

23   A   Well, it says on the accident report.

24   MR. RODRIGUEZ: Raymond, if you know what time the
25 accident happened, just say so. If you don't, just tell her.

CHARLES LEE RAYMOND

25

1   THE WITNESS: Okay.   It happened around 6:00 p.m. that evening.

2   Q   (BY MS. PEPPER)   How do you know what time it

3   happened?

4   A   Well, I know that I went straight to Red's

5   Tavern after work, and I couldn't have been there very long,

6   about an hour, so it must have been around 6:00 or 6:30 when

7   the accident happened.

8   Q   About how long after the accident happened

9   were you taken to the police station?

10   A   Fifteen, twenty minutes.

11   Q   How long did it take you to get to the police

12   station?

13   A   About ten minutes.   Not long.

14   Q   How long after you got to the police station

15   did you take the breathalyzer test?

16   A   Oh, they made me take that sucker right away.

17   Q   Do you remember what the results of the

18   breathalyzer test were?

19   A   Uh, no, not really.   It wasn't very much, though.

20   Q   If I told you that the officer's report says

21   that your score was .13 on the breathalyzer, would that

22   sound about right?

23   A   Is that what it was?   Well, I guess I was kinda

24   drunk then.   Sure didn't feel like .13 though, I can tell you.

25   Was that my score?

CHARLES LEE RAYMOND

26

1   Q   That is what the officer's report says your

2 breathalyzer results were. Do you dispute the results of

3 that test?

4   A   Well, no. I mean, I guess not. That is some-

5 thing my attorney had better answer for me.

6   MR. RODRIGUEZ: Go ahead and answer the ques-

7 tion, Charles.

8   THE WITNESS: Well, then, no, I don't dispute

9 what that officer says.

10   Q   (BY MS. PEPPER) Do you remember what the

11 results were?

12   A   No, but they put me in jail.

13   Q   Were you charged with anything?

14   A   They charged me with a DUI.

15   Q   So you were legally drunk?

16   A   That's what they seemed to think, but I could-

17 n't believe it. I still don't, even though that officer

18 says I was. I don't mean to say he's lying. I just can't

19 believe that I was legally drunk because I've been drunk. I

20 mean, I know when I'm drunk, you know. And I know I wasn't

21 drunk when that accident happened.

22   Q   Mr. Raymond, about how tall are you?

23   A   Huh?

24   Q   What is your height and weight?

25   A   Oh, I guess I'm about 5'8" and weigh somewhere

CHARLES LEE RAYMOND

27

1   around 180.

2   Q   Thank you. Okay. Now, back to your DUI for

3   this accident. Were you convicted?

4   A   Yes.

5   Q   What was the sentence?

6   A   Two years in prison.

7   Q   How much time did you actually serve?

8   A   About ten months, I think. They put this

9   breath thing on my car to keep me from drinking and driving,

10 you know, that thing you have to breathe into to get your

11 car to start. That's on there now and I guess I'll have to

12 put up with that for a while.

13   Q   Does that work? Does it keep you from driving

14 if you've been drinking?

15   A   Oh, I guess it does pretty much of the time.

16   Q   Okay. Did you get your car fixed?

17   A   The car that I had the accident in? No, I

18 sold it.

19   Q   Did you receive some proceeds from selling the

20 car and some insurance money that you know of?

21   A   Some what?

22   Q   Okay. Did the insurance company pay for the

23 damage to the car?

24   A   I'm not sure. My mom took care of all of that.

25   Q   Your mother took care of it?

         A   Yeah.

CHARLES LEE RAYMOND

28

1   Q   Okay. So would your mother have kept any doc-
2 umentation that could tell us how much money you got for
3 your car when you sold it? Was it paid for by check?
4   A   I have no idea. You'd have to ask her.
5   Q   Well, do you recall getting any money for the car?
6   A   Well, yeah. I mean, it was worth something
7 even though it got totalled. And I should have gotten more
8 than I did.
9   Q   Okay. So what did you get as payment for the car?
10   A   Oh, about $1,000, I think.
11   Q   About $1,000. Was that in cash?
12   A   Well, it was when my mom gave it to me.
13   Q   But you don't know if that was how much money you
14 got from the insurance people or where it came from, do you?
15   A   No. Like I told you, my mom took care of all
16 of that. She's got the time to mess with that stuff so she
17 just took care of it.
18   Q   Okay. Now, you have claimed that you were
19 injured in this accident; isn't that right?
20   A   Yeah.
21   Q   But you said earlier that you told people at
22 the accident — you're not sure whom — that you weren't hurt;
23 is that true?
24   A   Yes. I mean, I didn't know that I was hurt.
25 At least, not then.

CHARLES LEE RAYMOND

29

1   Q   I see. Did anyone offer any medical assistance

2   to you at the scene? Did anyone check you out to see if you

3   had been hurt?

4   A   Well, yeah. The ambulance guys, one of them

5   came over and asked me if I was okay. I told him I was

6   because I didn't know I could have injuries that wouldn't

7   show up till later.

8   Q   Okay. We talked earlier about what you

9   reviewed for this deposition, and you said that one of the

10   things you had reviewed was your answers to these interroga-

11   tories. Do you recall that answer?

12   A   Yes.

13   Q   Do you recall being asked in interrogatories

14   about whether you had any accidents or illnesses before this

15   accident happened? Do you recall that question?

16   A   Yes.

17   Q   Do you recall what answer you gave?

18   A   To what?

19   Q   When you answered the interrogatories, what

20   was your answer when you were asked whether you had been in

21   any other accidents or if you had any illnesses or medical

22   problems before the accident happened?

23   A   I believe I said that I had not been in any

24   prior accidents.

25   Q   But didn't you just tell us today that you had

CHARLES LEE RAYMOND

30

1   been in another accident in 1990?

2   A   Yes, ma'am. I had forgotten about it before,

3   the 1990 one. I mean, when I was answering those questions,

4   it must have slipped my mind.

5   Q   Okay. Had you suffered any other illnesses or

6   had any medical problems before this accident occurred?

7   A   Nothing out of the normal. I had been in a

8   few other accidents when I was younger, but I wasn't the

9   driver in those accidents.

10   Q   So as far as your answer, you had been

11   involved in at least one prior accident and have had some

12   prior illnesses; is that correct?

13   A   Yes.

14   Q   At the time of the accident, were you taken to

15   any hospital or any doctor for evaluation that evening?

16   A   No, ma'am. They took me straight to jail.

17   Q   Then what happened?

18   A   Well, my mom came and bailed me out.

19   Q   How soon after your arrest were you released?

20   A   I'm not sure. It didn't take very long though.

21   Q   What did you do then?

22   A   I went home with my mom, and she brought me an

23   ice pack for my neck because it was starting to feel kinda stiff

24   and sore. I sat with that ice pack on my neck for about half

25   an hour and then I went out and ate with some of my friends.

CHARLES LEE RAYMOND

31

1　I kept the ice pack with me in the car the whole time.　Then

2　I came home.

3　　　　Q　　Do you recall sitting in any police car and

4　giving statements that night?

5　　　　A　　I remember talking to the police officers, but

6　I don't remember sitting in any police car.

7　　　　Q　　If one of the officers at the scene said that

8　you were put in the back of his squad car for a time, would

9　you say that the officer wasn't telling the truth?

10　　　　A　　I don't know what to say except that I don't

11　remember sitting in no police car.　If he said I was there,

12　I was, but I don't remember it.

13　　　　Q　　Do you recall signing anything that night?

14　　　　A　　No.

15　　　　Q　　Who were the friends that you went out with

16　later that night?　What are their names?

17　　　　A　　I went out with my brother Rusty and Janet

18　Payne. There was one other person there, but I don't remem-

19　ber her name.

20　　　　Q　　Do you know their addresses and telephone numbers?

21　　　　A　　Well, Rusty's is the same as my mom's because

22　he lives there, too.　I have no idea where Janet and that

23　other girl live.

24　　　　Q　　Where did you go?

25　　　　A　　To eat.

CHARLES LEE RAYMOND

32

1   Q   Okay.

2   A   The Hooters on the Expressway.

3   Q   How long did you stay there?

4   A   I don't know.

5   Q   Would it have been before or after midnight

6   when you got to Hooters?

7   A   I'm sure that it would have been before mid-

8   night, because that's when they close.

9   Q   Okay. Now, did you go to work the day after

10   the accident?

11   A   I'm not sure. Was it a work day?

12   Q   Yes.

13   A   Then I probably did. I don't know.

14   Q   Okay. So that evening, the day the accident

15   happened, your neck started feeling sore?

16   A   Yes, it did.

17   Q   But you were able to go in to work the follow-

18   ing day?

19   A   I guess. I don't know.

20   MR. RODRIGUEZ: I object, Counselor. That

21   question has already been asked and answered.

22   MS. PEPPER: Okay. I'll withdraw the question.

23   Q   (BY MS. PEPPER) Mr. Raymond, do you know how

24   many days of work you have missed because of this accident?

25   A   Not exactly, no. You see, most of the time I do

CHARLES LEE RAYMOND

33

1   fine, but every now and then I twist or turn funny, it makes

2   my neck start hurting again.

3   Q   And you have sought medical treatment for this

4   injury?

5   A   Yeah. I've been going to my mom's chiropractor.

6   Q   What is the chiropractor's name?

7   A   Dr. Ted Kalousdian.

8   Q   Has Dr. Kalousdian been able to help you?

9   A   Oh, yeah. He's done me a lot of good.

10   Q   So you are still seeing him for this injury?

11   A   Yes. Like I said, it goes along okay until I

12   turn funny, and then my neck and back start hurting again.

13   Q   Have you had a chance to look at any of the

14   medical bills and reports that have come along with these

15   interrogatories that were sent to my office?

16   A   No.

17   Q   Okay.

18   A   I don't believe I have.

19   Q   There's a — something here from a department

20   store for $429.97. Do you recall what that was for?

21   A   I'm not sure.

22   Q   Okay. Did you have to buy any crutches or a

23   neck brace, anything like that?

24   A   No.

25   Q   Any orthopedic type clothing or aids at all?

CHARLES LEE RAYMOND

34

1	A	I bought an orthopedic bed.
2	Q	Was that on the recommendation of a doctor?
3	A	Yeah, to get off the waterbed.

4   Q   Okay. Since this accident, have you received
5 any kind of medical treatment that you believe is not relat-
6 ed to your accident?

7   A   Such as? I don't understand.

8   Q   Going to any dermatologist or going for just
9 routine —

10   A   I've had — I've gone to the doctor for aller-
11 gies, I believe it was — or I thought it was the flu, but it
12 turned out to be allergies real bad, and got some prescrip-
13 tion medicine from him. I believe that's the only time.

14   Q   I saw in some reports that you had some concern
15 about your eyes, or at one time your eyes got red and swollen.

16   A   Yes, that's right.

17   Q   Do you believe that was attributable to this
18 accident?

19   A   It could have been.

20   Q   Could it have been attributable to maybe your
21 contacts irritating your eyes, not being clean?

22   A   I don't know. You'd have to ask my doctor
23 about that.

24   Q   Do you recall what your eye doctor recommended
25 for this problem?

CHARLES LEE RAYMOND

35

1   A   I think he said that I had to wear my glasses

2 until it cleared up, but I'm not sure. I remember wearing

3 my glasses for a while.

4   Q   Did you doctor recommend that you get rid of

5 your old contacts and get a new prescription for new contacts?

6   A   He said that I should get rid of my old con-

7 tacts because they were contaminated.

8   Q   How do contacts get contaminated, do you know?

9   A   Well, from the eye infection I had.

10   Q   Okay. Have you had any problems since then?

11   A   No.

12   Q   Did you get new contacts?

13   A   Yes.

14   Q   In going through your medical records related

15 to this accident, I also noticed some bills from Dr.

16 Katherine Cox. Did you also see Dr. Cox for injuries from

17 this accident?

18   A   Yes.

19   Q   Do you recall telling Dr. Cox that you weren't

20 experiencing any more pain?

21   A   I don't remember. I know that I complained to

22 her about it, that's why I went to her was because of my neck,

23 but I don't remember if I ever told them that I wasn't sore

24 anymore. I don't remember if I ever told them that or not.

25   Q   Do you recall telling any doctor after the

CHARLES LEE RAYMOND

36

1   accident that you felt perfectly fine?

2   A   I never said I felt perfectly fine, I don't think.

3   Q   So it would be your testimony you've never

4   told a doctor that you haven't felt perfectly fine since the

5   accident?

6   A   I don't believe I've ever said I felt perfect-

7   ly fine, no.

8   Q   Do you recall any recommendation from any of

9   these doctors that you do some back strengthening exercises?

10   A   One of them put me on physical therapy for it

11   and made me do some exercises.

12   Q   Have you consistently tried to do those exercises?

13   A   Yes.

14   Q   Has it strengthened your back?

15   A   I guess so. It feels better than it did before.

16   Q   How often do you do them?

17   A   Oh, I guess about once a week. That seems to

18   be plenty.

19   Q   Mr. Raymond, have you been encouraged by your

20   attorney to seek out further medical care?

21   MR. RODRIGUEZ: I'm going to object to the

22   question and instruct Mr. Raymond not to answer. You're

23   asking questions that invade the attorney-client province.

24   Don't answer that question.

25   Q   (BY MS. PEPPER) Do you agree with what your

CHARLES LEE RAYMOND

37

1   attorney has just said?

2   A   Yes.

3   Q   Okay. Other than occasional visits you still

4   make to the chiropractor, are you receiving any other med-

5   ical care for injuries you received in this accident?

6   A   I consider that, yeah, I have to go see the doc-

7   tor every so often to see how I'm doing. I guess that's a yes.

8   Q   How long has it been since you have seen the

9   doctor?

10   A   Do you mean Dr. Cox?

11   Q   Yes.

12   A   I don't know how long it's been since I saw

13 her last. Probably months.

14   MS. PEPPER: All right. Mr. Raymond, I want

15 to take a short break while we go off the record.

16   (Brief recess)

17   CROSS EXAMINATION

18 BY MR. RODRIGUEZ:

19   Q   Charles, there are just a few things I want to

20 go over. I wasn't sure about your answer when Ms. Pepper

21 asked you about your speed as you entered the intersection.

22   You had come to a complete stop at the inter-

23 section of Childs and 14th, did you not?

24   A   Yes. I stopped for the red light.

25   Q   Were there any cars in front of you in line at

CHARLES LEE RAYMOND

38

```
 1   the intersection there on Childs?

 2          A       Any cars ahead of me?   No.   I was first in line.

 3          Q       All right.   Can you recall then what your

 4   speed was or give us your best estimate of your speed as you

 5   entered the intersection?

 6          A       Probably between five and ten miles per hour.

 7          Q       All right.   So it is your best estimate and

 8   recollection today that you accelerated to about five to ten

 9   miles per hour to go through the intersection?

10          A       Yes.

11                  MR. RODRIGUEZ:   Okay.   That's all I have.

12                          REDIRECT EXAMINATION

13   BY MS. PEPPER:

14          Q       Mr. Raymond, when you were sitting at the

15   intersection of Childs and 14th, did you notice that traffic

16   had stalled in the middle of the intersection?

17          A       No.

18          Q       You didn't see that the cars traveling on 14th

19   were backed up through the middle of the intersection?

20          A       No.   Like I said, your client ran the red

21   light and was in my right of way.   She should have yielded

22   to the red light like I did when I stopped at the intersec-

23   tion.   That's what you are supposed to do.

24          Q       Is it possible that the cars were backed up on

25   14th Street through the intersection and that you just didn't
```

CHARLES LEE RAYMOND

39

1 happen to notice it?

2   A   Well, I guess anything is possible. I don't

3 think that's what happened, but I guess it's possible.

4   Q   So if my client and other witnesses said that

5 traffic on 14th was backed up through the intersection on

6 14th and Childs, you wouldn't dispute that?

7   A   I wouldn't what?

8   Q   If there are other people who say that the

9 traffic had been backed up through the intersection blocking

10 the right of way, would those people be telling the truth?

11   A   Well, I can't tell you if someone is telling the

12 truth or not, especially people I don't know who they are. I

13 mean, I've never even met these people. How would I know?

14   Q   What I mean is, Mr. Raymond, if that is their

15 recollection of what happened, that traffic had backed up and

16 was blocking the intersection, that could be true, couldn't

17 it?

18   A   Well, I don't know. Maybe.

19   Q   Is it possible that my client didn't run a red

20 light, that she was left stranded in the middle of the

21 intersection when traffic in front of her stopped?

22   A   Well, like I said, anything is possible. I just

23 don't know whether that's really so or not. I mean, I would

24 have seen her if she had just been sitting there, wouldn't I?

25   Q   Mr. Raymond, how long do you think you sat at that

CHARLES LEE RAYMOND

40

1 red light? Was it red as you approached the intersection?

2   A   No. It started turning yellow as I was coming

3 up to the intersection and then changed to red just before I

4 got there.

5   Q   Okay. So you had to sit at the intersection

6 during a full red light?

7   A   Yeah, I suppose so.

8   Q   Do you have any idea how long that was?

9   A   Oh, I guess a couple of minutes. The normal

10 amount of time for a red light.

11   Q   So, during the time you sat waiting for the

12 light to change, what did you do?

13   A   What did I do? I sat there.

14   Q   Yes. I know you sat there. What I mean is, did

15 you look around, change the radio station, stuff like that?

16   A   Oh, I don't know. I can't remember.

17   Q   Okay. So whatever you did, you didn't notice

18 my client's car sitting in the middle of the intersection

19 during that time?

20   A   No.

21   Q   Okay. I have just a few more questions and

22 then we'll be finished, Mr. Raymond.

23   A   Good.

24   Q   Mr. Raymond, you testified earlier in this

25 deposition that your boss, Mr. Allegretti, knew about your

CHARLES LEE RAYMOND

41

1   drinking and your past driving record?

2   A   Yes.

3   Q   Would you say that he didn't care about it?

4   A   Oh, I don't know. I don't think he did.

5   Q   Why don't you think so?

6   A   Well, if he did, he wouldn't be asking me to

7   deliver stuff in his car, would he?

8   Q   Did Mr. Allegretti or any other supervisor at

9   Allegretti & Sons ever talk to you about your drinking?

10   A   What do you mean?

11   Q   Well, did any boss or supervisor ever counsel

12   you about not drinking on the job or when making deliveries?

13   A   Who? You mean Mr. Allegretti?

14   Q   Or any other supervisor.

15   A   I don't know. They might have. I remember

16   Mr. Allegretti asking me if I was okay to drive one time

17   when he wanted me to make a delivery, but I don't know that

18   we really talked about had I been drinking or anything.

19   Q   Is that the only instance you can recall when

20   a supervisor talked to you about drinking on the job?

21   A   Yes. It was just understood. As long as I

22   did my job, no one asked any questions.

23   MS. PEPPER: That's all the questions I have.

24   MR. RODRIGUEZ: When the deposition is over,

25   Charles, the court reporter will transcribe her notes and have

CHARLES LEE RAYMOND

42

1   it typed up in a booklet form like this that lists all the

2   questions that were asked and the answers that were given.

3   You have the right to take this deposition tran-

4   script, when yours is done, and read it through and check it

5   for errors or omissions. Then, if you do find any errors or

6   something that has been left out, you will write down those

7   corrections on a sheet of paper called an errata page.

8   You'll get blank errata pages with your deposition. Then

9   you will need to sign your deposition on the jurat page pro-

10   vided by the court reporter.

11   You have another option and that is you can waive

12   your signature and rely on the court reporter's expertise in

13   transcribing the testimony.

14   It's your decision to make and you need to tell the

15   court reporter what you wish to do. As your attorney, I'm

16   going to recommend that you read and sign it.

17   THE WITNESS: Okay. I'll read and sign it.

18   (Signature required; witness excused)

19   * * * * * *

20

21

22

23

24

25

CHARLES LEE RAYMOND

```
                                                              43
 1

 2

 3                        _____

 4                        CHARLES LEE RAYMOND

 5

 6   STATE OF OKLAHOMA        )

 7                            )   SS:

 8   COUNTY OF OKLAHOMA       )

 9          Subscribed and sworn to before me this _____

10   Day of _____, 1995.

11

12                        _____

13                        Notary Public, State of Oklahoma

14                        My Commission Expires: _____

15

16

17

18

19

20

21

22

23

24

25
```

CHARLES LEE RAYMOND

44

1   C E R T I F I C A T E

2   STATE OF OKLAHOMA   )
)   SS:
3   COUNTY OF OKLAHOMA   )

4

5   I, ELIZABETH J. CAMPBELL, CSR for the State of

6   Oklahoma, certify that CHARLES LEE RAYMOND was by me sworn

7   to testify the truth; that the deposition was taken by me in

8   stenotype and thereafter transcribed and is a true and cor-

9   rect transcript of the testimony of the witness; that the

10   deposition was taken on August 10, 1995, at 228 Robert S.

11   Kerr, Suite 110, Oklahoma City, State of Oklahoma; that I am

12   not an attorney for or a relative of either party, or other-

13   wise interested in this action.

14   Witness my hand and seal of office on this the 17th

15   day of August, 1995.

16

17

18   _____

19   ELIZABETH J. CAMPBELL, CSR, CP, RPR
     Oklahoma Certified Shorthand Reporter
20   Certificate No. 00162

21

22

23

24

25

$

$1,000 28:10,11
$429.97 33:20

&

& 2:4 12:23 41:9

*

* 2:18,18,18,18,18,18 3:15,15,15,
15,15,15 42:19,19,19,19,19,19

0

00162 44:20

1

1 20:22,24
10 3:5 44:10
110 1:25 44:11
12 6:23
122 2:8
13 25:21,24
14th 37:23 38:15,18,24 39:5,5
17th 44:14
180 27:1
1954 6:23
1985 16:5
1986 10:4,11 14:7
1990 7:16 9:17,17,21,22,23
10:10 12:14 13:5 14:7 30:1,3
1993 10:21 14:8
1995 3:5 44:10,15

2

219 7:8
228 1:25 44:10
2408 6:25

4

40 22:5
412 7:2

5

5'8 26:25

6

619 9:14
63rd 13:2
6:00 24:25 25:6

6:30 25:6

7

73107 2:5

A

able 12:7 32:17 33:8
about 4:12 5:24 7:4,14,168:18,18
9:16,25 11:17 12:21 13:10,20,22
14:1,7,8,12,13 15:14,22 16:13
21:23 22:13 23:17 24:21 25:5,
8,13,21 26:22,25 27:8 28:10,11
29:8,13 30:2,24 34:15,22 35:22
36:17 37:20,21 38:8 40:25 41:3,9,
12,18,20
absolutely 22:17
accelerated 38:8
accelerator 22:19
accident 11:20 12:10,13 15:25
19:16 21:1,4,22 22:17 23:10,15,17
24:5,21,22,24 25:7,8 26:21 27:3,17
28:19,22 29:15,22 30:1,6,11,14
32:10,14,24 34:4,6,18 35:15,17,25
36:5 37:5
accidents 13:23 29:14,21,24 30:8,9
across 18:23
action 44:13
actually 27:7
addicted 8:12
addiction 8:9,10
addictive 8:8
address 6:24 9:13,15
addresses 31:20
after 8:17 12:16 14:14 19:6 20:11
21:1 25:5,8,14 30:19 32:5,9 35:25
again 33:2,12
against 4:9 19:10
ago 17:3
agree 36:25
AGREED 3:2,8
agreement 3:7
ahead 26:6 38:2
aids 33:25
alcohol 8:21
ALLEGRETTI 1:6 12:23 13:9,16,
20 14:1,7,12 15:1,3,14,18 40:25
41:8,9,13,16
Allegretti's 13:2 16:6
allergies 34:10,12

Alley 21:20
along 15:16 33:11,14
already 32:21
always 14:15 24:4
ambulance 11:20 12:1,3 22:13
29:4
AMELIA 2:3 4:6
amount 40:9
another 10:4 11:10 17:4 30:1
42:11
answer 3:11 4:15 26:5,6 29:11,
17,20 30:10 36:22,24 37:20
answered 29:19 32:21
answering 30:3
answers 4:24 6:9,10,13 29:10
42:2
anybody 8:21
anymore 35:24
anyone 7:11 11:16 16:14 17:23
22:23 29:1,2
anything 5:22 6:6 14:12 15:10
16:24 17:21 18:3,5 26:13 31:13
33:23 39:2,22 41:18
anyway 8:13
apartment 7:1,2,9
APPEARANCES 2:1
applied 13:15
apply 22:14
approached 40:1
around 10:19 14:4 17:16 21:6
22:5 24:25 25:6 27:1 40:15
arrest 30:19
arrested 12:9
arrests 10:16,17
ask 4:14,23 5:4,15,16,19 12:21
24:3 28:4 34:22
asked 21:5 24:6,11 29:5,13,20
32:21 37:20 41:22 42:2
asking 5:18 36:22 41:6,16
assistance 29:1
assume 4:16 13:1
ate 30:25
attorney 4:7,11 5:11 10:25 26:5
36:20 37:1 42:15 44:12
attorney-client 36:23
attorneys 3:3,9
attributable 34:17,20
August 3:5 44:10,15
Austin's 19:24 20:2,11,18

CHARLES LEE RAYMOND

Avenue 2:8
avoid 22:17
away 13:14 25:16

B

babe 18:15 23:24
back 11:8 27:2 31:8 33:12 36:9, 14
backed 38:19,24 39:5,9,15
background 6:21
bad 34:12
bailed 30:18
bam 22:20
bar 15:12
bartender 16:17
Because 5:2,5   10:24
11:8,21,24,24 12:10 13:17 14:2
17:16,25 21:9 24:18 26:19 29:5
30:23   31:21   32:8,
24 35:7,22
bed 34:1
beer 16:20
beers 15:13 17:4
before 4:19 7:7,20 9:4 12:18
14:25 18:23 22:20 29:14,22 30:2,6
32:5,7 36:14 40:3
behalf 3:4
behind 11:11,12,22
believe 14:24 26:17,18 29:23
33:18 34:5,11,13,17 36:6
best 38:4,7
bet 21:23
better 5:1 14:16 26:5 36:15
between 3:2,8 14:18 38:6
big 14:10
bills 33:14 35:15
birth 6:22
bit 8:10 17:14
black 16:5 17:21
blank 42:8
blocking 18:16 39:9,16
blue 20:7,17
BMW 19:2
booklet 42:1
boss 14:25 40:25 41:11
both 5:2 11:1 23:3
bought 34:1
Boys 14:5
brace 33:23

braked 11:14
brakes 22:14
break 5:10,12 14:20,25 22:1 37:15
breath 27:8
breathalyzer 24:12 25:15,18,21
26:2
breathe 27:10
Brief 14:23 22:2 37:16
broke 12:18
brother 31:17
brought 30:22
Buechner 2:4
bump 11:24
bumped 11:10,12,15,23
business 11:19
buy 33:22

C

cab 18:6
call 18:6 21:6
called 11:19 42:7
calls 13:13 14:16
came 11:20 12:1 20:11,18 22:10,
13 28:14 29:4 30:18 31:2
Campbell 3:6 44:5,19
can 5:3,11,21 6:16 14:19 17:14
19:15 22:1 25:24 38:3 41:19 42:11
can't 5:5 16:16 18:3 26:18 39:11
40:16
car 11:6,10,15,24 15:19 16:4,
6,6 18:9 19:1,3,7,9,13,20,24 20:2,
4,11,18 21:2,5,8,11,16,17,21,22,
24 22:10 24:18 27:9,10,16,17,18,
22 28:3,5,9 31:1,3,6,8,11 40:18
41:7
care 18:7 24:18 27:23,24 28:15,17
36:20 37:4 41:3
Carla 9:6,7,8,21 12:18
carry 9:3
cars 20:12 37:25 38:2,18,24
cash 28:11
certainly 8:4 18:21
Certificate 44:20
CERTIFIED 2:14 3:6
certify 44:6
chance 4:11 22:14 33:13
change 12:20 40:12,15
changed 40:3
charged 26:13,14

CHARLES 1:6 3:4 4:1,22 26:7
37:19 41:25 44:6
check 8:22 28:3 29:2 42:4
checked 9:21
Childs 18:11   22:4,7   37:23
38:1,15 39:6
chiropractor 33:5 37:4
chiropractor's 33:6
Christmas 10:19,21
circle 20:16
cirrhosis 8:20
City 2:5 3:5 6:25 7:8 13:3 16:3
18:10 44:11
CIV-94-1742-H 1:5
claimed 28:18
clean 34:21
clear 18:23
cleared 35:2
client 14:21 21:23 23:24 38:20
39:4,19
client's 40:18
clients 6:2
close 32:8
closed 14:14
clothing 33:25
collided 20:12
come 12:3 33:14 37:22
coming 11:13 40:2
Commission 43:14
company 12:7 15:19 16:6 27:21
complain 11:17
complained 35:21
complete 37:22
complies 19:23
concern 34:14
condition 8:5
consider 37:6
consistently 36:12
contact 23:8,9
Contacts 23:13 34:21 35:5,5,6,
8,12
contaminated 35:7,8
convicted 17:3
convictions 10:12,13
copy 13:16
corner 19:11
correct 4:17 6:13 30:12 44:8
corrections 42:7
corrective 23:5

CHARLES LEE RAYMOND

CHARLES LEE RAYMOND

CHARLES LEE RAYMOND

CHARLES LEE RAYMOND

names 31:16

neck 30:23,24 32:15 33:2,12,22 35:22

need 5:10,11 11:21 14:20 18:1 42:9,14

needs 13:14

never 36:2,3 39:13

new 35:5,5,12

Next 18:15 20:20

night 31:4,13,16

nobody 18:1

nodding 5:5,7

normal 30:7 40:9

normally 23:12

North 6:25

Northwest 13:2

Notary 43:13

notes 41:25

nothing 22:16 30:7

notice 20:4 38:15 39:1 40:17

noticed 20:3 35:15

Now 9:20 12:20,22 19:20,24 20:10 27:2,11 28:18 32:9 33:1

Nowack 2:4

numbers 31:20

O

Oaktree 7:8

oath 4:24

object 32:20 36:21

objection 20:23

OBJECTIONS 2:17 3:10

occasional 37:3

occasionally 8:11

occasions 11:4

occur 24:21

occurred 30:6

off 18:10 34:3 37:15

offer 29:1

offering 20:22

office 33:15 44:14

officer 22:10 23:1,19 24:1,3,6, 15,17 26:9,17 31:9

officer's 25:20 26:1

officers 31:5,7

often 13:10,11 15:14 16:10 36:16 37:7

Oh 15:8,16 16:13 25:16 26:25 27:15 28:10 33:9 36:17 40:9,16 41:4

Okay 5:1,7,8,21 6:6,15 14:1,24 19:15 20:6,10,15,19 21:15 22:9,23, 24 24:25 27:2,16,21 28:1,9,18 29:5,8 30:5 32:1,9,14,22 33:11,17,22 34:4 35:10 37:3 38:11 40:5,17,21 41:16 42:17

Oklahoma 2:5,5 3:5,6,7 9:12 13:3 43:13 44:2,3,6,11,11

old 11:21 35:5,6

omissions 42:5

once 15:16,24 36:17

one 10:4,10,11 11:7,10,10 12:5,14 14:11 18:2 20:10 21:5,24 22:21 29:4,9 30:3,11 31:7,18 34:15 36:10 41:16,22

only 5:3 22:19 34:13 41:19

opportunity 5:12

option 42:11

orthopedic 33:25 34:1

other 10:11,12,16 17:5 18:2 23:2 24:17 29:21 30:5,8 31:18,22 37:3,4 39:4,8 41:8,14

otherwise 44:13

out 12:8,16,18 13:1,12,19 14:13 15:1,3,6,20 17:21 18:9 21:2,4,19 22:9 29:2 30:7,18,25 31:15,17 34:12 36:20 42:6

over 6:8,16 10:19 11:7,8 14:3 18:10 19:10 29:5 37:20 41:24

overreacts 8:21

owned 9:19

P

p.m 24:25

pack 30:23,24 31:1

Page 2:10,13,16 42:7,9

pages 42:8

paid 8:25 9:2 28:3

pain 35:20

paper 42:7

parking 18:9

part 13:7,17

parties 3:3,9

parts 16:2 18:10

party 44:12

past 15:1 41:1

pavement 11:25

pay 7:18 9:18 27:21

payment 28:9

Payne 31:17

pen 19:20 20:7,16,17

people 11:17 14:11 21:5 23:2 28:14,21 39:8,10,12,13

Pep 14:5

PEPPER 2:3 4:5,6 6:1,6 11:3 14:22,24 17:10 20:21 21:1 22:3 25:2 26:10 32:22,23 36:25 37:14,20 38:13 41:23

per 21:13,25 22:5 38:6,9

perfectly 36:1,2,4,6

perhaps 18:5

person 31:18

physical 36:10

picture 19:15

place 7:24

Plaintiff 1:4 2:2 3:5 4:7

Plaintiff's 20:22,24

play 15:6

played 15:9

please 5:16 9:9 20:10

pled 10:23 11:2

plenty 36:18

pole 19:11 20:16,19

police 10:20 11:7 21:6 22:10 23:1,17 24:1,15 25:9,11,14 31:3, 5,6,11

pool 15:7,9

possible 38:24 39:2,3,19,22

prepare 5:23 6:2,7

prescription 34:12 35:5

pretty 17:8,20 18:11 27:15

prior 29:23 30:11,11

prison 27:6

Probably 23:3 32:13 37:13 38:6

problem 5:10 8:7 14:22 34:25

problems 29:22 30:6 35:10

proceeds 27:18

propounded 4:3

provided 42:9

province 36:23

psychiatric 8:3

Public 43:13

pulled 10:19 11:7

purpose 4:12

purposes 20:25

pursuant 3:7

put 22:19 26:12 27:8,11 31:8 36:10

CHARLES LEE RAYMOND

CHARLES LEE RAYMOND

signature 42:12,18
signing 31:13
Simpson 16:16,25 17:23
Since 13:5 34:4 35:10 36:4 37:8,12
sit 40:5
sitting 20:14 22:18 31:3,6,11
38:14 39:24 40:18
sixty 21:25
slid 19:10
sliding 11:24
slipped 11:15 30:4
smack 18:16
soft 11:18
sold 27:17 28:3
some 5:1 6:21 12:21 13:12 15:9
16:2 19:2 21:21 27:18,19,20
30:11,25 34:12,14,14 35:15
36:9,11
someone 11:12,19 13:8,14 18:6
21:5 39:11
someplace 16:8
something 6:4,5 10:17 13:14
17:3,5 18:18 21:18 23:21 26:4
28:6 33:19 42:6
sometimes 13:8,13
somewhere 8:22 20:20 26:25
Sons 12:23 41:9
soon 30:19
sore 30:24 32:15 35:23
Sort 7:23
sorts 8:7,9
sought 33:3
sound 25:21
South 2:8 18:11
southwest 19:11
space 17:18
special 21:18
specialty 13:18
speed 22:3,7 37:21 38:3,4
spell 9:9
spent 12:14
squad 31:8
SS 43:8
stalled 38:16
standard 6:1
standing 21:6
start 27:11 33:2,12
started 18:10,13,19,23 32:15 40:2
starting 30:23

State 3:7 43:13 44:2,5,11
statement 24:2
statements 31:4
STATES 1:1
station 24:12,15 25:9,12,14 40:15
stay 8:6 9:2 32:3
stayed 9:4
staying 8:16
stenotype 44:8
stiff 30:23
still 26:17 33:10 37:3
STIPULATED 3:2,8
stop 5:10 11:13,14 19:13 37:22
stopped 11:9 13:24 14:11 16:8,9
21:10 37:24 38:22 39:21
store 33:19
straight 9:20 25:4 30:16
stranded 39:20
Street 9:14 11:14 12:11,12 18:11,
17 19:5 20:13,15,16 38:25
streets 19:17
strengthened 36:14
strengthening 36:9
stuff 11:18 15:20 28:16 40:15 41:7
subject 12:20
substance 8:8
such 9:2 34:7
sucker 25:16
sued 12:6
suffered 30:5
suggest 17:23
SUITE 1:25 44:11
supervisor 41:8,11,14,20
suppose 40:7
supposed 13:7 20:9 22:22 38:23
Sure 9:10 13:22 14:10,22 15:12
16:20,21 17:8,11 19:6,8 25:24
27:23 28:22 30:20 32:7,11 33:21
35:2 37:20
suspended 10:24 11:4,5 14:2,8
sweet 21:24
swollen 34:15
sworn 4:2 44:6

T

take 5:3 14:19 15:20 17:24 19:20
21:19 22:1 24:17 25:11,15,16 30:20
37:15 42:3
taken 3:4 5:25 25:9 30:14 44:7,10

taking 3:13
talk 4:11 5:11 14:20 23:17 41:9
talked 8:17 23:19 29:8 41:18,20
talking 31:5
tall 26:22
Tavern 15:8 16:9,12 25:4
taxi 17:24
technician 12:25
Ted 33:7
telephone 31:20
tell 5:11 13:22 16:23 18:1 22:23
23:23 24:24 25:24 28:2 29:25
39:11 42:14
telling 31:9 35:19,25 39:10,11
ten 25:13 27:8 38:6,8
test 24:12 25:15,18
testified 40:24
testify 44:7
testimony 36:3 42:13 44:9
Thank 27:2
That's 12:5,14 13:7 14:3,15
17:8,9,16 19:19 21:23 22:13 23:14
26:16 27:11 32:8 34:13,16 35:22
37:7 38:11,22 39:3,23 41:23
therapy 36:10
there's 5:10 24:5 33:19
thereafter 44:8
thing 18:15 20:10 27:9,10
things 8:18 22:12 29:9 37:19
think 6:17 9:24 10:6 16:19 17:3
19:2 20:19 26:16 27:8 28:10 35:1
36:2 39:2,25 41:4,5
thinks 14:12
Thirty 8:15
Those 6:15 11:1,3,6 17:11 30:3,9
36:12 39:10 42:6
though 15:22 25:19,24 26:17
28:7 30:20
thought 34:11
three 7:4 11:3
Thunder 21:20
ticket 10:17
ticketed 13:25
tickets 14:11
till 29:6
time 3:11,12,13 5:10,12 8:11,21
9:2,25 11:5,15 12:19 14:5,11,13
16:15 17:3,13 18:12 19:3 21:25
22:9,11,16 23:10,15 24:21,23 25:2

CHARLES LEE RAYMOND

27:7,15 28:16 30:14 31:1,8 32:25 34:13,15 40:10,11,19 41:16
times 13:24 15:2 16:11
tissue 11:18
titled 6:4
today 4:8 5:23 6:19 29:25 38:8
together 14:13 15:1,15
told 14:1,4,7 23:24 24:8 25:20 28:15,21 29:5 35:23,24 36:3
Tony 16:16 18:1
took 10:20 24:2 27:23,24 28:15,17 30:16
totalled 19:14 24:19 28:7
towed 24:18
town 14:3,4
traffic 14:11 18:24 22:21 38:15 39:5,8,15,21
Trans 16:5
transcribe 41:25
transcribed 44:8
transcribing 42:13
transcript 42:4 44:9
transmission 12:25 13:14
transmissions 13:9,18 14:6
traveling 38:18
treatment 33:3 34:5
trial 3:12
tried 23:25 36:12
true 28:23 39:16 44:8
trusted 15:18,21
truth 4:16 16:23 31:9 39:10,12 44:7
tuning 21:19
turn 18:12 19:21 33:1,11
turned 18:12 34:11
turning 40:2
twenty 25:10
twist 33:1
two 10:5,10 14:1 20:11 27:6
type 12:24 33:25
typed 42:1

U

uh-huhs 5:6
under 4:24
understand 4:14,15,23 5:16,17 34:7
understood 41:21
UNITED 1:1

until 3:11 5:17 7:16 9:21 20:4 22:10 33:11 35:1
up 5:7 8:16 11:13 12:18 19:10 20:11,19 27:11 29:6 35:2 38:19,24 39:5,9,15 40:2 42:1
us 5:2,11 14:18 28:2 29:25 38:4
use 20:17
used 4:8 8:11 14:12 21:19
usual 17:9
usually 13:11 15:8
utility 19:11

V

verbal 5:3
verbally 5:4
very 21:9 25:5,19 30:20
video 5:24
videotape 6:2
visits 37:3
vs 1:5

W

waited 18:12
waiting 19:21 40:11
waive 42:11
want 5:9 10:7 12:20 14:2 21:15 22:6 37:14,19
wanted 8:21 41:17
wasn't 8:12 11:9,20 12:12 17:9,12,20,25 24:9,14 25:19 26:20 30:8 31:9 35:23 37:20
waste 13:19
waterbed 34:3
way 16:8 18:21 19:5 22:17,20 24:19 38:21 39:10
we'll 40:22
wear 23:5,7,12 35:1
wearing 23:14 35:2
weaving 11:8
week 7:6 16:11 36:17
weeks 15:16
weigh 26:25
weight 26:24
well 7:21 8:5,17,17 10:19 11:17 13:20,22 14:10 15:6,8,12,17,20 17:2,14,17,20 18:5 19:13 20:4,8,13 21:3,9,17,18 22:8 23:21 24:22 25:4, 23 26:4,8 28:5,6,12 29:4 30:18 31:21 35:9 39:2,11,18,22 41:6,11

wet 11:14,25 12:11,12
wham 18:15
whatever 40:17
wherever 20:3
whether 18:22 29:14,20 39:23
whiplash 11:17
Whispering 7:25 8:1,14 9:4,22 12:17
who's 16:15
whole 31:1
whom 28:22
Wild 14:15,16
will 4:16,24 5:16 41:25 42:6,8
willing 24:11
wish 42:15
withdraw 32:22
without 10:8
WITNESS 17:8 19:23 24:25 26:8 42:17,18 44:9,14
witnesses 39:4
women 18:18
work 12:24 13:1,11 25:5 27:13 32:9,11,17,24
working 12:22 13:4
worried 8:18
worries 8:18
worth 28:6
wouldn't 12:11 17:2,15 29:6 39:6,7,24 41:6
wreck 11:6
wrecked 19:13
wrecking 21:24
write 42:6

Y

year 7:17 10:21
years 7:14 27:6
yellow 40:2
yet 17:21
yield 18:25 22:22
yielded 38:21
younger 30:8
yourself 17:24
yuppy 19:2

Z

zero 21:24

GLOSSARY

ABA Model Guidelines for the Utilization of Legal Assistant Services Guidelines outlining recommended standards for using legal assistants.

active voice The sentence form in which the subject is doing something.

administrative regulations Law created by administrative agencies.

advance sheet A pamphlet containing the most recently reported opinions of specific courts or the courts of several jurisdictions; the volume and page numbers usually are the same as in the subsequently bound volumes of the respective reporter series, which cover several numbered issues of the advance sheets.

adversarial An argument for one side or the other.

advice or opinion letter A letter addressing a client's question of law and containing legal authority to support its conclusion, which may also recommend a particular course of action.

affidavit A written declaration of facts made voluntarily and under oath before a person authorized to administer oaths, such as a notary public.

affirmed The declaration by an appellate court that the judgment, decree, or order of a lower court is valid and must stand as rendered; when used as parenthetical information to indicate prior or subsequent history, it is abbreviated as "aff'd."

affirmative defense A defense that raises matters not covered in the plaintiff's Complaint and that will defeat the plaintiff's claim even if the plaintiff is able to prove all allegations in its Complaint; matter asserted by defendants which, assuming the Complaint to be true, constitutes a defense to it; a type of defense asserting that the defendant had the legal right to do whatever the plaintiff has complained of in the Petition or Complaint.

allegation A statement of fact that one expects to prove.

alliteration The deliberate repetition of similar sounds in close succession to emphasize particular words.

Amended Complaint A modified or corrected Complaint filed after service of the original Complaint.

amicus curiae, amici Latin meaning "friends of the court" used to refer to persons or legal entities who are not actual parties to the lawsuit but who have shown some vital interest in its outcome.

annotated code The unofficial version of state statutes containing brief summaries of the law and facts of cases interpreting or applying those statutes, normally included following the text of the statute.

annotation Explanatory commentary designed to give the reader basic information on a statute, case, or regulation intended to illustrate or explain its meaning.

annotation history table A table indicating whether an annotation has been superseded or supplemented.

Answer Defendant's formal, written response to the allegations in the plaintiff's Complaint, denying the allegations in whole or in part or confessing them and alleging a new matter in avoidance, which should prevent recovery on the facts alleged by the plaintiff.

antecedent The word or idea to which the pronoun refers.

appellant The party who brings the appeal.

appellate brief A brief prepared by counsel for filing with an appellate court after a case has been decided in the trial court.

appellate court A court having jurisdiction of appeal and review of decisions made by a lower court.

appellee The party against whom an appeal is brought.

appositive phrase Nouns and their modifiers, which rename or describe other nouns that cannot stand alone as sentences.

Argument and Authorities The section of a brief that states the party's legal arguments and the authorities to support those arguments.

attorney, counsel of record The attorney who has filed a notice of appearance for a party in court stating that the attorney is representing that party in the lawsuit.

attorney work product Any notes, working papers, memoranda and mental impressions or personal recollections prepared or formed by an attorney and his or her staff for litigation or trial that are protected from discovery.

bar associations A national, state, or local association of members of the legal profession.

bar journal A regular publication by a state or the national bar association, which may contain, among other things, recently decided opinions by the appellate courts for that state, various announcements, changes or additions to court rules, and articles written by lawyers on a wide variety of legal subjects.

Bill of Costs A certified, itemized statement of the amount of costs incurred by one of the parties in a lawsuit; in federal coourts, costs are allowed as a matter of course to the prevailing party, unless the court directs otherwise.

block indentation Text that is normally single-spaced and indented on both margins, usually used for quoted material.

boilerplate forms Standard language that, if used in a particular type of form or pleading, retains the same specific meaning from form to form.

brackets Symbols used when indicating an omission of letters or words or when changing a letter from uppercase to lowercase, or vice versa.

brief Formal and adversarial legal document containing arguments and authorities filed with the court in support of, or in opposition to, some motion or other matter, written to educate and persuade the court to rule in favor of the writer's client.

Brief Answer A brief, clear answer to the Question Presented in a legal memorandum.

brief bank A form file and research tool in which briefs and legal research are filed and categorized for easy retrieval.

caption, style of the case The beginning of a pleading, motion, deposition, or other legal instrument which indicates the names of the parties, name of the court, and the docket or case number.

case The status of a noun or pronoun, referring to whether the noun or pronoun is the subject or the object of the sentence.

case at bar The case now before the court and under its consideration—the case being tried or argued.

case brief A summary of the salient facts of the case, together with a succinct account of the court's decision or holding, and especially, the rationale or reasoning by which the court reached that decision.

cases Judicial opinions that interpret statutes, regulations, and constitutional provisions.

case law Law created by decisions of the court; the body of reported cases interpreting statutes, regulations, and constitutional provisions; used to decide what the law is and what a court will do when facing a certain question in a particular fact scenario.

case number The number assigned to a lawsuit by the court clerk used on all subsequent documents in that lawsuit to distinguish it from others.

case synopsis, syllabus A brief statement summarizing the rulings of a court opinion which, unless written by the court itself, constitutes no part of the court's opinion but is prepared by the publisher for the convenience of the reader.

cause of action Also called a claim; the fact or facts that give a person a right to judicial relief against another; the legally accepted reason for suing.

Certificate of Service, Certificate of Mailing Written assurance that a copy of the document upon which the Certificate appears has been served upon counsel for all parties or pro se litigants in the lawsuit, commonly made in accordance with the Rules of Civil Procedure.

certiorari A Latin word meaning "to be informed of"; most commonly used to refer to supreme courts, which use the writ of certiorari as a discretionary devise to choose the cases they wish to hear.

chronological deposition summary A summary broken down by subject matter and stated in chronological order.

Circuit Courts In the federal judicial system, the first level of appellate review for cases from the federal district court whose jurisdiction extends over several federal districts.

citation The reference to, or quotation of, legal authority.

citations of authority Statutes, case law, regulations, or treatises cited in support of a legal argument.

citator A research book containing lists of references or cites to help you assess the current validity of a case, statute, or other law and to provide leads to additional laws.

cite A reference to, or quotation of, an authority; to name in citation or to mention in support, illustration, or proof of.

cite-check The process of proofreading every legal authority in a legal document to check it for accuracy and correct citation form and to verify that the authority cited is still "good" law.

civil action
An action to enforce private rights.

civil cover sheet A form sometimes required by federal courts to be filed with the Complaint.

claim Also called a cause of action; a legally accepted reason to sue and the facts that give a person the right to judicial relief against another.

code system A system by which statutes are organized in sections, often called "titles," according to subject matter rather than in chronological order.

codify To collect and systematically arrange by subject matter the laws, rules, or regulations of a particular geographic location, or a certain area of the law.

collective nouns Nouns that refer to more than one person or thing, and may take either a singular or plural verb (e.g., "group").

comma splice A punctuation error in which two independent clauses are joined by only a comma.

Complaint Sometimes called a "Petition" or "Bill of Particulars," the first step, and pleading, in any lawsuit that gives the opposing party, the defendant, notice of the grounds for the plaintiff's claim.

compound words Words made up of two or more words used together as one expression.

compulsory counterclaim   A counterclaim arising out of the same facts or transaction which gives rise to the allegations in the plaintiff's Complaint and are permanently waived if not included in the litigation.

Conclusion   Within a legal memorandum, a brief summary of the analysis of the Discussion and the answer to the Questions Presented; within a brief, the closing section that provides a summary of each major point made in the argument or discussion and restates the request for relief.

concurring opinion   A separate opinion in which one or more justices agree that the result reached by the majority or plurality opinion is correct, but wish to add their own thoughts on the reasons for the decision.

confidential   That which is meant to be held in confidence or kept secret.

confidentiality   The ethical and legal obligation not to disclose any oral or written communications made between a lawyer or his or her staff and the client.

conflict of interest   A situation in which an attorney's or legal assistant's regard for one duty could lead to the disregard of another duty.

contempt citation   A writ issued by a court which states that a party was acting with wilful disregard or disobedience of a public authority, including a court.

contention interrogatory   An interrogatory that inquires of the opinions and contentions of an adverse party.

contributory negligence   An affirmative defense that must be pleaded and proven by the defendant; in tort law, a plaintiff's unreasonable act or omission amounting to want of ordinary care which, together with a defendant's negligence, is the proximate cause of the injury.

controlling authority   Any law (predominately case law) in your case's jurisdiction, dealing with the same issue as yours, on which the court could rely in reaching its decision.

count   The statement of a cause of action, or a separate and independent claim, involving a single theory of recovery even though each is based on the same transaction or event.

Counterclaim   Sometimes called a Cross-Complaint, a cause of action or claim for relief by one or more defendants asserted against one or more plaintiffs in the same lawsuit.

course and scope of employment   Activities of an employee that fairly and reasonably may be said to be incident to his or her employment or logically and naturally connected with it. Activities of an employee in furtherance of duties owed to the employer where the latter is exercising or could exercise control over what the employee does; an employee is in the course of employment when, within the time covered by the employment, he or she is doing something at a proper place, which he or she might reasonably do while so employed.

court reporter   A person who transcribes testimony by shorthand or stenography during court or trial related proceedings, such as a deposition.

court rules   Rules promulgated and adopted by courts that have the force of law and govern practice and procedure.

cover letter   A letter mailed with another document to introduce that document.

cover page   A brief's first page that usually sets out the case number, the style of the case, the title of the brief, the name, address, and telephone number of the attorney filing the brief and which party that attorney represents, and the date the brief was filed. Appellate brief covers may also include the name of the trial judge and the jurisdiction from which the case came.

criticized   In a citator, a type of treatment of a case meaning that the soundness of reasoning in the cited case is criticized by subsequent opinions.

Cross-Claim   A cause of action or claim for relief by one or more defendants asserted against one or more co-defendants in the same lawsuit.

cross reference The second research tool found in the unofficial version of the federal code, U.S.C.A., which will lead to different, but related, sections of the Code.

damages Monetary compensation that may be recovered in court by someone who has suffered injury or loss to person, property, or rights through an unlawful act or omission of another.

dangling modifiers Modifiers that modify a noun placed either before the modifier or after the modifier.

dangling preposition A preposition left uncertain at the end of a sentence.

default judgment A judgment rendered against a party who has failed to defend against a claim that has been brought by another party.

defense The allegations of fact or legal theories offered to offset or defeat an opposing party's claims or demands.

Definitions Used to define the terms within that discovery so that the language is as comprehensive and unambiguous as possible.

delivery The act by which something is placed within the possession or control of another.

demand letter A form of legal correspondence sent to the opposing party in a controversy demanding whatever action or compensation that will satisfy the client; it speaks with an air of assurance and certainty, requiring the addressee to do something that the writer demands as a matter of right.

denial A declaration that something is not true, such as denial of the allegations in the plaintiff's Complaint; a type of defense in which the defendant denies one or more facts necessary to support the claim. The denial is based upon a different view of the same rule of law raised by the opponent. The party asserting the denial is saying that the rule of law on which the claim is founded cannot be established because the other party has failed to prove an essential element of that rule.

dependent clause A clause that begins with a subordinating word, such as *because, if, who,* or *that,* to express particular relationships between the clauses they introduce and the main clauses to which they are attached. A dependent clause never stands alone as a sentence.

deponent One who testifies in a deposition.

deposition A pretrial discovery device by which one party questions the other party or a witness whose answers are given under oath in the presence of a stenographer or court reporter who transcribes what is said. All or a part of a deposition can be used at trial.

deposition summary, index A concise summary of a deposition transcript used for various purposes by attorneys throughout the course of litigation and in preparation for trial.

deposition transcript An official copy of the deposition which is a word-for-word typing of everything that was said "on the record" during the deposition.

descriptive name A designated name used to describe the parties when there are multiple plaintiffs or defendants.

descriptive word index A tool used in legal research when using a digest to lead you to other areas and case law.

designation Abbreviated or short, clear names for each of the parties or other actors, or for some other important event, document, or thing, to make the document more readable and understandable; used whenever a particular person or thing appears repeatedly throughout a document. In text, the designation assigned to each party is enclosed in parentheses and quotation marks.

dictum, dicta A non-binding comment or observation made by a judge in an opinion that is *not* essential to the determination of the case.

digest Volumes organized by subject containing paragraph summaries (called headnotes) at the beginning of an opinion of each issue or point of law within that opinion which are primarily used as case finders.

Discussion   Within a legal memorandum, the section that gives an impartial analysis of the law as it applies to the question answered by the legal memorandum.

discovery   Pretrial devices that can be used by a party to obtain information and evidence from the other side to assist in preparing for trial.

discovery conference   A face-to-face meeting between opposing counsel to discuss disputes over discovery that is often required before the dispute is brought to the court.

discovery motion   A motion filed with the court that deals solely with discovery issues.

discovery plan   A strategic plan for using discovery devised to reap the most benefit for the client.

dismissal with prejudice   Conclusive of the rights of the parties having the same effect as a final adjudication and bars the plaintiff's right to bring a lawsuit later on the same cause of action.

dismissal without prejudice   No rights or privileges are waived or lost by dismissing the lawsuit, and the plaintiff is not barred from bringing a new lawsuit later on the same cause of action.

disposition   The final decision by the court.

dispositive motion   A motion that attacks the pleadings which, when ruled upon by the court, resolves the entire lawsuit or a portion of it.

disqualify   To render ineligible or unfit.

dissenting opinion   The explicit disagreement of one or more judges of a court with the decision passed by the majority. A dissent may or may not be accompanied by a dissenting opinion.

distinguish   When discussing case law, to point out an essential difference or to prove a case cited as applicable or inapplicable.

District Courts   Court of original jurisdiction where all evidence is first received and considered. In the federal judicial system, the trial courts with general federal jurisdiction over cases involving federal laws or offenses and actions between citizens of different states whose judgments are subject to appellate review; in state judicial systems, a trial court having full jurisdiction within its own jurisdictional area over both civil and criminal cases involving state laws or offenses whose judgments and decrees are subject to appellate review.

districts   The territorial areas into which an entire state or country, county, municipality, or other political subdivision is divided for judicial, political, electoral, or administrative purposes.

diversity of citizenship   Jurisdiction of federal courts extending to cases between citizens of different states or between a citizen of a state and an alien, for which a requisite jurisdictional amount must also be met.

docket number   The case number assigned by the court administration to identify each new piece of litigation.

double negative   Two negative words used in the same sentence. Two negatives make a positive.

ellipsis   Punctuation generally used to indicate the omission of a word or words to take the place of the omission.

entry of appearance   A document filed with the court stating that the attorney named is entering an appearance as counsel of record on behalf of a litigant which states that the attorney is representing that party in the lawsuit; a voluntary submission to a court's jurisdiction. An entry of appearance sometimes also reserves an additional twenty days for the defendant to file his or her Answer to the Complaint.

equitable relief   Relief sought from a court with equity powers, such as in the case of one seeking an injunction or specific performance instead of money damages.

essential facts   Yet another way to refer to key facts.

et al. A Latin abbreviation of et alii, meaning "and others" that is often added after the name of the first party (where there are multiple plaintiffs and/or defendants) to replace names of the remaining parties, e.g., John Smith et al. v. Concrete World, Inc. et al.

ethical canons State bar association regulations governing attorney conduct, including a lawyer's use of legal assistants.

et ux A Latin abbreviation meaning "and wife."

evidence Any kind of proof offered to establish the existence or nonexistence of a fact in dispute, e.g., testimony, writings, other material objects, and demonstrations.

exhibit A paper, document, or thing referred to and made a part of an affidavit, pleading, or other document, and also an item of physical/tangible evidence which is to be or has been offered to the court.

exhibit list A party's list of all prospective documents and things which that party expects to introduce as evidence at trial.

expert witness A witness who is retained or specially employed to provide expert testimony in the lawsuit or whose duties as an employee of the party regularly involve giving expert testimony.

ex rel. A Latin abbreviation for *ex relatione,* meaning upon relation or information; legal proceedings that are instituted by the attorney general (or other proper official for a state, county, etc.) in the name and on behalf of the state, but on the information and at the instigation of an individual who has a private interest in the matter, are said to be taken "on the relation" (*ex rel.*) of such person who is called the "relator": State *ex rel.* Doe v. Roe.

fact pleadings Formal allegations by the parties to the lawsuit that require identification of all facts which must be proved to win that claim to allege a valid cause of action.

fact witness A person who testifies to what he or she has seen, heard, or otherwise observed.

Federal Rules of Civil Procedure Procedural rules that govern civil actions in federal district courts.

Federal Rules of Evidence In federal courts, Court rules that govern the admissibility of evidence at trials and hearings.

filing fee The fee assessed by the clerk for filing any Complaint or Petition and other documents, or for issuing a summons or subpoena, regardless of whether the document is filed with, or issued from, a state or federal court.

final appealable order or judgment A judgment is considered final, and thus appealable, only if it determines the rights of the parties and disposes of all issues involved so that no future action by the court will be necessary to settle and determine the entire controversy except execute judgment.

footer A specific line of text, page numbers, or both, at the bottom of a page.

form books Collections of sample legal documents to be used as models for creating other documents.

form files, form bank Samples of pleadings and other documents that are organized and stored for easy retrieval.

forum The court to which the litigation is brought.

functional designations Descriptive names that indicate the relationship between the parties other than plaintiff and defendant.

good cause A legally sufficient ground or reason; in discovery, good cause is present if the discovery sought is material to the moving party's trial preparation and is ordinarily satisfied by a factual allegation showing that the requested documents are necessary to establish the movant's claim or that denial of production would cause moving party hardship or injustice.

header Information placed at the top lefthand corner of the second and subsequent pages of correspondence to identify them in case the pages are separated.

heading or caption   The section of a legal memorandum that identifies the person for whom the memorandum was prepared, the author, the date, what the memorandum is about, and the file to which it belongs.

headnote   A small paragraph summary found at the beginning of an opinion of each issue of point of law within an opinion; headnotes are written by the publisher, not the court which wrote the opinion.

hearing   A court proceeding with definite issues of fact or law to be resolved in which witnesses are heard, the parties confront each other, and an impartial officer presides, such as a judge or magistrate.

Historical Note   The first research tool found in the unofficial version of the federal code, U.S.C.A., that briefly summarizes how the present section got to look the way it does, including notes about what each amendment added or changed.

holding   The court's answer to, or resolution of, the legal issue before it; the legal principle to be drawn from the opinion (decision) of the court.

hornbook   Popular reference to a series of textbooks that review various fields of law in summary, narrative form, as opposed to casebooks that are designed as primary teaching tools and include many reprints of court opinions.

hyphen   Mark used either to divide a word or to form a compound word.

id.   An abbreviation meaning "the same" used to indicate reference to the immediately preceding authority; indicates an exact repetition of the last citation given.

imperative mood   The verb form used for commands. "Order in the court," said the judge.

implied preposition   A preposition that is not stated in the sentence, but is implied from the sentence.

incidental legal services test   A general test used by the court to define the unauthorized practice of law where the court considers whether the activity is frequently performed by laypersons depending upon and secondary to some other business transaction.

independent clause   A clause that can stand alone as a sentence.

indicative mood   The verb form used for ordinary statements. "The legal assistant drafted the discovery request."

infinitive   A predictive or future verb form (e.g., "to send").

in forma pauperis   The way in which an indigent person, unable to pay court costs and fees, may be permitted to sue without prepaying those costs and fees.

information letter   A standard type of letter used to give information.

injunctive relief   A court-ordered equitable remedy prohibiting someone from doing some specified act or commanding someone to undo some wrong or injury.

in personam jurisdiction   The power a court has over the defendant himself, that enables the court to issue an *in personam* judgment, in contrast to the court's power over the defendant's interest in property (quasi in rem) or power over the property (in rem).

in rem jurisdiction   Refers to an action taken directly against the defendant's property, or the power by a court over a thing which allows it to seize and hold the object for some legal purpose.

Instructions   Used as reminders to the answering party of the rules pertaining specifically to that type of discovery.

internal memorandum   Memorialized information of some aspect of the case, to be used only in-house.

interrogatories   A type of discovery consisting of written questions about the lawsuit from one party to another to be answered under oath.

interrogatory subparts   Subparagraphs to an interrogatory that, depending on the applicable court rules, may be are counted as separate interrogatories.

Introduction   An optional paragraph at the beginning of a legal memorandum or other document used to identify the parties and to explain briefly what has already happened in the case, how the issue arose, or the event which caused the document to be written.

introductory paragraph or sentence A concise statement at the beginning of a pleading or other document containing the name of the party, the party's designation, and the character of the pleading.

introductory signals Signals before a citation provided to show the purposes for which the citation is made and the degree of support the citation gives.

involuntary dismissal Under rules practice, may be accomplished on court's own motion for lack of prosecution or on motion of defendant for lack of prosecution or failure to introduce evidence of facts on which relief may be granted, and disposes of all of the party's rights. It is a "final" order that can be appealed.

issue A single certain and material point of fact or of law, created by the allegations and pleadings of the parties, which is disputed by the parties; the precise question the court is deciding.

issue-by-issue approach A specialized format using individual propositions to state the issues through which the reader is led in a logical, methodical way to the conclusion.

issues of pure law An issue of law arises where evidence is undisputed and only one conclusion can be draw from it.

joint stipulation for dismissal, joint motion to dismiss When both the plaintiff and defendant decide to dismiss the lawsuit.

judgment The official decision of a court in a case brought before it; the judicial determination of the rights and duties of parties growing out of litigation before a court. (The judgment was reversed.)

jurisdiction The power of a court to hear and determine a case.

jury instructions Directions given by the trial judge to the jury about the law of the case which the jury needs to reach a verdict. Sometimes referred to as a "charge" rather than instruction.

jury trial The trial of a matter before a judge and jury as opposed to a trial solely before a judge.

Jury Trial Demanded A statement made by a party filing the pleading demanding a jury trial on any claim triable by right before a jury to prevent the waiver of that right.

key fact A fact that is so crucial that, if it were changed, the holding of the opinion would also have changed.

key number A number identifying where a particular topic falls in West's outline of the law; West's key number system is the organizational principle used to classify small paragraph summaries of the opinions in the digests.

ladder, branching interrogatories Interrogatories that first ask a broad question, followed by specific questions relating to one or more possible responses.

law review A periodic publication of most law schools containing topical articles by law professors, judges, or attorneys, and case summaries by law review member-students.

lead case A case that has, because of its important character, demanded more than usual attention from the judges and, because of this, is frequently looked upon as having settled or determined the law upon all points involved in such cases, and serves as a guide for subsequent decisions.

leave of court Permission from the court to take a particular action that is otherwise prohibited without the court's consent.

legal advice Counsel given by attorneys to their clients consisting of an opinion or recommendation of a course of action.

legal authority The written material used to decide what the law is in a particular case, and from which you analyze what the probable result of that issue will be in your case.

legal conclusions A statement of legal duty without stating facts from which the duty arises.

legal encyclopedia A type of secondary authority that is a general source of information in which the fabric of the law is broken down into many subtopics, arranged alphabetically.

legal memorandum An internal memorandum written to solve a legal problem by applying pertinent cases and statutes.

legalese Outdated words, phrases, or other legal jargon that obscure meaning.

legal opinion A document or statement in which an attorney renders his or her understanding of the law as applied to the assumed facts, which may also recommend a course of action.

legal periodical A secondary authority, journal, magazine, or newspaper prepared by a private publisher containing recent decisions, notices of local court proceedings, and news of general interest to the legal profession published from various sources, including bar associations and commercial publishers.

legal relief A remedy available, under the particular circumstances of the case, in a court of law.

legal terms of art A word or phrase that has a fixed and known legal meaning.

legal theory A right recognized by the law which the plaintiff seeks to enforce; in litigation, either the cause of action, or claim, and the defense, all of which are always based upon one or more rules of law.

library reference The third research tool found in the unofficial version of the federal code, U.S.C.A., which leads to other reference materials within the West system.

limited In a citator, a treatment for a given case that means a later opinion restricts the decision of the cited case in duration, extent, or scope.

limiting paragraph In an opinion letter, a statement of the information upon which the opinion is based.

linking verbs Verbs that connect their subjects to the description that follows.

local court rules Court rules adopted by an individual court which supplement the Rules of Civil Procedure applicable to that court and which apply only to the court that creates them.

mandatory authority Any primary authority that a court must follow in reaching its decision.

majority opinion The opinion of an appellate court in which the majority of its members join; it may also refer to a view of a legal principle in which most jurisdictions concur.

malapropism The mistaken use of a word that sounds similar to the correct word but has a different meaning.

material fact One which is essential to the case, defense, application, etc., and without which it could not be supported; one which tends to establish any of the issues raised and one upon which the outcome of litigation depends.

materiality test Used to test evidence essential to the case, without which the lawsuit could not be supported, or used to test evidence that tends to establish any of the issues raised by the lawsuit.

Medical Authorization or Release A written statement by a patient of his or her intention to discharge another from the duty of confidentiality between physician and patient, and authorizing the production of his or her medical records to the requesting party.

modified The amendment or adjustment of a lower court's decision by an appellate court.

modifiers Any word or group of words which limits or qualifies the meaning of other parts of the sentence.

modifying phrase A group of words that alters the quality, degree, or meaning of another word in a sentence.

motion An application made to a court or other decision-making body to obtain a favorable action or decision, made usually for one of the following reasons: (1) to control information; (2) to control the final outcome; (3) to control the procedure; or (4) to control the parties.

Motion for Attorney Fees   A motion filed with the court requesting an award of attorney fees to be given to the prevailing party (the movant) pursuant to the American Rule (the winning party in litigation cannot obtain the costs of attorney fees from the losing party unless authorized by statute or unless the losing party acted in bad faith, vexatiously, wantonly, or for oppressive reasons).

motion for extension of time   A procedural motion in which the movant asks the court for additional time to file a document with the court or otherwise respond to an opposing party.

motion for judgment on the pleadings   A dispositive motion filed with the court requesting it to make a decision on the pleadings alone without a trial, on the ground that the material facts are not in dispute and only questions of law remain.

motion for protective order   A motion filed with the court requesting the court to enter a protective order to protect one party from abusive service of process or discovery by the opposing party or to order a party to cease some act or harassment, or to keep certain privileged documents or information confidential.

motion for sanctions   A motion filed with the court requesting that Rule 11 sanctions or penalties be awarded by the court upon the attorneys, law firms, or parties who have violated Rule 11(b) or who are responsible for the violation, which usually consist of the payment by the violator of opposing counsel's attorney's fees and costs.

motion for summary judgment   A dispositive motion asking the court to conclude that there is no genuine issue as to any material fact and that a judgment should be rendered in the movant's favor without the need for a trial.

motion in limine   A motion filed with the court, made before or after the beginning of a jury trial, for a protective order against the potential use of prejudicial statements, evidence, or questions by the other side.

motion to compel   A motion requesting the court to order the opposing party to respond to discovery requests.

motion to dismiss, demurrer   A motion usually made before trial begins that requests the court to dismiss the case because the pleadings of the other side are insufficient or because the Complaint does not state a claim for which the law provides a remedy.

National Association of Legal Assistants   One of the two major national legal assistant organizations.

National Federation of Paralegal Association   One of the two major national legal assistant organizations.

negative history   The subsequent history of a cited case indicating that the case has been vacated, reversed, overruled, limited, superseded, criticized, modified, distinguished, or questioned.

negligence   To omit doing something which a reasonable person, guided by those ordinary considerations that generally regulate human affairs, would do, or the doing of something which a reasonable and prudent person would not do.

nominalization   A noun made out of a verb.

non-restrictive clause   A clause that follows but does not define or limit a noun. Non-restrictive clauses always begin with the word *which*.

Notes of Decisions   The fourth and final research tool found in the unofficial version of the federal code, U.S.C.A., that provides short synopses—like headnotes—of cases that have interpreted this statute.

notice of hearing   Written notice of the date, time, and location of any motion set to be heard before the court which must be served on every party in the lawsuit at least five days before the date of the hearing according to the Federal Rules of Civil Procedure.

notice paragraph   A paragraph at the beginning of certain types of discovery that states to whom the discovery is directed.

notice pleadings Formal allegations by the parties to a lawsuit of their respective claims and defenses to provide notice of what is to be expected at trial.

Notice to Take Deposition Sometimes required by court rules, a written document filed with the court by one party to notify all other parties in the lawsuit that a deposition of a witness or party has been scheduled at a certain date, time, and location.

number The form of a word indicating the word's singular or plural status.

object, objection Argument or reason contending that the matter objected to is improper or illegal; used to call the court's attention to improper evidence or procedure.

offer of proof Telling the court what evidence a party proposes to present to obtain a ruling on admissibility.

official reporters One of three reporters containing opinions of the Supreme Court of the United States.

"on all fours" A case is that is exactly on point with another case as to result, facts, or both.

on point Or "on all fours," means the facts and issues of the opinion are the same as, or substantially similar, to your client's.

operative fact The most important facts of a case on which the court rested its opinion.

oral argument The verbal presentation by attorneys for each party before an appellate court of why the lower court's decision should be affirmed, modified, or reversed.

overruled An opinion is overruled when a later decision, rendered by the same court or by a superior court, expresses a judgment on the same question of law directly opposite to that which was given before, thereby depriving the earlier opinion of all authority as a precedent.

page-line deposition summary A page-by-page summary of a deposition transcript.

page-line-topic deposition summary A summary that states the page and lines being summarized, then the actual summary, and then a condensed one-word "topic."

page-only deposition summary A summary by page that is less detailed than other types of deposition summaries.

parallel citation A citation reference to another set of books or reporters in which the same case—word for word—can be located.

parallel construction Consistent word form and verb tense among particular words and/or sentences expressing two or more ideas using the same grammatical form.

parenthetical An abbreviated summary of the case's facts, holding, or reasoning, whichever is pertinent to the reason for citing the case, that is often used in string citations.

parenthetical comments Explanatory, supplementary, or transitional words or phrases usually set off by parentheses, commas, or dashes.

participial phrase A group of words that functions as a participle and refers to the subject of the sentence. "Hearing the woman's cry for help, the policeman ran to the scene of the crime."

passim A Latin word meaning simply "dispersed," that is, "here and there" used when an authority is cited on many pages.

passive voice The sentence form in which the subject has something done to him, her, or it.

per curiam A Latin phrase meaning "by the court."

per curiam opinion A phrase used to distinguish an opinion of the whole court as opposed to one from an opinion written by any one judge.

permissive counterclaim A counterclaim grounded in facts different from those in the main lawsuit, although the parties to both controversies are the same, not waived by failure to press them in the plaintiff's action, and may be filed as a separate lawsuit.

persuasive authority Non-mandatory, primary authority and any secondary authority that may influence or give guidance to the court or administrative tribunal by its arguments or reasons offered, but is not binding on the court.

Pertinent Statutes Those statutes that control the issues to be discussed in a legal memorandum.

pinpoint cites The second page number given in a full citation that gives the number of the page where the statement or quotation can be found in the cited original source.

pleadings A legal term of art describing documents that contain claims and defenses filed by the parties to a lawsuit with the court. Pleadings set out the issues to be tried.

pleonasm The use of more words than are necessary.

plurality opinion Where there are not enough agreeing justices to form a majority of the court, an opinion in which more justices join than in any concurring opinion.

pocket part A cumulative supplement in pamphlet form found in the back of a book that updates or consolidates all earlier volumes.

praecipe A document signed by a plaintiff or plaintiff's attorney requesting the court clerk to issue a summons to a defendant.

prayer, prayer for relief Also called a "demand for relief," or "wherefore clause," a requisite element of a pleading or motion that states the specific type of relief sought and the grounds in support of the request, costs, interest, attorney's fees, and any type of special damages to which the pleader deems him- or herself entitled; a formal request to the court made as the final closing paragraph of a document which asks for specific relief, damages, or process.

pretrial conference Meeting of counsel for all parties and the judge before the trial where they attempt, among other things, to narrow the issues to be tried, to obtain stipulations of facts or authenticity of documents, to identify witnesses and exhibits to be introduced by each party at trial, and to make a final effort to settle the case without a trial.

pretrial order An order jointly prepared by counsel for all parties that controls the future course of action at trial and lists, among other things, the parties' allegations and defenses, the witnesses and exhibits each party intends to introduce at trial, and the other side's objections to the same.

prima facie A Latin term meaning "on the face of it," pertaining to a fact that is presumed to be true unless disproved by some evidence to the contrary.

primary authority Any law on which a court could rely in reaching its decision, predominantly case law.

prior proceedings, prior history The stages of litigation that occurred before the cited opinion was written; the *Bluebook* requires that the prior history should be given in a citation only if it is significant or relevant to the point for which the case is cited.

privilege The client's right to confidentiality of oral or written communications exchanged within the attorney-client relationship; a special immunity enjoyed by a person, company, or class beyond the common advantages of other citizens. When certain communications are deemed privileged, this allows holders of that privilege to resist discovery attempts to disclose that information. A holder of the privilege can also enjoin other participants from disclosing the information.

procedural history The entire history, both prior and subsequent, of a given case that includes who sued whom and for what, and exactly what was decided by each court.

procedural issue A question dealing with the technicalities of bringing or defending the litigation, e.g., the format of the complaint, the jurisdiction of the court, or the admissibility of evidence.

process The means used by a court to acquire or exercise its jurisdiction over a person or over specific property.

process server A person authorized by law, such as a sheriff, to serve process papers.

professional judgment test   A general test used by the court to define the unauthorized practice of law where the court considers whether the activity requires legal skills, knowledge, and training beyond that of the average layperson.

pronoun reference   The noun to which the pronoun refers.

proof of service   Also known as "return of service," the evidence submitted service was properly made on a party or others.

proposed order   An order that is submitted with a motion for the court's execution to save the court from drafting the order itself.

proposition   A heading or subheading that consists of a succinct statement—normally a single sentence or sentence fragment—which states the question or issue to be discussed and answered in the discussion that follows.

protective order   A court order designed to protect one party from abusive service of process or discovery by the opposing party or to order a party to cease some act or harassment, or to keep certain privileged documents or information confidential.

proximate cause   That which, in a natural and continuous sequence, unbroken by any efficient intervening cause, produces injury, and without which the injury would not have occurred.

Public Law number   The number assigned to a law identifying the Congress from which the law came and the law's number.

punitive damages   Damages on an increased scale awarded to the plaintiff over and above what will compensate for his or her actual property loss, where the wrong was aggravated by violence, oppression, malice, fraud, or wanton conduct of the defendant.

Question Presented   A terse, clear statement of the legal question or questions the legal memorandum is intended to solve.

real party in interest   The one who, under applicable substantive law, has the right that the lawsuit seeks to enforce.

reasoning, rationale   In an opinion, the court's application of the law to the facts to solve the question before the court and the court's explanation of why it decided an issue as it did.

record   The official collection of pleadings, transcripts, exhibits, and so on, designated by the parties that constitutes the written memorial of all the acts and proceedings in a lawsuit in a court of record.

RE or subject line   A standard part of a letter or memorandum heading that states the subject matter of the correspondence or memorandum.

regional reporters   Volumes of state court opinions that collect the appellate opinions of several contiguous states in a single volume.

relevance   Applicability to the matter in question and having a logical tendency to prove or disprove a material fact.

relevancy standard   Testimony is *relevant* if reasonable inferences can be drawn from it regarding, or if any light is shed upon, a contested matter; evidence is *relevant* not only when it tends to prove or disprove precise fact in the issue, but when it tends to establish facts from which existence or nonexistence of facts in issue can be directly inferred.

remand   To send a case back to an inferior or lower court for some kind of further action or proceeding.

Reply   The plaintiff's response to the defendant's Answer.

reporters   The books that contain the opinions written by the courts.

Request for Admissions   A type of discovery consisting of written statements of fact submitted to an adverse party, which that party is required to admit or deny; statements that are admitted will be treated by the court as having been established and need not be proved at trial.

Request for Physical or Mental Examinations   A type of discovery used when the physical or mental condition of a party or person in the custody or legal control of a party is in controversy to determine the genuineness of that condition, its extent and causes, and to develop a prognosis.

Request for Production of Documents and Things A discovery tool through which a party requests another party to disclose documents or things in that party's exclusive knowledge or possession and necessary to the party seeking discovery as evidence to prove that party's allegations or defenses.

res ipsa loquitur A Latin phrase meaning "the thing speaks for itself" used in tort law. The event would not have happened without negligence.

restrictive clause A clause that follows and defines or limits a noun. Restrictive clauses generally begin with the word *that.*

return of service The evidence submitted showing that proper service was made on a party or others.

reversed A decision made by an appellate court to set aside or overturn the decision made by a lower court.

Rule 11, Federal Rules of Civil Procedure A court rule regarding the attorneys' and litigants' obligation to the court for their conduct which provides sanctions for violations and requires the attorneys' or litigants' signatures and certification that (1) the document is not presented for improper purposes; (2) the claims, defenses, or contentions are warranted by existing law; (3) the allegations have, or are likely to have, evidentiary support; and (4) the denial of any contention is reasonably based on a lack of information or belief.

Rules of Civil Procedure Procedural rules that govern civil actions in district courts.

Rules of Evidence Court rules that govern the admissibility of evidence at trials and hearings applicable in trial courts.

rule of short The shorter the sentence, the easier it is to understand.

run-on sentence Incorrect (or no) punctuation between main clauses in a sentence, resulting in a run-on sentence in which two thoughts are jumbled together.

sanctions Rule 11 sanctions or penalties awarded by the court upon the attorneys, law firms, or parties who have violated Rule 11(b) or who are responsible for the violation, which usually consist of the payment by the violator of opposing counsel's attorney's fees and costs.

scheduling conference A conference held by the judge and counsel for all parties in the lawsuit to determine the deadlines for the various stages of the litigation.

Scheduling Order An order issued by the court to set the deadlines for many stages of the litigation, such as amending the pleadings, joining other parties, filing motions, completing discovery, and filing witness and exhibit lists.

secondary authority Any non-law (e.g., treatise, legal encyclopedia, or law review article) on which a court could rely in reaching its decision.

seminal case A well-known case that subsequent cases regularly cite for the same issues you are discussing in your brief; an opinion cited repeatedly and with approval in subsequent decisions.

service of process The delivery or communication of writs, summonses, etc., or formal notice of parties' claims and defenses.

settlement demand letter Legal correspondence often found in personal injury litigation in which the plaintiff's attorney demands a sum settlement from the defendant or defendants.

Shepard's Citator The most widely used set of citators, it provides, through letter-form abbreviations or words, the subsequent judicial history and interpretation of reported decisions; it also denotes the legislative and amendment history, and cases that have cited or construed, constitutions, statutes, rules, regulations, etc.

shepardize To use the volumes of *Shepard's* to collect the research references provided for that item, such as the subsequent history of a particular case and how subsequent cases have cited or interpreted a particular case.

short or spot cite   Also called pinpoint cites; a citation that tells your reader the precise page in an authority on which the reference discussed by the author may be found.

signals   Indicators provided to show the purposes for which the citations are made and the degree of support the citations give.

signature block   The final section of the pleading or other document filed with the court containing the signature line, name, address, and telephone of the attorney of record or the pro se litigant, which also serves to meet the requirements of Rule 11.

signposting   A structural writing tool in which elements of a statement are categorized and numbered. The sentence is then structured by each enumerated point (i.e., "first," "second," and "third").

slip law   A legislative enactment that is promptly published in a pamphlet or in single sheets after it has been passed into law.

slip opinion   An individual court opinion published separately shortly after it is "handed down," or rendered, by the court.

special matters   The one exception to notice pleading format requirements requiring that some allegations, such as fraud, mistake, subject-matter jurisdiction, and special damages, must be pleaded "specifically" and "with particularity."

split infinitive   A predictive or future verb form. Infinitives are split when the article *to* is separated from the verb by another word or words. "He decided to quickly send the memo."

standard of care   The degree of care that a reasonably prudent person should exercise under the same or similar circumstances.

Statement of Facts   A section of a legal memorandum that provides all of the relevant facts necessary to the reader's understanding of the issues; the section of a brief containing a narrative of the pertinent facts needed to understand the issues discussed in the brief which, written correctly, can further educate the court about why your client should prevail.

Statement of the Case   The section of a brief that includes both facts and a procedural history of the case, when that history is important to the issues addressed within the brief or required by the court rules.

Statement of Uncontroverted Facts   The section of a motion for summary judgment or brief in support stating the material facts that are not in dispute in which each fact is supported by documentary evidence in the form of an exhibit, affidavit, or deposition excerpt.

statutes   Laws passed by the legislature at all levels—national, state, and local.

statutory law   Law created by acts of the legislature.

stipulation   A *stipulation* of expected testimony is an agreement by both sides that, if a witness were in court, he or she would testify substantially in the words of the stipulation.

string cite   A series of citations separated by semicolons which are often preceded by a signal and used to support a statement made in a brief, legal memorandum, law review articles, treatise, or legal encyclopedia; often used to emphasize a particular point in a legal memorandum or brief.

sua sponte   A Latin phrase meaning "of his or its own will or motion" or "without prompting or suggestion".

subdivision index   An index, in addition to the main index, for each of the major divisions (with Roman numerals).

subject-matter deposition summary   A summary which is broken down into particular topics, sometimes given in chronological order.

subject-matter jurisdiction   The court's power to hear and deal with the subject matter involved in the lawsuit.

subjunctive mood   The verb form used when writing about an uncertain condition or one that is contrary to fact or reality. "If I were the judge, I would overrule the objection."

subpoena   A command to appear at a certain time and place to give testimony upon a certain matter.

subpoena ad testificandum   Commonly called a subpoena, used to command someone who is not a party to the lawsuit to appear and testify in court or at a deposition.

subpoena duces tecum   A court process, initiated by a party in a lawsuit, compelling the production of certain specific documents and other items that are material and relevant to facts in issue in the lawsuit which are in the custody and control of the person or entity served with process.

subsequent history   The appellate court's treatment of the cited case after the date of the cited case; the stages of litigation which occurred after the cited opinion was written.

substantive issue   A question dealing with the actual law at hand, e.g., the pollution of a river, the breach of a contract, or the commission of a crime.

Summary of the Argument   A short, blunt summation of what the client wants and why the law says he should have it which immediately precedes the Argument and Authorities section.

summons   A means of acquiring jurisdiction over a party and notifying defendants that a lawsuit has been commenced against them.

superseded   When an appellate court suspended, canceled, or replaced a prior opinion or decision of a lower court.

supporting brief   The written legal arguments and authorities supporting a specific motion, or objection to another party's motion, and which states the party's grounds for bringing the motion, or objecting to it, and the reasons why the motion should be granted or denied.

Supreme Court of the United States   The highest appellate court, or court of last resort, in the federal judicial system, comprised of the Chief Justice of the United States and eight Associate Justices.

Table of Authorities or Table of Cases   An index of the citations for all of the authorities in the brief grouped by type of authority, e.g. case law, statutes, etc., that also indicates the page number(s) where each is cited within the body of the brief.

Table of Contents   An index of a brief's headings and subheadings that indicates the page number where each is found within the body of the brief.

tautology   Several words used together, each meaning the same thing.

10% Rule   The rule that any deposition or transcript summary or index to be one tenth of the actual deposition transcript.

The Bluebook   *The Bluebook, A Uniform System of Citation,* is a reference book for general and technical rules of legal citation and style. Published jointly by the Columbia Law Review, the Harvard Law Review, the University of Pennsylvania Law Review, and The Yale Law Journal.

Third-Party Answer   A pleading filed by the third-party defendant in response to the claims made by the defendant/third-party plaintiff in a Third-Party Complaint.

Third-Party Complaint   A complaint filed by a defendant against someone who is not presently a party to the lawsuit.

third-party defendant   The party against whom a Third-Party Complaint is filed by a defendant/third-party plaintiff.

third-party plaintiff   When a defendant files a Third-Party Complaint, the defendant then also becomes the third-party plaintiff to signify that party's adversarial relationship against the third-party defendant.

tickler   A reminder of things that must be done by certain dates.

tickler file   A system used to store and retrieve ticklers.

title   The name of the document, i.e., Complaint, Answer, etc., which should also identify the party to whom the document belongs; if the title to a motion or brief, it should also include the exact reason for the motion (e.g., Defendant's Motion for Extension of Time to Answer).

titles Under a code system, a unit or part of a statute, usually one of its major subdivisions devoted to a certain subject matter.

topic The general area of law in which a particular set of circumstances or issues falls; also a type of legal research that uses West's key numbers for researching digests.

traditional areas of practice test A general test used by the court to define the unauthorized practice of law where the court considers whether the activity would have been traditionally performed by an attorney or is commonly understood to be the practice of law.

transcript A word-for-word written record of everything that was said at a hearing, deposition, or trial, commonly taken in shorthand form by a court reporter who transcribes it into a typed transcript.

treatise A type of secondary authority that focuses on a particular area of the law.

trial brief A written statement and arguments prepared by counsel on the issues to be decided before, during, or after trial.

trial court A court of original jurisdiction where all evidence is first received and considered.

unauthorized practice of law When a non-lawyer performs acts that only a lawyer in good standing may perform, not limited to appearing in court or advising clients of an opinion or a recommended course of action.

Uniform Jury Instructions Model or pattern jury instructions that are required to be used, or substantially followed, by the trial judge.

United States Courts of Appeals The Circuit Courts; the first level of federal appellate courts which preside over well-defined areas of responsibility.

unofficial reporters Reporters published by commercial publishers containing the opinions.

vacated The decision of an appellate court to cancel or rescind a decision, or part of a decision, judgment, or decree made by a lower court.

venue The geographical area in which a court with jurisdiction may hear and determine a case.

verbatim To repeat something in exactly the same words; corresponding word for word to the original source or text.

Verification A sworn statement by the party that he or she has read the document and that all of the allegations, statements, or answers in it are true and correct to the best of his or her knowledge or belief.

versus A Latin word meaning "against"; the abbreviation for "versus" is "v."

voir dire Preliminary examination by the court and counsel for all of the parties of prospective jurors or witnesses to inquire into their competence.

voluntary dismissal Under rules practice, a voluntary dismissal may be accomplished by the plaintiff without leave of court if it is filed before the defendant's Answer or by stipulation signed by all of the parties after the defendant's Answer is filed.

witness list A document or documents prepared by a party listing all prospective witnesses which that party expected to introduce at trial.

witness fee The statutory per diem fee that must be paid to any non-party witness who testifies at a deposition or at trial.

writ of certiorari An order by the appellate court used by that court when it has discretion on whether to hear an appeal from a lower court.

INDEX